World War II and the Postwar Years in America

World War II and the Postwar Years in America

A Historical and Cultural Encyclopedia

VOLUME I: A–I

William H. Young and Nancy K. Young

ABC-CLIO

Santa Barbara, California • Denver, Colorado • Oxford, England

Copyright 2010 by ABC-CLIO, LLC

All rights reserved. No part of this publication may be reproduced, stored in a
retrieval system, or transmitted, in any form or by any means, electronic, mechanical,
photocopying, recording, or otherwise, except for the inclusion of brief quotations in
a review, without prior permission in writing from the publisher.

Library of Congress Cataloging-in-Publication Data

Young, William H., 1939–
  World War II and the postwar years in America : a historical and cultural encyclopedia /
William H. Young and Nancy K. Young.
     p. cm.
  Includes bibliographical references and index.
  ISBN 978-0-313-35652-0 (alk. paper)—ISBN 978-0-313-35653-7 (ebook)
 1. United States—History—1933–1945—Encyclopedias. 2. United States—
History—1945–1953—Encyclopedias. 3. World War, 1939–1945—
United States—Encyclopedias. I. Young, Nancy K., 1940– II. Title.
  E806.Y73 2010
  973.91—dc22   2010021470

ISBN: 978–0–313–35652–0
EISBN: 978–0–313–35653–7

14 13 12 11 10   1 2 3 4 5

This book is also available on the World Wide Web as an eBook.
Visit www.abc-clio.com for details.

ABC-CLIO, LLC
130 Cremona Drive, P.O. Box 1911
Santa Barbara, California 93116–1911

This book is printed on acid-free paper

Manufactured in the United States of America

Contents

VOLUME 1

Alphabetical List of Entries   vii
Guide to Related Topics   xi
Preface   xvii
Acknowledgments   xxi
Introduction   xxiii

The Encyclopedia, Entries A–I   1

Index   I-1

VOLUME 2

Alphabetical List of Entries   vii
Guide to Related Topics   xi

The Encyclopedia, Entries J–Y   417

Timeline for the 1940s   787
Selected Resources   801
Index   I-1

Alphabetical List of Entries

ABC (American Broadcasting Company)
Abstract Expressionism
Acuff, Roy
Advertising
All-Girl Orchestras
Andrews Sisters, The
Architecture
Art (Painting)
ASCAP vs. BMI Radio Boycott and the AFM Recording Ban
Atomic Bomb, The
Automobiles and the American Automotive Industry
Autry, Gene, and Roy Rogers
Aviation
Axis Sally and Tokyo Rose

Baby Boom
Baseball
Basie, Count
Basketball
Bebop (Bop)
Berlin Airlift, The
Best Sellers (Books)
Best Years of Our Lives, The (William Wyler)
Beverages
Black Market

Blackouts, Brownouts, and Dim-Outs
Bogart, Humphrey
Boogie-Woogie
Book Clubs
Bowling
Boxing
Boyd, William (Hopalong Cassidy)
Broadway Shows (Comedy and Drama)
Broadway Shows (Musicals)

Canteens
Cartoons (Film)
Casablanca (Michael Curtiz)
Children's Films
Citizen Kane (Orson Welles)
Civil Defense
Classical Music
Cold War, The
Cole, Nat King
Comedies (Film)
Comic Books
Comic Strips
Copland, Aaron
Costume and Spectacle Films
Country Music
Crime and Mystery Films
Crosby, Bing
Crosley Automobiles

Dance
D-Day
Design
Desserts, Candy, and Ice Cream
Disney, Walt
Drama (Film)
Drive-Ins: Movie Theaters, Restaurants, and Banks
DuMont Network

Edgar Bergen/Charlie McCarthy Show, The
Education
Eisenhower, General Dwight David
Ellington, Duke

Fads
Fashion
Fast Food
Film Noir
FM Radio
Folk Music
Food
Football
Frozen Foods

Games
GI Bill (Servicemen's Readjustment Act of 1944)
Godfrey, Arthur
Golf
Grocery Stores and Supermarkets

Health and Medicine
Hobbies
Hockey
Hope, Bob
Horror and Thriller Films
Horse Racing
Hot Rods and Drag Racing
House Un-American Activities Committee (HUAC)
Howdy Doody Show, The

Illustrators
Internment Camps (Relocation Centers)
It's a Wonderful Life (Frank Capra)

Jack Benny Program, The
Jazz
Jones, Spike
Jukeboxes
Juvenile Delinquency

Kinsey, Alfred C.
Kraft Television Theatre

Labor Unrest
Lawns, Lawnmowers, and Fertilizers
Leisure and Recreation
Levittown and Suburbanization
Lone Ranger, The
Louis, Joe

MacArthur, General Douglas
Magazines
Marshall, General George Catlett
MBS (Mutual Broadcasting System)
Miller, Glenn
Miranda, Carmen
Motorsports
Movies
Murphy, Audie
Musicals (Film)

Newspapers

Photography
Political and Propaganda Films
Posters
Pyle, Ernie, and Bill Mauldin

Race Relations and Stereotyping
Radio
Radio Programming: Action, Crime, Police, and Detective Shows
Radio Programming: Children's Shows, Serials, and Adventure Series
Radio Programming: Comedy Shows
Radio Programming: Drama and Anthology Shows
Radio Programming: Educational Shows
Radio Programming: Music and Variety Shows
Radio Programming: News, Sports, Public Affairs, and Talk

Radio Programming: Quiz Shows
Radio Programming: Soap Operas
Rationing
Religion
Restaurants
Rhythm 'n' Blues
Roller Derby
Roosevelt, Eleanor
Roosevelt, President Franklin Delano
Rosie the Riveter

Scrap Drives
Sculpture
Selective Training and Service Act of 1940 (Selective Service, or Draft)
Serial Films
Service Flags (Gold Stars and Blue Stars)
Seventeen
Shore, Dinah
Sinatra, Frank
Skating (Figure)
Skating (Roller)
Skiing
Smith, Kate
Softball
Songwriters and Lyricists
Spam
Spock, Dr. Benjamin O.
Steel Pennies (1943)
Superman

Swimming and Water Skiing
Swing

Technology
Television
Tennis
Terry and the Pirates (Milton Caniff)
Texaco Star Theater (Milton Berle)
Toast of the Town (Ed Sullivan)
Toys
Trains
Transportation
Travel
Truman, President Harry S.

UFOs (Unidentified Flying Objects)
United Nations, The
USO (United Service Organizations)

V-E and V-J Day
Victory Gardens
Voice of America

War Bonds
War Films
Westerns (Film)
"White Christmas" (Irving Berlin)
Women in the Military: WACs, WASPs, WAVES, SPARS, and Others

Youth

Guide to Related Topics

Art

    Abstract Expressionism
    Advertising
    Art (Painting)
    Comic Books
    Comic Strips
    Design
    Disney, Walt
    Fashion
    Illustrators
    Magazines
    Photography
    Posters
    Pyle, Ernie, and Bill Mauldin
    Sculpture

Architecture

    Architecture
    Design
    Drive-Ins: Movie Theaters, Restaurants, and Banks
    Levittown and Suburbanization
    Technology

Aviation

    Aviation
    Berlin Airlift, The
    Technology

    Transportation
    Travel

Comic Books and Strips

    Cartoons (Film)
    Comic Books
    Comic Strips
    Illustrators
    Newspapers
    Serial Films
    Superman
    Terry and the Pirates

Fads and Games

    Book Clubs
    Dance
    Fads
    Games
    Hobbies
    Hot Rods and Drag Racing
    Leisure and Recreation
    Radio Programming: Quiz Shows
    Skating (Roller)
    Swing
    Toys

Food and Drink

    Advertising

Beverages
Canteens
Desserts, Candy, and Ice Cream
Drive-Ins: Movie Theaters, Restaurants, and Banks
Fast Food
Frozen Foods
Grocery Stores and Supermarkets
Health and Medicine
Rationing
Restaurants
Spam
USO (United Service Organizations)
Victory Gardens

Government

Atomic Bomb, The
Civil Defense
Cold War, The
Education
GI Bill (Servicemen's Readjustment Act of 1944)
Health and Medicine
House Un-American Activities Committee (HUAC)
Illustrators
Internment Camps (Relocation Centers)
Labor Unrest
Photography
Political and Propaganda Films
Posters
Race Relations and Stereotyping
Rationing
Roosevelt, Eleanor
Roosevelt, President Franklin Delano
Rosie the Riveter
Scrap Drives
Selective Training and Service Act of 1940 (Selective Service, or Draft)
Service Flags (Gold Stars and Blue Stars)
Steel Pennies (1943)
Trains
Transportation
Truman, President Harry S.
UFOs (Unidentified Flying Objects)
United Nations, The

USO (United Service Organizations)
Victory Gardens
Voice of America
War Bonds
Women in the Military: WACs, WASPs, WAVES, SPARS, and Others

Individuals

Acuff, Roy
Andrews Sisters, The
Autry, Gene, and Roy Rogers
Axis Sally and Tokyo Rose
Basie, Count
Boyd, William
Cole, Nat King
Copland, Aaron
Crosby, Bing
Disney, Walt
Eisenhower, General Dwight David
Ellington, Duke
Godfrey, Arthur
Hope, Bob
Jones, Spike
Kinsey, Alfred C.
Louis, Joe
MacArthur, General Douglas
Marshall, General George Catlett
Miller, Glenn
Miranda, Carmen
Murphy, Audie
Pyle, Ernie, and Bill Mauldin
Roosevelt, Eleanor
Roosevelt, President Franklin Delano
Shore, Dinah
Sinatra, Frank
Smith, Kate
Spock, Dr. Benjamin O.
Truman, President Harry S.

Literature

Best Sellers (Books)
Book Clubs
Comic Books
Illustrators
Magazines
Newspapers
Seventeen

Magazines

Advertising
Illustrators
Magazines
Photography
Seventeen

Movies

Autry, Gene, and Roy Rogers
Best Years of Our Lives, The (William Wyler)
Bogart, Humphrey
Boyd, William (Hopalong Cassidy)
Casablanca (Michael Curtiz)
Children's Films
Citizen Kane (Orson Welles)
Comedies (Film)
Costume and Spectacle Films
Crime and Mystery Films
Crosby, Bing
Dance
Disney, Walt
Drama (Film)
Drive-Ins: Movie Theaters, Restaurants, and Banks
Edgar Bergen/Charlie McCarthy Show, The
Hope, Bob
Horror and Thriller Films
House Un-American Activities Committee (HUAC)
It's a Wonderful Life (Frank Capra)
Lone Ranger, The
Miranda, Carmen
Movies
Murphy, Audie
Musicals (Film)
Political and Propaganda Films
Race Relations and Stereotyping
Serial Films
Superman
Television
War Films
Westerns (Film)

Music

Acuff, Roy
All-Girl Orchestras
Andrews Sisters, The
ASCAP vs. BMI Radio Boycott and the AFM Recording Ban
Autry, Gene, and Roy Rogers
Basie, Count
Bebop (Bop)
Boogie-Woogie
Broadway Shows (Musicals)
Classical Music
Cole, Nat King
Copland, Aaron
Country Music
Crosby, Bing
Dance
Disney, Walt
Ellington, Duke
FM Radio
Folk Music
Jazz
Jones, Spike
Jukeboxes
Miller, Glenn
Miranda, Carmen
Race Relations and Stereotyping
Radio
Radio Programming: Music and Variety Shows
Rhythm 'n' Blues
Shore, Dinah
Sinatra, Frank
Smith, Kate
Songwriters and Lyricists
Swing
Television
"White Christmas" (Irving Berlin)

Musicians

Acuff, Roy
Andrews Sisters, The
Autry, Gene, and Roy Rogers
Basie, Count
Cole, Nat King
Copland, Aaron
Crosby, Bing
Jones, Spike
Miller, Glenn
Miranda, Carmen

Shore, Dinah
Sinatra, Frank
Smith, Kate

Newspapers

Advertising
Atomic Bomb, The
Blackouts, Brownouts, and Dim-Outs
Berlin Airlift, The
Civil Defense
Cold War, The
Comic Strips
Newspapers
Pyle, Ernie, and Bill Maudlin
Rationing
Roosevelt, Eleanor
Roosevelt, President Franklin Delano
Scrap Drives
Superman
Terry and the Pirates
Truman, President Harry S.
UFOs (Unidentified Flying Objects)
USO (United Service Organizations)
V-E and V-J Day
Victory Gardens
War Bonds

Organizations

All-Girl Orchestras
House Un-American Activities Committee (HUAC)
USO (United Service Organizations)
Voice of America

Radio

Advertising
ABC (American Broadcasting Company)
ASCAP vs. BMI Radio Boycott and the AFM Recording Ban
Edgar Bergen/Charlie McCarthy Show, The
FM Radio
Jack Benny Program, The
Leisure and Recreation
Lone Ranger, The
Radio
Radio Programming: Action, Crime, Police, and Detective Shows
Radio Programming: Children's Shows, Serials, and Adventure Series
Radio Programming: Comedy Shows
Radio Programming: Drama and Anthology Shows
Radio Programming: Educational Shows
Radio Programming: Music and Variety Shows
Radio Programming: News, Sports, Public Affairs, and Talk
Radio Programming: Quiz Shows
Radio Programming: Soap Operas
Religion
Roosevelt, Eleanor
Roosevelt, President Franklin Delano
Shore, Dinah
Smith, Kate
Superman
Technology
Voice of America

Social Issues

Baby Boom
Berlin Airlift, The
Fads
Folk Music
GI Bill (Servicemen's Readjustment Act of 1944)
Health and Medicine
Juvenile Delinquency
Kinsey, Alfred C.
Labor Unrest
Race Relations and Stereotyping
Radio Programming: News, Sports, Public Affairs, and Talk
Religion
Roosevelt, Eleanor
Rosie the Riveter
Spock, Dr. Benjamin O.
United Nations, The

Sports

Baseball
Basketball

Bowling
Boxing
Golf
Hockey
Horse Racing
Hot Rods and Drag Racing
Motorsports
Roller Derby
Skating (Figure)
Skating (Roller)
Skiing
Softball
Swimming and Water Skiing
Technology
Tennis

Suburbanization

Advertising
Architecture
Automobiles and the American Automotive Industry
Baby Boom
Best Sellers (Books)
Book Clubs
Design
Drive-Ins: Movie Theaters, Restaurants, and Banks
Education
Fast Food
Games
GI Bill (Servicemen's Readjustment Act of 1944)
Golf
Grocery Stores and Supermarkets
Lawns, Lawnmowers, and Fertilizers
Leisure and Recreation
Levittown and Suburbanization
Magazines
Newspapers
Radio
Radio Programming: Action, Crime, Police, and Detective Shows
Radio Programming: Children's Shows, Serials, and Adventure Series
Radio Programming: Comedy Shows
Radio Programming: Drama and Anthology Shows
Radio Programming: Educational Shows
Radio Programming: Music and Variety Shows
Radio Programming: News, Sports, Public Affairs, and Talk
Radio Programming: Quiz Shows
Radio Programming: Soap Operas
Skating (Figure)
Skating (Roller)
Technology
Television
Trains
Transportation

Television

ABC (American Broadcasting Company)
DuMont Network
Edgar Bergen/Charlie McCarthy Show, The
Hope, Bob
Howdy Doody Show, The
Jack Benny Program, The
Kraft Television Theatre
Leisure and Recreation
MBS (Mutual Broadcasting System)
Technology
Television
Texaco Star Theater (Milton Berle)
Toast of the Town (Ed Sullivan)

Theater

Broadway Shows (Comedy and Drama)
Broadway Shows (Musicals)
Copland, Aaron
Dance
Movies
Radio Programming: Drama and Anthology Shows
Songwriters and Lyricists
Texaco Star Theater (Milton Berle)

Travel

Automobiles and the American Automotive Industry

Aviation
Crosley Automobiles
Trains
Transportation
Travel

World War II

Advertising
All-Girl Orchestras
Atomic Bomb, The
Aviation
Axis Sally and Tokyo Rose
Berlin Airlift, The
Best Years of Our Lives, The (William Wyler)
Black Market
Blackouts, Brownouts, and Dim-Outs
Canteens
Civil Defense
Cold War, The
D-Day
Education
Eisenhower, General Dwight David
GI Bill (Servicemen's Readjustment Act of 1944)
Health and Medicine
Hope, Bob
Internment Camps (Relocation Centers)
Louis, Joe
MacArthur, General Douglas
Magazines
Marshall, General George Catlett
Miller, Glenn
Movies
Murphy, Audie
Newspapers
Photography
Political and Propaganda Films
Posters
Pyle, Ernie, and Bill Maudlin
Race Relations and Stereotyping
Radio
Radio Programming: News, Sports, Public Affairs, and Talk
Rationing
Roosevelt, President Franklin Delano
Rosie the Riveter
Scrap Drives
Selective Training and Service Act of 1940 (Selective Service, or Draft)
Service Flags (Gold Stars and Blue Stars)
Smith, Kate
Songwriters and Lyricists
Spam
Steel Pennies (1943)
Technology
Television
Toys
Trains
Transportation
Travel
Truman, President Harry S.
USO (United Service Organizations)
V-E and V-J Day
Victory Gardens
Voice of America
War Bonds
War Films
"White Christmas" (Irving Berlin)
Women in the Military: WACs, WASPs, WAVES, SPARS, and Others
Youth

Preface

The 1940s—a decade that witnessed a global conflict of massive proportions followed by unprecedented prosperity—has been, and will continue to be, examined and discussed by scholars, students, and history enthusiasts. The focus of this two-volume encyclopedia centers on one aspect of this decade: the interplay between everyday life and popular culture.

Throughout the many entries, readers will sense the presence of unlimited loyalty and patriotism on the part of U.S. citizens toward their country as it plunged into the war and also how they coped on the home front, working their jobs, carrying out their chores, and relaxing with the visual arts, movies, radio shows, pop music, best sellers, sports, and all those other elements that give zest and flavor to living. For example, under the entries "Fast Food," "Food," and "Restaurants," the inclusion of information about related radio programming, magazine and newspaper articles, and posters demonstrates how popular sources of entertainment informed and reinforced habits of healthy eating in a time of rationing and scarcity. The text will stress how scrap drives, victory gardens, and the purchase of war bonds involved everyone, often with the urging of celebrities from the entertainment and sports worlds.

When peace finally returned, articles such as "Baby Boom," "Drive-Ins: Movie Theaters, Restaurants, and Banks," "Lawns, Lawnmowers, and Fertilizers," and "Levittown and Suburbanization" explore the emerging postwar lifestyles. With prosperity, Americans acquired new cars, bought houses in the growing suburbs, traveled more, ate out more often, and became aware that new threats, in the form of a Cold War, hovered on the horizon. But even anxiety about Communism and the possibility of a nuclear confrontation could not dispel the overall optimism of the day. Science and technology made advances in all fields, the GI Bill sent thousands of veterans off to college, and religious leaders touted positive thinking. Despite a few clouds, the future looked bright.

The 179 entries in this encyclopedia deal in a variety of ways with the decade and are listed alphabetically, from "ABC (American Broadcasting Company)" through "Youth," with plenty of stops in between. If an individual merits an entry, that person's surname comes first, followed by the given name, so Duke Ellington's entry reads "Ellington, Duke" in the listing. Birth and death dates are noted parenthetically following the first mention of a name in the text, as "Cartoonist Al Capp (1909–1979) created the Shmoo." In the front matter of the book, the reader will find a Guide to Related Topics. This feature groups the articles as they pertain to broad areas of interest; for example, the topic Magazines has the following subheadings: "Advertising," "Art," "Comic Books," "Illustrators," "Magazines," "Newspapers," "Photography," and *"Seventeen"* receive mention as additional places for investigation. Twenty-three topic areas are identified.

Charts appear throughout the encyclopedia to provide easy-to-find details on a subject in a concise and readable format. For example, the article "Baseball" offers two: the first contains statistics on the World Series; the second lists the pennant and playoff winners in the World War II–era women's leagues. Other charts include radio programming, movie formats, hit songs, and the like. If needed, explanatory comments are provided within a given chart.

Ninety-nine photographs, carefully placed within the text, bring visual life to many articles. Portraits often accompany an entry about a specific person, such as Roy Acuff, Gene Autry, Roy Rogers, Count Basie, Duke Ellington, and Eleanor Roosevelt. A frame taken from *The Best Years of Our Lives* presents the stellar cast of that important movie, a shot of parked cars at a drive-in theater captures a popular entertainment of the day, and a picture of an early TV camera enhances the "Technology" entry. Other images help to familiarize the reader with aspects of life unique to the 1940s: bandleader Cab Calloway poses in a zoot suit, some pages from a book of ration stamps illustrate something everyone had to have during the war years, and a picture of a military plane emphasizes the impacts World War II had on the nation.

Within the text, whenever original monetary amounts receive mention, their 2008 equivalents follow parenthetically. The current-day numbers represent dollars adjusted for inflation, thereby showing approximately what an equivalent product would now cost. Because the worth of dollars has shifted dramatically over the years, the adjusted values have not surprisingly gone through many changes between the 1940s and the present, but the revised figures may be surprising to contemporary readers.

Each article contains words or phrases in **boldface** that indicate additional related entries. For example, the aforementioned "Levittown and Suburbanization" article mentions, in the course of its text, baby boom, design, the GI Bill, magazines, rationing, television, trains, transportation, and travel. Each of these terms appears in boldface upon first mention, a signal to the reader that additional information can be found in the encyclopedia under that entry. At the conclusion of each article, a boldface **See also** suggests other encyclopedia topics not specifically mentioned in the entry that may also prove helpful in the subject area. In this case, "Levittown and Suburbanization" includes, in addition to the bolded terms, cross-references to Architecture; Automobiles and the American Automotive Industry; Grocery Stores and Supermarkets; Lawns, Lawnmowers, and Fertilizers; Juvenile Delinquency; and Race Relations and Stereotyping.

Immediately following the **See also** recommendations, a listing called **Selected Readings** gives titles of useful books, articles, and Web sites about the entry subject. These mini-bibliographies provide a starting point for further research and should not be considered exhaustive. A much more extensive listing of selected audio and print resources, found immediately before the index, presents a wealth of additional LPs, CDs, books, articles, and Web sites covering a myriad of subjects dealing with the 1940s. Many of the citations in this section address relevant topics not discussed directly in any particular entry. In addition, a timeline covers, year by year, highlights from the decade in abbreviated form.

In the final pages of this encyclopedia, a detailed index locates information about topics or people not found under individual entries. For example, artist and illustrator Norman Rockwell does not appear in that category. Discussion of him and his influence will be found in articles such as "Illustrators" and "War Bonds"; he can nevertheless be located in the index under his own name. Similarly, the popular Studebaker automobile will not be found under a heading of that name but instead under "Automobiles and the American Automotive Industry" and elsewhere by name in the index.

It is the authors' hope that anyone interested in American life and activities during World War II and the five years following the conflict will find much helpful and informative material within these pages.

Acknowledgments

Any work of this scope requires the help of others. We have been fortunate that many individuals have contributed, directly and indirectly, knowingly and unknowingly, in the creation of this encyclopedia. Once again, our sincere thanks to everyone at the Lynchburg College Knight-Capron Library, always our starting point. Director Chris Millson-Martula made all the library's facilities available to us, turning what could have been an overwhelming task into something doable. Ariel Myers, the college archivist and the person to see for interlibrary loans, characteristically found items that some considered impossible to locate. Belinda Carroll, Elizabeth Henderson, Michael Ours, and Christa Poparad deftly handled research and Internet questions, dug out the answers, and did it with a smile.

Farther south, the staff at the Harman Center for Sales, Advertising, and Marketing History at Duke University guided us through the mysteries of this previously unused treasure, allowing us to find some splendid examples of ads from the 1940s. And, although we did not visit there in person, the online riches—virtually all digitalized and thumbnailed now—at the Library of Congress to the north once again demonstrated that this venerable institution stands out as one of the best uses of tax dollars to be found. The excellence of its electronic resources makes it altogether too easy to postpone actually visiting Washington, which becomes our loss, since the people staffing the various departments are such a pleasure to work with. Maybe next time.

At home, folks got tired, we're sure, of our pulling out obscure facts about the 1940s, and equally tired of incessant questions pertaining to the decade. Tired or not, we gained a wealth of information through our queries. But special mention must be made of Charles Worsham, who brought his considerable expertise to bear on our works dealing with the visual arts; Dr. James Wright did likewise with sections on health and medicine, along with pertinent observations on related topics.

Administrative Assistant Cheryl Pendergraft of the School of Education and Human Development at Lynchburg College provided excellent service in the production of this text; her willingness to salvage reams of used paper that still had one clean side allowed us to print our many drafts in an environmentally friendly way.

As we've come to expect, the people at the Greenwood Publishing Group readily extended helping hands. Editor Debby Adams, with whom we had worked before, got us started and then moved on. We miss her, but when Greenwood became a part of ABC-CLIO, the company gave Mike Hermann the reins and he followed the project through; we were glad to have him come on board. Both Debby and Mike assisted immeasurably with text preparation, a task more arduous than it might sound. Appreciation is expressed also to the people at Apex CoVantage; they assisted immeasurably with editing and related details; Robin Tutt of ABC-CLIO took on the task of ordering, organizing, and laying out pictures.

And so we offer to all who participated in this project our hearty thanks. Any errors of commission or sins of omission of course remain ours and ours alone.

Introduction

On January 1, 1940, headlines on the front page of the New York Times gave more attention to the growing conflict in Europe than to New Year's Eve revelries in the city. Articles about the activities of the Third Reich on the continent and the Russians in Finland underscored the tension building on the other side of the Atlantic Ocean. One column announced updated regulations for Americans living, working, or traveling abroad; new procedures required the addition of thumbprints to validate passports, documents now good for only six months. And yet, on that previous evening, New Year's Eve, as worried as some U.S. citizens might have been about the inevitable involvement of the United States in a worldwide conflict, about one and a quarter million of them withstood frigid weather—meteorologists estimated a nighttime temperature of 10 degrees below zero—to welcome in the New Year and a new decade in New York's Times Square.

One year later, on New Year's Eve, December 31, 1940, another million or so celebrants crowded into Times Square, despite continued discouraging news from abroad. By this time, eligible males faced a military draft with the passage of the Selective Training and Service Act 1940 in September of that year, but Americans put on a brave face. The December 7, 1941 bombing of Pearl Harbor thrust an ill-prepared nation into World War II, and still yet another million gathered in the famous square, welcoming still another year, a year certain to be fraught with danger.

Traditions die hard, and the last night of 1942 saw the crowd's numbers halved from the previous celebration, and the usual cheery lights and descending ball from atop the *Times'* tower were nowhere to be seen. Dim-out and blackout restrictions had by then been imposed and would remain in effect into 1944. Despite the darkened city, however, several hundred thousand hardy souls twice made the trek to Times Square to toast the arrivals of both 1943 and 1944. When civilian defense officials declared, in late 1944, the threat of enemy attacks had sufficiently lessened, the Great White Way could again glow.

The promise of ultimate victory brought out another huge throng of merrymakers on December 31, 1944. If milling crowds at Times Square can provide any measurement of the national mood, the millions of people who surged into the famed intersection of Forty-Second Street and Broadway for the 1945 surrenders of Germany in May and Japan in September demonstrated the depth of joy felt with victory and the return to peace.

For the remainder of the decade, with the gloomy clouds of war finally lifted, Times Square went back to a semblance of normalcy. With all the lights back on, storefronts glittered with consumer goods, restaurants offered full menus, and traffic snarls resumed. Hundreds of thousands still showed up for New Year's Eve celebrations, but the urgency of the war years had dissipated.

The 1940s might therefore be thought of as two decades—the World War II years, 1940 to 1945, and the postwar era, 1945 to 1949. The first part saw a nation preoccupied with winning the war; little else mattered. The conflict even manipulated time itself: War Time, passed by Congress in 1942, put the nation on year-round daylight saving time in an effort to conserve energy, particularly electricity; legislators did not end it until September 1945, and even then many states chose to retain at least parts of daylight time; most citizens enjoyed the change during the summer months.

No matter the time of day or night, no matter how grim the news in newspapers and on radio, American popular culture, as has always been the case, provided moments of respite, relaxation, and enjoyment for everyone. Soldiers on the battlefield and children back home followed the exploits of superheroes like Superman and Batman in comic books and serials; radio stations served up shows of every imaginable kind; and movie houses offered chills, thrills, and laughter to some 80 million patrons a week. Broadway, that main New York thoroughfare, may have been darkened for a few years of the war, but not the theaters. Playgoers, enthralled with dramas written by Tennessee Williams and Henry Miller, also saw musicals rise to new heights, led by the inventive pens of Richard Rodgers and Oscar Hammerstein. *Oklahoma!* played to full houses from its opening in 1943 until its closing in 1948, a new record. Country music gained ground when some of its most ardent supporters moved from rural locations to defense jobs scattered around the nation and introduced their favorite tunes to new fans. Swing, once king, lost its crown, while vocalists and singing groups rose in prominence and popularity.

The immediate postwar years can be seen as a period of rebuilding, of reclaiming what had been lost or put aside during the long years of overseas battles and home front deprivations. Radio grew—from a little over 700 AM stations in 1940 to almost 2,000 in 1949. Television, where available, gained enthusiastic viewers in the waning years of the decade, while another new kid on the block, FM broadcasting, boasted 726 stations by 1949. Many new approaches to the arts and culture, so long under wraps or ignored by the general public, began to appear—abstract expressionism, early rock 'n' roll, teenage idols, and youth lifestyles in general—but their impacts on American life proved gradual and would be heralded as benchmarks of the 1950s; the few years of innovation following the war were largely trampled in the rush to return to a more normal, modern, and peaceful way of life, and so in many ways, the late 1940s, the postwar years, serve as but prelude to the 1950s.

The peace that the Allies finally achieved in 1945 brought with it a difficult transition. Although most shortages and rationing came to an end, an inflationary spending binge resulted as people splurged with the money accumulated during the lean war years. The troops flooded home, married, and produced both a baby boom and a dearth of housing that changed demographics for generations to come. The typical suburb, with its rows of neat, landscaped houses, its comfortable distance from the perceived turmoil of the city, and its perceived retreat from contemporary problems, represented a nostalgic cocoon that would later become a symbol for years to come. The popularity of Early American decor—knotty pine furniture, ladder-back chairs, milk glass, hooked rugs, and so on—symbolized a mythic past emblematic of security and a willful forgetfulness about present-day concerns.

Amid this domestic change, foreign relations also went through a transition, as Communism replaced the Axis powers as an external threat. The Cold War led to congressional witch hunts and a new Red Scare, and artists and scholars employed "the Age of Anxiety" as a catchphrase to describe the attitudes of the new postwar world. Perhaps people thought making it through the war could be considered accomplishment enough, but they now had new challenges to face. But face them they did, and a 1948 runaway best seller bore the title *How to Stop Worrying and Start Living*.

And so, on December 31, 1949, the ball again made its stately drop down the *Times* building, and below, waiting to welcome 1950, stood some 750,000 revelers. The country, poised for the greatest prosperity it had ever experienced, bid adieu to the 1940s—a difficult decade but one that had tested the mettle of the United States. In retrospect, it came through with flying colors.

A

ABC (AMERICAN BROADCASTING COMPANY)

In 1941, the Federal Communications Commission (FCC) ordered the National Broadcasting Company (NBC) to divest itself of one of its two networks in order to prevent it from having too much of a **radio** monopoly. Out of this divestiture came a new network, ABC.

Since its founding in 1926, NBC had operated two networks, or "chains," a term then employed by many sources. Each affiliate station could thereby be viewed as a link in a metaphorical chain. Under its banner, the company owned NBC Red and NBC Blue. These two parts ran as separate entities, and each had its own staffs, programming, and affiliates. Because of their size, NBC's Red and Blue networks effectively controlled more than a quarter of the country's radio stations, with CBS (Columbia Broadcasting System) strongly in second place. The remaining stations were either affiliated with much smaller networks (Colonial, **Mutual,** Texas Quality, Yankee, and others), or operated independently. In the eyes of the FCC, too much influence jointly rested with the Red and Blue networks, particularly in a number of large cities where NBC controlled several stations. The FCC acted accordingly, citing violation of antitrust regulations, and ruled that NBC would have to reduce its holdings.

Both NBC and CBS reacted immediately to the FCC challenge, arguing that the agency went beyond the powers granted it, and that the decision impinged on their rights of free speech. The case went to trial, eventually ending up at the United States Supreme Court. In a landmark decision, the Court ruled that the FCC had acted within its jurisdiction and did not deny the networks the right to free speech.

NBC then made the corporate decision to shed its Blue network, traditionally the weaker of the two in programming, audience, and income. NBC Blue went on the block in the spring of 1943, and several parties expressed interest. Considerable bidding ensued for the property, but Edward J. Noble (1882–1958), who had made a fortune by purchasing, in 1913, the candy company responsible for Life Savers, came away with the network. He paid $8 million for the property (approximately $92 million in 2008 dollars adjusted for inflation) in July of 1943, buying it in the name of American Broadcast Systems, Inc., a company he owned. The FCC approved the terms of the sale in September, and a year later the American Broadcasting Company was born.

For his $8 million, Noble gained a network with an absence of big stars or shows. It also had fewer affiliates than either NBC or CBS, all of which translated as fewer listeners. Potential sponsors, keenly aware of this inequity, were reluctant to invest their dollars in ABC, so the fledgling operation faced challenging financial times during the mid- and late 1940s. But, as the underdog among networks, it gained the freedom to take chances and innovate.

For example, **Bing Crosby** (1903–1977), one of the most popular entertainers of the day, from 1936 on, had hosted NBC's *Kraft Music Hall*. But in the fall of 1946, Crosby and NBC suffered a break, and the vocalist moved to ABC. Crosby had wanted to prerecord the *Music Hall,* but NBC and Kraft adamantly refused. Tape recording remained a new technique in 1946, and both NBC and CBS resisted utilizing it, arguing that audiences would not like "canned" radio shows. But Crosby saw advantages in time and professionalism, since tape could be edited, eliminating flubs or questionable performances. Both sides refused to budge, so Crosby quit, and ABC, not as averse to tape, welcomed him.

From 1946 until the summer of 1949, Crosby starred on *Philco Radio Time,* his replacement version of the Kraft show. NBC continued with the original *Music* Hall, using veteran entertainer Al Jolson (1886–1950) as the primary host. In time, when the other networks saw that audiences did not object to prerecorded shows, and their stance weakened, tape recording eventually became a normal part of broadcasting.

Bing Crosby, however, proved to be only one of several entertainers ABC acquired in its early years. Milton Berle (1908–2002), a veteran comedian from the days of vaudeville, had a checkered career in radio. Most of his previous shows had, at best, mediocre runs before being canceled. An energetic, visual comic, his critics found the purely aural qualities of radio unsuited for his antic humor. But ABC, in need of attractions to fill its skimpy schedule, gambled on Berle and produced *The Texaco Star Theater* (1948–1949). This variety show did little better than his previous efforts, but it allowed him and his writers to polish routines that would distinguish his next venture, a nearly simultaneous **television** series bearing the same name that premiered in the fall of 1948 for NBC-TV. The ABC radio show failed, but its format paved the way for his enormously successful Texaco television series that ran until 1953. In the process, Berle emerged as one of the first major stars of the new medium.

Another radio comedian, Henry Morgan (1915–1994), came to ABC from the Mutual network in 1945, after a two-year hiatus from broadcasting. Always controversial, at least among the sponsors he constantly ribbed in his routines, Morgan's offbeat, acerbic humor attracted enough listeners that stations strove to get backing for his show. He remained at ABC, unsponsored, until 1948, when he moved on to NBC.

Groucho Marx (1890–1977) gained fame as one of the Marx Brothers of the **movies.** Appearing with brothers Chico (1887–1961) and Harpo (1888–1964) in a long string of Hollywood slapstick comedies, such as *Duck Soup* (1933), *A Night at the Opera*

(1935), and *A Day at the Races* (1937), the zany trio continued on into the 1940s, but the later films did not do well. After *Love Happy* (1949), the brothers broke up. But by that time, Groucho had moved into other interests, including radio.

For the 1947 fall season, ABC premiered *You Bet Your Life,* a comedy quiz show with Groucho as its wisecracking host. Following in the trend-setting footsteps of Bing Crosby, the producers put the show on tape, editing 60 minutes of banter into a tight 30-minute show. Any dead spots between Groucho and his contestants were cut, along with any questionable material (language, subject matter). It made for a fast-moving half-hour of humor and rapid-fire wit, with Groucho asking the questions and providing one quip after another. *You Bet Your Life* became an overnight hit, and ABC retained it for two years. With its success, CBS briefly obtained the show in late 1949, only to have NBC take it over in 1950, keeping the quiz on radio but also introducing a televised version. Both continued with high ratings, running on radio until 1956 and on television until 1961.

The success of *You Bet Your Life* led ABC to look into other quiz-show formats. The network found another winner with *Stop the Music,* a clever audience-participation production that had call-in contestants attempting to guess the correct titles of songs while a vocalist sang the lyrics but hummed the title. At some point in the song, emcee Bert Parks (1914–1992) halted the proceedings by shouting "stop the music!" An operator then placed a random telephone call to someone in the United States; a correct answer brought sizable prizes, so millions of people tuned in on the off chance they might be called.

Debuting in March 1948, the show became a sensation, going from nowhere in the ratings to one of the top 10 radio shows in the country. It played on Sunday nights at 8:00 against the seemingly invincible Fred Allen (1894–1956), at that time one of the most popular comedians on radio. But the chance at big prizes caused many listeners to tune into the new ABC quiz, and *The Fred Allen Show* dropped precipitously. The novelty of a chance telephone call eventually wore off, however, and *Stop the Music* faded in popularity; it left the air after a four-year run, despite having been one of ABC's most successful radio efforts. It also ran on ABC television during most of the same time period, a fact that added to its overall popularity.

The new network also gained an ongoing situation comedy when, in 1949, it landed *The Adventures of Ozzie and Harriet,* then running on NBC, which, in turn, had gotten it from CBS in 1948. A family-oriented series, the show had originated in 1944. It starred Ozzie Nelson (1906–1975; "Ozzie" derived from Oswald) and his real-life wife, Harriett Hilliard Nelson (1909–1994). The Nelsons had formerly been part of the Big Band Era, with Ozzie leading his own orchestra and Harriet serving as a vocalist. When ABC commenced running the series, the couple's two sons, David (b. 1936) and Ricky (1940–1985) joined the cast, making it a true family show.

It remained on the air until 1954; besides being a radio favorite, *The Adventures of Ozzie and Harriet* made an easy transition to television in 1952 on ABC-TV. It survived until 1966, making it one of television's longest-running sitcoms. A movie, *Here Come the Nelsons,* also played theaters in 1952.

Another 1949 addition to the network's schedule involved gossip columnist Walter Winchell (1897–1972). Once a widely read reporter, syndicated in hundreds of

newspapers, Winchell had been a fixture on radio since 1930. He made news into entertainment, especially anything concerning the lives of celebrities. The columnist usually opened his broadcasts with a staccato "Good evening, Mr. and Mrs. North America and all the ships at sea." As he spoke, he tapped a telegraph key for effect, a gimmick implying that he alone had important breaking news. Over the years, his manner of digging the dirt about famous names gained him a substantial audience, but he grew increasingly strident and opinionated, and many of his former fans drifted away.

After many years with NBC, he went to ABC just as anti-Communist hysteria was sweeping much of the nation. No supporter of **President Harry S. Truman** (1884–1972), Winchell railed about "Reds in government" and an administration "soft on Communism" (both popular phrases of the day). Despite declining ratings, Winchell continued to tap his telegraph key and claim to possess insider information on a host of subjects. His radio career ended in 1955, but, by that time, ABC had put him in its television schedule for 1952. He remained in that medium until 1958, hat pushed back, tie askew, and sleeves rolled up—the anachronistic picture of a reporter.

Edward Noble's new American Broadcasting Company did not have an easy time of it in the 1940s. Much of the network's programming consisted of radio hand-me-downs, entertainers and journalists whose best days were behind them when they moved to ABC. Lacking as many affiliates as its primary competitors claimed, and perennially in third place, it would not be until the later1950s that ABC boasted a first-class stable of shows and performers for its growing television audience. By that time, it had virtually dropped its involvement in radio, with the exception of news and sports.

See also: Advertising; Comedies (Film); Desserts, Candy, and Ice Cream

Selected Reading
Barnouw, Erik. *A History of Broadcasting in the United States.* Vol. 2, *The Golden Web.* New York: Oxford University Press, 1968.
Nachman, Gerald. *Raised on Radio.* Berkeley: University of California Press, 1998.
Quinlan, Sterling. *Inside ABC: American Broadcasting Company's Rise to Power.* New York: Hastings House, 1979.

ABSTRACT EXPRESSIONISM

This term came into limited use in 1946, coined by critic Robert Coates (1897–1973) for an article that appeared in *The New Yorker* magazine reviewing an exhibit by German-born painter and teacher Hans Hofmann (1880–1956). In **art,** abstraction means to achieve effects through forms, colors, and textures instead of picturing recognizable reality, whereas expressionism suggests depicting the inner world of emotion, usually through distortion or exaggeration. Taken together, abstract expressionism connotes subjective emotional experience, or states of feeling, expressed in a nonrealistic, nonliteral way.

Of all the arts—visual, literary, musical, dramatic—the abstract expressionist movement of the late 1940s and on into succeeding decades had virtually nothing to say about World War II. Most of its practitioners, for various legitimate reasons, did no military service and studiously avoided depicting the conflict, or anything else, for that matter, in their work. Abstract expressionism, transcends time and place, and exists solely for itself. The trends of the 1930s—regionalism, urban realism, social protest, precisionism—were seen as passé, out of date, and artistically empty by many of the abstract painters of the postwar years.

No new cultural movements, including those in painting, spring up completely by chance; a tradition of at least partial abstraction has long held an accepted place in American art, from Milton Avery's (1893–1964) muted shapes against bands of color to John Marin's (1870–1953) restless sea and cityscapes to Georgia O'Keeffe's (1887–1986) much-magnified flowers. The antecedents for abstract expressionism therefore abound; one need look only at earlier American and European cubists and modernists, at **advertising** with its bold colors and simplified forms, and at American Indian and Asian motifs, especially calligraphy. It might be expected, then, that the abstract expressionists would borrow from these roots, but the geometry and form found in older abstract works they rejected as sterile and irrelevant.

They instead followed two paths in their explorations for a new style. One, so-called color field painting, depends on large, seemingly simple expanses of resonant color devoid of shapes. The actual source of this term remains unknown; critic Clement Greenberg (1909–1994) later coined "post-painterly abstraction," which means much the same thing. This approach vied with action painting, a technique that relies on the rapid, forceful application of paint, usually with large brushes or directly from the tube (or, in some cases, the can). Often referred to as gestural, or drip painting, action painting did not enter the artistic vocabulary until 1952, when critic Harold Rosenberg (1906–1978) used it as part of an essay appearing in *ARTnews*. In his article, Rosenberg stressed the importance of the spontaneity of the creative act itself. The two paths sometimes intertwined, and elements of both color field and action painting can be found in individual works.

Whatever the terminology, this new movement in American art involved oversize canvases with no discernable subject and the creation of nonrepresentational, abstract images freed from both easel and frame. The bigger the painting, the less chance existed that anything could come between it and the observer, or so the theory said. Method became almost as important as the paintings, and the artists strove to immerse themselves in the work, making the act of creation override any overt subject matter or stylistic reference. Some critics characterized this approach as a form of automatism, or the use of unpremeditated automatic techniques—an act of spontaneity that would release the creative forces dwelling in the mind, a kind of visual **jazz,** not unlike an extended, improvised solo, and thus the term "action painting."

Even titles for canvases often lost most meaning, as if they might influence the viewer's reaction or interpretation, and consisted of numbers, such as *Number 1* or *Number 2* (and so on), or more simply, *Untitled*. The abstractionists felt a title might suggest meaning beyond the painting. By upending cultural traditions, the artists sought to focus attention only on the work, making sure that no referents existed outside the canvas. The movement thereby challenged the authority usually given works of art, and most expressionistic abstract art on the surface seems divorced from any social or historical currents.

The majority of artists interested in or practicing abstract expressionism during the 1940s could be found on the East Coast, specifically New York City. Some commentators lumped them together as the New York School, making the incorrect assumption that any painters working in New York studios were also abstract expressionists. In the early days of the movement, only a handful of painters were actively involved with this area of abstraction, and even in its heyday in the 1950s and 1960s, it remained small, with the vast majority of American artists continuing to follow other styles and genres.

During this formative period, two critics in particular—the aforementioned Clement Greenberg and Harold Rosenberg—championed abstract expressionism and frequently wrote reviews and essays about it, although they tended to be intellectual rivals at the time. Their intensely parochial discussions, along with those of their colleagues, were mainly confined to journals with small circulations or in lengthy personal exchanges and seldom received much recognition beyond the immediate New York City region. In addition, a number of these early commentators wrote in such an incomprehensible, complex, mumble-jumble style that it would be difficult to know exactly what they were saying or what they were defending. They successfully placed themselves outside the mainstream, presenting an elitist attitude of superiority to other, more popular, more accessible, artistic styles.

Life magazine, an immensely popular weekly journal that featured photo essays on the news of the week, occasionally ran stories on art and artists. In its August 8, 1949, issue, the magazine published a three-page illustrated article by Dorothy Seiberling (b. 1922) with the title "Jackson Pollock: Is He the Greatest Living Painter in the United States?" Thanks to this generous spread, some 4 million subscribers had their first glimpse of the work of Pollock (1912–1956), an artist establishing a name for himself in the area of abstract expressionism and probably the best-known artist then working in the genre. Those same readers also learned a bit about the movement, despite Seiberling's occasionally flippant tone. Accompanying black-and-white pictures show Pollock hard at work, and the color photographs give a glimpse of some of his paintings. Swift reader reactions appeared in the "Letters" section in subsequent issues and were overwhelmingly negative (e.g., "Is he a painter?").

As abstract expressionism gained both a foothold and increasing notoriety in the contemporary art world, cartoonists had a field day depicting befuddled viewers, usually at a show in a gallery, scratching their heads and trying to make sense of an artist's latest work. A spate of books and articles also began appearing, condemning the movement's stubborn refusal to adhere to the traditions of fine art. Even some members of Congress now and then rumbled about the vague threats presented by modern art in general and implied that perhaps these painters were part of a sinister Communist plot. For the average art lover, however, the response more likely involved confusion. **President Harry S. Truman** (1884–1972; president from 1945 to 1953), always a plain-spoken man, perhaps summed up much popular feeling in 1948: "It looks like scrambled eggs."

In time, abstract expressionism would gain acceptance and appreciation in the American art world, but during the 1940s, most people saw it at best as a cultural curiosity. For the average reader or museumgoer, it remained a mystery, a private luxury apparently enjoyed by the few but hardly a necessity available to the many.

TABLE 1. Selected Artists Associated with Abstract Expressionism during the 1940s

Artist and Dates	Comments
Josef Albers (1888–1976)	German-born; Albers came to the United States in 1933. An influential teacher and theorist, but usually not thought an abstract expressionist, he influenced numerous postwar artists. He began work on his extended *Homage to the Square*, his best-known work, in 1949.
William Baziotes (1912–1963)	More of a surrealist; worked with the Works Progress Administration/Federal Art Project (WPA/FAP).
Ilya Bolotowsky (1907–1981)	A founding member of the American Abstract Artists, a group formed in 1937 to promote abstraction in art. Also worked with WPA/FAP.
James Brooks (1906–1992)	A WPA/FAP muralist, later an abstract expressionist.
Willem de Kooning (1904–1997)	One of the most important figures in abstract expressionism. He fused several styles, so that abstract and figurative images can be seen in his work. Had his first show in 1948. His famous *Women* series began in 1950, but it would be years after that before it reached its conclusion.
Burgoyne Diller (1906–1965)	A WPA/FAP supervisor, founding member of American Abstract Artists.
Arshile Gorky (1904–1948)	An early figure in abstract expressionism, although he rejected the label. Allusive paintings with sexual imagery.
Adolph Gottlieb (1903–1974)	In the abstract expressionist vanguard; he claimed the style represented the chaos of modern times.
Peggy Guggenheim (1898–1979)	Not a painter but a wealthy patron of modern art. Her New York gallery, Art of This Century, which held shows and displayed many contemporary artists from 1942 to 1947, exhibited most of the rising abstract expressionists and gave the nascent movement much-needed support.
Hans Hofmann (1880–1956)	Born in Germany, he settled in the United States in 1932, becoming an influential teacher of many contemporary American artists; his painting career as an abstractionist blossomed in the mid-1940s.
Lee Krasner (1908–1984)	One of the few women active in abstract expressionism; also worked with WPA/FAP; married to Jackson Pollock.
Norman Lewis (1909–1979)	One of a few black abstractionists.
Robert Motherwell (1915–1991)	Helped establish the high intellectual tone associated with abstract expressionism.
Barnett Newman (1905–1970)	A leading abstract expressionist noted for his "zip," a vertical line splitting his otherwise spare canvases.
Jackson Pollock (1912–1956)	Probably the most prominent of the abstract expressionists; had his first show at Peggy Guggenheim's gallery in 1943. His drip technique got him some popular recognition, particularly in *Life* magazine in 1949.
Ad Reinhardt (1913–1967)	Began expressionistically but later pioneered minimalism, a cultural movement of the 1960s and 1970s that attempted to pare down art and music to the most basic essentials.

(continued)

TABLE 1. *(continued)*

Artist and Dates	Comments
Mark Rothko (1903–1970)	A leading abstract expressionist noted for his color field works featuring soft and luminous rectangular compositions. All representation is eliminated; instead he emphasizes the relationships between colors, shapes, and boundaries.
Clyfford Still (1904–1980)	An early abstract expressionist, Still had his first show at Peggy Guggenheim's gallery in 1944.
Mark Tobey (1890–1976)	Although he denied being an abstract expressionist, he is usually grouped with them. His paintings present a nervous dream world, employing "white writing" or calligraphic style.

See also: Magazines; Photography

Selected Reading

Haskell, Barbara. *The American Century: Art and Culture, 1900–1950.* New York: W. W. Norton, 1999.

Kleeblatt, Norman L., ed. *Action/Abstraction: Pollock, De Kooning, and American Art, 1940–1976.* New Haven, CT: Yale University Press, 2008.

Knott, Robert. *American Abstract Art of the 1930s and 1940s.* New York: Harry N. Abrams, 1998.

ACUFF, ROY

Singer Roy Acuff (1903–1992) had, by the early 1940s, earned the title "King of Country Music," and some even called him the "Backwoods Sinatra" because of his crooning style. Born in Maynardsville, Tennessee, he had aspired to be a professional baseball player in his youthful years, but severe sunstroke, suffered in 1929, followed by a nervous breakdown, ended those dreams. While recovering from these setbacks, he listened to recordings of **country music** and taught himself to play the fiddle. After a brief tour playing and singing to sell patent medicine with a local show traveling in the mountains of Tennessee and Virginia, Acuff formed the Tennessee Crackerjacks. He and his band secured a spot on **radio** station WNOX in Knoxville, changing their name to the Crazy Tennesseans in the process. The group recorded several songs for the American Record Company (ARC) in 1936, including "Wabash Cannonball" and "The Great Speckled Bird," two numbers that garnered immediate attention in the country music field.

For five years, Acuff unsuccessfully attempted to appear on the *Grand Ole Opry,* a weekly show broadcast from Nashville, Tennessee, on WSM. Persistence paid off, and he finally landed an invitation in 1938. Opry managers thought his performance to be inferior to other acts, but telegrams and letters poured into the station praising his rendition of "The Great Speckled Bird." Recognizing the importance of audience approval, the executives relented and invited him back. With each additional appearance, the fans' enthusiasm grew, and management quickly hired Acuff as the full-time host of a 30-minute Opry segment that aired on NBC radio, a nationwide network. Prince

Albert tobacco sponsored the Acuff portion. He then became *Grand Ole Opry*'s first solo singer, a new format for the show. By 1940, Acuff had gained star status, replacing Uncle Dave Macon (1870–1952) as the program's most prominent entertainer.

Once ensconced with the *Grand Ole Opry,* Acuff and the Crazy Tennesseans became Roy Acuff and the Smoky Mountain Boys, a name he considered more sophisticated. Making themselves different from the other country music acts dressed in cowboy garb, they wore plain sports clothing and presented a repertoire of primarily sacred and traditional mountain-style melodies. They enjoyed a string of country hits recorded on the Conqueror, Vocalion, Okeh, and Capitol labels. Some of the popular numbers that Acuff penned included "Beneath the Lonely Mound of Clay" (1940), "Precious Jewel" (1943), "Our Own Jole Blon" (1947), and "Midnight Train" (1948).

Throughout the decade, the band also performed and recorded numbers written by other composers. Some well-known ones included "Fireball Mail" (Floyd Jenkins [n.d.], composed and recorded 1942), "Night Train to Memphis" (Beasley Smith [1901–1968], Marvin Hughes [n.d.], and Owen Bradley [1915–1998], composed and recorded 1942), "Pins and Needles (In My Heart)" (Floyd Jenkins, composed and recorded 1943), "The Prodigal Son" (Floyd Jenkins, composed and recorded 1944), "I'll Forgive You But I Can't Forget" (Joe Frank [n.d.] and Pee Wee King [1914–2000], composed and recorded 1944), "Blue Eyes Crying in the Rain" (Fred Rose [1897–1954], composed and recorded 1945), "Wreck on the Highway" (Dorsey Dixon [1897–1968], composed and recorded 1946), "Wait for the Light to Shine" (Fred Rose, composed and recorded 1947), "Freight Train Blues" (John Lair [1894–1985], composed 1935, recorded 1947), and "Tennessee Waltz" (Pee Wee King and Redd Stewart [1923–2003] composed 1948, recorded 1949).

Acuff's quick rise to popularity on the *Grand Ole Opry* radio show led him to travel to California and appear in **movies.** In 1940, he portrayed himself in the film *Grand Ole Opry,* followed by roles in four others—*Hi, Neighbor* (1942), *O, My Darling Clementine* (1943), *Cowboy Canteen* (1944), and *Sing, Neighbor, Sing* (1944).

In the early days of his career, Acuff supplemented his income by compiling and selling songbooks containing his compositions. Based on this experience, he and songwriter Fred Rose founded Acuff-Rose Publishing Company in 1942, using their own songs as a base. The company, perhaps Acuff's most important venture, held two distinctions: the first Nashville-based music

Roy Acuff, sometimes called the "Backwoods Sinatra," gained star status as Grand Ole Opry's *first solo singer in the early 1940s. (Photofest)*

publishing establishment and the first one exclusively devoted to country music. Acuff-Rose signed Hank Williams (1923–1953), one of their most successful clients, to a contract in 1946. A year later, Williams' first chart hit, "Move It on Over," brought major recognition to both him and Acuff-Rose.

During the war years, Roy Acuff and the *Grand Ole Opry* became synonymous, and he, as well as many of the other performers, broadened their fame and fortune across the country through the Opry's Camel Caravan, sponsored by the R. J. Reynolds Cigarette Company. This traveling unit of performers entertained troops at military bases in the United States and the Panama Canal region. His records sold by the millions all over the world, and he appeared on the Armed Forces Radio Network (AFN) program *Country Style USA*. Some said that he reigned equally with vocalist **Bing Crosby** (1903–1977) and bandleader Benny Goodman (1909–1986) and that he became a part of a Japanese battle cry, "To hell with Roosevelt, to hell with Babe Ruth, to hell with Roy Acuff."

Acuff, with singing, acting, personal appearances, and the publishing company, earned $200,000 (a little over $2 million in 2008 dollars) in 1944, a most comfortable income for a hillbilly performer. He left the *Grand Ole Opry* in April 1946 and initially found himself in constant demand for personal appearances. That same year, he had a leading role in the movie *Night Train to Memphis*. Without regular network exposure, however, the performance requests began to dwindle, and in 1949 he returned to the Opry to reestablish himself as a major performer. He also traveled again to California and appeared in his final picture, *Home in San Antone,* in 1949.

Once back with the Opry, Acuff in 1949 participated in the company's first overseas tour. Along with Little Jimmy Dickens (b. 1920), Hank Williams, and others, he performed at military bases in England, Germany, and the Azores. Being especially conscientious about performing for U.S. servicemen, both during and after World War II, Acuff and the Smoky Mountain Boys also entertained troops during the Korean and Vietnam wars.

With the return to peace in 1945, Acuff briefly flirted with politics and three years later became the Republican nominee for governor of Tennessee. Capitalizing on his entertainment skills, he campaigned by performing concerts with the Smoky Mountain Boys. Despite his popularity as a country music star, he lost the election and subsequently returned to his career of writing, publishing, and performing. With the arrival of the 1950s and his reputation established, Acuff continued to write and tour, but his work as a major recording artist declined.

In 1962, Roy Acuff, widely respected as a fiddler and country music vocalist, became the first living artist elected to the Country Music Hall of Fame. A final, posthumous, accolade for his more than 50 years of contributions to the field of country music came in 2005, when the Library of Congress named his 1947 recording of "Wabash Cannonball" to its National Recording Registry.

Selected Reading
Peterson, Richard A. *Creating Country Music.* Chicago: University of Chicago Press, 1997.
Shestack, Melvin. *The Country Music Encyclopedia.* New York: Thomas Y. Crowell Company, 1974.
Young, William H., and Nancy K. Young. *Music of the World War II Era.* Westport, CT: Greenwood Press, 2008.

ADVERTISING

Following the Great Depression of the 1930s, American business faced the task of restoring public confidence in the economic system. Advertising in particular had been attacked on many fronts, with critics saying its messages could not be trusted, and terms like "ballyhoo," "bunk," "flimflam," "hoopla," and "hype" (verb only; the noun form did not enter common speech until the 1960s) were attached to numerous ad campaigns by a suspicious public.

Public relations experts wanted to recast the negative images associated with advertising, and the onset of World War II gave them a unique opportunity to accomplish just that. During the period 1941–1945, most commercial advertising strove to portray American business as foursquare behind the nation's war efforts, a mixture of crass commerce and civic virtue. While urging people to buy **war bonds** and support the troops, it also offered a vision of postwar America lush with consumer goods—but first the war must be won.

Just prior to the Japanese attack on Pearl Harbor, business leaders and advertising executives formed the Advertising Council in November 1941. During the conflict, it went by the name of the War Advertising Council and became an important advocate of national ad campaigns and public service announcements (PSAs) that continually reinforced the idea of patriotic connections between the private sector—American industry—and the government. Together, they would win the war, but the need to sell goods and services remained in order to "Keep 'em Flying" and "Keep 'em Rolling," two popular slogans of the day.

The War Advertising Council cooperated with the Office of War Information (OWI) when placing any public service ads, especially those that referred to **scrap drives, rationing,** and the need for women in defense jobs. The image of **Rosie the Riveter** emerged, and countless ads appeared that displayed women in turbans and defense-plant attire hawking all manner of nondefense goods. Despite their obvious attempts to sell products, they also encouraged acceptance of women in the workforce. Wrigley's gum, for example, claimed chewing gum calmed "war nerves" and urged people to buy a package. Then, returning to the necessity of sacrifice in wartime, their advertising cautioned users to ration that package of gum by chewing each stick longer to make it last; in that way, limited supplies would go around, and everyone could enjoy a stick of Wrigley's.

Many wartime advertisements featured a small square or rectangle, usually in a lower corner of the overall composition, which said such things as "Let's back the attack! Buy Extra War Bonds"; "For Victory, Buy United States War Bonds and Stamps"; or, in the case of specific products (in this case, Studebaker), "Peacetime Builder of Fine Cars and Trucks, Wartime Builder of Wright Cyclone Engines for Boeing Flying Fortresses." Pepsi-Cola and Coca-Cola, long-time soft drink rivals, ran numerous ads throughout the war years extolling the virtues of their **beverages.** The themes of a needed break and the energy boost sodas provided allowed for considerable copy. Coke, more so than Pepsi, created a long series of ads dedicated to service personnel the world over. With illustrations by leading artists and using its well-known phrase, "the pause that refreshes," the company stressed that having a Coke with other people made lasting friendships and helped in the cause of peace.

Frequently, the advertising copy apologized for shortages and attempted to explain why services were not always what the consumer might expect. The sponsors urged public patience with any inconveniences brought about by the conflict. In one classic case, copywriter Nelson C. Metcalf, Jr. (active 1940s) created the New Haven Railroad's "The Kid in Upper 4" in 1942. The New Haven (now defunct), which covered southern New England from New York City to Boston, daily carried thousands of commuters, but during the war it also transported large numbers of U.S. troops headed for seaports and combat abroad.

Magazines ran the New Haven ad, and an accompanying drawing shows a youthful soldier lying awake in his upper berth as the train carries him toward an unknown future. The text urges displaced commuters to be patient. "If you have to stand enroute—*it is so he may have a seat.* If there is no berth for you—*it is so he may sleep.*" Widely reprinted and distributed after its initial appearance, the print ad crossed over into other media. Comedian Eddie Cantor (1892–1964) read the text on his NBC network **radio** show and later recorded it, and Metcalf's words even got set to music.

Among the products most advertised during the early 1940s were alcoholic beverages and cigarettes. Beer ads stressed the idea that having a cold glass of beer improved morale, not just for the civilian drinking it, but somehow for the soldiers and sailors—"ours and his"—far away from such homely comforts. This patriotic link between consumption and the war effort became an important and often-utilized motif for advertisers.

Johnny Roventini (1910–1998), in his bell captain costume, cried out on radio, "Call for-r-r Philip Mor-r-rss," a popular brand of cigarette made by the Virginia-based Philip Morris & Company. In person, the diminutive Roventini gave out free cigarettes at **canteens** and **USO** clubs, another example of industry support for the armed forces. The big **swing** bands quickly landed various tobacco companies as underwriters of their radio programs and concerts. R. J. Reynolds Tobacco sponsored Benny Goodman (1909–1986) and his popular aggregation on *Camel Caravan;* Liggett & Myers carried **Glenn Miller** (1904–1944) on *Chesterfield Time;* Raleighs and Kools, made by Brown & Williamson, boasted Tommy Dorsey (1905–1956) on the NBC network; the P. Lorillard Company, manufacturers of Old Gold cigarettes, underwrote Artie Shaw (1910–2004) and his orchestra on CBS; and, most famously, Lucky Strikes, a product of the American Tobacco Company, sponsored *Your Hit Parade,* a popular music show that ran on both radio and, later, **television.** Without exception, all of these programs featured music popular with both military personnel and the civilian public, and scripts made constant reference to "the boys overseas," solidifying associations between smoking and patriotism.

One of the most prominent cases of a cigarette company maximizing its perceived support for the war effort involved Lucky Strikes. The name had originated in 1871 as a chewing tobacco and evolved into a cigarette brand that would do well into the 1950s. A pack of Luckies had traditionally come in a dark green wrapper with a red bull's eye in the center; gold banding finished it off. During the late 1930s, researchers discovered that the package colors did not appeal to women, an important part of the smoking market. When World War II brought about the rationing of strategic materials, the company found that chromium went into the production of its green ink and copper for the gold trim. With these materials in short supply, the packaging would have to be altered.

George Washington Hill (1884–1946), the imperious but canny president of the American Tobacco Company, the manufacturer of Lucky Strikes, saw an opportunity. He had earlier commissioned Raymond Loewy (1893–1986), the distinguished industrial designer, to produce new packaging for Lucky Strikes that would increase the cigarettes' appeal to women. Loewy's **design** eliminated both the traditional green and gold, substituting a sleeker, less masculine pack in white. Only the red bull's eye remained.

When the new packaging appeared, Hill introduced a promotional campaign that said, "Lucky Strike Green has gone to war." It stressed the scarcity of chromium and copper and suggested how many additional tanks and artillery shells could now be turned out, thanks to the sacrifice being made by Luckies. The ads, of course, made no mention of increasing appeal to women, but as a result of this brilliant strategy, Lucky Strike sales rose 38 percent. People could feel good about smoking Luckies knowing that they assisted in the nation's defense, never realizing that the looks of the new pack also appealed to them and helped determine their selection. When they lit their Luckies or Chesterfields or Old Golds—or whatever brand—even the tiny matchbooks had printed on their covers "V for Victory," "Remember Pearl Harbor," "Loose Lips Sink Ships," and many other slogans in miniature. Advertisers left no stone unturned in promoting patriotism and commerce.

In 1943, the War Advertising Council, financially supported by the private sector, and dominated and run by business leaders, succeeded in influencing Congress to slash the OWI budget. In the eyes of both the Ad Council and Congress, free enterprise should not be hamstrung by government interference, a charge leveled at the OWI. An executive order terminated the OWI in 1945. After that, all public service ads went through the council only, which meant most public service messages, the copy donated by the council's own members, often displayed a strong, pro-business slant. The group dropped the word "war" from its name and reverted to just the Advertising (or Ad) Council in 1945. It continued to stress public service ads, but now dealt with such peacetime topics as registering to vote, highway safety, and forest fires. For example, the Ad Council worked closely with the National Safety Council to reduce highway accidents and invented the iconic Smoky the Bear in the summer of 1944. Its public relations arm set out to portray businesses as benevolent providers and then strove to create wants for a multitude of goods and services.

When peace returned in 1945, and the hard economic times of the Great Depression and the recent war-imposed austerity of the first half of the decade had become history, American ad agencies faced the challenge of touting postwar prosperity. It quickly became a job they relished. No rationing, new cars, innovative appliances, fashionable clothes—in short, abundance, an advertiser's dream. In five years, 1945 to 1950, ad expenditures doubled, rising from $2.9 billion to $5.7 billion (or from $26 billion to $51 billion in 2008 dollars). The amounts invested in advertising would grow even more rapidly during the 1950s and 1960s, surpassing any other economic indicators.

Once **automobiles** again began rolling off Detroit's assembly lines, they led the advertising charge, surpassing cigarettes and packaged goods, the two leaders during the earlier 1940s. Not only did spending on ads increase in the United States, most larger agencies (J. Walter Thompson; Young & Rubicam; BBDO [Batten, Barton, Durstine & Osborn]; Foote, Cone, & Belding; and others) commenced a new conquest of war-torn Europe, opening or expanding offices abroad in order to promote American goods.

Domestically, postwar copy became shorter and simpler, with color and vivid, arresting visuals replacing black and white. Illustrations tended toward the realistic and representational, creating a nostalgia for the "good old days" before economic crises and war. The rambling essay, perhaps accompanied by a pleasant bucolic scene, gave way to large, aggressive lettering that said little of any substance. As communication philosopher Marshall McLuhan (1911–1980) would later famously say in 1967, "the medium is the message." He meant that the advertisement itself, regardless of product or service, carried an implicit invitation to consume, and all else served as window dressing. Although most Americans probably realized that fact at some level of consciousness, it did little to dim the effectiveness of a well-composed ad.

A good example of an ad concealed as something else occurred in 1948. *Louisiana Story* (1948), a quasi-documentary directed by the renowned Robert Flaherty (1884–1951) and underwritten by the Standard Oil Company, appears to celebrate the region and its people, but really serves as a public relations coup for the corporation. Underlying the evocative photography by Richard Leacock (b. 1921), a famous cinematographer, there runs a continuous paean to Standard Oil. A memorable, prize-winning score by composer Virgil Thomson (1896–1989) reinforces the positive aspects of drilling for oil in the Acadian swampland, often making the quest for petroleum a heroic endeavor. Thus, without overtly saying so, an image of the inevitability of industrial progress and the benevolence of Standard Oil color the film. The fact that land will be destroyed, people uprooted, and a distinctive culture ignored never receives mention. Clearly, this defined the approach to public service ads the council envisioned.

At the same time, advertising agencies, anxious to remain in the good graces of the public, worked to refine their research methods, increasingly referred to as MR (for motivational research). They studied consumer habits and preferences all through the immediate postwar years, a procedure that would see increasing use in the 1950s. They also collected lengthy statistical data on incomes, occupations, **education,** marital status, preferred neighborhoods, and a wealth of other information in order to predict more accurately what would sell to whom and what would not. The era of the agency copywriter who relied on instincts—possibly honed by years of experience and trial and error—about consumer preferences drew to a close during the 1940s, replaced by a more scientific approach for creating ad campaigns. In 1957, author Vance Packard (1914–1996) would pen a best-selling book about MR and consumer manipulation titled *The Hidden Persuaders.* Much of its content concerns methodologies introduced in the late 1940s.

Although the postwar years witnessed a significant increase in advertising in all media—print, film, radio, even television—it all paled with the explosion of marketing that took place in the 1950s. Consumers soon forgot the relative austerity of the war years and immediately thereafter in a flood of advertising that swept over the country with the advent of the new decade and a continuing spiral of prosperity.

See also: Classical Music; Fashion; Illustrators; Photography; Posters; Radio Programming: Comedy Shows; Radio Programming: Music and Variety Shows; Trains

Selected Reading

Fox, Stephen. *The Mirror Makers: A History of American Advertising and Its Creators.* New York: William Morrow, 1984.

Goodrum, Charles, and Helen Dalrymple. *Advertising in America: The First 200 Years.* New York: Harry N. Abrams, 1990.

Holme, Bryan. *The Art of Advertising.* London: Peerage Books, 1985.

Lears, Jackson. *Fables of Abundance: A Cultural History of Advertising in America.* New York: Basic Books, 1994.

ALL-GIRL ORCHESTRAS

Bandleaders may have thought World War II would have little effect on their orchestras, but the military draft (Selective Service), initiated in the fall of 1940, and its consequences deeply affected the music business. As more and more male musicians went into service, conscription created the phenomenon of women instrumentalists entering the ranks of previously all-male ensembles. As a rule, they encountered considerable resistance and discrimination from critics, the public, and often their own sidemen in the bands. A few, however, cracked the big time and achieved modest success.

Some of the women appearing with top-flight but mostly male organizations were vibraphonist Marjorie Hyams (b. 1923), who established her credentials with Woody Herman; Melba Liston (1926–1999), who played in the trombone section of the 1940s band led by Gerald Wilson (1918–2008); and guitarist Mary Osborne (1921–1992), who performed with several bands, including Joe Venuti (1903–1978) and Stuff Smith (1909–1967). Pianist Mary Lou Williams (1910–1981, nee Mary Elfrieda Scruggs) became, in the 1930s, a star in her own right, especially as a composer in the **boogie-woogie** vein. During the 1940s, Williams wrote, arranged, played, and generally became a mainstay for the groups led by Andy Kirk (1898–1992). Countless other women labored in relative anonymity, occasionally with well-known orchestras, more often with second- and third-tier groups. Some remained for long stays and others for brief stopovers, but virtually all of them possessed American Federation of Musicians (AFM) union cards and could more than hold their own with their male counterparts, despite an endless barrage of snide remarks about their abilities.

The declining pool of eligible male musicians also gave rise to the "girl bands," a situation where women formed commercial groups of their own. No one would have thought to say "women's bands" in those less gender-sensitive times; regardless of age, they were girls playing in all-girl aggregations. Not an entirely new phenomenon, a few girl bands had existed prior to World War II, groups that billed themselves as novelties and capitalized on gender.

Three pioneers in this area were Peggy Gilbert (1905–2007), Ina Ray Hutton (1916–1984; nee Odessa Cowan), and a man, Phil Spitalny (1890–1970). Gilbert, who both led the way and outlived them all, played saxophone and led a number of groups under her name. She started out leading her first band, the Melody Girls, in 1923.

The once virtually all-male preserve of commercial bands faced hard times during the war years, and the simultaneous rise of all-girl ensembles demonstrated how capable many of these groups could be. Phil Spitalny, a pioneer in this area, led his own orchestra, the Hour of Charm, beginning in the mid-1930s. He is seen here in the early 1940s, fronting his aggregation of women musicians. Spitalny insisted they always dress in formal gowns. (Photofest)

For the next 60 years, Gilbert fronted various **swing**-oriented aggregations and sometimes appeared on bills with the likes of Benny Goodman (1909–1986) and Louis Prima (1910–1978).

Hutton led one of the best of the early girl bands, the Melodears. The ensemble featured the nonplaying Hutton herself, billed as "the Blonde Bombshell of Rhythm." Attired in tight, slinky gowns, she exuded seductive sex appeal while waving her baton. She formed the Melodears in 1934, and the group prospered, appearing in several film shorts and a part in the full-length feature movie, *The Big Broadcast of 1936* (1935). Shortly after dissolving the orchestra in 1939, Hutton formed an all-male group that lasted until 1944—a curious decision, since men qualified to play in a professional band were in increasingly short supply, given the pressures of World War II. With this new group, she called herself "Queen of the Name Bands." Hutton continued in the music business in the postwar era, forming another all-girl group and then moving on to **television** in 1950. She also stars (as herself) in a low-budget 1944 movie musical titled *Ever Since Venus*. During the Swing Era, however, Hutton and the Melodears earned some well-deserved fame as the only prominent women's band of that period.

Entrepreneur Phil Spitalny (1890–1970), who had endured a nondescript career in popular music during the 1920s, emerged a pioneer in the area of promoting women for roles as competent, professional instrumentalists when he devised the gimmick—no other word adequately describes what he sought—of an orchestra comprised entirely of women. In 1934, the same year Hutton introduced her Melodears, he realized his dream when he unveiled a group that he immodestly called Phil Spitalny and His All-Girl Orchestra. Unlike Hutton's blatant sex appeal, Spitalny emphasized class and decorum in his productions, and it paid off. He landed a contract in 1935 with CBS **radio** for a music show that received the name "The Hour of Charm," a term quickly transferred to the aggregation itself. Despite the program's title, the broadcast ran only 30 minutes, but it earned good ratings throughout the year. Arch-rival NBC noted its success and picked up the show for the next decade, 1936–1946, only to have CBS regain it for another two years, 1946–1948.

Hardly a driving swing band, Spitalny's crew played light classics and a lot of schmaltz, all part of his concept of "musical femininity." The Hour of Charm Orchestra at times boasted a choir, and it always featured strings, harp, and piano, instruments that he considered more "ladylike" than brass or reeds—although the aggregation had the requisite trumpets, trombones, and saxophones, too. When on tour, the Hour of Charm staged elaborate production numbers. Aside from Spitalny himself, Evelyn Kaye Klein (1911–1990; sometimes listed as "Evelyn Silverstone" or "Evelyn and Her Magic Violin") took honors as star of the show. The "magic violin," reputedly a rare Italian model, received a workout from Evelyn, because she preferred virtuoso numbers. Radio success led to Hollywood, first for some shorts, and then parts in two features, *When Johnny Comes Marching Home* (1942) and *Here Come the Coeds* (1945). The novelty of his all-girl orchestra eventually wore off, especially in light of similar groups performing throughout the war years, but Spitalny and his ensemble helped break the ice and survived until the early days of television. In addition, he and Evelyn, who also served as concertmaster during the heyday of the organization, wed in 1946.

Gilbert, Hutton, and Spitalny legitimatized the idea of women performing professionally in orchestras. Their acceptance opened the doors for others, and the later 1930s and early 1940s, especially with the war, saw a number of new all-girl bands attempting to make a go of it. One of the best called itself the International Sweethearts of Rhythm. Originally an all-black orchestra, the group was formed in 1937 to raise funds for the Piney Woods Country Life School, a rural Mississippi institution for poor or orphaned minority girls. When the band toured, the members actually lived in their bus, given the racial segregation of the region. In time, their traveling took them to larger cities, and they received favorable reviews as a good, solid swing orchestra. In 1940, they severed their connection to Piney Woods School and moved to northern Virginia as a commercial act and took paid bookings at some of the best clubs in the East.

As the performance skills and professionalism of the Sweethearts of Rhythm increased, Eddie Durham (1906–1987), a former **Count Basie** (1904–1984) arranger, came aboard as the band's music director. He guided the outfit into the first rank of touring bands. Durham himself went on to become "The Sepia Phil Spitalny" by

TABLE 2. Some Other All-Girl Orchestras Active during the 1940s

Clora Bryant and the Queens of Swing	Joy Cayler and Her All-Girl Orchestra
Herb Cook's Swinghearts	Count Berni Vici's All-Girl Theater Band
Al D'Artega's All-Girl Orchestra	Dixie Rhythm Girls
Bonnie Downs' All-Girl Orchestra	Frances Grey's Queens of Swing
Harlem Play-Girls	Nita King and Her Queens of Rhythm
Ada Leonard's All-American Girl Orchestra	Betty McGuire's Sub-Debs
Jean Parks and Her All-Girl Band	Rita Rio and Her All-Girl Orchestra
The Sharon Rogers All-Girl Orchestra	The Freddie Shaffer All-Girl Band
Viola Smith and the Coquettes	The Swinging Rays of Rhythm
The Syncoettes	Virgil Whyte's Musical Sweethearts

working with the All-Star Girl Orchestra and the Darlings of Rhythm in the 1940s, two other swinging all-girl bands that went on the professional touring circuit.

At the end of the war, the International Sweethearts of Rhythm performed for U.S. troops in **USO** shows staged in Europe and also recorded for RCA Victor, a leading label. Despite problems with both racial and gender-based prejudice, this unusual all-woman organization, one of the most successful both commercially and artistically of its type, continued to entertain audiences until 1949.

In a similar vein, Prairie View A & M University, situated in southeast Texas, organized the Prairie View Co-eds in 1943, a band set up as the women's counterpart to the college's all-male Prairie View Collegians. When the wartime draft took most of the Collegians' musicians, the Co-eds became the dominant band on campus and went on tour. The youthful players at Prairie View, founded as a black school, had to face the same problems of segregation and prejudice the International Sweethearts of Rhythm endured. Despite their formidable musical skills, the Co-eds never enjoyed the perks of fame, such as bookings in posh nightclubs or movie contracts; they instead labored in relative obscurity, an endless succession of one-nighters in small towns, traveling in rickety buses to play in gyms, theaters, and small dance halls.

Even with the difficulties facing all-girl bands, the idea spread, and promoters found the talent they needed to form groups throughout the later 1930s and on into the war years. The following list does not begin to name every orchestra active during that period and serves instead to suggest the sheer numbers of women playing in organized musical ensembles.

Whether playing with bands of their own or with male-dominated orchestras, the strong presence of women in popular music lasted only for the duration of the conflict, or until the troops started coming home; with peace, returning sidemen picked up their dusty instruments and resumed their musical employment at the expense of those women who had, often to their dismay, only temporarily replaced them. For most women in the music field, second-class citizenship accompanied their chosen profession. The "real" musicians continued to be men, a situation that continued for the remainder of the 20th century.

See also: Bebop (Bop); Jazz; Musicals (Film); Race Relations and Stereotyping; Rosie the Riveter; Selective Training and Service Act of 1940 (Selective Service, or Draft)

Selected Reading

Dahl, Linda. *Stormy Weather: The Music and Lives of a Century of Jazzwomen.* Pompton Plains, NJ: Limelight Editions, 1989.

Tucker, Sherrie. *Swing Shift: "All-Girl" Bands of the 1940s.* Durham, NC: Duke University Press, 2000.

ANDREWS SISTERS, THE

When the **Swing** era big bands began to lose some of their steam in the late 1930s and early 1940s, smaller instrumental ensembles, along with countless vocal groups and vocalists, waited in the wings for their chance at fame and fortune. The bands had begun increasingly to feature arrangements that called for vocal accompaniment, making stars out of singers like Doris Day (b. 1924), Ella Fitzgerald (1917–1996), Dick Haymes (1918–1980), Peggy Lee (1920–2002), **Frank Sinatra** (1915–1998), and Jo Stafford (1917–2008). Among the vocal groups, none sparkled more brightly than the Andrews Sisters.

The trio consisted of real-life sisters LaVerne (1911–1967), Maxene (1916–1995), and Patty (b. 1918) Andrews. While growing up, they had listened closely to the family

The three Andrews sisters—LaVerne, Maxene, and Patty—rose to the top ranks of popular music during the 1940s. Often teamed with Bing Crosby, shown here, but important in their own right, their close harmony and impeccable rhythm gave them an unprecedented string of hits for a vocal group. (Photofest)

radio whenever a recording by the Boswell Sisters (Martha, 1905–1958; Connee, 1907–1976; and Helvetia, or "Vet," 1911–1988) played. A popular trio that rose to stardom during the late 1920s, the Boswell Sisters utilized close harmony and improvisation, skills that greatly influenced the jazzy style the Andrews Sisters developed in the mid-1930s.

They cut their first recordings in 1937 for Decca Records, one of the biggest American record companies, and late that year gained recognition with "Bei Mir Bist Du Schon (Means That You're Grand)," a tune that catapulted them into the front ranks of music stars. For that effort, they initially received a flat $50 (roughly $750 in 2008 dollars) with no subsequent royalties. But "Bei Mir Bist Du Schon (Means That You're Grand)" changed the sisters' circumstances, and Decca renegotiated, signing them to a more reasonable and retroactive contract. The company had previously boasted the Boswell Sisters on its label, but when that trio broke up in 1937, Decca wanted a replacement and found it with the Andrews Sisters.

No vocal group, past or present, has ever surpassed them in popularity, and they boasted record sales of approximately 100 million disks over their 36-year career. That total includes over 600 individual song titles. More remarkable still, at least 100 of their recordings made the charts, and almost 50 of them reached the top 10, with 19 of them achieving first place for a time.

TABLE 3. Top 10 Charted Songs Performed by the Andrews Sisters, 1938–1950

Year	Song	Highest Chart Position
1938	"Bei Mir Bist Du Schon (Means That You're Grand)"	No. 1
1939	"Hold Tight (Want Some Seafood, Mama)"	No. 1
1940	"Yodelin' Jive" [with Bing Crosby]	No. 3
	"Say 'Si Si' (Para Vigo Me Voy)"	No. 3
1941	"(I'll Be with You) In Apple Blossom Time"	No. 5
1942	"Strip Polka"	No. 2
1943	"Pistol Packin' Mama" [with Bing Crosby]	No. 1
1944	"Shoo-Shoo Baby"	No. 9
	"Don't Fence Me In" [with Bing Crosby]	No. 8
	"(There'll Be a) Hot Time in the Town of Berlin (When the Yanks Go Marching in)" [with Bing Crosby]	No. 6
	"Is You Is Or Is You Ain't (Ma' Baby)" [with Bing Crosby]	No. 1
1945	"Rum and Coca-Cola"	No. 10
	"Ac-Cent-Tchu-Ate the Positive" [with Bing Crosby]	No. 1
	"Along the Navajo Trail" [with Bing Crosby]	No. 1
1946	"South America, Take It Away" [with Bing Crosby]	No. 1
1947	"Near You"	No. 1
	"Civilization (Bongo, Bongo, Bongo)" [with Danny Kaye]	No. 2
1948	"Toolie Oolie Doolie (The Yodel Polka)"	No. 3
1948	"Underneath the Arches"	No. 1
1949	[No Charted Songs]	
1950	"I Can Dream, Can't I?"	No. 1
	"I Wanna Be Loved"	No. 2

As the preceding table indicates, with the exception of 1949, the trio made the top 10 charts every year from 1938 through 1950; their banner year proved to be 1944, with four hits, closely followed by 1945, with three big sellers. In all, they enjoyed 21 top-10 music hits during this period, with countless others also listed among the top 50 for each of those years, a remarkable accomplishment. Several recordings that later generations tend to associate with the Andrews Sisters—"Beer Barrel Polka" (1939), "Beat Me, Daddy, Eight to the Bar" (1940), "The **Boogie Woogie** Bugle Boy (of Company B)" (1941), and "Don't Sit Under the Apple Tree (with Anyone Else but Me)" (1942)—came relatively early in the trio's career and initially did not achieve high rankings on the hit charts. Over time, however, these tunes did extremely well and can now be counted among their most successful and enduring performances.

An auspicious, albeit informal, musical partnership between **Bing Crosby** (1903–1977) and the Andrews Sisters resulted in 47 recordings on which the four sang together. It commenced in 1940 with "Yodelin' Jive," a surprise hit. Although none of the sisters read music, they worked well with Crosby, and he soon asked for them at recording sessions. The pairing paid off: 23 of their collaborative efforts made the charts, and they continued to work together for many years.

In addition to their unparalleled success in the recording studio, they also appeared in 13 motion pictures, beginning with a Ritz Brothers comedy, *Argentine Nights* (1940), in which they play themselves. Universal Studios quickly signed them, and 12 more films featured the threesome between 1941 and 1948; their voices can also be heard on the soundtracks of numerous **movies** made after 1948. Although they substituted energy and good humor for polished acting skills, and most of the productions in which they appear fall into the B-picture category, the films nevertheless did well at the box office.

As they became established stars, the Andrews Sisters performed at night clubs, on stage, radio, and eventually on **television.** In the fall of 1944, they headlined *The Andrews Sisters Eight-to-the-Bar Ranch* on **ABC** radio. It ran for a year and evolved into *The N-K Musical Show* (the N-K stands for Nash-Kelvinator, the program's sponsors), which remained on the air until mid-1946. They were regulars also on *Club Fifteen*, a 15-minute musical variety show, throughout the later 1940s. In addition, they could frequently be heard on numerous other programs, making them a true presence on radio broadcasting of the day.

During the war years, the Andrews Sisters performed tirelessly to help the nation's efforts to support the troops and raise money for bonds. They traveled with **USO** shows and sang at **canteens,** their cheery manner a sure way to boost the morale of both civilians and military personnel. Able to sing in virtually any style, but especially in swing and boogie-woogie formats, they turned out to be the premier vocal group of the decade.

See also: *ASCAP vs. BMI* Radio Boycott and the AFM Recording Ban; Comedies (Film); Country Music; Jukeboxes; Radio Programming: Music and Variety Shows; War Bonds

Suggested Reading

Jones, John Bush. *The Songs that Fought the War: Popular Music and the Home Front, 1939–1945.* Waltham, MA: Brandeis University Press, 2006.

Young, William H., and Nancy K. Young. *American Music through History: The World War II Era.* Westport, CT: Greenwood Publishing Group, 2005.

ARCHITECTURE

The imposing government office buildings and monuments erected in Washington, DC, during the 1930s, along with Spanish haciendas and Tudor manors built as private residences in neighborhoods across the land, represented a long, last gasp of conservative architectural tradition. In a slightly more modern vein, art deco, with its chevrons and zigzags and seemingly so important in the 1920s and into the 1930s, had begun to peter out around 1940 and virtually disappeared in the immediate postwar years. Streamline moderne, art deco's likely successor, had a brief moment during the later 1930s and early 1940s, and then likewise went into a sudden decline.

Larger, nonresidential buildings of the 1940s. After making sporadic appearances during the Depression, the International Style waited in the wings to become the dominant commercial fashion of the 1940s. A manner of building that had gained popularity with progressive architects in Europe during the latter years of the 1920s, its geometric linearity and lack of surface adornment found appeal in some circles, especially for larger buildings. It looked sleek and modern, and the absence of applied decorative elements permitted considerable financial savings during the construction process.

The early 1930s had left a legacy of splendid commercial structures, including the art deco Chrysler Building (1930), the modernistic Empire State Building (1931), the soaring Rockefeller Center complex with it many uses (1931–1939), and the Philadelphia Savings Fund Society Building (1932) and its imaginative application of the International Style. The Great Depression stalled much construction for the next few years, but toward the end of the 1930s, Frank Lloyd Wright (1867–1959) reasserted his claim as one of America's greatest architects with the Johnson's Wax buildings (1936–1939) in Racine, Wisconsin. He followed that triumph some 10 years later with the streamlined Johnson's Research Tower (1948–1950, also Racine).

This photograph of Frank Lloyd Wright was taken in 1949, when the architect had reached an age that many associate with retirement. For Wright, however, his career would continue to soar until his death, and many significant commissions still lay ahead of him. (Photofest)

In 1939, Edward Durrell Stone (1902–1978), working with Philip Johnson (1906–2005), made the Manhattan site of the Museum of Modern Art fit the International Style mold, one of the few museums from that era to reflect modernist thinking. Albert Kahn (1869–1942), who had been a force in industrial architecture throughout much of the 20th century, in the early 1940s designed factories that placed considerable stress on window walls for maximum interior light, or what he called "the daylight factory." Perhaps unknowingly, Kahn presaged a striking characteristic of postwar contemporary buildings, structures sheathed in glass.

The New York World's Fair of 1939–1940, with its motto "Building the World of Tomorrow," promised a streamlined future, where everything would run smoothly. But World War II brought a sudden halt to most attempts to broaden the aesthetic boundaries of **design;** with both materials and manpower in short supply, and working under strict time limits, the construction that occurred during the war years (1941–1945) reflected the austerity of the period. And although the surrender of the Axis powers in 1945 would seem to have set the stage for significant advances in the styles of large buildings, much nonresidential construction following the war in actuality observed a spare, technological format. Architects, in a rush to fill overdue needs, omitted any romantic or decorative elements. They instead stressed practical services, such as air conditioning, heating, lighting, and acoustics, and these utilitarian amenities often became formal elements of the overall plan. New building types, such as larger airport terminals, shopping centers, parking garages, and even highways also became commonplace, but not in any great numbers until the 1950s. Landscaping and the retention of open space also received more attention; a building need not occupy every inch of its site, but these concerns proved slow in coming.

Little of architectural significance therefore transpired during the later 1940s; the great designs associated with the postwar era had to wait, for the most part, until the early 1950s. With the return to peace, the severe International Style slowly asserted itself, and smooth surfaces of glass and steel, along with aluminum and considerable concrete, would characterize office towers in years to come. The few exceptions between 1946 and 1949 included Pietro Belluschi (1899–1994), working in Portland, Oregon. He designed the Equitable Life Assurance Building in 1944 (final construction did not occur until 1948), a structure that provided a dramatic foretaste of the glass box commercial buildings of the 1950s. Similarly, Wallace K. Harrison (1895–1981), among others, in 1949 contributed the slablike **United Nations** Secretariat in New York City.

While the likes of Kahn, Belluschi, and Harrison created plans that served as predictors of later architecture, several of their counterparts challenged the prevailing red-brick Georgian and gray medieval gothic-style designs that had long influenced the look of American college campuses. Ludwig Mies van der Rohe (1886–1969), who came to the United States from Germany in 1939, almost immediately began planning a striking new campus for the Chicago-based Illinois Institute of Technology. Spare and modern in all respects, and a break in academic tradition, his project would continue into the mid-1950s. At about the same time, Frank Lloyd Wright received a commission to lay out a master plan for new buildings at Florida Southern College in Lakeland. As with Mies, Wright would pursue this undertaking until the 1950s, creating a distinctive work that defies categorization other than "Wrightian." Finally, Finnish architect Alvar Aalto (1898–1976), who had impressed everyone with his striking and influential Finnish Pavilion at the New York World's Fair in 1939, received an invitation from the Massachusetts Institute of Technology to design a dormitory along the banks of the Charles River in Cambridge. The resultant Baker House dorm (1947–1949) gave its residents views of the river from its undulating facade. His use of natural materials and respect for the site hinted at innovative approaches to building that only became commonplace some years later.

One other area of noncommercial, nonresidential architecture that in the 1940s began breaking with past traditions involved ideas for ecclesiastical, or church, architecture. In Columbus, Indiana, a small town that welcomed modernity in building, Eliel and Eero Saarinen (1873–1950; 1910–1961), father and son, designed the Church of Christ in 1940–1942. One of the first truly modern churches in the United States, it reflected the International Style in its stark linearity. Several years later, the always-pioneering Wright contributed the Unitarian Church in Madison, Wisconsin (1947–1951). The prow-like exterior of its sanctuary resembles for some a pair of hands raised in prayer and demonstrated again that Wright would never be tied to particular styles other than his own.

Only with the onset of the 1950s did the landmark buildings that have come to define modernity in commercial architecture begin to rise in any numbers. The firm of Skidmore, Owings & Merrill (better known as SOM; the initials stand for Louis Skidmore, Nathaniel Owings, and John Merrill; 1897–1962, 1903–1984, and 1896–1975, respectively) became a leader in the field. Thanks to the vision of Gordon Bunshaft (1909–1990), an important architect within the company, SOM in 1952 built the Lever House on New York's Park Avenue, an elegant glass box that features glass and stainless steel curtain walls surrounding the entire structure. It ushered in a period of unparalleled postwar commercial building. Mies van der Rohe designed the elegant Lakeshore Drive Apartments in Chicago at this time, and shortly thereafter he, along with Philip Johnson, would contribute the striking Seagram Building (1954–1958) to the New York skyline. Many other notable structures followed, but they all came after the 1940s.

Housing and residential building during the 1940s. Although the war curtailed the majority of commercial plans, it simultaneously created the need for large-scale housing projects. Thousands of workers found employment in huge new aircraft factories and ship-building facilities, as the "arsenal of democracy" that **President Franklin Delano Roosevelt** (1882–1945) had so famously promised in a speech given in December of 1940, took shape. Envisioned as planned communities, most wartime housing went up hurriedly, and architects seldom received the attention they deserved, with the result their ideas had little impact in the planning processes. Most planners that rose to prominence during the 1930s and 1940s persisted in thinking in terms of standardization and collectivism. The residents moving into these new housing and apartment tracts had to coordinate their individual needs to sometimes grandiose ideas about collective living.

Exceptions fortunately did occur. In New Kensington, a town near Pittsburgh, architects Walter Gropius (1883–1969) and Marcel Breuer (1902–1981), both recent European émigrés, in 1941 created workers' housing that earned considerable praise. Hugh Stubbins Jr. (1912–2006) did likewise in 1942 at Windsor Locks, Connecticut, planning 85 homes in a simplified Cape Cod style to house defense workers.

The aforementioned firm of Skidmore, Owings & Merrill, before it had made such an important name for itself in the 1950s, assisted in designing Oak Ridge, Tennessee, the community that had much to do with the development of the **atomic bomb.**

Between its founding in 1942 and 1946, Oak Ridge grew to 75,000 people, and SOM played an important role in that gargantuan task. Channel Heights, a community in San Pedro, outside Los Angeles, had been established near several shipyards. Richard Neutra (1892–1970) in 1943 designed 600 modernistic units for this equally fast-growing town. That same year, Henry Churchill (1893–1962) worked to create 350 units in the development of Aquackanonk, a section of Clifton, New Jersey. In 1944, San Lorenzo Village, located a short distance from San Francisco and Oakland and overseen by developer David Dewey Bohannon (1898–1995), saw 1,500 units erected to house defense workers in the Bay area.

In all, thousands of houses and apartments were rushed to completion around the nation during the war years, but only a minority boasted much architectural distinction for mass-produced housing. The end result had the effect of further separating wealthier Americans from poorer ones, at least in housing. For those who could afford a custom-designed home, the 1940s produced some individuality in upper-class neighborhoods, whereas a sense of sameness pervaded poorer ones.

In the aftermath of the war, a considerable deficit in needed residential building had occurred despite the attempts to provide adequate shelter. Overwhelming demands on supplies and labor showed that the arsenal of democracy could not be shut down overnight, and so the transition to full-scale consumer production took several years. In addition, archaic building codes and dated union rules paralyzed innovation so that builders could not put in place the very things architects said they wanted. Some wartime restrictions on building materials, especially steel, also persisted during 1947 and 1948, further slowing down residential construction. In the meantime, the soldiers came home, their wives had babies, the **GI Bill** provided mortgage money at favorable rates, and yet good housing proved hard to find.

By the later 1940s, however, the postwar building boom finally commenced. In their haste to satisfy demand, developers usually offered modern appliances and more spacious interiors than in the past, but exteriors tended to be bland, as if stamped out by cookie cutters. By and large, postwar housing lacked proportion, texture, and color. The picture windows looked out on sameness, not something attractive.

Once again, a handful of forward-looking architects bucked these trends. Out of this attitude emerged the contemporary ranch-style house. Americans have long been fascinated with their Western heritage. The 1930s and 1940s proved no exception. Music of the era had innumerable Western-themed pop songs, such as "Back in the Saddle Again" (1940) and "I've Got Spurs that Jingle Jangle Jingle" (1942), and compositions such as *Rodeo* (1942). **Western movies** featured such cowboy stars as **Gene Autry** (1907–1998), **Roy Rogers** (1911–1998) and **William Boyd** (1895–1972, but better known as Hopalong Cassidy), and kids emulated them with their own cowboy outfits and toy six-shooters. The exploits of Red Ryder and the Cisco Kid appeared in **comic books, comic strips,** and on **radio.** In short, American popular culture emphasized the West in many ways, and most people carried, consciously or subconsciously, an awareness of the country's Western myths.

It should therefore come as no surprise that architecture would also reflect this background, and the most obvious manifestation of the Western heritage for the 1940s appeared with the rise in popularity of the ranch-style home, although it would not achieve real dominance until the 1950s. Although few true ranch buildings ever looked too much like the thousands built after World War II, home buyers relished the symbolism they saw in these new homes. Long and low, with a front picture window looking out on the wide open spaces (more likely their neighbors' houses), with a patch of green grass and maybe an outdoor barbeque, it appealed to that streak of rugged individualism so dear to most Americans.

On the West Coast, William W. Wurster (1895–1973) quietly created houses that featured spacious, open interiors in a style he called soft modernism; Oregon-based Pietro Belluschi designed homes as early as 1941 that looked ahead to the ubiquitous ranch houses of the 1950s. Harwell H. Harris (1903–1990), displaying a sensitivity to materials, worked to blend the interior with the exterior, house and site. His Wyle House, built in Ojai, California, in 1948, also presaged ranch designs. A major California developer, Cliff May (1908–1989), even claimed himself to be "the father of the California ranch style," although it could be argued that others shared in that parentage. Another real estate developer, Joseph Eichler (1900–1974), built countless postwar homes in the Palo Alto area from 1949 onward, creating subdivisions known as Sunnyvale, Sunnymount, University Gardens, and others.

Several important California architects also attempted more modernistic designs for private residences. Richard Neutra, another European émigré, brought elements of the International Style to the justly famous Kaufmann House in Palm Springs and to the Tremaine House in Santa Barbara (both 1946). Neither of Neutra's plans found a wide audience; costly materials, unique sites, and a futuristic look deterred the average buyer. Charles and Ray Eames (1907–1978, 1912–1988) in 1949 built a modern house for themselves in Santa Monica. In order to hold down costs, they utilized readily available off-the-shelf components, but the Eames's house remained too ahead of its time for most tastes.

While architects based on the West Coast popularized the ranch-style home, Royal Barry Wills (1895–1962) made his own Eastern variations on the design. During the 1940s, he created houses based on the traditional New England Cape Cod plan, sometimes adding a salt box effect, also a New England tradition. But his long, low homes also relied heavily on the ranch patterns emerging in California. Wills thus created a hybrid that spoke to the long history of the Cape Cod on the East Coast and reflected the growing popularity of the Western-tinged ranch.

When developer William Levitt (1907–1994) began planning the first of his Levittowns, he used a basic Cape Cod design for his introductory models. In 1947, he and his planners chose an expanse of potato fields near Hicksville, Long Island, for this experiment in massive suburban building, and it proved a rousing success. He would later build other Levittowns in Pennsylvania (1952) and New Jersey (1955). As the Long Island development expanded, he broadened the style choices slightly, eventually adding ranch models in the early 1950s.

While either traditional housing or the ranch style became the primary choices of Eastern home buyers in the later 1940s, several architects, like their West Coast colleagues, experimented with more daring approaches to residential design. Mies van der Rohe planned a modern classic with the Farnsworth House (Plano, Illinois) in

1946. Essentially an elegant glass box, it was not constructed until 1951, but it reflects his thinking about plain, unadorned steel frames sheathed in glass, much as he would later do at the Illinois Institute of Technology. Marcel Breuer created the forward-looking Geller House in Lawrence, Long Island, also in 1946. Its "butterfly roofs," as he termed them, sloped toward the center of the structure, challenging tradition. He would go on to design dozens more modern houses, but seldom found popular acclaim. His personal dwelling in New Canaan, Connecticut, long and low, combines natural stone and glass; begun in 1947, its horizontality suggests a ranch in many ways.

Philip Johnson in 1949 created perhaps the most famous glass box house of the era with his own home in New Canaan. A rectangle, all in glass with minimal framing components, it offers unobstructed views of its wooded setting. As critics were quick to point out, it also offers equally unobstructed views of its interior to anyone outside the house. Despite these reservations, the Johnson House has become an icon of post-war modern design.

Any discussion of residential design must also consider the contributions of Frank Lloyd Wright, the master iconoclast of American architecture. The 1936 house he called Fallingwater (Bear Run, Pennsylvania) took the precepts of the International Style and ended up as one of his greatest designs. Wright then moved on to smaller, less expensive, less elaborate plans with a series of homes he labeled Usonian houses (the term, a neologism, combines U.S. and a "-nian" suffix suggesting a collective group, in this case, the citizens of the United States). Built during the late 1930s and into the 1940s, many of his Usonian designs incorporate strong ranch-style elements—one story, a stress on the horizontal, low roofs—that put him in league with the trends of the period.

The housing shortage of the later 1940s also generated interest in prefabricated residences. If the structural components of a building could be standardized, manufactured, and then shipped to a site, many felt that costs would be reduced and great savings achieved in the needed assembly time. Little came of these discussions, with one significant exception: the prefabricated Lustron House. Devised by inventor Carl Strandlund (1899–1974) in the mid-1940s, he foresaw a large market for an inexpensive ready-made house that combined attractiveness and durability. Strandlund cobbled together a small manufacturing facility in Columbus, Ohio, and began to promote his invention.

He initially quoted preproduction prices of his Lustron homes at about $7,000 (about $63,000 in 2008 dollars), which, depending on the model, made them competitive with traditional residences. Strandlund proposed to make all the necessary parts at his factory, ship them to the buyer's site, whereupon a new house could be assembled in just a matter of days. Instead of wood, his frame, walls, ceilings, and roof would be made of steel panels with a baked-on enamel finish available in eight muted pastel colors. Not only would a Lustron house be fire-, lightning-, rust-, and rodent-proof, it required little maintenance. Easy soap-and-water cleanup would keep it sparkling, inside and out, for years.

The company advertised four models ranging from just under 1,000 square feet to just over 1,200 square feet. Architecturally speaking, Lustron homes tended to be rather nondescript, a basic one-story box with little originality in its design, and prices eventually ranged from about $6,000 to $10,000 (or from $54,000 to about $90,000 in 2008 dollars), plus the lot chosen by the owner. Public curiosity nevertheless ran high, and Strandlund eventually had 20,000 units on order. Between 1949 and 1950, his company built about 2,500 houses. Lack of sufficient capitalization, delays in assembly and shipping, and flagging customer interest caused the firm to declare bankruptcy in 1950, thus ending the most concerted attempt to introduce prefabricated housing to the American market. Around the country, several dozen Lustron houses still exist, living up to their claims of exceptional durability

One final structure from the 1940s merits mention: the lowly Quonset hut. So named because many early models were fabricated at Quonset Point in Rhode Island, they have come to be one of the most enduring building types from the war years, although they seldom receive much attention in architectural histories. But these durable, all-purpose structures were assembled by the tens of thousands for Allied military forces around the world. An outgrowth of the similar British Nissan hut from World War I, Quonset huts constituted a rediscovery of sorts. Faced with a shortage of strong but portable structures for both personnel and materiel, officials looked to the past success of the Nissan hut, improved on it, and proceeded to mass produce the ungainly structure.

Built as a half-cylinder that would rest, curved side up, on either a foundation or, in battlefield conditions, bare earth, the exterior of a Quonset hut consisted of galvanized steel laid over a wooden frame. Precut plywood sections then sealed either end. The basic size for most huts measured 20 feet in width and 48 feet in length, which allowed for an approximate 10-foot height at it highest point. Many variations also became available. Following the conflict, the government sold the huts as war surplus, and untold numbers of private citizens bought them cheaply as farm outbuildings, storage units, garages, auto repair shops, and countless other uses. Some became temporary churches, and others served as school rooms. Users were limited only by their imaginations. Newly made Quonset huts can still be purchased economically through specialty catalogs, metal fabricators, and large building supply centers. Because so many were built during World War II, Quonset huts remain an enduring reminder of the 1940s.

For the average person, while the new commercial structures going up in postwar America were impressive, the greatest architectural impacts were felt in the countless suburban tracts filled with middle-class houses built with mass-produced materials and cookbook designs.

See also: Baby Boom; Children's Films; Classical Music; Copland, Aaron; Fashion; Lawns, Lawnmowers, and Fertilizers; Levittown and Suburbanization; Radio Programming: Children's Shows, Serials, and Adventure Series; Rationing; Serial Films; Technology

Selected Reading
Handlin, David P. *American Architecture.* London: Thames & Hudson, 1985.
Hess, Alan. *Ranch House.* New York: Harry N. Abrams, 2004.
Shanken, Andrew M. *194X: Architecture, Planning, and Consumer Culture on the American Home Front.* Minneapolis: University of Minnesota Press, 2009.
Stern, Robert A. M. *Pride of Place: Building the American Dream.* Boston: Houghton Mifflin, 1986.

ART (PAINTING)

Prior to the 1940s, American art, particularly in the area of painting, had been conservative and dominated by realism, both urban and rural. The regionalist painters of the 1930s, as well as those working in the areas of social consciousness and protest during the Great Depression commanded most critical and popular attention. Numerous aspects of more modern movements in art also persisted, quietly and less obviously, always in the background, ready to burst forth at some later time.

Regardless of style, the federal government had a hand in the directions art would follow, at least until the early 1940s. The Works Progress Administration, or WPA, had been created during 1935—a wide-ranging New Deal project that, among other things, provided employment for artists. Renamed the Work Projects Administration in 1939, it allowed many talented people to pursue their creative interests, especially in the form of the Federal Arts Project (FAP). Countless colorful murals, **posters,** booklets, and the like brightened a dreary Depression environment.

Because familiarity with art usually came through prints, reproductions, and illustrations, exposure to secondhand works caused most citizens to function as spectators instead of supporters of artistic endeavor. The influences of the FAP and allied agencies therefore proved far-reaching, making a considerable audience aware of original art and giving people access to imaginative work in many styles. The long tradition of aloofness between artist and community, between elite and popular culture, displayed some cracks. A number of localities saw the establishment of new museums and art schools toward the end of the 1930s, but just as they began to open their doors, the inexorable pressures of a world war absorbed all the nation's energies. Artistic endeavors were put on hold "for the duration," as many called the war years.

After 1941, with a world war raging and finances tight, Congress closed down the WPA in 1943, effectively ending the FAP. Local branches discarded hundreds of canvases, finished or not, and suddenly jobless artists had to fend for themselves. The war may have shuttered the FAP, but it also opened new opportunities. In 1942, the Office for Emergency Management (OEM), which had been established in 1940, issued a call for pictures dealing with the nation's defense efforts. Over 1,100 artists responded. Other agencies, such as the Red Cross, Civil Defense, the War Production Board, and the Office of War Information (OWI), along with commercial advertisers, sought patriotic posters and illustrations. *Artists for Victory,* a collaborative effort of about two dozen art societies, aided the war effort by holding exhibitions and competitions, and then auctioning off pictures by their members.

Despite assistance on many fronts, a survey undertaken in 1943 found that most artists in the United States made less than a living wage from their craft—and women artists made half as much as their male counterparts. Most had to rely on teaching, hack work, or other enterprises to keep food on the table. Nonetheless, after the demise of the FAP, the government remained opposed to federal support for the arts.

Museums retrenched, often holding retrospective shows built from their own collections. Restrictions on travel, especially gasoline **rationing,** precluded traveling exhibitions and made it difficult for people to visit distant shows, causing overall attendance to dwindle. The period 1941–1945 thus proved a bleak period for many artists, as far as

TABLE 4. Selected Shows Mounted by Museums during the War Years, 1940–1945

Year	Museum	Title or Subject
1940	Art Institute of Chicago	*50 Years of American Art*
	Metropolitan Museum	*American Watercolors*
	Museum of Modern Art (MoMA)	*War Comes to the People*
1941	Baltimore Museum of Art	Mary Cassatt (1844–1926) retrospective
	Metropolitan Museum	*WPA Exhibit*
	[The National Gallery of Art opens in Washington, DC, in 1941 but initially features no American artists in its shows]	
1942	Art Institute of Chicago	*The Hudson River School* (early- to mid-19th-century American painters)
	Metropolitan Museum	*Artists for Victory*
	MoMA	*Road to Victory* (posters)
1943	Art Institute of Chicago	Edward Hopper (1882–1967), Georgia O'Keeffe (1887–1986), and Charles Sheeler (1883–1965), all active during the 1940s
	Brooklyn Museum	*The Eight* (early 20th-century American painters)
	Guggenheim Museum	Jackson Pollock
	Metropolitan Museum	*War Art*
	MoMA	*Airways to Peace*
	Whitney Museum	*Front Line Paintings by War Correspondents*
1944	Boston Museum of Fine Arts	*Sporting Art*
	Metropolitan Museum	*Naval Aviation in the Pacific*
	Philadelphia Museum of Art	Thomas Eakins (1844–1916) retrospective
	Whitney Museum	Winslow Homer (1836–1910) retrospective
1945	Metropolitan Museum	*The War Against Japan;* William Sidney Mount (1807–1868) retrospective
	MoMA	Stuart Davis (1894–1964) retrospective
	Philadelphia Museum of Art	William Glackens (1870–1938), George Luks (1866–1933), Everett Shinn (1876–1953), and John Sloan (1871–1951) retrospective
	Whitney Museum	*Early American Art*

exhibiting or selling their work. Not until 1946, and a return to peace, did the outlook for the arts once again brighten.

In the meantime, many noted foreign-born artists, such as Josef Albers (1888–1976), Marc Chagall (1887–1985), Lyonel Feininger (1871–1956), George Grosz (1893–1959), Hans Hofmann (1880–1966), Ferdnand Leger (1881–1955), Piet Mondrian (1872–1944), and Yves Tanguy (1900–1955), had fled their native lands, seeking shelter from fascism and the unfolding war in Europe, and immigrated to the United States. After 1945, a number of these individuals decided to stay, providing a bracing infusion of new ideas, styles, and techniques for native talents to absorb. By and large, however, the realistic tradition—representational art—remained the popular favorite.

TABLE 5. Selected Shows Mounted by Museums during the Postwar Years, 1946–1950

Year	Museum	Show
1946	Art Institute of Chicago	George Bellows (1882–1925) retrospective
	MoMA	Georgia O'Keeffe retrospective
	Whitney Museum	*Pioneers of Modern Art*
1947	Metropolitan Museum	*Survey of American Art*
	MoMA	Ben Shahn (1898–1969) retrospective
1948	MoMA	Thomas Cole (1801–1848) retrospective
1949	Almost no American-themed shows of note are held at major museums; instead, they feature previously unavailable European treasures made available after World War II.	
1950	Boston Museum of Fine Arts	*American Art*
	Metropolitan Museum	*American Painting Today*
	Whitney Museum	Edward Hopper retrospective

Abstraction, particularly a postwar movement called **abstract expressionism,** tended to be misunderstood and rejected by bewildered onlookers and mainly widened the gap between modern artists and the public. The realistic motifs pursued during the 1930s had narrowed that gap, but those working in the most modernistic, or avant-garde, styles appeared to care little about popular opinion. On the other hand, in a carryover of themes explored in the 1930s, anything dealing with the "American scene" continued to appeal to many, especially if it possessed the aura of patriotism that colored so many endeavors while World War II raged.

Land- and seascapes, often referred to disparagingly as "calendar art," found a receptive public. The war fostered a yearning for a more peaceful, tranquil past. Scenes of a river or stream crossed by a picturesque bridge, children frolicking in a forest glade, or a cozy cottage nestled among flowers and trees brought about much mediocre painting disguised as nostalgic or patriotic statements. An inevitable by-product of those years of conflict, such consumer-oriented art sold well in cheap reproductions.

The two tables above briefly survey some of the exhibitions in major museums during the war and postwar years. They demonstrate the difficulties faced by many artists anxious to move forward, not backward. The first list, covering the period 1940–1945, reflects how much World War II dominated any public presentation of art or **photography.** With the exception of abstractionist Jackson Pollock (1912–1956) in 1943, younger artists, particularly abstractionists in any vein, usually had to rely on private galleries to be shown, a situation that limited them to larger cities and cut their potential audience sharply.

The second table identifies some of the larger public exhibitions presented from 1946 to 1950. The innate conservatism of most American museums at the time becomes apparent because of the relative absence of any notable modernists in the listing. Once again, it befell small, private galleries to give younger artists an opportunity to be seen by a limited public.

TABLE 6. Selected American Artists Active during the 1940s

Artist and Dates	Comments
Ivan Le Lorraine Albright (1897–1983)	Noted for his realistic depictions of human deterioration and decay, a form of exaggerated naturalism, Albright enjoyed a unique moment of renown when one of his paintings, *Dorian Gray* (1944), served as the centerpiece in the 1945 Hollywood movie *The Picture of Dorian Gray*, based on the 1890 tale by Oscar Wilde (1854–1900).
Milton Avery (1893–1964)	Avery maintained some continuity with European modernism by practicing what critics called figural abstraction. Working to eliminate all nonessential details, he created a distinctive style of flattened shapes and muted colors.
Romare Bearden (1914–1988)	A black modernist, his work was much influenced by cubism during the 1940s.
Thomas Hart Benton (1889–1975)	Often considered a regionalist, Benton created some hard-hitting paintings about the war and the nation's enemies that had nothing to do with fertile cornfields or the Midwest.
Isabel Bishop (1902–1988)	Bishop focused mainly on working women and their everyday lives in New York City, done in a style called social realism.
Peter Blume (1906–1992)	Working in a variety of styles, Blume created a surreal, metaphorical world that often included references to contemporary events.
Charles Burchfield (1893–1967)	A watercolorist, Burchfield depicted older, lonely, and decrepit neighborhoods and created a unique, expressionistic nature vocabulary in many paintings of trees and plants.
Paul Cadmus (1904–1999)	A veteran of the WPA/FAP programs, Cadmus worked in the area of social realism, often featuring controversial male figures.
Ralston Crawford (1906–1978)	A precisionist, his unusual studies of bridges offered new perspectives on the built environment; he gradually moved into more geometric abstraction.
Stuart Davis (1894–1964)	Employing a colorful mix of abstraction and realistic detail, Davis succeeded in portraying a real America but in abstract forms. An influence on many later painters, he was drawn to jazz, popular culture, and advertising as themes.
Arthur Dove (1880–1946)	One of the first American abstractionists, Dove continued to work in that style throughout his life, bringing the bright colors of nature to his canvases.
Philip Evergood (1901–1973)	Much concerned with social causes, Evergood came out of the WPA/FAP era with several murals to his credit; a figurative painter, his often cartoonlike characters symbolize his essential humanity.
Morris Graves (1910–2001)	After a brief stint with the WPA art projects, Graves turned inward. Employing mystical symbolism, especially in stylized birds rendered in a calligraphic style, he created his own expressionistic language.
William Gropper (1897–1977)	A committed radical, Gropper worked in both formal painting and cartooning. Strongly anti-Axis during World War II, he carried on by opposing the repressive political climate of the postwar era.

Philip Guston (1912–1980)	A noted muralist with the WPA/FAP, Guston early on displayed a strong social conscience; he leaned toward the abstract expressionists in the 1940s but later abandoned the style for a more representational approach.
Robert Gwathmey (1903–1988)	Among the first modern white painters to portray black life in the rural South in a dignified manner rather than a stereotypical way, Gwathmey worked in a highly stylized form of realism and attracted attention in the 1940s.
Marsden Hartley (1877–1943)	An important early abstractionist, Hartley reflected the European modernism of the day and prefigured some of the pop artists of the 1960s. By the late 1930s, he had turned to a muscular, almost primitive, realism focused on the farmers and fishermen of rural Maine.
Edward Hopper (1882–1967)	A traditional painter, respected by abstractionists and realists alike, Hopper was already at the peak of a long career when the 1940s decade began. In a series of outstanding paintings, he emerged as one of the premier artists of the 20th century. Many of his works show deserted city streets or near-empty theaters and restaurants. A portrayer of the anomie of the modern urban scene, he created the iconic *Nighthawks* in 1942, a painting that has taken on a life of its own. Through agreements reached with its owner, the Art Institute of Chicago, countless prints of *Nighthawks* have sold extremely well, as have parodies that substitute celebrities for the anonymous diners in the painting. A marriage of popular culture and elite art, *Nighthawks* brought Hopper out of the museum and into everyday life and greatly enlarged the audience for serious American art.
Peter Hurd (1904–1984)	A regionalist painter who focused on the Southwest, Hurd married into the famous Wyeth family of artists upon his union with Heniette Wyeth (1907–1997), a noted painter in her own right. Firmly realistic, Hurd served as an overseas artist with *Life* magazine during World War II.
Rockwell Kent (1882–1971)	An early American modernist grounded in realism, Kent also created distinctive pen-and-ink illustrations for a number of books, particularly *Moby-Dick*. He remains noted for his stylized, colorful landscapes, usually of distant, isolated locales.
Walt Kuhn (1880–1949)	A realist remembered for naturalistic studies of solitary individuals, often vaudeville performers and clowns.
Jacob Lawrence (1917–2000)	Painting in a flat, almost abstract, style that he called dynamic cubism, Lawrence became one of the most recognized and honored black American artists of the mid-20th century. Starting in the late 1930s, he commenced creating a monumental and cyclical historical work called *Migration of the Negro*, a series of some 60 paintings about the movement of blacks from the rural South to the more industrialized North.
Jack Levine (b. 1915)	A veteran of the WPA/FAP programs, Levine blended satire, searing social realism, and caricature in a series of paintings about U.S. politics, business, and corruption. In his later years, he turned increasingly to religious themes.
John Marin (1870–1953)	An early American abstractionist noted for his city and seascapes—particularly those dealing with the coast of Maine—paintings that always contain elements of realism. His work, fluid and filled with energy, places him in the tradition of American romantic individualism.

(continued)

TABLE 6. (continued)

Artist and Dates	Comments
Reginald Marsh (1898–1954)	Always recognizable, Marsh's considerable body of work celebrates the American City (New York) and all its squalor, vulgarity, beauty, and energy. An avowed populist, he created images of subways, burlesque shows, voluptuous sunbathers, and muscled acrobats at Coney Island, the down and out and dispossessed, along with the haughty rich. The murals he executed for the Department of the Treasury in the mid- to late 1930s continue that urban celebration.
Grandma (Anna Mary Robertson) Moses (1860–1961)	A self-taught, nonprofessional painter, "Grandma" Moses found herself a popular, sought-after folk artist in the late 1930s and through the next two decades. Discovered in 1938, her primitive, detailed scenes of bygone rural life in upstate New York were widely reproduced and also appeared in glossy magazine advertisements and graced the fronts of sentimental greeting cards. She referred to her art as memory painting, and it struck a chord with the public.
Georgia O'Keeffe (1887–1986)	No woman in the arts equaled the fame and influence achieved during O'Keeffe's long tenure as a distinctive American modernist. From the 1920s onward, her studies of buildings, flowers at close range, and a rugged, desert section of New Mexico where she eventually settled, became virtual trademarks. By the 1940s, her reputation established, O'Keeffe continued to follow a disciplined regimen of work, painting, expanding her palette, and refining her techniques. Many works from this period become increasingly abstract, with shape and color overriding any traditional content. O'Keeffe remained active until the last days of her life, a major figure in American art.
Maxfield Parrish (1870–1966)	A superb illustrator, particularly of children's books, Parrish developed a style of heightened realism that he then blended with fantasy. Skilled in the use of glazes and luminous colors, he achieved a level of success that allowed him to devote himself to landscape painting and only occasionally did calendars or advertisements in the 1940s.
Horace Pippin (1888–1946)	Injured in World War I, Pippin came to art in his thirties. A folk, or naïve, painter, he created pictures of everyday black life during the 1930s and 1940s. He included content that denounced segregation and injustice, all done in a flat, almost surreal, style.
Norman Rockwell (1894–1978)	The best-loved American artist of the 20th century, Rockwell worked primarily as an illustrator. He created hundreds of paintings, with 322 covers for the *Saturday Evening Post* alone, executing 71 of them during the 1940s. Rockwell also painted countless advertisements, calendars, posters, greeting cards, and magazine and book illustrations, with most of them done in a highly realistic style. Most of his paintings exemplified a narrative tradition and told stories, with the picture providing just enough information that audiences could fill in the missing details. Often blending sentiment and patriotism, especially during the war years, but with a sly sense of humor also permeating his work, he achieved enormous and continuing fame.
Ben Shahn (1898–1969)	A WPA/FAP muralist, Shahn early on included often radical political commentary and protest in his works of social realism. He also excelled at photography, working with Walker Evans (1903–1975) for the Farm Security Administration during the 1930s and documenting rural poverty. The war years found Shahn at the Office of War Information creating posters, although his antiwar biases prevented most of them from being published. Following the conflict, he protested nuclear testing along with labor and racial injustices.

Charles Sheeler (1882–1945)

A precisionist—a word he coined to describe his work and expanded to include other artists following similar themes and techniques—Sheeler's realistic paintings of factories and machinery resemble detailed photographic studies. Beneath the sharp edges and flat planes of color, his art possesses an underlying abstract structure. Accomplished in photography and filmmaking, he organized geometric forms into aesthetic composition. Many of Sheeler's paintings, devoid of human activity and any expressive brushwork, possess an aura of melancholy and stillness as he dispassionately described the manmade environment, not the world of nature.

Max Weber (1881–1961)

Frequently described as the artist that introduced cubism to the United States, Weber came to the United States from Poland as a child. His great years predated the 1940s. A cubist, an expressionist, a modernist—Weber defied category, but helped immensely in bringing the trends in European modernism to the attention of the American art community. By the 1940s, his work had settled into expressionistic studies of his religious past, especially Hasidic Jewish life.

Grant Wood (1892–1942)

Usually associated with the Midwestern regionalists of the 1930s, Wood's *American Gothic* (1930) has become familiar to many people and remains a recurring subject for parodies of all kinds. Wood, however, continued painting, a steadfast regionalist until his early death in 1942. He created scenes of rich Iowa fields, retellings of American historical events, and a number of portraits. But Wood's rugged nationalism did not find as ready an audience in the days of internationalist thinking leading up to World War II; he would have to await rediscovery in later years.

Andrew Wyeth (1917–2009)

Despite the opinions of a number of critics in the late 1940s, representational art was far from dead. Modernism and abstraction might be in the ascendancy, but well-done, realistically rendered paintings could also rally enthusiastic support. Andrew Wyeth, son of the famous illustrator N. C. Wyeth (1882–1945) proved this statement by becoming one of the most famous—and popular—traditional artists of the postwar era. Working with either egg tempera or watercolors in a spare, uncrowded style, and employing a muted palette, Wyeth focused on depictions of his immediate environments in Pennsylvania and Maine. Throughout the 1940s, barns, leafless tree limbs, barren fields, and an occasional neighbor comprise the basic elements found in many of his paintings. In an increasingly noisy, industrialized world, his admirers embraced this vision, demonstrating that artists need not be separated from their public, as is often the case.

An alphabetical list can be found above of some of the leading American painters of the 1940s. A rich period in terms of sheer numbers of artists, space does not permit including all the notable individuals active during the decade. Despite World War II, many continued to paint, although for the majority it would take time for their work to be seen by a significant public. Most of these artists avoided the war as an obvious subject in their work, but it undoubtedly had a psychological impact that manifested itself in less clear-cut ways.

Abstract art received considerable publicity during the 1940s; ironically, it also spurred a revival of interest in objective painting. Although the two approaches may have been at loggerheads, museum and gallery shows reflected public awareness of the arts in general, regardless of preferences.

The horrors of World War II, many of them only coming to light after the conflict ended, likewise influenced many painters. Escapism into a mythic past via nostalgia served as one approach, but the violence of the age also appeared in explosive abstract works in which the struggling inner mind of the artist attempted to comprehend recent events and express them on canvas. Somewhere in between, still other painters looked to beauty and controlled composition to describe the decade, often blending abstract shapes with realistic details. A transitional time, the 1940s in art provided something for everyone, but definitive answers about styles or techniques remained illusory.

See also: Advertising; Architecture; Magazines; Sculpture

Selected Reading

Graebner, William S. *The Age of Doubt: American Thought and Culture in the 1940s.* Boston: Twayne, 1991.

Green, Samuel M. *American Art: A Historical Survey.* New York: Ronald Press Company, 1966.

Haskell, Barbara. *The American Century: Art and Culture, 1900–1950.* New York: W. W. Norton, 1999.

Hughes, Robert. *American Visions: The Epic History of Art in America.* New York: Alfred A. Knopf, 1997.

ASCAP VS. BMI RADIO BOYCOTT AND THE AFM RECORDING BAN

With roots that go back many years, a curious, multifaceted chapter in American musical history played itself out during the early 1940s.

ASCAP vs. BMI

In 1914, a group of prominent composers and music publishers completed guidelines for an organization that would protect their creations from those who would perform them without acknowledgement and, more importantly, without paying any fees for the privilege. Known as ASCAP, or the American Society of Composers, Authors, and Producers, the new alliance signed agreements with those individuals who held copyrights for various musical compositions. ASCAP then collected fees from whoever used those compositions, distributing monies to the various artists and producers involved. The organization shortly gained a near-monopoly in American music circles, successfully demanding remuneration for any licensing of songs written, performed, or produced by its members. The payment structure increased, and, with no competitors, ASCAP became a prosperous, powerful force, jealously holding the performance rights to most of the sheet music and recordings created in the United States from 1914 to about 1940. Virtually all the major American music publishers belonged to ASCAP, collectively giving them control of more than 80 percent of the popular songs likely to be heard in the country.

With both **radio** and phonographs becoming growing carriers of music in the 1920s and 1930s, ASCAP took the position that playing a record over the air constituted a performance and demanded payment. Radio stations replied that broadcasting a recording equaled free **advertising,** because listeners might well purchase the record, and stations should not be required to pay royalties to ASCAP. Affected parties united in opposition to the ASCAP position and in 1923 formed their own interest group, the National Association of Broadcasters, or NAB. The new organization opposed any increases in licensing charges levied by ASCAP on stations or networks in order to gain the right to broadcast ASCAP music. For many years, however, ASCAP held sway in the continuing dispute, causing things finally to come to a head in 1939.

That year, ASCAP proposed increasing the fees charged stations for the right to play records by its members, a decision that included virtually all notable songwriters of the day. In the meantime, the dispute had been working its way through the courts. In a wide-ranging verdict, a judge ruled that radio stations could play recordings over the air and not pay any royalties to the musicians heard on them and that such use did not constitute infringement of copyright. The pronouncement, along with broadcaster dissatisfaction with ASCAP policies, set the stage for a showdown.

Appeals followed, but the United States Supreme Court in 1940 upheld the right of stations to play recorded music without royalties. The decision led to the hiring of countless disk jockeys around the country, because records constituted cheap programming—cheaper than retaining studio orchestras for live on-air performances. To be on the safe side, however, the three major networks—the Columbia Broadcasting System (CBS), the Mutual Broadcasting System (MBS), and the National Broadcasting Company (NBC)—along with the encouragement of the NAB, had created Broadcast Music Incorporated (BMI) in 1939. Established as a competitor to ASCAP, networks and their affiliates hoped its presence would counter the influence exerted by the older organization by setting rates and issuing licensing agreements.

But ASCAP responded by going ahead and raising its fee structure anyway, unilaterally dismissing the threat posed by BMI. As a result of this imperious approach, BMI, which until then existed mainly on paper, came into active being in February 1940; it immediately announced, with near-unanimous station and network support, a radio boycott of all ASCAP artists. This action meant the disappearance of most well-known popular music from commercial radio broadcasting, since ASCAP furnished over 80 percent of the songs heard on the air. People who wished to hear their favorite performers had to buy records, attend concerts, search out nightclubs and dance halls, or find other performance venues. Despite these predicted inconveniences, BMI did not back down.

BMI launched its boycott in January 1941; 660 broadcasters, out of almost 800 active stations, promptly signed with BMI, as did a few publishers. The Edward B. Marks Music Company, a publisher holding extensive catalogs of popular and Latin music, joined the new organization, as did the M. M. Cole Publishing Company and Ralph Peer (1892–1960), founder of the Southern Music Publishing Company. These two groups specialized in country-oriented compositions. Stations and disk jockeys therefore began playing considerably more **country music** than in the past, a situation that led to increased public exposure to this previously seldom-heard genre.

As BMI gained strength, ASCAP faced declining fees and public disappointment at the loss of many of their favorite performers on the air. ASCAP claimed to represent all musicians and had long collected their licensing and performance fees from stations and networks; in reality, it only disbursed royalties to those with whom it had contractual agreements. That exclusivity meant that non-ASCAP musicians might have their music performed over the air, but the organization did not recognize them as members and denied them royalties. This unfair practice made many artists more than ready for an organization like BMI, and the upstart group commenced an earnest search for people not directly signed with ASCAP. It also looked for songs in the public domain that possessed no copyright protection, numbers that could freely be played on the air by anyone.

As a result of the January boycott, American radio programming went through an abrupt change. Instead of the most current popular tunes, listeners now heard old favorites by the likes of Stephen Foster (1826–1864) or other 19th-century composers long out of copyright. For example, bandleader **Glenn Miller** (1904–1944) and his arrangers combed old song lists and unearthed a traditional Russian folksong, "The Volga Burlack's [Boatmen's] Song," that goes back at least to the 19th century. Arranger Bill Finegan (1917–2008) turned this morose piece into the swinging "Song of the Volga Boatmen" in 1941, and it soon became a major hit without being subject to any bans. Freddy Martin (1906–1983), leader of another **dance** aggregation, arranged Tchaikovsky's 1875 *Piano Concerto in B-Flat,* a non-ASCAP classical composition, for airplay and recording, calling it "Tonight We Love" (1941). Since it faced little contemporary competition, the new rendition spent a number of weeks on the hit charts.

Theme songs for several radio shows that fell under the ASCAP banner likewise underwent changes. *Amos 'n' Andy,* one of the most popular comedy series in radio history, dropped "The Perfect Song," written in 1915 and therefore still an ASCAP property. Producers replaced it with a melody from the 1860s called "Angels' Serenade." Comedian Eddie Cantor had to delete the ASCAP-licensed "One Hour with You" (1932), a melody penned by Richard A. Whiting (1891–1938), with lyrics by Leo Robin (1900–1984), with the old "Good Night Ladies" (1853; also known as "Merrily We Roll Along"). The boycott even affected commercials. Cigarette maker Philip Morris, which had excerpted composer Ferde Grofe's (1892–1972) readily identified "On the Trail" from his 1933 *Grand Canyon Suite* for its ads, substituted Tchaikovsky's *Andante Cantabile* in an adaptation from his String Quartet #1 of the 1880s.

In a search for usable, non-ASCAP songs, BMI investigators unearthed a number of more recent South American compositions by songwriters not connected with the organization. In 1941, tunes like "Amapola (Pretty Little Poppy)," "Green Eyes" (Aquellos Ojos Verde)," "Maria Elena," and "Yours (Quiereme Mucho)" attracted considerable attention in English translations, gained airplay, and ended up as American hits. Because these tunes had originally been written outside the United States, they did not fall under ASCAP jurisdiction. Many other Latin composers attempted to break into the profitable U.S. music market during this difficult time.

BMI hit additional pay dirt in its musical quest for usable music when it discovered that, over the years, ASCAP had regularly excluded most folk singers, country musicians, **jazz** and blues artists, along with many black performers connected with the growing field of **rhythm and blues.** ASCAP had instead sought mainstream performers, such as those in the areas of theater scores, movie soundtracks, classics, and popular songs. Relying on that focus, they tended to ignore more specialized or narrow avenues of expression. Almost immediately, BMI began signing up some of the best artists in these categories, building an enviable country, jazz, and rock 'n' roll catalog. For a large body of listeners, BMI gave them their first exposure to these formats, and its move in these directions proved a goldmine in subsequent years.

Seeing that their standoff led nowhere, both sides reluctantly reached some uneasy understandings; the boycott of ASCAP music effectively ended in late 1941, and many radio stations signed new licensing agreements. Although normalcy returned to the airwaves, BMI had in that short time established itself as a worthy rival to ASCAP. The early 1940s also signaled the beginnings of a transition from the traditional to a new era of pop and rock 'n' roll, and it would not take long for BMI to emerge in the postwar era as coequal with its once-invincible rival.

The AFM Recording Ban

Beginning in 1896, the American Federation of Musicians (AFM) served as the official bargaining agent for U.S. musicians with labor issues. In the summer of 1940, James C. Petrillo (1892–1984) won election as the national president of the AFM. At the time, he headed the Chicago local of the union. When he took office, he quickly set out to improve the lot of member musicians, especially in regard to compensation for recordings. Petrillo urged broadcasters that utilized phonograph records in their programming to pay fees to the AFM for this privilege. These charges would be in addition to anything already paid by stations to ASCAP or BMI for playing music of any kind. Under his plan, record companies would participate by reimbursing the union on a graduated scale based on the number of AFM musicians employed in a recording session. A contentious issue because of the costs involved, lengthy negotiations with the concerned parties ensued but broke down in June 1942.

A proud and stubborn labor leader, Petrillo, in retaliation for the collapse, ordered a complete ban on any recording activity by union instrumentalists or bands. He directed the ban to take effect at the beginning of August. Perhaps an oversight in retrospect, he did not prohibit radio stations from playing their libraries of older disks, despite his testy relationship with the broadcast industry. By keeping musicians out of the recording studios, Petrillo's ban doubtless hurt his membership as much as it hurt the record companies in the long run. He reasoned that the public's desire for recorded music, either over the air or through record sales, would force stations starved for new material, along with the manufacturers of recordings, to negotiate with the AFM and quickly reach a settlement. But when the ban commenced, everyone stood firm, displaying an unforeseen stubbornness.

The various manufacturers and distributors relied on existing stocks of recordings to meet public demand. Those inventories, however, all predated the union's ban, and consumers wanted new songs, music they heard live in concerts or on the soundtracks of movies. Since the ban did not include live performances, the public could still hear their favorite bands and musicians, provided they could find a venue that had booked them. No matter how much listeners might enjoy a particular song, however, unless it had been recorded prior to June 1942, they could not purchase a current recording of the title.

Petrillo displayed an unexpected attitude toward singers. The union did not block vocalists from making recordings, who as a rule did not belong to the AFM anyway. And although he expressly forbade bands and their sidemen to record, he made an exception of harmonicas. Petrillo declared it did not qualify as a musical instrument, so harmonicas can sometimes be heard on vocal recordings. Perhaps Petrillo later regretted his decision, but his exemption of vocalists meant that a number of a cappella sides were released by enterprising labels. **Frank Sinatra** (1915–1998), **Bing Crosby** (1903–1977), Dick Haymes (1916–1980), and other popular singers attempted a number of such arrangements, and consumers bought them up. Both Haymes and Sinatra, for example, recorded separate solo versions of "You'll Never Know" in 1943. The tune won a 1943 Academy Award in the category of Best Song, appearing in *Hello, Frisco, Hello*. By himself, Sinatra crooned "Close to You" that year, and few listeners seemed any the wiser. For his part, Haymes sang solo interpretations of "In My Arms" and "Wait for Me, Mary" in 1943. The Mills Brothers, a popular vocal quartet that had been around since the 1920s, similarly released "Paper Doll" in 1943, a revival of a 1915 song written by Johnny S. Black (active 1920s and 1930s). Even without any instrumentation, it emerged as the No. 2 song of the year. Other enterprising singers occasionally imitated instruments vocally in order to provide more of a backup to their musicianless performances.

With the country at war, pleas were made to Petrillo to lift the ban for the sake of morale, especially as regarded service personnel deprived of new recorded music. The uncompromising union president ignored the appeals, although he did agree to a government-run program of Victory Discs, better known as V-Discs. Under terms of an agreement struck with the armed forces, musicians could record virtually anything they wanted, provided the V-Discs were not made commercially or otherwise available within the United States and would not be played over the air. The average citizen at home thus never heard these recordings, although toward the end of the war, returning troops managed to smuggle in their favorites. Long after memories of the recording ban had disappeared, collectors located many of the wartime V-Discs, and most are now readily available.

The National War Labor Board (NWLB), which oversaw the utilization of manpower, in 1944 ordered the ban lifted, but Petrillo remained adamant, and, such was his power, nothing happened. Even **President Franklin Delano Roosevelt** (1882–1945), several months later urged the feisty labor leader to drop it, again to no avail. In the fall of 1943, the first cracks in the record companies' defense against the union had already appeared. For some time, Decca Records, along with several major radio stations, had been working behind the scenes to solve the impasse. They finally achieved a tentative agreement with the AFM in September 1943, some months prior to the public appeals made by the War Labor Board and Roosevelt. To AFM's benefit, most smaller labels likewise agreed to the terms, as did a number of broadcasters. Two recording giants, RCA Victor and Columbia, held out until the fall of 1944 before capitulating. Finally, after more than two years' duration, Petrillo in November lifted the last remnants of the recording ban, and new pressings began to come onto the market. Jubilant consumers flocked to record stores to purchase the latest disks, and things returned to normal in the world of American music. For the next several years, the victorious Petrillo continued to make demands, and relations among officials of ASCAP, BMI, music publishers, record companies, broadcasters, and the AFM remained cool at best. Petrillo's arrogant tactics eventually led to federal laws limiting the power of unions later in the decade, although he attempted, less successfully, another recording ban in 1948.

For the music industry, the onset of peace brought with it the unknown impacts of **television** and new recording technologies. For Petrillo and the AFM, the threat of government-led investigations into antitrust violations loomed in the immediate future. In short, the postwar era gave every indication of being as confusing and complex as the tumultuous years of the early 1940s.

See also: ABC (American Broadcasting Company); All-Girl Orchestras; Andrews Sisters, The; Basie, Count; Boogie-Woogie; Classical Music; Ellington, Duke; FM Radio; Folk Music; Jukeboxes; Labor Unrest; MBS (Mutual Broadcasting System; Radio Programming: Music and Variety Shows; Technology

Selected Reading

Jones, John Bush. *The Songs that Fought the War: Popular Music and the Home Front, 1939–1945.* Waltham, MA: Brandeis University Press, 2006.

Sanjek, Russell. *Pennies from Heaven: The American Popular Music Business in the Twentieth Century.* New York: Da Capo Press, 1996.

Smith, Kathleen E. R. *God Bless America: Tin Pan Alley Goes to War.* Lexington: University Press of Kentucky, 2003.

Young, William H., and Nancy K. Young. *American Music through History: The World War II Era.* Westport, CT: Greenwood Publishing Group, 2005.

ATOMIC BOMB, THE

In the gray half-light of dawn on a remote New Mexican desert site near Alamogordo, scientists pulled a switch on an experimental bomb nicknamed "The Gadget." An instant later, a flash of blinding white light, "a thousand suns," as one observer put it, brightened the sky for miles around. A thunderous roar and accompanying shock waves rumbled across the sands as a towering mushroom-shaped cloud rose into the sky. Abstruse theories, endless discussions, thousands of hours of experiments and planning, meticulous engineering details, and the expenditure of vast sums of money—everything came to fruition on Monday, July 16, 1945.

The successful detonation of this first nuclear bomb marked the true beginning of the Atomic Age. In a now-famous letter written to **President Franklin Delano**

Roosevelt (1882–1945) in August 1939, two distinguished physicists, Leo Szilard (1898–1964) and Albert Einstein (1879–1955), warned the president that German scientists were working feverishly to develop a working nuclear bomb and that the United States would be at risk if it did not also embark on such a project. Roosevelt heeded their words, but things moved slowly at first. After consulting other experts in the field, the president in 1940 ordered that a National Defense Research Committee (NDRC) be created. It soon grew into the Office of Scientific Research and Development (OSRD), with Vannevar Bush (1890–1974), a prominent academic and proponent of defense preparedness, chairing it.

From these initial actions came the Manhattan Project, or more formally, the Manhattan Engineer District (MED, 1941–1946). In reality, the MED had little to do with New York City, but since some of its early offices were located there, the name stuck, although much of the project's coordinating would eventually take place in Tennessee. A vast undertaking comprising both the civilian and military sectors, the Manhattan Project involved over 130,000 people and a cost in excess of $2 billion (approximately $24 billion in 2008 dollars). Its task: develop a practical, working atomic bomb. General Leslie R. Groves (1896–1970), with the Army Corps of Engineers, oversaw administrative duties, and J. Robert Oppenheimer (1904–1967), a leading theoretical physicist, took responsibility for the ongoing scientific research.

Working with a virtual blank check, personnel with the Manhattan Project created three top-secret sites to accomplish their goal. Oak Ridge, Tennessee, became the center for work on enriching uranium, one of the elements necessary for a nuclear weapon. Hanford (Richland), Washington, took on the challenge of producing plutonium, another essential component. Los Alamos, New Mexico, received the designation as the center for the actual mechanical design of the weapon. Numerous other cities also became part of the overall project, making it one of the largest, and most far-flung, undertakings in the annals of American science.

Atomic research, however, did not begin with the Manhattan Project; throughout the 1920s and 1930s, scientists from many countries had discovered a great deal about nuclear energy. Their work had spawned exciting stories in pulp **magazines** and other popular media about frightening weapons, laden with radioactivity, which might come about in the future. More serious mass-circulation periodicals, such as *Popular Mechanics* and *Popular Science,* foretold of engineering marvels powered by the atom (the details about how were always vague) that would release humankind from burdensome toil. But most of these articles more properly belonged in the realms of science fiction and fantasy. No one really knew the potential of nuclear power, and thus the public had some inklings about the concept but remained unclear as to specifics. The Manhattan Project went about its business under the tightest security possible, and few people even knew of its existence.

Under the forceful leadership of Groves, disparate groups of people, military and civilian, made significant advances. In a laboratory beneath the football stadium at the University of Chicago, Italian physicist Enrico Fermi (1901–1954) and his team achieved a controlled chain reaction in late 1942, a demonstration that indicated the feasibility of an atomic bomb. Encouraged, scientists moved ahead to devise ways to contain such a reaction and thereby trigger a nuclear explosion. Despite some dead ends and failures, the work progressed, always with the specter of Germany in the background, beating them to a deliverable weapon.

Finally, the team's work led to two types of possible bombs: one made from uranium-235, a rare isotope created from the more plentiful uranium-238, and one from plutonium-239, a synthetic that the Hanford plant could produce. Although a device made from uranium-235 presented fewer problems at the beginning, a shortage of that element caused most of the existing U-235 to go into a single prototype bomb. Two other bombs were also produced using the plutonium approach, giving the United States, in the summer of 1945, a total of three nuclear bombs, with more on the way.

Officials wanted a full-scale test of the plutonium mechanism, and they chose a remote area of New Mexico for this crucial exercise because of its desolation and relative proximity to the new Los Alamos facility. No equivalent test could be done with the uranium bomb because just one existed, and army personnel packed it for shipment to the Pacific. Japan would be the target, since Germany had surrendered in May, and everyone expected the Japanese to conduct a bloody, last-ditch defense of the home isles if the United State decided to mount an invasion. Perhaps a weapon more fearsome and destructive than anything yet seen would, in the long run, save untold thousands of American lives.

Military and civilian advisors presented this argument to **Harry S. Truman** (1884–1972), the new U.S. president, and he accepted their position. Scientists code-named their test Trinity, and the world's first atomic bomb exploded on schedule on July 16, 1945, vaporizing the steel tower from which the device had been suspended and melting the desert sand beneath it. For sheer destructive capability, it met expectations, delivering a blast equivalent to about 15,000 tons of TNT. But, except for a few curious people in rural New Mexico who, from miles away, had seen the flash from Trinity, nothing had outwardly changed.

Truman, hoping against hope for a quick peace, working in concert with Great Britain and China, made the Potsdam Proclamation on July 26, just 10 days after the test, to the Japanese government. In it, the Allies told Japan to surrender, unconditionally, or face the destruction of its homeland. The Japanese, however, rejected the ultimatum. Eleven days later, on August 6, 1945, the Trinity explosion still fresh in everyone's mind, a single American B-29 bomber, the *Enola Gay,* flew over the Japanese city of Hiroshima. It dropped one atomic bomb, the uranium-235 model. Nicknamed "Little Boy," the 9,700-pound device obliterated five square miles of the city, killing some 70,000 and injuring a like number. It also unleashed deadly radioactivity, and in the days and weeks to follow, thousands more perished.

When the Japanese government did not respond, another B-29, the *Bockscar,* dropped a plutonium-based bomb, this one nicknamed "Fat Man," on the city of Nagasaki on August 9, 1945. A 10,000-pound weapon, it killed some 40,000 people and injured an additional 60,000. Because hills ring Nagasaki, the destruction and resultant death toll were slightly less than what occurred at Hiroshima. Shortly thereafter, the Japanese government responded, agreed to Allied terms, and surrendered five days later.

The war had ended, but work on nuclear weapons continued unabated. Just under a year later, in July 1946, the United States conducted, for all the world to see, tests in the South Pacific. Using tiny Bikini Atoll as its primary site, scrapped naval vessels

The devastation caused by the blast of a single atomic bomb can be seen in the remains of the once-vibrant Japanese city of Nagasaki. This picture was taken shortly after the raid of August 9, 1945. (Photofest)

became targets for several demonstrations of atomic bombs. In an exercise called Operation Crossroads, two plutonium weapons, one in the air, one under the sea, were detonated in a spectacular show of destructive power.

The world, especially the United States, witnessed these events with a mix of fascination and anxiousness. The purveyors of popular culture, however, wasted no time in capitalizing on this new sensation, marketing all manner of products supposedly related to atomic energy. Cheap rings that purported to show atoms being split if the viewer peered through a tiny attached tube could be obtained for Kix cereal box tops, and hundreds of thousands of curious youngsters took the bait and sent for them. Similar ephemera, equally shoddy, could be found in five-and-dimes or ordered from the back pages of **comic books.** Several **movies** in production had hasty script revisions in order to make reference to "a-bombs" or "nuclear weapons," especially the idea of espionage in regard to military secrets, such as *Cloak and Dagger* (1946). *The Beginning or the End* (released in 1947, but made in 1946) stands as a quasi-documentary about the Manhattan Project and delivers a cautionary note about the potential for worldwide destruction now that the atom had been unleashed. In many ways, this motion picture reflects the public apprehensions about possible annihilation and the concurrent curiosity people had toward this new science.

The music business quickly released a number of pop songs that make reference to both these attitudes. Titles like "Atomic Cocktail" and "When the Atomic Bomb Fell" (both 1945) and "Atom Buster" and "Atom Polka" (both 1946) tend to convey a sense of relief that the war has ended, plus they support the idea that the nation's enemies would have done the same to the United States had they succeeded in developing such explosives first.

Perhaps the most unusual acknowledgement of the dawning nuclear age came from French engineer and part-time **fashion** designer Louis Reard (1897–1984). In 1946, he designed a bathing suit made from two miniscule pieces of fabric. In order to call attention to his revealing creation, he christened it a "bikini," suggesting that he had "split" previously more modest one-piece swimwear into something as small as atoms. And, since virtually everyone at the time had heard about the 1946 tests at tiny Bikini Atoll, his term seemed bizarrely appropriate. In reality, and despite reams of publicity, the bikini bathing suit took years to gain wide acceptance, long after the unique connections among atomic bombs, remote geographical locations, and swimsuits had been forgotten.

In the midst of these popular reflections about weapons of unparalleled destructiveness, the Atomic Energy Commission (AEC) replaced the Manhattan Project. This new group would oversee U.S. interests in the nuclear field, including testing. The spring of 1948 saw Operation Sandstone, this time at tiny, isolated Eniwetok Atoll in the Pacific, to further assess nuclear capabilities. Throughout these immediate postwar years, the United States basked in its weapons monopoly, and the various tests seemingly reassured an anxious public that the country maintained full control over its growing arsenal.

A number of concerned commentators and scientists, however, called for the country to investigate the idea of international control of all nuclear weaponry, arguing that such destructive power had made the idea of war obsolete and that no single nation should possess these devices. Evidence of the dangers of radiation, following the Japanese experiences at Hiroshima and Nagasaki, only heightened their distress. Public opinion also shifted during the postwar years. Overwhelming approval for dropping the bombs slowly swung toward a questioning of the wisdom of employing such devastating weapons. But the arguments largely fell on deaf ears while testing continued unabated and refinements were made in the growing U.S. arsenal.

Working closely with industry, the government—especially the AEC—began sponsoring educational seminars and fairs in the late 1940s. They addressed the subject of harnessing atomic energy but also attempted to allay public anxiety about nuclear destruction. The General Electric Company, an important defense contractor, helped defray the costs of publishing a much-seen, much-read cartoon book called *Dagwood Splits the Atom*. Featuring characters from the most popular **comic strips** and comic books of the day, it focuses on channeling the immense power of nuclear science for peaceful means, deftly assuaging citizen concerns about the military uses of such devices. Aimed primarily at school-age children, several million copies of the booklet were printed and distributed nationally at various exhibits touting an atomic future.

The United States' complacency received a rude awakening in August 1949; the Soviet Union, through espionage that had been ongoing almost from the birth of the

Manhattan Project and an accelerated research program of its own, detonated its first atomic bomb. The Germans had never come close to developing a nuclear weapon during World War II, but the USSR, working in great secrecy, achieved the goal in just four years following the end of hostilities. The **Cold War** had taken an ominous turn as the 1940s drew to a close, and the 1950s would witness a deadly race between the two superpowers for nuclear supremacy as each designed and built ever more powerful weapons.

See also: Aviation; Technology

Selected Reading
Atomic Bomb. www.atomicarchive.com/history/
Boyer, Paul. *By the Bomb's Early Light: American Thought and Culture at the Dawn of the Atomic Age.* New York: Pantheon Books, 1985.
Jungk, Robert. James Cleugh, translator. *Brighter Than a Thousand Suns: A Personal History of Atomic Scientists.* New York: Grove Press, 1958.
Winkler, Allan M. *Life under a Cloud: American Anxiety about the Atom.* Urbana: University of Illinois Press, 1999.

AUTOMOBILES AND THE AMERICAN AUTOMOTIVE INDUSTRY

In 1940, the population of the United States stood at 132 million people, with 27.5 million holding automobile registrations. These figures equal one car for every 4.8 persons, a monumental change from the 1910 ratio of 1:201 and 1920's 1:13. Just before the war, a new, medium-priced car cost around $800 (or about $12,300 in 2008 dollars) and averaged between 15 and 20 miles per gallon of gasoline, which then sold from 14 to 19 cents a gallon (approximately $2 to a little under $3 in 2008 dollars).

Transportation received major space in the Commerce and Industry Zone at the 1939–1940 New York World's Fair, a clear indication of the nation's fascination with automobiles. The primary American car manufacturers, Chrysler, Ford, and General Motors, familiarly known as the Big Three, created enormous and elaborate displays that presented a futuristic urban culture built around the automobile. By 1940, paved roads were commonplace throughout the United States: the Lincoln Highway, which ran 3,142 miles coast to coast; Route 66, with its 2,400 miles extending from Chicago to Los Angeles; and the recent opening of the first section of a superhighway in the East, the Pennsylvania Turnpike, served as examples of then-contemporary planning.

Despite the optimistic picture for the future presented by the fair, the U.S. government recognized the growing threat of Axis conquests occurring in Europe and Asia and began to press for increased industrial involvement to strengthen the country's military preparedness. In May 1940, industrial mobilization became the responsibility of an advisory committee, the Council of National Defense, chaired by William S. Knudsen (1879–1948), then president of General Motors. But little happened, and a year later **President Franklin Delano Roosevelt** (1882–1945) dismissed this group and created the Office of Production Management (OPM), also headed by Knudsen, along

Fords roll off the company's assembly line at its Edgewater, New Jersey, plant in October 1945. They offered the eager automobile shopper a slightly remodeled design of the company's 1942 cars. New models did not become available until 1949. (AP Photo)

with Sidney Hillman (1987–1946), president of the Amalgamated Clothing Workers. An attitude of no great urgency continued to prevail among many; in the automotive industry, the continuing manufacture of all kinds of motor vehicles proceeded under a banner of business as usual, and sales reached a little over 3.7 million cars in both 1940 and 1941, a 22 percent increase over 1939 totals and almost a 46 percent increase over 1938 figures.

The December 7, 1941, attack by Japan on Pearl Harbor, and the subsequent entry by the United States into World War II, threw the country into a state of frenzied concentration on defense tactics. The first major step occurred on February 22, 1942, when the U.S. government decreed a ban on the production of consumer automobiles and an immediate transition for auto manufacturers into the building of military equipment. Of all U.S. industries, the automobile companies, with their vast factories, proven assembly-line production, and huge labor pools, had the know-how to produce such work. From 1942 until the end of the war, they turned out $29 billion worth (a little over $99 billion in 2008 dollars) of military products and accounted for 20 percent of the nation's entire war-effort output.

With the energies of the Big Three directed toward military production, citizens on the home front had to adjust to getting along with old, worn-out cars, almost useless

TABLE 7. Automotive Industry War Commodities Output

Product	Percentage of Total Output
Complete Airplanes	10%
Machine Guns	47%
Carbines	56%
Tanks	57%
Armored Cars	100%
Scout Cars and Carriers	92%
Torpedoes	10%
Land Mines	10%
Naval Mines	3%
Helmets	85%
Aircraft Bombs	87%

Source: Rae, John B. *The American Automobile: A Brief History.* Chicago: University of Chicago Press, 1965, p. 158.

because of the **rationing** of tires, motor oils, and gasoline. A little-known ditty, written at this time by singer and songwriter Benny Bell (1906–1999) bears the title "The Automobile Song." Humorous lyrics run through a catalog of car parts and rely on sexual innuendoes to tell the story of an automobile mechanic asking his sweetheart if she will still love him as various components break down when he and his car age and wear out.

By late 1944, with victory in sight, the U.S. government and the country's industries began to plan for a return to peacetime production. The War Production Board (WPB) authorized resumption of civilian automobile manufacturing in mid-1945. The Ford Company used leftover body parts from its 1942 models and assembled the first of 39,910 Fords for the year in July 1945, thereby getting a jump start on the other companies. Those Americans eager to use their parked cars again welcomed the end of the rationing of gasoline and fuel oil that occurred on August 15, 1945, the same day that Emperor Hirohito (1901–1989) announced Japan's surrender. With this news, many Americans hopped in their old cars and drove to their dealers to place an order for a 1946 model. Tire rationing in the United States ended December 31, 1945.

For some prospective buyers, the choice would be a Studebaker. Prior to World War II, the Studebaker Corporation, at one time the largest wagon builder in the world and the manufacturer of automobiles under its own brand name since 1913, ranked fourth (after Chrysler, Ford, and General Motors) in the production of cars. Although the company turned out military trucks during the war, it returned to civilian production quickly. In 1947, Studebaker launched the nation's first all-new postwar automobile design, two full years ahead of the Big Three, who at first simply resumed turning out what were essentially their prewar models. Studebaker's innovative styling in their 1947 Champion Starlight Coupe featured a long rear deck and a wraparound rear window that extended to the sides of the car, providing a panoramic effect similar to a railroad observation car. This creation by Loewy and Associates designer Virgil Exner (1909–1973) caused viewers to joke, "Which way is it going?" The 1950 models added the famous bullet nose for the front grill, giving their cars a distinctive airplanelike appearance.

Studebaker managed to pull off this styling coup because of the wartime regulations that had been levied on the Detroit Big Three. As a part of mobilizing the automotive industry for military purposes, the U.S. government, in 1942, placed restrictions on in-house design departments, a step that prevented the three companies from officially working on civilian automobile designs during the war. An exception to the rule gave Indiana-based Studebaker an advantage. In the 1930s, the company had contracted with Loewy and Associates, a firm headed by designer Raymond Loewy (1893–1986), to fashion some modern automotive concepts. Because of this firm's independence from the Studebaker Corporation, the government policies did not apply; thus, the relationship continued throughout the war years. The loophole allowed Studebaker's early return to the postwar car market with new models. The company received favorable recognition in May 1946, when *Life* magazine printed a 10-page display and commentary titled "Studebaker, Its Assembly Line Is First to Produce a Postwar Auto." Interested consumers flocked to dealer showrooms, and the company enjoyed initially strong sales.

Even without the advantage of new designs, the Big Three, as well as the other top independent firms—Hudson, Nash, Packard, and Willys, along with Studebaker—anticipated big sales of their coupes, sedans, convertibles, and station wagons—and big sales they had, with a jump from the industry's cumulative sales of 100 vehicles in 1943 to 610 in 1944 and 69,500 vehicles in 1945. The numbers kept rising in the postwar years, with 5.1 million units by 1949. A marked slowdown of purchases in late 1948 and 1949 probably reflects the recession of 1948, which ran from November of that year to October 1949. Over the decade, the number of car registrations fluctuated up and down until 1946, when they again climbed rapidly. Overall, from 1941 to 1949, car registrations increased by about 22 percent.

Chrysler, Ford, and General Motors had early on established divisions in order to maximize sales by providing a number of models and a wide range of prices. In 1946, the low-end cars—a roomy, gas-guzzling Plymouth, Ford, or Chevrolet—carried an average price tag of $1,000 (a little over $11,000 in 2008 dollars). Even though this represented about 40 percent of median family income, the price did not deter sales. A step up to the next level of a Dodge, Mercury, or Pontiac meant a higher price of around $1,700 ($18,760 in 2008 dollars), cars that nonetheless readily sold.

TABLE 8. Postwar Automobile Factory Sales and Consumer Registrations

Year	New Passenger Car Sales	Percent of Preceding Year	Car Registrations
1941	3,799,600	n.d.	29,624,000
1942	222,800	5.86%	27,972,000
1943	100	.04%	36,009,000
1944	610	610%	25,566,000
1945	69,500	11,393%	25,796,900
1946	2,148,600	3,091%	28,217,000
1947	3,558,100	166%	30,849,300
1948	3,909,200	110%	33,355,200
1949	5,119,400	131%	36,457,900

Source: *Historical Statistics of the United States, Colonial Times to 1970.* Washington, DC: Census Bureau, U.S. Department of Commerce, 1975.

TABLE 9. Representative Postwar Automobiles from the Big Three

	Chrysler
Brand/Division	**Comments**
Plymouth P15S Deluxe	This model, along with the P15 Special Deluxe, became available in 1946 and included a four-door sedan, a two-door sedan, a club coupe, and a business coupe and featured 15-inch wheels and Goodyear Super Cushion tires.
P15 Special Deluxe	The model added a convertible coupe and a wood-body station wagon with exterior wood trim, removable second- and third-row seats, and the first all-steel body.
Dodge Custom D-24	The 1946 to 1948 cars remained similar in appearance and deviated from prewar models with front fender shapes that carried into the door panels.
Dodge Coronet D-30	Dodge's first major postwar design change offered three options: the Wayfarer, Meadowbrook, and Coronet. New improvements included a combination starter-ignition switch, sea-leg shock absorbers, and GyroMatic semiautomatic transmission.
DeSoto Deluxe	Used an improved Gyrol Fluid Drive and Tip-Toe Hydraulic Shift.
DeSoto Suburban	A nine-passenger car that offered a folding third seat, roof luggage rack, and two-tone paint sold from 1946 through the 1954 model year and comfortably transported passengers and luggage.
Chrysler Town & Country	A prewar issue, this woody added an all-steel roof after the war; super cushion tires became standard in 1948.
Chrysler Royal	This nine-passenger station wagon used a photographic transfer process to achieve a simulation of highly polished mahogany to cover the sheet metal.
Chrysler New Yorker	Known for many years as Chrysler's flagship model, the New Yorker first became available in 1939 and again in 1946. The next year saw a minor design change in tires, trim, and instrument panel.
Chrysler Imperial	First introduced in 1926, the Imperial served as Chrysler's answer to the most expensive Lincolns and Cadillacs. Large, heavy cars, they bespoke luxury.

	Ford
Brand/Division	**Comments**
Ford Custom	First built in the 1930s, this car represented the deluxe or upper range of Ford's offerings until the late 1940s.
1949 Ford	From the end of the war until the 1949 model year, Ford had only produced remodeled designs of its 1942 cars. The 1949 Ford, a sleek automobile for the day, broke away from all previous designs; as a totally new and different car on the marketplace, it gave Ford a much-needed strong seller.
Mercury Sportsman	This woody convertible, introduced in 1946, was nothing more than a gussied-up Ford trying to be different with solid maple or yellow birch framing and mahogany insert panels. It carried a steep price of $2,200 (almost $24,300 in 2008 dollars) and did not sell well.
Lincoln Cosmopolitan	This full-size sedan sold from 1948 to 1955 and featured a four-speed manual transmission and an aerodynamic hood ornament. The 1949 model used a one-piece curved windshield.

Lincoln Continental	Introduced in 1939, the Continental became available again in 1946 with no changes other than some new pieces of trim. Production stopped in 1948, and the car was reintroduced in 1955 as the Continental Mark II. In the 1940s, a new Continental cost in the neighborhood of $10,000 (or around $100,000 in 2008 dollars), making it one of the most expensive American cars of any make.

General Motors

Brand/Division	Comments
Chevrolet Master	Built from 1933 through 1942, this basic midsize car could be purchased in 1940 for as little as $659 (approximately $10,130 in 2008 dollars).
Chevrolet Suburban	This large personal version of a panel truck, first introduced in 1935, continues relatively unchanged in production today except for more modern exterior lines. The 1940s models had seating for up to eight people
Pontiac Streamliner	Initially available in early 1942, it reappeared on the market in 1946 with a full-width grill and decorative chrome fender strips to complement Pontiac's standard chrome trim on the hood and back. General Motors discontinued this model in 1948.
Pontiac Chieftain	Introduced in 1949 with four models: sedan, sedan coupe, business coupe, and deluxe convertible coupe, this brand came with a choice of V-6 or V-8 engines.
Buick Special	Represented the division's entry-level model.
Buick Super	First manufactured in 1940 and reintroduced in 1946, it rested on Buick's longest wheelbase, one shared by the Roadmaster and some Oldsmobiles.
Buick Roadmaster	Between 1946 and 1957, this model reigned as Buick's premier vehicle; from 1936 to 1948, it came in sedan, coupe, convertible, and station-wagon body styles. A hardtop coupe joined the model lineup in 1949. In 1948, Roadmaster models featured Dynaflow, an optional automatic transmission.
Oldsmobile 88	Popularly called "The Eighty-Eight" and first on the market in 1949, this full-size car ranked as one of the country's best-performing cars because of its relatively small size, light weight, and advanced V-8 engine.
Oldsmobile 98	In production since 1941 and reintroduced after the war, the Oldsmobile 98, the division's top-of-the-line model, rested on a Cadillac chassis.
Cadillac Fleetwood	Cadillac used the Fleetwood name for its premier offering starting in 1927 and introduced the Sixty Special Fleetwood and Series 75 Fleetwood in 1946.
Cadillac Series 62	The first Cadillac model to reenter production after World War II, this car came as a coupe or sedan with a four-door convertible version available in 1947. Two years later, it sported incipient tailfins, at that time the latest in Detroit styling.
Cadillac Coupe DeVille	Related to the Series 62 line, the DeVille—a two-door coupe with a hardtop showing chrome bows to simulate the ribs of a convertible top—entered the market in late 1949, and a real convertible was also available. One of the most expensive models of the series, it was luxuriously trimmed with leather upholstery. Popular throughout the 1950s, it became the company's best seller in 1961.

By the last years of the decade, the average cost in the lowest price range had risen to around $1,800 (a little over $16,000 in 2008 dollars), giving the consumer a car with an eight-cylinder engine of about 100 horsepower, a sleek body slightly longer and lower than prewar models, sealed-beam headlights, and a manual gearshift, although all makes offered automatic transmissions as extras. A heater and radio were optional, but few vehicles sold without them. A purchase at yet another level, a Chrysler, Buick or Oldsmobile, required a financial jump to an average cost of $2,500 ($22,600 in 2008 dollars). Those who desired the largest and most luxurious cars, such as Chrysler Imperials, Lincolns, or Cadillacs, paid around $3,500 (almost $32,000 in 2008 dollars), plus any optional accessories.

On the commercial side of automobile production, station wagons had served for years as taxis for travelers, especially those riding **trains,** because the modified back accommodated large amounts of luggage. In 1938, banking on a prestige aura that had developed around this vehicle primarily from articles in **magazines,** Dodge/Plymouth offered the P6 Westchester Suburban under the classification of a car. Chrysler followed in 1941 with its Town & Country station wagon, a forerunner of the modern-day minivan. It offered an optional nine-passenger seating arrangement, a rear hatch, and wooden exterior panels. Station wagons, affectionately known as woodies, could be purchased after the war from all the major car manufacturers, both with wooden construction and all-steel composition, a production technique learned during the war. Station wagons required a payment of around $2,500 (approximately $24,000 in 2008 dollars).

At the conclusion of World War II, pent-up demand and short supplies worked to the advantage of the automotive industry and the **advertising** world. Competition ran high as anxious consumers were ready to buy any and all varieties of cars. During the late 1940s and early 1950s, as car sales increased, owning a car no longer carried the social status of the prewar days. Advertisements took a new direction, trying to create market niches for various brands and models, suggesting that each car served as a symbol of the manufacturer as well as the owner's personality and psyche, thus establishing the buyer as an extension of the automobile company.

Popular culture outlets likewise linked the car to lifestyle. American songwriter Bobby Troup (1918–1999) composed the standard "(Get Your Kicks on) Route 66" in 1946. Recorded that same year by **Nat King Cole** (1919–1965), the lyrics follow the path of the famous highway, making reference to many of the cities and towns through which it passes. **Hot rods and drag racing,** a West Coast phenomenon born in the early 1940s, produced a number of songs, such as "Hot Rod Race." A recounting of a contest between a Ford and Mercury, it became a hit for Arkie Shibley (1914–1975) and presaged a string of tunes about hopped-up cars.

The comic strip *Gasoline Alley,* created by Frank King (1883–1969) and first published in1918, initially focused on America's love affair with automobiles through a cast of car-tinkering buddies. By the 1940s, *Gasoline Alley* had evolved into a family strip with the cast operating in real time. In addition to gracing the comics page of **newspapers,** the characters appeared in several **radio** adaptations with a 1948–1949 syndicated series focusing on the lead figure, Skeezix Wallet, who runs a gas station and garage, the Wallet and Bobble Garage, with a partner, Wilmer Bobble.

Toy cars had been popular with children since the automobile's inception, and prior to World War II they mostly came as die-cast metal replicas of the various brands then rolling off the manufactures' assembly lines. In mid-1942, production of all **toys** utilizing metal and rubber in their building ceased, and toy manufacturers, wanting to hold on to their markets, produced cars out of wood. Kits were also available, which required punching parts out of a piece of stiff paperboard and then assembling the motor vehicle. Not too long after the war, plastic became a favorite substance for the construction of a variety of toys.

Automobiles also entered the sports world. Official stock car racing first occurred in 1936 on the Daytona Beach Road Course. In 1938, William France Sr. (1909–1992), the owner of a car repair shop in Daytona, assumed management responsibilities of the annual event. As with many sports activities, these races came to a halt in 1942 and did not return until 1946. Once the races resumed, France saw a need for a business that would professionalize the sport as well as govern multiple car racing events. On February 21, 1948, he officially formed the National Association for Stock Car Auto Racing (NASCAR); the rest is history.

The closing years of the 1940s held promise for a bright future for most Americans. Their lifestyles now required owning a car, and automobiles allowed for more choices on where to settle and assisted in a massive migration of city dwellers to rapidly expanding suburbs. The car also became the means for shopping and expanded entertainment and recreational possibilities. The increased number of motor vehicles on the road soon required the states and the federal government to oversee the building of a countrywide system of intersecting super highways. Farm land not only gave way to paved roads but also to new businesses, such as **drive-ins,** motels, and gas stations, all to service the car and its occupants.

Detroit, striving for ways to continue to increase sales, provided remodeled exteriors on an annual basis, causing previous editions of the same car to look obsolete. Although the mechanics might change little, the one-year-old car had to be turned in for the newest and most enhanced version. With flashy chrome and ever-sleeker and longer bodies ending in tail fins, postwar American automobiles became objects of style and **art** that consumers wanted parked in their driveways.

See also: Architecture; Aviation; Comic Strips; Design; Fast Food; Hobbies; Leisure and Recreation; Levittown and Suburbanization; Radio Programming: Children's Shows, Serials, and Adventure Series; Radio Programming: Comedy Shows; Technology; Travel

Selected Reading
Flink, James J. *The Automobile Age.* Cambridge, MA: MIT Press, 1990.
Rae, John B. *The American Automobile, A Brief History.* Chicago: University of Chicago Press, 1965.
———. *The Road and the Car in American Life.* Cambridge, MA: MIT Press, 1971.

AUTRY, GENE, AND ROY ROGERS

Throughout the later 1930s and all of the 1940s, Gene Autry (1907–1998) and Roy Rogers (1911–1998) performed both as cowboy actors and singers in dozens upon dozens of **Westerns,** achieving a level of stardom and success that overshadowed anything

Horses and campfires played important roles in Western films. Roy Rogers and his horse Trigger frequently shared the spotlight in both movies and guest appearances. (Photofest)

their counterparts attempted. In terms of popularity, fame, or even life spans, the two closely matched one another. They both had network **radio** shows and, later, their own **television** series, plus their countless recordings sold in the millions. For over 15 years, they virtually defined what has come to be called the singing cowboy.

With the advent of sound **technology** in the late 1920s, the movies learned not only to talk, but also to sing. It broadened the possibilities of what could be included in films and, across the board, directors and sound engineers experimented with ways performers could effectively utilize their vocal skills. Even Westerns, one of the most traditional of Hollywood genres, looked for ways to introduce music and songs into their formats. How could a cowboy, usually at best a laconic figure, be made to sing and have the audiences go along with this break from tradition?

Montana Moon (1930), hardly a memorable Western by any estimate, marks the beginning of music in sound Westerns. It stars a young Joan Crawford (1906–1977) and Johnny Mack Brown (1904–1974) as a pretty flapper and a naïve cowboy. In the course of the story, the two get to sing, usually with a chorus of ranch hands accompanying them. It may all be pretty artificial, but *Montana Moon* paved the way to a new kind of Western, one featuring the singing cowboy. In short order, others followed, establishing such familiar scenes as the hero who would rather draw out his guitar than his six-gun, the musical cowpokes gathered around a campfire out on the range, and ranch romances couched in song. Even John Wayne (1907–1979), such a stalwart figure later in his career, had to play "Singin' Sandy Saunders" in some of his early movie outings (*Riders of Destiny*, 1933, and others). Such was the quality of his voice that Smith Ballew (1902–1984), later a minor star in his own right, dubbed Wayne's songs for him.

The singing cowboy films almost always fit the category of "B" Westerns—cheap, quickly made, repetitive movies that filled out a double feature or played primarily rural areas. Despite their deficiencies, they usually earned a modest amount of money throughout the 1930s and 1940s, finally disappearing from screens in the early 1950s with the rising competition of **television.** In their heyday, they kept both the studios, usually small and struggling, that produced them and the audiences that attended them happy. Second-tier players like Rex Allen (1920–1999), Dick Foran (1910–1979), Tex Ritter (1905–1974), Jimmy Wakely (1914–1982), Ray Whitley (1901–1979), and a host of others found steady employment, got to cut an occasional record, and created a subgenre of Westerns that flourished for about 20 years.

Gene Autry, born Orvon Grover Autry in rural Texas, had already made recordings, issued a cowboy songbook, and performed on radio's *The National Barn Dance* when he made his 1934 film debut as an uncredited player in two Ken Maynard (1895–1973) vehicles from Mascot Pictures: *In Old Santa Fe* and a 12-part serial, *Mystery Mountain*. His appearances apparently stirred audience enthusiasm, because more contracts awaited him. Despite some obvious deficiencies in acting, along with limited riding experience, Autry found himself getting top billing in another serial, *The Phantom Empire* (1935), in which he reprised a number he had earlier written called "That Silver-Haired Daddy of Mine" in no less than eight separate episodes. From then on, his association with **country music** was fixed, and promoters touted him as "the screen's new singing cowboy star." Incidentally, "That Silver-Haired Daddy of Mine," initially released in 1931, achieved some fame of its own, reputedly being among the first gold records that sold a million copies or more.

By 1940, Gene Autry enjoyed a strong career in the movies, radio, and recordings, but service with the U.S. Army interrupted his show business activities. Seen here after the war, Autry again experienced success in the entertainment field. (Photofest)

Autry also appeared in *Tumbling Tumbleweeds* (1935), a mix of music and adventure; it features his horse Champion (or a look-alike), destined to appear with him in all his subsequent pictures, and gravel-voiced Smiley Burnette (1911–1967), another regular in Autry's films. Burnette provides comic relief and serves as a loyal sidekick, a standard character in most B Westerns of the day. Between 1935 and the beginning of 1940, Autry made a remarkable total of 36 low-budget pictures, or some seven or eight each year. In all of them, he performs numerous songs, many his own compositions, in addition to maintaining law and order in the West.

As a measure of his success, merchandising giant Sears, Roebuck in the late 1930s offered a Gene Autry guitar in its catalog, the perfect gift for any aspiring singing cowboy. Autry found he often could make more money from product endorsements, such as toy cap pistols bearing his name, than from his movies and records combined. A radio show called *Gene Autry's Melody Ranch* debuted on the CBS (Columbia Broadcasting System) network at the beginning of 1940. As its theme song, Autry used "Back in the Saddle Again," a 1939 tune he had composed, and it remained forever associated with him.

Melody Ranch, a mix of music and stories, usually with comic Pat Buttram (1915–1994) as his bumbling pal, ran until 1956, except for a wartime break in 1943–1945.

TABLE 10. The Films of Gene Autry, 1940–1949

Year	Movie Titles	Actors
1940	*Carolina Moon*	Gene Autry, Smiley Burnette
	Gaucho Serenade	Autry, Burnette
	Melody Ranch	Autry, George "Gabby" Hayes
	Men with Steel Faces	Autry, Smiley Burnette
	Rancho Grande	Autry, Burnette
	Ride, Tenderfoot, Ride	Autry, Burnette
	Shooting High	Autry, Jane Withers
1941	*Back in the Saddle*	Autry, Smiley Burnette
	Down Mexico Way	Autry, Burnette
	Ridin' on a Rainbow	Autry, Burnette
	Sierra Sue	Autry, Burnette
	The Singing Hill	Autry, Burnette
	Sunset in Wyoming	Autry, Burnette
	Under Fiesta Stars	Autry, Burnette
1942	*Bells of Capistrano*	Autry, Burnette
	Call of the Canyon	Autry, Burnette
	Cowboy Serenade	Autry, Burnette
	Heart of the Rio Grande	Autry, Burnette
	Home in Wyomin'	Autry, Burnette
	Stardust on the Sage	Autry, Burnette
1943–1945	[Military Service]	
1946	*Sioux City Sue*	Autry, Lynne Roberts
1947	*The Last Round-Up*	Autry, Robert Blake
	Robin Hood of Texas	Autry, Lynne Roberts
	Saddle Pals	Autry, Roberts
	Trail to San Antone	Autry, Peggy Stewart
	Twilight on the Rio Grande	Autry, Sterling Holloway
1948	*Loaded Pistols*	Autry, Chill Wills
	The Strawberry Roan	Autry, Pat Buttram
1949	*The Big Sombrero*	Autry, Elena Verdugo
	The Cowboy and the Indians	Autry, Sheila Ryan
	Riders in the Sky	Autry, Pat Buttram
	Riders of the Whistling Pines	Autry, Smiley Burnette
	Rim of the Canyon	Autry, Nan Leslie
	Sons of New Mexico	Autry, Gail Davis

For its entire duration, Wrigley's Doublemint gum sponsored the program. Success on the airwaves also brought numerous guest appearances on the leading variety shows of the day, furthering his fame and popularity.

With World War II in the offing, Autry had just finished filming Republic Pictures' *Ridin' on a Rainbow* (1941). In the movie, he performs another of his compositions, "Be Honest with Me," and it received an Academy Award nomination for best song that year, a first for the versatile entertainer. The tune lost, however, to "The Last Time

I Saw Paris" (1940), a melancholy composition that reflected growing apprehensions about the war and featured in the musical *Lady Be Good* (1941).

Firmly established as a singing cowboy star by the opening of the 1940s, it seemed that nothing could slow down the entertainer. And nothing did, until the outbreak of World War II. A patriotic citizen, Autry enlisted in the Army Air Corps, a move that brought his movie career to a halt, but only temporarily. While in the service, and because of his widespread fame, army officials broke with military tradition and allowed him to wear his cowboy boots with his uniform. Occasions for photographic opportunities ("photo ops") abounded, and Technical Sergeant Gene Autry (later Flight Officer) could frequently be seen in **newspapers** and **magazines,** resplendent in fancy boots for good public relations. Following his honorable discharge in 1945, Autry immediately resumed his interrupted recording and movie careers.

Autry made 92 motion pictures (36 from 1935 to 1939, 33 from 1940 to 1949, and 23 from 1950 to 1953), an average of just over five movies a year. He appeared in none during 1943–1945 because of his military service. Note: *Men with Steel Faces* (1940) consists of edited segments taken from the 1935 serial *The Phantom Empire* and received a subsequent re-release as a standard 70-minute feature; it has not been counted as one of his 1940 efforts.

Of all the Western actors of the 1930s and 1940s, Gene Autry perhaps most deserves the title of singing cowboy. Along with his busy Hollywood schedule, he recorded many hits, such as "You Are My Sunshine" (1940), "(I've Got Spurs that) Jingle Jangle Jingle" (1942), "Don't Fence Me In" (1944 [a revival of a popular 1934 song]; "Sioux City Sue" (1945), "Here Comes Santa Claus" (1947), "Ghost Riders in the Sky" (1949), and "Peter Cottontail" (1949). Undoubtedly, the best-remembered, best-loved of his recordings was—and continues to be—"Rudolph the Red-Nosed Reindeer," a tune he cut in 1949. With the exception of Irving Berlin's (1889–1989) **"White Christmas"** (1942), no Christmas song has ever sold better.

Roy Rogers, born Leonard Franklin Slye in Cincinnati, Ohio, followed in the singing cowboy footsteps made by Gene Autry. Ironically, it was because of Autry that Rogers initially achieved success. When Autry's contract for renewal with Republic Pictures (Autry's former Mascot organization had been absorbed by Republic in a 1935 merger of several small studios) came up in 1938, the actor asked for more money. The Republic executives refused, and because of this dispute, Autry failed to report for his next movie, a tale to be called *Washington Cowboy*. But the studio expected this move and had scouted Hollywood for a replacement, which turned out to be Roy Rogers.

No newcomer to motion pictures, Rogers had appeared in 13 minor, mostly uncredited, film roles since 1935 but made little impact. He also participated as a member of a Western singing group that called itself the International Cowboys. From there he founded and led the Pioneer Trio along with Tim Spencer (1908–1974) and Bob Nolan (1908–1990). In 1934, the trio became the Sons of the Pioneers. Experiencing some success, the group appeared on radio shows and cut several records as a quartet, activities that gave Rogers exposure and a varied musical background.

He changed his professional name to Dick Weston in 1937–1938, but when Republic approached him, the Sons of the Pioneers had just signed a contract with another studio, Columbia Pictures. In order to work for Republic, Slye/Weston withdrew from the group and assumed the name Roy Rogers. With this new billing, he took the lead in

Washington Cowboy, and the studio retitled the feature *Under Western Stars* (1938). In its promotional material, Republic boasted that "a new Western star is born."

Pleased with Rogers' work, the studio released an additional 13 features between 1938 and the end of 1939 and continued to bill their newfound star as Roy Rogers. At some point, the company's publicity office even gave him the nickname "King of the Cowboys," and he retained it for the rest of his life. Although Rogers's career did not blossom as early as Gene Autry's, he quickly became the only rival to the more established cowboy star.

Rogers' pictures all serve up generous amounts of singing and light humor, and the early titles range from *Shine On, Harvest Moon* (1938) to *Jeepers Creepers* (1940), both of which typically include the title numbers. No big musical hits came from his efforts, just a steady stream of Western-tinged songs that sold steadily and well. With the advent of the 1940s, his movie output increased, although the formulaic storylines remained unchanged.

When Gene Autry temporarily sacrificed his movie career in 1942 to enlist in the Army Air Corps, Roy Rogers got his chance to become the top singing cowboy. He qualified for a draft deferment because he had three children. He did, however, participate in numerous **USO** tours, raising millions of dollars for the war effort through the sale of **war bonds.** But with Autry absent from movie theaters, Rogers achieved the status of the leading Western star at the box office. Through the decade, he made 60 motion pictures; coupled with his 13 movies from the late 1930s and 11 additional releases in the early 1950s, Rogers appeared in 84 Westerns. Only Autry, with 92 films, surpasses that number, and no other leading cowboy actors, singing or otherwise, come close.

Between 1940 and the end of 1943, the energetic Rogers churned out 26 Westerns; just as Gene Autry had Smiley Burnette for comic relief, most of Rogers' early 1940s pictures feature George "Gabby" Hayes (1885–1965), a longtime character actor who spent most of his professional acting career playing a cantankerous old curmudgeon. Hayes appeared alongside not just Rogers, but also with Gene Autry and **William Boyd (Hopalong Cassidy)** during the 1930s. A popular performer in his own right, once Hayes became associated with Rogers, he soon enjoyed second billing as the singer's crusty sidekick.

In addition to Gabby Hayes, mention must also be made of horses. Gene Autry boasted Champion, "the wonder horse of the West," whereas Roy Rogers rode Trigger, "the smartest horse in the movies." Although the actors and their publicists seldom mentioned the fact, several different horses appeared as both Champion and Trigger, and sharp-eyed fans could notice differences. Original or stand-in, both Champion and Trigger played integral roles in both actors' pictures. As tributes to their mounts, Autry featured Champion in *The Strawberry Roan* (1948), and Rogers used the original Trigger in *My Pal Trigger* (1946) and a younger version in *Trigger, Jr.* (1950).

Starting in 1944 with *The Cowboy and the Senorita,* Rogers also found another costar with whom he would spend increasing amounts of time, both on screen and off. Singer Dale Evans (1912–2001), a minor player in Republic's roster of performers, found for herself a comfortable niche playing the pretty girl that seems so necessary to the plots of Westerns involving singing cowboys. But life sometimes imitates art, and in 1947 the two married and Evans assumed a larger role in Rogers' movies; the couple frequently

TABLE 11. The Films of Roy Rogers, 1940–1949

Year	Movie Titles	Actors
1940	The Border Legion	Roy Rogers, George "Gabby" Hayes
	Carson City Kid	Rogers, Hayes
	Colorado	Rogers, Hayes
	The Ranger and the Lady	Rogers, Hayes
	Young Bill Hickok	Rogers, Hayes
	Young Buffalo Bill	Rogers, Hayes
1941	Arkansas Judge	Rogers, Spring Byington
	Bad Man of Deadwood	Rogers, Hayes
	In Old Cheyenne	Rogers, Hayes
	Jesse James at Bay	Rogers, Hayes
	Nevada City	Rogers, Hayes
	Red River Valley	Rogers, Hayes
	Robin Hood of the Pecos	Rogers, Hayes
	Sheriff of Tombstone	Rogers, Hayes
1942	Heart of the Golden West	Rogers, Hayes, Smiley Burnette
	Man from Cheyenne	Rogers, Hayes
	Ridin' Down the Canyon	Rogers, Hayes
	Romance on the Range	Rogers, Hayes
	Sons of the Pioneers	Rogers, Hayes
	South of Santa Fe	Rogers, Hayes
	Sunset on the Desert	Rogers, Hayes
	Sunset Serenade	Rogers, Hayes
1943	Idaho	Rogers, Smiley Burnette
	King of the Cowboys	Rogers, Burnette
	The Man from Music Mountain	Rogers, Sons of the Pioneers
	Silver Spurs	Rogers, Smiley Burnette
1944	Song of Texas	Rogers, Sons of the Pioneers
	The Cowboy and the Senorita	Rogers, Dale Evans
	Hands Across the Border	Rogers, Ruth Terry
	Lights of Old Santa Fe	Rogers, Evans, Hayes
	San Fernando Valley	Rogers, Evans
	Song of Nevada	Rogers, Evans
	Yellow Rose of Texas	Rogers, Evans
1945	Along the Navajo Trail	Rogers, Evans, Hayes
	Bells of Rosarita	Rogers, Evans, Hayes
	Don't Fence Me In	Rogers, Evans, Hayes
	Man from Oklahoma	Rogers, Evans, Hayes
	Sunset in El Dorado	Rogers, Evans, Hayes
	Utah	Rogers, Evans, Hayes
1946	Helldorado	Rogers, Evans, Hayes
	Home in Oklahoma	Rogers, Evans, Hayes
	My Pal Trigger	Rogers, Evans, Hayes

(continued)

TABLE 11. (continued)

Year	Movie Titles	Actors
	Out California Way	Rogers, Evans, Hayes
	Rainbow Over Texas	Rogers, Evans, Hayes
	Roll On Texas Moon	Rogers, Evans, Hayes
	Song of Arizona	Rogers, Evans, Hayes
	Under Nevada Skies	Rogers, Evans, Hayes
1947	Apache Rose	Rogers, Evans
	Bells of San Angelo	Rogers, Evans, Andy Devine
	On the Old Spanish Trail	Rogers, Devine
	Springtime in the Sierras	Rogers, Devine
1948	Eyes of Texas	Rogers, Lynne Roberts
	The Far Frontier	Rogers, Gail Davis
	The Gay Ranchero	Rogers, Andy Devine
	Grand Canyon Trail	Rogers, Devine
	Night Time in Nevada	Rogers, Devine
	Under California Stars	Rogers, Devine
1949	Down Dakota Way	Rogers, Dale Evans
	The Golden Stallion	Rogers, Evans
	Susanna Pass	Rogers, Evans

received joint billing on lobby cards and theater marquees as Roy Rogers and Dale Evans. She even shared royalty with the King of the Cowboys, becoming "Queen of the Cowgirls." For her part, Evans rode Buttermilk, another popular movie horse. All told, she eventually appeared with Rogers in 23 features from early 1944 through 1949. During this time, she also starred in three Republic pictures without Rogers—the musical *Hitchhike to Happiness* (1945) and two mysteries, *The Trespasser* (1947) and *Slippy McGee* (1948)—but by that time, her star was firmly hitched to Roy Rogers' career.

In the fall of 1944, **MBS (Mutual Broadcasting System)** commenced carrying *The Roy Rogers Show,* a musical variety offering, on its network of radio stations. The show changed networks off and on but ran without interruption until 1954. The Sons of the Pioneers, or similar Western groups, usually accompanied Rogers on the air. Dale Evans exhibited her songwriting talents when, in 1950, she penned "Happy Trails," a tune destined to become associated with the couple. They quickly adopted it as the closing theme for both their radio and later television productions. Evans and Rogers took the plunge into TV in 1951 with *The Roy Rogers Show;* it ran until 1957 and broadcast more than 100 episodes.

The singing cowboy movies offered audiences a nostalgic vision of the American West and proved to be a popular movie genre throughout the 1940s. They never claimed to be realistic, and their simple plots generally revolved around good people (or more likely a pretty girl) caught in predicaments brought about by villains of one sort or another. In the nick of time, a singing cowboy, usually surrounded by a group of well-rehearsed fellow musicians, takes control of the situation and calms everyone with a soothing song. In the end, he rides into the sunset with his trusty horse and guitar.

See also: Desserts, Candy, and Ice Cream; Photography; Toys

Selected Reading
Fenin, George N., and William K. Everson. *The Western: From Silents to Cinerama.* New York: Orion Press, 1962.
Green, Douglas B. *Singing in the Saddle: The History of the Singing Cowboy.* Nashville, TN: Vanderbilt University Press, 2002.
Turner, Lillian. "The Singing Cowboys: Real to Reel." www.bbhc.org/pointswest/
Young, William H., and Nancy K. Young. *Music of the World War II Era.* Westport, CT: Greenwood Press, 2008.

AVIATION

Brothers Orville and Wilbur Wright (1871–1948; 1867–1912) piloted the first powered flight in a heavier-than-air craft in 1903, giving birth to a mode of **transportation** that immediately experienced dramatic growth. Just 11 years after the Wrights' accomplishment, Tony Jannus (1889–1916) piloted the first U.S. commercial trip between St. Petersburg and Tampa, Florida. Despite the success of this venture and the appearance of other small airline companies across the country, passenger service for some time was sporadic. During the airline industry's infancy, the biggest source of business came from the United States Post Office; the agency awarded airmail delivery contracts to commercial bidders beginning in 1918.

To support the growth of aviation, the industry worked to develop bigger, faster, more comfortable airplanes. During the 1930s and continuing into the 1940s, various

A picture of a Grumman TBF/TBM Avenger in flight. The navy used this versatile aircraft, capable of carrying bombs or a torpedo, in the Pacific theater throughout World War II. (AP Photo)

aircraft manufacturers entered both production models and experimental prototypes of their speediest, most maneuverable planes in air races around the country. The makers of aviation-related products gladly sponsored these spectacles, as planes zipped around pylons mounted on towers or raced from point to point in the shortest time, all of which provided spectators displays of speed and piloting skills. The National Air Races incorporated several events, the two most important of which were the Bendix Trophy and Thompson Trophy competitions. The Bendix race, held between 1931 and 1962 (with time out for the war), emphasized the distance abilities of propeller-driven craft and also allowed a separate class for jets after 1946. The Thompson Trophy Races, usually presented in Cleveland, Ohio, employed a tight course marked by pylons, and pilots jockeyed for position. They continued until 1949, but were also halted during the war.

On the other hand, the more prosaic business of transporting passengers comfortably and safely fell to less glamorous airliners of various types. Leading into the 1940s, the twin-engine Douglas DC-3 airliner, which had become available in 1935, popularized cross-country travel; it needed only three fuel stops for a coast-to-coast flight and offered the convenience of sleeping berths and an onboard kitchen. The four-engine Douglas DC-4, initially built in 1938 to complement the company's successful DC-3, got diverted to the United States Army Air Forces because of the outbreak of World War II, becoming the C-54 Skymaster. Pan American Airway's Boeing-314 Yankee Clipper, a huge flying boat, made a trial flight across the mid-Atlantic, from Baltimore to Ireland, on March 26, 1939; by May it began regular mail service, and in June inaugurated the world's first transatlantic passenger service between New York and Marseilles, France. The Boeing 307 Stratoliner, a pressurized plane that allowed flying above 20,000 feet and bad weather conditions, offered flights in 1940 between New York and Los Angeles, as well as to locations in Latin America. With the onset of World War II, however, the heretofore steady growth of commercial aviation came to an abrupt halt.

Because of the exigencies of the conflict, military aviation grew in quantum leaps, while the airlines took a back seat. The war guaranteed massive support for research and development of new and improved aircraft. In the late 1930s, the army and the navy lacked modern airplanes, but new, sprawling aircraft manufacturing plants soon alleviated the shortages. Between 1940 and 1945, U.S. factories churned out some 300,000 military planes, an unprecedented number. This continuous flood of bombers, fighters, and everything in between, turned the tide of battle. By war's end in 1945, the nation faced a surplus of warplanes. Officials destroyed many of them, disassembled some for parts, and placed still others in aviation graveyards, huge expanses of open land, usually in dry desert climates, where they bake under the sun, never to fly again.

Table 12 outlines a few of the innumerable military airplanes used by the United States armed forces during World War II and likely to be known on the home front by name and reputation. Most of these planes went out of production with the conclusion of the war, although some continued to be built and utilized in the Korean conflict (1950–1953).

An immediate postwar benefit from the overnight expansion of aviation **technology** and industrial output accrued to commercial and civilian flying. Much of this wartime

TABLE 12. Representative U.S. Military Aircraft of the World War II Era, 1940–1945 (Alphabetical by Category)

Type of Airplane	Examples	Comments
Amphibious Aircraft	Consolidated PBY Catalina	A multipurpose plane used for patrolling, antisubmarine warfare, light bombing, mining, convoy escorts, search-and-rescue missions, and cargo transport. Its long range (over 3,000 miles in some models) made it invaluable in the vast Pacific; Consolidated manufactured over 4,000 Catalinas.
	Martin PBM Mariner	A naval patrol bomber designed to complement the PBY Catalina; it sank 10 German U-boats in the Atlantic; just over 1,200 built.
	Vought OS2U Kingfisher	The main ship-launched observation aircraft used by the U.S. Navy; it served on battleships and cruisers in both theaters. Over 1,500 were built.
Bombers, Attack	Douglas A-26 Invader	A rugged and dependable bomber, first introduced to combat in November 1944; also used in the Korean and Vietnam conflicts.
	Martin B-26 Marauder	First deployed in the Pacific in 1942, but then based mainly in Europe; initially it took heavy losses but became one of the most successful medium-range attack bombers. A little over 5,000 built before its retirement in 1945.
Bombers, Dive	Douglas SBD Dauntless	Served as the navy's main dive bomber until 1943, when it the SB2C supplanted it; almost 6,000 built.
	Curtis SB2C Helldiver (called "Shrike" in a version manufactured for the Army Air Force)	After 1943, the navy's prime dive bomber, replacing the Douglas Dauntless. It saw action until the end of the conflict; over 7,000 built.
Bombers, Heavy	Boeing B-17 Flying Fortress	One of the most famous aircraft ever built; best known for daylight strategic bombing of German industrial sites. Production ended in 1945 and totaled 12,726.
	Consolidated B-24 Liberator	Served as a heavy bomber, maritime patrol, and transport plane and deployed in every combat theater of World War II. Over 18,000 built, making it the most-produced U.S. military aircraft of the war.
	Boeing B-29 Superfortress	Designed as a long-range strategic bomber, it saw service in the Pacific theater. One, the *Enola Gay*, dropped the first **atomic bomb** on Hiroshima, Japan, on August 6, 1945; it was followed by *Bockscar*, which delivered a second nuclear weapon on Nagasaki three days later, effectively ending the war. Boeing manufactured almost 4,000 B-29s, some of which later saw action in the Korean conflict.

(continued)

TABLE 12. *(continued)*

Type of Airplane	Examples	Comments
Bombers, Medium	North American B-25 Mitchell	In 1942, B-25s were the first bombers to raid Japan. Launched from the aircraft carrier USS *Hornet,* they hit oil fields, factory areas, and military installations in the Tokyo area. North American Aircraft built almost 10,000 Mitchell bombers. Flying in fog on July 28, 1945, a B-25 crashed into the Empire State Building in New York City, hitting the structure between the 79th and 80th floors and killing 14 people, including the 3 occupants of the bomber.
Bombers, Torpedo	Grumman TBF Avenger	First saw action during the Battle of Midway, June 4–7, 1942. Late in the war, George H. W. Bush (b. 1924), who would later become the 41st president of the United States, piloted Avengers, and famed actor Paul Newman (1925–2008) served as a rear gunner on this kind of plane.
Cargo and Passenger Planes	Douglas C-47 Skytrain (also called a Dakota)	Adapted from the famous DC-3 commercial airliner and nicknamed the "Gooney Bird," the C-47 hauled cargo and personnel, towed troop-carrying gliders, and dropped paratroopers into enemy territory; over 9,000 built by the end of World War II.
	Curtiss-Wright C-46 Commando	Similar to the Skytrain but not as extensively produced, Curtis-Wright built over 3,000 Commandos. Because of its high-altitude capabilities, this aircraft primarily moved supplies to troops in China from bases in India and Burma by flying "the Hump," an aerial route over the Himalayan Mountains.
Fighters	Curtiss P-40 Warhawk (also known as Tomahawk, Kittyhawk)	The United States' foremost fighter when World War II began; it engaged Japanese aircraft during their attacks on Pearl Harbor and the Philippines. With fierce teeth painted on its nose, the P-40 gained fame as the primary fighter used by the Flying Tigers in China.
	Lockheed P-38 Lightning	Debuted in 1939 by flying from California to New York in a record seven hours; the Lightning was first used in World War II in 1942 as a long-range escort fighter and reconnaissance plane; by the end of production in 1945, almost 10,000 had been manufactured.
	Chance Vought F4U Corsair	This unique, gull-winged carrier-based fighter made its debut in 1942, and both the U.S. Navy and Marine Corps used it extensively; over 12,000 built.

Type of Airplane	Examples	Comments
	Republic P-47 Thunderbolt	Made its first flight on May 6, 1941, and later became one of the more famous aircraft active during the war, working both as a high-altitude escort fighter and a low-level fighter and bomber. Its sturdy construction allowed it to sustain severe battle damage and continue flying; more than 15,600 built.
	North American P-51 Mustang	This fast, maneuverable fighter provided high-altitude escort and destroyed 4,950 enemy planes in the air, more than any other aircraft in the European theater. It continued in active military service until 1984, and almost 16,000 were manufactured.
Helicopters	Sikorsky R-4	The world's first mass-produced helicopter and the first such craft to enter service with the U.S. Army Air Forces and Coast Guard; the 131 built primarily participated in rescue operations and ferried parts to aviation repair units in the South Pacific.
Jets	Lockheed P-80 Shooting Star	The first operational military jet produced for the United States; a few were sent to Europe shortly before the end of the hostilities in 1945, but they did not see any combat. In 1950, while in service for the Korean conflict, they engaged enemy aircraft, the first recorded jet-to-jet aerial combat.
Reconnaissance	Lockheed P-38 Lightning	Used for photo reconnaissance as well as long-range fighter escort duties; the P-38 saw action in every major combat area of World War II; almost 10,000 built.
	Piper L-4 Grasshopper	A military version of the popular civilian Piper J-3 Cub. Featuring larger windows for improved viewing and photography, over 5,000 of this versatile light plane saw service both in World War II and Korea.
Trainers	North American T-6 Texan	This single-engine aircraft filled the need for basic combat training for most Army Air Forces fighter pilots; almost 15,000 built.

Sources: "U.S. Army Planes of World War II." *Aviation-Central.com.* www.aviation-central.com/1940-1945/aeb00.htm; "Warbird Alley's Aircraft Information, Histories, Links and More." www.warbirdalley.com/acft.htm

know-how transferred to the private sector. In addition, the many pilots and technicians trained by the various armed services found careers in commercial aviation or pursued their love of flying with private planes of their own.

Even with the interruption to travel experienced by civilians during World War II, Table 13 shows continuous growth for the aviation field from 1934 to 1949. The number of certified airplane pilots and U.S. airports in operation increased for each year presented. The decrease in the number of air carriers in 1940 compared to 1934 can be

TABLE 13. Civil Aeronautics Administration (CAA) Statistics, 1934–1949

Description	1934	1940	1945	1949
Certified Airplane Pilots	13,949	69,829	296,895	525,174
U.S. Airports in Operation	2,297	2,331	4,025	6,484
Number of Air Carriers				
Domestic	24	19	20	37
International	2	3	4	13
Average Number of Seats				
Domestic	8.86	16.54	19.68	35.03
International	n.a.	18.28	18.91	36.00

Source: Historical Statistics of the United States, Colonial Times to 1970. Washington, DC: Census Bureau, U.S. Department of Commerce, 1975.

attributed to the buying of smaller companies by the larger ones, business transactions that created the major airlines. The change in the average available seats for domestic trips as compared to international flights reflects a rise in civilian interest in traveling by airplane both within the United States and abroad; the size of the planes for both domestic and international flights remained relatively the same.

Hollywood also contributed to public perceptions about aviation during the 1940s, releasing dozens of films filled with pilots and their planes. Even before World War II had started, Warner Bros. released *Dive Bomber* (1941), an Errol Flynn (1909–1959) vehicle that featured pre-WWII navy aircraft; it focused on a flight surgeon and pilot working together to solve the problem of altitude sickness, which causes blackouts at high altitudes. *Wings for the Eagle* (1942), starring Ann Sheridan (1915–1967), Dennis Morgan (1908–1994), and Jack Carson (1910–1963), takes place in a factory that manufactures military aircraft and deals with marital discord and men seeking defense work as a way to avoid the draft.

Several **movies** made shortly before the end of the war likewise focus on aviation topics. *A Wing and a Prayer* (1944) tells the story of the carrier war in the Pacific. It stars Don Ameche (1908–1993) and Dana Andrews (1909–1992). *Thirty Seconds over Tokyo* (1944) from Metro-Goldwyn-Mayer (MGM) gives a detailed account of the Doolittle raid led by Colonel Jimmy Doolittle (1896–1993), former air racer and stunt pilot. This attack on Japan took place on April 18, 1942, in retaliation for its bombing of Pearl Harbor on December 7, 1941. The unique feature of the raid, a highlight of the movie, involves the launching of 16 fully loaded B-25s from the USS *Hornet* in stormy seas, something no one thought possible at the time.

In 1945, the First Motion Picture Unit of the United States Army Air Forces distributed *Wings for This Man,* narrated by actor, and later president of the United States, Ronald Reagan (1911–2004). This documentary celebrates and tells the story of the pilots and crewmen trained at Tuskegee Air Field in Alabama. Known as the Tuskegee Airmen, these black troops were the first to serve as flight personnel in the U.S. armed forces during World War II. Also, in 1945, Consolidated Pictures Corporation issued a documentary, *The Story of Willow Run*. With a voice-over by Harry Wismer (1913–1967), this Ford Motor Company promotional film tells the story of the factory located at Willow Run, Michigan, and its manufacture of the B-24 Liberator heavy bombers. At peak capacity, the plant employed 42,000 workers and one complete, four-engine B-24 rolled out of the door every 55 minutes. Other wartime titles include such efforts as *Aerial Gunner, Bombardier, Pilot #5* (all 1943), and *God Is My Co-Pilot* (1945).

Once World War II ended, a number of U.S. citizens expressed an eagerness to **travel,** and commercial aviation again grew rapidly. The Lockheed Constellation, a four-engine propeller-driven aircraft, introduced in 1943 as the C-69 transport for the Army Air Force, and then acquired in 1945 by Trans World Airlines (TWA) for commercial passengers, substantially cut the flying time for both continental and ocean crossings. Its graceful lines and spacious interior added to the public interest in air travel. Also that year, the U.S. Civil Aeronautics Board granted permission to three airlines to operate air services across the North Atlantic. Pan American, which had held a monopoly over international air travel, was now joined by American and TWA, thus offering the consumer a competitive market for the first time.

The airline companies continued their research and development of bigger, better, and faster planes. The 1947 production of the Douglas DC-6, initially intended for military use as the C-118 Liftmaster and as the official aircraft for the U.S. president, signaled major changes in airliners. It was soon acquired by Pan American for transatlantic flights in the early 1950s. The Boeing 377 Stratocruiser, the airliner version of their military C-75 Stratofreighter transport, featured accommodations for between 55 and 100 passengers or 28 sleeping berths and five seats. In addition, the continuing evolution of jet-powered aircraft promised even greater changes for the coming decade.

Captain Charles E. (Chuck) Yeager (b. 1923) of the United States Air Force flew the rocket-powered Bell X-1 past the speed of sound in 1947 and awakened the United States and the world to the possibility of previously unimagined fast travel. Evidence grew when, on September 22, 1950, Air Force Colonel David C. Schilling (1918–1956) flew the first nonstop transatlantic jet flight from England to Limestone, Maine, in 10 hours 1 minute. With that accomplishment, fast air travel over great distances became a reality.

Since the epochal 1903 flight of the Wright Brothers, vast changes have come about in aviation. Aircraft soon ceased to be laboriously hand-crafted items, but instead rolled off the assembly lines of large companies such as Boeing, Douglas, Lockheed, Martin, and North American Aviation; air travel went from a privilege of the few to a means of transport for the many. When World War II broke out, the manufacture of aircraft underwent drastic changes—huge factories operated 24 hours a day, six to seven days a week. Women joined the workforce, bringing the aviation industry labor pool to a high of 2.1 million workers by the end of 1943. At the war's conclusion in 1945, about 300,000 military planes had been produced for the nation's armed forces and its allies. While endless planes were being built, countless pilots received training—193,000 between 1939 and 1945. During the 1940s, research and development led to faster, more powerful, and more durable airplanes; the sound barrier fell, heralding the arrival of the jet age that would make long-range travel efficient and comfortable.

TABLE 14. Representative U.S. Aircraft of the Postwar Era, 1945–1950 (Alphabetical by Category)

Type of Airplane	Examples	Comments
Commercial Airliners	Douglas DC-4	The civilian version of the military C-54 Skymaster; first developed in 1938 as a successor to Douglas's famed DC-3, but converted to a troop and cargo transport when the war began. Over 1,000 Skymasters rolled off production lines, many of which then went into the peacetime market after 1945, and numerous airlines adapted them.
	Lockheed Constellation	First introduced in 1943 as a military transport, the C-69 Constellation. In 1945, airlines, led by TWA, commenced using both C-69s and civilian models; fast and sleek, "Connies" personified modern air travel in the late 1940s. Over 800 (including C-69s) were manufactured.
	Douglas DC-6	An improved and larger version of the DC-4, the Navy and the Air Force also purchased large numbers of this transport plane, calling it the C-119 Liftmaster. Popular with many airlines, it continued in service until recently, with over 700 being built.
	Martin 202 (later 404)	Introduced in 1947 as a two-engine competitor to the aging Douglas DC-3; Martin's 202 gained popularity, but structural problems led to the development of improved models, the 303 and 404. The 404, which debuted in 1951, became a mainstay of many smaller, regional airlines. Over 100 were built, whereas the company produced only about 50 of its earlier 202s.
Small Private Aircraft	Beechcraft Bonanza	Introduced in 1947 as a general-purpose civilian aircraft, it proved so popular that the Beech Aircraft Corporation eventually manufactured some 17,000 in various models. It featured a distinctive V-tail assembly, making it quickly recognizable.
	Cessna 120, 140, and 170	Introduced in the immediate postwar years, this trio of light planes continued in production until the mid-1950s, making them some of the most popular private planes ever created, with over 7,000 manufactured.
	Piper J-3 Cub (plus many variations)	A plane that first appeared in 1937, the J-3 attempted to make aviation available to all. World War II interrupted this dream, but the Piper Company continued to produce aircraft, including a military version of the J-3 called the L-4, or "Grasshopper," which the Army used for reconnaissance, among many other duties. In the late 1940s, Piper introduced the Super Cub, an improved version of the classic J-3. Over 19,000 J-3s alone were manufactured between 1938 and 1947.
Bombers, Heavy	Boeing B-50 Superfortress	A revised (1947) version of the B-29, more powerful and capable of longer-range flights. In 1949, a B-50 called *Lucky Lady II* flew around the world nonstop (with aerial refueling), the first aircraft to do so. Over 350 delivered to the Air Force.

	Consolidated-Vultee (later Convair) B-36 Peacemaker	Introduced in 1949, the B-36 served as a transitional bomber between the propeller-driven Superfortress and the later jet-propelled bombers of the 1950s. It boasted an intercontinental range of over 6,500 miles, could fly at more than 400 miles per hour, and carried a bomb load of well over 72,000 pounds, meaning it could carry thermonuclear payloads on its missions. It served as the mainstay weapon of the Strategic Air Command during the **Cold War** days of the late 1940s and early 1950s.
Bombers, Medium	Northrop YB-49	A unique craft, the YB-49 was a "flying wing," a design that somewhat resembled a boomerang. Lacking a discernable fuselage and with four small rudders on its immense expanse of wing, its futuristic look captured the popular imagination. Because of recurring problems, however, it never got beyond the testing stage, and only a few were actually built.
	North American B-45 Tornado	The nation's first jet bomber, introduced in 1948. Never in widespread use—it would soon be replaced by the superior B-47 Stratojet in 1951—the B-45 served as an interim craft. Only about 140 were built.
	Boeing B-47 Stratojet	The Boeing B-47 began tests in 1947 but did not become a standard Air Force bomber until 1951. Its swept-wing design would greatly influence the look of commercial jets in ensuing years. Over 2,000 Stratojets became part of the Air Force arsenal, but with the delivery of the much larger B-52 Stratofortress in early 1955, they quickly became obsolete.
Fighters	Lockheed F-80 Shooting Star	The first military jet manufactured for the Army Air Force saw duty in mid-1945, too late to be a combatant. Soon rendered obsolete by constantly improving jet propulsion technology, the F-80 nonetheless served in the Korean conflict and performed well. Lockheed produced about 1,700 Shooting Stars, including a training version, the T-33.
	Republic F-84 Thunderjet	In the evolution of fighter jets, the F-84 replaced the F-80 and was in turn superseded by the F-86 Sabre. It came into active service in 1947 and compiled an outstanding record in the Korean war. Republic manufactured over 7,500 F-84s.
	North American F-86 Sabre	Introduced in 1949, the swept-wing Sabre proved a worthy opponent to the similar Soviet-built MIG aircraft in Korea. Because of its high speed—about 675 miles per hour—and reliability, almost 10,000 Sabres were built.
Helicopters	Bell 47	Introduced in 1946 and the successor to the Sikorsky R-4, the Bell model gained quick acceptance for both military and civilian uses. Over 5,600 were manufactured between 1946 and 1974. Its unusual, dragonfly-like appearance made the 47 instantly recognizable.
Transports	Fairchild C-119 Flying Boxcar	Developed in 1947 and accepted by the Air Force in 1949, the Flying Boxcar was an improved version of Fairchild's C-82 Packet, introduced in late 1945. A twin-boom transport, its voluminous center fuselage could carry just about anything, from tanks to troops—thus its nickname. Over 1,100 C-119s saw service.

See also: Automobiles and the American Automotive Industry; Civil Defense; Newspapers; Race Relations and Stereotyping; Rosie the Riveter; Trains; War Films

Selected Reading
Bilstein, Roger E. *Flight in America: From the Wrights to the Astronauts.* Baltimore: Johns Hopkins University Press, 1984.
Emde, Heiner. *Conquerors of the Air.* New York: Bonanza Books, 1968.
Rose, Mark H., Bruce E. Seely, and Paul F. Barrett. *The Best Transportation System in the World.* Columbus: Ohio State University Press, 2006.

AXIS SALLY AND TOKYO ROSE

Today, Axis Sally and Tokyo Rose exist as little more than footnotes in the multifaceted history of World War II, but at the time of the conflict, many people believed they posed a genuine threat to national morale. These two women (in the case of Tokyo Rose, possibly several individuals assumed her role) broadcast to Allied service personnel over Radio Berlin and Radio Tokyo, mixing news, popular music, and commentary. Following the end of the war, arrests were made, trials were held for treason, and convictions reached. But what seemed treasonous in the late 1940s has been moderated by time, and the principals in both cases eventually returned to private life, the furor over their actions long forgotten.

A photograph of Iva Toguri, better known as Tokyo Rose during the war years. Some individuals found her Japanese radio broadcasts treasonous, and a jury convicted her on one count. Cooler heads later prevailed, and she received a full pardon in 1977. (Hulton-Deutsch Collection/CORBIS)

The battles of World War II did not involve just military campaigns on land, sea, and air; each side also waged war psychologically, contesting for the minds of people. No previous conflict witnessed as much propaganda, misdirection, persuasion, exaggeration, and lies utilized in the various adversaries' causes. Neither the Axis powers—Germany, Japan, and Italy—nor the United States and its allies—Great Britain, the Soviet Union, China, France, and others—felt any compunctions about using every trick at their command to gain an advantage of any kind in any way.

Radio, a relatively new technological device in the years immediately following World War I, had emerged as one of the primary means of mass communication by the later 1930s. **President**

Franklin Delano Roosevelt (1882–1945) employed the medium to great effect during the grim days of the Great Depression. His famous Fireside Chats, delivered over the major commercial networks, reassured an anxious nation and demonstrated the persuasive power of radio. On the other hand, actor and producer Orson Welles (1915–1985) showed another side of broadcasting when he dramatized *The War of the Worlds* in 1938 and convinced many that Martians had landed somewhere in New Jersey. More than a few people panicked at the show's realism, another example of the power inherent in mass media.

Both the Germans and the Japanese well understood media and the uses of propaganda, becoming masters of it during the 1930s. Their technological resources—radio, film, **photography,** recording, journalism, publishing—had the firm backing of their governments, and those involved worked earnestly in getting pro-Axis messages out to friend and foe. Among the many approaches their efforts took, both nations employed the radio voices and talents of women they hoped would demoralize Allied soldiers, sailors, and airmen and convince them to question the war. Any seeds of discontent their scripted words could plant would be thought a psychological victory, possibly equal to one achieved on the battlefield.

For the Germans, Mildred Gillars (nee Sisk 1900–1988), a U.S. citizen and native of Maine, served as their propaganda star on Radio Berlin. She called herself "Midge at the Mike," but she apparently also liked the name "Axis Sally," one visited on her by the troops that heard her broadcasts, although some used more derogatory labels. Gillars had come to Germany in the 1930s and found employment with the national network as an announcer. With the war, Nazi propagandists saw an opportunity to undermine the morale of Allied soldiers by creating a show built on loneliness and nostalgia. They called the production *Home Sweet Home*. Gillars played current popular music and, using a sultry voice, raised questions about distant loved ones. But she also dropped in anti-Semitic remarks and often attacked Roosevelt as a warmonger. Most damning of all, in the eyes of later inquisitors, she tried to convince Allied troops to desert or disobey orders in the face of German opposition and sometimes posed as a Red Cross worker when visiting hospitals in order to get interviews with wounded U.S. servicemen that she later incorporated into her broadcasts.

The Japanese, on the other hand, enlisted Iva Toguri (b. Ikuko Toguri, 1916–2006), another U.S. citizen, born of Japanese immigrant parents in California. She found herself stranded in Japan visiting relatives when the war broke out in 1941. The Japanese government prevented Toguri from returning to the United States and denied her a ration card because she refused to denounce the United States, which made her suspect and a victim of police harassment throughout her years in Japan. Desperate for work, she joined a news agency as a typist and later moved to Radio Tokyo. Toguri soon thereafter participated in a show called *Zero Hour*, a production put together by Allied prisoners of war. The format of the show limited her role to a few comments, written by others and usually consisting of light banter, that she made before and after playing American recordings. At first, Toguri called herself "Ann" and later "Orphan Ann," a reference to the popular newspaper comic strip and radio serial *Little Orphan Annie* and to her status as an isolated U.S. citizen living in wartime Japan. The name Tokyo Rose, as with Axis Sally, came about from her audience, and she did not personally use the term to introduce herself. At times, apparently, other women announcers with the station took her role, but little in *Zero Hour* can be considered seditious. Most of the show dealt with music, news, and nostalgia, and Allied prisoners prepared the scripts, not Japanese officials.

U.S. authorities arrested Toguri in 1945 and Gillars in 1948; they held Toguri in Japan and promptly returned Gillars to the United States. The two women would face separate trials for treason. The evidence against Gillars, based on recordings of her broadcasts, proved overwhelming. Her defense attorneys said she did no actual harm, but the jury thought otherwise and convicted her on one count of treason in 1949. She received a prison sentence of 10 to 30 years but gained parole in 1961. Despite her past, Gillars lived a quiet life after that and died in 1988.

Toguri's arrest occurred at war's end, but the FBI did not find sufficient evidence for a trial and released her in 1946. Still in Japan, she lobbied to return to the United States, but several journalists by this time had heard about her case. Walter Winchell (1897–1972), a popular investigative reporter who delighted in gossip and scandal, used his considerable influence to have her forcibly returned to the States where new charges awaited her. Accused of giving aid and comfort to the enemy, her trial began in the summer of 1949, a period when anti-Japanese sentiment still lived in the minds of many people. An all-white jury found Toguri guilty on a single count of treason, whereupon the court levied a fine and sentenced her to 10 years in prison. She received parole at the beginning of 1956 and moved to Chicago.

Over time, many questioned Toguri's punishment, because little evidence supported any of the charges. The *Chicago Tribune* and television's *60 Minutes* looked into the case in 1976 and found that several key witnesses had lied under oath, apparently pressured by federal authorities to do so. Toguri appealed to President Gerald Ford (1913–2006), and with considerable support from various organizations, he granted her a pardon in January 1977. Her citizenship restored and her case vindicated, a number of groups honored her as a patriotic American, gestures that came too late to help her when she needed them. Toguri continued to live in Chicago until her death in 2006.

See also: *ASCAP vs. BMI* Radio Boycott and the AFM Recording Ban; Comic Strips; Newspapers; Television

Selected Reading

Bernstein, Adam. "Iva Toguri D'Aquino, 90: 'Tokyo Rose' in WWII." www.washingtonpost.com/wp-dyn/content/article/2006/09/27/ar2006092700133.html

Duus, Masayo. *Tokyo Rose: Orphan of the Pacific.* New York: Kodansha Amer, 1979.

Fuller, M. Williams. *Axis Sally.* Santa Barbara, CA: Paradise West, 2004.

Harper, Dale P. "Mildred Elizabeth Sisk: American-Born Axis Sally." www.historynet.com/mildred-elizabeth-sisk-american-born-axis-sally.htm

B

BABY BOOM

This term, coined around 1941, describes a spike in the ongoing birth rate. As more and more U.S. soldiers departed for war, social scientists began noting increasing numbers of pregnancies and births throughout the country. When these same soldiers returned home after the German and Japanese surrenders in 1945, the numbers grew even more sharply in the postwar years. The number of live births in the United States swiftly climbed from 2,858,000 in 1945 to 4,027,000 in 1964, and the decennial census counts show that the once typical American family of two children had almost doubled by the early 1960s, the peak years of the baby boom. The 76 million infants born over this period therefore came to be labeled the baby boomer generation. Similar conditions also prevailed in much of Europe, Asia, and Australia, although not at the pace displayed in the United States.

Economic conditions and the war influenced this population explosion. Prior to the baby boom years, financial hardships created by the Great Depression of the 1930s caused some engaged individuals to postpone marriage and those newly married to delay having children. With the United States' entry into World War II on December 7, 1941, attitudes about marriage and babies quickly changed. Couples rushed to the altar, resulting in a wartime high in 1942 of 1.77 million ceremonies and a corresponding high of 2.99 million live births. The aftermath of the war produced even higher numbers: 2.29 million marriages and 3.4 million live births in 1946. After that year, the marriage figures decline, but live births continue to escalate because couples opted for two, three, or four children in rapid succession.

The following table shows the number of marriages, live births, and the nation's population for each year of the decade. Live birth rates continued to rise after 1949 and finally peaked in 1957 at 4.3 million. They then declined until 1961, a year that

TABLE 15. Marriages, Live Births, and U.S. Population, 1940–1949 (in thousands)

Year	Number of Marriages	Number of Live Births	Population
1940	1,596,000	2,559,000	132,122,000
1941	1,696,000	2,703,000	133,402,000
1942	1,772,000	2,989,000	134,860,000
1943	1,577,000	3,104,000	136,739,000
1944	1,452,000	2,939,000	138,397,000
1945	1,613,000	2,858,000	139,928,000
1946	2,291,000	3,411,000	141,389,000
1947	1,992,000	3,817,000	144,126,000
1948	1,811,000	3,637,000	146,631,300
1949	1,580,000	3,649,000	149,188,000

Source: Historical Statistics of the United States, Colonial Times to 1970. Washington, DC: Census Bureau, U.S. Department of Commerce, 1975.

recorded a second high of 4.2 million. In 1965, the number dropped below 4 million and proceeded to plunge to 3.1 million by 1973. By 1989, live births once again exceeded 4 million and some refer to the years 1980–1999 as an echo baby boom.

A return to peacetime industrial output commenced in 1945, and postwar prosperity thereafter supported the baby boom and changed the economic and sociocultural landscape of the United States. Financial incentives contained in the 1944 Serviceman's Readjustment Act, better known as the **GI Bill,** specifically assisted veterans in a number of ways. Money for a college **education** and job training enabled returning service personnel to obtain work that paid more than jobs that did not require education and training. For families, this translated as well-paid husbands and fathers. Wives and mothers, many of whom worked during the war, could now remain at home, and the couple could afford several children with the bonus of a stay-at-home mom.

New families with growing numbers of children of course needed a place to live. To address this situation, the federal government granted veterans low interest rates on home mortgage loans. This led to the construction of thousands upon thousands of new dwellings in open suburban spaces located away from traditional downtowns. Prospective homeowners quickly perceived these developments as ideal places to raise families.

The baby boom also created jobs, an important factor in maintaining postwar prosperity. In addition to new housing, Americans needed new **automobiles** to drive to work and the grocery store. Baby food, educational **toys,** playgrounds, furniture, and diaper service became big business. The new suburban homes boasted modern appliances; the installation and upkeep of the lawns necessitated special products and equipment. An enlarged and improved highway system had to be built to handle increased motor vehicle traffic. To accommodate manufacturers who wanted to make consumers aware of all of these new buying possibilities, the **advertising** world likewise experienced rapid growth.

Along with dealing with the material aspects of the baby boom, new parents expressed anxiety and concern about how to best raise their children. In a fortunate stroke of timing, **Dr. Benjamin O. Spock** (1903–1998) came to the rescue with his 1946 book, *The Common Sense Book of Baby and Child Care.* In opposition to the past strategies of rigid schedules for feeding, weaning, sleeping, and toilet training, Spock's text, in easy-to-understand words, advises parents to employ flexible schedules, show lots of affection, see their children as individuals, and enjoy them. He offered a new direction in child rearing at a time when the country was rapidly experiencing a number of changes, and his ideas caught on immediately.

The book initially sold for 25 cents (approximately $2.65 in 2008 dollars) and circulated an astonishing 750,000 copies in its first year, followed by 4 million copies during its first six years. *Baby and Child Care* went through seven editions, saw translations into 39 languages, and influenced millions of parents.

In addition to housing, **transportation,** and parenting, the baby boom had a huge effect on educational systems across the country. A need to enlarge or build new facilities and obtain teachers for the increased numbers of schoolchildren quickly became apparent. In 1947, statisticians estimated that more than 5 million children would enter elementary school during the next 10 years, and junior and senior high school enrollments would skyrocket in due time.

Most communities found it economically difficult to address these challenges. In a meeting of the National Education Association (NEA) in July 1948, 3,000 teachers, superintendents, and college officials called on **President Harry S. Truman** (1884–1972) to summon a special session of Congress to approve a bill for federal aid to education. First introduced by Ohio Senator Robert A. Taft (1889–1953) in 1946, it had been released from committee in 1947. Despite its 1948 passage by the Senate and outcries for help from the NEA and other organizations, political differences on a number of topics caused the bill to stall in the House of Representatives twice, 1948 and 1949. Thus much-needed financial assistance for education, especially construction and teachers' salaries, did not come from the federal government in the 1940s. The struggle continued throughout the 1950s with a substantial federal aid to education bill coming close to passage in 1959, making educational aid a major issue in the presidential campaign of that year.

World War II and the postwar years created significant changes in family life in the United States. During the conflict, many families moved in order for some members to obtain defense jobs or to be close to a military base. Many couples faced separation because of the war; understanding its life and death realities, they married and had their first child.

With postwar prosperity, husbands and wives reunited and became optimistic and looked forward to the future. They celebrated with increases in family size and the onset of the baby boom. This prosperous period of American history reflects a decline in economic hardships that had kept people from marrying and having children prior to the war. Peace allowed couples to comfortably raise children and spouses to return to traditional roles.

See also: Grocery Stores and Supermarkets; Lawns, Lawnmowers, and Fertilizers; Leisure and Recreation; Levittown and Suburbanization

Selected Reading
"Education and the Baby Boom." *New York Times,* July 11, 1948. www.proquest.com
Kaledin, Eugenia. *Daily Life in the United States, 1940–1959: Shifting Worlds.* Westport, CT: Greenwood Press, 2000.
Kizer, George A. "Federal Aid to Education: 1945–1963." *History of Education Quarterly* 10 (1) (Spring 1970): pp. 84–102.
Spock, Benjamin, Dr. www.drspock.com/about/drbenjaminspock/0,1781,00.html
Historical U.S. Population Growth by Year 1900–1998. NPG Facts & Figures. www.npg.org/facts/us_historical_pops.htm

BASEBALL

Until World War II, baseball had long enjoyed nationwide popularity and deserved its title of the national pastime. In 1939, the National Baseball Hall of Fame had opened in Cooperstown, New York. To underscore the importance of this event, the United States Post Office issued a three-cent (about 44 cents in 2008 money) commemorative stamp to acknowledge the sport. Annual attendance at major league games for 1940 stood at almost 10 million spectators, the highest since 1931.

Baseball, however, faced extreme hardships during the subsequent war years as the draft and enlistments stripped the teams of eligible players. The numbers of people present at games dropped slightly, bottoming out at about 7.5 million for the 1943 season. When hostilities ended, the nation witnessed the return of thousands of veterans eager to recoup lost time and enjoy themselves. As a result, baseball, like many other aspects of life in the United States, experienced a postwar boom. By 1949, a little over 20 million fans, or twice as many as in 1940, cheered their favorite teams; the period represented a time of unprecedented change and growth.

As evidence of its continuing popularity, songwriters throughout the 20th century penned several hundred tunes extolling the game in one way or another. The 1940s certainly had its share of baseball-oriented music, with at least 40 melodies available for fans. For example, the decade saw some six compositions about the Brooklyn Dodgers alone, the beloved "Bums of Flatbush." They ranged from 1943's "Leave Us Go Root for the Dodgers, Rodger" to 1947's "Dodger Polka" and finally to 1949's "Brooklyn Baseball Cantata." Few, if any, however, achieved the lasting fame of a song like "Take Me Out to the Ball Game," composed in 1908.

The film industry likewise utilized baseball as thematic material in a number of movies. 1942's *Pride of the Yankees* stars Gary Cooper as Lou Gehrig (1903–1941), the former Iron Man of the New York Yankees. Actor William Bendix convincingly plays the immortal Babe Ruth in the biographical *Babe Ruth Story* (1948). That same year, MGM offered *Take Me Out to the Ball Game,* a musical comedy showcasing Frank Sinatra (1915–1998), Esther Williams (b. 1921), and Gene Kelly (1912–1996). Some B movies with weak plots, such as *It Happened in Flatbush* (1942) and *It Happens Every Spring* (1949) also deal with baseball themes. An offbeat 1949 picture, *The Stratton Story,* highlights a true story. It tells of Monty Stratton (1912–1982), a pitcher who lost his leg in a hunting accident; he stunned fans when, in 1946, he returned to the sport with a minor league team. James Stewart (1908–1997) plays Stratton, and June Allyson (1917–2006) portrays his wife. On a lighter side, Bud Abbott (1895–1974) and Lou Costello (1906–1959) perform their famous comedy routine, "Who's on First?" in Universal Pictures' 1945 *Naughty Nineties*.

American **advertising** also capitalized on the surging popularity of the national game, and many businesses offered trading cards, player photographs mounted on stiff cardboard, as a means of stimulating sales of their products. This practice had originated early in the 20th century, when tobacco companies and gum and confectionary enterprises spurred sales by giving away similar cards. The Goudey Gum Company reigned as the primary card distributor from 1933 to 1941, offering attractive designs with full-color line drawings on thick stock. The war, however, brought an abrupt end to the manufacture of baseball cards because of paper shortages. Production resumed in 1948, when the Bowman Gum Company issued a set of black-and-white prints, giving one card with each piece of gum for a penny (about 9 cents in 2008 money), and the Leaf Company offered a set of colorized picture cards with its chewing gum.

The war may have ended baseball cards but not baseball. On December 7, 1941, while the citizens of the United States briefly reeled in shock from the Japanese attack on Pearl Harbor, the commissioner of baseball, Judge Kenesaw Mountain Landis (1866–1944), approached **President Franklin Delano Roosevelt** (1882–1945) for guidance on whether to suspend the sport in light of the national emergency. Roosevelt, after brief consultation with Clark Griffith (1869–1955), owner of the locally based Washington Senators, urged its continuance, because he believed the game could provide a much-needed diversion for war-weary citizens. A longtime fan of baseball himself, Roosevelt continued through the early years of the decade to be a faithful spectator at the Senators' home games.

Despite this official sanctioning of the game, baseball struggled to maintain any semblance of its former identity, both in retaining players and attracting spectators. The armed forces depleted most rosters of both the major and minor league teams. Two top-ranked players happened to be among the first inductees: the Detroit Tigers' star first baseman Hank Greenberg (1911–1986), who joined the army, and the Cleveland Indians' ace pitcher Bob Feller (b. 1918), who went with the navy.

The entry of Greenberg (also known as "Hammerin' Hank") into professional baseball had not been easy. Jews, blacks, and other outsiders encountered prejudicial obstacles qualifying for the major leagues, but after spending three years in the minors, the Detroit Tigers finally signed Greenberg to a contract. He played with them from 1933 until 1946, with the years 1940 to 1945 out for service. He then joined the Pittsburgh Pirates for the 1947 season before retiring. In 1949, Greenberg, along with pitcher Satchel Paige (1906–1982) and 15 members of the Indians' team, appeared in a Republic Pictures movie, *The Kid from Cleveland*. A more significant achievement occurred for Greenberg in 1954, when he became the first Jewish player elected to the National Baseball Hall of Fame.

Feller, known as "Bullet Bob" and "Rapid Robert," in 1940 became the first American League pitcher to throw a complete no-hitter on the opening day of a season. Just one year later, he was fighting in the war. He had joined the Cleveland Indians in 1936 and remained with them until his retirement in 1956. After serving from 1941 to 1945, he returned to major league baseball, regained his dominance on the mound, and in 1962 was inducted into the Hall of Fame.

Other notable baseball players who saw active duty included Joe DiMaggio (1914–1999) and Ted Williams (1918–2002). DiMaggio entered semipro ball in 1932 and in 1941 achieved a 56-game hitting streak, an unbroken record. When war broke out, he held the position of center fielder for the New York Yankees, for whom he played from 1936 until 1951. He joined the U.S. Army Air Force in 1943 but never saw action. Instead he worked as a physical education instructor and played baseball during his 31-month stint. He appeared in his last game on September 30, 1951, and entered the Hall of Fame in 1955. A pop song of the day, "Joltin' Joe DiMaggio" (1941), celebrates his prowess at the plate. Bandleader Les Brown (1912–2001), with a vocal by Betty Bonney (active 1940s), recorded the tune and it claimed some modest success.

Ted Williams, the "Splendid Splinter," at bat for the Boston Red Sox, a team for which he played from 1939 to 1960. (Photofest)

Ted Williams, the star left fielder for the Boston Red Sox, played 19 seasons with the team. In his peak year, 1941, the "Splendid Splinter" batted .406, a feat no one has since equaled or surpassed. Military service as a Marine Corps pilot interrupted his career twice, first in World War II and again during the Korean conflict. Williams led the American League in batting average, runs batted in, and home runs in both 1942 and 1947, a feat that earned him baseball's Triple Crown, the prestigious award for a hitter who leads in those three statistics. Williams entered the Hall of Fame in 1966.

These outstanding players provide the briefest of sketches about career interruptions and their impacts on the sport because of the war; in total, more than a thousand professional baseball players served in the armed forces. But from these hardships came opportunities for others. As teams with members off to war jockeyed to maintain full rosters, older major-leaguers suddenly found that they could extend their careers, while rookies got an unexpectedly early chance to play. It also opened doors for women who could play well, although they never competed directly with men on the field.

Philip K. Wrigley (1894–1977), chewing gum magnate and owner of the Chicago Cubs, established the All-American Girls Professional Baseball League in 1943. Each team consisted of 15 players, a coach, a business manager, and a chaperone who instructed the members in proper posture, etiquette, and appropriate responses whenever they had a called third strike. Their distinctive uniforms included short skirts that offered some modesty but little protection when sliding into home plate. Like their male counterparts, they donned the traditional brimmed beanie caps. Initially, 60 women received the honor of being the first to play professional baseball on one of four inaugural teams: the Kenosha Comets and Racine Belles in Wisconsin, the Rockford Peaches in Illinois, and the South Bend Blue Sox in Indiana.

By 1948, the number of teams had grown to 10, with attendance reaching a peak of nearly a million spectators turning out for their games. Spring training took place in distant locations such as Havana, Cuba, and Opa-Locka, Florida. Postseason tours to Cuba and South America were planned in hopes of creating an International League of Girls Baseball, while the All-American League cities organized Junior Leagues for young women 14 years and older. After 1945, however, the men started coming home, and fans returned to the tried and true. Enthusiasm for women's baseball slowly waned, attendance declined, competition from the men's teams overshadowed them, and the televising of big-league games finally brought the women's league to a close in 1954. Columbia Pictures Corporation immortalized this unique moment in baseball history with *A League of Their Own* (1992).

The table below shows the top two All-American Girls League teams for each season. The Racine Belles and the Rockford Peaches, two of the original four teams, clearly dominated during the 1940s. The Milwaukee Chicks had formed in 1944 and got off to a very successful start. The Grand Rapids Chicks joined the league in 1945 and the Muskegon Lassies in 1946.

Women were not the only ones who had difficulty entering the world of baseball. In the racially segregated United States, blacks could not join white professional leagues even though they had played on military, college, and company teams. A few Midwestern team owners organized the Negro National League in 1920, and soon a second one, the Negro American League, formed in 1937. The all black East-West All-Star Game, first played in 1933, served as the premier annual event for the players in these leagues. In 1946, Hollywood acknowledged the presence of the black leagues when Image Entertainment produced a documentary, *Negro Leagues Baseball.* The film featured two teams, the Indianapolis Clowns and the Kansas City Monarchs. A later commercial movie, *The Bingo Long Traveling All-Stars & Motor Kings* (1976), humorously chronicles life on the road for a fictionalized black team during the 1930s.

Although racial segregation remained in force throughout baseball until the later 1940s, several people of considerable importance in the major leagues had tried to

TABLE 16. Women's League Pennant and Playoff Winners, 1943–1949

Year	Pennant Winner	Playoff Winner
1943	Racine Belles	Racine Belles
1944	Milwaukee Chicks	Milwaukee Chicks
1945	Rockford Peaches	Rockford Peaches
1946	Racine Belles	Racine Belles
1947	Muskegon Lassies	Racine Belles
1948	Grand Rapids Chicks	Rockford Peaches
1949	Rockford Peaches	Rockford Peaches

Source: Lahman, Sean. "The All American Girls Professional Baseball League." *The Baseball Archive.* www.baseball1.com/bb-data/bbd-wb1.html

end this practice in the sport, but to no avail. Branch Rickey (1881–1965), president and general manager of the National League's Brooklyn Dodgers, was instrumental in assisting Jackie Robinson (1919–1972) to break the color barrier. Robinson, who had played with the Negro League's Kansas City Monarchs, took this momentous step in 1947 when he signed a contract to play for the Dodgers at second base. Racist pressures pummeled him from the day he donned his new uniform, but his athletic abilities, outgoing personality, and calm disposition prevailed; he soon won respect and became a symbol of black opportunity. *The Sporting News* magazine had opposed blacks in the major leagues, but nonetheless recognized Robinson with its first Rookie of the Year Award in 1947, an award renamed for Robinson in 1987.

Hollywood recounted this historic moment with a 1950 biopic, *The Jackie Robinson Story,* that stars the Dodger star as himself. Songwriters offered "Jackie Robinson" (1947) and "Did You See Jackie Robinson Hit that Ball?" (1949). He won election to the Hall of Fame in 1962.

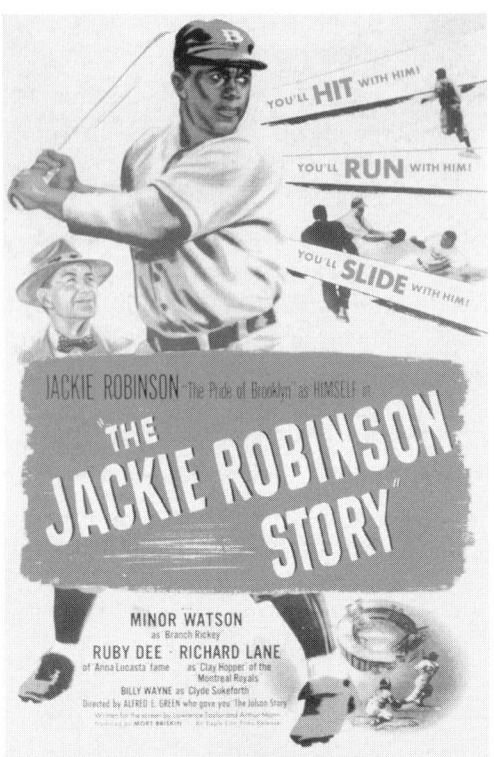

Jackie Robinson, the first black major league baseball player, broke the color barrier in 1947. He had gained enough popularity by 1950 to play himself in Legend Film's The Jackie Robinson Story. *(Kisch / Photofest)*

Just 11 weeks after Robinson's entry into previously all-white professional baseball, Larry Doby (1923–2003) from the Newark Eagles joined the Cleveland Indians to play center field. As such, he became the second black player to join the majors and the first on an American League team. A fine addition to the Indians' lineup, Doby was inducted into the Hall of Fame in 1998.

Satchel Paige ("The Ageless"), yet another outstanding star, had played with several Negro League teams during the 1920s and 1930s. In 1948, just one year after Robinson's and Doby's historic moves, he became, at age 42, the third black player to join this growing revolution. Paige moved from the Kansas City Monarchs to the Cleveland Indians and broke records as the first black pitcher to throw in the World Series when he started game 5 of the 1948 World Series against the Boston Braves. The Indians went on to win the series 4 to 2. He continued to pitch actively until 1956, and then made occasional appearances on the mound until 1967. Four years later, at the age of 65, Paige was elected to the Hall of Fame.

Since 1903, the primary goal of National and American League teams has been to win the season's culminating event, the World Series. Each year the country asks, "Which rivals will meet in this championship race and emerge victorious from the

TABLE 17. The World Series, 1940–1949

Year	Teams	League	Wins
1940	CINNCINNATI REDS	National League	4
	Detroit Tigers	American League	3
1941	NEW YORK YANKEES	American League	4
	Brooklyn Dodgers	National League	1
1942	ST. LOUIS CARDINALS	National League	4
	New York Yankees	American League	1
1943	NEW YORK YANKEES	American League	4
	St. Louis Cardinals	National League	1
1944	ST. LOUIS CARDINALS	National League	4
	St. Louis Browns	American League	2
1945	DETROIT TIGERS	American League	4
	Chicago Cubs	National League	3
1946	ST. LOUIS CARDINALS	National League	4
	Boston Red Sox	American League	3
1947*	NEW YORK YANKEES	American League	4
	Brooklyn Dodgers	National League	3
1948	CLEVELAND INDIANS	American League	4
	Boston Braves	National League	2
1949	NEW YORK YANKEES	American League	4
	Brooklyn Dodgers	National League	1

Source: Wallechinsky, David. *Wallechinsky's Twentieth Century History with the Boring Parts Left Out.* Boston Little, Brown, 1995, pp. 681–682.
*In 1947, cameras televised the World Series for the first time.

best-of-seven contest?" The table shows the World Series results during the 1940s and lists the participating teams and final winners (in caps), each team's respective league, and the number of wins for each. During the decade, the American League captured 6 of the 10 events, with the New York Yankees winning 4 of those 6 championships. In the National League's 4 wins, the St. Louis Cardinals dominated with 3.

During the 1940s, the nation experienced baseball perhaps as in no other decade and provided the sport with many important firsts: the first Jewish superstar, the first women to play professional baseball, the first black to join a previously all-white major league team, and the first black to pitch in the World Series. But good things sometimes come to an end, and, eventually, the uncontested televising of professional **football,** along with the inclusion of other spectator sports, brought baseball down from the heights it had achieved in the 1940s.

See also: Movies; Race Relations and Stereotyping; Radio Programming: News, Sports, Public Affairs, and Talk; Technology; Television

Selected Reading
All-American Girls Professional Baseball League. www.aagpbl.org/league/history.cfm
Baseball Songs. www.loc.gov/rr/perform/baseballbib.html
Marshall, William. *Baseball's Pivotal Era, 1945–1951.* Lexington-Fayette: University Press of Kentucky, 1999.

Rader, Benjamin G. *Baseball, A History of America's Game.* Chicago: University of Illinois Press, 2002.

Wallechinsky, David. *Wallechinsky's Twentieth Century History with the Boring Parts Left Out.* New York: Little, Brown, 1995.

BASIE, COUNT

Born William James Basie (1904–1984) in Red Bank, New Jersey, this outstanding pianist and bandleader enjoyed a long and storied career. A natural piano player, he quickly learned to improvise and picked up odd jobs playing along with silent **movies** while still in his teens. After dropping out of junior high school and "scuffling" (a popular term among musicians, meaning to move from one job, or "gig," to another) around New Jersey as best he could, he eventually landed in Harlem during the early 1920s. There he met many of the leading **jazz** players of the day, including pianist Willie "the Lion" Smith (1893–1973), who advanced his piano skills, and pianist Fats Waller (1904–1943), who taught him to play the organ.

Basie toured with several traveling vaudeville shows in the mid-1920s, employment that took him to the Midwest. He joined the Tulsa-based Blue Devils band, led by

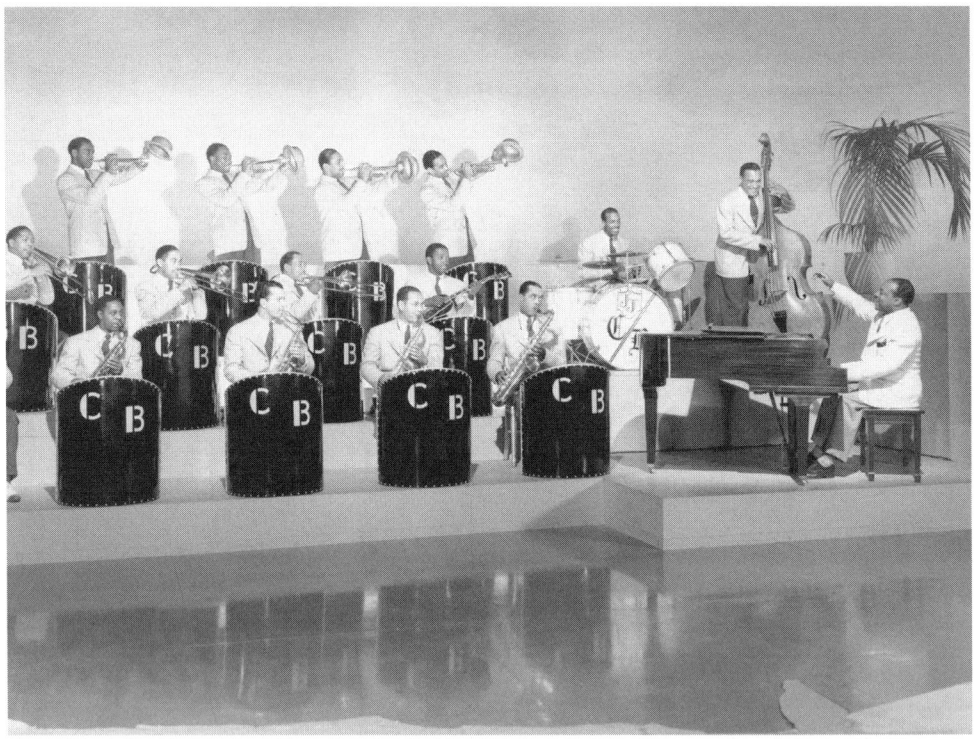

Leader of some of the greatest jazz and swing bands of all time, William "Count" Basie began his career in the 1920s. Many consider the orchestra he led from the mid-1930s to the mid-1940s to be his best group. An accomplished pianist, he had the knack of attracting outstanding musicians of the day. (Photofest)

bassist Walter Page (1900–1957), in 1928. Around this time, someone, possibly himself, anointed him "Count," and the title/name stuck. The following year, he became an arranger in pianist Bennie Moten's (1894–1935) orchestra based in Kansas City. Page also joined Moten. Basie played so impressively that he soon became the group's pianist, and Moten served as leader.

Moten had pioneered a riffing style in which brief musical lines are repeated, and it would come to characterize Basie's later orchestras, especially those of the late 1930s and 1940s. In addition, Page's powerful, rhythmic bass—called a "walking bass" because it helped propel the band—and Basie's short, but effective, piano fills gave the aggregation a new, light, modern sound. Moten died in 1935 and Basie strove to keep the band going, but it folded. He then formed the first Count Basie Orchestra and used a number of players from the defunct group and recruited the inimitable tenor saxophone player Lester Young (1909–1959), a move that contributed immeasurably to the sound of the Basie band in upcoming years.

The new Basie ensemble, in addition to playing Kansas City clubs, also participated in nighttime **radio** broadcasts. An announcer christened the group Count Basie and His Barons of Rhythm, and noted **music** writer and talent scout John Hammond (1910–1987), traveling in Chicago, happened to hear one of these programs on his car radio in 1936. He quickly journeyed to Kansas City to hear them in person. Shortly thereafter, Hammond brought a quintet from the band into a recording studio to cut several memorable sides as "Jones-Smith Incorporated" (Basie, piano; Walter Page, bass; Lester Young, tenor sax; Jo Jones [1911–1985], drums; and Carl "Tatti" Smith [1908–?], trumpet), because prior commitments to Decca Records forbade them recording under Basie's name. In 1937, the band as a whole began recording for Decca, a major label, turning out dozens of sides. After years of scuffling, Count Basie and his gifted associates were on their way.

The later 1930s found the rising band ensconced in New York City, playing the best venues: the Apollo Theater, the Famous Door, the Roseland Ballroom, the Savoy Ballroom, and others. Famed singer Billie Holiday (1915–1959) performed with them, but contractual conflicts prevented her from recording. Bluesman Jimmy Rushing (1901–1971) and vocalist Helen Humes (1913–1981) took care of singing chores, top arrangers like Jimmy Mundy (1907–1983) and Eddie Durham (1906–1987) contributed charts, and a string of successful records gained the band a popular following. Basie himself wrote many of the orchestra's numbers, and his "One O'Clock Jump," first recorded on Decca in 1937, made the charts, giving the band its first national hit; it soon became the group's theme song.

At the urging of Hammond, Basie left Decca and in 1939 signed a contract with Columbia Records, a growing label that would soon become a leader in **swing** and big-band recordings. The addition of Basie to its roster of artists only burnished that reputation. During the early 1940s, before the draft took some of its best players, the orchestra's personnel reads more or less—some shifting occurs, as with any band—as seen in Table 18.

In the judgment of most critics, a truly all-star lineup, this orchestra skillfully melded jazz, the blues, swing, and even popular music into a distinctive formula. Unlike many bands, Basie managed to retain high-caliber musicians year in and year out, and people noticed the consistently high morale of the orchestra as a whole. The

TABLE 18. The Count Basie Orchestra, Early 1940s (an approximation)

Instrument	Musician
Trumpets	Buck Clayton (1911–1991)
	Al Killian (1916–1950)
	Harry "Sweets" Edison (1915–1999)
	Ed Lewis (1909–1985)
Trombones	Vic Dickenson (1906–1984)
	Dickie Wells (1907–1985)
	Dan Minor (1909–1982)
Reeds	Earle Warren (1914–1995; alto)
	Lester Young (tenor)
	Buddy Tate (1913–2001; tenor)
	Jack Washington (1910–1964; baritone)
The "All-American Rhythm Section," as many referred to it	Basie (piano)
	Freddie Green (1911–1987; rhythm guitar)
	Walter Page (bass)
	Jo Jones (drums)
Vocals	Jimmy Rushing or Helen Humes

hits on Columbia rolled out, even given the recording ban of 1942–1944, which hurt all big bands. "Tickle Toe" (1940), "Goin' to Chicago Blues" (1941), and a definitive version of "One O'Clock Jump" in 1942 constituted just a few of the many successes that Basie enjoyed.

Since he could not make new recordings during the bans, Basie looked to Hollywood and guest appearances in movies. No stranger to film, he had made several musical shorts in the early 1940s. He struck gold in 1943, appearing with his orchestra in six features, including such titles as *Hit Parade of 1943, Reveille with Beverly,* and *Stage Door Canteen.* If people could not buy his records, they could at least hear and see him and the band on screen. He also toured with the **USO;** cut V-Discs (recordings made expressly for the armed forces and not available commercially during the war; most have subsequently appeared in various anthologies); and, if all that were not enough, the band spent much of its time on the road, going from one appearance to another.

The postwar era turned out to be one of transition for the music business. As the big-band era drew to a close, vocalists and small groups vied for the public's attention, chilling the climate for swing orchestras. Basie, however, cut several more successful disks in the mid-1940s, including such classics as "Avenue C" and "Rambo." He even had an unexpected 1947 hit with the novelty tune, "Open the Door, Richard!" It features an unusual vocal from trumpeter Harry Edison and went briefly to No. 1 on the charts. But reacting to the economic realities facing big bands, Basie reduced the size of his orchestra, playing mainly with sextets or octets. He signed with RCA Victor in 1947, but most of the sides veer away from his usual swinging style, heading in the direction of more modern jazz and **bebop,** such as 1949's "Normania" (also known as "Blee Blop Blues") or "Futile Frustration" (1947)—an emotion he perhaps felt as he moved away from his Kansas City roots.

Undiscouraged, Basie returned with a reconstituted big band in 1952, which some fondly nicknamed a "swing machine," allowing old and new audiences to rediscover—or discover for the first time—his ability to play in all styles. He landed new recording contracts, hired new arrangers, added a number of young musicians to the aggregation's ranks, toured Europe, and moved into the 1950s, 1960s, and beyond a popular living legend of jazz.

See also: ASCAP *vs.* BMI Radio Boycott and the AFM Recording Ban; Race Relations and Stereotyping

Selected Reading
"Count Basie." www.rutgers.edu/ijs/cb/index.html
Dance, Stanley. *The World of Count Basie.* New York: Charles Scribner's Sons, 1980.
Schoenberg, Loren. *Count Basie: The Columbia Years.* Booklet accompanying *Count Basie and His Orchestra: America's #1 Band!* Columbia/Legacy C4K 87110. 4 CDs. 2003.
Shapiro, Nat. "William 'Count' Basie." In *The Jazz Makers,* eds. Nat Shapiro and Nat Hentoff, 232–242. New York: Grove Press, 1957.

BASKETBALL

As with many activities, basketball struggled as a viable sport during World War II but experienced stability and growth during the postwar years. The game had been created in 1891 by James Naismith (1861–1939), a Canadian physical **education** professor and instructor at the Young Men's Christian Association Training School in Springfield, Massachusetts. Naismith wanted to provide his students vigorous exercise during the long, cold New England winters. He finalized 13 basic rules that described appropriate handling and throwing of the ball, fouls, scoring, length of play, and the role of a referee and umpire. He nailed a wooden basket 10 feet above the floor and oversaw the first official game with a handful of players on January 20, 1892.

Students at the training school moved on to jobs across the country, teaching the game wherever they went, and soon a number of American colleges added it to their roster of athletic offerings. In 1906, the Intercollegiate Athletic Association of the United States (IAAUS) was formed to govern the rules of eligibility for college athletics, including basketball; the organization changed its name four years later to the National Collegiate Athletic Association (NCAA).

By the mid-1930s, basketball had gained enough prominence to hold its own against **baseball** and **football** as a popular pastime. New York City's Madison Square Garden hosted its first college basketball contests in 1934; the sport made an official appearance as an Olympic game in Berlin in 1936; a rule change in 1938 removed a mandatory jump ball at the center of the court after every basket, thereby adding speed and nonstop action to the game; and the NCAA held its first collegiate basketball tournament in 1939.

Momentum continued when W2XBS, an experimental **television** station affiliated with NBC (the National Broadcasting Company) in New York City, broadcast the first college basketball game on February 28, 1940, and **MBS (Mutual Broadcasting System)** followed suit on national **radio** with the 1941 NCAA tournament final. Basketball had spread beyond college campuses and regional interests; in neighborhoods and schools, games took place in gymnasiums as well as outside when weather allowed. High school and college administrations appreciated the game's modest equipment requirements and quickly added it to their sports programs.

With the onset of World War II, player shortages caused by able-bodied men joining the military forced many colleges to either drop team sports for the duration of the war or enlist freshmen not yet old enough for the draft. Soon after the Japanese attack on Pearl Harbor, the American public voiced concern about continuation of their favorite athletic contests. In response, **President Franklin Delano Roosevelt's** (1882–1945) endorsed carrying on professional baseball—and, by extension, other major sports—as long as eligible players did not avoid the draft. He proposed that a good game would provide brief relief to a war-weary country.

The wartime depletion of white players in all sports opened the door for participation by minorities. Prior to 1940, teams had been segregated, both in their member composition and games. Black teams had no league organization for scheduling games or guaranteeing fairness and safety in their play. Nevertheless, the New York Renaissance, or Rens, formed in 1923, crisscrossed the country playing any team that would take them on, and in 1939 entered the World Basketball Tournament held in Chicago. They defeated a white team from Wisconsin, the Oshkosh All-Stars, becoming the first black team to win a world championship.

Despite many disadvantages, another all-black basketball team, the Harlem Globetrotters, organized in 1927, rose to prominence because of their display of extraordinary skills and high level of entertainment. In 1941, they took the world championship away from the Rens. One year later, the Chicago Studebaker Flyers, funded by the United Auto Workers, and the Toledo Jim White Chevrolets, affiliated with an Ohio automotive company, became the first members of the National Basketball League (NBL) to integrate their teams, a step that led the way for other blacks to assert themselves in basketball at both the college and professional levels.

After the war, soldiers returned home and enrolled or reenrolled in college on the **GI Bill** and, in turn, advanced basketball to another level for both whites and blacks. Exceptionally physically fit players enthusiastic for the sport joined college teams, and extremely tall players became more of a norm. The number of fans increased as the game moved from one of speed and agility on the court to include shooting and defensive skills under the basket. For the first time in history, two teams won the NCAA championship two years in a row; Oklahoma A&M in the 1945–1946 and 1946–1947 seasons, followed by the Kentucky Wildcats in 1947–1948 and 1948–1949. These victories generated publicity for basketball as a major college sport and paved the way for a growing interest in professional teams.

The NBL, established in 1898, had been the first pro league, but it lasted only five years before disbanding. A number of loosely organized groups muddled through the early decades of the 20th century, and in 1937 a second NBL formed. In 1949, the NBL and the Basketball Association of America (founded in 1946) merged to create the National Basketball Association (NBA). As a part of the merger, rule changes such as allowing for one-on-one plays, along with a format for championship playoffs, went into effect, all in an attempt to attract large numbers of fans by creating the most exciting game possible.

Over the years, the NBA has featured many famous players, and three, Joe Fulks (1921–1976), George Mikan (1924–2005), and Bob Cousy (b. 1928), began their careers as the 1940s drew to a close. Fulks, who joined the Philadelphia Warriors, was considered the greatest offensive player of his day. On February 10, 1949, he scored 63 points, at the time the most for an individual in an NBA game and a figure generally higher than a winning team score. He held the record for 10 years and became the first player to be enshrined in the Naismith Memorial Basketball Hall of Fame.

George Mikan played for one year with the NBL's Chicago American Gears team before signing in 1947 with the NBA's Minneapolis Lakers; he retired after an outstanding eight-year career with the latter team. With an unusual height for the time, (6 feet, 10 inches), superior coordination, and a fierce competitive spirit, Mikan led the Lakers to five championships and became professional basketball's first superstar by being voted by the Associated Press (AP) in 1950 as the Basketball Player of the Half-Century.

Bob Cousy began his career playing college basketball in the late 1940s. Known for his outstanding passing ability, he joined the Boston Celtics in 1950 and, during the course of his career, played in 13 straight NBA All-Star Games. In the process, Cousy helped build the Celtics into one of basketball's greatest teams during the 1950s and 1960s.

As interest in professional basketball grew, the sport began integrating in 1950, when Charles "Chuck" Cooper (1926–1984) joined the Boston Celtics and later moved to the Milwaukee Hawks. At almost the same time as Cooper's entry into the NBA, Earl Lloyd (b. 1928) went with the Washington Capitols. It turned out that, although Cooper was the first black to sign a contract, Lloyd was the first to play in a game. The New York Knicks added Nathaniel "Sweetwater" Clifton (1922–1990) to their roster after he completed his 1950 contract with the Harlem Globetrotters, bringing the total of black players in the NBA to three.

Basketball has the distinction of being one of the few games that developed in tandem for men and women. Just a few months after Naismith's first official game in 1892, Senda Berenson Abbott (1868–1954), a physical education teacher at Smith College, adapted his rules for women and the game spread from the East Coast of the United States to the West via women's colleges and the playing of intercollegiate games. Abbott, to remove the possibility of overexertion and the "vapors"—popular ideas about women at the time—introduced changes that included shortening the court by half, limiting dribbling to just three bounces, and not allowing players to run, conditions that continued until 1971.

Over the decades, women's basketball teams formed at colleges and high schools but did not gain league and championship status until well after the 1940s. National collegiate championship games got under way in 1969; women's basketball qualified as an Olympic game in 1976; and the Women's Professional Basketball League (WBL), the first such league for women, was organized in 1978; it unfortunately folded three years later.

The men playing in the NBA took a different route. The prosperity that followed the war, along with the development of television, led to the merchandising of their games in order to attract revenue from sources other than ticket sales. By the late 1950s, men's basketball had become a big business, providing untold hours of armchair athletics for Americans, while creating heroes who could be used to sell goods.

See also: Race Relations and Stereotyping; Radio Programming: News, Sports, Public Affairs, and Talk

Selected Reading
Batchelor, Bob, ed. *Basketball in America: From the Playgrounds to Jordan's Game and Beyond.* New York: Haworth Press, 2005.
McCallum, John D. *College Basketball, USA, Since 1892.* New York: Stein and Day, 1978.
Pluto, Terry. *Tall Tales: The Glory Years of the NBA, in the Words of the Men Who Played, Coached, and Built Pro Basketball.* New York: Simon & Schuster, 1992.
Thomas, Ron. *They Cleared the Lane: The NBA's Black Pioneers.* Lincoln: University of Nebraska Press, 2002.

BEBOP (BOP)

In the early 1940s, and in their after hours, many young and enterprising **jazz** musicians who would later come to fame throughout the 1940s went to a place called Minton's Playhouse. A small club in Harlem that had opened in 1940, Henry Minton (active 1940s) owned it; he hired Teddy Hill (1909–1978), a musician, in 1941 as manager. Regulars at the club made for a veritable who's who of modern jazz. The brass players included Roy Eldridge (1911–1989) and Fats Navarro (1923–1950), while Lester "Prez" Young (1909–1959), Coleman Hawkins (1904–1969), and Budd Johnson (1910–1984) could be counted among the reed players; pianists Thelonious Monk (1917–1982), Mary Lou Williams (1910–1981), and George Wallington (1923–1993); drummers Kenny "Klook" Clarke (1914–1985), and Max Roach (1924–2007); bassists Milt Hinton (1910–2000) and Oscar Pettiford (1922–1960); and guitarists Danny Barker (1909–1994) and Charlie Christian (1916–1942) made up an enviable rhythm ensemble. On any given night, some of these musicians could be found in attendance, experimenting with new sounds in contemporary American music.

While these artists were jamming at Minton's, other up-and-coming artists congregated at the many jazz clubs then lining New York City's Fifty-Second Street between Fifth and Seventh Avenues. This locale, often called "Swing Street," or more simply "the Street," had reigned as a jazz mecca for musicians black and white, traditional and modern, since the mid-1930s. Just as Minton's had attracted artists in Harlem, most of the clubs on the Street likewise encouraged impromptu jam sessions where players could test their skills in a competitive but friendly atmosphere.

Some of the clubs featured traditional jazz, or Dixieland, but they were in the minority. The music most likely to be heard in the early 1940s came to be called "bebop." A few at first referred to it as "rebop," but both forms soon came to be shortened to "bop." Etymologically, bebop-rebop-bop probably derives from the music itself. A musician might take several bars and rhythmically play them be-bop, be-bop, and so on. Singers, instead of articulating words when imitating instruments, might also use these terms as part of their scat singing, improvisational vocalizing that replaces regular speech with made-up syllables, such as "oop boop bop sha bam." Whatever its roots, bop became the commonplace term when referring to this new jazz format.

Amid all this club activity, veteran pianist Earl Hines (1903–1983), a virtuoso performer in almost any style, formed a band under his own name during the 1942–1943 period. Hines hired many young musicians as his sidemen, including John Birks "Dizzy" Gillespie (1917–1993), a trumpet virtuoso from South Carolina, and Charlie "Bird" Parker (1920–1955), an alto saxophone player from Kansas City. Gillespie already had some band experience, playing with the Cab Calloway (1907–1994) band, and Parker had arrived in New York with the Kansas City–based Jay McShann (1916–2006) group earlier in 1942.

John Birks "Dizzy" Gillespie, a gifted trumpeter, was one of the unofficial leaders of a new movement in jazz that came to be called bebop. His colorful personality made him a favorite of club audiences, and a series of recordings he cut—often alongside Charlie Parker—introduced countless listeners to this innovative music during the mid- and late 1940s. (Photofest)

Both Gillespie and Parker were destined to become two of the leading lights in the development of modern jazz, especially bebop. An equally youthful Sarah Vaughan (1924–1990) doubled on vocals and occasional piano, and Billy Eckstine (1914–1993), the "sepia Sinatra," as some labeled him, carried the male singing duties. In all, the Hines band featured a remarkable lineup of jazz innovators and would come to perform some of the now-classic tunes associated with the musical changes of the early 1940s. For example, Gillespie's "A Night in Tunisia," composed in 1942 by the trumpeter, could be found in Hines's repertoire; it would eventually become a jazz standard, and countless musicians would perform and record it.

Perhaps encouraged by his work with Hines, Billy Eckstine branched out with his own band in late 1943. Starting out at the Onyx, a nightclub located on Fifty-Second Street, this pivotal orchestra featured some top modern innovators, presaging many of the changes ahead for traditional **swing** bands and also for jazz. He hired Gillespie and Parker, along with reed players Lucky Thompson (1924–2005) and Gene Ammons (1925–1974). George Wallington sat at the piano, Max Roach first kept time on the drums, followed by Art Blakey (1919–1990), and Sarah Vaughan returned to the bandstand as vocalist alongside Eckstine. Most importantly, the leader counted among his arrangers Tadd Dameron (1917–1965), Boyd Raeburn (1913–1966), Budd Johnson, and Gillespie—a stellar group of writers in the evolving jazz idiom. In no way did this orchestra qualify as a traditional swing ensemble. Thanks to recording contracts with the DeLuxe and National labels, two pioneering independents, Eckstine's group survived the war years and looked toward the second half of the decade with some optimism.

Bop mixes swing, gospel, stride, and the blues, but it also has silences, starts and stops, unusual rhythms, unexpected chord changes, and flatted fifths. It will mix 12-bar blues and 32-bar popular songs, as players create intricate solos that completely disguise the original melody. Whereas most swing bands relied on a steady 4/4 beat, in bop the drummer employs the top cymbal to carry the beat, and the bass drum (or snare) drops "bombs"—explosive accents. The brass and reeds then build solos on long improvisational lines instead of short bits, but perform them in a rapid-fire manner that often consists of eighth notes. In the early 1940s, it all sounded like nothing that had come before. And not everyone liked it. Traditionalists and other nay-sayers called the music dissonant, nervous, even frantic, and deemed it unlistenable. On the other side, the boppers called those who opposed their music "moldy figs"—people stuck in a musical rut, unable to move ahead.

At first, bop attracted mainly young black musicians, most of whom expressed disdain for swing, calling it "too white," too arranged, too predictable." They had also grown restive with the artificial racial restrictions they saw around them, especially in the segregated South. In time, however, a number of white artists also found it

An artistic and performing colleague of Dizzy Gillespie, Charlie "Bird" Parker played alto saxophone and helped revolutionize the modern jazz of the 1940s. Unusual chord progressions and a complete mastery of his instrument marked his playing, but a troubled personal life unfortunately took him early in the bop movement. (Photofest)

attractive, although much of the integration in bop occurred during the postwar years. Black or white, the players turned their backs on tradition and challenged their audiences to discard the past and come along with them. Bop was revolutionary, a musical expression by **youth.** In the eyes of many, however, especially commercial promoters, the biggest downside to bop rested with the fact that people could not dance to it.

Some of the smaller independent record labels—Blue Note, Dial, Guild, Keynote, Manor, Musicraft, Savoy, and several others—emboldened by Decca's capitulation to the AFM's (American Federation of Musicians) terms during the 1942–1944 recording ban, began capturing this new music in late 1943, so at least some of it got preserved. Also, a few individuals in possession of recording equipment taped a number of early performances. In some instances, their efforts eventually turned up in commercial markets, sometimes long after the event took place. For the most part, these early recordings, both professional and amateur, tended not to be the best examples of bop. They often possess inferior sound quality, the performances tend to be uneven, and so they display an art in its formative period as the musicians struggle with this often unfamiliar music.

Finally, in the fall of 1945, a few of the leading interpreters of bebop—Dizzy Gillespie, Charlie Parker, Max Roach, and several others—created some timeless examples of early bop when they gathered at the recording studios of Savoy Records. A teenaged Miles Davis (1926–1991) even participated in a session or two, but his fame still lay years ahead of him. Among the tunes, Dizzy Gillespie's "Salt Peanuts" and "Groovin' High," and a song with a prescient title, Charlie Parker's "Now's the Time," were destined to become jazz classics, although they did not receive that kind of praise immediately. Several tunes took their structure from older, more established numbers: Parker's "Ko Ko" originated with the chord changes found in the 1938 swing classic "Cherokee," written by bandleader Ray Noble (1903–1978). It should not be confused with the 1940 tune bearing the same title but composed by **Duke Ellington** (1899–1974). In a similar vein, Parker's "Ornithology" can be traced to the chord structure of the 1940 tune "How High the Moon" and Tadd Dameron's "Hothouse" grew out 1930's "What Is This Thing Called Love?" written by Cole Porter (1891–1964). These songs received new names in order not to pay ASCAP licensing fees for the originals, a common practice in bop during those formative days. Plus, most casual listeners probably would not recognize them in their reinvented form.

In 1947, Gillespie formed his own orchestra. Although it had to struggle against ingrained tastes in jazz, the aggregation nonetheless managed to translate into a big-band setting many of the experiments that he and others had attempted in small groups. In addition, Gillespie finally had an opportunity to explore Afro-Cuban music, an interest he had held for some years. He met Chano Pozo (1915–1948), a brilliant Cuban-born percussionist, and the two collaborated on several compositions. Working with arranger/composer George Russell (b. 1923), Gillespie unveiled "Cubano Be/Cubano Bop," a classic vehicle that showcased Pozo's rhythmic skills. Pozo also contributed the melody for "Manteca" in late 1947, another important Cuban-influenced number for the band. Although Latin tunes had been around for years, Gillespie's use of them in a jazz setting ushered in a new musical element heretofore limited to novelties.

In addition to being a force in the development of bop (by the mid-1940s, most fans and commentators had dropped the prefix "be-" from the term), Gillespie also became the much-publicized face of the music. Onlookers soon associated the tuft of hair beneath his lower lip, beret, horn-rimmed glasses (sometimes sunglasses), and other sartorial accoutrements with the music. His on-stage antics and hipster-style talk warmed audiences to the band, adding to the mystique of the modern jazz musician.

Woody Herman's "Second Herd," which he formed in 1947 in response to the publicity bop was receiving, played a number of boppish arrangements, most notably "Four Brothers," composed by Jimmy Giuffre (1921–2008), one of the members of Herman's sax section. Even Benny Goodman (1909–1986), the King of Swing himself, dipped his clarinet into some bop-style arrangements during 1947–1949, when he recorded for Capitol Records. That period's "Undercurrent Blues," written by Chico O'Farrell (1921–2001), typifies the Goodman approach—not as daring as the things Gillespie, Parker, and others attempted, but a far cry from his swing work of the 1930s and early 1940s.

As bop became another piece in the multipatterned mosaic that is jazz, it lost much of its controversy. A sign of the growing acceptance acceded bop occurred in late 1949. The Clique Club on 52nd Street closed its doors only to reopen them as Birdland, a new jazz venue named in honor of Charlie "Bird" Parker. "Lullaby of Birdland," penned by pianist George Shearing (b. 1919) and one of the anthems of the new music, came out in 1952. Birdland in its heyday regularly booked the best jazz musicians to be found, and that included many players associated with the bop movement. But the club's openness to any and all meant that it existed as a jazz club, not a place for boppers only.

The intense scrutiny and reams of criticism—both pro and con—that bop received throughout the decade waned in time, and it began to be accepted as yet another addition to the jazz palette. Herman broke up the Second Herd in 1950, Goodman returned to swing, and many other musicians disassociated themselves from playing bop exclusively. The revolution, so fiery and insistent for a while, came to an end in the early 1950s. In its heyday, however, bebop signaled a musical impatience, particularly from young black artists, to move ahead. It had bubbled just beneath the surface of the wartime swing years, and in the second half of the decade it finally burst forth. With peace, new music of every description, from country to classical, found an audience ready to shed the past. Bebop—fast, frantic, and esoteric for the noninitiated—served as only one manifestation of this restlessness, but it gained more than its share of publicity from critics and audiences alike.

See also: ASCAP *vs.* BMI Radio Boycott and the AFM Recording Ban; Classical Music; Country Music; Race Relations and Stereotyping; Radio Programming: Music and Variety Shows; Rhythm 'n' Blues

Selected Reading
DeVeaux, Scott. *The Birth of Bebop: A Social and Musical History.* Berkeley: University of California Press, 1997.
Feather, Leonard. *Jazz.* Los Angeles: Trend Books, 1957.
Giddens, Gary. *Visions of Jazz: The First Century.* New York: Oxford University Press, 1998.
Ward, Geoffrey C., and Ken Burns. *Jazz: A History of America's Music.* New York: Alfred A. Knopf, 2000.

BERLIN AIRLIFT, THE

Instead of peace and harmony, tensions grew between Russia and the other Allied powers after the conclusion of World War II. The world drifted into a protracted era of anxiety as the USSR sought to extend its sphere of influence over Eastern Europe, while Britain, France, and the United States looked for ways to block any Communist expansion. This post-1945 period, which soon came to be called the **Cold War** era, saw the adversaries waging a continuous battle of words and threats, as each side strove to gain an advantage over the other. Although the political posturing stopped just short of actual warfare, it at times threatened to escalate into situations that diplomacy might not be able to contain. The 1948 Soviet blockade of Berlin serves as a case in point.

At the cessation of hostilities in Germany in May 1945, U.S. and British armies controlled most of the western part of the country, while Soviet forces occupied the eastern sections. For a number of reasons, most of them political instead of military, the Americans and their allies stopped short of Berlin, ceding the city to the Soviet armies advancing from the east. An agreement hammered out by the victors partitioned the conquered city into four zones: U.S., British, French, and Soviet, although the location of Berlin itself placed it deep within Soviet–controlled territory. It thus existed as an occupied island of sorts, surrounded by hostile Soviet forces. The terms of the treaty creating a divided Berlin guaranteed the Western Allies specified routes through Eastern Germany, granting them ground, water, and air access to the city. Just over three years later, on the flimsy pretext that Western-approved German currency had not received Russian acceptance, Soviet forces, on June 23, 1948, blocked all **trains,** vehicles, and barge traffic headed toward the occupied city. They did not, however, forbid Western aircraft from flying into Berlin.

With the city effectively blockaded, the Western powers had to decide: should they force their way militarily into the beleaguered city, thus risking war with the Soviet Union, or should they give in to Russian demands and surrender any effective control of Berlin? The U.S. president, **Harry S. Truman** (1884–1972), in his typically blunt way, probably spoke for the majority when he said of the Western allies, "We are going to stay. Period." How they would manage to do so remained undecided. Three years after the end of World War II, Europe again seemed poised to go into battle over politics and disputed territory.

In reality, a third course of action existed, one hardly entertained at the beginning of the blockade; it involved supplying the British, French, and American zones by air. When continuing negotiations with the Soviet Union went nowhere, the three powers reluctantly agreed that this latter strategy would be followed. General Lucius Clay (1897–1978), the commander of U.S. forces in Europe and the military governor of the American zone in West Germany, responded to the Soviet threat by cobbling together a fleet of transport aircraft, mainly veteran C-47 Skytrains and C-54 Skymasters. Much of the once-mighty Allied air armada had been dismantled after 1945, so suitable planes were initially in short supply, and pilots had to be hurriedly assigned to the mission. Almost immediately, planes began to ferry in desperately needed **food,** fuel, and medicines to the citizens living in the Western zones. In an airlift dubbed Operation Vittles, they flew along three narrow corridors over the Soviet zone, landed at Berlin's

Tempelhof and Gatow airports, unloaded their cargoes, and then took off and returned to West Germany, only to repeat the procedure again and again.

At first, the U.S. Air Force pilots and their Royal Air Force (RAF) counterparts managed just over 1,000 tons of supplies each day, which would not be sufficient to satisfy the city's needs. Then, throughout August 1948, they boosted their average to 4,000 tons of cargo per day, a bare subsistence load. But colder weather would soon arrive, making flying more difficult and necessitating greater tonnage to satisfy living requirements in the months to come. In the meantime, the Soviet Union worked to make its zone completely separate from its Western counterparts. Before long, the city's British, French, and American zones came to be thought of as West Berlin, whereas people called the Soviet sector East Berlin—names that remained in place for years to come.

The summer eventually drew to a close, but the nonstop flights continued. Neither the Western powers nor the Soviets could reach any agreements, and Berliners looked toward a long and difficult winter. But General Clay had received more and larger aircraft, the French joined in, and January and February saw 5,500 tons become the new daily average. March and April raised the total again, to over 8,000 tons a day, exceeding what had previously been brought in by rail in preblockade times, and more than enough to sustain the city and its inhabitants.

In the spring of 1949, a frustrated Soviet Union, faced with strong negative opinion from much of the world and knowing full well that the now-successful airlift could go on indefinitely, returned to serious discussions about the fate of the divided city. In early May, the four powers announced that restrictions on **travel** to and from West Berlin would be relaxed. Shortly thereafter, on May 12, 1949, the Berlin blockade officially ended, a humiliating failure for Soviet planners and a solid victory for Allied resolve. Flights continued until September, however, while the Allies built up surplus supplies in case the Soviets should choose to block access to the city again.

Understandably, such a humanitarian undertaking caught the imagination of the American people. Journalists filled columns with reports of plane after plane landing on the tarmac, just minutes separating one from another. They told of grateful Berliners turning out by the thousands to upgrade dated runways and helping to unload the priceless supplies that were keeping the city alive. Photographers captured the drama of a transport coming in out of the clouds, landing lights blazing, with another close behind. Press microphones picked up the roar of the engines and the cheers of the waiting crowds. These sounds and images played in newsreels shown nightly in U.S. theaters, and people read about the continuing airlift in their **magazines** and daily **newspapers.**

Some of the transport crews carried candy bars, other sweets, and small **toys,** which they had purchased with their own money. They would drop them from their planes, often utilizing tiny, homemade parachutes, as they came in toward Tempelhof or Gatow. Children, many still clad in worn clothing left over from the war, scrambled after the goodies, and the West could not have asked for better propaganda. This unofficial act of generosity soon gained the approval of air force commanders, and Americans reacted in kind. Children in the United States contributed candy, and several large confectioners likewise made donations. The popularity of this movement gained it the name Operation Little Vittles; in all, it logged over 275,000 flights and carried almost 2.5 million tons of food and other essentials, a number that equates to almost a ton apiece for every citizen then dwelling in West Berlin.

Authorities had envisioned the airlift lasting, at most, three weeks before agreements could be reached with the Soviet Union. It instead lasted almost 11 months. Operation Vittles was not without cost; over 100 Allied pilots, crewmen, and airfield personnel died during the course of the operation, including 31 Americans. A commercial movie, *The Big Lift,* came out in 1950 and uses the background of the Berlin Airlift as the basis for its fictional plot.

See also: Aviation; Desserts, Candy, and Ice Cream; Movies; Photography

Selected Reading
Diggins, John Patrick. *The Proud Decades: America in War and Peace, 1941–1960.* New York: W. W. Norton, 1988.
Gaddis, John Lewis. *The Cold War: A New History.* New York: Penguin Press, 2005.
Knapp, Wilfred. *A History of War and Peace: 1939–1965.* New York: Oxford University Press, 1967.

BEST SELLERS (BOOKS)

The term "best seller" entered the language in the late 19th or early 20th centuries. It applies to anything that sells in large numbers, a meaning that has been largely restricted to the book trade, although exceptions can also be found (best-selling automobiles, best-selling records, and so on). It generally refers to those books that have sold in significant numbers in a brief span of time. Because so many different types of books, genres of literature, audiences, and countless other variables apply, it would be difficult to attach a precise, quantitative meaning to best seller. As a result, publishers have freely employed the term to generate interest—a best-selling novel, but according to what standards?

Some books sell remarkably well when first issued, but the novelty soon wears off and they disappear, forgotten over time. Other books, however, sell only moderately well at any given period, but they continue that pattern over many years. Most classics of literature eventually sell far more copies than a momentarily popular book does in its brief moment of fame or acclaim.

A publicity shot of author Mickey Spillane whose I, the Jury *(1948) became one of the biggest fiction best sellers in the history of American publishing; the paperback edition has sold millions of copies. (Bettmann/CORBIS)*

American book publishing underwent a number of significant changes with the onset of the 1940s. Paperback (also known as paperbound, softbound, and soft cover) books rose to become a powerful force in the industry, with most titles outselling their traditional hardback (clothbound, hardbound, and hard cover) counterparts by the thousands—and even millions, on occasion. In 1939, the beginning of the modern paperback era, dealers sold about 3 million softbound books; by 1949, sales exceeded 175 million copies. Conversely, traditional book (hardback) sales in 1939 totaled approximately 11 million copies; in 1949, this category had not changed significantly, with about 12 million hardcover books sold. In the space of a decade, the marketplace had profoundly changed.

Paperback publishers achieved their remarkable sales by utilizing the distribution channels favored by **newspapers** and **magazines.** These inexpensive volumes could be found at newsstands and kiosks, supermarkets and drug stores, variety and department stores, as well as venues like airports and bus stations. The country supported about 5,000 traditional book stores in 1950, but over 100,000 establishments sold paperback books. Glued spines instead of sewn bindings kept costs down, as did cheap papers and inks; and colorful, eye-catching, often lurid, covers further boosted sales.

In June 1939, publishing giant Simon & Schuster created a subsidiary firm called Pocket Books. Led by Robert de Graff (1895–1981), who had studied the ongoing success of paperback publishing in Europe, Pocket Books initially issued 10 paperbound reprints of existing hardbound books pricing them at 25 cents each (about $3.85 in 2008 dollars), compared to the average $2 to $4 most hardcover books cost then (or about $31 to $62 in 2008 dollars). True to their name, these volumes, roughly 4-1/4 inches by 6-1/2 inches, fit easily into a jacket pocket, unlike a larger, bulkier hardcover book.

In quick succession, competing publishers took the plunge, anxious to have a share of the vast, untapped American paperback market. Penguin Books, an established English firm already in the paperback business, set up New York offices just a month after de Graff's Pocket Books had made its debut and began issuing titles under its imprint shortly thereafter. Avon Books came along in 1941, Popular Library (originally Popular Books) in 1942, Dell Books in 1943, Bantam Books in 1945, New American Library (Signet and Mentor imprints) in 1948, Pyramid Books and Harlequin Books (the latter a Canadian enterprise specializing in romance novels) in 1949, along with a number of smaller houses in the later 1940s.

As a rule, most paperback titles published during the decade tended toward lighter, middle-brow fare, with mysteries, Westerns, and self-help books leading the way in sales. Movie tie-ins soon became commonplace. Pioneering Pocket Books soon learned that mystery novelists Erle Stanley Gardner (1889–1970) and Agatha Christie (1890–1976) consistently ranked as their overall top sellers for many years, although individual titles by either writer seldom made any best-seller lists. Regardless of author, initial print runs by the 1940s averaged 200,000 copies, considerably more than the normal number of hardcover copies for a title. And although they had, at best, wafer-thin profits, the new paperback publishers strove to retain the 25-cent cover price; not until the 1950s did the industry begin charging more for the average title.

While paperbound books were establishing a strong foothold in the American marketplace, the many publishers of clothbound titles—Appleton-Century-Crofts; Crown;

TABLE 19. Best-Selling Books, Fiction and Nonfiction, 1940–1950

Year	Title and Author; Those Books Most Often Found on Best-Seller Lists	Title and Author; Other Significant Books, Not Often Found on Best-Seller Lists
1940	*Fiction* 1. *How Green Was My Valley*, Richard Llewellyn (1906–1983) 2. *Kitty Foyle*, Christopher Morley (1890–1957) 3. *Mrs. Miniver*, Jan Struther (1901–1953; b. Joyce Anstruther) 4. *For Whom the Bell Tolls*, Ernest Hemingway (1899–1961) 5. *The Nazarene*, Sholem Asch (1880–1957) *Nonfiction* 1. *I Married Adventure*, Osa Johnson (1894–1953) 2. *How to Read a Book*, Mortimer Adler (1902–2001) 3. *A Smattering of Ignorance*, Oscar Levant (1906–1972) 4. *Country Squire in the White House*, John T. Flynn (1882–1964) 5. *Land Below the Wind*, Agnes Newton Keith (1901–1982)	*Fiction* *Journey into Fear*, Eric Ambler (1909–1998) *Farewell, My Lovely*, Raymond Chandler (1888–1959) *And Then There Were None*, Agatha Christie (1890–1976) *The Ox-Bow Incident*, Walter van Tilburg Clark (1909–1971) *The Hamlet*, William Faulkner (1897–1962) [an important American author rarely found on any best-seller lists] *The Heart Is a Lonely Hunter*, Carson McCullers (1917–1967) *New Adventures of Ellery Queen*, Ellery Queen (pseudonym of Frederic Dannay and Manfred Lee, 1905–1982 and 1905–1971) *The Grapes of Wrath*, John Steinbeck [published in 1939 but still selling well in 1940; Steinbeck would go on to win the Nobel Prize for Literature in 1962] *You Can't Go Home Again*, Thomas Wolfe (1900–1938) [a major American writer, but seldom a top seller] *Native Son*, Richard Wright (1908–1960) [the debut novel of a significant black writer] Comment: The above books also reflect the growing importance of mysteries and related themes (Ambler, Chandler, Christie, and Queen), plus the lack of recognition given major writers at the time.
1941	*Fiction* 1. *The Keys of the Kingdom*, A. J. Cronin (1896–1981) 2. *Random Harvest*, James Hilton (1900–1954) 3. *This Above All*, Eric Knight (1897–1943) 4. *The Sun Is My Undoing*, Marguerite Steen (1894–1975) 5. *For Whom the Bell Tolls*, Ernest Hemingway (1899–1961) [Hemingway's most topical novel, it sold well and enjoyed the boost of a popular 1943 movie] *Nonfiction* 1. *Berlin Diary*, William L. Shirer (1904–1993) 2. *The White Cliffs*, Alice Duer Miller (1874–1942) 3. *Out of the Night*, Jan Valtin (1905–1951) 4. *Inside Latin America*, John Gunther (1901–1970) 5. *Blood, Sweat and Tears*, Winston S. Churchill (1974–1965)	*Fiction* *Young Dr. Kildare*, Max Brand [Frederick Faust] (1892–1944) [Brand, normally thought a writer of Westerns, also created the immensely popular Kildare] *Mildred Pierce*, James M. Cain (1892–1977) *The Patriotic Murders*, Agatha Christie (1890–1976) *Above Suspicion*, Helen MacInnes (1907–1985) *My Friend Flicka*, Mary O'Hara (1885–1980) *Strange Woman*, Ben Ames Williams (1889–1953)

(*continued*)

TABLE 19. (continued)

Year	Title and Author; Those Books Most Often Found on Best-Seller Lists	Title and Author; Other Significant Books, Not Often Found on Best-Seller Lists
1942	*Fiction* 1. *The Song of Bernadette*, Franz Werfel (1890–1945) [another book made into a successful 1943 film] 2. *The Moon Is Down*, John Steinbeck (1902–1968) [a powerful novel about World War II] 3. *Dragon Seed*, Pearl S. Buck (1892–1973) 4. *And Now Tomorrow*, Rachel Field (1892–1942) 5. *Drivin' Woman*, Elizabeth Pickett (1896–1984) *Nonfiction* 1. *See Here, Private Hargrove*, Marion Hargrove (1919–2003) [the misadventures of a raw recruit in the U.S. Army] 2. *Mission to Moscow*, Joseph E. Davies (1876–1958) 3. *The Last Time I Saw Paris*, Elliot Paul (1891–1958) 4. *Cross Creek*, Marjorie Kinnan Rawlings (1896–1953) 5. *Victory Through Air Power*, Alexander P. de Seversky (1894–1974)	*Fiction* *The High Window*, Raymond Chandler (1888–1959) *Go Down Moses and Other Stories*, William Faulkner (1897–1962) [the collection included his story "The Bear," considered one of his best] *Damon Runyon Favorites*, Damon Runyon (1880–1946) *Nonfiction* Comment: Most nonfiction during 1942 and 1943 concerned itself with the war or related topical subjects.
1943	*Fiction* 1. *The Robe*, Lloyd C. Douglas (1877–1951) 2. *The Valley of Decision*, Marcia Davenport (1903–1996) 3. *So Little Time*, John P. Marquand (1893–1960) 4. *A Tree Grows in Brooklyn*, Betty Smith (1896–1972) 5. *The Human Comedy*, William Saroyan (1908–1981) *Nonfiction* 1. *Under Cover*, John Roy Carlson (1909–1991) 2. *One World*, Wendell L. Willkie (1892–1944) 3. *Journey Among Warriors*, Eve Curie (1904–2007) 4. *On Being a Real Person*, Harry Emerson Fosdick (1978–1969) 5. *Guadalcanal Diary*, Richard Tregaskis (1916–1973)	*Fiction* *Silvertip's Roundup*, Max Brand [Frederick Faust] (1892–1944) [even with the success of Dr. Kildare, Brand continued to turn out popular Westerns] *The Lady in the Lake*, Raymond Chandler (1888–1959) *Claudia*, Rose Franken (1895–1988) *Kitty*, Rosamond Marshall (1902–1957) *The Fountainhead*, Ayn Rand (1905–1982) *Nonfiction* Comment: Whereas much of the fiction of 1942 and 1943 provided escapism for war-weary readers, nonfiction remained basically topical.

1944 *Fiction*
1. *Strange Fruit*, Lillian Smith (1897–1966) [a controversial indictment of racism by a white writer]
2. *The Robe*, Lloyd C. Douglas (1877–1951)
3. *A Tree Grows in Brooklyn*, Betty Smith (1896–1972)
4. *Forever Amber*, Kathleen Winsor (1919–2003) [one of the decade's biggest sellers, it sold over 3 million copies]
5. *The Razor's Edge*, W. Somerset Maugham (1874–1965)

Nonfiction
1. *I Never Left Home*, Bob Hope (1903–2003)
2. *Brave Men*, Ernie Pyle (1900–1945)
3. *Good Night, Sweet Prince*, Gene Fowler (1890–1960)
4. *Under Cover*, John Roy Carlson (1909–1991)
5. *Yankee from Olympus*, Catherine Drinker Bowen (1897–1973)

Fiction
Dangling Man, Saul Bellow (1915–2005) [Bellow would eventually win the Nobel Prize for Literature in 1976]
Dragonwyck, Anya Seton (1904–1990)

1945 *Fiction*
1. *Forever Amber*, Kathleen Winsor (1919–2003)
2. *The Robe*, Lloyd C. Douglas (1877–1951)
3. *The Black Rose*, Thomas B. Costain (1885–1965)
4. *The White Tower*, James Ramsey Ullman (1907–1971)
5. *Cass Timberlane*, Sinclair Lewis (1885–1951)

Nonfiction
1. *Brave Men*, Ernie Pyle (1900–1945)
2. *Dear Sir*, Juliet Lowell (1901–1998)
3. *Up Front*, Bill Mauldin (1921–2003) [a collection of cartoons about World War II, much beloved by both service personnel and civilians]
4. *Black Boy*, Richard Wright (1908–1960) [an autobiographical book about growing up in a segregated society]
5. *Try and Stop Me*, Bennett Cerf (1998–1971)

Fiction
If He Hollers Let Him Go, Chester Himes (1909–1984) [Himes, like Richard Wright before him, remained an often-neglected black author]
Cannery Row, John Steinbeck (1902–1968)

(*continued*)

TABLE 19. (continued)

Year	Title and Author; Those Books Most Often Found on Best-Seller Lists	Title and Author; Other Significant Books, Not Often Found on Best-Seller Lists
1946	*Fiction* 1. *The King's General*, Daphne du Maurier (1907–1989) 2. *This Side of Innocence*, Taylor Caldwell (1900–1985) 3. *The River Road*, Frances Parkinson Keyes (1885–1970) 4. *The Miracle of the Bells*, Russell Janney (1884–1963) 5. *The Hucksters*, Frederic Wakeman (1909–1998) *Nonfiction* 1. *The Egg and I*, Betty MacDonald (1908–1958) 2. *Peace of Mind*, Joshua L. Liebman (1907–1948) 3. *As He Saw It*, Elliott Roosevelt (1910–1990) 4. *The Roosevelt I Knew*, Frances Perkins (1882–1965) 5. *Last Chapter*, Ernie Pyle (1900–1945)	*Fiction* *God's Little Acre*, Erskine Caldwell (1903–1987) [this book originally came out in 1933 and did little; not until its 1946 paperback edition did it take off—over 4.5 million copies sold] *The Member of the Wedding*, Carson McCullers (1917–1967) *Tales of the South Pacific*, James A. Michener (1907–1997) *The Street*, Ann Petry (1908–1997) [another neglected black author] *All the King's Men*, Robert Penn Warren *The Foxes of Harrow*, Frank Yerby [his first of many appearances, although not in the top five] *Nonfiction* *The Common Sense Book of Baby and Child Care*, Dr. Benjamin Spock (1903–1998) [an American standard, this title has sold in the millions over the years]
1947	*Fiction* 1. *The Miracle of the Bells*, Russell Janney (1884–1963) 2. *The Moneyman*, Thomas B. Costain (1885–1965) 3. *Gentleman's Agreement*, Laura Z. Hobson (1900–1986) 4. *Lydia Bailey*, Kenneth Roberts (1885–1957) 5. *The Vixens*, Frank Yerby (1916–1991) *Nonfiction* 1. *Peace of Mind*, Joshua L. Liebman (1907–1948) 2. *Information Please Almanac, 1947*, John Kieran, editor (1892–1981) 3. *Inside U.S.A.*, John Gunther (1901–1970) 4. *A Study of History*, Arnold J. Toynbee (1889–1975) 5. *Speaking Frankly*, James F. Byrnes (1882–1972)	*Fiction* *The Victim*, Saul Bellow (1915–2005) *I, the Jury*, Mickey Spillane (1918–2006) [the paperback release in 1948, along with subsequent editions, has sold more than 6 million copies, making it one of the all-time best sellers in the United States] *Nonfiction* *Merriam-Webster Pocket Dictionary* [the paperback edition of this reference work has sold millions]

1948 *Fiction*
1. *The Big Fisherman*, Lloyd C. Douglas (1877–1951)
2. *The Naked and the Dead*, Norman Mailer (1923–2007)
3. *Dinner at Antoine's*, Frances Parkinson Keyes (1885–1970)
4. *The Bishop's Mantle*, Agnes Sligh Turnbull (1888–1982)
5. *Tomorrow Will Be Better*, Betty Smith (1896–1972)

Nonfiction
1. *Crusade in Europe*, Dwight D. Eisenhower (1890–1969)
2. *How to Stop Worrying and Start Living*, Dale Carnegie (1888–1955) [a book destined to be a perennial best-seller]
3. *Peace of Mind*, Joshua L. Liebman (1907–1948)
4. *Sexual Behavior in the Human Male*, Alfred C. Kinsey (1894–1956) et al. [sequel, *Sexual Behavior in the Human Female*, 1953; both become known as *Kinsey Reports*]
5. *Wine, Women and Words*, Billy Rose (1899–1966)

Fiction
Other Voices, Other Rooms, Truman Capote (1924–1984)
Intruder in the Dust, William Faulkner (1897–1962) [one of the few appearances of Faulkner in any listing, this novel sold relatively well]
The Amboy Dukes, Irving Shulman (1913–1996)
Comment: T. S. Eliot (1888–1965) wins the 1948 Nobel Prize for Literature, boosting his own sales and poetry in general

1949 *Fiction*
1. *The Egyptian*, Mika Waltari (1908–1979)
2. *The Big Fisherman*, Lloyd C. Douglas (1877–1951)
3. *Mary*, Sholem Asch (1880–1957)
4. *A Rage to Live*, John O'Hara (1905–1970)
5. *Point of No Return*, John P. Marquand (1893–1960)

Nonfiction
1. *White Collar Zoo*, Clare Barnes Jr. (active 1940s)
2. *How to Win at Canasta*, Oswald Jacoby (1902–1984)
3. *The Seven Storey Mountain*, Thomas Merton (1915–1968)
4. *Home Sweet Zoo*, Clare Barnes Jr. (active 1940s)
5. *Cheaper by the Dozen*, Frank B. Gilbreth Jr. (1911–2001) and Ernestine Gilbreth Carey (1908–2006)

Fiction
The Little Sister, Raymond Chandler (1888–1959)
Comment: William Faulkner wins the 1949 Nobel Prize for Literature, significantly boosting his subsequent sales

Nonfiction
Canasta, the Argentine Rummy Game, Ottilie H. Reilly; *Canasta*, Josephine Artayeta de Viel and Ralph Michael
[together with Jacoby's books, both below and on the following page, these titles illustrate the runaway popularity of Canasta in the late 1940s]

(continued)

TABLE 19. (continued)

Year	Title and Author; Those Books Most Often Found on Best-Seller Lists	Title and Author; Other Significant Books, Not Often Found on Best-Seller Lists
1950	*Fiction* 1. *The Cardinal*, Henry Morton Robinson (1898–1961) 2. *Joy Street*, Frances Parkinson Keyes (1885–1970) 3. *Across the River and into the Trees*, Ernest Hemingway (1899–1961) [one of his lesser novels; Hemingway would, however, win the Nobel Prize for Literature in 1954] 4. *The Wall*, John Hersey (1914–1993) 5. *Star Money*, Kathleen Winsor (1919–2003) *Nonfiction* 1. *Betty Crocker's Picture Cook Book* (creation of General Mills) 2. *The Baby* (creation of Pet Milk Company) 3. *Look Younger; Live Longer*, Gaylord Hauser (1895–1984) 4. *How I Raised Myself from Failure to Success in Selling*, Frank Bettger (1888–1981) 5. *Kon-Tiki*, Thor Heyerdahl (1914–2002) [the story of an expedition in the Pacific aboard balsa rafts]	*Fiction* *My Gun Is Quick*, Mickey Spillane (1918–2006) [shunned by critics, Spillane nonetheless became a popular favorite, selling millions of copies, particularly during the 1950s] *Nonfiction* *Oswald Jacoby's Complete Canasta*, Oswald Jacoby (1902–1984) *The Flying Saucers Are Real*, Donald Keyhoe (1897–1988) [yet another book reflecting faddish news of the day]

Doubleday; Harcourt; Harper Brothers; Houghton-Mifflin; Little, Brown; Macmillan; McGraw-Hill; Prentice Hall; Random House; and Vanguard, to name just some of the larger ones—continued to release new titles in all fields, despite the difficulties imposed by wartime **rationing** (particularly a scarcity of quality paper) and uncertain, changing public tastes. Reading served as a popular **leisure** pastime, both during the war and into the prosperous postwar years. In addition, publishers, working with the government, made over 1,000 titles in free, paperbound editions, available to those in active military service, with some 125 million copies distributed worldwide during the war years. Most firms participated, using the slogan, "Books Are Weapons." Homefront drives called Victory Book Rallies collected still more reading materials for service personnel. The 1940s also saw the growth of **book clubs** that kept the public abreast of the newest best sellers.

When assessing what people read and which books topped the best-seller lists, expectations and actualities seldom agree. The preceding lists, of necessity, focus on those best sellers available in hardbound format; rankings of paperbacks based on sales did not appear with any regularity until the 1970s.

Best sellers in the book trade should not be considered infallible barometers of the nation's reading tastes; they do provide, however, a snapshot of popular trends. For the 1940s, most fiction kept the war at a distance, providing a blend of escapism and inspiration, with sex and crime adding spice to the mix. Many deserving works escaped notice at the time of publication, and their worth only became known in later years. On the nonfiction side, the reverse held true, with many titles tackling the issues of war and peace, providing readers with information on many sides of current issues. But biographies, self-help, and discussions of popular pastimes also appealed to readers.

See also: Leisure and Recreation; Movies

Selected Reading
Hackett, Alice Payne, and James Henry Burke. *80 Years of Best Sellers, 1895–1975.* New York: R. R. Bowker, 1977.
Hart, James D. *The Popular Book: A History of America's Literary Taste.* Berkeley: University of California Press, 1961.
Lupoff, Richard. *The Great American Paperback: An Illustrated Tribute to Legends of the Book.* Portland, OR: Collectors Press, 2001.

BEST YEARS OF OUR LIVES, THE (WILLIAM WYLER)

Winner of seven Academy Awards (eight, counting a special honorary award), *The Best Years of Our Lives* (1946) captures some of the problems faced by veterans in the first years following World War II. The film grew out of a 1945 short novel written by MacKinlay Kantor (1904–1977). After hearing about difficulties encountered by returning GIs, famed Hollywood producer Samuel Goldwyn (1879–1974) urged Kantor to do a possible story treatment about the difficulties of readjusting to civilian life. The author responded by writing, in blank verse, a novella called *Glory for Me* just as the war entered its last days.

Best Years of Our Lives, The *(William Wyler)*

Two powerful performances from The Best Years of Our Lives *(1946) involve newcomer Harold Russell, a veteran himself and a double amputee from war wounds, and Cathy O'Donnell, who plays his understanding girlfriend. Russell's role has him as a man attempting to deal with his special circumstances, and he brings a touching realism to the part. (RKO / Samuel Goldwyn / Photofest)*

The distinguished playwright Robert E. Sherwood (1896–1955) then converted *Glory for Me* into a workable screenplay. During this adaptation, prose replaced Kantor's previous verse construction, and a new, more meaningful, title was found. Working quickly in order to be as topical as possible, Goldwyn secured William Wyler (1902–1981) as director and cast the popular Fredric March (1897–1975) and Dana Andrews (1909–1992) for two of the three male leads. A newcomer to the screen, Harold Russell (1914–2002), received the nod for the remaining role. A number of other familiar stars rounded out the cast, including Hoagy Carmichael (1899–1981), Myrna Loy (1905–1993), Virginia Mayo (1920–2005), and Teresa Wright (1918–2005).

The Best Years of Our Lives had its American release in November 1946, little more than a year after the final surrenders marking the end of World War II had occurred. The picture earned immediate critical praise and did well at the box office. At the 1946 Academy Award ceremonies, it earned top honors for best picture, best actor (Fredric March), best supporting actor (Harold Russell), best director (William Wyler), best screenplay (Robert Sherwood), along with Oscars for scoring (Hugo Friedhofer, 1901–1981) and editing (Daniel Mandell, 1895–1987). In addition, Harold Russell, a double amputee (he had lost both hands in a war-related accident and wore prostheses), won an honorary Academy Award for being an inspiration to other wounded veterans. Unknown to the Academy of Motion Picture Arts and Sciences at the time—and doubtless much to its surprise—Russell also won the supporting actor award for which he had been nominated, the only person ever to win two Academy Awards for the same role. Until 1946, only 1939's *Gone with the Wind* had accumulated eight victories, putting *The Best Years of Our Lives* in select company. During the 1950s and beyond, however, a handful of other motion pictures have accumulated as many—and more—Oscars, but *The Best Years of Our Lives* stood alone during the 1940s in total awards.

The movie's plot focuses on events in the lives of three servicemen returning to their home town, the fictitious Boone City, a typical community located in the Midwest. One of the three, Dana Andrews, had been a captain in the air force and thinks he can easily get a commercial flight, but it ends that he must rely on the military's Air Transport Command. Thus, he meets the other two veterans of the story, and they board a B-17 bomber ferrying people and supplies for the long trip home. In conversation, the trio reveals a collective nervousness about being stateside again, and justifiably so. Andrews' character has a wife he knows little about, March worries about a reunion with his family, and Russell dreads people seeing his "hooks."

Nothing goes well at first, and the veterans encounter a United States not overly eager to have them back. No heroes' welcome awaits them, and their service to their

Critically acclaimed, The Best Years of Our Lives *(1946) could not have been more topical, dealing with the problems faced by veterans returning to an unfamiliar civilian world; Fredric March portrays a former sergeant who has begun to drink too much, and Myrna Loy plays his patient wife. (RKO / Samuel Goldwyn / Photofest)*

country seems to count for little. Andrews discovers his war-bride wife has cheated on him, March cannot comfortably step back into his former life, and Russell finds it hard to believe that the girl he left behind might accept his prostheses. All of this takes place at a leisurely pace; *The Best Years of Our Lives* runs for almost three hours, far more than the usual 90-minute film of that day. But this tempo allows for extended character development and social commentary.

Time passes as the three veterans try to come to grips with their changed lives. Andrews cannot find a good job ("no qualifications," despite his service), March must bend to the ways of a hard-hearted banking system and reject the loan applications of men on the **GI Bill,** and Russell slowly learns to deal with his handicap and his sweetheart's acceptance of it. Several memorable scenes highlight these predicaments: Andrews wandering a vast field of abandoned military aircraft and wondering if he, too, has been similarly discarded; March giving a speech, while drunk, to fellow bankers about how they have lost sight of human needs in their quest for profits; and Russell taking his girl to his bedroom and revealing to her how the prostheses function.

In the end, resolution occurs. It could be argued that the movie's conclusion sugarcoats the preceding problems, but, in so doing, it paints an optimistic picture of postwar America. Opportunity—financial, occupational, romantic—awaits those willing to strive for it, a message most people wanted to believe in 1946. And things did get better for most veterans after the first rocky adjustments to civilian life. Later in the 1940s and 1950s, several members of congressional committees investigating Communist infiltration into the movie industry criticized *The Best Years of Our Lives* for being anti-American and antagonistic toward a capitalist economic system. But their complaints had little impact; few critics and film buffs saw the arguments as legitimate, and the film continued to ride on its reputation as a meaningful and ultimately positive exploration of the transitional period between war and peace.

Over the years, a consensus has arisen about two American films from the 1940s. Much of the critical community has declared **Casablanca** (1942) to be the best film about the actual war years, even though it has no battle scenes; by the same token, *The Best Years of Our Lives* may well rank as the outstanding motion picture about the difficult postwar aftermath.

See also: Drama (Film); House Un-American Activities Committee (HUAC); Political and Propaganda Films

Selected Reading

Dixon, Wheeler Winston, ed. *American Cinema of the 1940s: Themes and Variations.* New Brunswick, NJ: Rutgers University Press, 2006.

McLaughlin, Robert L., and Sally E. Perry. *We'll Always Have the Movies: American Cinema during World War II.* Lexington: University Press of Kentucky, 2006.

Muller, Jurgen. *Movies of the 40s.* Cologne, Germany: Taschen, 2005.

BEVERAGES

Water clearly serves as the best way to quench thirst. Nonetheless, there has always been a market for other beverages, including tart and sweet, simple and complex, and alcoholic and nonalcoholic varieties. Because of World War II, the beverage industry, as did most industries and citizens, faced economic challenges during the first half of the decade, followed by postwar prosperity.

Soft drinks. Sometimes called soda or pop and originally made of sugar or another sweetener, carbonated water, and flavorings, these beverages date back to the early 1800s and the first days of drug store soda fountains. Sold then primarily for medicinal uses, enterprising pharmacists during the first decades of the 20th century succeeded in adding more interesting flavors; soon all ages enjoyed them simply for their pleasant taste. Mass production followed, and, by 1940, several brands could be bought in virtually any part of the United States. Two manufacturers, the Coca-Cola Company, founded in 1886, and Pepsi-Cola, in 1898, clearly ranked as the primary pro-

"The pause that refreshes" served as an advertising phrase for Coca-Cola, a popular soft drink during the 1940s. The company actively supported the war effort by supplying five-cent Cokes to U.S. troops everywhere. (Photofest)

ducers, although 7-Up and Nehi's Royal Crown Cola offered some competition. Others—Dr. Pepper, Orange Crush, Canada Dry, Kist, Cheer Up, A&W Root Beer, and Moxie, to name a few—lingered in the background, but also had their fans.

During the 1930s, Coca-Cola and Pepsi engaged in escalating **advertising** wars as each attempted to achieve sales supremacy. Sparing no expense, Coca-Cola had artists such as Norman Rockwell (1894–1978) and Haddon Sundblom (1899–1976) provide images for its massive marketing efforts through **magazines,** billboards, calendars, and giveaways—depictions that made Coca-Cola as much an icon in American culture as the Statue of Liberty or apple pie. Pepsi also employed artists, such as cartoonist Otto Soglow (1900–1975), to assist with advertisements appearing in magazines. The company gained renown by introducing a short jingle on **radio** and premiering skywriting at the 1939 New York World's Fair as an advertising tool.

Coca-Cola entered the 1940s anticipating continued growth and financial success. Its 1941 advertising budget of over $10 million (about $141 million in 2008 dollars) exceeded any previous year in its history. As proof of the success of this extraordinary marketing effort, the nickname Coke, which had been used by customers for many years, now appeared on all the bottles.

Pepsi-Cola's 1939 newspaper advertising cartoon strip, *Pepsi & Pete,* had introduced a marketing theme, "Twice as Much for a Nickel," which made reference to the fact that Pepsi came in a 12-ounce bottle for just a nickel (about 75 cents in 2008 money), double the amount of refreshment that any other soft drink companies gave for the same price at the time. This campaign led to the development of the company's famous advertising jingle titled "Pepsi-Cola Hits the Spot." Commonly known as "Nickel, Nickel," two songwriters adapted it from the 1890 English song, "John Peel." It was the first advertising jingle to be broadcast nationwide, a history-making opportunity for Pepsi. "Nickel, Nickel" eventually became a popular record with translations into 55 languages.

When the United States joined its allies in the battles of World War II, soft drink companies, as well as many other industries, suddenly found their businesses limited by wartime restrictions and regulations. The **rationing** of sugar, a key ingredient in a soft drink, caused a severe curtailment of production and the possibility of zero growth for most producers. Pepsi-Cola proved the exception. Unlike Coca-Cola and others that sold a sugary syrup to bottlers, Pepsi provided a concentrated substance, and the bottlers added the sugar in their plants. Most of Pepsi's people were able to find supplemental supplies of sugar, sometimes by reducing their production of other soft drink lines. In 1943, Pepsi president Walter S. Mack (1897–1990) purchased a sugar plantation in Cuba, an effective and profitable way to further strengthen the company's position in dealing with the rationing of sugar and its bottlers.

Shortly after the bombing of Pearl Harbor, in an extraordinary show of patriotism, and what turned out to be a financial boon for the company, Coca-Cola board chairman Robert W. Woodruff (1889–1985) announced that throughout the conflict all servicemen and women could buy a bottle of Coke for 5 cents (about 71 cents in 2008 money) no matter where they were, no matter what the cost to the company. New slogans, such as "It's the real thing," "Coca-Cola goes along," and "That Extra Something!" along with pictures of individuals in the military, spoke to GIs far away from home.

Not surprisingly, Coca-Cola struggled throughout 1942 with fulfilling this promise. Before the war, it had gone international with distribution of its soda fountain syrup for bottling plants in 44 countries. But now it lacked the necessary sugar for production both at home and abroad. Also, to reach American GIs in significant numbers, the company needed more bottling plants, especially ones close to the battlefields. To Coca-Cola's relief, because of its intention to support the troops, the War Production Board (WPB) increased its allotment of sugar and eventually placed the company on the list of industries that provided military necessities, thereby allowing production to meet demand.

A final business boost occurred in 1943, when **General Dwight David Eisenhower** (1890–1969) asked for 10 Coca-Cola bottling plants and enough syrup to provide his men in North Africa with 6 million bottles a month. Despite protests from Pepsi and accusations that the army had created a monopoly, Army Chief of Staff **General George Catlett Marshall** (1880–1959), gave not just Eisenhower, but all theater and area commanders, full discretion to set up soft drink bottling operations and to request personnel to operate the facilities. He also authorized government payment to cover the transportation expenses of entire Coca-Cola bottling plants.

Military personnel followed through on all these allowances, and 250 Coca-Cola technical observers, or TOs, followed the troops to every continent except Antarctica to make sure that all those in service, as well as the local inhabitants, had Coke to drink. By the end of the war, the number of international Coca-Cola bottling plants had increased to 108, growth that cost Coca-Cola very little money. The TO program continued until 1948, further establishing the selling of Coke in the areas housing bottling plants, steps that cemented worldwide recognition and the expansion of Coca-Cola's international trade throughout the decade and years to follow.

On the home front, returning veterans brought home a preference for the drink as supported by a 1948 survey conducted by *American Legion Magazine.* The report had 63.67 percent of the respondents preferring Coke as a soft drink, with Pepsi showing a low 7.78 percent. This same year, the Coca-Cola Company had a gross profit of $126 million (a little over $1 billion in 2008 dollars), compared to the Pepsi Company's $25 million (a little over $215 million in 2008 dollars—hardly a paltry figure itself). Coca-Cola had turned a world war into a marketing boom with a secure future and had become a firmly established American icon, along with strengthening the soft drink market for all brands.

The Pepsi-Cola Company, even with the challenges of wartime restrictions and Coca-Cola's runaway success, stayed in business and made significant competitive headway. Likewise looking for ways to support the war effort and to show its patriotism, Pepsi changed the color of its bottle caps to red, white, and blue—pieces that eventually became collectors' items. The company established three integrated military service centers, unlike the segregated U.S. Army versions. Located in New York City at Times Square, Washington, DC, and San Francisco, these **canteens** assisted millions of armed forces personnel during the war and earned favorable recognition for Pepsi-Cola.

After the war, Pepsi experimented with selling its product in steel cans instead of glass bottles, and, by 1948, the company had its drink in a 12-ounce, lined, cone-top can at a price of three for a quarter. But the interior lining failed, resulting in leaky cans on grocery and pantry shelves. It would not be until the late 1950s and the introduction of aluminum cans that this problem would be solved.

Pepsi's international business, along with its U.S. trade, grew, but more historic was the effort made by Pepsi in 1947 to hire an all-black sales force to sell its soft drink to this underserved minority market. To head up this work, Walter Mack hired Edward F. Boyd (1914–2007) from the National Urban League. Mack had already created a business internship program in 1940 with a nationwide essay contest for college graduates; it took a step toward breaking racial barriers by including 2 blacks in the first 13 winners.

Even more significant steps on this matter occurred through Boyd's advertising campaigns of 1948, 1949, and 1951, when the image of the black U.S. citizen changed from a caricature to an attractive, everyday, middle-class individual. The sales team, working in the days of Jim Crow segregation laws, met with resistance in some parts of the country; they had to ride at the back of buses and in separate train cars and had to look for **restaurants** and establishments that would serve them. They persevered, however, producing double-digit sales. Both soft drink companies grew and increased sales during the 1940s and following years, and the Pepsi-Coke competition continues unabated into the present.

Coffee. Soft drinks may have provided "the pause that refreshes," but it was coffee that got the day started. *Adventures in Good Eating,* by Duncan Hines (1880–1959), appeared on best-seller lists in 1939 and included a good cup of coffee as a requirement for a restaurant to receive his stamp of approval. Three years earlier, coffee-producing countries had funded the formation of the Pan American Coffee Bureau, an organization with the sole intent to promote coffee consumption in North America. By 1941, the United States imported 70 percent of the world's coffee crop, up from 50 percent in 1934.

Starting in September 1942, First Lady **Eleanor Roosevelt** (1884–1962) aired "Over Our Coffee Cups" on NBC's (National Broadcasting Company) Blue Network on Sunday evenings. Sponsored by the Pan American Coffee Bureau, the radio program offered a discussion of current events over a cup of coffee. The show ran until April 1942. *Time* magazine, in May of that year, described coffee "as typical of U.S. life as gasoline," and in October, when the WPB announced its November rationing regulations, lovers of the brew rushed to stores and swept the shelves clean. For some unknown reason, even non-coffee-drinking citizens became enamored of the beverage.

During the brief period of rationing, November 1942 to July 1943, the allowance of one pound every five weeks left many grabbing at a variety of substitutions. Newspaper articles published a number of recommendations, such as brewing coffee grounds twice. They also suggested the addition of roasted chicory root, a New Orleans favorite, to an amount of coffee smaller than usual, along with recipes for several mixtures, some containing coffee and grains and others using just grains. Barley, figs, malt, chick peas, and molasses seemed the most popular. Postum, a caffeine-free roasted grain beverage sold since 1895 as a coffee substitute, experienced a resurgence in sales.

World War II energized the coffee industry. Defense factory workers were allowed time to drink coffee (a rest period in the work routine but not called a coffee break until the 1950s), and military commanders regarded the drink as essential to successful warfare. Producers of instant coffee, such as Maxwell House, Nescafe, and George Washington Coffee, provided lightweight aluminum foil packets of soluble coffee in soldiers' K rations. Maxwell House introduced this product to the public after the war as Instant Maxwell House coffee.

In Europe, 300 Red Cross "clubmobiles" dispensed coffee and doughnuts to troops; volunteers across the United States provided the same in canteens, as well as met troop trains to do likewise. Even those stationed in the far Pacific and North Africa enjoyed coffee on a regular basis.

By 1944, coffee drinking on the home front had risen beyond prewar levels. Annual per capita consumption in 1941 stood at 15.9 pounds and increased to 19.8 pounds by the end of 1945; coffee had become a standard product on grocery shelves. After the war, chain restaurants, such as Howard Johnson's, increased the number of their sites and advertised coffee shops. Chase and Sanborn sponsored ***The Edgar Bergen/Charlie McCarthy Show*** on the NBC radio network. It starred ventriloquist Edgar Bergen (1903–1978) and his dummy Charlie McCarthy and ran from 1937 until 1948.

Tea. During America's colonial days, tea surpassed coffee in popularity, but a national shift began to occur following World War I. With Prohibition, iced tea served as an alternative to illegal beer, wine, and liquor; with Repeal in 1933, tea remained popular well into the 1940s, particularly in hot weather. In the South, it became a year-round beverage. By the 1940s, coffee, however, had clearly won out over tea. Many people, perhaps mostly men, avoided drinking tea, because they mistakenly assumed it to be a beverage for clubwomen and their annual charity teas, spinsters, those of British or Asian origin, or the sick and weak.

Because of shipping difficulties during World War II, the tea supply for the United States, which came from India and Ceylon, meant black tea only; the war had cut off the possibility of tea from the Dutch East Indies, Formosa, China, and Japan, making teas such as oolong, jasmine, and green unavailable. During the first year of the war, supplies of tea in the United States had been reduced to about 75 percent of prewar amounts. By July 1943, however, all kinds of tea once again began to arrive in the United States, and, by the end of the war, the annual per capita consumption rose to the peacetime rate of three-quarters of a pound or 150 cups.

Constant Comment appeared on the market as a new postwar tea product. This innovation came out of the New York kitchen of Ruth Bigelow (1896–1966), who, along with her husband David (d. 1970), was struggling to make ends meet. Intrigued by the tea business and looking for something that would solve their money problems, Ruth experimented with blending teas to create unique new products. She soon settled for a combination of black tea, orange peel, and spices. The couple succeeded in convincing neighborhood gourmet and gift shops, along with Bloomingdale's department store, to carry their tea. By 1950, the business had moved out of the kitchen and into a factory in Norwalk, Connecticut; Constant Comment eventually became a top-selling specialty tea in the United States.

Juice. Frozen concentrated orange juice offers another success story with roots in World War II. Early in the conflict, the Boston-based National Research Corporation (NRC) developed high-vacuum evaporation processes for dehydrating, among other things, penicillin and blood plasma for use in the war effort. The military asked that this technological advance also be applied to food, especially orange juice, and, in early 1945, NRC organized Florida Foods Corporation to provide powdered orange juice to the army. When the war ended, however, the army cancelled the order. The focus of the company immediately shifted to the commercial market and away from a powder to a frozen orange juice concentrate. In hopes of conveying convenience and ease of preparation, the firm adopted the brand name Minute Maid, and the first shipment of this revolutionary product took place on April 15, 1946, the same month the company changed its name to Vacuum Foods Corporation.

Once established as a popular juice, money became available for extensive advertising. In 1948, the company launched a radio campaign with singer Bing Crosby (1903–1977) endorsing Minute Maid frozen orange juice on his daily transcribed show. Although the Philco Corporation had Crosby under exclusive contract, they agreed to let him be Minute Maid's man as long as he also included a daily kind word for Philco products. Purchases of Minute Maid across the country increased dramatically from 1946 to 1951.

Miscellaneous beverages. Americans consumed other beverages during the 1940s, with many improving in quality and increasing in sales after the war. By 1940, milk came in a homogenized form. Kool-Aid, first distributed nationwide to grocery stores in 1929, ceased expansion during the war because of the rationing of fruit and dextrose. After 1945, Kool-Aid accelerated in growth and, by 1950, produced nearly 1 million packets each day. A&W Root Beer offers another example of postwar growth, greatly increasing the number of its drive-in stands throughout the 1940s.

Alcoholic beverages. The liquor industry, like many U.S. operations, experienced operational difficulties because of wartime restrictions. The production of beverage alcohol came to a halt in late 1942, but distillers immediately informed the drinking public that the available stock of whiskey could easily satisfy the nation's thirst for at least four years. Wine production also had to be curtailed in order to have sufficient grapes to increase the quantity of raisins available for men and women in the armed forces. Breweries had lower production rates but not to the extent of distilleries and vineyards. Unable to convert their plants to war production, beer establishments continued to receive the necessary ingredients needed for making their brew.

Cocktails and cocktail parties, encouraged by liquor advertisements and already a common social event, grew in popularity during the 1940s, especially in the years following the war. For those needing help in planning a party, pamphlets and books could be consulted. For example, G. F. Heublein & Bros., a food and beverage importing firm, published *The Club Cocktail Party Book* in 1941. Just one year earlier, James Beard (1903–1985), chef, writer, and promoter of American cuisine had authored *Hors d'Oeuvre and Canapes.* He also contributed to Broadway producer and author Crosby Gaige's (1882–1949) *The Standard Cocktail Guide* (1944). Morrison Wood (active 1930s–1960s), food writer with the *Chicago Tribune,* published *With a Jug of Wine* in 1949.

Even though the singing group the **Andrews Sisters** (Patty [b. 1918], Maxene [1916–1995], LaVerene [1911–1967]) recorded "Rum and Coca-Cola," which hit No. 1 on the popular music charts in 1945, many sources reported martinis, followed by Manhattans, whiskey sours, rickeys, fizzes, Collinses, and old-fashioneds as America's favorite party drinks. A new lemon-lime nonalcoholic beverage called Mountain Dew, slang for moonshine, created by brothers Barney (d. 1949) and Ally Hartman (n.d.), owners of Hartman Beverage bottling plant in Knoxville, became known as a good mixer with Tennessee whiskey.

By 1940, the American beer industry had regained the production levels enjoyed prior to Prohibition, but with fewer breweries. More and more small operations closed as their sales lagged, with the bulk of consumer business going to the larger ones, such as Anheuser-Busch, Coors Brewing Company, and Pabst Brewing Company. At the end of the decade, the *New York Times* reported all-time high sales of beer.

Beer producers made large contributions to the war effort. In 1942, each member of the armed forces in North Africa received a pound of beef or chicken and an American beer for a special Christmas meal. In 1943, 15 percent of beer production went to the armed forces. Throughout the war, all cans of Pabst Blue Ribbon beer, exclusively made for the troops because of tin rationing, came painted a military green.

The war years were difficult ones for the beverage industry; it struggled to recover and, in the postwar period, did achieve a comeback. Growth for the soft drink branch became easier after the Second World War, when the government set aside 50,000 pounds of sugar for each returning veteran willing to open a soft drink bottling plant, and GI loans allowed many to do so. Vending took a giant leap forward as machines, which previously had been considered suitable only for the workplace, started appearing in **grocery stores and supermarkets** and other retail outlets. At the end of the decade, about 70 percent of the milk sold came in homogenized form, up from 33 percent in 1940. Frozen orange juice concentrate reached new sales highs in 1949. Whatever the preferred alcoholic beverage during the 1940s, industry revenue grew by $2 billion ($21 billion in 2008 dollars) between 1945 and 1947. These events set the stage for fierce competition within the nonalcoholic and alcoholic drink industries and the introduction of a host of new beverages during the 1950s.

See also: Best Sellers (Books); Comic Strips; Newspapers; Race Relations and Stereotyping; Radio Programming: Comedy Shows; Radio Programming: Music and Variety Shows; Television

Selected Reading
Allen, Frederick. *Secret Formula: How Brilliant Marketing and Relentless Salesmanship Made Coca-Cola the Best-Known Product in The World.* New York: Harper Business, 1994.
Beverages. *New York Times.* November 4, 1941; January 6, 1942; March 30, 1942; April 3, 1942; July 22, 1942; November 8, 1942; November 18, 1942; December 25, 1942; January 3, 1943; July 22, 1943; July 31, 1945; October 5, 1948; August 4, 1949. www.proquest.com
Pendergrast, Mark. *For God, Country, and Coca-Cola: The Unauthorized History of the Great American Soft Drink and the Company That Makes It.* New York: Charles Scribner's Sons, 1993.
———. *Uncommon Grounds: The History of Coffee and How It Transformed Our World.* New York: Basic Books, 1999.
Trager, James. *The Food Chronology: A Food Lover's Compendium of Events and Anecdotes from Prehistory to the Present.* New York: Henry Holt, 1995.

BLACK MARKET

In times of war, natural or manmade disasters, economic dysfunctions, or other instances where prolonged shortages of essential goods emerge as a problem, black markets will begin to appear. Not stores or merchandisers in the conventional sense, these businesses function outside the law and supply items otherwise not available. They rely on genuine scarcity or because government controls or taxes have priced certain items beyond the means of many consumers. Black marketeers operate in one of two ways, either by charging exorbitant prices for articles they stock or undercutting legally sanctioned prices.

Although the practice of offering goods illegally has been around since time immemorial, the actual term "black market" first came into use around 1931, in the waning days of Prohibition and the onset of the Great Depression. No credence has been given to the notion that it once referred to slavery or somehow carries other racial connotations, although that belief has persisted, even into contemporary times. The word "black" in this instance refers to anything extralegal or underhanded, giving the phrase the literal meaning of an illegal market or an establishment that avoids any regulations.

To cite a classic example: during the 1920s and early 1930s, the U.S. government attempted, unsuccessfully, to ban the sale of alcohol under the terms of the Eighteenth Amendment to the Constitution. Prohibition, as most Americans called it, set up a flourishing black market for intoxicating beverages of all kinds, and people openly flouted the restrictions. By 1933, the Twenty-first Amendment repealed Prohibition, and with the sale of alcohol once again legal in most areas of the country, the once-pervasive black markets for liquor effectively withered and died.

When the nation entered World War II, the government immediately put in place extensive **rationing** programs and set price controls on a wide range of goods. Beginning in early 1942, the federal Office of Price Administration (OPA) oversaw these efforts. Automotive goods, such as tires and mechanical parts, practically disappeared from the open market because the war effort needed the materials used in their manufacture. Almost overnight, clandestine dealers in these articles appeared. For a price, a new or used tire might be obtained if an individual knew the right people. The OPA restrictions also limited how much gasoline one could purchase, but there always seemed to be someone who knew someone who had an extra supply of the precious fuel hidden away somewhere. Of course, that illegal gallon or two would cost far more than the price posted at a legitimate station pump. And it might have impurities, might even be diluted, but that was part of the risk when dealing with the black market.

The motion picture industry, always quick to exploit the latest in criminal ventures, in 1942 released *Boss of Big Town* through PRC Studios, no strangers to fast, cheap movies. Racketeers take over "Big Town's" **food** distribution system and hope to make exorbitant profits, but a crusading city market manager (played by John Litel, 1892–1972) soon gets to the bottom of things. A second-rate picture, but the topic reflects national concerns about the existence of black marketers and consequent threats to food supplies.

Although Hollywood simplified a complex situation, nylon stockings, silk lingerie, medicines, extra train reservations, and a host of other goods became increasingly scarce with the war. A butcher might obtain some additional meat (best not to ask from where or how—horsemeat as a main course was not unheard of) and tell longtime customers they need not use their valuable ration stamps to buy it, although a surcharge might be added to the off-the-record price. Government inspectors, despite their best efforts, could not possibly keep up with these small exchanges and expended most of their efforts on catching professional criminals moving in on this lucrative trade.

One of the more popular rackets involved printing counterfeit ration stamps. Although both seller and buyer ran the risk of getting caught, the advantages to the buyer—access to otherwise restricted goods—and the monetary gains to the seller kept counterfeiters busy throughout the war. Estimates place the amount of gasoline purchased with fake stamps at 1 to 2 million gallons per week, and several thousand service stations around the country lost their business licenses when authorities found them violating rationing guidelines. And, in shades of Prohibition, bootlegging and moonshining again flourished. Distillers, limited to stocks on hand, could not keep up with demand, and so thirsty consumers looked to alternative suppliers. If needs could not be met legally, and if someone had what a buyer wanted, beating the system did not present too much of a moral dilemma for many, no matter how law abiding they were in other matters.

Shortages did not magically end in 1945 and the return to peace. In the waning days of the war, meat and some clothing, especially shoes, remained in short supply. The delay meant that black marketeers stayed busy until scarce items again became available at reasonable prices. In the meantime, cattle were rustled and sold under the counter to cooperating retailers. Truckloads of shoes destined for stores were stolen and then reappeared in selected shops; such activities kept the OPA active into 1946 as farmers and industry shifted to civilian production schedules. The OPA price controls remained in place to prevent inflationary pressures from elevating prices to a point that black market alternatives might appear attractive to consumers. In time, however, legitimate suppliers again filled shelves, once-scarce items reappeared, and the need, real or perceived, for a black market disappeared.

See also: Civil Defense; Grocery Stores and Supermarkets

Selected Reading
Lingeman, Richard. *Don't You Know There's a War On? The American Home Front, 1941–1945.* New York: Thunder's Mouth Press, 1970.
Manchester, William. *The Glory and the Dream: A Narrative History of America, 1932–1972.* 2 vols. Boston: Little, Brown, 1974.

BLACKOUTS, BROWNOUTS, AND DIM-OUTS

Journalist Edward R. Murrow (1908–1965), reporting for CBS (Columbia Broadcasting System) in a nightly radio newscast picked up in the United States and Canada, stood atop tall buildings in London and vividly described, with the explosions audible in the background, the destruction wrought by the Germans during the Blitz of 1940. On the American home front, civilians grew increasingly apprehensive about the possibility of enemy aircraft appearing over their cities carrying deadly loads of bombs, especially after hearing and reading about the extensive damage and loss of life. The December 1941 bombing of Pearl Harbor heightened those fears, and one of the first measures put into effect following the attack consisted of darkening much of the West and East Coasts.

Under government orders, cities and towns, when threatened with aerial attack, had to extinguish all visible nighttime lighting, both exterior and interior. This directive included homes and apartments, commercial and industrial buildings, and streetlights and advertising signs. "Blackout" came to be the term used to describe such an event, one first used in a military sense during the later 1930s. At night, a blacked-out city provides a much more difficult target to aircraft than a brightly lit one. Plans

The Federal Arts Project created this poster in the early 1940s to remind citizens about their responsibilities during any kind of air raid warning. (Library of Congress)

called for warning sirens to signal the approach of enemy planes and the immediate need for people to eliminate all possible artificial illumination that might be visible from the air.

Confusion marred some of the early efforts to achieve blackouts, such as many cities lacking the sirens needed to signal imminent danger and having a trained staff on hand to explain to worried citizens what was happening. But time and experience overcame these logistical problems. City dwellers acquired opaque blackout curtains and shades, and localities put into action a system of air raid wardens who worked to see that extraneous lights were darkened. Before long, and in the absence of any actual enemy attacks, cities across the country learned how to plunge themselves into comparative darkness quickly and efficiently.

Many of these approaches to blacking out U.S. cities were already in the planning stages in the months preceding Pearl Harbor. Federal, state, and local officials had worked to create **civil defense** councils, correctly anticipating the country's entry into the war. The groups recruited thousands of citizens to act as zone and block wardens in their respective neighborhoods. Federal and state funding supplied them with World War I-era helmets painted white and emblazoned with a civil defense emblem, along with countless identifying armbands. The wardens had the authority to knock on doors and remind offenders about "lights out" or, more emphatically, "douse those lights!" By 1942 and 1943, well over 600,000 individuals nationwide, all volunteers, stood ready to take to the streets upon hearing the insistent call of the warning siren.

In time, practice blackouts—unannounced, unexpected—became a part of nighttime America in cities across the land. Most of them occurred in communities situated near key defense industries, because they were thought to be prime targets for the enemy. At times, searchlights would probe the skies, their white beams crisscrossing one another. Inside the darkened buildings, people often used masking tape or thumb tacks to seal unruly curtains or ill-fitting shades. They would retreat to interior rooms, away from windows and the possibility of flying glass, and read or play games by candlelight or a low-wattage bulb. Since virtually everyone knew (or hoped they knew) that these blackouts were practice alerts and not the real thing, the time spent waiting for the all-clear signal could be a pleasant experience.

Along the coasts, a different kind of darkening took place. Even before the formal declarations of hostilities in December 1941, German submarines had been harassing shipping in the Atlantic. Since Germany had been at war with England since September 1939, ships destined for the British Isles, especially those with Lend-Lease supplies, became targets for roving U-boats (for *Unterseeboot,* or undersea boat). When the Nazi government declared open war against the United States, all U.S. ships risked attacks, and they shortly occurred with deadly regularity off the Atlantic coast. At first, the cost in lost shipping and crews proved horrendous. Almost daily, a fresh column of smoke off New Jersey or Virginia or Florida indicated another freighter or tanker had been torpedoed. Most of these sinkings took place at night, and onlookers marveled at the accuracy of the German sailors.

And then the answer came to officials: glittering coastal cities, automobile headlights shining toward the sea, garish beach amusements—any kind of bright land lights tended to silhouette ships at sea, particularly for submariners lurking farther out and looking back toward the illuminated coastline. They became easy targets—sitting ducks—for torpedoes, with the result that over 300 Allied ships were sunk during 1942–1943 (this figure also includes losses in the Caribbean and the Gulf of Mexico, and not all went down at night).

Civil defense and military personnel moved quickly to slow this carnage, with the result that the coastal portions of the continental United States underwent a dusk-to-dawn brownout on a nightly basis. Starting in March 1942, no one could display bright lights along the immediate shoreline and up to 10 to 15 miles inland; any illumination likely to be observed offshore had to be dimmed, a fact that led to the additional term "dim-out" to describe the situation. This order included vehicles of all kinds: a car or truck had to use parking lights and should avoid aiming them directly toward the ocean. This sweeping edict included streetlights and advertising signs; New York City, home of the Great White Way, protested, but to no avail. For over two years, until officials relaxed the order in 1944, when much of the German U-boat fleet had retreated or lay at the bottom of the ocean and no longer presented such a threat, coastal cities existed in a murky half-light designed to foil the undersea raiders.

Fortunately, no air raids occurred and no bombs fell, but the vigilance of thousands of civil defense volunteers undoubtedly reassured the nation that every precaution had been taken to avoid another sneak attack. But despite all the precautions against surprise, everyone gave a sigh of relief when any blackout, practice or otherwise, came to a close and the mournful whine of the all-clear sirens announced the lights could again come on. Such an exhibition of community spirit further bound the country in its quest for total victory.

See also: Black Market

Selected Reading
Hoopes, Roy. *Americans Remember the Home Front: An Oral Narrative.* New York: Hawthorn Books, 1977.
Lingeman, Richard. *Don't You Know There's a War On? The American Home Front, 1941–1945.* New York: Thunder's Mouth Press, 1970.
McCutcheon, Marc. *The Writer's Guide to Everyday Life from Prohibition through World War II.* Cincinnati: Writer's Digest Books, 1995.

BOGART, HUMPHREY

The epitome of the hard-boiled movie tough guy, yet capable of playing sympathetic, conflicted characters as well, Humphrey Bogart (1899–1957) was born into a wealthy New York City family and seemed destined for a career in medicine, his father's profession. But 1920 found him drifting after his discharge from the navy, and he ended up working for a theatrical company on Broadway. Bogart played a variety of bit parts to no great acclaim until late 1934, when he landed the role of gangster Duke Mantee in Robert Sherwood's (1896–1955) play *The Petrified Forest*. The show ran for almost 200 performances, and Bogart received favorable notices.

Warner Bros. Pictures acquired rights to the production and in the winter of 1936 released a movie version of the play with stars Bette Davis (1908–1999) and Leslie

One of the top movie stars of the 1940s, Humphrey Bogart epitomized the hard-boiled hero. This advertisement shows him with Mary Astor in The Maltese Falcon *(1941); Bogart plays Sam Spade, a private detective. (Warner Bros. Pictures/Photofest)*

Howard (1893–1943), plus Bogart in a re-creation of his stage role. A modest success, it led the studio to sign the actor to a contract, which in those days guaranteed work but not necessarily stardom. He played in two dozen films between 1936 and 1940, but few worth mentioning. Relegated to supporting roles, and usually typecast as a gangster, Bogart played second fiddle to Warner's stable of male leads, such as James Cagney (1899–1986), Pat O'Brien (1899–1983), Edward G. Robinson (1893–1973), and George Raft (1895–1980).

Elusive top billing finally came to the actor with *High Sierra* in 1941, a mystery costarring Ida Lupino (1914–1995). Bogart plays "Mad Dog" Roy Earle, an escaped criminal who meets his defiant end atop a California mountain. Bogart's fatalism, his acceptance of things as they are, created a new side to his character, one that worked well for him. Outwardly an amoral, insouciant type, always ready with a sardonic remark, the rough exterior hides a more sensitive and complex personality within; he has deliberately erected a wall between himself and others. As a tribute to his acting ability, Bogart allows the audience to see bits of this inner man, while the other players remain unaware of him. This kind of characterization made Bogart one of the first of what came to be popularly called antiheroes, reluctant protagonists who often exhibit nonheroic traits such as cynicism and avoidance of responsibility. Its attributes go back in literature and the arts, but "antihero" in fact first found widespread use as a critical term in the early 1940s.

TABLE 20. The Films of Humphrey Bogart, 1940–1949

Year	Movie Titles	Actors
1940	*Brother Orchid*	Humphrey Bogart, Edward G. Robinson
	It All Came True	Bogart, Ann Sheridan
	They Drive by Night	Bogart, George Raft
	Virginia City	Bogart, Errol Flynn, Randolph Scott
1941	*All Through the Night*	Bogart, Conrad Veidt
	High Sierra	Bogart, Ida Lupino
	The Maltese Falcon	Bogart, Mary Astor
	The Wagons Rolls at Night	Bogart, Sylvia Sidney
1942	*Across the Pacific*	Bogart, Mary Astor
	The Big Shot	Bogart, Irene Manning
	Casablanca	Bogart, Ingrid Bergman
1943	*Action in the North Atlantic*	Bogart, Raymond Massey
	Sahara	Bogart, Bruce Bennett
1944	*Passage to Marseille*	Bogart, Claude Rains
	To Have and Have Not	Bogart, Lauren Bacall
1945	*Conflict*	Bogart, Alexis Smith
1946	*The Big Sleep*	Bogart, Lauren Bacall
1947	*Dark Passage*	Bogart, Lauren Bacall
	Dead Reckoning	Bogart, Lizabeth Scott
	The Two Mrs. Carrolls	Bogart, Barbara Stanwyck
1948	*Key Largo*	Bogart, Lauren Bacall, Edward G. Robinson
	The Treasure of Sierra Madre	Bogart, Walter Huston
1949	*Knock on Any Door*	Bogart, John Derek
	Tokyo Joe	Bogart, Alexander Knox

Realizing they had a winning property, Warner Bros. soon followed *High Sierra* with *The Maltese Falcon* (1941). Based on a memorable 1930 novel of the same name by Dashiell Hammett (1894–1961), it introduced moviegoers to Sam Spade, the archetypal private detective. Spade had previously appeared on film in 1931, when an early *Maltese Falcon* came out with Ricardo Cortez (1899–1977) in the lead. Virtually impossible to find today, the movie suffers in comparison to the 1941 version, because Cortez's performance lacks the intensity of Bogart's. In 1936, *Satan Met a Lady* reinterpreted the story, but Spade becomes Ted Shayne, and the little-known Warren William (1894–1948) plays the Spade/Shayne character too lightly for good effect. It therefore befell Humphrey Bogart to create the definitive private eye.

Warner Bros. paired the actor with John Huston (1906–1987), an untried director making his debut with the Hammett story, one that he also scripted. Both apparently took to one another, and the 1941 *Maltese Falcon* ranks as an American film classic. A fine supporting cast—Mary Astor (1906–1987), Elisha Cook Jr. (1903–1995), Sidney Greenstreet (1879–1954), and Peter Lorre (1904–1964)—adds to the richness of the production. Dark and moody, an early example of the **film noir** stylistics that would dominate the **crime and mystery films** of the decade, the picture proceeds briskly and economically and avoids much overt violence, relying instead on intelligent dialogue and solid acting.

Following several forgettable films, Bogart endeared himself to audiences with one of his most memorable performances, that of night club owner Rick Blaine in *Casablanca* (1942). A romantic classic about World War II, it won Academy Awards for best picture, best director (Michael Curtiz, 1886–1962), and best screenplay. Five additional nominations included Claude Rains (1889–1967) for best supporting actor and Bogart himself for best actor, but he lost to Paul Lukas (1891–1971) for *Watch on the Rhine*.

A bittersweet romance and perfect for the war years, *Casablanca* tells a love story about Rick and Ilsa (played by Ingrid Bergman, 1915–1982). Bogart, typically seen with a drink in one hand and a cigarette in the other, loves Ilsa, but she happens to be married, and his personal code of honor will not allow him to interfere in that relationship. Under other circumstances, perhaps the lovers would have a chance, but Ilsa's loyalty to her husband and to the anti-Nazi resistance causes Rick to step away in a classic ending, as she tearfully boards a waiting plane and he helplessly watches her go.

What sounds like a soap opera plot works in this dark, smoke-filled drama; duty overrides affairs of the heart, especially in time of war, the looming background for *Casablanca*. For audiences in the grim year of 1943, it gave an inescapable message: citizens everywhere have to make sacrifices, and anything less would be selfish and unpatriotic. Later generations of audiences might view *Casablanca* as a sad tale of love denied, but their context would differ markedly from those who endured the countless deprivations, both personal and material, brought about by World War II.

Despite the success of *The Maltese Falcon* and *Casablanca*, Warner Bros. persisted in giving Bogart roles in mediocre pictures. In addition, the ongoing war affected all of Hollywood; the studios felt pressure to produce patriotic **movies,** and they often sacrificed quality to churn out tales featuring all-American heroes up against the evil Axis forces. And so with *Action in the North Atlantic, Sahara* (two 1943 motion pictures but with the latter produced by Columbia; studios occasionally loaned out their contract players), and *Passage to Marseille* (1944), Bogart gets to play a merchant marine officer, a tough army sergeant, and a French journalist. In each picture, he portrays his by-now characteristic reluctant hero; he does not look for conflict, but he accepts it, and in time rallies to the cause with the expected good results.

The actor regained his stride that same year with *To Have and Have Not* (1944), a loose adaptation of American writer Ernest Hemingway's (1899–1961) 1937 novel. Warner Bros. had given the story to William Faulkner (1897–1962), another famous novelist, for scripting, and then hired Howard Hawks (1896–1977) as director. Hawks and Faulkner proceeded to create a drama that may not be great literature (Hemingway played no role in the adaptation, and book and movie share little other than the same title), but it remains a motion picture that critics continue to dissect today.

The movie also introduces audiences to Bogart's costar, a young Lauren Bacall (b. 1924) making her film debut. Legend has it that sparks erupted on the shooting stage almost daily, as Hawks, Bacall, and Bogart, along with a number of other players, provided a steady supply of fodder for the Hollywood gossip columnists. Shortly thereafter, Bogart divorced his third wife and married Bacall, a match that would endure until his death in 1957.

On screen, the chemistry between the two seems palpable, and Bacall proves herself an equal to Bogart. The wisecracks and innuendoes fly thick and fast, and understanding the complex plot becomes secondary to watching the two stars play off one another. Ostensibly it revolves around the Caribbean island of Martinique during 1940, the dark days preceding the full-blown outbreak of World War II. Bogart plays Harry Morgan, a politically apathetic captain of a charter fishing boat, while Bacall portrays Slim Browning, a stranded American anxious to get back to the States. With obvious shades of *Casablanca,* these two characters must contend with the Gestapo and appear neutral, but of course Bogart eventually must make choices and drop the pretense of not caring and finds he has fallen in love and also taken sides.

The commercial success of *To Have and Have Not* led Warner Bros. to pair up the team of Bogart and Bacall for other pictures. *Conflict* (1945) stands as below-average even for his most devoted fans. By this time, however, Humphrey Bogart commanded the box office; posters **advertising** his films usually had his name in print larger than that promoting the titles of his features. Virtually anything he appeared in drew a crowd. So it was that marquees were soon flashing "Bogart-Bacall!" for a new picture directed by Howard Hawks. *The Big Sleep* (1946), a mystery opus based on a similarly titled 1939 novel by Raymond Chandler (1888–1959) and Bogart's first postwar effort, boasts screenplay credits by none other than William Faulkner, just as in *To Have and Have Not.* Bogart plays Philip Marlowe, the battered and slightly worn private detective whom Chandler had introduced in his book, a character not unlike Dashiell Hammett's Sam Spade from *The Maltese Falcon.* Bacall takes the role of the rich daughter of the even wealthier man who hired Marlowe.

Raymond Chandler seemingly created Philip Marlowe in 1939 with Bogart in mind, although the actor had hardly established his movie persona at that time, and the movie version of *The Big Sleep* lay six years in the future. But Marlowe, a reluctant knight-errant who holds off a world of cheats, liars, and frauds through weary cynicism and a detached view of his surroundings, reads on the printed page much like Bogart performing on the silver screen.

Several lesser movies followed *The Big Sleep* in what seemed a recurring cyclical pattern of two or three mediocre pictures and then an outstanding one. In this instance, Bogart resumed his winning ways with *The Treasure of the Sierra Madre* (1948), an adventure film that reunited him with director John Huston for the third time, a fruitful collaboration. With this motion picture, Huston won an another Academy Award for best director, and his father, Walter Huston (1884–1950), a fine actor who costars with Bogart, won best supporting actor from the Academy, making them the first father-son pairing to be so honored.

The story, for which John Huston also wrote the screenplay—and won yet an additional Academy Award for his efforts—originated in a novel by the enigmatic American author B. Traven (ca.1882–1969). First published in 1927 in a German edition, it received an English translation during the early 1930s. In 1947, the novel caught director Huston's eye, and the film, now a classic, appeared in theaters the following year.

Focusing on greed and what it does to otherwise decent people, the movie shows the disintegration of Fred C. Dobbs (played by Bogart) and his two companions, played by Walter Huston and Tim Holt (1918–1973), while searching for gold in a remote, mountainous section of Mexico. After striking it rich, but pursued by bandits and victims of their own incompetence and distrust, they lose everything. A bleak, uncompromising picture, with Bogart playing against type, it did not initially do well at the box office. In time, however, audiences came to appreciate the superior acting and tight storyline, and *The Treasure of the Sierra Madre* has long since joined a select group of motion pictures deemed among the best of the 20th century.

The team of Warner Bros., John Huston, and Humphrey Bogart immediately followed *The Treasure of the Sierra Madre* with *Key Largo* (1948). This film also features Lauren Bacall and a classic movie villain, Edward G. Robinson, here portraying a gangster reminiscent of some of the characters he played over a decade earlier, especially *Little Caesar* (1931). He was Rico then, and now he becomes (Johnny) Rocco. The plot gathers the cast in a seedy, semitropical hotel on the Florida Keys, and it all becomes rather stagy, as well it should, since Huston based his picture on a 1939 Broadway play by the renowned Maxwell Anderson (1888–1959). Bogart plays his alienated, reluctant antihero well; Bacall adds a note of glamour; and Robinson steals the show, sneering and snarling his way through the entire production.

Key Largo captures some of the disappointment the country experienced in the immediate postwar years. After successfully fighting a world war, returning veterans—the role taken by Bogart—found that numerous problems such as crime and inequality—still plagued the nation. The promise of the peacetime era continued to elude some citizens, and the disillusionment that marks many of his film characterizations constitutes a significant part of this motion picture.

Humphrey Bogart closed out the 1940s as one of the biggest stars in American movies; his presence in a picture practically guaranteed at least some box office success. As a result, in 1949 he broke with Warner Bros. and formed his own production company, Santana Pictures Corporation (distributed by Columbia), in order to have more control over his material and the roles he played. Unfortunately, his new enterprise got off to a disappointing start with *Knock on Any Door* and *Tokyo Joe* (both 1949). Despite some effective film noir **photography,** two-dimensional characters and didactic plotting serve mainly to create a gloomy mood that Bogart's presence does little to lessen.

Made in 1949 but not released until early 1950, *Chain Lightning* traded on his name as a star, but Bogart gives a listless performance playing a test pilot and World War II veteran. Not in any league with *The Maltese Falcon, Casablanca,* or *The Big Sleep,* it only adds to a short string of mediocre films he appeared in during the close of the decade.

With the 1950s, things picked up again for the actor. United Artists released *The African Queen* in 1951, one of those enduring movies that deserves the term "classic." Not really a film of the 1940s but one that gives Bogart a meaty role to show off his skills, it finally earned him a much-deserved Academy Award for best actor and capped off over a decade of extraordinary filmmaking. Of all the big-name male movie stars of the 1940s, perhaps none summed up, for the times, an attitude, an approach to life, better than Humphrey Bogart. He became an icon for the war and postwar years, one of a handful of stars who can be thought representative of the 1940s. His cynicism, his outsider stance, may act as barriers to keep others at a distance and block involvement, but, like most masks, beneath those traits, a more traditional, involved protagonist can be found.

See also: Radio Programming: Action, Crime, Police, and Detective Shows

Selected Reading
Schickel, Richard, with George Perry. *Bogie: A Celebration of the Life and Films of Humphrey Bogart.* New York: St. Martin's Press, 2006.
Ursini, James. *Humphrey Bogart.* Los Angeles: Taschen, 2007.

BOOGIE-WOOGIE

No one knows, with any precision, where or how the term "boogie-woogie" originated or evolved. Theories abound: from the French *bouger,* to move or stir; from West African *bogi,* to dance; a 19th-century slang term, "boogie," used by rural Southern blacks for syphilis; and another black term, this time a verb, for either partying or having sex ("going to boogie"). All the foregoing possibilities doubtless possess elements of truth, some probably more than others. The addition of "woogie," possibly a nonsense word in itself, made a duplication of sounds when combined with boogie. The first documented used of boogie-woogie as a musical term occurred in the late 1920s, appearing in a tune called "Pinetop's Boogie-Woogie" (recorded in 1928), and written by pianist Clarence "Pinetop" Smith (1904–1929).

Essentially a piano player's music, boogie-woogie enjoyed its greatest commercial success during the 1940s. Shown here is Pete Johnson, a popular boogie-woogie stylist; he frequently teamed up with blues singer "Big Joe" Turner for a series of recordings. (Photofest)

Regardless of its linguistic origins, boogie-woogie emerged as a distinctive musical style for piano, one marked by a strong, percussive beat that encouraged unrestrained dancing. The pianist's left hand played a repeated bass line while the right created the melody. A sensual music, almost primitive in its simplicity, its incessant beat and suggestive pauses contained sexual overtones, particularly in the hands of skilled performers. Growing out of traditions found in ragtime, barrelhouse piano, and early **jazz,** it became enormously popular in the late 1930s and early 1940s.

George Thomas (1885–1930) can be counted a pioneer in the idiom; he created an early form of boogie-woogie in his "New Orleans Hop Scop Blues" (1916). Following that groundbreaking work, a group of talented black pianists, including Albert Ammons (1907–1949), Charles Edward "Cow Cow" Davenport (1894–1955), Pete Johnson (1904–1967), and Meade "Lux" Lewis (1905–1964), all of whom played piano in the 1920s and on into the 1940s, took Thomas's innovations and created the format that took the country by storm a few years later.

When aficionado and producer John Hammond (1910–1987) staged two concerts at Carnegie Hall in 1938 and 1939, promoters called them *From Spirituals to Swing*. The programs featured boogie-woogie, among many other types of blues, jazz, and **swing,** and helped bring about increased public awareness of the style. Pete Johnson, along with singer "Big Joe" Turner (1911–1985), roused the audience with "Roll 'Em, Pete"; Meade "Lux" Lewis executed "Honky Tonk Train Blues," and Albert Ammons offered "Swanee River Boogie." For many in the audience, these performances introduced them to boogie-woogie.

Country artists, intrigued by the insistent boogie-woogie beat, experimented with combining it with traditional Western music. Johnny Barfield (1909–1974), a regional favorite in the South, recorded his own version of Pinetop Smith's "Boogie Woogie" in 1939; its success led to groups such as the Delmore Brothers (Alton, 1908–1964, and Rabon, 1916–1952) issuing titles like "Freight Train Boogie," "Boogie Woogie Baby," "Mobile Boogie," and "Hillbilly Boogie." Bob Wills (1905–1975), one of the leaders of Western Swing, also experimented with the format.

Meanwhile, the leading swing bands made up mainly of white performers, began putting boogie-woogie numbers in their repertoires, since dancers liked them so much. Tommy Dorsey (1905–1956) and his band in 1938 had scored with "Boogie Woogie," an adaptation of the Pinetop Smith chestnut. A new ensemble emerged when two sidemen from the big bands of the 1930s joined forces in 1939. They called their creation Will Bradley and His Orchestra, featuring Ray McKinley. Bradley (1912–1989; ne Wilbur Schwichtenberg), a trombonist, and McKinley (1910–1995), a drummer, quickly capitalized on the craze for boogie-woogie by stringing together a succession of hits with titles like "Beat Me, Daddy, Eight to the Bar," "Scrub Me, Mama, with a Boogie Beat" (both 1940), and "Bounce Me, Brother, with a Solid Four" (1941). They received invaluable assistance in these efforts from their pianist, Freddie Slack (1910–1965), himself a virtuoso interpreter of the boogie-woogie style. The Bradley-McKinley orchestra enjoyed its biggest hit, however, with a novelty number incongruously called "Celery Stalks at Midnight" (1940); as imaginative as it sounds, the title, conceived on the spot, really means nothing beyond its playfulness. But listeners liked its bouncy rhythm, and "Celery Stalks at Midnight" served as one of the few charted tunes produced by this clever but swinging band.

The popular **Andrews Sisters** (LaVerne, 1911–1967; Maxene, 1916–1995; Patty, b. 1918) created a wartime classic with "The Boogie Woogie Bugle Boy (of Company B)." Freddie Slack, who had formed his own band featuring vocalist Ella Mae Morse (1924–1999), likewise struck gold with "Cow Cow Boogie" in 1943. Shortly thereafter, however, the boogie-woogie craze began to fade, and soon became a relic of the musical past.

Although the greatest commercial successes with boogie-woogie were scored by white swing bands, their version of the style drained the music of its elemental force, diluting it into a form of bland popular music. The sensuality—the sexuality—inherent in authentic boogie-woogie had disappeared. But, like later protests about rock 'n' roll in the 1950s, these "cleaned up" (i.e., white, commercial, mass market) versions assuaged nervous critics, convinced that no good could come from such a suggestive form of music.

See also: Country Music; Radio Programming: Music and Variety Shows

Selected Reading
Boogie-Woogie. www.boogiewoogie.com/index.php/history/
Silvester, Peter J. *A Left Hand Like God: A History of Boogie-Woogie Piano.* New York: Da Capo, 1989.

BOOK CLUBS

Membership in a book club offered people an easy way to decide what to read and a convenient way to purchase a book. It proved particularly attractive to readers who lived in rural areas and small communities during World War II, a time of gasoline **rationing.** A 1946 article in the *New York Times* estimated that most of the mailings from the nation's two largest book clubs, Book-of-the-Month Club (BOMC), founded in 1926, and the Literary Guild, which began in 1927, went to people who resided in towns and cities of fewer than 100,000 residents and 10 miles from a book store. These two mail-order operations survived the Great Depression, flourished in the second half of the 1930s, and entered the 1940s expecting even greater success. They were not disappointed. With other commodities in short supply and cash in abundance because of the war, a book craze transpired. Americans read as never before, with about 50 different clubs offering memberships, a wide variety of choices, and bargains.

The BOMC's selections tended to be more literary, while the Literary Guild, despite its name, offered lighter reading. Other clubs specialized with volumes tailored to varying tastes: the Catholic Children's Book Club, Classics Club, Executive Book Club, History Book Club, Limited Editions Club, Mystery Book Club, Non-Fiction Book Club, and Scientific Book Club, to mention a few. Readers who could not find a topic to satisfy their preferences from all of these choices could join the Surprise Package Book Club and perhaps enjoy whatever arrived in the mail.

Doubleday & Company, one of the nation's largest publishing houses, dating back to the 19th century, purchased the Literary Guild in 1934, and during the 1940s added three additional clubs: Junior Literary Guild, Dollar Book Club, and Book League of America. Particularly successful was its One Dollar Book Club, introduced in 1930. Ten years later the name had been shortened to the Dollar Book Club, and selections consisted of reprints of **best sellers.** To secure membership, Doubleday advertised its clubs heavily in **newspapers** and **magazines.** Large display ads for the Dollar Book Club highlighted the benefits of membership; for example, one that appeared in the *New York Times* during 1942 shows a book that originally cost $2.75 (approximately $35 in 2008 dollars) in stores and the club's bargain price of $1 (approximately $13 in 2008 dollars).

In 1943, Sears, Roebuck and Company, Simon & Schuster, and Consolidated Book Publishers jointly created the People's Book Club, evidence that such ventures had attained the status of a big business. This partnership correctly predicted the existence of a market for books not yet reached by other clubs, one that could be tapped through Sears' catalog and retail outlets. The club operated on a membership plan already tested by the pioneers, one that offered subscribers a bonus gift book for joining, required the purchase of at least four selections a year at the price of $1.66 each (approximately $20 in 2008 dollars), and a free book for every four bought, a good deal for readers when looked at in its entirety.

But the People's Book Club differed from the older clubs, as promised by its name. The monthly selections for the organization came from the results of surveys conducted by the Gallup Poll, not from a panel or committee of literary experts. With members regularly asked about their reading interests and backgrounds, the club could honestly advertise its selections as "The People's Choice."

The Sears-backed club claimed a membership of 300,000 in 1946, with women making up 80 percent of the total. Sixty-six percent of all members resided in towns with populations under 10,000 people, and they averaged 35 years in age. **Education** levels were mixed: 60 percent had attended high school, and 40 percent had some college experience. After just three years of existence, the People's Book Club attained fourth place in total members to the Literary Guild's 1,100,000, the Book-of-the-Month Club's 900,000, and the Dollar Book Club's 600,000. Doubleday, noting the success of the Sears project, started promoting the Literary Guild in the 1946 spring catalog for Montgomery Ward, another large mail-order retailer.

Many factors contributed to an increase in the number of readers and the proliferation of book clubs during the 1940s. Inexpensive paperback reprints of hardcover best sellers made their appearance at the beginning of the decade and could be found at a variety of shopping locations in addition to bookstores—newsstands, supermarkets, cigar stores, and novelty shops. At an average price of 25 cents each ($3.53 in 2008 dollars), a large number of people purchased them, increasing the number of active readers across the country.

Throughout World War II, most **USO** (United Service Organizations) clubs included libraries that quickly became well stocked with thousands of volumes donated through Victory Book Rallies held weekly across the United States. Soldiers, frequently with time on their hands and looking for something to do, regularly visited USO clubs and became accustomed to picking up a book, reading it, and then trading it for another. When the war ended, they took this habit home.

As the country adjusted to a peacetime existence and families reunited, some recreational pursuits were briefly put on hold. In this atmosphere, book clubs experienced a drop in membership even though returning veterans and others were eager to read. An increase in the costs of publishing and distribution through the mail also contributed to the decline. Once businesses and industries retooled for postwar production, however, a boom began on many fronts, including book clubs. By late 1947, with more discretionary money in their pockets, countless Americans easily supported a wave of new publications, the reprinting of old standards, and the offerings from the clubs. In fact, in 1949, BOMC shipped its 100 millionth book and continued trying out new services such as the Classical Music Club. Other book clubs also prospered and their growth continued throughout the 20th century.

See also: Advertising; Hobbies; Leisure and Recreation

Selected Reading
Tebbel, John. *A History of Book Publishing in the United States.* Vol. 4, *The Great Change, 1940–1980.* New York: R. R. Bowker, 1981.
West, James L. W., III. *American Authors and the Literary Marketplace since 1900.* Philadelphia: University of Pennsylvania Press, 1988.

BOWLING

By 1946, tenpin bowling had become a well-established American sport, a pleasurable recreational activity for men, women, and children. A study for *Bowling* magazine reported the number of bowlers in the United States to be somewhere between 10 million and 15 million, a higher figure than for any other competitive sport and considerably greater than that reported by the U.S. government (slightly over 1 million). Whichever can be considered the correct statistic, the number of bowlers dramatically increased from 1940 to 1949 as Americans fell in love with the game. What had once been an activity for working-class men of modest means now attracted women in significant numbers and had attained participation for both genders across occupational categories and income levels.

Brought to the New World by the earliest European settlers and usually played on lawns outside taverns, bowling involves throwing a heavy ball down a cleared lane in an attempt to knock over wooden pins. By the early 1800s, bowling had gained popularity among working-class men, and New York City saw the country's first indoor alley in 1840. The original nine-pin game between two players or teams frequently served as a means of gambling and because of this component was outlawed in 1841. From the wording of the prohibition, the addition of a 10th pin made the game legal. By the late 1800s, this new form of bowling, now a more respectable activity, had advanced from just a passing recreational pastime to a recognized American sport.

Around the turn of the 20th century, a few women and children also played the game. During World War I, participation by women, mainly those holding factory jobs, grew and bowling prospered. Commercial establishments began to sponsor women's teams and tournaments, and the Women's National Bowling Association, later renamed the Women's International Bowling Congress (WIBC), formed in 1916. Nevertheless, men still represented two out of every three bowlers.

In the early decades of the 20th century, most bowling alleys were located in sleazy downtown buildings or off back alleys. But during the 1930s and 1940s, various community groups recognized the game's social and health benefits, and bowling alleys started to appear in church basements, lodge halls, student unions, industrial plants, and in respectable facilities built specifically for the game. The proliferation of alleys proved helpful in making the game available to many during wartime gasoline rationing, a condition that forced people to seek leisure and recreational outlets near their homes.

World War II touched off another surge for women bowlers. As they replaced men on industrial assembly lines, they formed their own company leagues. Bowling alley managers claimed that women accounted for 60 percent of their business. The WIBC supported the war effort and provided money for a bomber christened *Miss WIBC* and then raised funds for the purchase of an ambulance and three ambulance planes, activities that brought national attention to bowling, especially women bowlers.

Military administrators also recognized the importance of soldiers being able to continue to engage in their favorite sports and also encouraged the taking up of new ones. The installation of more than 3,000 alleys at military bases in the United States and overseas enabled seasoned bowlers to continue to play and introduced this pastime to thousands of newcomers. The Bowlers Victory Legion, founded in 1942 to raise money for recreational equipment for men and women in the armed forces, assisted in these efforts. Also, the National Bowling Congress (NBC) arranged for special tournaments and matches to raise funds for the war effort.

After the war, Americans gained more leisure time; bowling, as an inexpensive and easy-to-learn sport with no age or gender restrictions, entered its golden age. It received a huge boost as a universally popular pastime when, in 1947, **President Harry S. Truman** (1884–1972) had lanes installed in the White House. That same year, the first televised coverage of bowling occurred, an event that had a significant impact on the future popularity of this game as a healthy family outing. Whereas in the 1930s **newspapers** devoted space to individual games and players' averages and scores, and **magazines** provided cover stories on the sport, it took **television** in the late 1940s and early 1950s to popularize bowling on a national scale. Easy and inexpensive to shoot with the clumsy equipment that characterized the early days of TV, the medium offered Americans an intimate view of this developing activity.

But a technological innovation, the automatic pinsetter, patented by Gottfried Schmidt (n.d.) in 1946, perhaps provided the tipping point that transformed bowling alleys from seedy operations to family centers. First shown to the public at the national championships sponsored by the American Bowling Congress (ABC) in 1946, they did not become available for widespread use until the early 1950s. Schmidt's invention eliminated the need for pin boys and made pin setting and ball retrieval safer, faster, and more reliable. Since the alleys no longer needed schoolboys for the operation of the alleys, the establishments could present a more respectable appearance, making bowling more attractive to housewives during the day while their husbands were at work.

Throughout the later 1940s, bowling alley proprietors, in order to fill their alleys, provided a clean and attractive venue; formed leagues for men, women, families, and youth; and sponsored industrial leagues and tournaments. The Bowling Proprietors' Association of America supported these efforts by holding sanctioned tournaments as a way to create national champions, legitimize the sport, and bring even more people to the alleys. These tournaments and subsequent challenge matches featured notables such as Hank Marino (1889–1976), Andy Varipapa (1891–1984), and Ned Day (1911–1971), three of the professional stars of the era.

Varipapa and Day also served as goodwill ambassadors, advancing bowling as both a sport and a family game. Some time prior to the 1940s, Varipapa developed a unique style of trick shot bowling and in 1934 starred in the first bowling film short, Metro-Goldwyn-Mayer's *Strikes and Spares*. The studio featured him again in 1948 with another short feature, *Bowling Tricks*. In addition to working as an instructor and exhibition bowler, Varipapa won the 1946 and 1947 all-star tournaments and was recognized as the bowler of the year in 1948. Day, in addition to obtaining championship status, toured widely promoting the sport. In 1948, he authored a book titled *How to Bowl*. That year, Day also journeyed to the White House to give President Truman a bowling demonstration.

The American Bowling Congress contributed to these efforts by instituting a hall of fame in 1941; only baseball (1936) and golf (1940) have older halls of fame. Eleven inductees made the grade that year, including past greats such as Gilbert Zunker (1901–1938) and 1940s tournament champion Hank Marino. Ned Day finally received the honor in 1952 and Andy Varipapa in 1957.

By the end of the 1940s, the working man's game had changed to an activity for everyone. But marketing often focused on middle-class women by **advertising** beauty salons and other shopping opportunities for the convenience of its female clientele. The establishments continued to host leagues and tournaments as they simultaneously evolved into family entertainment centers that contained game rooms for children along with snack bars and other amenities. By 1949, over 6,000 bowling centers dotted the nation and demonstrated extraordinary growth and change. Affordable and playable by all, the United States Bowling Congress, an organization formed in 2005 by a merger of the American Bowling Congress, Women's International Bowling Congress, Young American Bowling Alliance, and USA Bowling, currently governs and sanctions the sport.

See also: Leisure and Recreation; Technology

Selected Reading
Bowling. www.bowl.com/aboutUSBC/history/
Grinfelds, Vesma, and Bonnie Hulstrand. *Right Down Your Alley: The Complete Book of Bowling.* West Point, NY: Leisure Press, 1985.
Hurley, Andrew. *Diners, Bowling Alleys, and Trailer Parks: Chasing the American Dream in Postwar Consumer Culture.* New York: Basic Books, 2001.
Weiskopf, Herman. *The Perfect Game: The World of Bowling.* Englewood Cliffs, NJ: Prentice Hall, 1978.

BOXING

Despite setbacks created by World War II, the 1940s were a popular period for boxing. Champions became war heroes as they fought in battles on foreign soil, helped sell **war bonds** back home, and posed for defense posters. Championships were won and lost; world heavyweight champion **Joe Louis** (1914–1981) received both civilian and military awards for sportsmanship and extraordinary service and sacrifice; middleweights Rocky Graziano (1922–1990) and Tony Zale (1913–1997) formed a rivalry often described as one of the fiercest in boxing history.

130 | Boxing

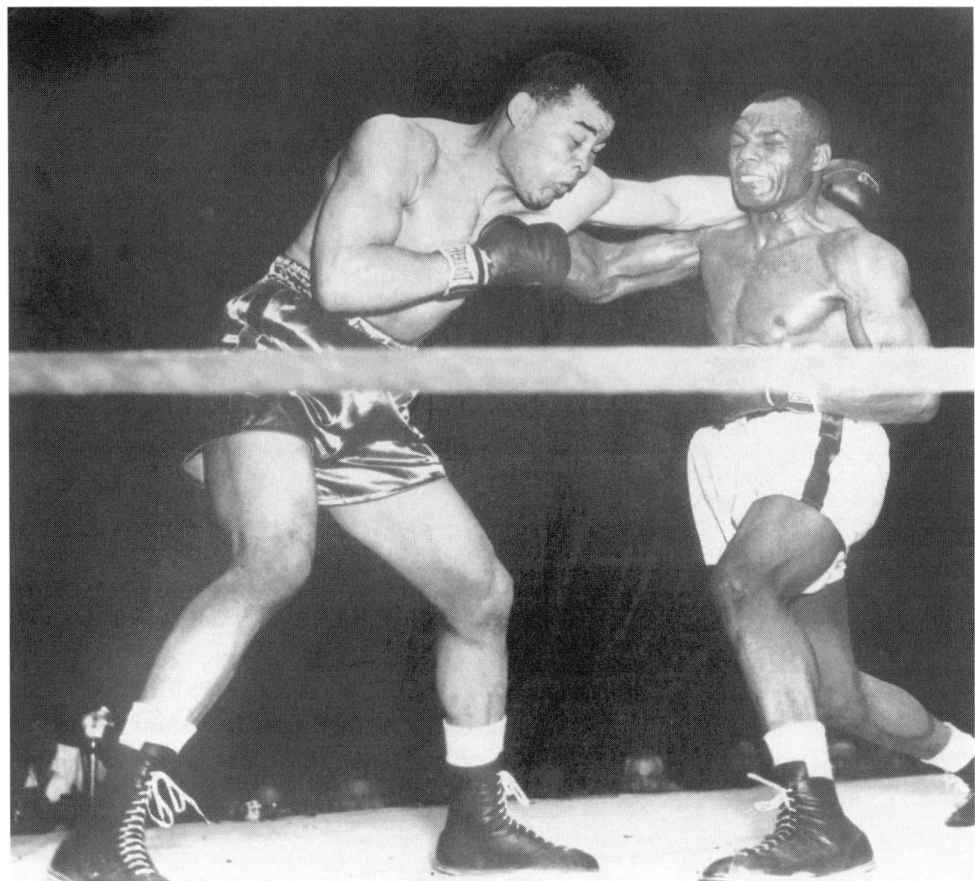

Following three years of service in the U.S. Army, heavyweight champion Joe Louis returned to the ring. He electrified the boxing world with this close win against Jersey Joe Walcott (above, right) in 1948. (Photofest)

Fistfighting can be traced to ancient times, and bare-knuckle bouts for the sake of holding an event frequently occurred throughout the United States during its early history. A reputation of lawlessness surrounded these matches, usually held at gambling establishments and accompanied by drinking and spectators having their own fights. The introduction of rules and gloves in the mid-1800s gradually changed the nature of boxing. Further legitimizing occurred in 1921 with the founding of the National Boxing Association (NBA), renamed the World Boxing Association (WBA) in 1962. Since then, three other groups—the World Boxing Council (WBC; 1963), the International Boxing Federation (IBF; 1983), and World Boxing Organization (WBO; 1988)—have also formed to sanction official matches and award world championship titles at the professional level.

The popularity of prizefighting declined in the early 1930s, but the ascendancy of Joe Louis, champion from 1937 until his retirement in 1949, brought new life and enthusiasm to boxing events. A June 18, 1941, match between Louis, "The Brown

Bomber," and Billy Conn (1917–1993), "The Pittsburgh Kid," at the Polo Grounds in New York, has come to be known as one of the greatest fights of all time. Conn gave up his light heavyweight title in order to qualify as a heavyweight. In this match, Louis outweighed Conn by 30 pounds, but the doughty challenger often outboxed and outslugged the champion. When Conn left his corner for the 13th round, he led in points; the two boxers parried, but then Louis unleashed a flurry of devastating blows that knocked Conn to the canvas; he tried to get up, but with two seconds remaining in the round, the referee counted him out and Louis retained his heavyweight crown.

Soon after this event, World War II practically froze boxing activities while many fighters entered military service. In December 1943, the *New York Times* reported that 4,019 boxers including active and inactive world champions Billy Conn (light heavyweight, army), Jack Dempsey (1895–1983, heavyweight; coast guard), Beau Jack (b. Sidney Jack, 1921–2000, lightweight, army), Joe Louis (army), Bob Montgomery (1919–1998, lightweight, army), Sugar Ray Robinson (1921–1989, welterweight and middleweight, army), Barney Ross (1909–1967, lightweight and welterweight, U.S. Marines), and Tony Zale (1913–1997, middleweight, navy) were fighting the Axis powers instead of each other. Dempsey and Louis never saw combat but served as instructors of physical education instead.

Boxing promoters quickly joined the athletes in supporting the war and staged tournaments to sell war bonds, often holding them in the early morning hours for the benefit of night-shift defense workers. Exhibition bouts regularly occurred at military training camps. Joe Louis fought Buddy Baer (1915–1986) on January 9, 1942, and gave his entire purse to the Navy Relief Fund. In a fight with Abe Simon (1913–1969) on March 27, 1942, he again gave his winnings to the war effort, this time to the Army Emergency Relief Organization.

After the war, Joe Louis resumed professional boxing and dominated both his division and the sport, while other notable American boxers won championships in their respective divisions. This new group of boxers attracted larger and larger crowds and rose to stardom by the end of the decade.

Each of the champions listed in Table 21 managed to gain individualized fame during the 1940s. Rocky Graziano, who fought for 10 years and held the title of world middleweight champion for less than a year, came the closest to being as famous as Joe Louis. As a professional boxer, he received heavy publicity because of a combination of boxing successes and a colorful lifestyle that included imprisonment for being AWOL (Absent With Out Leave) from the army and a suspension by the New York State Athletic Commission for failure to report an alleged bribery attempt.

The highpoint of Graziano's career came over a 21-month period that included three fiercely competitive fights against Tony Zale for the middleweight title. Zale, nine years Graziano's senior, knocked out Graziano in the sixth round in 1946 before a crowd of over 39,000 fans at Yankee Stadium. Graziano likewise stopped Zale in six rounds in 1947 in Chicago, only to lose the third match, held in 1948 at Ruppert Stadium in Newark, New Jersey, on a third-round knockout. Zale met defeat three months later when he lost the championship to French boxer Marcel Cerdan (1916–1949). Graziano and Zale retired shortly thereafter with similar records—Graziano, 67 wins

TABLE 21. Representative Titled American Boxers, 1940–1949, Sanctioned by the World Boxing Association

Name	Turned Professional	Year(s) Held World Title	Nickname	The Ring magazine's Fighter of the Year
Heavyweight Division (Over 175 pounds)				
Joe Louis	1934	1937–1949	Brown Bomber	1941
Ezzard Charles	1940	1949–1950	Cincinnati Cobra	1949
Light Heavyweight Division (Between 160 and 175 pounds)				
Gus Lesnevich	1934	1941; 1946–1948	None	1947
Middleweight Division (Between 147 and 160 pounds)				
Rocky Graziano	1940	1947–1948	The Rock	
Tony Zale	Late 1930s	1941–1947; June 1948–September 1948	Man of Steel	1946
Jake LaMotta	1941	1949–1951	Bronx Bull and Raging Bull	
Welterweight Division (Between 135 and 147 pounds)				
Sugar Ray Robinson	1940	1946–1950	Sugar Ray.	1942 1951
Lightweight Division (Between 126 and 135 pounds)				
Beau Jack	1940	1943–1944	No nickname	1944
Ike Williams	1940	1945–1951	No nickname	1948
Featherweight Division (118–126 pounds)				
Willie Pep	1940	1942 June 1946–October 1948 February 1949–September 1950	Will o' the Wisp	1945
Sandy Saddler	1944	October 1948–February 1949	No nickname	

out of 83 matches and Zale, 67 out of 87. Graziano wrote a somewhat fictional autobiography, *Somebody Up There Likes Me,* in 1955, which became a 1956 movie starring Paul Newman (1925–2008) as the fighter.

Another popular boxer, Jake LaMotta (b. 1921), gained renown for his immense punching power. Early in his career, he adopted a fighting style of staying physically close and stalking his opponent. With this approach, he managed to defeat Sugar Ray Robinson in 1943, the first upset for Robinson as a professional after 40 consecutive wins. LaMotta, known as the "Bronx Bull," wrote a memoir, *Raging Bull: My Story* (1970), which gave him a second nickname. It served as the basis of a 1980 movie of the same name starring Robert De Niro (b. 1943) in an Academy Award–winning performance.

Ranked among the top three welterweight and middleweight boxers of his era, and frequently cited as one of the greatest boxers of all time, Sugar Ray Robinson held the welterweight title for six years during the 1940s and won the middleweight title five times between 1951 and 1960. In the early 1940s, having just turned professional, Robinson attracted some of the largest crowds ever assembled for a fight. While in the army, he served with Joe Louis. Each went on tours performing exhibition bouts in front of U.S. troops. *The Ring* magazine named him the fighter of the decade for the 1950s. Robinson retired in 1965 after a career of 25 years and a record of 174 wins, 19 losses, and 6 draws.

Willie Pep fought for 26 years and lays claim to the most wins in boxing history—230 out of 242 bouts. Known for his speed and finesse, he was likened to a tap dancer in boxing gloves and earned the nickname "Will o' the Wisp." He achieved his first world championship just two years after becoming a professional in 1940. Three years later, he had a record of 61–0 when he met defeat for the first time in a contest with Sammy Angott (1915–1980). A favorite boxing legend has it that, in 1946, in a match with a relatively unknown Jackie Graves (1915–2005), "The Austin Atom." Pep won the third round without throwing a punch, although contemporary reports show otherwise. Fable or truth, Pep won with a knockout in the eighth round.

As reigning world featherweight champion, Pep boasted a record of 134–1–1 with 43 knockouts when he met Sandy Saddler on October 29, 1948. Saddler had a knockout victory in the fourth round, giving Pep his second defeat and taking the featherweight crown away from him. Saddler went on to be best known for a four-bout series with Pep, who recaptured the title in February 1949, but lost again to Saddler in 1950 and 1951. This last fight, reported to be one of the dirtiest championship fights ever fought at that time, caused the referee to stop it in the 10th round. Saddler retired in 1956 and Pep in 1960.

Hollywood started producing motion pictures with boxing plots during the silent movie days. The 1930s saw many stories of this sport come to the screen, such as *Winner Take All* (1932) with James Cagney (1899–1986) in the lead and *They Made Me A Criminal* (1939) starring John Garfield (1913–1969). Studios produced only a few such pictures during the war years. In the postwar period, features on the topic included *Joe Palooka, Champ* (1946), based on the heavyweight boxer in cartoonist Ham Fisher's (1901–1955) highly successful comic strip creation, *Joe Palooka*. It ran in **newspapers** from 1930 to 1984, with new artists taking it over after Fisher's death.

In the boxing world, the term "palooka," which predates Fisher's series, describes a mediocre prizefighter. Other films from this time dealing with the sport of boxing include *Body and Soul* (1947), *In This Corner* (1948), *The Fight Never Ends* (1949), and *The Set-Up* (1949). Plots tend to revolve around boxers either breaking into the profession or those over the hill. Beautiful girlfriends or sexy wives plead with them to quit as shady promoters and managers lurk in the background.

The popularity of boxing grew in the 1940s, thanks to crowd-pleasing and record-breaking fighters, but also because of the availability of **television.** Because of the ease of televising events in the ring, this new technological phenomenon featured prizefighting in its early years. Over time, televised bouts elevated many boxers to household names. Despite the brutality and physical dangers that could now be viewed on a TV screen, the number of fans grew. Although television brought boxing to the attention of more people, it also contributed to a significant decline in ringside attendance in the 1950s.

See also: Comic Strips; Movies; Radio Programming: News, Sports, Public Affairs, and Talk; Technology

Selected Reading

Boxing events. www.youtube.com, Marcel Cerdan vs. Tony Zale, 1948; Zale vs. Graziano, 1948; Rocky Graziano vs. Tony Zale III; Sugar Ray Robinson Fights Jake Lamotta 1; Sugar Ray Robinson Highlights; Ike Williams vs. Beau Jack, July 12, 1948; In This Corner—Willie Pep; Willie Pep vs. Sandy Saddler.

Sammons, Jeffrey T. *Beyond the Ring: The Role of Boxing in American Society.* Chicago: University of Illinois Press, 1988.

Sugar, Bert Randolph, and the Editors of *Ring* Magazine. *100 Years of Boxing.* New York: Galley Press, 1982.

BOYD, WILLIAM (HOPALONG CASSIDY)

As a young man, William Boyd (1895–1972) journeyed to Hollywood in the 1920s in search of fame and fortune. The celebrated director Cecil B. De Mille (1881–1959) took notice of the actor, and thereafter his star rose quickly. Boyd soon became a dashing leading man in a number of big-budget silent pictures, including top billing in *The Volga Boatman* (1926). A good speaking voice led Boyd into sound **movies,** and his future looked bright, but a publicity mix-up with another actor named Boyd dimmed his hopes and he soon had to search for lesser roles, including **Westerns.**

Fortune again smiled in 1935, when he won the lead in a new cowboy film then in the planning stages. That year, Boyd appeared in *Hop-Along Cassidy* (1935; retitled in 1951 as *Hopalong Cassidy Enters*), the first release in a long-running series of motion pictures that would endure until 1948 and *Strange Gamble,* the last feature-length entry in the saga of Hopalong Cassidy.

These events transpired because Harry Sherman (1884–1952), an independent Hollywood producer with a good eye for potential properties, discovered both Boyd and the writings of Clarence E. Mulford (1883–1956). In 1907, Mulford had published a book of his short Western tales that had previously appeared in **magazines.** He called the collection *Bar 20,* and in it he featured a ranch foreman named Buck Peters. Readers, however, were intrigued by a whiskey-drinking, tobacco-chewing, foul-mouthed, mean-spirited character who worked at the Bar 20 named Hop-a-Long Cassidy (later simplified to "Hopalong"). This generally disreputable cowhand had earned his unusual first name because of a gunshot wound in the thigh that created a unique gait.

Mulford wisely sensed that Cassidy should play a larger role in subsequent works, and the author created 27 additional novels that ran until 1941 and *Hopalong Cassidy Serves a Writ*. During those 34 years, the books sold well. In fact, after a nine-year absence from bookstores, Cassidy reappeared in a print format, but this time Mulford did not do the writing. In 1950, and employing the pen name of Tex Burns, Louis L'Amour (1908–1988), later a best-selling author of Western novels himself, wrote four additional Cassidy tales for paperback distribution. His publishers timed their release to capitalize on the enormously popular *Hopalong Cassidy* show then playing on the NBC (National Broadcasting Company) **television** network; aside from payment at the time, however, L'Amour neither received nor took credit for his work.

This picture, taken in 1940, shows actor William Boyd (1895–1972). He made his fame and fortune portraying Hopalong Cassidy, an upright cowboy that appeared in a string of Hollywood B Westerns made between 1935 and 1948. His greatest popularity came in the late 1940s, when these movies played on early television. (Photofest)

With Mulford's continuing success, Harry Sherman gained movie rights to them and convinced Paramount Pictures to distribute any motion pictures that might result. He then proceeded to search for the proper leading man to play Cassidy. Although several actors sought the role, the handsome Boyd, now prematurely gray and suitably mature, landed the part.

During the 34 years Mulford worked on the series, the once-notorious Cassidy had evolved into a nondrinking, nonsmoking, well-spoken, generous cowboy who sought justice and fair play in the West. Almost from the beginning of his association with Sherman, William Boyd made it clear he had his own ideas about the development of the character, although Cassidy's cinematic evolution mirrored in many ways Mulford's literary approach. Despite the many similarities in characterization, only the first few movies in the series were derived directly from Mulford's stories; within a short time, professional script writers had taken on the task of writing new adventures and refining the film persona of Hopalong Cassidy to better fit the ways in which Boyd perceived him.

Between 1935 and 1948, the duration of the movie series, Boyd made a remarkable 66 Hopalong Cassidy feature films. Of these, 26 came out in the 1930s, and the remaining 40 saw release in the 1940s, which means that Boyd averaged over 4 new productions a year for some 15 years. With an eye to television, Boyd in the late 1940s bought up the rights to all 66 motion pictures, since the Hollywood studios thought they had run their course and saw no use for such a large stock of B Westerns. The move cost him dearly—he sold virtually everything he owned, including his ranch, to acquire them—but it paid substantial rewards in due time. Television stations were hungry for usable motion pictures, and the movie industry displayed a reluctance to release anything to this erstwhile competitor.

Boyd, however, harbored no such reluctance, and in a brilliant move edited many of his earlier movies, which usually ran an hour or so, so that they played for 30 minutes, making them extremely attractive to television stations around the country. In order to have an ample supply of material, he also appeared in an additional 52 new 30-minute productions specifically designed for the small screen. These efforts paid off handsomely for Boyd. At first he leased his movies to individual stations, but, as the medium evolved, he found a taker with NBC-TV. Beginning in the summer of 1949, the network carried *Hopalong Cassidy* to its affiliates, a relationship that continued until the end of 1951 and made its star a household name. In 1952–1953, the show went into syndication, whereby any station, network or not, could rent Boyd's films, a move that only heightened Cassidy's popularity.

Since interest in Hopalong Cassidy never flagged during the decade, Boyd also moved into the medium of **radio.** In 1948, he agreed to work with a small specialty radio company, Commodore Productions, based in California. He prepared sample transcription disks that were sent to numerous independent stations, and slowly a handful responded positively. Audiences liked these early shows, and they received good ratings. The small **MBS (Mutual Broadcasting System)** agreed to carry *Hopalong Cassidy* at the beginning of 1950, and in the fall of that year, CBS (Columbia Broadcasting System), a much larger network, picked up rights to the show. It ran nationally until March 1952.

If all that were not enough, Boyd endorsed products of every description during the late 1940s and early 1950s. Lunchboxes, comic books, pens and pencils, coloring books, cowboy outfits, pajamas—all bore the smiling countenance of "Hoppy" (as his fans called him). Even Clarence Mulford's books, long out of print, came back with new covers, along with some editing to keep events true to the character Boyd had created, and a new generation of readers thrilled to adventures at the Bar 20 ranch. This celebrity also made Boyd a wealthy man, and he retired to a comfortable life.

As the list in Table 22 indicates, Boyd used only a few actors as his regular cinematic companions. They play sidekicks to the paternal Cassidy. James "Jimmy" Ellison (1910–1993) led the way, Russell Hayden (1912–1981) followed, and Andy Clyde (1892–1967) finished the series, although George "Gabby" Hayes (1885–1969), one of the most famous and popular character actors in the history of Westerns, also filled this role at times.

By and large, the Boyd/Cassidy Westerns subscribe to a formula: the hero (Cassidy) learns of problems or troubles somewhere nearby. He investigates, clad in his trademark black outfit with white piping (some maintain it was actually dark blue, but would photograph as black since camera crews shots all his movies on black-and-white stock), his shiny plated pistols and spurs, and accompanied by Topper, his splendid white horse. This leads to a showdown with the miscreants, usually after a furious chase and possibly a shootout, and justice prevails.

TABLE 22. The Hopalong Cassidy Films, 1935–1948

Year	Movie Titles	Actors
1935	*Bar 20 Rides Again*	William Boyd, James Ellison
	The Eagle's Brood	Boyd, Ellison
	Hop-Along Cassidy	Boyd, Ellison
1936	*Call of the Prairie*	Boyd, Ellison
	Heart of the West	Boyd, Ellison
	Hopalong Cassidy Returns	Boyd, George "Gabby" Hayes
	Three on the Trail	Boyd, James Ellison
	Trail Dust	Boyd, Ellison
1937	*Borderland*	Boyd, Ellison
	Hills of Old Wyoming	Boyd, George "Gabby" Hayes
	Hopalong Rides Again	Boyd, Hayes
	North of the Rio Grande	Boyd, Hayes
	Rustlers' Valley	Boyd, Hayes
	Texas Trail	Boyd, Hayes
1938	*Bar 20 Justice*	Boyd, Russell Hayden
	Cassidy of Bar 20	Boyd, Hayden
	The Frontiersmen	Boyd, George "Gabby" Hayes
	Heart of Arizona	Boyd, Hayes
	In Old Mexico	Boyd, Hayes
	Partners of the Plains	Boyd, Russell Hayden
	Pride of the West	Boyd, George "Gabby" Hayes
1939	*Law of the Pampas*	Boyd, Russell Hayden
	Range War	Boyd, Hayden
	The Renegade Trail	Boyd, Hayden
	Silver on the Sage	Boyd, Hayden
	Sunset Trail	Boyd, George "Gabby" Hayes
1940	*Hidden Gold*	Boyd, Russell Hayden
	Santa Fe Marshall	Boyd, Hayden
	The Showdown	Boyd, Hayden
	Stagecoach War	Boyd, Hayden
	Three Men from Texas	Boyd, Hayden
1941	*Border Vigilantes*	Boyd, Hayden
	Doomed Caravan	Boyd, Hayden
	In Old Colorado	Boyd, Hayden
	Outlaws of the Desert	Boyd, Andy Clyde
	Pirates on Horseback	Boyd, Russell Hayden
	Riders of the Timberlane	Boyd, Andy Clyde
	Secret of the Wastelands	Boyd, Clyde
	Stick to Your Guns	Boyd, Clyde
	Twilight on the Trail	Boyd, Clyde
	Wide Open Town	Boyd, Russell Hayden
1942	*Lost Canyon*	Boyd, Andy Clyde
	Undercover Man	Boyd, Clyde

(continued)

TABLE 22. (continued)

Year	Movie Titles	Actors
1943	*Bar 20*	Boyd, Clyde
	Border Patrol	Boyd, Clyde
	Colt Comrades	Boyd, Clyde
	False Colors	Boyd, Clyde
	Hoppy Serves a Writ	Boyd, Clyde
	Leather Burners	Boyd, Clyde
	Riders of the Deadline	Boyd, Clyde
1944	*Forty Thieves*	Boyd, Clyde
	Lumberjack	Boyd, Clyde
	Mystery Man	Boyd, Clyde
	Texas Masquerade	Boyd, Clyde
1945	**no releases**	
1946	*The Devil's Playground*	Boyd, Clyde
1947	*Dangerous Venture*	Boyd, Clyde
	Fool's Gold	Boyd, Clyde
	Hoppy's Holiday	Boyd, Clyde
	The Marauders	Boyd, Clyde
	Unexpected Guest	Boyd, Clyde
1948	*Borrowed Trouble*	Boyd, Clyde
	The Dead Don't Dream	Boyd, Clyde
	False Paradise	Boyd, Clyde
	Silent Conflict	Boyd, Clyde
	Sinister Journey	Boyd, Clyde
	Strange Gamble	Boyd, Clyde

If any love interest develops, it takes place between other performers; Hopalong never kisses the girl nor gets involved in any way. He can be friendly and offer sage advice, but he avoids romance, just as he avoids liquor, cussing, smoking, and bad grammar. Boyd envisioned Cassidy as a paragon of virtue and portrays him in that manner. Somehow, Cassidy escapes being a wooden, two-dimensional do-gooder and instead comes across as a vigorous, affable cowboy, and therein lies the success of this series and also the success of William Boyd.

Selected Reading
B Westerns. www.b-westerns.com/
Boyd, William. www.hoppyandthebar-20.50megs.com
Hopalong Cassidy. www.hopalong.com/home.asp
Nevins, Francis M. *Bar-20: The Life of Clarence E. Mulford, Creator of Hopalong Cassidy.* Jefferson, NC: McFarland, 1993.

BROADWAY SHOWS (COMEDY AND DRAMA)

Broadway, a major thoroughfare of New York City, runs from the southern tip of Manhattan to the city limits in the Bronx and cuts diagonally through Times Square, an area known worldwide for its wealth of theaters, both stage and movie. During the 1930s, the Federal Theatre Project (FTP), a New Deal program that ran from 1935 to 1939, provided playwrights opportunities to have their works produced not only in New York but in other cities and communities across the country. Controversies and politics brought the FTP to an abrupt end, and, coupled with the war during the early 1940s, the number of plays appearing in Broadway theaters diminished. Attendance nonetheless rose, more so at musicals and comedies than at dramas. Wartime defense workers had extra money to spend and could join already committed theatergoers for an evening on the town, including a Broadway play or movie.

Comedies and musicals proved to be popular throughout the decade. At this time of high anxiety and concern for the country and its soldiers, sailors, and airmen, Americans looked for an escape, a couple of hours of relaxation without reminders of the turmoil occurring around the globe.

Arthur Miller's Broadway hit, All My Sons, ran in 1947. This cover of Playbill features cast members (from the left) Arthur Kennedy, Karl Malden, Beth Merrill, Ed Begley, and Lois Wheeler. (Photofest)

With the end of World War II, an atmosphere of celebration prevailed and theatergoers continued to be interested in light entertainment. Three of the four comedies in the 1940s with over 1,000 performances were produced during the war years: *Harvey* (1944) with 1,775 shows, *The Voice of the Turtle* (1943) at 1,557, and *Arsenic and Old Lace* (1941), 1,444. The fourth hit, *Mister Roberts,* opened in 1948 and achieved 1,157 performances before closing in 1951. In the musical genre, four also topped the 1,000 mark with *Oklahoma!* (1943) in the No. 1 spot for all plays of any type at 2,212 shows, *South Pacific* (1949) boasted 1,925, *Annie Get Your Gun* (1946) 1,147, and *Kiss Me Kate* (1948) 1,070. Only one drama, *Angel Street* (1941), made it to this league with 1,295 performances. Table 23 identifies 42 plays—comedies and dramas holding high attendance records and/or receiving awards.

Stage actors, like most Americans, immediately supported the war effort in a number of ways. The American Theatre Wing, an organization started by seven women during World War I, regrouped under the leadership of renowned performers Gertrude Lawrence (1898–1952), Josephine Hull (1886–1957), Lucile Watson (1898–1952), Ruth Gordon (1896–1985), Helen Hayes (1900–1993), Vera-Ellen (1921–1981), and Edith Atwater (1911–1986). One of their first and largest projects involved the establishment of the Stage Door Canteen, housed in the 44th Street Theatre. Like other **canteens** across the country, it offered a place for those in service to gather and enjoy food, companionship, and entertainment.

In addition to their work at the canteen and assisting with the selling of **war bonds,** the theater community continued its efforts to provide the best theater possible. Once rehearsals and staging had been completed, many plays tested the market with a short run outside New York, often Boston, New Haven, or Philadelphia. If successful, they came to Broadway. After closing in New York, some went on to tour the country. Broadway shows, however, remained a form of entertainment enjoyed primarily by New York City residents and visitors to the area. With limited exposure, Broadway shows cannot be considered a major component of national popular culture. They, nevertheless, serve as an important part in the total realm of entertainment.

Recognition of the best playwrights, performers, and others necessary to the successful production of a play not only acknowledges their accomplishments but also provides publicity for the plays and Broadway. In 1935, 15 professional theatrical critics formed the New York Drama Critics Circle Awards. Initially, they announced an annual winner for the best American play and the best foreign play. In 1945, the critics added best musical as a third category. Six dramas won as the best American play during the 1940s: *Watch on the Rhine* by Lillian Hellman (1905–1984) for the 1940–1941 season, *The Patriots* by Sidney Kingsley (1906–1995) for 1941–1942, *The Glass Menagerie* by Tennessee Williams (1911–1983) for 1944–1945, *All My Sons* by Arthur Miller (1915–2005) for 1946–1947, *A Streetcar Named Desire* by Williams for 1947–1948, and *Death of a Salesman* by Miller for 1949–1950. The judges could not reach agreement about winners for the 1942–1943, 1943–1944, and 1945–1946 seasons.

Two additional ways of celebrating theatrical performances commenced in the 1940s. The Theatre World Award, first given in 1945 for the 1944–1945 season and each season thereafter, goes to six actors and six actresses for outstanding debut performances. Four recipients, Margaret Phillips (1923–1984) in *The Late George Apley* (1944), Patricia Neal (b. 1926) in *Another Part of the Forest* (1946), Ralph Meeker (1920–1988) in *Mister Roberts* (1948), and Cameron Mitchell (1918–1994) in *Death of a Salesman* (1949), appeared in shows found in the table below.

The Tony Award, bestowed annually since the 1946–1947 Broadway season, honors achievements in several theatrical categories. Named for one of the founders of the American Theatre Wing, Antoinette Perry (1888–1946), this prestigious theater award, the equivalent to Hollywood's Oscar, the music industry's Grammy, and **television**'s Emmy, can be given to more than one individual in each category. One or more persons affiliated with 14 of the plays in the table below received Tony Awards, and those plays and the categories are so noted.

Three playwrights from the 1940s stand out as exceptional: Eugene O'Neill (1888–1953), Tennessee Williams, and Arthur Miller. O'Neill, one of the first American playwrights to consider the stage appropriate for presenting serious ideas, wrote about the difficulties of family life, the growing pains of an adolescent boy, and a man's search for identity along with his need to hope for a better life. O'Neill won the Nobel Prize in Literature in 1936 and had completed most of his major work by 1940, with many of his one-act and full-length plays having been already staged on Broadway. The characters, especially in his later pieces, tend to engage in sordid behavior and live

TABLE 23. Representative Broadway Dramas and Comedies, 1940–1949

Year	Play Titles and Tony Awards	Performances	Playwrights	Major Cast Members	Revival History on Broadway and Movie Production(s) as of 2009
1940	*My Sister Eileen* Comedy	864	Joseph Fields 1895–1966, Jerome Chodorov (1911–2004)	Shirley Booth, (1898–1992), Jo Ann Sayers (b. 1918)	No revival. 1942 movie: Rosalind Russell (1907–1976), Janet Blair (1921–2007)
	Separate Rooms Comedy	613	Alan Dinehart (1890–1944), Joseph Carole (active 1940s)	Alan Dinehart, Glenda Farrell (1904–1971)	No revival.
	The Corn Is Green Drama	533	Emlyn Williams (1905–1987)	Ethel Barrymore (1879–1959), Rhys Williams (1897–1969), Edmond Breon (1907–1951)	Two revivals. 1945 movie: Bette Davis (1908–1989), Rhys Williams, Nigel Bruce (1895–1953)
	The Time of Your Life Comedy	217	William Saroyan (1908–1981)	Eddie Dowling (1895–1976), Julie Haydon (1910–1994), William Bendix (1906–1964), Celeste Holm (b. 1919)	Three revivals. 1948 movie: James Cagney (1899–1986), Jeanne Cagney (1919–1984), William Bendix
	There Shall Be No Night Drama	181	Robert Sherwood (1896–1955)	Alfred Lunt (1893–1977), Lynn Fontaine (1887–1983)	No revival. 1957 movie for TV
1941	*Arsenic and Old Lace* Comedy	1,444	Joseph O. Kesselring (1902–1967)	Josephine Hull (1886–1957), Boris Karloff (1887–1969), John Alexander (1897–1982), Jean Adair (1873–1953), Allan Joslyn (1901–1981)	One revival. 1944 movie: Cary Grant (1904–1986), Josephine Hull, John Alexander, Jean Adair, Raymond Massey (1896–1983)
	Angel Street Drama	1,295	Patrick Hamilton (1904–1962)	Judith Evelyn (1913–1967), Leo G. Carroll (1892–1972), Vincent Price (1911–1993)	Two revivals. 1946 movie for TV
	Claudia Comedy	722	Rose Franken (1898–1988)	Donald Cook (1901–1961), Dorothy McGuire (1916–2001)	No revival. 1944 movie: Dorothy McGuire, Robert Young (1907–1998)
	Watch on the Rhine Drama	378	Lillian Hellman	Lucille Watson (1879–1962), Paul Lukas (1891–1971), Mady Christians (1900–1951), John Lodge (1903–1985)	One revival. 1943 movie: Bette Davis, Paul Lukas
	Junior Miss Comedy	n.a. [ran until 1943]	Joseph Fields, Jerome Chodorov	Francesca Bruning (active 1930s, 1940s), Alexander Kirkland (active 1930s, 1940s, and 1950s), Patricia Peardon (1924–1993)	No revival. 1945 movie: Peggy Ann Garner (1932–1984), Allyn Joslyn, Mona Freeman (b. 1926)

(continued)

TABLE 23. (continued)

Year	Play Titles and Tony Awards	Performances	Playwrights	Major Cast Members	Revival History on Broadway and Movie Production(s) as of 2009
1942	*The Doughgirls* Comedy	671	Joseph Fields	Arlene Francis (1907–2001)	No revival. 1944 movie: Ann Sheridan (1915–1967), Alexis Smith (1921–1993), Jack Carson (1910–1963)
	Janie Comedy	642	Herschel V. Williams (active 1940s and 1950s), Josephine Bentham (active 1930s, 1940s, and 1950s)	Gwen Anderson (active 1940s and 1950s), Herbert Evers (1922–2005)	No revival. 1944 movie: Joyce Reynolds (b. 1925), Robert Hutton (1920–1994)
	Uncle Harry Drama	430	Thomas Job (1901–1947)	Joseph Schildkraut (1895–1964), Eva Le Gallienne (1899–1991), Karl Malden (1912–2009)	No revival.
	The Eve of St. Mark Drama	307	Maxwell Anderson (1888–1959)	William Prince (1913–1996), Aline MacMahon (1899–1991)	No revival. 1944 movie: Vincent Price (1911–1993), Anne Baxter (1923–1985), William Eythe (1918–1957), Michael O'Shea (1906–1973)
1943	*The Voice of the Turtle* Comedy	1,557	John Van Druten (1901–1957)	Margaret Sullavan (1911–1960), Elliott Nugent (1900–1980), Audrey Christie (1911–1989)	No revival. 1947 movie: Ronald Reagan (1911–2004), Eleanor Parker (b. 1922), Eve Arden (1908–1990)
	Harriet Drama	377	Florence Ryerson (active 1940s), Colin Clements (1895–1948)	Helen Hayes (1900–1993)	One revival.
	The Skin of Our Teeth Comedy	359	Thornton Wilder (1897–1975)	Tallulah Bankhead (1902–1968), Fredric March (1897–1975)	Two revivals. 1983 movie for TV
	The Patriots Drama	181	Sidney Kingsley (1906–1995)	Raymond Edward Johnson (1911–2001), Cecil Humphreys (1883–1947), House Jameson (1902–1971), Madge Evans (1909–1981)	No revival.

Year	Title / Genre	Runs	Author	Cast	Notes
1944	*Harvey* Comedy	1775	Mary Chase (1907–1981)	Frank Fay (1897–1961), Josephine Hull	One revival. 1950 movie: Jimmy Stewart (1908–1997), Josephine Hull
	Anna Lucasta Drama	957	Philip Yordan (1914–2003)	Hilda Simms (1920–1994)	One revival. 1949 movie: Paulette Goddard (1910–1990)
	I Remember Mama Comedy	713	John Van Druten	Mady Christians, Oscar Homolka (1898–1978)	No revival. 1948 movie: Irene Dunne (1898–1990), Oscar Homolka; basis for TV series, 1949–1957
	Ten Little Indians Drama	426	Agatha Christie (1890–1976)	Estelle Winwood (1883–1984), Halliwell Hobbes (1877–1962), Claudia Morgan (1912–1974), Michael Whalen (1902–1974)	No revival. 1945 movie as *And Then There Were None*: Walter Huston (1884–1950), Barry Fitzgerald (1888–1961); 1965 movie: Hugh O'Brian (b. 1923), Shirley Eaton (b. 1937)
	Jacobowsky and the Colonel Comedy	417	S. N. Behrman (1893–1973) (Adapted from the play by Franz Werfel, 1890–1945)	Louis Calhern (1895–1956), Oscar Karlweis (1894–1956), Annabella (1904–1996)	No revival. 1958 movie, *Me and the Colonel*: Danny Kaye (1918–1987)
	The Late George Apley Comedy	384	John P. Marquand (1893–1960), George S. Kaufman (1889–1961)	Leo G. Carroll (1892–1972), Janet Beecher (1884–1955), Margaret Dale, Margaret Phillips (1923–1984)	No revival. 1947 movie: Ronald Coleman (1891–1958), Vanessa Brown (1928–1999), Richard Haydn (1905–1985)
1945	*State of the Union* Comedy	765	Howard Lindsay (1889–1968), Russel Crouse (1893–1966)	Ralph Bellamy (1904–1991), Ruth Hussey (1917–2005)	No revival. 1948 movie: Spencer Tracy (1900–1967), Katharine Hepburn (1907–2003), Van Johnson (1916–2008), Angela Lansbury (b. 1925)
	The Glass Menagerie Drama	563	Tennessee Williams (1911–1983)	Laurette Taylor (1884–1946), Eddie Dowling (1895–1976), Julie Haydon, Anthony Ross (1909–1955)	One revival. 1950 movie: Jane Wyman (1917–2007). Kirk Douglas (b. 1916), Gertrude Lawrence, Arthur Kennedy; 1987 movie: Joanne Woodward (b. 1930), John Malkovich (b. 1953), Karen Allen (b. 1951) 1966, 1973 TV adaptations

(continued)

TABLE 23. (continued)

Year	Play Titles and Tony Awards	Performances	Playwrights	Major Cast Members	Revival History on Broadway and Movie Production(s) as of 2009
1946	*Happy Birthday* Comedy Tony: Best Actress	563	Anita Loos (1888–1981)	Helen Hayes	No revival.
	O Mistress Mine Comedy	482	Terence Rattigan (1911–1977)	Lynn Fontaine (1887–1983), Alfred Lunt (1893–1977)	No revival.
	Years Ago Drama Tony: Best Actor	206	Ruth Gordon (1896–1985)	Fredric March, Florence Eldridge (1901–1988)	No revival. 1953 movie as *The Actress*: Spencer Tracy, Jean Simmons (b. 1929)
	Joan of Lorraine Drama Tony: Best Actress	199	Maxwell Anderson	Ingrid Bergman (1917–1982)	No revival. 1948 movie: Ingrid Bergman
	Another Part of the Forest Drama Tony: Best Featured Actress and Best Costumes	182	Lillian Hellman	Patricia Neal (b. 1926), Mildred Dunnock (1901–1991), Margaret Phillips (1923–1984), Leo Genn (1905–1978), Percy Waram (1881–1961)	No revival. 1948 movie: Fredric March, Dan Duryea (1907–1968), Edmond O'Brien (1915–1985), Ann Blyth (b. 1928)
1947	*A Streetcar Named Desire* Drama Tony: Best Actress	855	Tennessee Williams	Jessica Tandy (1909–1999), Marlon Brando (1924–2004), Kim Hunter (1922–2002), Karl Malden (1912–2009)	Seven revivals. 1951 movie: Vivien Leigh (1913–1967), Marlon Brando, Kim Hunter, Karl Malden
	John Loves Mary Comedy	423	Norman Krasna (1909–1984)	Nina Foch (1924–2008), William Prince (1913–1996), Tom Ewell (1909–1994)	No revival. 1949 movie: Ronald Reagan, Jack Carson, Patricia Neal
	All My Sons Drama Tony: Best Costumes Tony: Best Director	328	Arthur Miller (1915–2005)	Ed Begley (1901–1970), Beth Merrill (1892–1986), Arthur Kennedy (1914–1990), Karl Malden	No revival. 1948 movie: Edward G. Robinson (1893–1973), Burt Lancaster (1913–1994), Mady Christians, Howard Duff (1913–1990)
	Medea Drama Tony: Best Actress	214	Euripides (ca. 480 B.C.E.–406 B.C.E.); adaptation by Robinson Jeffers (1887–1962)	Judith Anderson (1898–1992), Florence Reed (1883–1967), John Gielgud (1904–2000)	An ancient Greek tragedy, this was the first of six Broadway revivals. It originally opened in 1920. 1951 movie: Pauline Letts (1917–2001), Robert Speaight (1904–1976) 1988 Danish movie.

Year	Title / Category	Perf.	Author	Cast	Notes
	Antony and Cleopatra Drama Tony: Best Actress	126	William Shakespeare (1564–1616)	Katharine Cornell (1898–1974), Godfrey Tearle (1884–1953), Lenore Ulric (1892–1970), Kent Smith (1907–1985)	Fourth of five revivals. A theater classic, it first appeared on Broadway in 1846.
1948	*Mister Roberts* Drama Tony: Best Actor, Best Play, Best Producer, and Best Authors	1,157	Thomas Heggen (1918–1949), Joshua Logan (1908–1988)	Henry Fonda (1905–1982), William Harrigan (1893–1966), Robert Keith (1898–1966), David Wayne (1914–1995), Ralph Meeker (1920–1988)	One revival. 1955 movie: Henry Fonda, James Cagney (1899–1986), William Powell (1892–1984), Jack Lemmon (1925–2001)
	Goodbye, My Fancy Comedy Tony: Best Featured Actress	446	Fay Kanin (b. 1917)	Shirley Booth, Madeline Carroll (1906–1987), Joe Boland (1903–1987)	No revival. 1951 movie: Joan Crawford (1905–1977), Robert Young, Frank Lovejoy (1912–1962), Eve Arden (1908–1990)
	The Madwoman of Chaillot Comedy Tony: Best Actress	368	Jean Giraudoux (1882–1944)	Martita Hunt (1900–1969)	No revival. 1969 movie: Katharine Hepburn, Paul Henreid (1905–1992)
	Anne of the Thousand Days Drama Tony: Best Actor and Best Scenic Design	288	Maxwell Anderson	Rex Harrison (1908–1990)	No revival. 1969 movie: Richard Burton (1925–1984), Genevieve Bujold (b. 1942), Irene Papas (b. 1926)
	Edward, My Son Drama	260	Noel Langley (1911–1980)	Shirley Booth	No revival. 1949 movie: Spencer Tracy, Deborah Kerr (1921–2007)
1949	*Death of a Salesman* Drama Tony: Best Play, Best Supporting Actor, Best Author, Best Director, Best Scenic Designer, Best Producer	742	Arthur Miller	Lee J. Cobb (1911–1976), Mildred Dunnock (1901–1991), Arthur Kennedy, Cameron Mitchell (1918–1994)	Four revivals. 1951 movie: Frederic March, Mildred Dunnock, Kevin McCarthy (b. 1914), Cameron Mitchell. 1966, 1985, 1996, and 2000 TV adaptations.
	Clutterbuck Comedy	218	Benn W. Levy (1900–1973)	Arthur Margetson (1887–1951)	No revival. No movie.

outside society's conventional expectations. Hopes and aspirations usually give way to despair.

O'Neill completed some of his plays years before their production. For example, *The Iceman Cometh*, written in 1939 and published in 1940, did not open until October 1946 and closed March 1947, after 136 performances. He completed two plays in 1941: *Hughie,* which opened in 1959, and *Long Day's Journey into Night.* This autobiographical play, acclaimed as one of his greatest accomplishments, did not make it to the stage until 1956, three years after his death, as he had requested. *A Touch of the Poet* (1942) went into production in 1958. *A Moon for the Misbegotten* opened and closed in Columbus, Ohio, in 1947, not arriving on a New York stage until May 1957.

Tennessee Williams and Arthur Miller made their New York debuts in the 1940s and, like O'Neill, developed realistic plots that usually involve tragic circumstances. Williams' debut on Broadway came with *The Glass Menagerie.* From a successful run in Chicago in 1944, the play opened in New York on March 31, 1945. With a gripping story about the daydreams of a mother for her crippled and withdrawn daughter, coupled with an outstanding performance by Laurette Taylor as the mother, the play easily ran for over a year with 563 performances and captured the New York Drama Critics Circle Award as the best play of the season. Williams quickly followed in 1947 with a second powerful play, *A Streetcar Named Desire,* which brought him a Pulitzer Prize for drama. A superb cast, led by Jessica Tandy as Blanche and Marlon Brando as Stanley, portrays a cultural clash between Blanche, who desperately tries to hold on to an illusion of being an aristocratic woman from the old South, and Stanley, a rising member of the industrial urban class. Williams continued to write plays for Broadway; several became **movies** produced by Hollywood, starting with *The Glass Menagerie* in 1950.

Arthur Miller's first Broadway appearance, *The Man Who Had All the Luck* (1944) closed after four performances. Three years later, he returned with *All My Sons,* which opened to critical acclaim and won him a Tony Award for best author of the season. In 1948, he wrote *Death of a Salesman* in six weeks. It opened on Broadway on February 10, 1949, won the Pulitzer Prize for drama, and today is considered his masterpiece. It tells the story of Willy Loman, a man who spends more time dreaming the postwar American dream of success than acting on making it come true. Audiences found the downfall and suicide of this ordinary middle-aged man to be a riveting story. Lee J. Cobb (1911–1976) played Willy, and Mildred Dunnock (1901–1991) had the role of Linda, a wife who tries to shield her husband from the reality of his lost dreams. Miller's career spanned more than seven decades; he wrote screenplays, fiction, nonfiction, and **radio** dramas in addition to stage plays.

Other playwrights, such as Lillian Hellman, William Saroyan, Maxwell Anderson, and Thornton Wilder, already had established reputations by 1940 and continued with meaningful works throughout the decade. The plots of their plays dealt primarily with families, frustrations, and private disillusionment.

Comedic playwrights offered zany plots, uproarious situations, a parade of oddball characters, scatterbrained teenagers, and misunderstandings around romance and love in hopes of drawing crowds to the theater; and they did. Joseph Kesselring completed the writing of *Arsenic and Old Lace* in 1939 shortly before it opened in January 1940.

The plot focuses on a drama critic whose two spinster aunts poison lonely old men with a glass of homemade elderberry wine laced with arsenic. He also has a brother who believes he is Teddy Roosevelt, creating uproarious situations and many welcome laughs.

In 1944, the laughs became especially loud and long when, in Mary Chase's *Harvey,* Elwood P. Dowd constantly attempts to introduce his imaginary friend Harvey, a six-foot, three-and-half-inch tall rabbit to his mother and sister's society friends. Mrs. Dowd, in turn, attempts to institutionalize her son, a man who is liked by everyone he meets. Rapid, funny dialogue proved to be the tonic war-weary audiences needed.

Four years later and two and a half years after the surrender of Japan, Broadway experienced a huge success with a hilarious production about World War II titled *Mister Roberts.* Based on a 1946 novel with the same name by Thomas Heggen, the story takes place in the South Pacific aboard the US AK-601, an unimportant navy cargo ship far from any action. Henry Fonda played Mr. Roberts, a young first officer who longs for reassignment to a combat vessel. He reprised his role in a successful 1955 movie.

The Time of Your Life (1940), written by William Saroyan, was the first drama to win both the New York Drama Critics Award and Pulitzer Prize in the same year. Pulitzer Prizes, named for Joseph Pulitzer (1847–1911), were first given in 1917, and drama has been a category since 1918. The other Pulitzer recipients during the 1940s include Robert Sherwood's *There Shall Be No Night,* 1941; Thornton Wilder's *The Skin of Our Teeth,* 1943; Mary Chase's *Harvey,* 1945; Russel Crouse and Howard Lindsay's *State of the Union,* 1946; Tennessee Williams's *A Streetcar Named Desire,* 1948; and Arthur Miller's *Death of a Salesman,* 1949. Sherwood had previously won a Pulitzer in 1936 for *Idiots Delight* and in 1939 for *Abe Lincoln in Illinois,* as had Wilder in 1938 for *Our Town.* Tennessee Williams would be the recipient again in 1955 for *Cat on a Hot Tin Roof.*

Shortly after their successful runs on Broadway, almost three-quarters of the plays listed in the table became movies to be enjoyed by filmgoers across the country. With the subsequent growth of television, some also were adapted to that medium. Many of the playwrights worked on the film version of their play, and a few of the Broadway actors and actresses traveled to Hollywood to repeat their role in the movie. For the most part, however, Hollywood had its own ideas about who to contract for the parts. For some of the Broadway actors, the movie opportunity turned into a career. *I Remember Mama* afforded Marlon Brando his debut on Broadway, and, after an outstanding performance in *A Streetcar Named Desire* (1949), he moved to Hollywood and henceforth worked exclusively in film.

One Broadway comedy, *Junior Miss* (1941), aired on CBS radio in 1942, with Shirley Temple (b. 1928) as Judy Graves, a typical radio teenager. CBS radio reinstated the show on a continuing basis for the years 1948 to 1950, with Barbara Whiting (1931–2004) taking on the title role.

Throughout the 1940s, the number of Broadway productions remained lower than previous decades, and, by the last years of the 1940s, television had joined the movies in stealing audiences. But fresh new talents emerged, and gripping dramas and amusing comedies had successful runs. The artistic quality of most musicals and musical comedies increased substantially. Tennessee Williams's *A Streetcar Named Desire* and

Arthur Miller's *Death of a Salesman* analyzed people, not politics, an approach that intrigued theatergoers, while the lightweight comedies such as *Harvey* brought laughter from the first line to the closing curtain, and *Mister Roberts* dared to make war look ridiculous.

See also: Blackouts, Brownouts, and Dim-Outs; Broadway Shows (Musicals); Comedies (Film); Drama (Film); Radio Programming: Comedy Shows; Radio Programming: Drama and Anthology Shows; USO (United Service Organizations)

Selected Reading
Atkinson, Brooks, and Albert Hirschfeld. *The Lively Years, 1920–1973.* New York: Association Press, 1973.
Foertsch, Jacqueline. *American Culture in the 1940s.* Edinburgh, Scotland: Edinburgh University Press, 2008.
Harris, Andrew B. *Broadway Theatre.* New York: Routledge, 1994.

BROADWAY SHOWS (MUSICALS)

The word "Broadway" refers to both a main thoroughfare that runs diagonally through Manhattan and a small district near Times Square, where the majority of theatrical productions take place in playhouses clustered in that area. In the 1940s, some 25 Broadway theaters presented a variety of shows, including many musicals. Revues featured a series of unrelated comic skits, dances, and songs, while musical comedies added a plot, usually revolving around a tale of romance. Story and character development came to hold as much importance as the music.

Many shows, regardless of type, first had a brief trial run outside New York City, often in New Haven, Boston, or Philadelphia. If successful, they came to Broadway, and a long-running musical might eventually go on a national tour once it closed, although with less elaborate sets and lacking the original cast. Even with a Broadway run and pre- and post-performances, only a limited number of people had the opportunity to see one of these productions, a factor that reduces Broadway's validity as a carrier of true mass culture. That does not, however, change the pleasure of good music and big laughs enjoyed by those lucky enough to see a Broadway show.

Other media outlets—specifically **radio,** recordings, and the **movies**—brought some of the Broadway productions, or at least selected aspects of

Cole Porter's Panama Hattie *provided Ethel Merman her first solo billing on Broadway in 1940. (Photofest)*

them, to the level of national entertainment. Songs receiving an enthusiastic response from audiences usually got recorded and then aired on radio, and some gained enough popularity to be considered standards, such as "Bewitched, Bothered, Bewildered" (*Pal Joey,* 1940), "People Will Say We Are in Love" (*Oklahoma!* 1943), or "You'll Never Walk Alone" (*Carousel,* 1945), to name but a few. Hollywood, aware of the appeal of the more successful Broadway musicals, made a number of them into films. Rarely, however, did the New York actors and actresses who initially propelled the show to fame find themselves cast in Hollywood's version, because the film studios had their own rosters of stars.

In 1940, the Broadway season included a black folk musical titled *Cabin in the Sky* by composer Vernon Duke (1903–1969), with lyrics by John La Touche (1914–1956). A fantasy about love and faith among people living in the South, the show carried a serious story line. With a brief run of 156 performances, *Cabin in the Sky* does not qualify as a big hit, but it served as an unusual event for Broadway with its all-black cast that included Ethel Waters (1900–1977) and dancer-choreographer Katherine Dunham (1909–2006). The score had several distinguished tunes, including the title song and "Taking a Chance on Love." But blacks on Broadway remained a rare occurrence, not the norm.

A new feature for musicals occurred in 1943 with the successful run of *Oklahoma!* the first Broadway production by the new team of Richard Rodgers (1902–1979) and Oscar Hammerstein II (1895–1960), both veterans of the stage musical. In *Oklahoma!* the singing served as a continuation of the dialogue; in previous shows, a song tended to stop the action of the play and stood as an event unto itself. The innovation gave this production a dramatic richness and quality, and historians would later refer to the 1940s as the golden age of musical theater.

Richard Rodgers' musical career had begun in the 1920s, and until 1943 he partnered with lyricist Lorenz Hart (1895–1943) on 31 projects. After collaborating on *Pal Joey* (1940) and *By Jupiter* (1942), a disagreement led to a breakup in 1943, and Rodgers then began working with Oscar Hammerstein II on *Oklahoma!* Hammerstein, like Rodgers, had written his first Broadway show in the early 1920s. For the remainder of his career, he teamed with many composers, including Jerome Kern, with whom he had an extended and successful partnership, with the classic *Showboat* (1927) as their biggest hit.

In the fall of 1943, Rodgers again joined forces with Hart on a revival of *A Connecticut Yankee.* It opened on November 17, 1943, just five days before Hart died of pneumonia. Needing a new partner, and with their success with *Oklahoma!* fresh in everyone's minds, Rodgers resumed his collaboration with Hammerstein. In addition to *Oklahoma!* the duo turned out three more Broadway hits in the 1940s: *Carousel* (1945), *Allegro* (1947), and *South Pacific* (1949)—along with original music for a film titled *State Fair* (1945), a remake of a 1933 nonmusical movie. They continued their successful collaboration until 1959 and *The Sound of Music.* Hammerstein died the following year, but Rodgers remained active until ill health forced him to retire in the 1970s.

At the onset of World War II, the theater community did its part to support the war effort. Years earlier, during World War I, seven theater women had started an organization known as the Stage Women's War Relief. In 1940, with another world war imminent, they reactivated the organization, renaming it the American Theatre Wing. Shortly thereafter, the women inaugurated the famous Stage Door Canteen, housing it in the 44th Street Theatre. Throughout the conflict, stars from Broadway and Hollywood provided men in uniform **food,** conversation, songs, and dance. The Theatre Wing also produced entertainment programs for veterans' hospitals, **USO** clubs, and troops overseas, while actors and actresses participated in drives to sell **war bonds.**

During World War II, as had been the case with the Great Depression just a few years earlier, the number of plays produced in a single season decreased. But even with fewer shows, Broadway experienced an increase in both attendance and revenue throughout the 1940s. Two factors contributed. The war had provided high-paying jobs to both men and women, giving them a new level of prosperity and the financial means to have a night on the town, including a play. Also, most forms of entertainment, especially radio broadcasts, the movies, and newsreels, along with print media, provided constant reminders of the war. The 1940s musicals and comedies, for the most part, avoided topical issues, giving war-weary theatergoers a form of escapism and a couple of hours of relief. Wartime precautionary measures of a mandatory dimming of all city lights from April 29, 1942, until the end of the war, along with frequent blackout drills, did not deter those intent on seeing a play from traveling to a dimmed midtown Manhattan for an evening at the theater.

After victory had been achieved in 1945, the economic prosperity in the United States soared, and those seeking entertainment at Broadway theaters came expecting a comparable change in the caliber and quality of the shows. Sets and costumes became more elaborate, adding visual excitement to productions. Increased attention to the importance of the **dance** routines provided opportunities for choreographers such as Martha Graham (1894–1991), Agnes de Mille (1905–1993), and Jerome Robbins (1918–1998) to create more complex and dramatic numbers.

Throughout the decade, a number of seasoned Broadway composers and lyricists including Harold Arlen (1905–1986), Irving Berlin (1888–1989), Dorothy Fields (1905–1974), Ira Gershwin (1896–1983), Oscar Hammerstein II, Lorenz Hart, Jerome Kern (1885–1969), Jimmy McHugh (1895–1969), Cole Porter (1893–1964), Richard Rodgers, and Sigmund Romberg (1887–1951) reached new heights of accomplishment. Established performers such as Eve Arden (1908–1990), Ray Bolger (1906–1987), Ethel Merman (1909–1984), and Victor Moore (1876–1962) guaranteed the highest quality of singing and acting.

Four composers experienced the thrill of having their first hits occur in musicals of the 1940s: Leonard Bernstein (1918–1990) for *On the Town* (1944), George Forrest (1915–1999) for *Song of Norway* (1944), Jule Styne (1905–1994) for *High Button Shoes* (1947), and Charles Gaynor (1909–1975) for *Lend an Ear* (1947). Three lyricists also enjoyed successful debuts: Betty Comden (1919–2006) and Adolph Green (1915–2002) for *On the Town* and Sammy Cahn (1913–1993) for *High Button Shoes.* The hit musicals of the 1940s offered major roles for aspiring actors and actresses that included June Allyson (1917–2006) in *Best Foot Forward* (1941), Carol Channing (b. 1921) in *Let's Face It!* (1941), Danny Kaye (1913–1987) in *Lady in the Dark*

(1941), Gene Kelly (1912–1996) in *Pal Joey* (1940), and Mary Martin (1914–1990) in *One Touch of Venus* (1943).

Recognition for outstanding accomplishments has long been an American tradition, and the 1940s were no exception. In 1935, 15 professional theatrical critics organized the New York Drama Critics Circle Awards with two categories: best American play and best foreign play. Beginning with the 1945–1946 season, they added a third category, best musical. During the years 1946 to 1949, *Carousel* (1946), *Brigadoon* (1947), and *South Pacific* (1949) received these first awards. Some discord and disagreement among the members of the Critics Circle caused no award to be given in 1948.

Two other ceremonies for theatrical performances were organized in the 1940s. The first, the Theatre World Award, has been given annually since 1945 to six actors and six actresses for outstanding debut performances either on or off Broadway. Seven of the musical shows in the following table—*On the Town* (1944); *Carousel, Brigadoon, Oklahoma! Finian's Rainbow* (1947); *High Button Shoes* (1947); *Where's Charley?* (1948)—and three revues—*Call Me Mister* (1946), *Lend an Ear* (1948), and *Inside U.S.A.* (1948)—had the honor of one or more of their cast members receiving Theatre World recognition.

Since 1947, the American Theatre Wing has given a Tony Award, named in honor of one of its founders, Antoinette Perry (1888–1946), in a number of categories. For Broadway productions, the Tony ranks with the film community's Oscar, the Grammys in the music industry, and the Emmys for **television.** In 1947, a Tony for best choreography went to Agnes de Mille for *Brigadoon* and Michael Kidd (1915–2007) for *Finian's Rainbow*. The next year, Jerome Robbins captured the Tony for his dance routines in *High Button Shoes,* and, in 1949, choreographer Gower Champion accepted the award for his work in *Lend an Ear*. Also in 1949, *Kiss Me Kate* (1948) dominated the season with five Tony wins: best musical, best author, best composer and lyricist, best costume designer, and best producer. *South Pacific* topped that in 1950 by winning in nine categories: best musical, best libretto, best original score, best actor, best actress, best featured actor, best featured actress, best producer, and best director.

The table below identifies 31 musicals that opened in the 1940s and achieved 300 or more performances before closing. Nineteen of them exceeded 500 performances, with *Oklahoma!* leading the pack with 2,212 performances, a long-standing record. Fifteen have had successful revivals on Broadway since the 1940s, and 22 appeared again as Hollywood movies, although they often underwent significant changes in the transition.

One successful musical, Irving Berlin's *This Is the Army,* which tells about military life through songs and skits, will not be found in the table. When the United States entered World War II, Berlin decided to rework and update his World War I camp revue *Yip Yip Yaphank* (1918). The new version, the only production on Broadway that centered on life as a member of the armed forces when the country was at war, opened July 4, 1942, to play a limited 12-week engagement. It closed August 26, 1942, having sold out all 113 performances. It raised $10 million (approximately $132 million in 2008 dollars) for the Army Emergency Relief Fund. Along with Burl Ives (1909–1995) and a cast of over 300 soldiers assigned to this special Broadway production unit, composer and lyricist Berlin appears on stage to sing "Oh, How I Hate to Get Up

TABLE 24. Thirty-Two Broadway Musicals with Over 300 Performances, 1940–1949

Year	Musical Title	Ranking and Number of Performances	Composer; Lyrist	Major Cast Members	Representative Popular Songs	Revival History on Broadway as of 2009 and Movie Production
1940	*Panama Hattie* (Ethel Merman's first solo billing)	19th, 501	Cole Porter (1893–1964)	Ethel Merman (1909–1984), June Allyson (1917–2006), Betty Hutton (1921–2007), Vera-Ellen (1921–1981)	"Make It Another Old-Fashioned, Please"	No revival; 1942 movie: Red Skelton (1913–1997), Ann Sothern (2001)
	Louisiana Purchase (first show after seven-year absence)	23rd, 444	Irving Berlin (1888–1989)	Vera Zorina (1917–2003), Victor Moore (1876–1962)	"Fools Fall in Love"	No revival; 1941 movie: Bob Hope (1903–2003), Zorina, Moore
	Pal Joey	27th, 374	Richard Rodgers (1909–1979); Lorenz Hart (1895–1943)	Gene Kelly 91912–1996), June Havoc (b. 1913), Van Johnson (1916–2008)	"Bewitched, Bothered, Bewildered," "I Could Write a Book," others	Four revivals; 1957 movie: Rita Hayworth (1918–1987), Frank Sinatra (1915–1998)
	Let's Face It!	15th, 547	Cole Porter	Danny Kaye (1913–1987), Eve Arden (1908–1990), Nanette Fabray (b. 1920), Carol Channing (b. 1921), understudy		One revival; 1943 movie: Bob Hope, Betty Hutton (1921–2007)
1941	*Lady in the Dark*	21st, 467	Kurt Weill (1900–1950); Ira Gershwin	Danny Kaye, Victor Mature (1913–1999), Gertrude Lawrence (1898–1952)	"My Ship"	No revival; 1944 movie: Ginger Rogers (1911–1995), Ray Milland (1905–1986)
	Best Foot Forward	29th, 326	Hugh Martin (b. 1914); Ralph Blane (1914–1995)	June Allyson (1917–2006), Nancy Walker (1921–1992)	"Buckle Down, Winsocki," "Ev'ry Time"	No revival; 1943 movie: Lucille Ball (1911–1989), Allyson, Walker
1942	*By Jupiter* (last Rodgers and Hart show)	24th, 427	Richard Rodgers; Lorenz Hart	Ray Bolger (1906–1987), Constance Moore (1920–2005), Vera-Ellen, Nanette Fabray	"Nobody's Heart"	No revival; no movie version
1943	*Oklahoma!* (Rodgers and Hammerstein's first effort together)	1st, 2,212	Richard Rodgers; Oscar Hammerstein II (1895–1960)	Alfred Drake (1914–1992), Joan Roberts (b. 1918), Celeste Holm (b. 1919)	"Oklahoma," "Oh, What a Beautiful Mornin'," "People Will Say We Are in Love," many more	Four revivals; 1955 movie: Gordon MacRae (1921–1986), Gloria Graham (1923–1981)

	One Touch of Venus	14th, 567	Kurt Weill; Ogden Nash (1902–1971) and S. J. Perelman (1904–1979)	Mary Martin (1914–1990)	"Speak Low"	1948 movie: Robert Walker No revivals; (1918–1951), Ava Gardner (1922–1990), Dick Haymes (1916–1980)
	Carmen Jones (based on the 1845 opera by Bizet (1838–1875)	18th, 502	Georges Bizet (1838–1875); Oscar Hammerstein II	Luther Saxon (active 1930s–1940s), Muriel Rahn (1911–1961)		Two movies; 1954 movie: Harry Belafonte (b. 1927), Dorothy Dandridge (1922–1965)
	The Merry Widow	29th, 322	Franz Lehar (1870–1948); Adrian Ross (1859–1933) and Robert Gilbert (1899–1978)	Jan Kiepura (1902–1956), Marta Eggerth (1912–1966)	"I Love You So" ("The Merry Widow Waltz")	Five revivals with this production being the fifth; original in 1907–1908. Three Hollywood versions: 1925 (silent), 1934, and 1952 with Lana Turner (1921–1995), Fernando Lamas (1915–1982)
1944	Follow the Girls	6th, 882	Philip Charig (1902–1960), Dan Shapiro (active 1940s–1950s), and Milton Pascal (active 1930s–1940s)	Jackie Gleason (1916–1987), Gertrude Niesen (1910–1975)	"I Wanna Get Married"	No revival; no movie version
	Song of Norway	7th, 860	(loosely based on music by Edvard Greig (1843–1907); Robert Wright (1914–2005), George Forrest (1915–1999)	Lawrence Brooks (active 1940s–1950s), Helena Bliss (b. 1919)	"I Love You," "Piano Concerto in A Minor"	No revival; 1970 movie: Toralv Maurstad (b. 1926), Florence Henderson (b. 1934)
	Bloomer Girl	12th, 654	Harold Arlen; E. Y. Harburg (1896–1981)	Celeste Holm, Nanette Fabray	"When the Boys Come Home," "Right as the Rain"	One revival; no movie version
	On the Town	22nd, 663	Leonard Bernstein (1918–1990); Betty Comden (1919–2006), and Adolph Green (1915–2002)	John Battles (b. 1921), Adolph Green, Cris Alexander (b. 1920)	"New York, New York," "Lonely Town"	Two revivals; 1949 movie: Gene Kelly, Frank Sinatra, Vera-Ellen, Betty Garrett (b. 1919)

(continued)

TABLE 24. (continued)

Year	Musical Title	Ranking and Number of Performances	Composer; Lyrist	Major Cast Members	Representative Popular Songs	Revival History on Broadway as of 2009 and Movie Production
	Mexican Hayride (movie version dropped Porter songs)	20th, 481	Cole Porter	Bobby Clark (1888–1960)	"Count Your Blessings," "I Love You"	No revival; 1948 movie: Bud Abbott (1895–1974), Lou Costello (1906–1959)
1945	*Carousel* (played across the street from *Oklahoma!* 1945–1947)	5th, 890	Richard Rodgers; Oscar Hammerstein II	John Raitt (1917–2005), Jan Clayton (1917–1983)	"June Is Bustin' Out All Over," "You'll Never Walk Alone," "If I Loved You," many more	Four revivals; 1956 movie: Gordon MacRae, Shirley Jones (b. 1934)
	The Red Mill	16th, 531	Victor Herbert (1860–1924); Henry Blossom (1867–1919) and Forman Brown (1901–1996)	Eddie Foy Jr. (1905–1983), Michael O'Shea (1906–1973), Dorothy Stone (1905–1974), Odette Mytril (1898–1978)		A revival of the 1906–1907 original; 1927 silent movie
	Up in Central Park	17th, 504	Sigmund Romberg (1887–1951); Dorothy Fields (1905–1974)	Maureen Cannon (b. 1926), Wilbur Evans (1905–1987)	"Close as Pages in a Book"	One revival; 1948 movie: Deanna Durbin (b. 1921), Dick Haymes (1916–1980)
1946	*Annie Get Your Gun*	3rd, 1,147	Irving Berlin	Ethel Merman	"There's No Business Like Show Business," "The Girl That I Marry," "They Say It's Wonderful," many more	Two revivals. 1950 movie: Betty Hutton (1921–2007), Howard Keel (1919–2004)
	Show Boat (also known as *Showboat*)	26th, 418	Jerome Kern; Oscar Hammerstein II		"Ol' Man River," "Can't Help Lovin' Dat Man," "Why Do I Love You?" many more	Six revivals, with this production being the second; originally produced in 1927–1929

Year	Show	Rank, Perfs	Composer/Lyricist	Cast	Songs	Revivals/Movies
1947	*High Button Shoes*	10th, 727	Jule Styne; Sammy Cahn (1913–1993)	Nanette Fabray, Phil Silvers (1911–1985)	"Papa Won't You Dance with Me?"	No revivals; no movies
	Finian's Rainbow	11th, 725	Burton Lane (1912–1997); E. Y. Harburg	Albert Sharpe (1885–1970)	"How Are Things in Glocca Morra?" "Old Devil Moon"	Three revivals; 1968 movie: Fred Astaire (1899–1987), Petula Clark (b. 1932)
	Brigadoon	13th, 581	Frederick Loewe, (1904–1998); Alan Jay Lerner (1918–1986)	David Brooks (1917–1999), George Keane (1917–1995), Marion Bell (1919–1997)	"Almost Like Being in Love," "The Heather on the Hill"	Four revivals; 1954 movie: Gene Kelly, Van Johnson (1916–2008), Cyd Charisee (1921–2008)
	Allegro	30th, 315	Richard Rogers; Oscar Hammerstein II	John Battles	"The Gentlemen Is a Dope"	No revival; no movie
1948	*Kiss Me, Kate*	4th, 1,070	Cole Porter	Alfred Drake, Patricia Morison (b. 1915), Lisa Kirk (1925–1990), Harold Lang (1920–1985)	"Too Darn Hot," "Always True to You (In My Fashion)," many more	Two revivals. 1953 movie: Kathryn Grayson, Howard Keel (1919–2004), Ann Miller (1923–2004), Tommy Rall (b. 1929)
	Where's Charley? (based on Brandon Thomas's 1856–1914 *Charley's Aunt* (1893)	8th, 792	Frank Loesser (1910–1969); George Abbott (1882–1995)	Ray Bolger	"Once in Love with Amy," "My Darling, My Darling"	Two revivals; 1952 movie: Ray Bolger, Allyn Ann McLerie (b. 1926)
	As the Girls Go	26th, 420	Jimmy McHugh; Harold Adamson (1906–1980)	Bobby Clark	"Nobody's Heart But Mine"	No revival; no movie
1949	*South Pacific* (opened to largest advance sale on record, in its second year played to standing audiences, and second musical to win a Pulitzer Prize)	2nd, 1,925	Richard Rodgers; Oscar Hammerstein II	Mary Martin, Ezio Pinza (1892–1957)	"A Cockeyed Optimist," "I'm Gonna Wash That Man Right Out of My Hair," "Some Enchanted Evening," many more	Two revivals. 1958 movie: Rossano Brazzi (1916–1994), Mitzi Gaynor (b. 1931)
	Gentlemen Prefer Blondes	9th, 740	Jule Styne; Leo Robin (1900–1984)	Carol Channing	"Diamonds Are a Girl's Best Friend," "Bye, Bye, Baby"	One revival; 1953 movie: Jane Russell (b. 1921), Marilyn Monroe (1926–1962), Charles Coburn (1877–1961)
	Miss Liberty	32nd, 308	Irving Berlin	Eddie Albert (1908–2005)	"Let's Take an Old-Fashioned Walk"	No revival; no movie

in the Morning." The cast, after completing its Broadway run, set out on a tour starting in Washington, DC, and ending in Los Angeles. Once in California, Warner Bros. added George Murphy (1902–1992) and Ronald Reagan (1911–2004) to the military cast for a filmed version released in August 1943. After completing the film, the revue toured overseas until October 1945.

Four other musical revues deserve mention. *Call Me Mister* (1946), with a theme of servicemen readjusting to civilian life, had a cast of veterans and former USO entertainers and presented a good-humored and optimistic view of military life and demobilization. With 734 performances, it can be called a hit—so much so that Hollywood added a plot and released it in 1951, starring Betty Grable (1916–1973) and Dan Dailey (1913–1978). *Lend an Ear* (1948), billed as "an intimate musical revue," written, directed, and choreographed by Charles Gaynor, marked the Broadway debut of Carol Channing and ran a little over one year for 460 performances. Also opening in 1948 and led by comedian Sid Caesar (b. 1922), *Make Mine Manhattan* in its 429 performances took a light-hearted look at life in New York's most prominent borough. Richard Lewine (1910–2005) provided the music and Arnold B. Horwitt (1918–1977) the lyrics. An all-American revue, *Inside U.S.A.* (1948), with music by Arthur Schwartz (1900–1984) and lyrics from Howard Dietz (1896–1983), boasted 399 performances during its almost one-year engagement on Broadway. Beatrice Lillie (1898–1989) and Jack Haley (1902–1976) provided the comedy along with an itinerary that covered various regions of the United States. *Inside U.S.A.* was the last of seven revues from the pens of Schwartz and Dietz.

Beginning in the 1940s and continuing into the 1950s, plays on Broadway—especially musicals that rose to new heights in both artistic achievement and commercial success—drew enthusiastic audiences. Rodgers and Hammerstein's *Oklahoma!* set new standards for American musicals, and between 1943 and 1959, six out of nine shows from this prolific team became hits, four of them appearing on Broadway before 1950. Contemporaries of Rodgers and Hammerstein, including Irving Berlin, Lorenz Hart, Jerome Kern, and Cole Porter, likewise wrote songs that became standards. New composers—Leonard Bernstein, Frank Loesser, Frederick Loewe, and Jule Styne—also accepted the challenge and adopted the new approach on scores, which brought them well-deserved recognition. Finally, thanks to technological advances, the bountiful richness of the golden age of the American musical went beyond New York to larger audiences by way of cast recordings, radio, and film.

See also: ASCAP vs. BMI Radio Boycott and the AFM Recording Ban; Blackouts, Brownouts, and Dim-Outs; Broadway Shows (Comedy and Drama); Canteens; Radio Programming: Music and Variety Shows; Technology

Selected Reading

Blum, Daniel. *A Pictorial History of the American Theatre, 1900–1950.* New York: Greenberg, 1950.

Foertsch, Jacqueline. *American Culture in the 1940s.* Edinburgh, Scotland: Edinburgh University Press, 2008.

Green, Stanley, and Kay Green. *Broadway Musicals, Show by Show.* Milwaukee: Hal Leonard, 1994.

Jones, John Bush. *Our Musicals, Ourselves: A Social History of the American Musical Theatre.* Hanover, MA: Brandeis University Press, 2003.

C

CANTEENS

The word "canteen," derived from the French *cantine* and the Spanish and Italian *cantina,* all of which mean a tavern or wine shop, one frequently located in or near a military barracks or garrison, has a number of English definitions. In the context of the U.S. military, canteen can denote a snack bar or small cafeteria at a base, a flask for carrying drinking water, or a soldier's mess kit. During World War II, the term often designated temporary or mobile eating places found at train stations and close to military installations, facilities that proved to be a valuable asset at the time. They made significant contributions to the morale, comfort, and well-being of millions of service personnel and provided citizens on the home front a way to be involved, as well.

Following the Japanese attack on Pearl Harbor on December 7, 1941, the federal government, recognizing a need to transport large numbers of troops, obtained the permission and cooperation of the country's railroads to use passenger **trains** for this purpose, first for training and then deployment to either the European or Pacific theaters. Civilians, eager to participate in the war effort, influenced the creation of unique canteens along the routes of these trains.

Volunteers, mainly women, who lived in nearby communities saw an opportunity for service. Steam locomotives pulled most of the trains being used to transport military personnel and had to stop at some stations for as much as 10 to 20 minutes while they took on water, allowing the troops to disembark and stretch their legs. Local residents soon organized and awaited the soldiers at these stops, offering a distraction, a smile, a friendly word, and some home-cooked **food.**

Since the war, reports about these train-track canteens have focused on one in North Platte, Nebraska, and others in six Ohio towns. In North Platte, Rae Sleight (nee Wilson, 1916–1986), inspired to support the troops traveling through her town, solicited friends, businesspeople, and civic leaders to assist her in the establishment of

Movie stars (from the left) Jack Carson, Jane Wyman, John Garfield, and Bette Davis star in Warner Bros.' 1944 Hollywood Canteen. It tells the story of two soldiers on sick leave spending three nights at the Hollywood Canteen and also sends a message of praise for the war effort and canteens across the United States. (Warner Bros./Photofest)

a community canteen at their train station. Many readily agreed, and the organizers obtained permission from the U.S. War Department and the Union Pacific Railroad to set up shop. On December 25, 1941, several young women greeted the first of over 6 million GIs who would travel through North Platte from that day until April 1, 1946. With as many as 20 trains a day and sometimes 7,000 to 8,000 GIs on board, the town of 12,000 people soon needed help and recruited citizens from 125 farming communities in and around the region to join them in staying up all night to cook chickens and make thousands of sandwiches. It has been reported that 55,000 volunteers worked with the renowned North Platte Canteen, a wartime effort celebrated in a 2003 book, *Once Upon a Town: The Miracle of the North Platte Canteen,* by Bob Greene (b. 1947), and a PBS (Public Broadcasting System) **television** documentary, *The Canteen Spirit,* shown in 2005.

Similar stories and statistics have been reported for the Ohio towns of Bellefontaine, Crestline, Dennison, Lima, Marion, Springfield, and Troy. For example, Dennison volunteers had met over 1.3 million troops by the end of the war; Lima accounted for a total of 2.5 million; and in Crestline, 32,500 trains stopped and the troops consumed 600,000 pounds of food. Other canteens in other states likewise fed and assisted many soldiers. Achieving these results required the work of many people. Canteen workers came from all socioeconomic groups, with the wives of railroad employees and the mothers, wives, and sisters of soldiers frequently accounting for the largest numbers.

Gold Star mothers, those whose sons had been killed in action, took a particularly active role.

At the canteens, the volunteers initially delivered the refreshments to the soldiers and sailors in hand-carried baskets or on teacarts that could be wheeled beside the train. Another simple approach used tables near the train tracks to hold trays of sandwiches and donuts. If time was scarce, soldiers could simply reach out a window to be handed some food. As the popularity of the canteens grew, some station operators donated a room for serving, while others allowed the construction of various shelters, ranging from simple lean-tos offering little protection from the weather to more substantial buildings with a roof and walls, along with preparation and eating areas. For most canteens, the volunteers prepared the food elsewhere and brought it each day to the station.

The refreshments offered generally included sandwiches, with bologna, egg salad, and ham the most popular. Varied desserts, along with cookies, donuts, fruit, candy bars, popcorn, and chewing gum, filled out the bill of fare. Coffee, milk, and a few other choices served as **beverages.** At holidays, extra efforts usually produced special treats in keeping with the occasion, and the grateful troops would respond with songs. Many wrote letters and poetry in repayment for the kindness they experienced.

As the war dragged on and shortages set in across the country, the Office of Price Administration (OPA) mandated **rationing** of a number of food items, and canteen menus had to be adjusted. Community members frequently offered their rationed foods at the canteen as well as items from their pantries and **victory gardens,** making it possible to always have enough to give something to every soldier on each train. Donations from local businesses helped to fill in any gaps.

The workers at most canteens quickly discovered that the GIs could use more than food, so **magazines,** paperback books, cigarettes, **newspapers,** razor blades, and stationery became standard additions. Some facilities even added a piano in order to provide music for dancing, and the soldiers and volunteers often took to the floor. Frequently, popcorn balls contained small slips of paper with the addresses of young unmarried women for the soldiers to write to, and doubtless many followed the suggestion.

The basic idea of such services for military personnel was not a new one. The American Red Cross had established canteens in World War I, when thousands of soldiers journeyed by train between their homes and military camps or to ships that took them overseas. Even before the onset of World War II, six national nonprofit organizations formed the **USO (United Service Organizations)** in response to a request from **President Franklin Delano Roosevelt** (1882–1945) to provide recreation and boost the morale of the armed forces. The Stage Door Canteen in Times Square, New York City and the Hollywood Canteen in Los Angeles became the best-known of these USO clubs because entertainers from stage, screen, and **radio** worked as volunteers. They performed for the soldiers, talked with them, and served refreshments or a meal. Two **movies,** *Stage Door Canteen* (1943) and *Hollywood Canteen* (1944), star performers as themselves and celebrate the activities provided at these clubs.

In addition to the cooperative USO efforts, the Red Cross set up canteens somewhat like the community ones, mainly near military installations, ports of embarkation, at military airfields, and sometimes at train stations. Under its Services to the Armed Forces branch, the Red Cross operated what it called a Club Service for American troops overseas. These ranged from simple canteens in outdoor settings consisting of tables stacked with trays of sandwiches, donuts, and hot cups of coffee and called Donut Dugouts by the soldiers and Fleet Clubs by the sailors, to former hotels located in large cities that provided meals, overnight accommodations, and amenities such as barbershops and laundries.

In 1942, the American Red Cross introduced Clubmobiles in Great Britain and later set up some on the European continent. Usually converted half-ton trucks and single-deck buses, workers equipped these vehicles to be traveling units that served donuts with coffee and distributed newspapers, chewing gum, and other small items. Some contained phonographs and loudspeakers to play music, and a few, outfitted with movie projectors, became known as Cinemobiles. As with the community canteens, the American Red Cross achieved some remarkable statistics. Through its many services, including canteens, clubs, and recreational facilities, the organization had contact with every air base, army camp, and naval station in the United States and overseas.

Another group, the Salvation Army, actively rendered a wide variety of services to Allied soldiers, including 3,000 War Service Units for worship and assistance and 1,000 mobile canteens. Within the commercial world, the Pepsi-Cola Company opened a service center for military men in three U.S. cities—San Francisco, Washington, DC, and New York City. These centers provided overnight accommodations, facilities for showering and shaving, stationery and envelopes for writing letters, and a voice letter recording booth. The Pepsi-Cola Times Square Service Men's Center reported at the end of its first year of operation that 2 million men from all the country's armed forces had visited the center. In connection with its second anniversary, this same center assisted one soldier with a complete wedding ceremony and gave another the perfect furlough, which consisted of lunch at the Ritz, a ride in Central Park, a swim at Jones Beach, dinner at the Stork Club, and tickets for Broadway's *Oklahoma!*

With the country's entry in World War II, U.S. citizens and service organizations asked the questions how can we help and what can we do, and they organized in a number of ways to support the war effort. For the various members of the USO, it became a matter of providing entertainment, recreation, nourishment, and solace for those away from home—an approach that necessitated that the organizations communicate and coordinate their work and resources.

For individuals on the home front, such support required active participation. The decision to prepare and serve food at canteens demanded a person's time on an ongoing basis. Yet thousands of citizens, especially those in towns where the troop trains regularly traveled, established and worked at community canteens. Throughout the war, they offered nourishment, friendship, and compassion to soldiers on passenger trains, troop trains, and wounded GIs on hospital trains. The statistics from this work easily reveal that a large number of people participated and had an immeasurable impact on the soldiers' lives.

See also: Desserts, Candy, and Ice Cream; Transportation

Selected Reading
Greene, Bob. *Once Upon a Town: The Miracle of the North Platte Canteen.* New York: Harper, 2003.

The Canteen Spirit. PBS Home Video, 2006.
"Ohio Canteens." www.canteenbooks.com
"Pepsi-Cola Canteens." *New York Times,* March 1, 1943; July 22, 1943; July 22, 1944. www.proquest.com

CARTOONS (FILM)

A staple of movie theater bills almost from their inception early in the 20th century, cartoons had earned a measure of respect and profitability by the 1940s. Many of the major studios, such as MGM, Paramount, and Warner Bros., boasted full-time cartooning staffs and could mass produce short, animated features in quantity. Most of the people connected with cartooning labored in relative anonymity; the characters they conceived—Bugs Bunny, Felix the Cat, Heckle and Jeckle, Mighty Mouse, Tom and Jerry, Woody Woodpecker, to mention but a few—achieved far greater renown than the individuals who drew them. Warner Bros. marketed its Looney Tunes/Merrie Melodies cartoons so successfully that it had emerged, by 1940, a power in the field of animation, but only a few people could name who created and produced them. Only **Walt Disney** (1901–1966) emerged as a well-known figure in his own right, his name as identifiable as Mickey Mouse, Donald Duck, and all his other cartoon creations.

Walter Elias Disney broke into the animation business in 1919, mastering the craft by producing animated commercial messages for a Kansas City company. By the end of the 1930s, Disney had long since left the Midwest and settled in Hollywood, California. At the same time, he had achieved the position of a leader in the field of motion picture cartooning and become a household name. With the dawn of the 1940s, the term "Walt Disney" signified a brand, a measure of excellence, providing him and his studio monetary security and a level of fame that continued to grow significantly during the next several decades.

The Walt Disney studio commenced its march to success by producing a seemingly endless run of short cartoons throughout the 1920s and 1930s, a march that did not slow down in the war years. For the period 1940 to 1949, Disney artists turned out 149 cartoons, or almost 15 new titles a year. Slightly over half of these star Donald Duck, far surpassing Mickey, Pluto, Goofy, or any of the company's other familiar characters. During the war years, Disney and his artists dedicated numerous cartoons to the cause of victory, with titles like "Donald Gets Drafted" (1942), "Victory Vehicles," "Home Defense" (both 1943), "How To Be a Sailor," and "Commando Duck" (both 1944). Credit for the best-known of the short wartime cartoons must go to "Der Fuehrer's Face," a 1942 production.

Originally titled "Donald Duck in Nutziland," the studio promptly changed it to "Der Fuehrer's Face" to capitalize on the growing popularity of the cartoon's similarly named theme song. Spike Jones and His City Slickers, a raucous band that specialized in satire and parodies, recorded the politically incorrect tune shortly before the movie's release, and it quickly climbed the charts. Jones's recording differs slightly from the soundtrack version (some of the musical sound effects come across as ruder than those heard in the movie), but both poke uninhibited fun at the German dictator.

In the movie, Donald dreams he labors for the Nazis under terrible conditions; the dream turns into a nightmare until he finally awakens safe in his own bed. The song went on to become a major hit for Jones and his musical satirists, and the cartoon became a Disney classic. At the 1942 Academy Awards, Hollywood agreed and bestowed a best short subject/cartoon Oscar on the film. With the nation at war with Germany, both the song and the movie summed up American feelings toward Hitler.

As entertaining and popular as his short cartoons were, Disney and his talented staff wanted to put more of their time and effort into full-length animated feature films. The company had first explored the possibilities of this area of moviemaking with *Snow White and the Seven Dwarfs,* a picture that premiered at the end of 1937. Already in the works were two more films, *Pinocchio* and *Fantasia,* both of which went into theaters in 1940.

Pinocchio enjoys the same high quality of drawing as *Snow White,* and it likewise derives from a well-known story. Who can forget Pinocchio's nose growing longer and longer when he tells a lie? *Fantasia,* on the other hand, displays even more technical innovation and daring, but it failed initially to attract the appreciative audiences that flocked to *Snow White* and *Pinocchio.* It cannot claim a familiar story, no instantly popular songs like "Whistle While You Work" (*Snow White*) or "When You Wish Upon a Star" (*Pinocchio*) enliven its soundtrack, its plot is episodic, and word at the time had it that the movie was just too "artsy."

Part of this complaint concerned the picture's structure: *Fantasia* attempts to popularize classical music by means of animation. Narrator Deems Taylor (1885–1966), for many years the radio voice of the New York Philharmonic Orchestra, provides a learned running commentary on the eight musical pieces that constitute the film. Conductor Leopold Stokowski (1882–1977), noted for leading the Philadelphia Symphony Orchestra, takes studio musicians through the selections, ranging from Bach's *Toccata and Fugue in D Minor* to Schubert's *Ave Maria,* and appears, as himself, at points during the movie.

High art and popular culture meet as Disney accompanies the music with animation for each selection. Mickey Mouse, one of the many cartoon characters that appears in this innovative motion picture, portrays the Sorcerer's Apprentice in a memorable appearance set to Dukas's music. At other times, hippos dance; goldfish perform ballet; unicorns, centaurs, and fauns romp; and a host of other creatures have their moments on screen. To do justice to the music of *Fantasia,* studio engineers created "Fantasound," one of the first uses of stereophonic sound recording in the movie industry. Theaters that booked *Fantasia* had to be equipped with special audio devices in order to reproduce the thunderous score properly, a factor that severely held back national distribution of the film. Not until 1942 did *Fantasia* go into general release without the stereophonic effects. Since the picture cost well over $2 million (almost $35 million in 2008 dollars) to produce, it would take some time for the studio to recoup its investment. Despite these obstacles, Walt Disney Productions, using RKO Radio Pictures as a distributor, went ahead with the project. Only with the passage of time and several re-releases and fancier packaging has it earned the studio a profit, and in the ensuing years, the film has been elevated into a classic motion picture.

Undeterred by the less than rousing success of *Fantasia,* the Disney organization continued to produce animated, feature-length movies. *The Reluctant Dragon* and *Dumbo* came out in 1941, followed by the immensely popular *Bambi* in 1942. *Saludos Amigos* (actually four short films strung together to extol hemispheric harmony in time of war) and *Victory Through Air Power* (another propaganda piece whose title says it all) marked 1943, a time when everyone in Hollywood was turning out movies that supported the war effort.

The Three Caballeros (1945) picks up from *Saludos Amigos,* with Donald Duck mixed in with live action. *Make Mine Music* and *Song of the South* both graced marquees in 1946, although the live-action sequences in the latter might discomfit contemporary audiences because of their racial stereotyping. The cartoon segments, however, would offend no one and stand among Disney's best.

Four additional features round out Disney's work in the 1940:, *Fun and Fancy Free* (1947), *Melody Time* (1948), *So Dear to My Heart,* and *The Adventures of Ichabod and Mr. Toad* (both 1949). These films, labeled as package features because they combine both cartoons and some live action, seldom receive much mention in the Disney canon. Competent and entertaining, they represent attempts to minimize production costs and maximize box office profits in order to give the studio the flexibility to undertake more significant projects. Show business celebrities such as vocalist Dinah Shore (1916–1994), ventriloquist Edgar Bergen (1903–1978) and his dummy Charlie McCarthy, actors **Roy Rogers** (1911–1998), Burl Ives (1909–1995), Bobby Driscoll (1937–1968), and many others make appearances in these pictures.

Despite Walt Disney's acclaim during the 1940s, other artists also strove for recognition. Max Fleischer (1883–1972) probably stood as Disney's chief competition in the early days of movie animation. Coming into cartooning at about the same time as Disney, and usually working closely with his director brother Dave (1894–1979), Fleischer initially enjoyed the greater success. But he turned out to be less of a businessman and promoter, so that by the 1940s Disney and his powerhouse studio had eclipsed him.

With *Gulliver's Travels* (1939; because it did not go into theaters until late December, many people consider this film a 1940 release), the two brothers crafted a feature-length cartoon that rivals anything the Disney artists could do at the time. The Fleischers followed *Gulliver's Travels* with *Mr. Bug Goes to Town* (1941), another excellent, full-length animated work, but it suffered the misfortune of opening on December 9, 1941—two days after the attack on Pearl Harbor and the country's entry into World War II. Amid the confusion of those dark days, the cartoon essentially disappeared. Only in later years have Fleischer fans discovered its qualities.

Fleischer also made a last-gasp attempt to capture an audience with a spin-off from the growing popularity of **Superman.** The Man of Steel made his first appearance in comic books, the 1938 creation of Jerry Siegel (1914–1996) and Joe Shuster (1914–1992). An immediate hit with the public, the series went into newspaper comic syndication late the following year, and a radio version came on the air in 1940, where it would remain until 1951. It therefore seemed reasonable that a movie version should also be attempted. The Fleischer studios responded in 1941 with nine cartoon episodes of *Superman,* a feat achieved some seven years before the release of the first live-action feature movie. Many consider this work the best Fleischer ever turned out, although he will probably be best remembered for three pre-1940s cartoon characters: Ko-Ko the Clown (ca. 1920), Betty Boop (1930), and Popeye (1933), the last adapted from Elzie Segar's (1894–1938) popular newspaper comic strip called *Thimble Theatre.*

Despite their quality, none of these later works achieved any significant box office success, and a disappointed Paramount Pictures finally released both Max and Dave Fleischer from their contracts. The studio, however, retained the brothers' staff and remained in the cartoon business. It kept Popeye and obtained rights to *Little Lulu,* a magazine panel series drawn by Marge (b. Majorie Henderson Buell, 1904–1993) that enjoyed a large print readership. But basically Paramount coasted through most of the decade, seemingly uninterested in creating anything truly new or innovative.

The premature departure of the Fleischers left the cartoon field wide open, and challengers aplenty waited in the wings. If Disney completely dominated the feature-length animated movie, the quality of *Gulliver's Travels* notwithstanding, Warner Bros. worked earnestly to establish a firm foothold for itself with the classic short cartoon. Beginning in the 1930s, several artists, some of them Disney alumni, financed and encouraged by producer Leon Schlesinger (1884–1949), cobbled together a new firm they called Looney Tunes, a name inspired by the Disney organization's musical shorts that collectively went by the title Silly Symphonies.

At first, most Looney Tunes productions resembled Disney products, but with support from Warner Bros., the fledgling operation added Merrie Melodies and began to expand. Young, ambitious artists like Fred "Tex" Avery (1908–1980), Bob Clampett (1913–1984), Fritz Freleng (1905–1995), and Chuck Jones (1912–2002) came on board during the 1930s, as well as Mel Blanc (1908–1989), "the man of a thousand voices," and composer-arranger Carl W. Stalling (1891–1972) and proceeded to give the cartoon studio its distinctive flavor.

Combining their talents, Looney Tunes/Merrie Melodies in the 1940s forged a new dimension in American cartooning. They threw out older concepts of tempo and content, replacing them with a frenetic pace and stories that stressed an anarchic sense of humor. Stallings' typically hectic music, which often borrows snippets from popular songs already in the vast Warner Bros. library, complements this approach perfectly, as does Blanc's repertoire of voices. Porky and Petunia Pig led this revolution at first, although Petunia virtually gets written out of most 1940s-era cartoons. Daffy Duck soon joined the entourage in 1937, the inimitable Bugs Bunny in 1938, Elmer Fudd in 1940 (who evolved from an earlier cartoon character called Egghead), Tweety Bird in 1942, Yosemite Sam in 1944, Foghorn Leghorn in 1946, and Sylvester the Cat in 1947. The decade ended with two more enduring entries in the Looney Tunes/Merrie Melodies list: Wile E. Coyote and the Road Runner (both 1949). Although the Road Runner series' primary fame lay ahead in the 1950s, the pair easily fit in among the other characters, because the criteria always remained the same at Warner's: breakneck plotting and total disregard for older cartoon conventions, qualities that left most of the competition in the dust.

During the war, the Looney Tunes/Merrie Melodies crew fought the Axis just as earnestly as their Disney counterparts. In "Confusions of a Nutzy Spy" (1942; the spoofing title comes from *Confessions of a Nazi Spy,* a 1939 picture that just happens to be a Warner Bros. release), Porky hunts for bomb-bearing Nazi spies amid endless atrocious puns. "Scrap Happy Daffy" (1943) takes place on the home front, and it ostensibly encourages saving metal items for the war effort. But Hitler sends a billy goat to devour Daffy's accumulated scrap, with the usual mayhem the result, including an unflattering appearance by Hitler himself. "Bugs Bunny Nips the Nips" (1944), which may have been hilarious to a war-weary nation at the time of its release, stars the wisecracking hare against viciously stereotyped Japanese foes. The reduction of an enemy to subhuman status, an unfortunate wartime practice in all cultures, makes this cartoon uncomfortable—and unfunny—for contemporary audiences, but it does illustrate one way in which the entertainment industry participated in the war effort. Although patriotism and victory might be underlying themes in the many Warner Bros. cartoons of the period, audiences remember the nonstop jokes and puns, the sight gags, the disregard for authority, and always the madcap pace of the story.

Other talented people also contributed to the popularity of cartoons during the 1940s, but they lacked the combination of merchandising and business acumen essential to the kind of success enjoyed by the Disney and Warner Bros. organizations. For example, Paul Terry (1887–1971) created Terrytoons in 1929 and, with a limited staff, began producing cartoons under his own name. His best years occurred during the 1940s, when he had *Gandy Goose, Heckle and Jeckle,* and *Mighty Mouse* as his properties. Mighty Mouse actually made his debut in 1942 as Super Mouse, a spoof on the ongoing popularity of *Superman* in all its formats. After a year or so, "Super" became "Mighty," and a more identifiable character resulted. The magpies Heckle and Jeckle began entertaining audiences in 1946, and the two jokesters experienced immediate success. But repetition haunted the Terrytoons, and sameness prevented their ever achieving the enduring popularity of the Disney or Warner characters.

In a similar vein, Walter Lantz (1899–1994) had his own studio throughout the 1930s, but his most memorable character, Woody Woodpecker, did not come into being until 1940 in a cartoon called "Knock Knock." The tapping noise of the title comes about because of Woody's presence on a roof. This brash bird, not unlike Donald Duck, Daffy Duck, Bugs Bunny, and Heckle and Jeckle, quickly intrigued audiences grown accustomed to too many overly cute animals of various species. His signature laugh has been endlessly imitated and even served as the focus of "The Woody Woodpecker Song" (1948), a brief hit. But Lantz never found another character to equal Woody, although the gentle Andy Panda did have a following, especially among younger children. Comfortable with his small share of the animation pie, Lantz continued to turn out Woody Woodpecker cartoons throughout the decade and beyond.

Metro-Goldwyn-Mayer entered the cartoon production arena in the mid-1930s, but in a half-hearted way. The giant studio had no outstanding cartoon series under contract, and much of its early production consisted of well-drawn but tepid stories taken from an ongoing comic strip called *The Captain and the Kids.* Drawn for the **newspapers** by Rudolph Dirks (1877–1968), MGM did little with its crossover variation. But while the studio floundered in the animation arena, it gained the service of two young cartoonists, William "Bill" Hanna (1910–2001) and Joe Barbera (1911–2006). The pair worked up a sample called "Puss Gets the Boot" in 1940. An auspicious start, it features a nameless cat and mouse and their shenanigans. Nominated for an Academy Award, MGM urged them to create a sequel, and thereafter the series called the cat Tom and the mouse Jerry. The animals' slapstick antics quickly made them major stars in the cartoon world, and throughout the 1940s, the *Tom and Jerry* franchise competed with the best from Disney or Warner's, as evidenced by seven Academy Awards between 1943 and 1953.

MGM also hired Tex Avery, who had been with Leon Schlesinger at Warner's, in 1942. He brought with him the anarchic humor that characterized so many Looney Tunes/Merry Melodies productions. Despite a handful of delightful films and the creation of Droopy, a charming basset hound, too many MGM cartoons lacked imagination, and, by the mid-1950s, the operation had reached the end of the line, closing in 1957. With that turn of events, Hanna and Barbera moved to the new medium of **television,** where they found fame. Their production company created numerous TV cartoon series, with *The Flintstones* (1960–1966) probably being the most famous.

In retrospect, the 1940s marked a golden age in cartooning, both for short films and full-length feature productions. By the end of the 1940s, however, disturbing trends had begun to infiltrate the once-freewheeling world of movie cartoons. Expenses, both for new technology and personnel, had risen, and the studios put pressure on the production companies to keep costs down. Television, not yet really a competitor to film in the late 1940s, nonetheless worried people. Movie attendance fell off throughout the decade, and so the warning signs became more obvious. A number of the smaller cartooning studios closed their doors, leaving the field to Disney, Warner Bros., and a few others. Good, quality work would continue to be created, but the golden age had rapidly lost its luster by 1949.

See also: Children's Films; Classical Music; Comic Strips; Games

Selected Reading
Barrier, Michael. *Hollywood Cartoons: American Animation in Its Golden Age.* New York: Oxford University Press, 1999.
Gifford, Denis. *The Great Cartoon Stars: A Who's Who!* London: Jupiter Books, 1979.
Maltin, Leonard. *Of Mice and Magic: A History of American Animated Cartoons.* New York: McGraw-Hill, 1980.

CASABLANCA (MICHAEL CURTIZ)

In the summer of 1940, as the fury of World War II mounted in Europe, playwrights Murray Burnett (1911–1997) and Joan Alison (1902–1992) collaborated on *Everybody Comes to Rick's*. The drama revolves around a popular bar, Rick's Café Americain in Casablanca, French Morocco, and the varied people that congregate there. Burnett and Alison tried to find a producer willing to put their work on stage but failed to secure any backing. Good fortune, however, came their way when Warner Bros., a major Hollywood film studio, expressed interest in *Everybody Comes to Rick's*. The moviemakers purchased rights to the play in 1941 and assigned three screenwriters, Howard Koch (1902–1995), Julius Epstein (1909–2000), and Philip Epstein (1909–1952), the job of translating the book into cinematic format.

Casablanca *(Michael Curtiz)* | 167

One of the most popular films to come out of World War II, the cast of Casablanca *features Humphrey Bogart and Ingrid Bergman as star-crossed lovers in the exotic North African city as this lobby card shows. (Warner Bros. Pictures/Photofest)*

By the spring of 1942, director Michael Curtiz (1886–1962) had been hired to oversee the proposed picture, and Warner Bros. had to make choices about whom to cast in the major roles. Eventually, the studio decided the romantic leads should be **Humphrey Bogart** (1899–1957) as Rick and Ingrid Bergman (1915–1982) as Ilsa. A stellar supporting cast—Paul Henreid (1905–1992), Claude Rains (1889–1967), Sidney Greenstreet (1879–1954), Peter Lorre (904–1964), and others—ably complement the two stars. Film composer Max Steiner (1888–1971) created the accompanying score. Shooting commenced in May 1942 and finished by early August. By this time, *Everybody Comes to Rick's* had received a new title, *Casablanca,* but much of Burnett and Alison's storyline survived intact, although they received virtually no credit.

In the movie, Bogart plays the expatriate Rick as a weary cynic, wary of politics and beholden to no side in the growing conflict between the Axis powers and the Allies. The city of Casablanca, an outwardly neutral location under the governance of Vichy, France, serves as home or transit point for a passing gallery of disparate characters. Eventually, of course, Rick must take sides, a choice complicated by his continuing love for Ilsa, a woman married to Lazslo, a Czech Resistance fighter, played by Paul Henreid.

Set in late 1941, just weeks or days before the December 7 attack on Pearl Harbor and the entry of the United States into the war as an active combatant, tensions nevertheless run high at Rick's Café Americain. Movie audiences would naturally grasp the significance of mentioning the date and how events would shortly impact on all the characters. The script makes no attempt to hide its pro-American, pro-Resistance point of view. It symbolically depicts, through Rick, the need for the United States to throw off its professed neutrality and come into the conflict on the side of the Allies. Good people must stand up to bullies, personal considerations must be sacrificed so that individuals can unite against evil, and in their unity they will win. Rick, who has a background of fighting fascism, knows this, but he still desires Ilsa. But to be true to the democratic values the movie professes, Rick must lose Ilsa and allow her and her husband to flee the clutches of the Nazis.

In the early days of World War II, no other attitude would have been acceptable, especially in the eyes of the Office of War Information (OWI), a government body that oversaw film content. Although it exerted no real censorship powers, the OWI commented and advised on current **movies**—as did the various branches of the U.S. military—and Hollywood did not wish to run afoul of any such groups. The mere threat of censorship proved sufficient.

To qualify for the 1943 Academy Awards, Warner Bros. gave the film its premiere in late November 1942 for New York City audiences (Academy Awards are granted for cinematic excellence displayed during the preceding year). Then, in February 1943, the movie received national and international distribution. As a result, some people consider *Casablanca* a 1942 release, while others classify it as a 1943 offering. More importantly, its November release coincided with the Allied landings in North Africa, including French Morocco. With headlines daily announcing the progress of U.S. forces, the setting for the film takes on added meaning. At the time of *Casablanca*'s national issuance, the U.S. Army had secured the city and one of the first meetings of Allied leaders took place there with the January 1943 Casablanca Conference. History and military strategy had provided a fortuitous series of events that added to the picture's topical prominence.

The film did well at the box office, and it won the prestigious Academy Awards for best picture, best director, and best screenplay (shared by Koch and the Epsteins). In addition, it collected nominations for best leading actor (Bogart) and best supporting actor (Rains), along with best original dramatic score (as opposed to best song), best black-and-white cinematography, and best editing. But that proved only the beginning; the sad love story and the interplay between real events and a fictional plot give the picture added resonance, and it has continued, for many, as the definitive World War II movie. For the 21st century, *Casablanca* remains a crowd-pleasing favorite, a true cult movie for a wide range of fans who know its every scene and can quote numerous passages from the script; it plays frequently on **television,** and video stores know to keep it stocked on their shelves.

Although Max Steiner composed much of the background music in *Casablanca,* someone else's melody serves as a leitmotif throughout the film. As a young man, playwright Burnett had been attracted to a romantic ballad entitled "As Time Goes By," and Steiner skillfully incorporates both its melody and lyrics into his score. Composer-lyricist Herman Hupfeld (1894–1951) had originally written the number in 1931 for *Everybody's Welcome,* a forgotten musical then struggling to garner attention on Broadway. Although the play enjoyed moderate success with 139 performances, Hupfeld's contribution eventually fell by the wayside of forgotten songs, and he moved on to other projects.

In 1932, he wrote "Let's Put Out the Lights and Go to Sleep," and the topical "Are You Makin' Any Money?" in 1933. The latter went nowhere, suggesting the public did not want musical reminders about the crisis. Hupfeld had earlier written "Sing Something Simple" in 1930, and the nonsense song "When Yuba Plays the Rhumba on the Tuba," a minor hit in 1931. Despite these less than smashing successes, the composer will endure in the annals of American popular song for "As Time Goes By."

Fortunately, vocalist Frances Williams (1902–1959) recorded the number in 1931, as did bandleaders Jacques Renard (n.d.; active 1920s–1930s) and Rudy Vallee (1901–1986). Burnett adapted Williams' rendition for *Everybody Comes to Rick's*. When Hupfeld penned "As Time Goes By" in the early 1930s, a period marked by the Great Depression and all its resultant woes, the music's lyrics spoke to many of the hopes and dreams of Americans; more than a decade later, when they faced the new challenges accompanying World War II, the words again addressed their concerns. Certainly in *Casablanca,* "As Time Goes By" is a song that Rick and Ilsa recognize as their own.

In the film, musician Dooley Wilson (1886–1953), a drummer by trade, appears to play the piano while he sings Hupfeld's song to remarkable effect, both for the lead actors and the audience. Thus, this seemingly forgotten tune, along with Wilson's performance, provides a movie moment that everyone who has seen it remembers and allows a 1930s song to emerge as a major, enduring hit for the wartime years.

By presenting images and ideas appealing to Americans in the early days of World War II, *Casablanca* creates a mythic time and place where older concepts of isolationism can be discarded. The gradual transformation of Rick, his realization that he cannot escape responsibilities, and, no matter how alluring the thought of romantic love, his need to take a stand against those who would destroy anything good, propels this simultaneously sad but optimistic motion picture.

See also: Broadway (Musicals); Drama (Film); Political and Propaganda Films; War Films

Selected Reading
Anobile, Richard J., ed. *Michael Curtiz's Casablanca.* New York: Flare Books, 1974.
Dick, Bernard F. *The Star-Spangled Screen: The American World War II Film.* Lexington: University Press of Kentucky, 1985.
McLaughlin, Robert L., and Sally E. Perry. *We'll Always Have the Movies: American Cinema during World War II.* Lexington: University Press of Kentucky, 2006.
Zinsser, William. *Easy to Remember: The Great American Songwriters and Their Songs.* Jaffrey, NH: David R. Godine, 2000.

CHILDREN'S FILMS

Generally speaking, children's films appeal to viewers ranging in age from preschool to early adolescence. As **movies,** they must, above all, be entertaining. Hallmarks usually include slapstick, action (with lots of visual mayhem but no real violence or damage), exaggerated characterizations, and plotting that can be easily followed. In addition, they often possess a family orientation, and studios frequently market them as motion pictures that reinforce existing cultural mores and values.

Over the years, the film industry has never forgotten children. The early two-reel silent comedies of Charlie Chaplin appealed as much to youngsters as to their elders. Shirley Temple (b. 1928) reigned as one of Hollywood's most popular—and highest-paid—stars throughout the 1930s, and her movies exemplify bright, light children's fare. More recently, pictures like *Mary Poppins* (1964), *E.T.: The Extra-Terrestrial* (1982), and *The Lion King* (1994) have provided contemporary models of the genre, and film studios annually release a handful of new motion pictures with this audience in mind.

The 1940s proved no exception to these patterns, although the war years witnessed a dramatic drop in output aimed at boys and girls. That difficult period, 1941 to 1945, saw Hollywood focusing a major part of its energies on war-related films, not children's fare. The studios coped with an unwritten mandate to churn out as many morale-boosting pictures as possible, a supposition that left children's movies a neglected category. Not only did the industry produce a limited number of such films, those that were shown in theaters seldom depict the war in any way. Most suggest a background of peace and normality or refer to the conflict in such vague terms that it hardly intrudes on the story, if at all.

Taking the decade as a whole, despite the absence of topicality in both peacetime and war, a number of fine movies for the younger set came out during the 1940s. Since the studios released several hundred feature-length motion pictures each and every year, setting aside room for 15 or 20 productions for a selected audience did not place that great a burden on the industry. Plus, a few children's productions each year met with better-than-average box office success, and this fact alone justified the continuation of the genre.

A number of performers achieved their first success as child actors in films of the 1940s. Although some went on to long careers in the movies, others did not make the jump from child roles to adult stars. Among the more popular and successful of the youthful actors from this period, mention should be made of the following: Robert Blake (b. 1933), Claude Jarman Jr. (b. 1934), Margaret O'Brien (b. 1937), Dean Stockwell (b. 1936), Elizabeth Taylor (b. 1932), and Natalie Wood (1938–1981). Other youthful stars, such as Freddie Bartholomew (1924–1992), Jackie Cooper (b. 1922), Judy Garland (1922–1969), Roddy McDowall (1928–1998), Mickey Rooney (b. 1920), and Shirley Temple (b. 1928) hardly qualified as children with the onset of the 1940s. Popular in films during the 1930s, Hollywood still had them playing characters younger than their years in the early 1940s, although they quickly graduated to teen or young adult roles as time passed.

The table below does not attempt to list every child-oriented release marketed to young audiences during the 1940s but instead presents a sampling of some of the better-known examples. The many cheap B Westerns featuring **Gene Autry** (1907–1998), **Roy Rogers** (1911–1998), and others might have been included in the list, and they did indeed claim an enthusiastic youthful following during those years, but such movies fall more accurately into the **Westerns (Film)** category and therefore receive discussion under that heading.

TABLE 25. Representative Children's Films, 1940–1949

Year	Live-Action Films	Stars	Feature-Length Animated Films
1940	The Biscuit Eater	Billy Lee, Cordell Hickman	Fantasia
	The Bluebird	Shirley Temple, Spring Byington	Pinocchio
	The Swiss Family Robinson	Thomas Mitchell, Freddie Bartholomew	
	The Thief of Bagdad	Sabu, Conrad Veidt	
	Young Tom Edison	Mickey Rooney, Fay Bainter	
1941	How Green Was My Valley	Roddy McDowall, Walter Pidgeon	Dumbo
The Reluctant Dragon (also live action)
1942			Bambi
1943	Lassie Come Home	Elizabeth Taylor, Roddy McDowall	
	My Friend Flicka	Roddy McDowall, Preston Foster	
1944	Home in Indiana	Lon McCallister, Walter Brennan	
	Meet Me in St. Louis	Elizabeth Taylor, Margaret O'Brien	
	National Velvet	Elizabeth Taylor, Mickey Rooney	
1945	Christmas in Connecticut	Barbara Stanwyck, Dennis Morgan	
	The Enchanted Forest	Edmund Lowe, Billy Severn	
	Our Vines Have Tender Grapes	Edward G. Robinson, Margaret O'Brien	
	Son of Lassie	Lassie, Peter Lawford	
	Thunderhead, Son of Flicka	Roddy McDowall, Preston Foster	
	A Tree Grows in Brooklyn	Dorothy McGuire, Joan Blondell	
1946	Black Beauty	Mona Freeman, Richard Denning	Make Mine Music
	Courage of Lassie	Lassie, Elizabeth Taylor	
	Gallant Bess	Marshall Thompson, George Tobias	
	Great Expectations	John Mills, Valerie Hobson	
	It's a Wonderful Life	James Stewart, Donna Reed	
	Smoky	Fred McMurray, Anne Baxter	
	The Yearling	Gregory Peck, Claude Jarman Jr.	
1947	Cynthia	Elizabeth Taylor, George Murphy	Fun and Fancy Free
	Miracle on 34th Street	Natalie Wood, Edmund Gwenn	
	The Return of Rin Tin Tin	Rin Tin Tin, Robert Blake,	
1948	Abbott and Costello Meet Frankenstein	Bud Abbott, Lou Costello	Melody Time
So Dear to My Heart—(also live action)
	The Boy with Green Hair	Dean Stockwell, Pat O'Brien	
	The Green Grass of Wyoming	Charles Coburn, Robert Arthur	
	Hills of Home	Lassie, Edmund Gwenn	
	Oliver Twist	Alex Guinness, Robert Newton	

(continued)

TABLE 25. (continued)

Year	Live-Action Films	Stars	Feature-Length Animated Films
1949	Challenge to Lassie	Lassie, Edmund Gwenn	
	A Connecticut Yankee in King Arthur's Court	Bing Crosby, William Bendix	
	Little Women	June Allyson, Elizabeth Taylor, Margaret O'Brien	
	The Red Pony	Robert Mitchum, Peter Miles	
	The Secret Garden	Margaret O'Brien, Dean Stockwell	
	The Story of Seabiscuit	Shirley Temple, Barry Fitzgerald	
	The Sun Comes Up	Lassie, Jeanette Mac Donald	

Likewise, almost any of the Abbott and Costello (Bud Abbott [1895–1974]; Lou Costello [1906–1959]) comedies of the period would also be appropriate for youngsters, as would the popular short features of the Three Stooges. Both teams employ antic slapstick humor bound to bring laughter to legions of children. Further discussion of both Abbott and Costello and the Three Stooges can be found under **Comedies (Film).**

Among other series that can fit several categories, the nine *Tarzan* films that came out during the 1940s should be also noted. They range from *Tarzan's Secret Treasure* (1941) to *Tarzan's Magic Fountain* (1949), and their jungle hokum always appealed to children. They are discussed under **Costume and Spectacle Films.**

For the early adolescent set, the *Andy Hardy* pictures with Mickey Rooney recount growing up in the United States during the late 1930s and early 1940s; they receive coverage under comedies More family oriented, but still popular among children, the many *Blondie* movies, adapted from the newspaper comic strip pioneered by cartoonist Chic Young (1901–1973), cover the antics of Dagwood and Blondie Bumstead. They, too, can be found under comedies.

All children love **cartoons,** and the innumerable short animated features released by the likes of the Walt Disney Studio (Mickey Mouse, Donald Duck, Pluto, etc.), Warner Bros. (Bugs Bunny, Daffy Duck, Porky Pig, etc.), and others are discussed under cartoons. The Disney organization more or less dominated the longer feature-length cartoon genre throughout the decade, and that area of specialization can be found above on the table.

Finally, the many **serial films**—those multipart movie sagas that feature a rousing story broken into a dozen or so installments, with each one shown separately in order to assure audiences would keep returning to find out what happens next—had become established by the 1940s. They possessed great appeal for children, given their simple plots, almost nonstop action, and cliffhanger endings, so no Saturday matinees at neighborhood theaters would be complete without the latest installments. Given the unique qualities of serials, they are covered as a separate film genre.

Although children's films constituted but a small part of Hollywood's vast film output during the 1940s, they enjoyed a guaranteed, ready-made audience. As such, all the studios produced them, albeit only a few per year in terms of overall production. Seldom marketed like a movie with big-name stars or an audience-getting plot that promised sex, violence, and other adult themes, children's movies showed a quieter side to Hollywood's usual flamboyance.

See also: Comic Strips; Juvenile Delinquency; Newspapers; Youth

Selected Reading
Jackson, Kathy Merlock. *Images of Children in American Film.* Metuchen, NJ: Scarecrow Press, 1986.
Wojcik-Andrews, Ian. *Children's Films: History, Ideology, Pedagogy, Theory.* New York: Garland, 2000.
Zierold, Norman J. *The Child Stars.* New York: Coward-McCann, 1965.

CITIZEN KANE (ORSON WELLES)

A motion picture that appears on virtually every listing of all-time best films (the prestigious American Film Institute ranked it No. 1 out of 100 American **movies**), *Citizen Kane* first played on theater screens in 1941. The picture has as its producer, director, writer, and star Orson Welles (1915–1985), the enfant terrible of American **radio** ("War of the Worlds," 1938; *The Mercury Theatre on the Air,* 1937–1941), stage (*Julius Caesar, The Cradle Will Rock,* both 1937), and film (in addition to *Citizen Kane,* accolades for *The Magnificent Ambersons,* 1942; *The Lady from Shanghai,* 1947; and *The Third Man,* 1949).

The picture received nine Academy Award nominations (best film, director, actor, original screenplay, musical scoring, art direction, cinematography, editing, and sound recording) but won only for best original screenplay. Welles shared this honor with veteran screenwriter Herman J. Mankiewicz (1897–1953). Although Mankiewicz wrote most of the original story, Welles contributed ideas and the two worked together on the final editing. *How Green Was My Valley,* however, won for best picture, as did its director John Ford (1894–1973). Gary Cooper (1901–1961) beat out Welles for the acting laurels with his performance in *Sergeant York.* Gregg Toland (1904–1948), who has been widely lauded over the years for his superlative black-and-white camera skills, provided *Citizen Kane* with much of its atmosphere. He nonetheless lost out in the cinematography category to Arthur C. Miller (1895–1970), who filmed *How Green Was My Valley.*

In retrospect, the Academy members slighted a masterpiece, but at the time, with World War II just beginning, a warm, nostalgic picture like *How Green Was My Valley* doubtless held great emotional appeal, just as Cooper's rousing portrayal of Sergeant York gave a reassuring portrayal of a U.S. soldier in combat. So many subsequent awards and honors have been heaped on both Welles and *Citizen Kane* that the Academy oversight has faded with time.

The Citizen Kane of the title refers to Charles Foster Kane, a fictional character based loosely on newspaper tycoon William Randolph Hearst (1863–1951). Hearst, a jingoist, a demagogue, and very much alive when Welles made the movie, expressed outrage over the liberties the young filmmaker had taken with his life story. He did not allow the Hearst **newspapers** to publish reviews of the new film, nor would he permit

Many critics consider landmark film Citizen Kane *one of the most visually exciting productions of all time. Cameraman Gregg Toland, working closely with director Orson Welles, justly won an Academy Award nomination for his cinematography. In this striking shot, Kane (Welles) campaigns for political office. (Photo by Apic/Getty Images)*

any **advertising** about it, including theaters and show times. He threatened the studio, RKO Radio Pictures, with ruin and warned Welles of possible legal repercussions. But much of Hearst's wrath consisted of bluster and he could accomplish little, although a number of his friends in the movie industry brought pressure to bear on both RKO and theaters to pull the film and thus reduce its availability for audiences. Hearst need not have worried; the film initially did poorly at the box office, despite positive critical reviews; it would eventually do better as it established a reputation as a cinematic work of genius, but it took years.

The film begins with the death of Kane and then flashes back to tell, in essentially chronological order, of his life. His lonely childhood; his rise to success as a publisher; the accumulation of great wealth; and then the long, slow deterioration of all his personal affairs—at its most simplistic, a grandiose, albeit acidic, retelling of the Horatio Alger myth, but without the happy ending. *Citizen Kane* argues that, contrary to popular belief, great wealth and material success do not always bring happiness. It thus becomes in many ways a melodrama, an attempt to appeal to a large public anxious to see the rich and powerful cut down to size.

As Kane lies dying, he utters the cryptic "Rosebud." The tale that follows may or may not be summed up in Rosebud. As it turns out, Kane longed for simplicity in his life, such as sledding as a child. But wealth has distanced him from these pleasures, proving that one cannot go home again and recapture the past. But Rosebud itself has become an established part of American popular culture; for example, cartoonist

Charles Schulz (1922–2000) more than once used the term in *Peanuts,* his widely circulated comic strip. Most people reading the strip do not see it as some arcane reference, but instead make connections between Rosebud and *Citizen Kane.* The association has become established and no longer requires having seen the movie and knowing the role the term plays in the film.

A study in contrasting private life with public life, much of the movie employs the kind of tabloid journalism that Hearst's papers—the *San Francisco Examiner,* the *New York Journal,* the *Boston American,* the *Detroit Times,* and numerous others—featured. Very much a newspaper-based motion picture, *Citizen Kane* utilizes reporters as a method of telling its story, and portions of the dialogue paraphrases statements, real or apocryphal, attributed to Hearst.

Kane achieves ever greater wealth during the first third of the 20th century; his inflated sense of self-importance, however, causes him to lose longtime friends and associates. But he also gains a mistress, partially based on Hearst's lengthy affair with Hollywood actress Marion Davies (1897–1961). In the film, Davies becomes Susan Alexander (played by Dorothy Comingore, 1913–1971), actually a composite of several women plus the imaginations of Mankiewicz and Welles. Portrayed as a mediocre opera singer, several scenes purport to show how Kane builds her a Chicago opera house and just how dismally she sings, none of which applies to the real Marion Davies.

Hearst did, however, build San Simeon, a vast castle on the California coast north of Santa Barbara. Construction began in 1919 and continued for many years while he tinkered with details of the structure and poured millions into it. The castle served as a palatial getaway for himself and Davies as well as the site of many lavish social events. Furnished with fine art and antiques acquired by the boatload from Europe and designed by the noted American architect Julia Morgan (1972–1957), it stands as an ostentatious monument to wealth and the absence of taste. But its very exuberance makes San Simeon perfect for a visual medium like motion pictures.

In *Citizen Kane,* San Simeon becomes Xanadu, even more vulgar than the actual San Simeon, and allows cinematographer Toland to utilize unique photographic effects. Already an Academy Award winner for his work in 1939's *Wuthering Heights* and a nominee in 1940 for *The Long Voyage Home,* Toland desired the latitude, promised to him by Welles, to try new techniques. In addition, advances in Kodak film allowed for heightened dark and light contrasts without graininess. He particularly wanted to work with deep focus shots, wherein everything—foreground, middle ground, background—in the frame remains sharply in focus instead of blurring, thus forcing the observer to take in all aspects of a scene instead of concentrating only on certain parts. Shots of Kane and Susan Alexander in the vast rooms of Xanadu achieve a remarkable power thanks to Toland's dramatic and imaginative **photography.**

Because RKO, in its contract with Welles, allowed him complete artistic freedom on the set, his entire crew, not just Toland, felt confident to try new approaches instead of hewing to studio rules or Hollywood traditions. Welles also brought his considerable experience in radio, an aural medium, and used it to advantage with *Citizen Kane.* For many old sound pros then working in Hollywood, the radio engineers introduced them to many new techniques. The same holds for composer Bernard Herrmann (1911–1975), who had previously worked with the Mercury Theatre radio shows. He brought an individualistic approach to musical scoring for a film: after reading the script, he would write the music first, and then Welles and his editors faced the task of arranging the images accordingly. The technique obviously worked; Herrmann received an Academy Award nomination for his *Citizen Kane* score but lost to himself because he had been similarly nominated in that category for his score to *The Devil and Daniel Webster* (also known as *All That Money Can Buy*), an unusual occurrence in the annals of the Academy Awards. This utilization of the talents of experienced, skilled personnel, along with Welles's own inexperience in making a movie, makes *Citizen Kane* a truly collaborative effort.

With the passage of years, *Citizen Kane* has come to rival, if not overshadow, two other excellent pictures from the 1940s: **Casablanca** (1942) and **The Best Years of Our Lives** (1946). Immensely more popular at their release, they represent the best of topical moviemaking and have endured extremely well. But *Citizen Kane* transcends time; the tumultuous events of the first 40 years of the 20th century certainly provide a background, but they play little role in the telling of Charles Foster Kane's biography. Along with its technical brilliance, this particular American tragedy speaks to all generations—past, present, and future—by removing the audience from the constraints of a particular era. It allows them to see Kane—and Kane alone, because of his complete dominance of every frame within the motion picture—as a man doomed by his own quest for the unattainable.

See also: Drama (Film)

Selected Reading
Carringer, Robert L. *The Making of Citizen Kane.* Berkeley: University of California Press, 1985.
Gottesman, Ronald, ed. *Focus on Citizen Kane.* Englewood Cliffs, NJ: Prentice Hall, 1971.
Kael, Pauline. *The Citizen Kane Book.* New York: Limelight Editions, 1988.
Leming, Barbara. *Orson Welles: A Biography.* New York: Viking Penguin, 1985.

CIVIL DEFENSE

The concept of modern civil defense had its birth in World War I, when concern about protecting citizens and property from indiscriminate bombing gave rise to mobilizing means to thwart or minimize the effects of such attacks. By the late 1930s, military and government leaders in the United States realized that technological advances in warfare, especially long-range bombers, removed geographical security the North American continent might have once felt. As the specter of World War II and eventual U.S. involvement loomed, these officials looked to the British for ideas about protecting civilian populations.

Although England, especially London, would not experience the horrors of the German Blitz until late 1940 and early 1941, the British had already been working vigorously toward a nationwide approach to civil defense, given their experiences in both World War I and the early days of World War II. American observers took note of how the English prepared for aerial bombardment, and in March 1940, **President Franklin Delano Roosevelt** issued an executive order directing the federal government to move ahead with the first contingency plans for civilian defense. Shortly thereafter, and in anticipation of enemy attacks, the government created the Office of Emergency Management (OEM) in May of that year.

This agency at first functioned as a liaison office and clearinghouse among various national defense agencies. The OEM had within its divisions the Office of Civilian Defense (later the Office of Civil Defense; OCD), created in May 1941, a year following the formation of OEM. It attempted to coordinate the efforts of numerous state and local defense councils, because most had been operating independently with a resultant haphazard patchwork of civil defense policies. A few people realized that soon,rather than later, the United States would be drawn into the growing conflict abroad, and they made attempts to organize a civilian cadre of volunteers trained in first aid and responses to disaster situations, but it took the debacle at Pearl Harbor in December 1941 to awaken a sleeping nation.

The colorful mayor of New York City, Fiorello La Guardia (1882–1947), received appointment as the first head of the OCD early in 1941. An enthusiastic and vocal supporter of civil defense, La Guardia found it difficult to balance his roles as New York's mayor and as a federal administrator. He eventually resigned, and James M. Landis (1899–1964) took over the position from early 1942 until the end of 1943; William N. Haskell (1878–1952) in turn followed Landis and guided the organization until the end of the war. With peace, **President Harry S. Truman** (1884–1972) phased out the agency. Despite the leadership turnovers at the OCD, work continued unabated, particularly during 1940 and 1941, and gradually a framework for actions to be taken in case of attack evolved.

This poster, created in 1941, when the threat of war and enemy attacks was growing, found wide distribution across the country. The circular Civil Defense emblem became familiar to everyone and the text urges citizens to join with their neighbors in becoming part of an organized cadre of volunteers. (Library of Congress)

For cities and towns, the agency urged a system of volunteer air raid wardens. Following intensive training, they would be placed on duty to assist in any needed ways before, during, and after an enemy raid. Their responsibilities included overseeing the rules for **blackouts,** particularly the need to extinguish any visible sources of illumination. They also received instruction about dealing with incendiary devices, fire fighting, the proper use of gas masks in the event of chemical warfare, and basic first aid techniques. At the neighborhood level, they could direct people to the nearest air raid shelters, sturdy structures usually marked with a yellow *S,* and they would see to it that those needing assistance received it. Their greatest value, however, lay in their ability to calm a worried public. In the spring of 1942, the OCD christened this first line of defense the United States Civilian Defense Corps, and it eventually enrolled over half a million people, men and women, young and old.

Plans for civil defense, however, went beyond wardens fulfilling their duties during blackouts or other war-related events. The Civil Air Patrol (CAP) had come into being in the late 1930s with the realization that neither the Army Air Corps nor the air arms of the U.S. Navy and Marines possessed sufficient aircraft and manpower to patrol the nation's coastlines in addition to their more purely military missions. Government officials decided to take advantage of the 128,000 certified pilots residing in the United States and the 25,000 light civil aircraft in their possession.

The aviation community responded enthusiastically, and, by 1943, membership in the Civil Air Patrol numbered about 75,000 individuals. Flying their own small private planes, CAP pilots daily patrolled the shores along the Atlantic, Pacific, and Gulf of Mexico, looking for any suspicious activity. They also flew out to sea, sometimes over 100 miles from land and usually unarmed, looking for enemy submarines. This latter activity proved invaluable, because a submarine, even submerged, is far more visible from the air than from aboard a ship. Their orders were to report any sightings, but a few even engaged the foe by feigning an attack until assistance could arrive. They reportedly drove off a number of submarines using this tactic and eventually received permission to carry bombs; the lightest planes often took a 100-pound bomb aloft, and larger ones could manage one or two depth charges (explosive devices designed to detonate underwater and damage or destroy a submarine). In the course of their patrols, CAP pilots received credit for sinking two German submarines.

Over the duration of the war, Civil Air Patrol pilots flew over 86,000 coastal patrol missions, logging countless hours in the air and covering millions of square miles. The group's activities were not without cost: 65 pilots or observers lost their lives, and over 90 planes were destroyed. By venturing so far offshore, fuel shortages or mechanical problems could occasionally doom the tiny, single-engine aircraft they flew, causing them to go down at sea with the loss of both the crews and their planes.

Authorities moved the Civil Air Patrol from the Office of Civil Defense to the War Department in the spring of 1943, and made the organization an auxiliary of the Army Air Corps. This shift did not, however, end CAP's civil defense responsibilities. Its pilots continued to fly reconnaissance missions, plus they performed search and rescue duties for downed aircraft. They also carried mail, light cargo, and occasional passengers for the military services. The end of the war raised the issue of what to do with CAP, but in light of its exemplary service, no one wanted to disband it. With the creation of the United States Air Force in 1947, the Civil Air Patrol became an official auxiliary of the new service branch. Emphasis was placed on education and maintaining a viable cadet corps, a function it continues to maintain.

In addition to air raid wardens and the activities of the Civil Air Patrol, the Ground Observer Corps (GOC) served as a third leg in a growing system designed to alert localities in the event of an attack by air. Overseen by the War Department and the Army Air Force, the GOC put thousands of people on rooftops, in towers, on beaches and fields, and anywhere else one could get a reasonably clear view of the sky, rain or shine, day and night. Formed in 1942 and at its peak a year later, some 600,000 aircraft spotters scanned the horizons looking for suspicious aircraft. Armed with a telephone hook-up to their community, identification books, and spotter cards—decks of cards containing silhouettes of many different airplanes, both friend and foe, that allowed for quick identification of anything flying overhead—these civilian observers maintained a continuous vigil throughout the war.

The money for the spotters came from local sources, not the government. Towns held bake sale, raffles, and other fundraisers to buy materials necessary for constructing shacks, crude towers, and the like to provide their volunteers a modicum of protection from the elements. At first, overly zealous observers reported both flocks of crows and friendly aircraft, but they soon adapted to the job's requirements, plus they learned to differentiate Allied from enemy aircraft.

The Pearl Harbor attack had demonstrated to an unsuspecting nation that the United States was not impregnable. Hawaii might be far from any land mass, and vast oceans separated the continental United States from much of the rest of the world, but with a world war erupting on two fronts—the Japanese in the Pacific, Germany and Italy threatening from the Atlantic—a rush to organize some kind of home front defense system supplanted complacency. Within days of the bombing, civilians rushed to volunteer for various duties connected with protecting the home front from enemy attack and sabotage. In an unparalleled display of community solidarity, Americans everywhere responded by taking responsibility for their own defense against enemy actions.

When, however, the hostilities ended in 1945, people wanted to forget about war and air raids, and civil defense as a part of everyday life languished. The spotters and the block wardens put away their identification books and helmets; the Civil Air Patrol returned to routine, peacetime activities; and President Truman deactivated the Office of Civil Defense. But no one had counted on the **Cold War** commencing almost as soon as the soldiers laid down their arms. Tensions rose between East (Soviet Union) and West (the United States and its allies) and the saber rattling began anew.

With its monopoly on nuclear weapons and industrial base virtually intact, the nation felt relatively secure in the immediate postwar period. The Truman administration supported forming the National Security Resources Board (NSRB) in 1947, an umbrella agency that would oversee, among many things, the implementation of any new civil defense measures, should they be necessary. But times change, as does **technology**. The Air Force had added the B-36 bomber, a six-engine behemoth capable of delivering atomic bombs anywhere on the planet. The Soviet Union, however, also built up its long-range air capabilities, utilizing designs quite frankly stolen from American models, and could conceivably strike North America within hours of takeoff. An arms race between the two powers had begun—one that would endure for decades.

To the shock of the man on the street, on August 29, 1949, **newspapers** announced that the USSR had successfully detonated an atomic bomb of its own. Thanks to captured German scientists and documents, prolonged espionage in most Allied nations, and its own scientific establishment, the Communist country had completely altered the balance of power between East and West. The announcement also brought about a flurry of activity in Washington, and civil defense again became a topic for serious discussion at various levels of government.

President Truman quickly activated the Office of Civil Defense Planning, an extension of the old Office of Civil Defense from the war years. As officials discussed ways of coping with the unthinkable—a nuclear attack from Soviet bombers directed at U.S. cities—other experts decreed that a new agency would be necessary to deal with the threat. In December 1950, and after the North Korean invasion of South Korea in June, the Office of Defense Mobilization (ODM) came into being—a new and powerful agency designed to coordinate many levels of national preparedness, including civil defense. Thereafter, with the development of hydrogen bombs on both sides, intercontinental missiles capable of reaching the continental United States cities within minutes, instead of the hours required of conventional bombers, the ODM eventually coalesced into the Office of Civil and Defense Mobilization (OCDM) in 1958. In light of new and ever more deadly threats, U.S. civil defense once again had a high priority.

See also: Atomic Bomb; Aviation; Political and Propaganda Films; Youth

Selected Reading
Civil Air Patrol. www.CAP.gov/documents/arch8_history_of_cap.pdf
Hoopes, Roy. *Americans Remember the Home Front: An Oral Narrative.* New York: Hawthorn Books, 1977.
Lingeman, Richard. *Don't You Know There's a War On? The American Home Front, 1941–1945.* New York: Thunder's Mouth Press, 1970.
Winkler, Allan M. *Under a Cloud: American Anxiety about the Atom.* Urbana: University of Illinois Press, 1999.

CLASSICAL MUSIC

The *New Oxford American Dictionary* (2001) offers several definitions for the word "classical," including "typically a form of art regarded as representing an exemplary standard long-established in form or style." Well into the 20th century, enthusiasts of classical music used the criterion for determining excellence and concluded that the only good **music** came from Europe, in blatant disregard for American composers who wanted to incorporate local flavor into their works.

Even Walt Disney's (1901–1966) movie *Fantasia,* which premiered at New York's Broadway Theatre on November 13, 1940, to great critical acclaim, acknowledged this infatuation with composers from other countries. In this feature, animators set cartoons to classical compositions, such as *The Sorcerer's Apprentice* (1897; Paul Dukas, 1865–1935)*, Nutcracker Suite* (1892; Peter Tchaikovsky, 1840–1893), *Night on Bald Mountain* (1886; Nikolay Rimsky-Korsakov, 1844–1908), and *Rite of Spring* (1913; Igor Stravinsky, 1882–1971), all non-Americans.

Although typical classic music listeners in the United States purported to prefer the above, along with Bach (1685–1750), Beethoven (1770–1827), and Brahms (1833–1897), some American composers dared to experiment with writing pieces that came from their experiences in the New World, not their ancestral origins. For example, Charles Ives (1874–1954), born in Connecticut, readily used hymns and popular tunes rooted in New England life when crafting his sonatas, symphonies, and other concert music written in the early decades of the 20th century. Health conditions prevented him from composing after 1922, but he enjoyed public performances of his works until his death, and saw several composers follow his lead.

Aaron Copland (1900–1990), Roy Harris (1898–1979), Virgil Thomson (1896–1996), William Grant Still (1895–1978), and Morton Gould (1913–1996) all searched for a uniquely American sound and, by 1940, had become significant native composers. Of these five, Copland became the most successful, especially through three well-received ballets: *Billy the Kid* (1938), *Rodeo* (1942), and *Appalachian Spring* (1944). Each deals with American themes and incorporates simple musical motifs, such as cowboy and folk tunes, reflective of the country's culture. Copland's 1946 *Third Symphony* continues in this format, with some tunes suggestive of folksongs. He also composed for the **movies,** with five films from the 1940s to his credit: *Our Town* (1940), *The North Star* (1943), *The Cummington Story* (1945), *The Red Pony* (1949), and *The Heiress* (1949).

Roy Harris, in his 1940 *Folk Song Symphony,* embodied traditional folk themes such as "When Johnny Comes Marching Home Again," as well as two other Civil War tunes. For this effort, Harris received a citation from the U.S. Treasury Department in 1941 for distinguished and patriotic services to the country. After the war, he held teaching positions with various colleges and universities and produced a violin concerto in 1949.

In the meantime, Virgil Thomson moved from Paris back to New York City in 1940, working as a music critic for the *Herald Tribune.* His composing included a piece for an Office of War Information (OWI) documentary titled *Tuesday in November* (1945), an examination of a free and fair presidential election in a country at war. An opera, *The Mother of Us All* (1946), focuses on the life of suffragette Susan B. Anthony (1820–1906) and uses a variety of musical sources ranging from medieval church music to folk hymns and ballads. Thomson also traveled to Hollywood and wrote the score for *Louisiana Story* (1948), a documentary about changes to life on the bayous when the oil industry arrived.

As did Copland, Harris, and Thomson, William Grant Still reflects and pays homage to his cultural background in works such as *And They Lynched Him on a Tree* (1940) and *In Memoriam: The Colored Soldiers Who Died for Democracy* (1944). Known as the"Dean of African American Composers," Still provided arrangements for musicians who performed popular music; he also wrote and produced programs for **radio** networks. During the 1940s, he penned scores for 14 B-grade Hollywood films without credit, such as *The Secret Seven* (1940), *The Missing Juror* (1944), *The Millerson Case* (1947), *Phantom Valley* (1948), and *Rim of the Canyon* (1949). A truly versatile composer, he also offered an opera, *A Bayou Legend,* which premiered in 1941, followed by a suite, *Pages from Negro History,* in 1943. His *Festive Overture* (1944) won the Jubilee Prize given by the Cincinnati Symphony Orchestra for the best overture to celebrate its jubilee season that year.

Morton Gould (1913–1996), another composer active during the 1940s, frequently featured well-known American themes integrating folk, blues, **jazz,** gospel, and Western elements as can be heard in *Spirituals* (1941), *Latin American Symphonette* (1941),

Cowboy Rhapsody (1942), and *Fall River Legend* (1947). He gained recognition across the country through arranging and conducting for network radio, particularly the Columbia Broadcasting System's *Chrysler Hour* and Mutual's *The Cresta Blanca Carnival of Music*. For Broadway, he created the scores for *Billion Dollar Baby* in 1945 and *Arms and the Girl* in 1950. Hollywood credits include the documentary *Ring of Steel* (1942) and the musical *Delightfully Dangerous* (1945), in which he appeared leading an orchestra.

Other composers writing notable compositions during the 1940s, but making their biggest marks in the decades following, include Samuel Barber (1910–1981), Paul Creston (1906–1985), William Schuman (1910–1992), Norman Dello Joio (1913–2008), David Diamond (1915–2005), Elliott Carter (b. 1908), and Gian Carlo Menotti (1911–2007). In 1943, Schuman won the inaugural Pulitzer Prize for music with his cantata *A Free Song,* adapted from Walt Whitman's (1819–1892) poetry. Menotti's *Amahl and the Night Visitors* (1951) gained fame as the first opera written expressly for and performed on **television.**

Mention should also be made of Howard Hansen (1896–1981), Walter Piston (1894–1976), and Roger Sessions (1896–1985). They worked primarily as educators, conductors, and promoters of other composers. Hansen, as head of the Eastman School of Music at the University of Rochester, presented some 1,500 works by 700 composers. From 1946 to 1962, he was active in the **United Nations** Educational, Scientific, and Cultural Organization and composed a piece for its 1949 world conference in Paris.

Piston, in his compositions during the World War II era, occasionally incorporated the rhythms of jazz and American country dance music, but none became well known or popular. His Third Symphony, written in 1948, received the Pulitzer Prize in music. He authored three significant music textbooks, two during the 1940s: *Harmony* (1941) and *Counterpoint* (1947).

Although Roger Sessions wrote many pieces (five during the 1940s), no orchestras at the time regularly performed his compositions. He remains best known for his teaching at institutions such as Princeton University; the University of California, Berkeley; and the Juilliard School; along with being able to count among his former students such eminent composers as David Diamond (1915–2005) and others.

Even before the United States' entry into World War II in December 1941, a patriotic fervor had spread across the country that continued throughout the conflict. Musicians from all genres, including both the famous and the unknown, participated in the war effort in a number of ways. For example, the popular **swing** clarinetist Benny Goodman (1909–1986) appeared as a soloist in the Mozart (1756–1791) *Clarinet Concerto* with the New York Philharmonic Symphony Orchestra in October 1940, while the Symphony Orchestra of the National Youth Administration (NYA, a New Deal program) for New York City presented free Sunday afternoon concerts in the summer of 1940 with programs that included both European and American classical music.

Interested in boosting morale on the home front through radio and recordings, conductor and arranger Andre Kostelanetz (1901–1980) requested submissions of musical portraits of great Americans that could be performed with various orchestras. The four pieces commissioned by him in 1942 included *Portrait for Orchestra: Mark Twain* by Jerome Kern (1885–1945), *Mayor La Guardia Waltzes* and *Canons for Dorothy*

Thompson by Virgil Thomson, and the *Lincoln Portrait* by Aaron Copland. He penned two additional wartime pieces, *Fanfare for the Common Man* (1944) and *Letter from Home*. *Fanfare* premiered on March 12, 1943, under the baton of Sir Eugene Goossens (1893–1962), resident conductor for the Cincinnati Symphony Orchestra. **ABC (American Broadcasting Company)** commissioned *Letter from Home* for its national programming; a short number, it deals with American GIs off fighting the war.

Other composers and musicians likewise capitalized on their talents to become involved with the war. In 1939, Nelson Eddy (1901–1967), a classically trained baritone who achieved fame starring in light movie operettas, performed in a concert to benefit Polish war relief. After that, he frequently appeared at the Hollywood Canteen; broadcast for the Armed Forces Radio (AFR); and, in 1943, traveled to South America, Africa, Egypt, and Persia (now Iran) to entertain U.S. troops.

Ferde Grofe (1892–1972), best known from his "On the Trail," a segment of his *Grand Canyon Suite* (1931) and used in Philip Morris cigarette advertisements, supported the war through radio and the film industry. He served as the maestro for a wide variety of radio shows; collaborated on a number of Hollywood films, including *Strike up the Band* (1940), *Thousands Cheer* (1943), and *Rhapsody in Blue* (1945); participated in **USO (United Service Organizations)** shows; and, at times, held the baton for military bands. In fact, classical music proved to be so popular with service personnel that the USO in 1942 set up a concert division devoted exclusively to arranging for these kinds of shows.

More direct assistance came from composer Marc Blitzstein (1905–1964), who joined the army and served as musical director of the government-run American broadcasting facility in London. While there, he wrote *Freedom Morning,* a symphonic poem for orchestra, which opened in London in 1943. The United States Air Force commissioned him to produce a choral piece that he titled *Airborne Symphony;* it had a notable performance in New York City in 1946, with Orson Welles (1915–1985) as narrator and Leonard Bernstein (1918–1990) conducting. It received a lukewarm reception, however, because most Americans wanted to put all reminders of the war behind them.

Gail Kubik (1914–1984), composer and musical advisor for NBC radio, wrote the score for an OWI film called *The World at War.* Arturo Toscanini (1867–1957), also affiliated with NBC as the conductor of its symphony orchestra, in 1943, revived Giuseppe Verdi's (1813–1901) *Hymn of the Nations,* composed in the early 1860s, for inclusion in an OWI documentary film about Italian Americans aiding the Allies during World War II. Toscanini added a bridge to Verdi's work to include arrangements of the anthems of the United States and the Soviet Union. Originally produced for European distribution, the movie was released in the United States in April 1946.

An increased interest in classical music became just as evident at home. Despite the challenges of wartime **rationing,** the San Francisco Ballet Company in 1944 produced the first complete U.S. performance of Tchaikovsky's *The Nutcracker,* composed in 1890–1891. Uniforms for the toy soldiers had to be made out of old Cort Theater curtains. Support for classical music by some citizens across the country did not abate with an end to fighting. On May 4, 1946, the first of seven weeks of concerts focusing on popular modern composers and performed by members of the New York

Philharmonic Orchestra, was held at Carnegie Hall in New York City. To promote their 1947 **baseball** schedule, the New York Yankees sponsored a program of symphonic music every afternoon during the season on a local radio station. At the same time, Chicago offered Grant Park concerts free and brought the finest of classical music to the Windy City.

Before, during, and after World War II, radio offered a wide variety of programming, and among classical music professionals, Andre Kostelanetz became one of its most popular personalities. He came to the United States from his native Russia in 1922, and two years later made his radio debut conducting an orchestra. In 1929, he joined CBS and performed until 1946 with symphony orchestras on a number of shows beginning with *Andre Kostelanetz Presents.* He reached his greatest recognition from his arranging and recording of light classical music pieces intended for mass audiences and recorded by Columbia Records from the 1940s until 1980.

Some of Kostelanetz's success, and that of subsequent radio musical programs and recordings, came from his recommendations concerning microphone placement and sound mixing, a technique that became the standard for both mediums. A significant boost for the selling of classical records occurred in 1948, when Columbia Records introduced the long-play album (33-1/3 revolutions per minute [rpm]) in both 10-inch and 12-inch disks. The company reserved its 12-inch recordings for higher-priced classical compositions, because, with its playing time of 17 minutes to a side (most 78-rpm records could accommodate only 3 to 4 minutes per side), the disks allowed many of these to be played without interruption.

Kostelanetz, professionally active in many ways, made numerous recordings over the course of his career, including a series of easy listening instrumental albums on Columbia Records, conducting the New York Philharmonic in pops concerts and recordings. He encouraged the orchestra in 1943 to engage a youthful Leonard Bernstein as conductor, thus, giving him his first big break. On a nonmusical note, Kostelanetz also assisted in the development of **technology** that enabled Allied ships and submarines during World War II to differentiate their own craft from enemy vessels.

Prior to employing Kostelanetz, CBS in 1929 formed an in-house orchestra for a show called *The Columbia Symphony Orchestra,* which aired irregularly and closed in 1938. Meanwhile, in 1937, NBC (National Broadcasting Company) engaged the most renowned conductor in the world, Arturo Toscanini (1867–1957), to lead its studio orchestra for a weekly program called *The NBC Symphony Orchestra,* a show that played continuously until 1954. It, along with other classically oriented shows, provided rich offerings for the few who listened.

Of the two networks, NBC took the lead in hours and money invested for classical programming and experienced more success with its studio orchestra than did CBS. In Table 26, NBC leads CBS by seven to three programs airing throughout the 1940s.

World War II created shortages and cutbacks on a number of fronts, including musical programming for radio. While some shows endured the interruptions of war, others did not fare as well and ceased soon after the United States' entry into the conflict. In addition, Table 27 reveals that NBC did not cancel as many shows as CBS.

Devotees of classical music also had other sources from which to choose. Large metropolitan areas, such as New York, Boston, and Chicago, prided themselves on

TABLE 26. A Sampling of Classical Music Radio Shows on the Air during the 1940s

Program Title	Dates	Network
The New York Philharmonic Orchestra	1927–1963	CBS
The Music Appreciation Hour (a groundbreaking educational program for children)	1928–1942	NBC
The Voice of Firestone (began as *The Firestone Hour*)	1928–1954	NBC
	1954–1957	ABC
The Metropolitan Opera	1931–1958	NBC
The NBC Symphony Orchestra	1937–1954	NBC
Philadelphia Symphony Orchestra	Late 1930s and early 1940s	NBC and CBS
The Boston Symphony Orchestra	1932–1956	NBC and ABC
The Telephone Hour, also called *The Bell Telephone Hour*	1940–1958	NBC
Philadelphia Symphony Orchestra Children's Concerts	1945–1948	CBS
Carnegie Hall	1948–1950	ABC

Source: Adapted from Dunning, John. *On the Air: The Encyclopedia of Old-Time Radio.* New York: Oxford University Press, 1998.

TABLE 27. A Sampling of Classical Music Radio Shows That Left the Air during World War II

Program Title	Dates	Network
The Cincinnati Conservatory Symphony	1935–1941	CBS
The Curtis Institute Musicale	1933–1941	CBS
The Ford Sunday Evening Hour	1934–1942	CBS
The Radio City Music Hall of the Air	1932–1942	NBC
The Rochester Civic Orchestra	1929–1942	NBC
The Rochester Philharmonic Orchestra	1929–1930	NBC
	1935–1937	
	1939–1942	
The Indianapolis Symphony Orchestra	1937–1938	Mutual
	1938–1943	CBS

Source: Adapted from Dunning, John. *On the Air: The Encyclopedia of Old-Time Radio.* New York: Oxford University Press, 1998.

promoting fine music and art. The United States boasted five prominent symphony orchestras: the New York Philharmonic, founded in 1842; the Boston Symphony Orchestra, 1881; the Chicago Symphony Orchestra, 1891; the Philadelphia Orchestra, 1900; and the Cleveland Orchestra, 1918. All remained active during World War II; in addition to their annual concert series performed in their respective cities, they regularly broadcast on network radio.

The musicians with these symphony orchestras and others across the country tended to be male. The Chicago Symphony Orchestra featured a female harpist in its first season of 1892 to 1893, a rare exception, and the Cleveland Orchestra included four women in 1923. Perceptions that they lacked the physical strength required for playing instruments other than the piano or harp, that they did not have the stamina needed for lengthy rehearsals, that they could not rehearse regularly because of their duties at home, and that they might look less than ladylike while performing, coupled with a general resistance for women to work outside the home, barred them from membership in most groups. The rapid growth of American music schools and conservatories in the late 19th century created an excess of capable female players who wanted to work professionally. They secured positions in amateur and semiprofessional orchestras but generally not the major ones. The formation of all-women ensembles became an alternative, particularly during the 1920s and 1930s.

During World War II, these musicians stood ready to join the major orchestras as more and more men either enlisted or were drafted into military service, causing a serious need for competent instrumentalists. Despite their eagerness to play, however, few women actually performed. Eighteen joined the Pittsburgh Orchestra in 1942 and 24 more in 1944. But a report prepared for the National Commission on the Observance of International Women's Year 1975 noted that, even with this pressure to engage female players for instruments other than the piano or harp, the most renowned American orchestras employed fewer than 10 women in all, with the exception of Pittsburgh. Generally, positions offered to women were understood to be temporary, not employment on a regular contractual basis.

Despite widespread efforts during the 1940s to promote an appreciation for classical music through public concerts and programs on national radio networks, this particular genre never gained the popularity experienced by many other kinds of music. World War II caused all aspects of everyday life in the United States to slow down or change, but composers such as Copland, Harris, Thomson, Still, and Gould strove to promote classical music possessing an American sound and gained some moderate success. At the same time, Kostelanetz brought classical music to millions of Americans through radio and recordings. Two large record companies—RCA Victor and Columbia—had classical recordings in their inventory, and, in 1949, Capitol Records joined them, leaving Decca alone of the big four companies producing only popular fare. Toscanini and the NBC Orchestra stayed on the air with sizeable audiences for 17 years, and groups such as the New York Philharmonic Orchestra and the San Francisco Symphony began to tour the country, exposing even more people to this genre.

See also: Advertising; All-Girl Orchestras; Broadway Shows (Musicals); Canteens; Country Music; Musicals (Film); Newspapers; Rosie the Riveter

Selected Reading

Ammer, Christine. *Unsung: A History of Women in American Music.* Westport, CT: Greenwood Press, 1980.

Cooper, Martin, ed. *The New Oxford History of Music: The Modern Age, 1890–1960.* London: Oxford University Press, 1974.

Horowitz, Joseph. *Classical Music in America: A History of Its Rise and Fall.* New York: W. W. Norton, 2005.

Struble, John Warthen. *The History of American Classical Music: MacDowell through Minimalism.* New York: Facts on File, 1995.

COLD WAR, THE

The death of **President Franklin Delano Roosevelt** (1882–1945), just beginning his fourth term in office in April, thrust Vice **President Harry S. Truman** (1884–1972) into the international spotlight. Relatively inexperienced in foreign affairs, Truman had to deal with the closing months of World War II and an increasingly troublesome relationship with the Union of Soviet Socialist Republics (USSR) and its difficult leader, Joseph Stalin (1879–1953). Truman and the American public may not have realized it at the time, but before the final peace treaties had been signed, and with the former Axis countries lying in ruins, the opening volleys of a new kind of war—a cold war, as opposed to a "hot" one with bombs and soldiers in combat—had begun.

Less than a year after Truman assumed the presidency, during a speech delivered at tiny Westminster College in Fulton, Missouri, on March 5, 1946, former British Prime Minister Winston Churchill (1874–1965) invoked the image of an iron curtain descending, separating Eastern and Western Europe. With Truman in attendance, Churchill in his message said that the Soviets wanted to divide East and West into two blocs, Communist and non-Communist, and that the two entities were like enemies in an undeclared war, meaning that those countries falling under the yoke of Communist rule will be isolated from the Free World by an impenetrable military and ideological barrier or "curtain."

In keeping with the tensions aroused by deteriorating relations between the United States and the Soviet Union, Hollywood released a number of anti-Communist films during the late 1940s. This scene comes from The Iron Curtain *and shows Dana Andrews and Gene Tierney in a somber moment. (Twentieth Century-Fox Film Corporation/Photofest)*

On April 16, 1947, just over a year later, financier and longtime presidential advisor Bernard Baruch (1870–1965) employed the term "cold war" in comments given in South Carolina. (It should be noted that English author George Orwell (1903–1950) probably first used the term in a 1945 essay, but it gained little notice.) Shortly after Baruch's speech, columnist Walter Lippmann (1889–1974) used the phrase in a series of published articles, giving it a considerably larger audience. Instead of pitched battles between massed armies, a cold conflict involves diplomatic, ideological, political, and economic rivalry—an armed truce—in an attempt to achieve geographic and military dominance. Both "cold war" and "iron curtain" became metaphors that gave Americans a slightly better grasp of the postwar era. This colorful imagery describing deteriorating postwar Soviet-U.S. relations henceforth enjoyed widespread use in popular conversation.

The roots that produced the Cold War remain tangled, with many interpretations that attempt to explain the postwar world situation in 1945. In brief, the Big Three—Roosevelt representing the United States, Churchill the United Kingdom, and Stalin the USSR—in July 1945 met at Potsdam, in Russian-occupied Germany, to discuss the map of Europe following the war. The Allies, with the addition of France, took control of the western section of Germany, while the Soviet Union took the eastern part. The victors divided Berlin, the traditional capital that lay well within the eastern sector, into four sections of military control. But much of the remainder of the devastated continent at first leaned neither toward either side, in effect creating a power vacuum. All that shortly changed, however, proving the accuracy of Churchill's words at Westminster College. An Eastern European bloc of Soviet-controlled satellite states, including Albania, Bulgaria, East Germany, Poland, Romania, and later Czechoslovakia and Hungary, disappeared behind the Iron Curtain.

In the midst of these changes, George F. Kennan (1904–2005), serving as deputy chief of the U.S. mission in Moscow under Ambassador W. Averell Harriman (1891–1986), in spring 1946 sent a lengthy, secret telegram to the Department of State outlining what he saw as the reasons behind the deteriorating relations with the USSR. Using the pseudonym "Mr. X" in the fall 1947 issue of *Foreign Affairs,* Kennan published "The Sources of Soviet Conduct," an expansion of his earlier correspondence with the State Department, since called "the long telegram." In both documents, he championed the containment of the Soviet Union, saying that the country should not be allowed to expand its areas of influence beyond what it had already attained.

Other officials, searching for a middle ground, supported a theory of convergence that said, in effect, the United States had to recognize the legitimacy of Soviet conquests, and that "spheres of interest" were a realistic response to the geopolitics of the time. Columnist Walter Lippmann served as Kennan's primary dissenter. In his aforementioned *The Cold War* (1947), Lippmann argued that both sides—the United States and the Soviet Union—should withdraw their forces from Europe and allow the uncommitted nations to pursue their own destinies. He claimed that containment would prove untenable and so expensive it would drain U.S. resources. Kennan's approach nevertheless won over many in Washington and motivated the conduct of the nation's international policies for the remainder of the decade.

While others debated ways of dealing with the Soviet Union, President Truman, in a speech given in March 1947, articulated to Congress what his approach to foreign affairs would be. He said the country would aid any nation threatened by Communism, and pundits promptly labeled his plans as the Truman Doctrine, a term that stuck. Soon thereafter, the president requested and received $400 million (approximately $3.6 billion in 2008 dollars) in aid to Turkey and Greece, two unaligned countries strategists saw as threatened by Communist forces, both internal and external. Truman's actions marked the formal entry of the United States into the Cold War.

Together, the Truman Doctrine and George F. Kennan's containment policies had an immediate effect, and probably helped to save Italy, France, Austria, and Greece from Communist takeovers. Josip Broz Tito (1892–1980), the leader of Yugoslavia, played both sides, accepting arms and money but never committing to one or the other. U.S. planners feared the Soviet Union would invade the Balkan nation, and thus gave Yugoslavia considerable aid for many years. Because a sense of urgency drove the Cold War policies of the United States, they went essentially unchallenged and emboldened the country to intervene indiscriminately in the affairs of other nations, always with the excuse that Communism needed to be stopped whenever and wherever it seemed to threaten U.S. security.

As 1947, a key year, progressed, a number of other events increased public awareness of the complexities associated with the Cold War. Under the leadership of **General George Catlett Marshall,** acting in his capacity as secretary of state, the European Recovery Plan took shape. Better known as the Marshall Plan, it consisted of an unprecedented outpouring of aid and funds to war-torn Europe. Marshall and Truman recognized that a reinvigorated Europe would better resist any attempts by Communist groups to seize power; plus, on a more selfish level, the United States was anxious again to have strong European trading partners. The Soviet Union and its satellites, sensing that the Marshall Plan functioned as a cover-up while the United States strove to establish capitalism instead of socialism and increase trade, thereby making economic policies a driving force behind the Marshall Plan, declined to participate. The Soviets called the European Recovery Plan an "imperialist plot," claiming its implementation would further heighten tensions.

In light of the USSR's rejection of the Marshall Plan, Sewell Avery (1873–1960), the chairman of Montgomery Ward, the huge merchandising firm, proposed shipping millions of mail-order catalogs directly to the USSR, allowing its citizens to see the array of goods available through capitalism. Another individual urged the government to air-drop millions of nylon stockings on the unsuspecting Russian citizens, causing them to look more favorably toward the material wealth of the West. Neither suggestion received any official government sanction.

Although it might have been unimpressed with catalogs and nylons, Congress did, however, pass the National Security Act in July 1947. Under its provisions, the Department of Defense replaced the old War Department, and two new agencies, the National Security Council (NSC) and the Central Intelligence Agency (CIA), were born, both of which would eventually play pivotal roles in the Cold War. Additionally, propaganda agencies, such as **Voice of America** (VOA), Radio Free Europe (RFE), and the United

States Information Agency (USIA), saw sharp budget increases as the government increasingly utilized this form of psychological warfare, or what some called "perforating the Iron Curtain." At the same time, the Soviets and their satellites, in a seesaw battle with the West, attempted to purge all evidence of American mass culture within their borders. Soon thereafter, the two sides began arresting alleged spies and hurling threats and accusations back and forth.

During the summer of 1948, the first major postwar crisis between East and West occurred when Soviet authorities raised blockades to shut down transportation routes into Berlin, the now-isolated German capital managed by the victorious Four Powers (France, Great Britain, the Soviet Union, and the United States). Beginning in July, Soviet barriers effectively sealed off from the outside world that portion of Berlin managed by the three Western powers. In an amazing turn of events, Allied pilots daily flew hundreds of flights from Western Europe into the beleaguered city. The **Berlin Airlift,** as it came to be called, electrified the Free World and saved the city, while the Soviet Union suffered a humiliating propaganda defeat and reopened access to Berlin by land traffic in May 1949.

That same month, the United States Great Britain, and France, working with the West German government, created the autonomous Federal Republic of Germany; almost simultaneously, the Soviet Union proclaimed the German Democratic Republic (GDR) for the eastern section of Germany. Overnight, West Germany and East Germany split the old nation in two, and it would be decades before reunification occurred.

As tensions rose, and fearful of an overwhelming Soviet attack against Western Europe, military and political officials in the Allied nations lobbied for a military pact that would unite them in defending their territories. These countries clearly looked to the United States, thousands of miles from Europe's shores, for leadership, aid, and, most importantly, troops and arms. Out of these discussions came NATO (North Atlantic Treaty Organization) in the spring of 1949. Working from the premise that an armed attack against one constitutes an armed attack against all, its participants saw the organization as a military shield with integrated forces from all 12 member nations. It also meant that European affairs had become U.S. affairs—the final end of any pretense of isolationism. Although an overwhelming majority (83 percent) of Americans opposed going to war against the Soviet Union, some 75 percent wanted the nation to beef up its armed forces and thus were generally supportive of NATO, despite the USSR's distrust of long-range Allied intentions.

While the problems in Europe festered and drew considerable attention, the Cold War took a less prominent turn in Asia. In 1946, troops commanded by Ho Chi Minh (1890–1969), a Communist-leaning revolutionary, commenced guerilla warfare against the colonial army in the northern section of French Indochina (or *Indochine,* the French term for present-day Vietnam). The conflict dragged on, but the French finally met defeat in 1954, an event that paved the way for the later Vietnam War that would eventually involve the United States.

At roughly the same time, and after a protracted civil war in China, Mao Zedong (1893–1976), more commonly called Chairman Mao, in 1949 successfully defeated the forces of Nationalist leader Chiang Kai-shek (1887–1975). Mao declared the formation of the People's Republic of China. An ardent Communist, Mao enjoyed Soviet support, whereas Chiang Kai-shek's Kuomintang party had the backing of many Western governments. The loss of both Vietnam and China to Communism caused great consternation in U.S. diplomatic circles and led to countless political recriminations against Truman and his advisors.

To add to the administration's woes, that same year the United States lost its coveted nuclear monopoly in late August, when the Soviet Union exploded its own **atomic bomb.** This event signaled a new balance of terror as far as concerned weaponry, and both sides embarked on extensive testing of nuclear arms. Just three years later, in 1952, the United States announced the development of a much more powerful hydrogen bomb; in August 1953, the Soviets claimed their own hydrogen **technology.** In no time at all, the arms race between East and West had reached a dangerous new level.

On the home front, the public did not at first seem unduly alarmed about the news, but vocal critics of national security claimed the country's tolerance of Communism and fellow travelers were to blame for the Soviet Union obtaining nuclear weapons. Soviet spies and their confederates, they said, had made the unthinkable possible—and a measure of truth lived in this claim. Revelations about spying, the passing of secrets, and lax security at supposedly secret atomic facilities all came to light. Politicians from both parties angrily demanded immediate investigations into how this could have happened; clearly, Russian spies ran rampant at the highest levels of government, cried the more vociferous critics. The official clamor and dire predictions about Soviet intentions led to rising concern among citizens, concerns that led to a general paranoia about the Soviet Union and the A-bomb.

In short order, schools were conducting "duck and cover" drills for children, the prescribed action to take in the event of a Soviet nuclear strike. **Civil defense** was reborn, and sturdy buildings bore yellow signs designating them as havens during an attack. Many people, convinced World War III could break out at any moment, feverishly excavated their backyards for fallout shelters. Entrepreneurs advertised fallout kits, and do-it-yourself magazines provided plans for various defenses against bombs of all kinds.

Public fears continued to grow in the late 1940s, and with good reason. In military circles and among civilian planners, there emerged the theory of mutual assured destruction (MAD). In this scenario, any nuclear attack (a first strike) would lead to an equally deadly response or massive retaliation (a second strike), which could mean the obliteration of both sides in such a conflict. But, these theorists argued as a kind of reassurance, MAD means that neither side would dare launch such an attack, a deterrent posture that leads to a nuclear standoff and the avoidance of a first strike altogether. As Americans learned their leaders entertained these kinds of options in their strategic thinking, small wonder they worried about the likelihood of war.

People's fears found reinforcement in the actions of the House Committee on Un-American Activities (better known and remembered as the **House Un-American Activities Committee (HUAC),** a standing congressional committee that came into being in 1945, an outgrowth of similar panels dating back to the 1930s. Throughout the latter years of the decade, this committee subpoenaed countless individuals in a quest to root out Communists wherever they might be found. In many ways a rebirth of the infamous "red scare" following World War I, it utilized trial by innuendo, and those summoned by HUAC would seldom know the exact accusations nor could they confront their accusers. The federal government had already, in March 1947, required loyalty oaths from government workers to sign, and the procedures of HUAC only added to the worries of ordinary citizens.

For example, HUAC demanded that the reading lists used in selected high school and college classes be reviewed in order to purge any questionable titles that might support Communist ideology. Meek administrators, instead of stirring up trouble or arousing suspicion, frequently went along with these requests. The committee's activities became daily newspaper fodder when, in the summer of 1948, HUAC initiated a series of hearings investigating the alleged infiltration by Communist agents into many quarters of American life. Whittaker Chambers (1901–1961), an admitted Soviet spy during the 1930s and at the time of the hearings an editor with *Time* magazine, testified that State Department official Alger Hiss (1904–1996) had been a Soviet agent. Chambers charged, Hiss denied, and their confrontation became the show trial of the day. Congressman Richard M. Nixon (1913–1994), a member of HUAC only since 1947, doggedly pressed the issue and finally assisted in getting Hiss accused of perjury. Interested spectators included Wisconsin Senator Joseph McCarthy (1908–1957), who would gain notoriety in the early 1950s for his zealous hunts for Communists at all levels of government.

With the hearings attracting attention amid unchecked fears of Communists lurking almost anywhere, enterprising publishers rushed into print a stream of books with titles like *American Capitalism vs. Russian Communism, American Communism, Communism and the Conscience of the West, The False Christ of Communism and the Social Gospel, Iron Curtain, The Red Plotters, The Soviet Spies, Why They Behave Like Russians,* and such. Given national concerns about the escalating Cold War, most of these books did reasonably well in sales. **Magazines** and **newspapers** likewise ran countless articles about the perceived red menace.

The congressional purges reached into the film industry, accusing it of placing pro-Communist content in many of its releases. The investigation resulted in contempt of Congress charges against ten screenwriters and directors, the so-called "Hollywood Ten." In response, the studios hurriedly produced and released several anti-Communist **movies** during the late 1940s, including *The Iron Curtain* (1948), *The Red Menace* (1949), and *I Married a Communist* (1949). They obviously hoped such films would demonstrate the film capital's opposition to subversive elements, and they continued to crank out many more anti-Communist motion pictures during the early 1950s.

In retrospect, 1947 can be seen as an epochal year in the early history of the Cold War. Few political scientists or historians challenged the official U.S. line about the conflict's origins until well into the 1960s, when a generation of revisionist scholars began to question details. Until then, aggressive Soviet expansionism served as the accepted primary cause. The arguments and differing points of views have continued into the present. Public concerns engendered by the Cold War, however, did not reach their peak until the 1950s, with the Korean War, the McCarthy witch hunts and hearings, the Rosenberg executions, an ever-escalating arms race, and innumerable other high-profile events demonstrated how completely Cold War hysteria had enveloped the nation. This period in American history did not come to an end until the dissolution of the Soviet Union in 1991, and even then vestiges of the conflict stubbornly clung to aspects of foreign policy and national defense. The 1940s served but as prelude.

See also: Crime and Mystery Films; Drama (Film); Eisenhower, General Dwight David; Political and Propaganda Films; Radio Programming: News, Sports, Public Affairs, and Talk; Selective Training and Service Act of 1940 (Selective Service, or Draft); United Nations, The

Selected Reading
Diggins, John Patrick. *The Proud Decades: America in War and Peace, 1941–1960.* New York: W. W. Norton, 1988.
Graebner, William S. *The Age of Doubt: American Thought and Culture in the 1940s.* Boston: Twayne, 1991.
Hixon, Walter L. *Parting the Curtain: Propaganda, Culture, and the Cold War.* New York: St. Martin's Press, 1998.
Rose, Lisle. *The Cold War Comes to Main Street.* Lawrence: University Press of Kansas, 1999.

COLE, NAT KING

This popular pianist and vocalist, born Nathaniel Adams Coles in Alabama, will always be remembered as Nat King Cole (1919–1965). The epitome of a smooth, **jazz**-inflected singer, Cole began performing in the 1930s, achieved a modicum of fame during the 1940s, and then became a major entertainer in the 1950s, his star continuously rising until his untimely death in 1965.

The Coles family moved to Chicago while Nathaniel was still a child; he learned to play piano and organ and became interested in jazz after hearing many famous instrumentalists play at the clubs that flourished in the Windy City at the time. In the mid-1930s, he formed a small group of his own and used the name Nat Cole. At some point, companions added "King," probably because of the nursery rhyme about Old King Cole. His older brother, Eddie Coles, who had played bass for several bands, meanwhile decided to organize a small jazz group, Eddie Coles' Solid Swingers, and invited young Nat to sit in on piano. And, because of Eddie's prior connections, the Solid Swingers even got to record several sides for Decca in 1936. Nothing ever came of these early recordings, but they pointed Nat toward a career in jazz.

During the later 1930s, Cole landed the job of piano accompanist for a road revival version of Eurbie Blake's (1887–1983) *Shuffle Along,* a Broadway show originally written in 1921. The production went broke on the West Coast, and Cole decided to remain there. Southern California had an active jazz club scene, so after accepting every playing job he could find, Cole asked guitarist Oscar Moore (1916–1981) and bassist Wesley Prince (1907–1980) to join him in establishing the Nat King Cole Trio. The combination of piano-bass-guitar worked well and would function successfully, both commercially and artistically, throughout the 1940s. Bassist Johnny Miller (1915–1988), replaced Prince in 1942, when the latter got drafted.

At first, the trio played mainly instrumental numbers, although Cole would sometimes do a vocal over his own piano playing, and occasionally Moore and Prince would add their voices for a unison effect. Some early Decca tracks, along with some sides

Nat King Cole's fame began to rise during the 1940s. His velvety voice and exemplary piano stylings made him both a jazz and pop star, and he enjoyed a number of hits in the postwar years. This publicity photo shows him as a suave entertainer, an image he perpetuated in the years to come. (Photofest)

for small independent labels recorded in 1940 and 1941, show that Cole already had become a modestly talented singer, although his voice had yet to mature into the velvet baritone people came to know in the years ahead. Most of the time, however, the interplay of piano and guitar overshadows any vocalizing and displays the strong roots in contemporary jazz the trio had developed. **Bebop** (or bop) had begun to make inroads on **swing** at that time, and many younger black musicians displayed a growing interest in this new jazz format. Cole's lyrics to tunes like "Gone with the Draft" (1940), "Are You Fer It?" and "Hit That Jive, Jack" (both 1941) come across as dated novelty numbers, much in the manner of popular performers like Cab Calloway (1907–1994) and Louis Jordan (1908–1975), but they also pay their respects to the jive talk that often went along with the imagery of bebop.

During this time, Cole also demonstrated considerable facility in composing and arranging. One of his tunes, written in 1943, he called "Straighten Up and Fly Right," and many consider it his best work. Possibly based on a sermon he heard when young, or completely of his own making, it tells a fable about deceit and power., A person found misbehaving or doing his or her job improperly or with the wrong attitude may be told to "straighten up and fly right." If nothing else, his lyrics added a colorful phrase to World War II–era language. Movie fans got to hear the tune and see it performed by the trio in a minor 1943 musical called *Here Comes Elmer.*

That same year, Cole signed a contract with fledgling Capitol Records, a Hollywood-based label with which he would remain until his death. Founded in 1942 by composer-lyricist Johnny Mercer (1909–1976), songwriter and producer Buddy DeSylva (1895–1950), and businessman Glenn Wallichs (1910–1971), the new company quickly developed a varied roster of artists, one that included a heavy emphasis on contemporary jazz and vocals. Cole fit right in with Capitol's plans, and in the 1950s he would emerge as one of the label's most reliable and successful stars.

His piano skills won Cole considerable esteem in jazz circles. *Metronome* magazine, a well-respected monthly music journal that focused on jazz and swing, in 1939 inaugurated an annual readers' poll to select the top instrumentalists and vocalists of the day. The magazine continued the custom until 1961, and unlike other polls, *Metronome* attempted to gather each year's winners in a studio for a recording session. In 1946, Cole received top *Metronome* honors for piano. Backed by first-class sidemen, he recorded "Sweet Lorraine," a tune he would perform many times in the years ahead but with **Frank Sinatra** (1915–1998), voted that year's best male vocalist, singing the lyrics. At that same session (December 1946), Cole sings with June Christy (1925–1990), the winner as best female vocalist, on "Nat Meets June," a trifle but one that nonetheless displays his smooth vocal manner. Cole repeated in the piano category for 1947 and recorded "Leap Here," an all-instrumental piece that featured some of the best instrumentalists of the time. He also won similar polls conducted by *Down Beat* magazine from 1944 until 1947 and the *Esquire* jazz survey in 1946 and 1947, sure evidence of his high standing among those readers, although he had yet to build the tremendous popular following that would characterize his work after 1950.

That hoped-for popular following, however, began to materialize in 1946 when Cole recorded "I Love You (for Sentimental Reasons)." Performed by the trio, jukebox and airplay catapulted it to No. 8 for the year on the *Billboard* charts. He also enjoyed a lesser hit at that time with "The Christmas Song (Merry Christmas to You)," a composition destined to become a perennial holiday favorite. Originally penned in 1945 by singer Mel Torme (1925–1999) and songwriter Bob Wells (1922–1998), Cole and his group made their first recording of the tune in 1946. Later in the year, they added a small string section, and Capitol released this new interpretation; it did well during the 1946 holiday season. Over time, "The Christmas Song" became a seasonal standard, and Cole recorded it yet again in 1953 with a large orchestra, and that version eclipsed his earlier interpretations of the tune. It may be Mel Torme's composition, but most people associate the song with Nat King Cole.

A busy performer, Cole's threesome played jazz concerts and could be heard frequently as guests on top-name **radio** shows. In 1948, he hit the charts again with "Nature Boy," a curious song about a "strange, enchanted boy" written by Eden Ahbez (1908–1995), a Brooklyn-born eccentric who chose to live simply in Los Angeles parks and the Hollywood hills. Based on an old Yiddish melody, "Nature Boy" came out in 1947 on the B side of a Capitol single; no one held any great expectations for the tune. But listeners loved it and it became Cole's biggest hit up to that time, establishing itself as the No. 4 song for 1948.

Performed without the trio, but with a large studio orchestra, "Nature Boy" showed company executives that Cole possessed the potential to become a major pop vocalist along the line of Bing Crosby (1903–1977) and Frank Sinatra. The early 1950 release of "Mona Lisa," another syrupy, romantic ballad that ended up at No. 6 for the year confirmed the company's hopes and completed the transformation of Cole from innovative jazz pianist and ensemble player to vocal interpreter of contemporary love songs. He had already dissolved his famous trio at the end of the decade and began recording prolifically in front of orchestras and strings. He also appeared in **movies** (he had done some cameos with the trio in several forgettable musicals during the 1940s) and eventually moved to **television**. In that new medium, he could be seen as a frequent guest on various programs and graduated to host his own variety show in 1957, one of the first black entertainers to achieve so many levels of success.

See also: Broadway Shows (Musicals); Jukeboxes; Magazines; Musicals (Film); Race Relations and Stereotyping

Selected Reading
Epstein, Daniel Mark. *Nat King Cole.* New York: Farrar Straus and Giroux, 1999.
Gourse, Leslie. *Unforgettable: The Life and Mystique of Nat King Cole.* New York: St. Martin's Press, 1991.

COMEDIES (FILM)

In a period of war, people still need to laugh, just as they would in peacetime. Grim headlines, tense **radio** broadcasts, separation from loved ones, plus all the other daily reminders of the conflict make this need especially great, and World War II Hollywood rose to the occasion. From silly slapstick to slick, urbane tales of sophisticated characters in amusing situations, the movie comedies of the era offered everything from knowing grins to robust guffaws.

When the 1940s opened, the nation wanted very much to stay out of overseas wars. Isolationism sounded appealing to many, and the idea of intervention had few followers. For the most part, the prewar movie comedies took a decidedly neutral path and avoided European and Asian situations or any other hint of topicality.

For 1939 to 1941, that gray period before the nation's entry into World War II, a number of dramas, on the other hand, had already chosen sides. As early as 1939, serious films like *Confessions of a Nazi Spy* made no efforts to conceal their allegiances, and, as the conflict drew nearer, *Escape* (1940), *Man Hunt* (1941), and a number of others continued to show the Axis powers as the enemy. *Caught in the Draft* (1941), one of the few comedies to hint at the growing drumbeats for war, masked reality through humor. A Bob Hope (1903–2003) feature, he plays a character trying to evade the recently enacted draft. Released in the summer of 1941, Selective Service and the disruptions it brought to civilian life were still fair game for comedy, but that attitude would not last long.

As the table below suggests, by and large Hollywood provided lots of laughs on an almost weekly basis, with romantic comedy, cheerful music, and slapstick humor glossing over most reality.

In 1942, Jack Benny (1894–1974), whose fame resided primarily in radio, starred in *To Be or Not to Be,* a mix of Shakespeare and anti-Nazi humor. Supposedly set in Warsaw, the picture tells how an acting troupe (led by Benny, of course) sabotages the Gestapo with wit and sly humor, demolishing, along the way, any lingering ideas about "the Master Race."

Hail the Conquering Hero (1944), a clever satire on celebrity worship, has hometown boy Eddie Bracken (1915–2002) mistaken for a military hero. Not really about the war, it deals more with American attitudes and the gullibility of crowds. *The Miracle of Morgan's Creek* (1944), another dark comedy that addresses situations removed from the war, stars Bracken in his second 1944 appearance and Betty Hutton (1921–2007). Since great numbers of soldiers passed through cities and towns while on their way to postings, the occasional civilian pregnancy took place, and that subject, daring for its time, creates the plot. Very much an adult comedy about a potentially unfunny subject, it manages to avoid moralizing and still provides an ending the censors of that day could approve.

TABLE 28. Representative Film Comedies, 1940–1949

Year	Film Titles	Stars
1940	An Angel from Texas	Jane Wyman, Ronald Reagan
	Arise, My Love	Claudette Colbert, Ray Milland
	Brother Orchid	Edward G. Robinson, Humphrey Bogart
	Christmas in July	Dick Powell, Ellen Drew
	The Doctor Takes a Wife	Ray Milland, Loretta Young
	The Great McGinty	William Demarest, Brian Donlevy
	His Girl Friday	Cary Grant, Rosalind Russell
	My Favorite Wife	Irene Dunne, Cary Grant
	The Philadelphia Story	Katharine Hepburn, Cary Grant, Jimmy Stewart
	The Shop Around the Corner	James Stewart, Margaret Sullavan
1941	Ball of Fire	Barbara Stanwyck, Gary Cooper
	Bedtime Story	Fredric March, Loretta Young
	The Bride Came C.O.D.	James Cagney, Bette Davis
	The Devil and Miss Jones	Jean Arthur, Robert Cummings
	Hellzapoppin'	Olsen, Johnson
	Here Comes Mr. Jordan	Robert Montgomery, Claude Rains
	The Lady Eve	Barbara Stanwyck, Henry Fonda
	Skylark	Claudette Colbert, Ray Milland
	Topper Returns	Joan Blondell, Roland Young
1942	George Washington Slept Here	Jack Benny, Ann Sheridan
	I Married a Witch	Fredric March, Veronica Lake
	Larceny, Inc.	Edward G. Robinson, Broderick Crawford
	The Major and the Minor	Ginger Rogers, Ray Milland
	The Male Animal	Henry Fonda, Olivia de Havilland
	The Man Who Came to Dinner	Monty Woolley, Billie Burke
	The Palm Beach Story	Claudette Colbert, Joel McCrea
	Sullivan's Travels	Joel McCrea, Veronica Lake
	The Talk of the Town	Cary Grant, Jean Arthur
	To Be or Not to Be	Jack Benny, Carole Lombard
1943	Best Foot Forward	Lucille Ball, Tommy Dix
	Crazy House	Olsen, Johnson
	Heaven Can Wait	Don Ameche, Gene Tierney
	The Human Comedy	Mickey Rooney, Frank Morgan
	A Lady Takes a Chance	Jean Arthur, John Wayne
	The More the Merrier	Jean Arthur, Joel McCrea
	Mr. Lucky	Cary Grant, Laraine Day
	Never a Dull Moment	The Ritz Brothers
	No Time for Love	Claudette Colbert, Fred MacMurray
	Young and Willing	William Holden, Eddie Bracken
1944	Arsenic and Old Lace	Cary Grant, Josephine Hull
	The Canterville Ghost	Charles Laughton, Robert Young
	Casanova Brown	Gary Cooper, Teresa Wright
	Hail the Conquering Hero	Eddie Bracken, William Demarest
	It Happened Tomorrow	Dick Powell, Linda Darnell
	The Miracle of Morgan's Creek	Betty Hutton, Eddie Bracken
	Mr. Winkle Goes to War	Edward G. Robinson, Robert Mitchum
	Once Upon a Time	Cary Grant, Janet Blair
	Rosie the Riveter	Jane Frazee, Frank Albertson
	See Here, Private Hargrove	Robert Walker, Donna Reed

(continued)

TABLE 28. *(continued)*

Year	Film Titles	Stars
1945	*Blithe Spirit*	Rex Harrison, Kay Hammond
	Brewster's Millions	Dennis O'Keefe, Helen Walker
	Christmas In Connecticut	Barbara Stanwyck, Dennis Morgan
	Getting Gertie's Garter	Dennis O'Keefe, Marie McDonald
	The Kid from Brooklyn	Jack Benny, Alexis Smith
	Kiss and Tell	Shirley Temple, Robert Benchley
	Murder, He Says	Fred MacMurray, Helen Walker
	Pardon My Past	Fred MacMurray, Marguerite Chapman
	A Thousand and One Nights	Cornel Wilde, Evelyn Keyes
	What Next, Corporal Hargrove?	Robert Walker, Keenan Wynn
1946	*Because of Him*	Deanna Durbin, Charles Laughton
	The Bride Wore Boots	Barbara Stanwyck, Robert Cummings
	Cluny Brown	Jennifer Jones, Charles Boyer
	The Kid from Brooklyn	Danny Kaye, Virginia Mayo
	Our Hearts Were Growing Up	Gail Russell, Diana Lynn
	People Are Funny	Jack Haley, Philip Reed
	Rendezvous with Annie	Eddie Albert, Faye Marlowe
	So Goes My Love	Myrna Loy, Don Ameche
	Two Guys from Milwaukee	Jack Carson, Dennis Morgan
	Without Reservations	Claudette Colbert, John Wayne
1947	*The Bachelor and the Bobby Soxer*	Cary Grant, Shirley Temple
	The Bishop's Wife	Cary Grant, Loretta Young
	The Egg and I	Claudette Colbert, Fred MacMurray
	The Farmer's Daughter	Loretta Young, Joseph Cotton
	The Ghost and Mrs. Muir	Gene Tierney, Rex Harrison
	The Late George Apley	Ronald Colman, Peggy Cummins
	Life with Father	William Powell, Irene Dunne
	Monsieur Verdoux	Charlie Chaplin, Mady Correll
	The Perils of Pauline	Betty Hutton, Billy De Wolfe
	The Secret Life of Walter Mitty	Danny Kaye, Virginia Mayo
1948	*The Bride Goes Wild*	June Allyson, Van Johnson
	Every Girl Should Be Married	Cary Grant, Franchot Tone
	A Foreign Affair	Marlene Dietrich, Jean Arthur
	The Fuller Brush Man	Red Skelton, Janet Blair
	Mr. Blandings Builds His Dream House	Cary Grant, Myrna Loy
	My Dear Secretary	Laraine Day, Kirk Douglas
	One Touch of Venus	Ava Gardner, Robert Walker
	Romance on the High Seas	Jack Carson, Doris Day
	That Wonderful Urge	Tyrone Power, Gene Tierney
	Unfaithfully Yours	Rex Harrison, Linda Darnel
1949	*Adam's Rib*	Spencer Tracy, Katharine Hepburn
	Always Leave Them Laughing	Milton Berle, Virginia Mayo
	The Beautiful Blonde from Bashful Bend	Betty Grable, Rudy Vallee
	Everybody Does It	Paul Douglas, Celeste Holm
	I Was a Male War Bride	Cary Grant, Ann Sheridan
	Inspector General	Danny Kaye, Walter Slezak
	It Happens Every Spring	Ray Milland, Paul Douglas
	Kind Hearts and Coronets [English]	Alec Guinness in nine roles
	A Kiss for Corliss	Shirley Temple, David Niven
	Ma and Pa Kettle	Marjorie Main, Percy Kilbride

Among some of the other noteworthy comedies in the chart above: Edward G. Robinson (1893–1973), who often plays a menacing gangster, in 1944 starred in *Mr. Winkle Goes to War,* a touching picture about how the draft eventually affected all lives, including Robinson's character. *See Here, Private Hargrove* (1944) and *What Next, Corporal Hargrove?* (1945) humorously relate a series of anecdotes about an army enlisted man. And Cary Grant (1904–1986), whose name appears frequently in any list of films from the 1940s, stars in *Mr. Blandings Builds His Dream House* (1948), a rollicking tale about the frustrations of moving to and building in the newly fashionable suburbs of the postwar era. Grant also takes the lead in *I Was a Male War Bride* (1949), a screwball comedy about war brides, women from foreign countries who marry U.S. servicemen and thus gain the privileges of U.S. citizenship. The problem explored in this film revolves around the fact that Cary Grant claims to be the bride and the confusion that results.

In addition to the many individual comedy **movies** produced during the 1940s, a remarkable number of comedy series flourished. For example, the enormously popular Andy Hardy movies had begun in 1937 with *A Family Affair;* that film stars Mickey Rooney (b. 1920) as Andy and features Lionel Barrymore (1878–1954) as the wise, kindly Judge Hardy. Barrymore, however, would be replaced by Lewis Stone (1879–1953) for all the subsequent pictures, and Stone soon became identified with the role. Since the first outing did well, MGM released seven additional Andy Hardy titles during the last years of the 1930s. The studio's franchise continued its winning ways into the 1940s, and, between 1940 and 1946, MGM produced seven more motion pictures in the series.

The long-running series ostensibly concluded with *Love Laughs at Andy Hardy,* but MGM gathered much of the original cast yet again for a "family get-together in" 1958, *Andy Hardy Comes Home.* Between 1937 and 1958, the Andy Hardy movies totaled 16 features, and Mickey Rooney starred in them all.

The major radio networks, as well as some syndicating services, often took popular movie series and adapted them for broadcast. Between 1949 and 1953, Rooney and much of the original movie cast could be heard on *The Hardy Family,* a group of original radio scripts that continued the well-received stories about Andy, his household, and his pals in half-hour segments.

Pretty much forgotten today, but popular in the early 1940s, the character of Henry Aldrich provided competition for the better-known Andy Hardy. The series grew out of

TABLE 29.   The Andy Hardy Movies, 1940–1946

Year	Film Titles	Stars
1940	*Andy Hardy Meets Debutante*	Mickey Rooney, Judy Garland (1922–1969)
1941	*Andy Hardy's Private Secretary*	Rooney, Kathryn Grayson (b. 1922)
	Life Begins for Andy Hardy	Rooney, Garland
1942	*The Courtship of Andy Hardy*	Rooney, Donna Reed (1921–1986)
	Andy Hardy's Double Life	Rooney, Esther Williams (b. 1921)
1944	*Andy Hardy's Blonde Trouble*	Rooney, Lee and Lyn Wilde (twins, b. 1922)
1946	*Love Laughs at Andy Hardy*	Rooney, Lina Romay (b. 1922)

a 1938 Broadway play by Clifford Goldsmith (1899–1971) called *What a Life*. It deals with the ups and downs of being a teenager. Several entertainment figures saw promise in the production, and soon thereafter Paramount Pictures had secured rights to it. With an eye to offering a choice between the Andy Hardy films, which rival MGM owned, and their own adolescent series, Paramount cast the likeable Jackie Cooper (b. 1922) as Henry.

What a Life did well enough that the studio in 1941 ordered a sequel, *Life with Henry*, again featuring Cooper. Audiences also enjoyed the youthful shenanigans of the main character, even with the direct competition of Mickey Rooney in the ongoing MGM pictures, and thus was born a new series. Nine more Henry Aldrich movies came out between 1941 and 1944, with Jimmy Lydon (b. 1923), who replaced Cooper, playing Henry in all of them. By the last one, *Henry Aldrich's Little Secret*, the stories had run out of steam, and Paramount wisely let the series die.

Movie producers were not the only ones interested in Goldsmith's *What a Life*. The National Broadcasting Company (NBC) also acquired rights to the characters in the play. The network introduced *The Aldrich Family* in the summer of 1939; it remained with NBC until 1944, when the Columbia Broadcasting System briefly ran the show from 1944 until 1946. In the world of broadcasting, changes occurred frequently, and NBC regained *The Aldrich Family* later in 1946, keeping the property until 1953, when the networks dropped almost all continuing programming in the face of **television.**

A humorous series, the show witnessed a constantly changing cast, especially during the war years, when many young men were drafted and had to go into service. One constant, however, remained through most of its history: for over a dozen years, Jell-O sponsored the broadcasts. Perhaps the best-remembered part of *The Aldrich Family* came at the opening, when a stern-sounding woman's voice cried out, "Hen-ree, Henry Aldrich!" A squeaky adolescent male voice would then reply, "Coming, Mother." Both the movies and the radio show recalled a simpler, more innocent time in the nation's history.

Cartoonist Murat "Chic" Young (1901–1973) in 1930 created a newspaper comic strip he called *Blondie*. Within a few years, this domestic comedy about Dagwood and

TABLE 30. The Henry Aldrich Movies, 1939–1944

Year	Film Title	Stars
1939	*What a Life*	Jackie Cooper
1941	*Life with Henry*	Jackie Cooper
	Henry Aldrich for President	Jimmy Lydon
1942	*Henry and Dizzy*	Jimmy Lydon
	Henry Aldrich, Editor	Jimmy Lydon
1943	*Henry Aldrich Gets Glamour*	Jimmy Lydon
	Henry Aldrich Swings It	Jimmy Lydon
	Henry Aldrich Haunts a House	Jimmy Lydon
1944	*Henry Aldrich, Boy Scout*	Jimmy Lydon
	Henry Aldrich Plays Cupid	Jimmy Lydon
	Henry Aldrich's Little Secret	Jimmy Lydon

Blondie Bumstead had attracted an immense readership, making it the most popular strip of its day, a position it would hold throughout the 1940s. The couple's daily adventures have continued into the present, under different writers and artists, in hundreds of **newspapers.** Surprisingly, it took Hollywood several years to realize the potential inherent in the series. Not until 1938, when Columbia Pictures acquired movie rights to the strip from King Features, did the transition from newspaper page to theater screen at last take place.

In a stroke of casting genius, Penny Singleton (1908–2003) received the part of Blondie, while Arthur Lake (1905–1987) played Dagwood. The two fit their roles perfectly, giving birth to one of the longest-lived series in movie history. Beginning with the release of *Blondie* in 1938, Columbia churned out an additional 27 features, and did

TABLE 31. The Blondie Movies, 1938–1950

Year	Film Titles
1938	*Blondie*
1939	*Blondie Meets the Boss* *Blondie Takes a Vacation* *Blondie Brings Up Baby*
1940	*Blondie on a Budget* *Blondie Has Servant Trouble* *Blondie Plays Cupid*
1941	*Blondie Goes Latin* *Blondie in Society*
1942	*Blondie Goes to College* *Blondie's Blessed Event* *Blondie for Victory*
1943	*It's a Great Life* *Footlight Glamour*
1945	*Leave it to Blondie*
1946	*Life with Blondie* *Blondie's Lucky Day* *Blondie Knows Best*
1947	*Blondie's Big Moment* *Blondie's Holiday* *Blondie in the Dough* *Blondie's Anniversary*
1948	*Blondie's Reward* *Blondie's Secret*
1949	*Blondie's Big Deal* *Blondie Hits the Jackpot*
1950	*Blondie's Hero* *Beware of Blondie*

not end the cycle until 1950 and the release of the last movie, *Beware of Blondie*. These numbers average out to just over 2 new releases a year, and 22 of the 28 were produced during the 1940s. Throughout the entire run, Singleton kept her role as Blondie and Lake his as Dagwood, giving each actor over a decade of steady employment but also severely limiting their availability for any other parts.

Back in 1930, Young initially created his character Blondie as a featherbrained, Roaring Twenties flapper; with the onset of the Great Depression just a few months later, such a figure seemed dated and out of place, and he wisely changed her into a struggling (but funny) middle-class housewife. Singleton plays her as the latter, but lets her flapper roots show through every so often. Both the comic strip and the many movies portray Dagwood as the stereotypical American husband, earnest and good-hearted, but bumbling and always a bit befuddled.

The radio networks, just as they had with Andy Hardy and Henry Aldrich, quickly developed a situation comedy series based on both the movies and the comic strip. *Blondie* premiered in 1939 on CBS. Although network affiliations shifted about during its run, *Blondie* remained on the air until 1950. Penny Singleton and Arthur Lake reprised their movie roles, and sound effects substituted for the sight gags on the comic strip and movies.

Paramount Pictures in 1940 released a spirited comedy called *Road to Singapore*. It features two of the studio's biggest stars, Bing Crosby (1903–1977) and Bob Hope (1903–2003). For insurance, the picture also has the comely Dorothy Lamour (1914–1996), often clad in a sarong, an outfit that became something of a trademark for the actress. The trio made a winning combination and produced an unexpected box office hit. Paramount wasted no time and in 1941 put the three stars in *Road to Zanzibar* (1941) and thereby started a series that would have audiences laughing throughout the 1940s and beyond. The following year, 1942, saw *Road to Morocco* and, after a slight pause, *Road to Utopia* in 1945. Crosby-Hope-Lamour closed out the decade with 1947's *Road to Rio*. But the Road pictures came back in 1952 with *Road to Bali* and, a decade later, the three, considerably longer in the tooth by then, romped through *The Road to Hong Kong* (1962), the final entry in this successful venture.

In these seven movies, a sensible plot takes a back seat to the steady stream of one-liners, sight gags, slapstick, and songs that characterize the series. Hope and Crosby, out of money and stranded in exotic locales—usually Paramount lots or other sites in Southern California—bicker over the favors of Lamour while at the same time scheming to get some quick cash and outsmarting villains who likewise ogle their lovely costar. Silly, zany stuff, formulaic in the extreme, but good, escapist fun, particularly during the dark war years, the Road pictures offered an effective antidote to the grim headlines of the day.

Bing Crosby, Bob Hope, and Dorothy Lamour could also be seen in many other pictures at this time. Most were light musical comedies, such as *Birth of the Blues* (1941), *Blue Skies* (1946), and *Top o' the Mornin'* (1949) for Crosby, to name just a few. And Crosby could be heard on the radio almost daily, because many of his recordings became hits and received considerable airplay. Although he could not boast top-selling recordings, Hope nevertheless starred in comedic vehicles like *Caught in the Draft* (1941), *Monsieur Beaucaire* (1946), and *Sorrowful Jones,* among many others. Almost as busy as her two costars, Dorothy Lamour had featured roles in movies like *Beyond the Blue Horizon* (1942), *Masquerade in Mexico* (1945), *the Lucky Stiff* (1949), and more. The Road pictures, however, marked a high spot in American comedy, and most of the credit for that success goes to the three stars.

In addition to the several comedy series that played theaters in the 1930s, an offshoot—the comedy team—also attracted considerable attention. At times, teams and series went together, as with Bob Hope, Bing Crosby, Dorothy Lamour, and the Road pictures. The three actors can be thought of as a team (although each undertook projects in which the other two did not play a part), and the Road format can be a series.

Most comedy teams, however, linked two or three players together; the movies they made might have no discernable connection beyond humor. For example, comedians Bud Abbott (1895–1974) and Lou Costello (1906–1959) had both worked in vaudeville and burlesque but did not meet until 1931, when Abbott substituted for another performer in Costello's vaudeville act. They then teamed up, with Abbott playing the ostensible straight man in their routines and Costello acting the clown. Some success in radio led to a movie contract with Universal Pictures, and the two made their screen debut in 1940 with *One Night in the Tropics,* a runaway box office hit.

Success begets more movies, and the now-hot team of Abbott and Costello began turning out one Universal comedy after another, and the ticket-buying public could not get enough of their jokes, puns, and slapstick antics. The team early on even made a trio of movies honoring the services in their own hilarious way. With *Buck Privates* (1941; the army), *In the Navy* (1941; the navy), and *Keep 'em Flying* (1941; the Army Air Corps), the pair are shown as enlistees in each of these branches. While they do their best to upset military routine, the pictures ultimately salute the armed services and might have seemed reassuring just prior to the outbreak of hostilities.

As Table 32 suggests, with 25 feature films during the 1940s, Abbott and Costello must have been as busy as Penny Singleton and Arthur Lake laboring over at neighboring Columbia Pictures with an almost equal number of *Blondie* comedies. Although several of the titles intimate that the war might play some role in the plotting, for the most part these particular tales simply mean that military subjects have become grist for their comedy mill. In no way do the pictures ever become topical. With the various armed services a part of everyday American life, the comedians utilize them for laughs, not for any serious treatment of wartime hardships.

More madcap, more slapstick than even Abbott and Costello were the endless shorts churned out by the Three Stooges. (A short, in movie parlance, usually runs 10 to 25 minutes in length and thus plays for a briefer time than the usual 60- to 90-minute feature film.) A trio of comedians that initially made its mark in the vaudeville circuit during the 1920s, the original Stooges consisted of Moe Howard (1897–1975), his brother Shemp Howard (1895–1955), and Larry Fine (1902–1975). Shemp moved on to other comedic roles elsewhere in the early 1930s, and a third brother, Curly Howard (1903–1952), replaced him. But Curly suffered a stroke in 1947, an occurrence that caused Shemp to rejoin the group for the remainder of the decade. Beset with health problems and the deaths of both Curly and Shemp in the early 1950s, the troupe struggled. Other comedians stepped into the vacant roles, but the Three Stooges came to an end as an active attraction in 1970.

During the 1930s, they made over 40 pictures and established their appeal among both young and old. The 1940s saw them working at a furious pace, releasing 76 shorts in a

TABLE 32. Representative Abbott and Costello Movies, 1941–1949

Year	Film Titles
1941	Buck Privates
	In the Navy
	Keep 'em Flying
	Hold That Ghost
1942	Ride 'Em Cowboy
	Rio Rita
	Pardon My Sarong
	Who Done It?
1943	It Ain't Hay
	Hit the Ice
1944	In Society
	Lost in a Harem
1945	Here Come the Co-Eds
	The Naughty Nineties
	Abbott and Costello in Hollywood
1946	Little Giant
	The Time of Their Lives
1947	Buck Privates Come Home
	The Wistful Widow of Wagon Gap
1948	The Noose Hangs High
	Abbott and Costello Meet Frankenstein (costarring Bela Lugosi and Lon Chaney Jr.)
	Mexican Hayride
1949	Africa Screams
	Abbott and Costello Meet the Killer, Boris Karloff (costarring Boris Karloff)

brief 10 years. They hardly rested during the 1950s, with 72 additional titles, and finally slowed down only in the 1960s. In all, the Three Stooges made close to 200 films—too numerous to list here—all of them shorts and always with the same studio, Columbia Pictures. The totals also do not include the guest appearances they made in many other movies. The Stooges focused on broad, physical humor—the thumb in the eye, the twisted nose or ear, and gags galore, usually accompanied by their trademark laugh, "Nyuk, nyuk." During the war, the Stooges actually made a few movies with topical overtones. At the Axis' expense, titles like *You Nazty Spy* (1940), *I'll Never Heil Again* (1941), *They Stooge to Conga* (1943), and similar groaning puns pricked the pomposity of Hitler and his cronies. For the most part, however, the team laughed at the world in general and themselves in particular, and the moviegoing world laughed with them.

Popular for over 30 years, the Stooges have attained a certain cult status in more recent times. Their many films enjoy renewed life on television and as DVD rentals and purchases. Boxed sets that chronologically track their output have proved particularly popular.

Other comedy teams likewise strove to satisfy the public's seemingly bottomless desire to be amused. The Marx Brothers—Groucho (1890–1977), Harpo (1888–1964), and Chico (1887–1961—such big hits in the 1930s, soldiered on with *Go West* (1940), *The Big Store* (1941), *A Night in Casablanca* (1946), and *Love Happy* (1949), but age had caught up with them, at least for physical comedy. Tepid affairs, the manic humor that had characterized their earlier efforts was gone.

Similarly, the great team of Stan Laurel (1890–1965) and Oliver Hardy (1892–1957) tried a few additional films in the 1940s—*Great Guns* (1941), *Air Raid Wardens* (1943), *Jitterbugs* (1943), and others—but few of their efforts measured up to the comedy shorts they had been making for the previous quarter century, both silents and talkies. Like their contemporaries the Marx Brothers, Laurel and Hardy had passed their prime.

On the other hand, the East Side Kids, who metamorphosed into the later Bowery Boys, seemed ageless and made dozens of pictures between 1940 and 1958. This group of unruly teens started their movie lives as the Dead End Kids, making their screen debut in 1937 in a film adaptation of the decidedly unfunny 1935 play, *Dead End,* by Sidney Kingsley (1906–1995). Success led Warner Bros., their parent studio, to produce an additional six pictures, with more and more of their antics played for laughs. At the same time, much of the cast split their talents as Little Tough Guys (12 movies, plus 3 serials), a rival series from Universal, with their last effort coming in 1943.

Monogram Pictures, a small studio specializing in cheap Westerns and crime stories, saw opportunity with this format and offered contracts to most of the original players and proceeded in 1940 to create the East Side Kids, an obvious spin-off of all the foregoing material. Audiences apparently enjoyed these movies about youthful street gangs, because Monogram released 22 East Side Kids features. In 1946, the studio dropped the property, only to rush into production a new series with many of the same actors called the Bowery Boys. Far and away the most successful of these youth-oriented comedy-dramas, new features with the Bowery Boys played in theaters until 1958, with a total of 48 titles.

Through all the name and studio changes, a handful of actors performed in the majority of these movies. Chief among them, and probably the best remembered, would be Leo Gorcey (1917–1969). He devised the idea for the Bowery Boys and starred in 41 features. By 1945, the East Side Kids were no longer kids (most were at least in their mid-twenties), and Gorcey proposed a new series that reflected these changes. The emphasis would be more on comedy, not poverty and youthful disagreements with parents. Huntz Hall (1919–1999) costarred with Gorcey, the two playing Slip and Sach, and they wore suits and hung out at an ice cream parlor, not in tatters on the East River docks as in the earlier series. Billy Halop (1920–1976) and Bernard Punsly (1923–2004), familiar faces from the Dead End and East Side Kids days, did not make the change to the Bowery Boys, but the equally well-known Gabriel Dell (1919–1988) and Bobby Jordan (1923–1965) did, and they became regulars. In all, the Dead End Kids, the Little Tough Guys, the East Side Kids, and the Bowery Boys could claim a combined total of 89 motion pictures.

One final comedy team merits brief mention: Martin and Lewis. In the spirit of Abbott and Costello, crooner Dean Martin (1917–1995) teamed up with writer-comedian Jerry Lewis (b. 1926) in the late 1940s. They made their joint film debut in 1949 in

TABLE 33. Representative Titles in the Dead End Kids, Little Tough Guys, East Side Kids, and Bowery Boys Film Series, 1937–1958

Year	Movie Title	Studio	Actors
The Dead End Kids			
1938	*Angels with Dirty Faces*	Warner Bros.	Leo Gorcey, Huntz Hall, Billy Halop, Bernard Punsly, Gabriel Dell, Bobby Jordan
1939	*The Angels Wash Their Faces*	Warner Bros.	Gorcey, Hall, Halop, Punsly, Dell, Jordan
The Little Tough Guys			
1940	*You're Not So Tough*	Universal	Hall, Halop, Punsly, Jordan
1942	*Tough as They Come*	Universal	Hall, Halop, Punsly
The East Side Kids			
1943	*Ghosts on the Loose*	Monogram	Gorcey, Hall, Jordan
1944	*Block Busters*	Monogram	Gorcey, Hall, Dell
The Bowery Boys			
1946	*Bowery Bombshell*	Monogram	Gorcey, Hall, Jordan
1949	*Angels in Disguise*	Monogram	Gorcey, Hall, Dell
1953	*Jalopy*	Monogram	Gorcey, Hall

My Friend Irma, a less than dazzling picture adapted from the popular radio show of the same name. Billed below Marie Wilson (1916–1972), who also played Irma on radio, their antics—Martin served as the straight man to Lewis's clown—garnered them enough recognition to do another Irma movie in 1950. After that, 14 more Martin and Lewis comedies followed, and the two took off as one of the hottest new acts in show business. They stayed together until 1956, hardly a lengthy partnership, but their style echoed all the best Hollywood comedy teams of the past.

Despite a war and despite the readjustments of the postwar period, Hollywood dispensed a steady stream of comedy films. Seldom topical, these pictures show why some referred to the movie industry as a dream factory. For the 75 or 90 minutes of a feature film, audiences could escape the harsh realities of a war-torn world.

See also: ASCAP vs. BMI Radio Boycott and the AFM Recording Ban; Broadway Shows (Comedy and Drama); Comic Strips; Football; Serial Films; Westerns (Film)

Selected Reading
Dale, Alan. *Comedy Is a Man in Trouble: Slapstick in American Movies.* Minneapolis: University of Minnesota Press, 2000.
Dunning, John. *On the Air: The Encyclopedia of Old-Time Radio.* New York: Oxford University Press, 1998.
Durgnat, Raymond. *The Crazy Mirror: Hollywood Comedy and the American Image.* New York: Dell, 1969.
Harvey, James. *Romantic Comedy in Hollywood.* New York: Da Capo Press, 1998.

COMIC BOOKS

Scholars and fans alike agree: the 1940s stand as a high point—some go so far as to call the period a golden age—in the evolution of the American comic book. The combined influences of newspaper **comic strips,** existing comic books, pulp **magazines,** and Big Little Books in the early 1930s; the popularity of movie and **radio** serials in mid-decade; along with unparalleled character innovation in the later years brought about the success of this new form of periodical. A brief discussion of this fruitful time will place the rapid rise of the 1940s comic book in context.

During the earlier years of the 20th century, attempts had been made to reprint popular newspaper comics in booklet form, but there existed no concerted effort to market and popularize comic books. The 1933 publication of *Funnies on Parade,* a giveaway featuring several popular cartoon characters then running in daily papers, proved a milestone, but it existed as a one-shot publication. *Funnies on Parade* did, however, lead other publishers to consider similar collections, but not necessarily for free. These occasional publications tended to be expensive, costing from 25 cents to 75 cents an issue (approximately $3.75 to $11.35 in 2008 dollars), and thus their appeal remained limited. The content they took from the **newspapers** covered the whole gamut of series, from humorous (*The Katzenjammer Kids, Mickey Mouse, Mutt and Jeff, Smitty,* many others) to serial (*The Gumps, Little Annie Rooney, Little Orphan Annie, Winnie Winkle,* others) to adventure (*Buck Rogers, Smilin' Jack, Tarzan,* **Terry and the Pirates,** others).

In the meantime, *Famous Funnies* appeared on newsstands in 1934. The periodical generally accepted as the first modern comic book, *Famous Funnies* carried a cover price of a dime; not cheap, but a manageable sum (approximately $1.55 in 2008 dollars). It contained 64 pages, mainly reprints from Sunday newspapers, and fared well. Publishers and the public accepted both the price and the length, thus creating standards for comic books that carried into the 1940s. Soon, titles like *Ace Comics, The Comics, Comics on Parade, Crackajack Funnies, The Funnies, King Comics, New Comics, Popular Comics, Super Comics,* and *Tip Top Comics* were tempting customers, mainly youngsters with change in their pockets. Most of these newcomers offered a mix of newspaper reprints and new, original material, and they all contained bright, garish color, another quality of this unique popular art form.

By 1938, the combined sales of comic books exceeded 2 million yearly copies. To meet this demand, publishers continued to cannibalize the newspaper strips, they raided the files of Big Little Books, and they adapted and illustrated the plots of numerous B Westerns then playing theaters. Wisely, they also hired cartoonists and writers, many of them veterans from the newspaper strips and pulp magazines that then flourished and allowed these staffers to create "All New! All Original!" comic books.

The break from reprinting previously published material marked a significant change. For example, the newspaper popularity of *Dick Tracy* prompted *Detective Comics* in 1937. Instead of copying runs of the famous policeman's exploits, the publishers ran completely new stories created by their own staff. Similarly, *New Comics,* which premiered in 1935, altered its name to *New Adventure Comics* a year or so later and finally dropped the "*New*" in 1938 to become *Adventure Comics.* More and more, comic books turned their attention to action and suspense with tales that read like illustrated versions of pulp fiction. Two young men, writer Jerry Siegel (1914–1996) and artist Joe Shuster (1914–1992), could be found on the roster of publishers working within this innovative area. Functioning as a team, their early creations only hinted at where they would eventually go in the industry, but they typified the eager newcomers moving into comic book art.

In the early 1930s, Siegel and Shuster had created a character they called Superman, but editors were not ready for such a protagonist; the concept languished and the two cartoonists took on other series to make ends meet. Finally, *Action Comics,* accurately sensing that readers liked larger-than-life heroes, decided to give **Superman** a chance in the June 1938 issue. The cover shows him attired in blue tights and a flowing red cape, single-handedly lifting a car over his head, but his name remains conspicuously absent, and the publishers buried the story within the pages of the comic book. The issue sold reasonably well (an original copy has today become a priceless collectible), and in 1939 the first solo *Superman* comic rolled off the presses.

Soon after that pioneering issue of *Action Comics,* other oddly costumed crime fighters started to appear on the pages of the adventure comics, setting the stage for the 1940s. A comic book called *Funny Pages*—although some of its stories could hardly be called funny—featured *The Arrow* in the fall of 1938. Written and drawn by Paul Gustavson (1916–1977), the Arrow turned out to be a skillful archer who went around in a shapeless shroud in order to hide his identity. At about the same time, *The Green Hornet,* a popular afternoon radio serial that had premiered in 1936 (it would run until 1952), caught the attention of cartoonist Jim Chambers (n.d.). The man called the Green Hornet, loosely based on **The Lone Ranger** of both radio and later comic fame, has a secret identity, wears a distinctive outfit, and has access to sophisticated weaponry. With that character clearly in mind, Nodell drafted *The Crimson Avenger* for *Detective Comics* in 1938. A twin to radio's *Green Hornet,* the Avenger wears a mask and a flowing cape. The Avenger might have lacked Superman's extraordinary physical powers, but he nonetheless resembled the Man of Steel in many ways. Little did these pioneer artists realize they had initiated a new trend in comic books.

Reluctant to miss what appeared a sure bet, *Wonder Comics* introduced Wonder Man in May of 1939, but his comic life proved short. The publishers of *Superman* claimed copyright infringement and promptly squashed the new hero. But *Detective Comics,* already the owners of *Superman,* felt free to introduce *The Batman* (the publishers soon dropped the article from the title) in early 1939. Created by Bob Kane (1915–1998), this mysterious Batman, also called the Caped Crusader, possesses no superhuman traits but instead relies on superb physical skills and soon emerged a favorite in the 1940s and beyond.

The Batman, in reality wealthy playboy Bruce Wayne, prowls Gotham City (at first identified as New York City but dropped in favor of the more generic "Gotham City" in later adventures) at night, the nemesis of any criminals. In 1940, he gains a faithful companion in Robin, the Boy Wonder, who serves as a pint-sized version of Batman himself. More acrobats than superheroes, the two battle some memorable villains, such as Catwoman, the Joker, the Penguin, and the Riddler. In no time, *Batman* comics had established a niche for yet another larger-than-life character.

Thus, when the new decade opened, a small army of comic book characters granted amazing attributes competed for attention. Marvel Comics, premiered late in 1939 with several characters, such as the Human Torch and Sub-Mariner. Usually associated with action-filled adventures, Marvel promptly entered into competition with DC Comics, the label that had introduced Superman. But by mid-1941, over 100 different titles vied for customer dimes, and the total continued to grow. Blackhawk, Bulletman, Captain America, Captain Marvel, Minute-Man, The Sandman, Spy Smasher, Wonder Woman, along with a much larger number who remain forgotten, constituted this burgeoning branch of the comic book business. Their roots may have been initially planted in the early 1930s and an emphasis on fighting crime, but they soon took on the Axis in the days following the attack on Pearl Harbor. These characters embody most of the dominant themes of action-oriented comic books during the first half of the 1940s. Superman and his force of super cohorts would see to it that the country made it through both World War II and any postwar threats.

Given the chaotic nature of the comic book business, accurate dates for a character's debut or ultimate demise are notoriously hard to come by. In many cases, the dates listed above reflect generalizations based on the comments of scholars and fans or publicity releases from publishers. Many characters seemingly disappear from comic books only to be reincarnated in later editions. In the dates supplied, "present" means these characters reappeared in the 1990s and the first decade of the 21st century, but significant gaps in chronology have doubtless occurred. It would be incorrect to surmise that *Blackhawk,* et al., had unbroken publishing runs from the 1940s until now.

To maximize their characters' visibility, publishers would often link superheroes in joint adventures. In addition, their many youthful comrades—Bucky, Domino, Robin, Sandy, Toro, and so on—occasionally enjoyed exploits independent of their more mature counterparts. For example, *Young Allies* and *Boy Commandos,* comic titles that sold well on newsstands during World War II, recount the escapades of daring bands of boys, led by the likes of Captain America's Bucky and the Human Torch's Toro, as they take on Axis forces.

The deeds of all these heroes, young and old, soon seemed pretty tame and repetitious with such a glut of new characters. Despite steadily rising sales for comic books throughout the decade, publishers grew fearful that buyers would weary of too many superheroes. They became hard to differentiate—what unusual gimmick would a new entry have that had not already been attempted in an earlier comic? Plus they lost a convenient enemy when the Axis went down to defeat in 1945—and so the industry searched for new avenues to explore. The conflict nevertheless lingered in many comics as publishers sought to use up a backlog of war-related stories, but changes also became apparent.

Pretty girls, usually in distress and in provocative clothing and poses, began to populate postwar comic books, always a sure lure for older male readers. Beautiful women dressed in leopard skins also appeared among the many new titles coming out in the second half of the decade. *Sheena, Queen of the Jungle* probably stands out as the most successful of this particular approach to cartooning. Clearly, in an attempt to broaden their audience, publishers gave a medium originally intended for children some distinctly adult overtones. Amid mounting criticism from parents and critics, however, the

TABLE 34. Some Representative Superheroes of the 1940s

Name	Features	Approximate Dates
Black Cat	The alter ego of fictional screen star and stuntwoman Linda Turner, this fast-paced adventure series debuted in 1941. "The Cat" rides a motorcycle and boasts a black belt in judo. Most of her adventures involve battling spies and saboteurs, but she provided some gender contrast from all the male superheroes then beginning to populate comic books.	1941–1950s
Blackhawk	Created in 1942 as one of many characters in *Military Comics* ("Stories of the Army and Navy"). A refugee Polish pilot, Blackhawk joins with others that have escaped Axis terror and launches a guerilla war; he and his cohorts fly in exquisitely drawn aircraft (Grumman XF5F Skyrockets) sure to fascinate youthful male readers. Not until the 1950s did he acquire his first jet aircraft. For many years, Blackhawk was accompanied by Chop-Chop, a stereotyped Chinese sidekick.	1942 to present
The Blue Beetle	Wears an invulnerable chain-mail costume, takes Vitamin "2X" for his powers.	1939 to present
Bulletman	Clad in tights and with a bullet-like helmet of his own design, this hero can fly and deflect oncoming bullets. He has a companion, Bulletgirl.	1940 to present
Captain America	One of the more successful superheroes of the decade. This red-white-and-blue-clad warrior, called Steve Rogers in civilian life, symbolized the patriotic fervor surrounding World War II. Bucky Barnes serves as his fearless boy companion.	1941 to present
Captain Marvel	Nicknamed "The Big Red Cheese" by his arch-foe, Dr. Sivana, this slightly self-satirical character proved to be one of the most popular creations of the decade, even outselling Superman in some years. Drawn by C. C. Beck (1910–1989), the plot reveals that Captain Marvel is in reality a boy named Billy Batson, who, by uttering the magical word "SHAZAM!" becomes a superhero, complete with the requisite tights and cape. Billy's sister joined the series in late 1942 as Mary Marvel, and there was even a Captain Marvel Junior, another boy about Billy's age. Captain Marvel's favorite expression is "Holy moley!"	1940 to present
Captain Midnight	Adapted from a successful radio serial, the comic book version thrusts Midnight into war against the Axis powers. More human than most superheroes, Midnight relies on an array of exotic weapons for his battles. Also a 1942 movie serial.	1941–1948
The Flame	Controls his own body temperature to the point that he bursts into flames and burns through barriers; also able to transport himself anywhere in the form of fire. Not surprisingly, his most dangerous foe is water. He is often accompanied by Flame Girl, a young woman possessing similar powers.	1939–1942
The Flash	Endowed with blinding speed, he wears a small helmet with wings, just like Mercury of mythology.	1940–1949

Name	Features	Approximate Dates
The Green Mask	Despite an unusual costume, the hero relies on guns as much as feats of derring-do. Later in the series, exposure to "Vita Rays" endows him with superpowers. He has a youthful companion, Domino.	1939–1941
The Human Torch	A "synthetic man," he ignites in the presence of oxygen. Toro, his young assistant, accompanies him. In the 1940s, he often appeared alongside Sub-Mariner.	1939 to present
Plastic Man	An amusing, if not surreal, character, expertly drawn by Jack Cole (1914–1958). Plastic Man can stretch himself to ludicrous shapes and sizes, and his adventures are billed as "Packed with thrills, chills, and laffs!"	1941 to present
The Sandman	The alter ego of Wesley Dodds, the Sandman dispenses justice by spraying criminals with a gas that puts them to sleep. In 1939, he had no costume (he wears a business suit) and no extraordinary powers, but in subsequent reincarnations, he metamorphoses into a superhero.	1939 to present
The Spirit	Created by renowned cartoonist Will Eisner (1917–2005), this figure first appeared in newspaper strips and entered the world of comic books in 1942. A crime fighter dressed in a suit, tie, and fedora, his costume consists of gloves and a tiny mask. His adventures, often against the evil Octopus, tend to be more oriented to adults than children. *The Spirit* has become one of the most enduring and endearing titles in comics.	1940 to present
Sub-Mariner	An angry hero named Prince Namor from beneath the sea, he wants revenge on humanity for destroying his home. During the World War II, however, he uses his powers, often in tandem with other Marvel characters, to wreak havoc on the Axis powers.	1939 to present
Wonder Woman	One of the few women in the comics with any staying power, Wonder Woman was created by William Moulton Marston (1893–1947; writing as Charles Moulton), a psychologist who wanted to depict strong women as a counter to the feminine stereotypes of the day. A bizarre series in every sense, from her bullet-deflecting bracelets to her Magic Lasso, Wonder Woman has nevertheless outlasted most of her competitors, male or female.	1941–1990s

"girlie" (a popular term from the 1940s, meaning teasing and alluring) comics began to disappear as the decade drew to a close.

Less oriented to pinup art, the countless comics devoted to romance, favorites among adolescent girls, flourished in the years following the war. Growing out of the popularity of radio soap operas, confession magazines, and romantic **movies,** titles like *Life Story, Sweethearts, Young Love,* and *Young Romance* quickly gained huge audiences anxious for something more adult than superheroes and funny animals. The stories followed the tried-and-true soap opera path: love, obstacles, and eventual resolution, but not before even more complications extended the anguish of the lovers.

In 1946, a little-heralded comic titled *Eerie* appeared on newsstands. Network radio had been enjoying considerable success with scary series such as *Escape, Inner Sanctum,*

Lights Out, Suspense, and *The Whistler.* Most of these radio shows had premiered in the early 1940s and continually boasted healthy ratings, a fact not unnoticed by comics editors. Horror had not been explored much by writers and cartoonists, aside from the predictable violence enacted in the superhero tales, and that tends to be so exaggerated—whack! thud! cra-a-ck! bang!—and relatively bloodless that it offended few readers. Plus the heroes always win, they will vanquish evil until the next issue, when order must again be restored. *Eerie* and its myriad successors would change all that.

The publishers moved warily into this new ground. *Eerie* existed as a single issue, not to reappear until the 1950s and the heyday of the horror comics. Instead, realistic crime stories made their appearance in the mid-1940s, with gore, murder, and death more graphically displayed than in the past. *Crime Does Not Pay* led the field, but titles like *Crime and Punishment, Crime Case Comics, Crimes by Women, Official True Crime Cases, Real Clue Crime Stories, True Crime Comics,* and a host of others with similar titles tempted buyers.

A relatively new organization, EC Comics (it had initially meant Educational Comics and then Entertaining Comics), raised the level of realism in crime—and later, horror—comics. Overseen by William M. Gaines (1922–1992), the company released *Crime SuspenStories* at the end of the decade. Featuring explicit frames of violence, both real and implied, along with drawings of maimed bodies, it set the stage for the onslaught of horror comics that characterized the early 1950s and helped lead to sensational books linking comics with **juvenile delinquency** and psychological ills, set off congressional investigations, and caused the industry to establish the Comics Code Authority in 1954 to fend off the massive backlash of criticism about the content of these once-innocuous 10-cent periodicals.

Despite the rocketing popularity of caped and masked superheroes during the early 1940s and the rise of crime and horror comics after that, many publishers stayed with tradition, at first mixing reprints and original materials and focusing on humor as their primary content. The terms "funnies" and "comics," used initially to describe newspaper offerings, summed up the thrust of most strips until the 1930s, when detectives like *Dick Tracy* and *Secret Agent X-9,* along with adventurers such as *Smilin' Jack* and *Wash Tubbs,* changed the tenor of the funny pages. But gags and humorous characters, plus countless anthropomorphic animals, continued to play a significant role in publishing, generating consistently strong sales throughout the 1940s.

For example, the Walt Disney (1901–1966) organization, boosted by a string of popular animated cartoons, branched into comic books in 1935 with Mickey Mouse. Reprints of the company's newspaper strips soon followed, and by 1943, original adventures with Donald Duck, Mickey and Minnie, Pluto, and the rest of the Disney menagerie vied for sales. During the 1940s, artist Carl Barks (1901–2000) gained renown for his portrayals of Donald Duck.

The Warner Bros. film studio, witnessing Disney's success, entered the publishing field in 1941 with comic book versions of its Looney Tunes and Merrie Melodies theatrical cartoons. Familiar characters like Bugs Bunny, Porky Pig, Elmer Fudd, and the other zanies from the studio enlivened a long-running series of comic books.

Similarly, Woody Woodpecker, Mighty Mouse, and Henry Aldrich moved from movie theaters to the pages of comic books. In the later 1940s, in an attempt to attract more teenaged readers that might be put off by characters from animal cartoons, publishers also added a number of new titles, like *Andy Hardy, Archie Andrews, Buzzy, Candy,* and *Hi-Jinx,* that starred high school adolescents as their main characters.

Collectively, all these influences coalesced to create a new national literature. Only a handful of comic book titles existed at the beginning of the 1940s, but by 1949, anywhere from 500 to 650 titles were issued monthly, making them a significant component of American popular culture. Legions of sociologists and critics have commented on the roles of such characters in American lives and fantasies, and much of their learned commentary concerns World War II and its aftermath. In all, comic books appealed to a broad audience, they played on basic American themes, and they proved enormously successful.

See also: Westerns (Film), Youth

Selected Reading
Daniels, Les. *Comix: A History of Comic Books in America.* New York: Bonanza Books, 1971.
Goulart, Ron. *Over Fifty Years of American Comic Books.* Lincolnwood, IL: Mallard Press, 1991.
Jones, Gerard. *Men of Tomorrow: Geeks, Gangsters, and the Birth of the Comic Book.* New York: Basic Books, 2004.
Savage, William W., Jr. *Comic Books and America, 1945–1954.* Norman: University of Oklahoma Press, 1990.

COMIC STRIPS

The golden age for the American newspaper comic strip took place during the 1930s and continued on into the 1940s. The funnies (as people usually referred to a newspaper's comic pages at that time) boasted a daily audience that reached into the millions, and even more readers perused the brightly colored Sunday comic supplements. Barely a half-century old in the 1940s, comic strips ranked among readers' favorite newspaper sections, holding their own against headlines and sports. No one wanted to be in the dark as far as the exploits of their favorite characters were concerned.

Although **comic books,** the younger siblings of the more venerable comic strips, received more publicity and stirred more controversy than did newspaper comics in the 1940s, they could not begin to match the estimated readership for the strips, even though they sold in the millions. By virtue of appearing as a regular part of a typical newspaper, far more people were exposed to comic strips than comic books could ever claim. With close to 1,800 different American **newspapers** published daily throughout the 1940s, and with collective circulation figures exceeding 50 million issues each and every day (and it must be assumed that many papers had more than one reader), a major proportion of the population received more or less constant exposure to a vast array of strips.

For ease of discussion and arrangement, the comics have been divided into three broad categories that have become accepted for the period: (1) humor, (2) family/continuity, and (3) action/adventure. At the turn of the century, most cartoonists presented humorous characters and situations, thus giving the medium the names funnies and comics. In time, strips with continuing story lines emerged, as did those that depicted both the serious and humorous sides of family life. By the late 1930s, a relatively

In 1930, cartoonist Chic Young created Dagwood and Blondie Bumstead as characters in a new daily newspaper comic strip. It skyrocketed to popularity, and movies about the family began appearing in 1938, with over 20 produced during the 1940s. This illustration shows a typical lobby card advertising one of the Blondie features. (Columbia Pictures/Photofest)

new kind of strip made deep inroads on the others when action and adventure stories featuring strong heroes caught the public fancy.

In their formative years, the funnies remained fiercely nontopical, but the Great Depression of the 1930s and the gathering clouds of World War II could not be completely ignored, and artists and writers began to throw off some of their neutrality. When the United States entered the conflict in December 1941, countless comic strips promptly sided with the Allied cause. Cartoonists did what they could to encourage support for the war, and for some that meant being drafted or personally enlisting. For example, Gus Arriola (1917–2008), George Baker (1915–1975), Dave Breger (1908–1970), and Alex Raymond (1909–1956) were among the many who served their country. If not on active duty themselves, they involved their characters in events, either on the home front or on distant battlefields. Buz Sawyer, Captain Easy, Skeezix (from *Gasoline Alley*), both Snuffy Smith and Barney Google, and Terry Lee (of **Terry and the Pirates**) publicly joined the service in the course of their stories, and Tillie the Toiler became a WAC (Women's Army Corps), to name just a few.

These fictional characters fought enemy forces, engaged spies and saboteurs or, if too young for that sort of thing, worked with scrap drives and hospitals in the war effort. Popeye served as the official "spokescharacter" for the U.S. Navy; beginning in mid-1941; the colorful sailor appeared in newspaper ads urging young men to enlist. Al Capp (1909–1979), creator of *Li'l Abner,* drew features for the Red Cross and Treasury Department in 1942. Cartoonist Harold Gray (1894–1968) had Little Orphan Annie encouraging thousands of youngsters to join her Junior Commandos and collect scrap, rubber, and discarded newspapers for defense industries. Some strips, however—especially the humorous ones—went their merry way and avoided direct references to ongoing events, but, given the overriding popularity of comics, no one complained. Plus they offered a pleasant respite from the grim realities of the war years.

An unintended consequence of related shortages and **rationing** involved shrinking the published size of a comic strip. With printing ink in limited supply and newsprint on ration lists, papers had to make do with less. That meant dropping less-popular strips and making the survivors smaller in order to take up less space. Large comic strips, so characteristic of the 1920s and 1930s, became a thing of the past. Layout staffs squeezed as many comics as they could onto a single page, a process that did not cease with the resumption of peace. By 1948, the price of newsprint had doubled from its wartime level, and cost-conscious editors cut every corner they could, a practice that has continued to the present.

The postwar years witnessed a gradual decline in the action/adventure genre; without a common enemy, many of the swashbuckling heroes had lost their primary reason for being. A number of strips came to an end; others did the best they could in peacetime. Audiences rediscovered humor strips—a gag a day—and many of the old originals kept on, while a host of new, more modern, series came along to fill in any gaps. In retrospect, the comics enjoyed a postwar boom, with over 100 new titles introduced in 1946 alone, and only about 40 being permanently dropped. In many ways, the American comic strip reinvented itself in the years following 1945. Anthropomorphic animals, silly characters in silly situations, and visual jokes made a return and gained immense popularity.

A number of classic series carried on from the early days of the genre. George McManus (1884–1954), who had begun drawing *Bringing Up Father* (known to many as *Maggie and Jiggs*) in 1913, continued his tales about a family of Irish immigrants in New York City in the early days of the 20th century. Deliberately nostalgic, he did not shatter reader expectations with sudden topicality. In like manner, both *The Katzenjammer Kids* (debuted in 1897) and *The Captain and the Kids* (1914) chronicled the endless shenanigans of Hans and Fritz, two boisterous lads forever embroiled in mischief. As the chart suggests with its dates, a number of other, older humorous comic strips also flourished during the 1940s; as long as their gags tickled enough funny bones and caused circulation to remain high, age seemed no drawback.

On the other hand, Krazy, Ignatz, and Offissa Pupp, the trio that stars in *Krazy Kat* and inhabits the delightfully imaginary Coconino County somewhere in the desert Southwest, said good-bye to millions of disappointed readers when cartoonist George Herriman (1880–1944) died. Thanks to syndication, many strips outlive their creators and seemingly go forever, but his genius could not be duplicated, a rarity in the world of comics. *Krazy Kat* has been preserved in a number of print anthologies, but it ceased appearing in newspapers in the mid-1940s.

Despite the loss of Herriman's work, several new and innovative strips came along that regaled a host of readers. *Barnaby,* a frankly experimental series by Crockett Johnson (1906–1975), told about a precocious little boy named Barnaby and his fairy godfather, Mr. O'Malley. As is often the case in stories of this type, adults—specifically, Barnaby's parents—deny the existence of O'Malley, a situation that leads to consternation, child psychology, and a number of other serious themes unusual in a humor strip. It ran for a decade and enjoyed many devoted followers, particularly older readers.

Walt Kelly (1913–1973), another poet of the funny pages, created his unique *Pogo* in 1949. The denizens of the Okefenokee Swamp—Pogo Possum, Albert the Alligator, Howland Owl, Churchy LaFemme, P. T. Bridgeport, and roughly several hundred other characters—serve as either regulars or drop-ins in this often satirical and political strip. Only *Li'l Abner* came close in the use of sarcasm and lampooning the high and mighty. Kelly had introduced some of his menagerie in comic books during the early 1940s, and he had also drawn editorial cartoons for a time. But *Pogo* remained a new and different creation and successfully ran for over a quarter of a century, proving that topicality could sell, even in a humor strip.

Finally, the comics had early on identified teenagers as a potential audience. As far back as 1912, with the introduction of Cliff Sterrett's (1883–1964) *Polly and Her Pals,* the world of adolescents emerged as a popular focus. Merrill Blosser (1892–1983) created *Freckles and His Friends* in 1915, and 1919 saw the debut of Carl Ed's (1890–1959) *Harold Teen.* With teenagers receiving increasing attention in the late 1930s and early 1940s, strips like Hilda Terry's (1914–2006) *Teena* in 1941, Harry Haenigsen's (1900–1991) *Penny* in 1943, and Bob Montana's (1920–1975) *Archie* in 1946 attested to the growing importance given teens, albeit in the form of humor.

The family and continuity strips—that is, stories with continuing characters and plots that usually carry over from day to day—gained increasing popularity in the years following World War I. Much in the spirit of **radio** soap operas, these tales moved at a sluggish pace, so if readers missed an episode or two, they could catch up in the days following with no real gaps in the storylines. The slow tempo, however, allowed fans to become familiar with the personalities and quirks of the people within the comic strip. It was not at all unusual for irate fans to write letters to editors complaining about the treatment of a figure within a story, or for birthday or holiday gifts to arrive at newspaper offices addressed to Orphan Annie or Blondie Bumstead because of reader identification with particular characters.

In 1945, a newspaper delivery strike in New York City prevented people from getting their daily comics. Never averse to a bit of publicity, Mayor Fiorello LaGuardia (1882–1947) rose to the occasion and read the funnies aloud over a city radio station, focusing especially on the continuity strips. Stations in other parts of the country often had staffers read the comics on Sunday mornings, more evidence of the enthusiastic mass audience these features enjoyed during the 1940s.

Among the leaders in continuity strips at this time were *Little Orphan Annie* and her look-alike, *Little Annie Rooney.* Orphan Annie has her dog Sandy, and Annie Rooney has Zero. Both are around 12 years in age, always on the move in order to escape cruel or evil adults, but Orphan Annie boasts a healthy right-wing cynicism about those around her, whereas Annie Rooney remains blissfully ignorant about the realities of the world. Of the two, Orphan Annie garnered more readers, and during the war years even dealt with all manner of Axis types. In the postwar era, mealy mouthed liberals and Communist sympathizers incur her not inconsiderable wrath.

After debuting in the Depression years as *Apple Mary,* a doughty older woman selling apples on a street corner, Mary Worth slowly rose in the world and evolved into a tireless solver of the romantic dilemmas of others. Clearly drawn from the immensely popular radio soap operas of the 1940s, *Mary Worth* found its niche among the funnies and has remained with the formula until the present.

In terms of longevity and consistency, few strips have ever come close to *Blondie.* As much a daily gag series as a family/continuity series, the trial and tribulations of Dagwood Bumstead, its real star, ran in more than 1,200 American newspapers at mid-century, a record. Created by Chic Young (1901–1973) in 1930, *Blondie* chronicled middle-class American family life during the 1940s as well and as accurately as any comic strip of its day. A long-running series of *Blondie* motion pictures (1938–1950), 28 **movies** in all, points to the strip's remarkable popularity.

TABLE 35. Representative American Humorous Comic Strips Published during the 1940s

Title	Artists/Writers during the 1940s	Total Years Published
Archie	Bob Montana (1920–1975)	1946 to present (comic book began in 1941)
Barnaby	Crockett, Johnson (b. David Johnson Leisk, 1906–1975)	1942–1952
Bringing Up Father (Maggie & Jiggs)	George McManus (1884–1954)	1913–2000
Bugs Bunny	Leon Schlesinger (1884–1965) credited, but (Roger Armstrong (1918–2007) ghosted the strip	1942–1993
Cap Stubbs and Tippie	Edwina Dumm (1893–1990)	1918–1966
The Captain and the Kids	Rudolph Dirks (1877–1968)	1914 (initially as *Hans und Fritz*)–1979
Debbie	Cecil Jensen (1902–1976)	1946 (initially as *Elmo*)–1961
Donald Duck	Walt Disney (1901–1966) credited, but Bob Karp (1911–1975) and Al Taliaferro (1905–1969) ghosted the strip	1934 to present
Etta Kett	Paul D. Robinson (1898–1974)	1925–1974
Felix the Cat	Otto Messmer (1892–1983)	1923–1967
Gordo	Gus Arriola (1917–2008)	1941–1985
Harold Teen	Carl Ed (1890–1959)	1919–1959
Henry	Carl Anderson (1965–1948) until 1942; thereafter, John J. Liney (1913–1982) on dailies, and Don Trachte (1915–2005) on Sundays	1934–1995
Hubert	Dick Wingert (1919–1993)	1945–1994
Just Kids	Ad Carter (1895–1957)	1923–1957
The Katzenjammer Kids	Harold H. Knerr (1882–1949)	1897 to present
Krazy Kat	George Herriman (1880–1944)	1913–1944
The Little King	Otto Soglow (1900–1975)	1934–1975
Little Mary Mixup	R. M. Brinkerhoff (1880–1958)	1917–1957
Male Call	Milton Caniff (1907–1988)	1942–1946
Mickey Mouse	Walt Disney (1901–1966) credited, but Floyd Gottfredson, (1907–1986) ghosted the strip	1930 to present
Mopsy	Gladys Parker (1910–1966)	1939–1965
Mutt and Jeff	Al Smith (1902–1982)	1907–1982
Nancy	Ernie Bushmiller (1905–1982)	1933 (initially as *Fritzi Ritz*) to present
Oaky Doaks	Ralph B. Fuller (1890–1963) and Bill Dyer (n.d.)	1935–1961
Penny	Harry Haenigsen (1900–1991)	1943–1970
Pete the Tramp	Charles D. Russell (1895–1963)	1932–1963
Pogo	Walt Kelly (1913–1973)	1948–1975
Private Breger	Lt. Dave Breger (1908–1970)	1942–1970 (renamed *Mr. Breger* in 1945)
Reg'lar Fellers	Gene Byrnes (1889–1974)	1917–1949

(continued)

TABLE 35. *(continued)*

Title	Artists/Writers during the 1940s	Total Years Published
Right Around Home	Dudley Fisher (1890–1951)	1938–1965 (Fisher added *Myrtle* to the series in 1941)
The Sad Sack	Sgt. George Baker (1915–1975)	1942–1958
Skippy	Percy L. Crosby (1891–1964)	1919–1945
Smitty	Walter Berndt (1899–1979)	1922–1974
Smokey Stover	Bill Holman (1903–1987)	1935–1973
Teena	Hilda Terry (1914–2006)	1941–1964 (initially as *It's a Girl's Life*)
Thimble Theatre Starring Popeye	Tom Sims (n.d.) and Bill Zaboly (1910–1985)	1919 to present
Toonerville Folks	Fontaine Fox (1884–1964)	1915–1955

Note: n.d. = no data available.

Three other women who made names for themselves in the comics were Winnie Winkle, Dixie Dugan, and Tillie Jones. Each personifies a working woman, a fitting topic during World War II, when millions of wives and girlfriends who had not previously been employed, took on defense jobs. But these three characters were pioneers as far as portraying strong, independent women. *Winnie Winkle the Breadwinner* first appeared in newspapers in 1920; *Tillie the Toiler* closely followed suit in 1921, whereas *Dixie Dugan* premiered in 1929. Young men, romance, and families concern them more than their occupations, but the workplace background gives them a particular relevance during the war. A 1926 silent feature, *Happy Days,* along with a number of shorts during that time, make up the *Winnie Winkle* filmography. *Tillie the Toiler,* released in 1941, attracted little notice (she had also been the subject of a 1927 silent film), nor did *Dixie Dugan* in 1943. Despite their lack of box office success, the mere fact that Hollywood attempted to create movies about these three characters again demonstrates the wide audience that followed their adventures.

Li'l Abner, the 1934 creation of cartoonist Al Capp, grew in popularity throughout the 1930s and 1940s. An inventive genius and a master of marketing, Capp carefully controlled anything that alluded to his hillbilly strip. His Sadie Hawkins Day, which first took place in 1937, skyrocketed in popularity during the 1940s, particularly on college campuses. His Shmoo, a lovable creature introduced in 1948, made millions as dolls and other salable paraphernalia. A movie version of the strip played theaters in 1940 and did a respectable business, although a series of cartoon shorts produced in 1944 did not fare as well. Broadcasters even attempted a *Li'l Abner* radio serial in 1939–1940, but something so visual did not successfully translate to the aural medium.

Relative newcomers to the comic pages, action/adventure strips quickly became familiar to millions during the 1930s and 1940s. As indicated in the chart below, a remarkable number of new series came along in the mid-1930s. Led by the likes of *Dick Tracy* (crime), *Flash Gordon* (science fiction), *The Phantom* (fantasy), *Terry and the Pirates* (adventure), and *Secret Agent X-9* (espionage), these newcomers brought realistic drawing to their frames and violence to their stories. Their humorous counterparts

TABLE 36. Representative American Family/Serial Continuity Comic Strips Published during the 1940s

Title	Artists/Writers during the 1940s	Years Published
Alley Oop	V. T. Hamlin (1900–1993)	1933 to present
Barney Google and Snuffy Smith	Billy DeBeck (1890–1942) until 1942; thereafter Fred Lasswell (1917–2001)	1919 to present
Blondie	Chic Young (1901–1973)	1930 to present
Bobby Sox	Marty Links (b. Martha Arguello, 1917–2008)	1944–1979
Boots and Her Buddies	Edgar Martin (1898–1960)	1924–1969
The Bungle Family	Harry J. Tuthill (1886–1957)	1918–1945
Clarence	Frank Fogarty (1887–1978) and Weare Holbrook (1896–1985)	1924–1949
Dixie Dugan	J. P. McEvoy (1929–1966) and John H. Striebel (1891–1962)	1928 (initially as *Show Girl*)–1966
Ella Cinders	Fred Fox (1902–1982) and others during the decade	1925–1961
Freckles and His Friends	Merrill Blosser (1892–1983)	1915–1971
Gasoline Alley	Frank King (1883–1969)	1918 to present
The Gumps	Gus Edson (1901–1966)	1917–1959
Jane Arden	Russell Ross (n.d.) and Monte Barrett (n.d.)	1928–1968
Li'l Abner	Al Capp (1909–1979)	1934–1977
Little Annie Rooney	Brandon Walsh (1883–1955) and Darrell McClure (1903–1987)	1929–1966
Little Orphan Annie	Harold Gray (1894–1968)	1924 to present
Mary Worth	Allen Saunders (1899–1986) and Ken Ernst (1918–1985)	1934 (initially as *Apple Mary*) to present
Mickey Finn	Lank Leonard (1896–1960)	1936–1976
Moon Mullins	Frank Willard (1893–1958)	1923–1993
Mr. and Mrs.	Clare Briggs (1875–1930) credited, but ghosted by various artists in the 1940s	1919–1963
Polly and Her Pals	Cliff Sterrett (1883–1964) credited, but ghosted by various artists in the 1940s	1912–1958
Tillie the Toiler	Russ Westover (1886–1966)	1921–1959
Tiny Tim	Stanley Link (1894–1957)	1931–1958
Toots and Casper	Jimmy Murphy (1892–1965)	1918–1956
Winnie Winkle	Martin Branner (1888–1970)	1920–1996

Note: n.d. = no data available.

continued to delight readers, but the action/adventure series offered novel-like complexities and a dark, shadowy environment, one that suggested the realities of the worrisome days leading up to World War II.

When the conflict embroiled the United States in 1941, these strips leaped into the fray, their heroes going full-blast against the Axis powers. Barney Baxter flew his airplanes in dogfights, Buz Sawyer did likewise for the navy, Flyin' Jenny became an ace test pilot, and superheroes like Superman and Batman took care of any villains the other characters might have overlooked.

TABLE 37. Representative American Action/Adventure Comic Strips Published during the 1940s

Title	Artists/Writers during the 1940s	Years Published
Barney Baxter	Frank Miller (1898–1949) until 1942; Bob Naylor (1910–n.d.), 1942–1946; Frank Miller, 1946–1949	1935–1950
Batman and Robin	Bob Kane (1916–1998) and Bill Finger (1914–1974)	1943–1946
Brenda Starr	Dale Messick (b. Dalia Messick, 1906–2005)	1940 to present (Sundays) 1945 to present (dailies)
Brick Bradford	William Ritt (1901–1972) and Clarence Gray (1911–1957)	1933–1987
Broncho Bill	Harry F. O'Neill (n.d.)	1928–1950
Buck Rogers	Dick Calkins (1895–1962) and Rick Yager (1912–1995)	1929–1967 (dailies) 1930–1967 (Sundays)
Buz Sawyer	Roy Crane (1901–1977)	1943–1989
Captain Easy	Roy Crane (1901–1977) until 1943; thereafter Leslie Turner (1899–1988)	1933–1988 (Sundays only; Easy was also a continuing character in Crane's daily *Wash Tubbs*)
Connie	Frank Godwin (1889–1959)	1927–1944
Dick Tracy	Chester Gould (1900–1985)	1931 to present
Dickie Dare	Coulton Waugh (1896–1973)	1933–1957
Don Winslow of the Navy	Frank V. Martinek (1895–1971) and Leon A. Beroth (1905–n.d.)	1934–1955
Flyin' Jenny	Russell Keaton (1910–1945) until 1945; thereafter Marc Swayze (n.d.) and Glenn Chaffin (1897–1978)	1939–1952
Flash Gordon	Alex Raymond (1909–1956) Sundays until 1944; then Austin Briggs (1909–1973) until 1948; then Mac Raboy (1916–1967); Briggs did the dailies 1940–1944	1934–2003
Invisible Scarlet O'Neil	Russell Stamm (1915–1969)	1940–1956
Joe Palooka	Ham Fisher (1901–1955)	1930–1984
Johnny Hazard	Frank Robbins (1917–1994)	1944–1977
Jungle Jim	Alex Raymond (1909–1956) until 1944; then John Mayo (n.d.) until 1948; Paul Norris (1914–2007) thereafter	1934–1954
Kerry Drake	Alfred Andriola (1912–1983)	1943–1983
King of the Royal Mounted	Jim Gary (1905–n.d.)	1935–1954
Little Joe	Bob Leffingwell (n.d.)	1933–1969
The Lone Ranger	Charles Flanders (1907–1973) and Fran Striker (1903–1962)	1938–1971
Mandrake the Magician	Lee Falk (1912–1999) and Phil Davis (1906–1964)	1934 to present
Mark Trail	Ed Dodd (1902–1991)	1946 to present
Miss Fury	Tarpe Mills (b. June Mills, 1915–1988)	1941 (Sundays only)–1952

Title	Artists/Writers during the 1940s	Years Published
Patsy	Charles Raab (n.d.) until 1942; followed by several others, and then Bill Dyer (n.d.)	1935–1956
The Phantom	Lee Falk (1912–1999) and Ray Moore (1905–1984); Moore left in 1941, replaced by Wilson McCoy (1902–1961)	1936 to present
Prince Valiant	Hal Foster (1892–1982)	1937 to present (Sundays only)
Radio Patrol	Eddie Sullivan (n.d.) and Charlie Schmidt (1917–1958)	1933–1950
Red Ryder	Fred Harmon (1902–1982) and Russ Winterbotham (1904–1971)	1938–1964 (Sundays) 1939–1964 (dailies)
Rip Kirby	Alex Raymond (1909–1956)	1946–1999
Scorchy Smith	Frank Robbins (1917–1994) until 1944; various artists followed	1930–1961
Secret Agent X-9	Mel Graff (1907–1975)	1934–1996
Smilin' Jack	Zack Mosley (1906–1993)	1933–1973
The Spirit	Will Eisner (1917–2005)	1941–1944
Steve Canyon	Milton Caniff (1907–1988)	1947–1988
Steve Roper	Allen Saunders (1899–1986) and Elmer Woggon (1898–1978); also several ghost artists in the 1940s	1936 (initially as *Big Chief Wahoo*; later *Steve Roper and Wahoo,* then *Steve Roper,* and *Steve Roper and Mike Nomad*)–2004
Superman	Wayne Boring (1916–1986)	1939–1966
Tarzan	Burne Hogarth (1911–1996), Sundays; Rex Maxon (1892–1970), dailies	1929–1972 (dailies), 2000 (Sundays)
Terry and the Pirates	Milton Caniff (1907–1988) until late 1946; George Wunder (1912–1987) thereafter	1934–1973
Tim Tyler's Luck	Lyman Young (1893–1984)	1928–1996
Wonder Woman	William Moulton Marston (1893–1947) and Harry G. Peter (1880–1958)	1941 (comic book) 1945–1946 (comic strip)

Note: n.d. = no data available.

In the meantime, cartoonist Chester Gould (1900–1985) enjoyed a field day creating grotesque adversaries for Dick Tracy to overcome. Many fans maintain the 1940s marked a highpoint for this strip, with evocatively named characters like B. B. Eyes, Flattop, Gargles, Measles, Mumbles, Pruneface, and Wormy doing their worst to get away with all kinds of crimes. Naturally, they never succeed, at least for long. Escapism all the way, yet Gould and *Dick Tracy* seldom missed an opportunity to inject topicality into the series, whether the subjects be Nazis, bureaucrats, or Communist sympathizers.

Police adventures also occupied Kerry Drake, an investigator created in 1943 by Alfred Andriola (1912–1983). But whereas Dick Tracy's world involves flying bullets and bizarre criminals, Drake's revolves around methodical detection, coolness under pressure, and a realistic drawing style that avoids the exaggerated stylistics favored by Gould.

With change in the air, Milton Caniff (1907–1988), who had created, in *Terry and the Pirates,* a memorable hero with Terry Lee, dropped the series in 1946 and instead introduced Steve Canyon, a suave adventurer for the postwar years. Able to hold his own in any situation and always ready with a quip, Canyon represents a change for action/adventure comics. With the war behind them, they must adapt to a new world, no less dark and threatening, but without the convenient Axis enemies. Alex Raymond (1909–1956) followed suit with *Rip Kirby,* and Allen Saunders (1899–1986) and Elmer Woggon (1898–1978) reinvented *Steve Roper,* an older series, so that it would more closely fit this new model that relies less on violent action and two-dimensional characters.

Because the activities of the action/adventure heroes were presented so visually—fights, airplanes, various weapons, explosions, and so on—many of them moved from the newspapers to radio and film. Dick Tracy appeared in feature movies, plus the hawk-nosed detective had a regular radio serial. Both Brick Bradford and Don Winslow also boasted movie serials. *Jungle Jim* patrolled the rain forests of Asia, *Terry and the Pirates* visited exotic locales, *King of the Royal Mounted* got his man in the Arctic wastes, and listeners could hear them all in long-running radio serials. And who could forget the "Hi-Yo Silver!" of *The Lone Ranger,* a radio series that began in 1933 and actually predated the comic strip of the same name? It stayed on the air until 1954 and on the comic pages until 1971.

American newspaper comic strips provided a national literature to be shared by all, young and old, regardless of race, class, or any other divisions. They could make people laugh, get their fans involved in fictional relationships, thrill them with daring adventures, or simply entertain with their easy story lines and black-and-white drawings. Hundreds of different comics appeared each and every day in papers around the country; some enjoyed huge circulations and audiences, others walked a shaky line between success and failure. Following the tremendous growth the medium experienced in the 1930s, the comic strips of the 1940s showed no signs of slowing down or losing their inventiveness; they continued as a unique expression of popular culture.

See also: Fads; Radio Programming: Action, Crime, Police, and Detective Shows; Radio Programming: Children's Shows, Serials, and Adventure Series; Radio Programming: Comedy Shows; Radio Programming: Soap Operas; Youth

Selected Reading
Goulart, Ron, ed. *The Encyclopedia of American Comics.* New York: Facts on File, 1990.
Horn, Maurice, ed. *100 Years of American Newspaper Comics.* New York: Gramercy Books, 1996.
Walker, Brian. *The Comics: Before 1945.* New York: Harry N. Abrams, 2004.
———. *The Comics: Since 1945.* New York: Harry N. Abrams, 2002.

COPLAND, AARON

A composer of orchestral, choral, and film music, as well as a teacher, conductor, speaker, author, and accomplished pianist, Aaron Copland (1900–1990) wrote his first song for his mother at age 8. When 11, he offered an opera scene of seven bars of music he called *Zenatello*. Two years later, he began music lessons and by 15 had decided on a composing career. Instead of going to college as his father desired, Copland went to Paris in 1921 and studied for three years with the renowned composer-conductor-teacher Nadia Boulanger (1887–1979). Upon returning to the United States in 1924, he wrote in what can best be described as a symphonic jazz motif, creating pieces that were hard to listen to and play. He gradually recognized a growing distance between this music and the American public and discarded the approach to search for a more accessible style.

In the late 1930s, when commissioned by Lincoln Kirstein (1907–1996) to write a ballet, Copland settled on a simplified approach that incorporated folk influences in a piece titled *Billy the Kid*. It premiered in Chicago on October 16, 1938. Performed by Ballet Caravan, with Eugene Loring (1911–1982) as choreographer, *Billy the Kid* played to enthusiastic audiences. The story follows the life of the infamous outlaw Billy the Kid (1859–1881) and features cowboys, pioneers, outlaws, and the open prairie of the West with numbers such as "Goodby, Old Paint," "Great Granddad," and "Old Chisholm Trail." All date back to the 19th century, and the last two had been recorded in the early 1930s by **Gene Autry** (1907–1998), a popular cowboy singer. *Billy the Kid* went on to its first New York performance on May 24, 1939, at the Martin Beck Theatre.

A second ballet, *Rodeo,* premiered at New York's Metropolitan Opera House on October 16, 1942, and also drew on cowboy tunes and the spacious landscape of the American prairie. Its well-known theme of "Hoe-Down" comes from an old folk song called "Bonyparte," or "Bonaparte's Retreat," frequently heard at square dances. Like *Billy the Kid, Rodeo* deals with an outsider, this time a cowgirl who is just one of the boys, but nevertheless yearns for romance. The Ballet Russe de Monte Carlo, a dance company that had moved to the United States because of war in Europe, performed the episodes choreographed by Agnes de Mille (1905–1998), who played the cowgirl on opening night. In 1943, Copland condensed the score into *Four Dance Episodes from "Rodeo."* Both versions experienced more success than *Billy the Kid* and did much to promote the careers of both Copland and de Mille.

Appalachian Spring, a third ballet from the composer, experienced immediate success with both audiences and critics and earned Copland the 1945 Pulitzer Prize for music. It opened at the Library of Congress in Washington, DC, on October 30, 1944, and tells a story of celebration about pioneers in the early 1800s, specifically two young newlyweds at their newly built farmhouse, not out West, but on the western Pennsylvania frontier. Created at the request of dancer Martha Graham (1894–1991), who choreographed the piece and played the leading role on opening night, this ballet features square dance rhythms, revivalist hymns, and country fiddle tunes. The last movement includes a well-known Shaker song, "Simple Gifts" (1848; words and music by Elder Joseph Brackett, 1797–1882). In 1945, Copland rearranged *Appalachian Spring* as an orchestral suite. These three ballets, reflective of American culture, pushed Copland to the forefront of the nation's composers at the time, a position that he continued to hold throughout the 1940s.

The success of these ballets notwithstanding, Copland reached an even larger audience through music written for a number of Hollywood **movies.** Beginning with the

Composer, teacher, conductor, speaker, author, and pianist Aaron Copland wrote Rodeo, *the second of three successful ballets, in 1942. The story, told through cowboy tunes, highlights the spacious landscape of the American West and benefits from Agnes de Mille's brilliant choreography. (Photofest)*

soundtracks for *Of Mice and Men* and *The City* in 1939, he provided the scores for four 1940s features: *Our Town* (1940), *North Star* (1943), *The Red Pony* (1949), and *The Heiress* (1949), plus a short, *The Cummington Story* (1945). He wrote *Music for the Movies* in 1942 as an orchestra concert suite of five movements from the original scores for the films *The City* (1939), *Of Mice and Men* (1939), and *Our Town*. It premiered on February 17, 1943, at Town Hall in New York City.

In addition to ballets and scores for movies, Copland penned pieces intended to help rally the nation, to support the call for patriotism by all U.S. citizens during World War II. *Lincoln Portrait* (1942) composed for narrator and orchestra and also for concert band resulted from a commission by composer-conductor Andre Kostelanetz (1901–1980), who wanted to acquire musical portraits of several great Americans. Copland's piece, one of the more serious contributions, honored Abraham Lincoln (1809–1865). It includes fragments of *Camptown Races* (1850) by Stephen Foster (1826–1864) and numbers popular during the American Civil War (1861–1865), along with material from the 16th president's speeches and letters. *Lincoln Portrait* premiered on May 14, 1942, with Kostelanetz conducting the Cincinnati Symphony Orchestra and actor William Adams (1887–1972) narrating. Shortly thereafter, a **radio** broadcast aired from the Hollywood Bowl with renowned poet Carl Sandburg (1878–1967) in

Adams's place. The piece continues today as a standard for patriotic holidays such as the Fourth of July, Memorial Day, and President's Day.

Almost one year later, Copland penned *Fanfare for the Common Man* at the request of the English composer-conductor, Sir Eugene Goossens (1893–1962), resident conductor for the Cincinnati Symphony Orchestra. First performed on March 13, 1943, this piece presents a musical statement of love for the United States and celebrates the labors and sacrifices made by those citizens not on a battlefield. It became an instant American classic, and today *Fanfare for the Common Man* can be heard at civic and national events, sometimes including presidential inaugurations, and is perhaps Copland's most often played composition. Another patriotic piece, *Letter from Home,* written by Copland in 1944, suggests the emotions that might be experienced by a soldier receiving and reading a letter from home.

Copland's simpler pieces composed during the first half of the decade supported a thesis he presented in his book *Our New Music* (1941). He wrote of a new audience for music that had developed as a result of the popularity of radio and record players and suggested that new compositions should reflect the existence and use of this **technology.** A year earlier, he had joined the Berkshire Music Center at Tanglewood as a teacher and chairman of the faculty and held those positions until 1965. He urged his many students, one of the most successful being Leonard Bernstein (1918–1990), to write in a simple, contemporary, American way.

Music written by Copland during the 1940s includes orchestral works such as *John Henry* (1940); *Danzon Cubano* (1944); the *Third Symphony* (1946), which incorporates *Fanfare for the Common Man;* and *Preamble for a Solemn Occasion* (1949). He also composed *Las Agachadas* (1942) and *In the Beginning* (1947) for chorus, along with *Violin Sonata* (1943) for violin, *Midsummer Nocturne* (1947) for piano, and *Clarinet Concerto* (1948) for clarinet and string orchestra with harp. This last work, commissioned by **swing** clarinetist Benny Goodman (1909–1986), demonstrates his versatility. Between 1940 and 1949, Copland wrote a total of 26 pieces and throughout his career he frequently toured the world to promote his music.

Along with composers Virgil Thomson (1898–1996) and Roy Harris (1898–1979), Aaron Copland dominated the public perception of American **classical music** during the 1930s and 1940s. Clearly a populist composer, his music glorified American culture. He reached the peak of his career in the 1940s, and none of his pieces after that ever made as great an impression with the public as did his three ballets along with *Lincoln Portrait* and *Fanfare for the Common Man,* all written during the late 1930s and 1940s. Despite his public acceptance, in 1953, Senator Joseph McCarthy's (1908–1957) infamous Senate subcommittee investigating the composer's possible Communist activities during the 1930s called Copland to testify. McCarthy viewed his liberal attitudes as suspect, but many notable individuals rallied to his support and McCarthy failed to implicate him in any way.

Copland stands as one of the country's most successful and prestigious composers, having created a true American style. He retired from composing in 1973 but continued to conduct until memory loss kept him confined to his home.

See also: Cold War, The; House Un-American Activities Committee (HUAC)

Selected Reading

Ballet performances in New York City. *New York Times,* May 25, 1939; October 17, 1942; November 1, 1944. www.proquest.com

Horowitz, Joseph. *Classical Music in America: A History of Its Rise and Fall.* New York: W. W. Norton, 2005.

Struble, John Warthen. *The History of American Classical Music: MacDowell Through Minimalism.* New York: Facts on File, 1995.

COSTUME AND SPECTACLE FILMS

Since the earliest days of commercial film production, the motion picture industry has capitalized on its ability to enthrall audiences with elaborate dress and settings. Nothing can beat the sweep of costume and action-filled sequences on the big screen. From *The Birth of a Nation* (1915) to the burning of Atlanta in *Gone with the Wind* (1939) to any of the *Star Wars* films (1977 and onward) to *Avatar* (2009), the large-scale movie has long been an identifiable genre in its own right. But such undertakings require huge amounts of money, equipment, and supplies; the studios might have had the money, but the materials could not be not readily obtained in the straitened 1940s.

Just weeks after the war began in earnest for the United States, the newly created Office of Price Administration (OPA) commenced creating a list of goods that would be restricted in their availability to the public. In short order, the OPA announced that such items as tires, gasoline, and a long list of foodstuffs would henceforth be rationed. In addition, many commodities not explicitly listed became scarce, and Americans had to manage with less.

These federal edicts also affected the movie industry. A showy costume drama could no longer indulge in lovely silken gowns; almost immediately rationed, silk could hardly be found at all, because the manufacture of parachutes demanded great quantities of it. Virtually all synthetics, such as nylon or rayon, also disappeared from the marketplace. In addition, uniform makers required wool and cotton, plus the government considered the dyes used to color clothing as strategic since they went into the production of explosives. Even lowly metal buttons had disappeared from suppliers.

Heedlessly expending gasoline, either for spectacular special effects (explosions or fires) or for **transportation** to exotic locales, became a difficult proposition with its scarcity. Tires were almost irreplaceable, and the construction of elaborate sets presented unexpected difficulties given the shortages of many building materials. Crowd scenes with lots of youthful male players posed a problem, since men, too, were in short supply. In short, Hollywood had to scale back for the duration of the war and employ flimsy sets and less sumptuous costumes, and producers settled for shooting on studio back lots and sound stages.

With the return to peace in late 1945, the studios may have begun planning new cinematic extravaganzas, but the immediate postwar years witnessed a continuation of some scarcities while the nation readjusted the channels of supply to civilian needs. Not until the later 1940s did a sense of normality again descend on the movie capital. With 1949, peace and prosperity combined to put Hollywood back on track for expensive, elaborately staged pictures. That year saw *The Prince of Foxes* and *Reign of Terror,* both of which consumed endless yards of once-rationed silk in fancy costumes, and sets that

TABLE 38. Representative Costume and Spectacle Films of the 1940s

Year	Film Titles	Stars
1940	Hudson's Bay	Paul Muni, Gene Tierney
	The Mark of Zorro	Tyrone Power, Basil Rathbone
	Northwest Passage	Spencer Tracy, Robert Young
	One Million B.C.	Victor Mature, Lon Chaney Jr.
	Pride and Prejudice	Greer Garson, Laurence Olivier
	The Santa Fe Trail	Errol Flynn, Olivia de Havilland
	The Sea Hawk	Errol Flynn, Claude Rains
	The Thief of Bagdad	Sabu, Conrad Veidt
	Victory	Fredric March, Cedric Hardwicke
1941	Blood and Sand	Tyrone Power, Linda Darnell
	The Corsican Brothers	Douglas Fairbanks Jr., Akim Tamiroff
	The Sea Wolf	Edward G. Robinson, Ida Lupino
	The Son of Monte Cristo	Louis Hayward, George Sanders
	That Hamilton Woman	Laurence Olivier, Vivien Leigh
1942	Arabian Nights	Sabu, Jon Hall
	The Black Swan	Tyrone Power, Maureen O'Hara
	The Jungle Book	Sabu, Joseph Calleia
	Reap the Wild Wind	John Wayne, Ray Milland
	Son of Fury: The Story of Benjamin Blake	Tyrone Power, George Sanders
1943	Forever and a Day [English]	Cedric Hardwicke, Brian Aherne
	Jack London	Michael O'Shea, Susan Hayward
	Phantom of the Opera	Claude Rains, Nelson Eddy
1944	The Adventures of Mark Twain	Fredric March, Alexis Smith
	Ali Baba and the Forty Thieves	Jon Hall, Maria Montez
	Frenchman's Creek	Joan Fontaine, Basil Rathbone
	Gypsy Wildcat	Jon Hall, Maria Montez
	Jane Eyre	Orson Welles, Joan Fontaine
	Kismet	Ronald Colman, Marlene Dietrich
	Summer Storm	Linda Darnell, George Sanders
	Wilson	Alexander Knox, Geraldine Fitzgerald
1945	A Song to Remember	Cornel Wilde, Paul Muni
	The Spanish Main	Paul Henreid, Walter Slezak
1946	Anna and the King of Siam	Irene Dunne, Rex Harrison
	The Bandit of Sherwood Forest	Cornel Wilde, Edgar Buchanan
	Caesar and Cleopatra	Janet Leigh, Stewart Granger
	Devotion	Ida Lupino, Olivia de Havilland
	Great Expectations [English]	John Mills, Alec Guinness
	Henry V [English]	Laurence Olivier, Robert Newton
1947	Captain from Castile	Tyrone Power, Jean Peters
	Green Dolphin Street	Van Heflin, Lana Turner
	The Macomber Affair	Gregory Peck, Joan Bennett
	Sinbad the Sailor	Douglas Fairbanks Jr., Maureen O'Hara
	Tycoon	John Wayne, Cedric Hardwicke
	Unconquered	John Wayne, Paulette Goddard

(continued)

TABLE 38. *(continued)*

Year	Film Titles	Stars
1948	*Adventures of Don Juan*	Errol Flynn
	Hamlet [English]	Laurence Olivier, Jean Simmons
1948	*Joan of Arc*	Ingrid Bergman, Jose Ferrer
	Macbeth	Orson Welles, Jeanette Nolan
	Saraband	Stewart Granger, Joan Greenwood
	Scott of the Antarctic	John Mills, Derek Bond
	The Swordsman	Larry Parks, Ellen Drew
	The Three Musketeers	Gene Kelly, Lana Turner
	Wake of the Red Witch	John Wayne, Gail Russell
	The Woman in White	Sidney Greenstreet, Agnes Moorehead
1949	*The Blue Lagoon*	Jean Simmons, Donald Houston
	The Heiress	Olivia de Havilland, Montgomery Clift
	Little Women	June Allyson, Margaret O'Brien
	Madame Bovary	Jennifer Jones, Van Heflin
	Might Joe Young	Terry Moore, Ben Johnson
	Pirates of Capri	Louis Hayward, Binnie Barnes
	Prince of Foxes	Orson Welles, Tyronne Power
	Reign of Terror	Robert Cummings, Arlene Dahl
	Samson and Delilah	Victor Mature, Hedy Lamarr

bespoke the availability of supplies. The decade culminated with producer-director and master showman Cecil B. DeMille (1881–1959), famed for making one visual spectacle after another in the prewar years (*King of Kings* [1927], *Cleopatra* [1934], many others), returning to his old form with *Samson and Delilah* (1949), a biblical epic that pulled out all the stops and presaged the big-budget blockbusters of the 1950s.

From the list above, a few generalizations can be made regarding costume and spectacle films: The average number of motion pictures fitting this category declined during the war years, 1941 to 1946. Of those **movies,** the majority depend more on costume than they do on scope. Most fit the category of character studies or, in the case of actual figures from history, "biopics" (biographical pictures), a descriptive neologism created shortly after World War II. An unusually large proportion involve swashbucklers, swordsmen displaying their skills on a limited stage. In this way, period dress and simple sets substitute for elaborate crowd scenes and sweeping vistas. Most films utilized traditional black-and-white stock, both cheaper and more readily available than color at the time.

Toward the end of the 1940s, however, the number of productions increased, sets became more elaborate, and camera crews favored on-location shooting (i.e., away from Hollywood and studio lots). When feasible, Technicolor replaced black-and-white **photography.** But wide-screen projection, such as CinemaScope and Cinerama, along with enhanced sound and other technological advances, did not occur during the 1940s; these changes would have to wait until the 1950s.

Theater attendance remained high—60 to 80 million weekly patrons—throughout the war and early postwar years. A slight decline became evident over the decade, but few reckoned with the plunge it would take during the 1950s with the advent of **television** and its overnight rise in popularity. In 1949, most people continued their weekly visits to a neighborhood theater for the latest movies and special features. And as far as concerns lavish, big-budget motion pictures, the 1940s can be seen as an era of relative calm, with the 1940 to 1949 period a time for restraint. Only in the final years of the decade did the industry return to its more freewheeling ways of the past.

See also: Fashion; Rationing; Technology

Selected Reading
Richards, Jeffrey. *Swordsmen of the Screen.* London: Routledge & Kegan Paul, 1977.
Swashbuckling. www.classicalfencing.com/articles/swash.php

COUNTRY MUSIC

With themes of love and loss, mothers and sweethearts, and hope and heartbreak, country music advanced in popularity and acceptance as an American musical form during the 1940s. No longer denigrated as backwoods hillbilly music, it covered a wide gamut of styles: traditional country, the string band sound, bluegrass, Western, honky-tonk, and Western Swing. In 1942, *Billboard* magazine, a music trade journal that reports the top-selling songs for the week, introduced a column on country music. The journal added a folk records chart in 1944 and changed the name to Hillbilly in 1947. It arrived at the final name of Country and Western Chart in 1949, a sure sign that the genre was evolving and holding its own with mainstream music. At this same time, another boost came as popular artists such as **Bing Crosby** (1903–1977), **The Andrews Sisters** (Patty [b. 1918], Maxene [1916–1995], LaVerne [1911–1967]), and Margaret Whiting (b. 1924) began to record their own versions of the songs that had risen to the top of the country chart.

Other earlier events contributed to country music's climb to success. Two **radio** broadcasts, *National Barn Dance* (1924–1960) and *Grand Ole Opry* (1927 to present), initially served limited areas of the nation. In 1939, the Opry, a Saturday evening live broadcast of country music from station WSM in Nashville, Tennessee, obtained network status as a 30-minute weekly program on the NBC (National Broadcasting Company) network. Sponsored by Prince Albert Tobacco, it moved to coast-to-coast programming in 1940, and suddenly the show and its stars became known outside its regional boundaries of the southeastern United States. By 1944, more than 600 country music radio shows filled the airwaves, some local or regional and some national.

Prior to this time, record companies had come to this Appalachian Mountain area in search of new singers. For example, by the 1940s RCA Victor had established a hillbilly catalog and aggressively publicized their disks; from the late 1940s, Decca Records represented a number of country music artists. **Jukeboxes** located in ice cream and soda shops and small dance halls served as a prominent recording industry marketing tool because they exposed the public to new releases, especially in the country music field. At the same time, Hollywood featured some country artists in a number of Westerns with singing cowboys, thereby bringing country music to even more audiences.

In this early 1940s photograph, a proud Ernest Tubb holds the guitar of his idol, country music pioneer Jimmie Rodgers. By 1943, Tubb had switched to an electric model, the first country artist to do so. It earned a spot for him on the Grand Ole Opry, where he reigned as one of its stars for 39 years. (Photofest)

World War II probably served as the most significant event of all in the establishment of country music as a national phenomenon and big business. Because of the draft and wartime industries, major population shifts occurred as new soldiers moved to training camps and workers sought defense jobs. For some, their families followed to nearby towns. Those enamored of country music and its songs carried them to places like Los Angeles, Detroit, Cincinnati, Chicago, and Baltimore. The concentration of men in military installations and the mass migration of workers created a new market for country and hillbilly music. People unfamiliar with these formats now heard them on local radio stations, at public gatherings, and at concerts.

During the war, country music stars participated in **USO (United Service Organizations)** Camp Shows both in the United States and Europe, exposing even more people to their music. Likewise, singers and musicians connected with the Opry gained recognition for themselves and their music through the *Grand Ole Opry*'s Camel Caravan, underwritten by the cigarettes of the same name. This traveling unit of performers entertained troops at military bases in the United States and the Panama Canal region. Other radio barn dance shows such as Chicago's *National Barn Dance,* Cincinnati's *Boone County Jamboree,* and Kentucky's *Renfro Valley Barn Dance* kicked off tours that frequently played before crowds in excess of 5,000 people. Through these various activities and events, anyone previously unacquainted with country music now regularly heard it, and some became new fans.

Many of the country music artists who claimed star status during the 1940s had entered the field through the *Grand Ole Opry.* **Roy Acuff** (1903–1992), host and solo performer for the show, as well as a composer, publisher, and recording artist, had, by the early 1940s, earned the title of King of Country Music. His success as a recording artist peaked in the 1940s, and he, along with composer Fred Rose (1897–1954), opened a country music publishing business in Nashville. After 1950, his recording career ceased, but until his death he continued to write and perform.

With Acuff as a member of the *Grand Ole Opry,* the show's emphasis moved from instrumental performances to solo star appearances. Comedy, along with costumes, had always been a part of the barn dance shows, and when, in the fall of 1940, Sarah Ophelia Colley (1912–1996) made her debut on the *Grand Ole Opry* as comedian Minnie Pearl, another country star was born. By 1942, Minnie Pearl, with her trademark

"How-dee-e-e!" and wearing a big hat with the price tag of $1.98 (approximately $29 in 2008 dollars) dangling off the side, had created her enduring stage personality. Audiences never seemed to tire of her portrayal of a small-town spinster preoccupied with chasing men and gossiping about her family and neighbors. Minnie Pearl remained in Nashville until 1991, when she suffered a debilitating stroke.

Another rising performer, Eddy Arnold (1918–2008), the "Tennessee Plowboy" with a crooner's style of singing, joined the Opry in 1940 as the lead vocalist for Pee Wee King's (1914–2000) band. He obtained solo star status in 1943 and cut his first disk in 1944. Recording for the RCA Victor label, Arnold's renditions of "That's How Much I Love You" in 1946, followed by three No. 1 hits in 1947—"It's a Sin," "What Is Life Without Love," and "I'll Hold You in My Heart (Till I Can Hold You in My Arms)"—pushed him to the top. Success for Arnold and Victor continued with four singles in the top 5 in 1948—"Bouquet of Roses" (No. 1 for 19 weeks), "Anytime," "Just a Little Lovin'," and "Texarkana Baby"—and two in 1949—"Don't Rob Another Man's Castle" and "I'm Throwing Rice at the Girl I Love." He had edged out Ernest Tubb (1914–1984), Red Foley (1910–1968), and even Roy Acuff as the nation's best-known country singer.

National Barn Dance, the other famous country music radio show, also made significant contributions to the genre. Its most popular performers included the husband-wife team of Scotty Wiseman (1909–1981) and Lula Belle (b. 1913), Patsy Montana (1914–1996), and Louise Massey (1902–1983). **Gene Autry** (1907–1998) appeared on the show from 1932 to 1934 and by 1940 boasted his own radio program, *Melody Ranch* (1940–1956). Autry and **Roy Rogers** (born Leonard Slye, 1911–1998) hold the distinction of being the best-known and most successful singing cowboys. *National Barn Dance* also featured a well-known comedy team, the Hoosier Hot Shots. In addition to providing laughs for the audience, this group appeared in a number of movies—Westerns, musicals, and comedies—including a cinematic version of *National Barn Dance,* released in 1944.

Clyde "Red" Foley, who had joined and left *National Barn Dance* during the 1930s, returned in 1940 and one year later signed with Decca, where he hit it big with his first recording, "Old Shep," a song about a dog he owned as a child. As did many country composers and singers, Foley performed before military audiences throughout the war years. In 1944, he held the No. 1 spot on the *Billboard* folk (country) chart for 13 consecutive weeks with a recording of a patriotic number titled "Smoke on the Water." One year later, he became the first major country performer to record in Nashville, a city that was rapidly gaining a reputation for being the heart of country music. Foley's 1946 entry as a regular member on the Prince Albert Tobacco segment of *Grand Ole Opry* broadened his career to include that of master of ceremonies, hosting both singers and comedians. He ended the decade with a string of hits: "M-I-S-S-I-S-S-I-P-P-I," "Goodnight Irene," and "Birmingham Bounce" (all 1949) and went on to issue "Chattanoogie Shoe Shine Boy" in 1950, a No. 1 hit for 13 weeks and considered by many to be his signature song.

While these individual performers worked their way to stardom and advanced the popularity of country music, various groups of country musicians likewise added their innovations and contributed to the growing interest. The Monroe Brothers—Bill

(1911–1996) and Charlie (1903–1975)—achieved popularity during the 1920s and 1930s as a duet performing songs with a hard-driving beat; they went their separate ways in the late 1930s to form their own bands.

Bill Monroe, who played the mandolin, became the more successful of the two, organized the Blue Grass Boys and, in turn, popularized a music style that had originated with string bands of the 1920s. Similar to the Monroe Brothers' duet style, this group played at a faster tempo than traditional country music; they called it bluegrass after their group's name. Sometimes the Blue Grass Boys featured vocalists who offered high-pitched singing that emphasized multiple vocal parts. They became one of *Grand Ole Opry*'s strongest attractions and cut disks for RCA Victor's Bluebird label during 1940 and 1941.

The group did not record again until 1945, when Monroe signed with Columbia Records. The label issued "Kentucky Waltz" (which Monroe had written in 1934) and "Footprints in the Snow." At this time, the Blue Grass Boys added two new members: Earl Scruggs (b. 1924), a banjo player who employed a distinctive, three-finger style of picking, and rhythm guitarist and singer of heartfelt vocals Lester Flatt (1914–1979). Music historians generally agree that the musical style, talents, and innovativeness offered by Flatt and Scruggs solidified the bluegrass sound. "Blue Moon of Kentucky," written by Bill Monroe and recorded by the Blue Grass Boys in 1947, became a bluegrass standard and entered the National Recording Registry at the Library of Congress in 2002. Monroe's music clearly defined the bluegrass sound, and many consider him the father of that particular style.

Flatt and Scruggs left Monroe in 1948 and formed the Foggy Mountain Boys. They added a dobro, a metal-topped resonator guitar with a slide placed on the strings on the instrument's neck to produce a sound similar to that of a Hawaiian band sound. In 1949, they recorded "Foggy Mountain Breakdown" for Mercury Records; it featured Scruggs's unique playing style and gave them their first hit. Flatt and Scruggs and the Foggy Mountain Boys had clearly joined Bill Monroe and the Bluegrass Boys as major forces in spreading bluegrass music across the United States. In 2004, their "Foggy Mountain Breakdown" joined "Blue Moon of Kentucky" in the National Recording Registry.

Along with the development of bluegrass, a style known as Western Swing also gained recognition in the country music field. In the early 1930s, Bob Wills (1905–1975) and his Texas Playboys along with Milton Brown (1903–1936) and his Musical Brownies, added the amplified steel guitar and other electrified instruments to their string bands and offered traditional country music with a hint of the "**swing**" and jazz played by big bands in urban ballrooms at the time. In 1940, Wills assembled a band of 18 musicians playing saxophones, trumpets, clarinets, and drums, along with the usual guitars, and recorded "New San Antonio Rose," a repeat of his 1938 tune, "San Antonio Rose." Its success enhanced the future of Western Swing and it quickly gained favor with dancers in Texas, Oklahoma, and other western states. "New San Antonio Rose" became known as a Western Swing classic, and, like many other successful country tunes, Bing Crosby recorded it.

In 1940 and 1941, Bob Wills and his Texas Playboys appeared in two **movies** as themselves and 13 more Westerns before the decade ended. Wills enlisted in the army in 1942 and received a medical discharge the following year. He then moved to

California and reorganized his band, removing most of the brass and reeds and relying more on fiddles, a decision that allowed him to retain a fairly strong following even after the big bands dipped in popularity. In 1945, Wills and his group recorded "Smoke on the Water," the same song cut in 1944 by Red Foley (not to be confused with the 1972 hit of the same name by the rock group Deep Purple). Will's version hit No. 1. Postwar successes for Wills included "New Spanish Two-Step,""Roly-Poly" (both 1946), and "Sugar Moon" (1947).

Pee Wee King, songwriter, recording artist, band leader, and **television** entertainer, along with fellow band member Redd Stewart (1923–2003), penned what some believe to be the song that guaranteed country music's prosperity, "The Tennessee Waltz." (1947). Originally recorded in 1948 by King and the Golden West Cowboys, vocalist Patti Page (b. 1927) achieved No. 1 on the pops chart in 1951, and within six months sold 5 million copies with her version. In 1965, the state of Tennessee adopted it as its official song.

King and his band had joined *Grand Ole Opry* in 1937 and immediately set some new standards. They dressed in stylish Western outfits specifically designed for them and introduced an array of new instruments to the program's stage, including trumpet, drums, and electric guitar. Initially polka and waltz rhythms characterized most of their songs, but they soon produced smoother, danceable sounds and became more of a Western Swing band. In 1947, King and his Golden West Cowboys left the Opry for a weekly radio show on WAVE in Louisville, Kentucky. One year later, they transferred to affiliate WAVE-TV where they had a television show until 1957.

New genres of country music during the 1940s did not stop with bluegrass and Western Swing. For a little over a decade, laborers in Texas and Louisiana had gathered at the end of the day in small local taverns, called honky-tonks, a slang term derived from honk-a-tonk, which means a cheap saloon that served alcohol, both legally and illegally. There, they would drink, socialize, listen to music, and dance. Al Dexter (1905–1984), a singer and writer of a 1937 song titled "Honky Tonk Blues," operated such a bar in Texas and reportedly originated the music called honky-tonk, songs that lament the workers' good and bad times and epitomize the spirit of drinking and hard living, of loving and losing at love.

This music, when played on electric instruments, had a louder sound and a heavier beat than other country styles and offered bold lyrics. In 1944, Dexter's "Pistol Packin' Mama" (written 1942), "Rosalita," "So Long Pal," and "Too Late to Worry, Too Blue to Cry" all scored No. 1 on *Billboard's* country chart. In addition to Dexter, Bing Crosby and the Andrews Sisters, as well as Frank Sinatra, recorded "Pistol Packin' Mama." Three movies of the decade featured the song—*Pistol Packin' Mama* (1943), *Strange Affair* (1944), and *Beautiful But Broke* (1944)—while another movie, *Frontier Fugitives* (1945), offered his "Too Late to Worry, Too Blue to Cry" and "I'll Wait for You Dear."

The years 1945 through 1948 continued to be profitable ones for Dexter. Three recordings hit No. 1: "I'm Losing My Mind over You" (1945), "Guitar Polka," and "Wine, Women, and Song" (both 1946). "I'll Wait for You Dear," the B side of "I'm Losing My Mind Over You," made it to the No. 2 spot. But his success did not stop there. "Triflin' Gal" and the B side, "I'm Lost Without You" (1945), along with "It's Up to You," "Kokomo Island," and "Down at the Roadside Inn," recorded in 1946–1947, made it to the top five. Finally in 1948, "Rock and Rye Rag" and "Calico Rag" scored in the top 15. In all, Dexter received 12 gold records for million-sellers from 1943 to 1948.

Along with Al Dexter's promotion of honky-tonk music, two southwestern country artists, Floyd Tillman (1914–2003) and Ted Daffan (1912–1996), also contributed significantly to its development. Both versatile artists, Tillman worked as a singer and songwriter and frequently performed his own numbers rather than the compositions of others, and Daffan excelled as a guitarist, band leader, singer, and songwriter.

Floyd Tillman's success began in 1939 with "It Makes No Difference Now," recorded by Western swing bandleader Cliff Bruner (1915–2000) and also by Bing Crosby in 1940, a number considered by many to be the first classic honky-tonk piece. Tillman served as a radio operator during World War II, and being stationed near Houston enabled him to continue to record. Two 1944 compositions, "Each Night at Nine" and "They Took the Stars Out of Heaven," gained popularity because they appealed to people separated from loved ones, whatever the reason.

After 1945, Tillman wrote some of the best honky-tonk songs of the postwar period, including "I Love You So Much It Hurts" (1948), "Slipping Around" (1949), and a follow-up song to the same melody, "I'll Never Slip Around Again" (1949). One of the first pieces to address adultery and considered the most recognized country song about cheating, Capitol Records decided to also cut a duet version of "Slipping Around" by pop vocalist Margaret Whiting (b. 1924) and the multitalented Jimmy Wakely (1914–1982). Their rendering ranked No. 4 on the country chart and No. 5 on *Billboard's* Hot 100 for 1949.

Ted Daffan hit it big in 1940, thanks to the success of Cliff Bruner's recording of Daffan's "Truck Driver's Blues." Song titles by Daffan such as "Worried Mind" (1940), "Born to Lose," and "No Letter Today" (both 1943 and written under the pseudonym of Frankie Brown), as well as "Headin' Down the Wrong Highway" (1945) certainly convey the moods glorified in honky-tonk music. Both "Born to Lose" and "No Letter Today" sold a million copies. Over the years, "Born to Lose" has been recorded by a variety of musicians, including Ray Charles (1930–2004), Dean Martin (1917–1995), and Ella Fitzgerald (1917–1996).

Hank Williams (1923–1953), frequently referred to as the Father of Contemporary Country Music, wrote most of the songs that he sang and also advanced the honky-tonk style. He formed the first version of his band, the Drifting Cowboys, when only 16 years old. By the early 1940s, while still a teenager, he played one-night gigs at clubs across Alabama. A move to Nashville in 1946 put him in contact with Fred Rose, co-owner of Acuff-Rose Publishing, who arranged for Williams to record for Sterling Records. The success of two singles, "Never Again" and "Honky Tonkin'," garnered the attention of MGM, a newly formed recording subsidiary of the giant Metro-Golden-Mayer film studio.

Under contract with MGM, Williams cut "Move It on Over," in 1947. An immediate hit, it climbed to No. 4 on *Billboard's* country singles chart. During 1948, he performed for *Louisiana Hayride* tours and appeared on its WKWH radio program carried nationally from Shreveport, Louisiana, by the CBS (Columbia Broadcasting Company).

In 1949, Williams reorganized his Drifting Cowboys and, at different times during the year, had five songs to rank in the top five of *Billboard's* Hot Country Singles:

"Wedding Bells," "Mind Your Own Business," "You're Gonna Change (Or I'm Gonna Leave), "My Bucket's Got a Hole in It," and, the most successful of all, "Lovesick Blues," a 1922 Tin Pan Alley song that claimed the No. 1 spot. *Grand Ole Opry* immediately invited him to join the show, and, at his first appearance, the audience insisted on six encores of his yodeled closing line of "Lovesick Blues." In 2004, the National Recording Registry selected this famous song for its archives.

Five more singles made it into the top 15 during the last two years of the decade. His fame soared, and Williams moved from regional success to national stardom. He continued to record hit after hit in the early 1950s and died on January 1, 1953, at the age of 29 in the back seat of his Cadillac while being driven to a concert in Canton, Ohio. The exact cause of his death is debatable, with some attributing it to his serious problems with alcohol, morphine, and painkillers, and others reporting that he had a heart attack.

Another honky-tonk performer, Ernest Tubb, became the first country artist to employ an electric guitar at the Opry, where he reigned as one of its major stars for the next 39 years. Perhaps most associated with one of his early compositions and recordings, "Walking the Floor Over You" (1942), a country classic, he frequently appeared on best-selling charts. His hits from the 1940s included "Soldier's Last Letter" (1944), "Tomorrow Never Comes" and "It's Been So Long Darling" (both 1945), and "Rainbow at Midnight" and "Filipino Baby" (both 1946).

Tubb headlined the first *Grand Ole Opry* show presented at Carnegie Hall in September 1947 and recorded "I'm Biting My Fingernails and Thinking of You" with the Andrews Sisters in 1949. That same year, he had six other hits, including "Have You Ever Been Lonely." In addition to his Opry work and recording, he toured the country constantly and appeared in three Hollywood Westerns: *Fighting Buckaroo* (1943), *Jamboree,* and *Riding West* (both 1944). He was one of many country stars playing themselves in *Hollywood Barn Dance* in 1947, the same year that he opened the Ernest Tubb Record Shop in Nashville, the first major all-country music store, and hosted the *Midnight Jamboree,* which followed the Opry on WSM.

Some country artists of the 1940s did not align themselves with just one popular genre. For example, Merle Travis (1917–1983) came from a traditional background and played music derived from folk music he had heard growing up in Kentucky. In the mid-1930s, he appeared with local bands around Evansville, Indiana, and in 1937 joined the Drifting Pioneers, a group that performed on WLW in Cincinnati until the outbreak World War II.

After a brief stint with the Marines and subsequent discharge, Travis settled in California and recorded for Capitol Records. His biggest successes came from singing Western and honky-tonk songs. In 1946, he wrote two numbers that focused on the lives of coal miners, "Sixteen Tons" and "Dark as a Dungeon," with the former becoming a No. 1 country hit for Tennessee Ernie Ford (1919–1991) in 1955. Other notable compositions included "Divorce Me C.O.D." (1946), "Three Times Seven," and "So Round, So Firm, So Fully Packed" (both 1947); the last-named climbed to the No. 1 position on the country charts and gave him national prominence. For his friend Tex Williams (1917–1985), Travis wrote what in 1947 became Capitol's first million-selling hit: "Smoke! Smoke! Smoke! (That Cigarette)." *Billboard* listed it as No. 5 in a category called the Hot 100 for 1947. But Travis did not limit himself to composing and recording. During the 1940s, he appeared as a singer in three movies, had acting roles in 11, and portrayed himself in a movie short, *When the Bloom Is on the Sage* (1945).

With the success of many country music singers and musicians and the accompanying growth of the country music industry, hot spots for playing and listening to the music appeared throughout the country. In addition to acting and recording opportunities, Hollywood provided live performances at the Los Angeles County Barn Dance at Venice Pier. Eastern Pennsylvania and West Virginia likewise witnessed a lot of activity thanks to the *Wheeling Jamboree* broadcast over WWVA in Wheeling, West Virginia. But no place compared to Nashville, the country music center of the United States, whatever the style. The town clearly contained all elements of the country music industry—performances, recording, publishing, and marketing.

The 1940s witnessed a rapid and broad growth in both the development and popularity of various genres of country music. The styles and performances changed as more and more country musicians electronically amplified their guitars and talented vocalists using a microphone stepped out to front the bands. Promoters and booking agents became active in advancing the careers of the aspiring stars and brought country music to a larger audience. In tribute to these efforts, the Smithsonian Institution, in 1981, released *The Smithsonian Collection of Classic Country Music.* It contains 143 tracks deemed to be significant to the history of country music. Thirty-six, or one-fourth of these tracks, come from the time period 1941 to 1953. An additional 18 represent a separate category of bluegrass tunes.

See also: Westerns (Film)

Selected Reading
Malone, Bill C. *Country Music, U.S.A.* Austin: University of Texas Press, 1968.
Peterson, Richard A. *Creating Country Music: Fabricating the Authentic.* Chicago: University of Chicago Press, 1997.
Shestack, Melvin. *The Country Music Encyclopedia.* New York: Thomas Y. Crowell, 1974.
Tyler, Don. *American Music through History: Music of the Postwar Era.* Westport, CT: Greenwood Publishing Group, 2008.

CRIME AND MYSTERY FILMS

A well-done mystery movie can also serve as superlative drama, although only a fraction of dramatic motion pictures can be called mysteries. Precise plotting, interesting characters, and evocative sets all contribute to the carefully wrought mystery film. Crime stories, which stand slightly apart from mysteries, usually focus more on the act itself and less on characterization. The line separating the two genres, however, can easily be blurred, as has frequently happened in cinematic history. A strong director, working with a good screenplay, can make even the most mundane tale of crime into a gripping mystery. The reverse, of course, also holds true: a lesser director, a weak screenplay, can make a shambles of a mystery, a product far inferior to many straight-ahead crime pictures.

Any survey of **movies** from the 1940s will show that studios released a great number of both crime and mystery pictures, which suggests an abundance of fans. An unusual and often overlooked aspect of this genre during the 1940s concerns series films. A particular sleuth—Sherlock Holmes, Charlie Chan, the Saint, the Falcon, and numerous others—appears in a movie and audiences respond positively—that is, it does well at the box office. This prompts the studio to produce a sequel, and if that draws well, too, a series will often ensue. For the 1940s, a disproportionate number of crime and mystery series flourished, with some continuing for years. At the same time, each and every year of the decade saw many individual (nonseries) crime and mystery films released. These ranged from action-oriented thrillers to intellectual exercises in crime solving.

A small sampling of such titles follows and illustrates the broad range they covered. In addition, several of the more popular series also receive discussion (**Film noir,** a separate category of crime and mystery movies, can be found elsewhere in this encyclopedia).

TABLE 39. Representative Crime and Mystery Films, 1940–1949

Year	Film Titles	Stars
1940	*Angel Street* [also known as *Gaslight*]	Anton Walbrook, Diana Wynyard
	Busman's Honeymoon	Robert Montgomery, Robert Newton
	The Invisible Man Returns	Cedric Hardwicke, Vincent Price
	Johnny Apollo	Tyrone Power, Dorothy Lamour
	The Letter	Bette Davis, Herbert Marshall
	The Man with Nine Lives	Boris Karloff, Roger Pryor
	Raffles	David Niven, Olivia de Havilland
	Rebecca	Joan Fontaine, Laurence Olivier
	Stranger on the Third Floor	Peter Lorre, Elisha Cook Jr.
	They Drive By Night	George Raft, Humphrey Bogart
1941	*The Black Cat*	Basil Rathbone, Bela Lugosi
	Dressed to Kill	Lloyd Nolan, William Demarest
	High Sierra	Humphrey Bogart, Ida Lupino
	Johnny Eager	Robert Taylor, Van Heflin
	Lady Scarface	Judith Anderson, Dennis O'Keefe
	Law of the Tropics	Constance Bennett, Regis Toomey
	The Maltese Falcon	Humphrey Bogart, Mary Astor
	Out of the Fog	John Garfield, Ida Lupino
	Shadows on the Stairs	Paul Cavanagh, Miles Mander
	Suspicion	Joan Fontaine, Cary Grant
1942	*The Big Shot*	Humphrey Bogart, Irene Manning
	Crossroads	William Powell, Hedy Lamarr
	Eyes in the Night	Edward Arnold, Donna Reed
	Fingers at the Window	Basil Rathbone, Lew Ayres
	The Glass Key	Alan Ladd, Veronica Lake
	Grand Central Murder	Van Heflin, Tom Conway
	I Live on Danger	Chester Morris, Jean Parker
	Kid Glove Killer	Van Heflin, Marsha Hunt
	Lucky Jordan	Alan Ladd, Marie McDonald
	This Gun for Hire	Alan Ladd, Veronica Lake

(continued)

TABLE 39. *(continued)*

Year	Film Titles	Stars
1943	*Adventures of Tartu*	Robert Donat, Valerie Hobson
	Appointment in Berlin	George Sanders, Gale Sondergaard
	The Black Raven	George Zucco, Wanda McKay
	Boss of Big Town	John Litel, Florence Rice
	Eyes of the Underworld	Richard Dix, Lon Chaney Jr.
	The Ghost Ship	Richard Dix, Lawrence Tierney
	Lady of Burlesque	Barbara Stanwyck, Michael O'Shea
	The Leopard Man	Dennis O'Keefe, Jean Brooks
	The Seventh Victim	Tom Conway, Kim Hunter
	Shadow of a Doubt	Teresa Wright, Joseph Cotton
1944	*Dangerous Passage*	Robert Lowery, Phyllis Brooks
	Double Indemnity	Barbara Stanwyck, Fred MacMurray
	Gaslight	Ingrid Bergman, Charles Boyer
	Laura	Gene Tierney, Dana Andrews
	The Lodger	Merle Oberon, George Sanders
	The Mask of Dimitrios	Peter Lorre, Sidney Greenstreet
	Ministry of Fear	Ray Milland, Dan Duryea
	Murder, My Sweet	Dick Powell, Claire Trevor
	The Phantom Lady	Franchot Tone, Elisha Cook Jr.
	Roger Touhy, Gangster	Preston Foster, Victor McLaglen
1945	*And Then There Were None*	Barry Fitzgerald, Walter Huston
	Crime, Inc	Tom Neal, Leo Carillo
	Danger Signal	Zachary Scott, Faye Emerson
	Dangerous Partners	James Craig, Signe Hasso
	Dillinger	Lawrence Tierney, Edmund Lowe
	Fallen Angel	Alice Faye, Linda Darnell
	The House on 92nd Street	Lloyd Nolan, Signe Hasso
	Johnny Angel	George Raft, Claire Trevor
	Leave Her to Heaven	Gene Tierney, Cornel Wilde
	Spellbound	Gregory Peck, Ingrid Bergman
1946	*The Big Sleep*	Humphrey Bogart, Lauren Bacall
	The Black Angel	Dan Duryea, Peter Lorre
	The Blue Dahlia	Alan Ladd, Veronica Lake
	Crack-Up	Pat O'Brien, Claire Trevor
	Criminal Court	Tom Conway, Steve Brodie
	The Dark Corner	Lucille Ball, Clifton Webb
	Deadline at Dawn	Susan Hayward, Paul Lukas
	The Killers	Burt Lancaster, Ava Gardner
	The Postman Always Rings Twice	Lana Turner, John Garfield
	The Verdict	Peter Lorre, Sidney Greenstreet
1947	*The Accused*	Loretta Young, Robert Cummings
	Boomerang!	Dana Andrews, Jane Wyatt
	Born to Kill	Lawrence Tierney, Claire Trevor
	Framed	Glenn Ford, Barry Sullivan
	The Gangster	Barry Sullivan, Akim Tamiroff

Year	Film Titles	Stars
	Kiss of Death	Victor Mature, Richard Widmark
	Lured	George Sanders, Lucille Ball
	Moss Rose	Victor Mature, Vincent Price
	The Red House	Edward G. Robinson, Judith Anderson
	Song of the Thin Man	William Powell, Myrna Loy
1948	The Big Clock	Ray Milland, Charles Laughton
	Call Northside 777	James Stewart, Lee J. Cobb
	Cry of the City	Victor Mature, Richard Conte
	The Dark Past	Lee J. Cobb, William Holden
	He Walked by Night	Richard Basehart, Scott Brady
	Key Largo	Humphrey Bogart, Edward G. Robinson
	The Naked City	Howard Duff, Barry Fitzgerald
	The Night Has a Thousand Eyes	Edward G. Robinson, Gail Russell
	The Street with No Name	Mark Stevens, Richard Widmark
	T-Men	Dennis O'Keefe, Wallace Ford
1949	The Big Steal	Robert Mitchum, William Bendix
	The Bribe	Robert Taylor, Ava Gardner
	Criss Cross	Burt Lancaster, Yvonne DeCarlo
	Gun Crazy	Peggy Cummins, John Dall
	Johnny Stool Pigeon	Howard Duff, Shelly Winters
	The Man on the Eiffel Tower	Charles Laughton, Franchot Tone
	Take One False Step	William Powell, Shelley Winters
	Tension	Richard Basehart, Audrey Totter
	Thieves' Highway	Richard Conte, Lee J. Cobb
	White Heat	James Cagney, Virginia Mayo

The Crime Series

In addition to the foregoing, a remarkable number of crime and mystery series existed, testifying to their popularity with audiences. They usually featured a sleuth, often accompanied by a humorous sidekick, and they could run for years at a time. Even the most mediocre ones apparently had their fans, although some series lasted only for a few pictures. Probably the best-known and most popular of the several mystery series running during the 1940s based its episodes on the character of Sherlock Holmes. Not that it lacked for challengers: Charlie Chan, Boston Blackie, the Saint, the Falcon, The Lone Wolf, and many others also appeared on movie screens and illustrate the popularity enjoyed by this type of film.

The Sherlock Holmes pictures. In 1888, Sir Arthur Conan Doyle (1859–1930) published his first Sherlock Holmes story, *A Study in Scarlet,* and it found an immediate, enthusiastic audience. He wrote many more novels and short stories about this detective, penning his last tale in 1927. By that time, the man in the deerstalker cap had long since been adapted to the stage, and the first Holmes movie came along in 1900.

Dozens more Holmes motion pictures followed, so that by 1939, Sherlock Holmes existed as a well-established fictional character, known to millions.

In that year, Twentieth Century-Fox, a major Hollywood studio, released a new Holmes film, *The Hound of the Baskervilles,* based on a 1902 novel by Doyle. It stars Basil Rathbone (1892–1967) as the pipe-smoking detective and Nigel Bruce (1895–1953) as the bumbling Dr. Watson for comic relief. The picture did so well that Fox promptly produced a sequel, *The Adventures of Sherlock Holmes,* using the same two leads.

With the beginning of the 1940s, Universal Pictures obtained the Holmes franchise, and it became a goldmine for them. Retaining both Rathbone and Bruce, the studio released 12 titles between 1942 and 1946 and, in the process, wandered rather far from the Victorian roots of Doyle's original stories. A number of the pictures have Holmes and Watson battling Nazi spies and saboteurs in contemporary settings, and the films usually end with Rathbone waxing eloquent about the close ties between England and the United States and the need to fight for victory over fascism. Hollywood hokum, but even with the changes to the Doyle canon, the pictures developed a loyal cadre of fans, and Rathbone and Bruce have endured to the present as entertaining embodiments of the fictional pair.

In light of their success, NBC (National Broadcasting Company), and later MBS (Mutual Broadcasting System), carried *Sherlock Holmes* from 1939 until 1946, which means the **radio** shows were on the air during the same period the films played theaters. With many more broadcasts than movies, scriptwriters had to create countless half-hour cases for the legendary sleuth to solve. Bruce narrated the series in his humorous style, and sound effects experts gave the shows atmosphere.

The Boston Blackie pictures. Boston Blackie, a semireformed safecracker turned sleuth, first entertained readers in 1914 in a series of short stories written by Jack Boyle (1881–1928). Adapted to film during the silent era, Blackie returned in a long-running (1941–1949) group of inexpensive sound pictures that enjoyed an enthusiastic following. Columbia Pictures tapped Chester Morris (1901–1970), an actor who had had an up-and-down career in the 1930s, mainly in gangster movies, to play Blackie. He took sole possession of the part for the series' duration.

TABLE 40. Sherlock Homes Movies from Universal Pictures, 1942–1946

Year	Movie Titles	Stars
1942	*Sherlock Holmes and the Secret Weapon* *Sherlock Holmes and the Voice of Terror*	Basil Rathbone, Nigel Bruce
1943	*Sherlock Holmes Faces Death* *Sherlock Holmes in Washington*	Basil Rathbone, Nigel Bruce
1944	*Sherlock Holmes and the Spider Woman* *The Pearl of Death* *The Scarlet Claw*	Basil Rathbone, Nigel Bruce
1945	*The House of Fear* *The Woman in Green* *Pursuit to Algiers*	Basil Rathbone, Nigel Bruce
1946	*Terror by Night* *Dressed to Kill*	Basil Rathbone, Nigel Bruce

Morris fit the role of the wisecracking crook-detective well, eventually appearing in 14 features. Formulaic B movies, they start with the commission of a crime; Blackie gets blamed because of his questionable past, and so he must find the perpetrator. Some fisticuffs, a gunshot or two, and then the tale ends with the arrest of the real criminal. In the heyday of the double feature, the Boston Blackie pictures, seldom more than 70 minutes long (and sometimes shorter), fit the lower half of the bill perfectly.

As with the Holmes adventures, Boston Blackie made the transition to radio, running from 1944 to 1950, mainly in syndication. Chester Morris did the voice of Blackie at first, but other actors took on the assignment in 1945.

The Charlie Chan pictures. Almost as well-known as Sherlock Holmes, at least to moviegoers, Charlie Chan began his fictional career in 1925 in a series of tales written by novelist-playwright Earl Derr Biggers (1884–1933). The first of these, *The House Without a Key,* introduced readers to his Honolulu detective of Chinese descent, and soon thereafter the author penned five more Chan novels, the last of which, *Keeper of the Keys,* came out in 1932, shortly before Biggers's death.

The novelty of an Asian detective soon intrigued Hollywood moviemakers, and 1931 saw the first Charlie Chan opus, *Charlie Chan Carries On,* a product of the Fox Film Corporation (later to become Twentieth Century-Fox). It stars Warner Oland (1879–1938), a Swedish-born actor who, thanks to exaggerated makeup, would play the Chinese character in 16 low-budget movies until 1937. White actors frequently portrayed Asian characters, a comment on racial attitudes of the time.

With the series well established and popular, Fox hired Sidney Toler (1874–1947), another white performer, to portray the detective in *Charlie Chan in Honolulu* (1938). Toler took to the role and played Chan in a total of 22 features that ran until 1947 and *The Trap.* By this time, Monogram Pictures, a lower-tier studio that specialized in cheap productions, had taken over the long-running franchise and wanted to continue it. The studio brought in yet another non-Asian actor, Roland Winters (1904–1989), as

TABLE 41. Boston Blackie Movies from Columbia Pictures, 1941–1949

Year	Movie Titles	Stars
1941	*Confessions of Boston Blackie* *Meet Boston Blackie*	Chester Morris
1942	*Alias Boston Blackie* *Boston Blackie Goes Hollywood*	Chester Morris
1943	*After Midnight with Boston Blackie* *The Chance of a Lifetime*	Chester Morris
1944	*One Mysterious Night*	Chester Morris
1945	*Boston Blackie Booked on Suspicion* *Boston Blackie's Rendezvous*	Chester Morris
1946	*Boston Blackie and the Law* *A Close Call for Boston Blackie* *The Phantom Thief*	Chester Morris
1948	*Trapped by Boston Blackie*	Chester Morris
1949	*Boston Blackie's Chinese Venture*	Chester Morris

Toler's replacement. Although it had deteriorated in quality, the series lasted another six movies, finally ending with *The Sky Dragon* in 1949.

In all, the Oland-Toler-Winters movies totaled 44 Charlie Chan features. Of these, 24, or more than half, came out during the 1940s.

Purely formulaic B movies, these pictures nonetheless developed a core of devoted fans. Charlie either gets assigned a case or stumbles upon a crime. His sons—usually referred as "Number One Son," "Number Two Son," and so on—attempt to assist "Pop," but they usually get in the way and muddle the clues. But Charlie carries on, quoting supposedly Chinese proverbs as he does so. Humor soon becomes a standard offering in the series, and audiences loved it. Eventually, however, the jokes and aphorisms lost their punch, and Charlie Chan seemed a dated figure in a postwar world.

At about the same time *Charlie Chan Carries On* began playing theaters, NBC radio broadcast a serialized version of *The Black Camel*, a 1929 Chan novel written by Biggers. Other extended works followed, but the shows had an erratic schedule in the 1930s. Finally, in 1944, NBC introduced *The Adventures of Charlie Chan,* with Ed Begley (1901–1970) playing Charlie. In both the movie and radio versions, the detective speaks with a patois neither Chinese nor English but one that patronizes, in a stereotyped way,

TABLE 42. Charlie Chan Movies from Fox and Monogram, 1940–1949

Year	Movie Titles	Stars
1940	*Charlie Chan at the Wax Museum* *Charlie Chan in Panama* *Charlie Chan's Murder Cruise* *Murder Over New York*	Sidney Toler
1941	*Charlie Chan in Rio* *Dead Men Tell*	Sidney Toler
1942	*Castle in the Desert*	Sidney Toler
1944	*Charlie Chan in Black Magic* *Charlie Chan in the Secret Service* *The Chinese Cat*	Sidney Toler
1945	*The Jade Mask* *The Red Dragon* *The Scarlet Clue* *The Shanghai Cobra*	Sidney Toler
1946	*Dangerous Money* *Dark Alibi* *Shadows Over Chinatown* *The Trap*	Sidney Toler
1947	*The Chinese Ring*	Roland Winters
1948	*Docks of New Orleans* *The Golden Eye* *Shanghai Chest* *The Feathered Serpent*	Roland Winters
1949	*The Sky Dragon*	Roland Winters

any Asian for whom English is a second language. Unfortunately, this kind of characterization becomes especially apparent on radio. The show ran until 1948.

Although the series never really competed with the Charlie Chan movies, Monogram Pictures at the close of the 1930s released *Mr. Wong, Detective.* An obvious attempt to challenge Fox's Charlie Chan, the plot came from a popular sequence of short stories by Hugh Wiley (1884–1968) that ran in *Collier's* magazine. The studio managed to land Boris Karloff (1887–1969), the actor famed for his roles in horror pictures, to play Mr. Wong. Through the magic of makeup, Karloff made a passable Chinese character.

Two more Mr. Wong pictures came along in the 1930s, and another pair—*The Fatal Hour* and *Phantom of Chinatown*—in 1940, but they never rivaled Charlie Chan. In the final picture, *Phantom of Chinatown,* an Asian actor named Keye Luke (1904–1991) replaced Karloff and portrayed Mr. Wong, something of a first for American movies. Luke also on occasion played one of Charlie Chan's sons on screen.

The Saint pictures. Author Leslie Charteris (1907–1993) in 1928 created a character unique among the mystery/detective figures of the day. He named him Simon Templar, but readers knew him better as the Saint. A skilled thief, but also an amateur detective, the roguish Simon Templar likes fast cars and beautiful women and lives on the fringes of the law. Frequently blamed for crimes committed by others, he uses his sleuthing skills and underworld contacts to solve cases and preserve his innocence. In time, over 100 novels featuring the Saint were published, although writers other than Charteris wrote the later ones. As with the other series discussed above, commercial radio chronicled a number of Saint movies during the late 1930s and early 1940s.

For whatever reasons, these films never achieved any great box office success or critical renown; when actor George Sanders (1906–1972) took on the role in 1939, he gave Templar a smooth, sophisticated air, but the movies remained B pictures on the lower half of a double bill. Interestingly, when Sanders agreed to appear in the later Falcon films mentioned below, he changed his screen persona hardly at all; only the most dedicated fan could distinguish Sanders' Saint from Sanders' Falcon. In fact, Charteris threatened legal action against RKO on account of the films' similarity, charging infringement on artistic property. The Saint movies expired in 1943, whereas the Falcon pictures continued until 1949.

On radio, Charteris's creation fared only a little better; NBC ran a show called *The Saint* in 1945, although CBS quickly acquired it, with broadcasts until 1948. After

TABLE 43.   Saint Movies from RKO Radio, 1938–1943

Year	Movie Titles	Stars
1938	*The Saint in New York*	Louis Hayward
1939	*The Saint Strikes Back*	George Sanders
	The Saint in London	
	The Saint Takes Over	George Sanders
	The Saint's Double Trouble	
1941	*The Saint in Palm Springs*	George Sanders
	The Saint's Vacation	Hugh Sinclair
1943	*The Saint Meets the Tiger*	Hugh Sinclair

that, a media merry-go-round kept shifting networks, times, and players, but *The Saint* could still be heard as late as 1951. Of the numerous actors who played Templar, Vincent Price (1911–1993) probably remains the best known for his portrayals in the late 1940s and early 1950s.

The Falcon pictures. Featuring another wealthy, sophisticated character who skirts the law on occasion, the Falcon movies came from the pen of writer Michael Arlen (1895–1956). He created the Falcon expressly for the screen in 1941. RKO Radio Pictures, already the owner of rights to *The Saint,* bought Arlen's concept and proceeded to produce *The Gay Falcon* that same year. Without missing a beat, the studio cast the debonair George Sanders (1906–1972) as Gay Lawrence, or the Falcon (which explains the use of "gay" in the title). Fresh from his role as the Saint, Sanders moved easily into the role of this new character,

Sanders' first appearance as the Falcon received applause from most people who saw it. RKO convinced him to do another, which then led to yet another. In late 1942, however, Sanders tired of the character and wanted to leave the series in order to move on to other parts. In the fourth episode, *The Falcon's Brother,* the script has Gay Lawrence killed and his place taken by his brother Tom, played by Tom Conway (1904–1967). A device, certainly, but intriguing because Tom Conway was, in real life, George Sanders's brother. Born Thomas Sanders, he changed his name to avoid confusion with his younger sibling.

In *The Falcon Strikes Back* (1943), Conway assumes the solo lead and carries on the name "the Falcon," a role he would proceed to play for another nine pictures. In his final appearance, in late 1946 as the suave character in *The Falcon's Adventure,* many thought the entertaining series had come to an end. But in 1948, a studio calling itself Falcon Pictures Corporation released *Devil's Cargo.* In this low-budget movie, actor

TABLE 44. Falcon Movies from RKO Radio and Falcon Pictures Corp., 1941–1949

Year	Movie Titles	Stars
1941	*A Date with the Falcon*	George Sanders
	The Gay Falcon	
1942	*The Falcon Takes Over*	George Sanders
	The Falcon's Brother	George Sanders, Tom Conway
1943	*The Falcon and the Co-Eds*	Tom Conway
	The Falcon in Danger	
	The Falcon Strikes Back	
1944	*The Falcon in Hollywood*	Tom Conway
	The Falcon in Mexico	
	The Falcon Out West	
1945	*The Falcon in San Francisco*	Tom Conway
1946	*The Falcon's Adventure*	Tom Conway
	The Falcon's Alibi	
1948	*Appointment with Murder*	John Calvert
	Devil's Cargo	
1949	*Search for Danger*	John Calvert

John Calvert (b. 1911) plays a man billed as Michael "the Falcon" Waring. Subpar in all respects, the film nevertheless signaled the return of the Falcon. Calvert made two additional appearances in the role, and then the series truly did expire.

Naturally, radio executives displayed interest in the successful Falcon series. NBC created the first shows in 1943, then Mutual carried *The Falcon* from 1945 until 1950, whereupon it reverted to NBC until 1952, and finally back to Mutual for a two-year run. Various actors played the Falcon, but not George Sanders nor Tom Conway, and the airwaves missed their mellifluous voices.

The Lone Wolf pictures. Yet another crime-mystery series involving a solitary operator who happens to be an expert jewel thief, independently wealthy with a dapper way about him, the Lone Wolf can outwit both the police and criminals. He bears the name Michael Lanyard, but people appropriately call him the Lone Wolf. The character grew out of a series of novels by Louis Joseph Vance (1879–1933), a prolific American writer. In 1914, he wrote *The Lone Wolf;* its success led him to write several more featuring Lanyard. By 1917, a silent movie had been made of *The Lone Wolf,* launching one of the very first detective cycles on film. Throughout the 1920s and 1930s, additional titles played theaters, but they featured various performers taking the part of Michael Lanyard, and not until 1939 did a well-defined series go into production.

Warren William (1894–1948), himself a suave, urbane actor comfortable in many roles, initially portrayed the Lone Wolf for *The Lone Wolf Spy Hunt.* He reprised the part an additional eight times. Released by Columbia Pictures, the Lone Wolf signaled the arrival of a new series to compete with all the other crime/mystery pictures then attempting to attract audiences. Gerald Mohr (1914–1968) replaced William in 1946, and Ron Randell (1918–2005) came aboard in 1949 for the conclusion to the series.

Among the many other crime and detective series that showed in theaters during the 1940s, a few of the other favorites include *Crime Doctor,* starring Warner Baxter

TABLE 45. The Lone Wolf Pictures from Columbia, 1939–1949

Year	Movie Titles	Stars
1939	*The Lone Wolf Spy Hunt*	Warren William
1940	*The Lone Wolf Strikes* *The Lone Wolf Meets a Lady*	Warren William
1941	*The Lone Wolf Keeps a Date* *The Lone Wolf Takes a Chance* *Secrets of the Lone Wolf*	Warren William
1942	*Counter-Espionage*	Warren William
1943	*One Dangerous Night* *Passport to Suez*	Warren William
1946	*The Notorious Lone Wolf*	Gerald Mohr
1947	*The Lone Wolf in Mexico* *The Lone Wolf in London*	Gerald Mohr
1949	*The Lone Wolf and His Lady*	Ron Randell

Note: Films are arranged chronologically.

(1889–1951), which ran from 1943 until 1949 and came from a radio show with the same name. *Inner Sanctum Mysteries,* another radio spin-off, starred Lon Chaney Jr. (1906–1973) and leaned more toward horror than detection. It ran from 1943 until 1945. Bulldog Drummond, a detective created during the 1920s, appeared in a few pictures during the 1940s; a radio show also ran, off and on, from 1941 until 1949. Even Dick Tracy, who had first appeared in a 1931 comic strip by Chester Gould (1900–1985), had his moment in the movies. He served as the main character in a number of serials from the late 1930s and early 1940s; the mid-1940s saw several features with the hawk-nosed detective.

All in all, crime and detective movies have proved to be among the most popular and enduring forms of film entertainment for the 1940s. From B movies like the Boston Blackie and Saint series to elegant whodunits like *The Maltese Falcon* and *The Big Clock,* the genre displayed great depth and variety. Proof of its popularity can be found among the many radio adaptations of such motion pictures.

See also: Best Sellers (Books); Bogart, Humphrey; Comic Strips; Drama (Film); Radio Programming: Action, Crime, Police, and Detective Shows; Radio Programming: Children's Shows, Serials, and Adventure Series; Serial Films

Selected Reading
Clarens, Carlos. *Crime Movies: From Griffith to the Godfather and Beyond.* New York: W. W. Norton, 1980.
Dunning, John. *On the Air: The Encyclopedia of Old-Time Radio.* New York: Oxford University Press, 1998.
McArthur, Colin. *Underworld U.S.A.* New York: Viking Press, 1972.

CROSBY, BING

A native of Tacoma, Washington, Harry Lillis Crosby (1903–1977) would eventually emerge as arguably the most popular male vocalist of the 20th century. The family moved to Spokane in 1906, and around 1910 a childhood friend nicknamed him Bingo because of his early fondness for a comic strip called *The Bingville Bugle,* written and illustrated by humorist Newton Newkirk (1870–1936). Friends soon shortened it to Bing, and the name stuck. He enrolled in Spokane's Gonzaga University and joined a local band, the Musicaladers, led by Al Rinker (b. Alton, 1907–1982). After a handful of paying jobs with the Musicaladers, Crosby found the lure of show business irresistible and dropped out of college in 1924, his senior year, to join forces with Rinker. During the group's performances, Crosby would frequently sing through a megaphone, as did numerous vocalists then in order to be heard. His singing nonetheless provided a hint about the direction his career would take.

The advent of electronic sound amplification and improved condenser microphones allowed him to discard the megaphone and intimately caress the lyrics. Fans and critics soon dubbed this style "crooning," meaning to hum or sing softly directly into an electrical microphone, first in a melancholy way, but finally just singing without putting much force behind it, be it sad or happy. Crooners seldom performed at concerts or in dance halls, since these venues tended to be too big and too noisy; they at first existed on and for **radio** and later dominated recordings.

The popular bandleader Paul Whiteman (1890–1967), a man always on the lookout for talent, heard about Crosby and Rinker in 1926; soon the two found themselves part of Whiteman's extensive organization, a giant step in their careers. Crosby met many individuals who would influence his artistic growth as a vocalist; he also associated with movie and radio stars and built a network of friends that would contribute to his flowering as a show business personality.

Later that year, Crosby and Rinker met another young musician, Harry Barris (1905–1962). The three formed an instant rapport, and out of that came a trio they called The Rhythm Boys. Whiteman again took notice and installed the threesome in his orchestra, giving them remarkable freedom; they could record and perform independently when not tied to prior commitments. The bandleader even landed them several recording contracts.

Bing Crosby and songwriter Johnny Mercer (on the left) engaging in some patter, probably on Crosby's radio show, given the NBC initials on the microphone. Over the years, Crosby recorded a significant number of Mercer's compositions. (Photofest)

The Rhythm Boys moved from Whiteman to work with bandleader Gus Arnheim (1887–1955). They cut a number of recordings, appeared on his radio show, and received featured billing with the aggregation. Crosby's voice dominates these performances and marks his inevitable emergence as a star in his own right. He parted from The Rhythm Boys in the early 1930s and become a single; he soon achieved acclaim as a crooner and signed with Brunswick Records, a major label.

Jack Kapp (1901–1949) led Brunswick, and he encouraged Crosby at every turn, serving as mentor and friend. Many of the early tunes Crosby cut for his new employer quickly became hits, the first of hundreds he would record throughout the upcoming years. In 1934, following a convoluted transaction, a new record label appeared on the U.S. market—Decca, a name previously associated with an English recording company. Crosby moved from Brunswick to Decca and promptly rose to the top of the company's roster of performers and quickly made Decca a leader in the industry: one-third of all the singles sold during the late 1930s and early 1940s bore the Decca label.

Whereas most male vocalists in the popular field at that time tended to be tenors, Crosby possessed a warm baritone, and most of his output focused on the romantic side of life. In later recordings, he lowered his pitch slightly and dropped some of the vibrato, which allowed him to branch out into other genres. He recorded Western songs, blues, and **jazz,** moving away from straight romantic crooning. He often injected some humor into his inimitable style, usually with light-hearted banter, always a part of his personality. Crosby's unending flow of recordings—he eventually cut almost 2,000 titles during his career, most of them for Decca—coupled by their widespread acceptance and sales in the hundreds of millions, made him the biggest star in popular music throughout the 1930s and 1940s.

In addition to recordings, Crosby moved to radio in 1931, when CBS (Columbia Broadcasting System) programmed *Fifteen Minutes with Bing Crosby*. While there, he helped write "Where the Blue of the Night (Meets the Gold of the Day)" (1931); it quickly became his enduring theme song. For the next 40 years, the tune would be associated with him and few other singers would even attempt it. In 1936, he became the host on NBC's (National Broadcasting Company) *Kraft Music Hall*. Already a successful show, it soon became a Thursday night ritual for millions of radio listeners, and Crosby would remain there until 1946. His radio personality came over the airwaves as that of a nice, easygoing guy, someone people would like for their neighbor. The casualness might be studied, but it worked.

His continuing radio success allowed him to invite his favorite musicians and vocalists as guests on the show, and that translated as popular standards, along with some good jazz and **swing.** Although the *Kraft Music Hall* might seem as relaxed as its host, Crosby demanded high levels of professionalism. A significant part of the show involved comedy, and that meant frequent visits from **Bob Hope** (1903–2003), his costar in numerous motion pictures that played throughout the 1940s. Of course, the

TABLE 46.   Bing Crosby Feature Films, 1940–1949

Year	Film Titles	Notes
1940	*Road to Singapore*	with Bob Hope and Dorothy Lamour
	If I Had My Way	with Six Hits and a Miss
	Rhythm on the River	with Mary Martin
1941	*Road to Zanzibar*	with Bob Hope and Dorothy Lamour
	Birth of the Blues	with Mary Martin
1942	*Don't Hook Now*	with Bob Hope
	Holiday Inn [Academy Award for best song, "White Christmas"]	with Fred Astaire
	Road to Morocco	with Bob Hope and Dorothy Lamour
	Star Spangled Rhythm	with many popular stars
1943	*Dixie*	with Dorothy Lamour
1944	*Going My Way* [Academy Award for best song, "Swinging on a Star"]	[Academy Award for best actor for Crosby]
	Here Comes the Waves	with Betty Hutton
1945	*The Bells of St. Mary's*	with Ingrid Bergman
1946	*Road to Utopia*	with Bob Hope and Dorothy Lamour
	Blue Skies	with Fred Astaire
1947	*Welcome Stranger*	with Barry Fitzgerald
	Road to Rio	with Bob Hope and Dorothy Lamour
1948	*The Emperor Waltz*	with Joan Fontaine
1949	*A Connecticut Yankee in King Arthur's Court*	with William Bendix
	Top o' the Morning	with Barry Fitzgerald

main ingredient remained music, whether performed by Crosby himself or one of the many talented guests.

Along with extensive radio exposure, Crosby churned out numerous films that capitalize on his easygoing style. Usually sustained by wafer-thin plots, they provide Crosby ample opportunity to sing, and he eventually appeared in 79 **movies,** including 20 full-length features during the 1940s. His motion pictures also demonstrated how different media—radio, recording, and film—can interconnect for a major entertainer.

If the films mentioned above were not enough, between 1950 and 1974 Crosby would make 17 more features, including two additional Road pictures with Bob Hope and Dorothy Lamour—*Road to Bali* (1952) and *The Road to Hong Kong* (1962).

During the war years, Crosby toured overseas, entertaining troops everywhere, and soldiers loved his relaxed shows. He also made film shorts supporting **war bonds,** plus many personal appearances for bonds, **scrap drives,** and anything else that might help the war effort on the home front. When all is said and done, however, singing remained Crosby's primary strength.

As Table 47 shows, Bing Crosby visited the hit charts regularly, with 41 songs between 1940 and 1949 (1947 proving the exception). He enjoyed his best year in 1944, with 10 songs listed, almost one-quarter of the total. More remarkable still, out of the top 20 songs for the year, Crosby claimed seven, or roughly one-third of them. Over his lengthy recording career—from 1926 until 1977—he scored more than 300 hits out of the several thousand songs he performed.

Crosby also enjoyed a good working relationship with the popular **Andrews Sisters,** an effervescent trio of siblings with whom he regularly recorded. They appear eight times on Table 47, although that counts only charted songs. He also made other, less commercially successful, recordings with them; not every tune can be a top hit.

For his *Kraft Music Hall* radio show on December 25, 1941, Crosby introduced "**White Christmas,**" a seasonal tune written by Irving Berlin (1888–1989). It attracted little more than passing attention at the time, and apparently the program failed to be preserved in any way. In the late summer of 1942, Paramount Pictures released *Holiday Inn,* a cheery musical with Crosby and Fred Astaire (1899–1987). The picture enjoyed immediate box office success and became a Christmas favorite, even though it hit theaters long before the start of the holiday season. Paramount had not marketed *Holiday Inn* as a Christmas movie, since the picture recognizes a number of other traditional celebrations in the course of its story. But during the film, Crosby sings "White Christmas." Following the movie's premiere, Decca put on sale a soundtrack recording of the score, and this time around, "White Christmas" became an overnight hit.

Although accurate figures do not exist, "My Blue Heaven," as recorded in 1927 by an early crooner name Gene Austin (1900–1972), had gained the reputation of being the best-selling American recording of all time—or at least until Crosby unseated it with his rendition of Berlin's song. By October, Crosby's recording had rocketed up the charts, quickly establishing itself as the No. 1 song for 1942, and its good fortune did not end with the start of a new year. It reappears as a hit in 1945 and 1946, an unprecedented occurrence. By the end of the 20th century, "White Christmas" had accumulated sales of over 100 million records, both singles and albums.

On the heels of "White Christmas," Crosby followed that success with 1943's "I'll Be Home for Christmas." For many holiday seasons thereafter, this nostalgic offering

TABLE 47. Top-Rated Songs Performed by Bing Crosby, 1940–1949

Year	Song	Notes
1940	"Only Forever"	
	"Sierra Sue"	
	"The Singing Hills"	
	"Trade Winds"	
	"Yodelin' Jive"	with the Andrews Sisters
1941	"Dolores"	
	"Shepherd Serenade"	
1942	"White Christmas"	
	"Deep in the Heart of Texas"	
1943	"Sunday, Monday or Always"	
	"Pistol Packin' Mama"	with the Andrews Sisters
	"People Will Say We're in Love"	with Trudy Erwin
	"I'll Be Home for Christmas (If Only in My Dreams)"	
	"Moonlight Becomes You"	
	"Oh! What a Beautiful Mornin'"	with Trudy Erwin
1944	"Swinging on a Star"	
	"Don't Fence Me In"	with the Andrews Sisters
	"(There'll Be a) Hot Time in the Town of Berlin (When the Yanks Go Marching In)"	with the Andrews Sisters
	"San Fernando Valley"	
	"I Love You"	
	"I'll Be Seeing You"	
	"Amor"	
	"Is You Is or Is You Ain't (Ma' Baby)"	with the Andrews Sisters
	"Poinciana (Song of the Tree)"	
	"Too-La-Loo-Ra-Loo-Rai (That's an Irish Lullaby)	
1945	"I Can't Begin to Tell You"	
	"It's Been a Long, Long Time"	
	"White Christmas" (originally 1942)	
	"Ac-Cent-Tchu-Ate the Positive"	with the Andrews Sisters
	"On the Navajo Trail"	with the Andrews Sisters
	"You Belong to My Heart"	
	"On the Atchison, Topeka and the Santa Fe"	
1946	"White Christmas" (originally 1942)	
	"South America, Take It Away"	with the Andrews Sisters
	"Sioux City Sue"	with the Jesters
	"Symphony"	
1947	[no songs charted]	
1948	"Now Is the Hour"	
1949	"Far Away Places"	
	"Galway Bay"	
	"Some Enchanted Evening"	
	"Mule Train"	

also attracted substantial sales, and it continues to show up in various Christmas anthologies. Reflecting the sadness felt by many Americans, both those with loved ones in service and those far away longing to be home, the title effectively summarizes the dilemma faced by millions during wartime.

In the process of becoming a multimedia star, Crosby and the people around him created a persona—that of the easygoing, likable guy, someone of inherent modesty and enduring optimism. For the Depression years, the World War II period and the postwar era, this image appealed to millions. In reality, an astute businessman who had to practice his air of casualness, few people realized how powerfully Crosby influenced show business and American popular music.

See also: Comic Strips; Country Music; Musicals (Film); Radio Programming: Music and Variety Shows

Selected Reading
Crosby, Bing. *Bing Crosby: It's Easy to Remember.* 4 CDs. Proper Records, 2001.
Giddins, Gary. *Bing Crosby: A Pocketful of Dreams; The Early Years, 1903–1940.* Boston: Little, Brown, 2001.
Grudens, Richard. *Bing Crosby: Crooner of the Century.* Stony Brook, NY: Celebrity Profiles, 2004.

CROSLEY AUTOMOBILES

A visionary, Powel Crosley Jr. (1886–1961) dreamed of creating a small, inexpensive automobile available to all. Born into relative affluence in Cincinnati, Ohio, he began the preliminary work on his first car, which he called a Marathon Six, in 1907. Although this first venture failed, he took jobs in Indiana with other modest, automotive-oriented companies and learned more about motorcars. At this time, the auto industry had by no means chosen Detroit as its manufacturing center; dozens of entrepreneurs around the country tinkered in shops large and small, hoping to design and develop cars that would catch the public eye.

In 1916, Crosley decided that better fortunes lie with accessories for **automobiles**. With his brother, Lewis Crosley (1888–1978), as his astute business manager, he developed several successful gadgets for motorists and began to establish the Crosley name for quality products. The rise of the **radio** receiver business following World War I, coupled with high prices, led him to build a cheap radio of his own. By the early 1920s, he and Lewis had formed both the Crosley Broadcasting Corporation and the Crosley Radio Corporation; his cheap Pup radios soon led all competitors. Selling for under $10 in 1925 (about $120 in 2008 dollars), whereas most other company's models sold in the $100 range (about $1,225 in 2008 dollars), his firm dominated the market for several years. He also demonstrated the first practical car radio in 1930.

Success with radio endeavors led the Crosleys to branch out into home appliances, including the best-selling Shelvador refrigerator (the door held shelves, unheard of at the time) in the early 1930s. Powel Crosley even built several airplanes but did not pursue this line. His personal fortune continued to accrue during this period, and investments in yachts, land, and innovative home building techniques—he even acquired the Cincinnati Reds **baseball** team—occupied his hours, but the early dream of an inexpensive automobile never left his mind.

Finally, in 1939, he introduced his first Crosley car, a diminutive vehicle that weighed less than 900 pounds, which he manufactured at plants in Indiana. He first showed it at the 1939–1940 New York World's Fair and the Indianapolis Speedway, and it drew thousands of curious onlookers. In an ingenious scheme, he allowed those department stores that carried his appliances to also market the Crosley automobile. Its list price averaged $250 (or slightly less than $3,900 in 2008 dollars). His appliance experience had taught Crosley about mass production techniques, and so in 1940 he built over 400 Crosleys, available in both convertible coupe and sedan models, most of which sold.

The basic car boasted a 12-horsepower Waukesha engine, had an 80-inch wheelbase (or just over six feet long), and measured a narrow 48 inches wide, meaning it could manage the doors of most commercial establishments where it might be displayed. In addition, its tiny motor could nurse 50 miles out of a gallon of gas, far more than the cars manufactured by any other American companies at that time. Many other technological achievements resided in the little automobile, and Crosley held high hopes for his creation. In 1941, he produced almost 2,300 cars before World War II intervened. The last American car manufacturer to cease production in 1942, he managed to turn out an additional 1,000 or so Crosleys, which buyers took because of gas **rationing** and the vehicle's good mileage figures. The company had added a pickup truck, a panel truck, and several other models by this time.

With the end of the war in 1945, Crosley stood poised to resume production. He changed motors, introducing the CoBra (copper brazed) engine in 1946; it put out 26 horsepower, or more than double that of previous models. He manufactured over 22,500 Crosleys in 1947 and followed with almost 25,000 vehicles in 1948, his best year. But despite those numbers, his venture began to slide sharply in 1949. A redesigned engine, the CIBA (cast iron block assembly), more reliable than its predecessors, did little to help the struggling company. The introduction of still more models, including the Hot Shot Roadster—billed as the first American sports car—and the Super Sport, also could not stop the decline, and in 1952 the company ceased operations.

Times had changed; the postwar rush to consume material goods did not include purchasing tiny cars. With newfound prosperity, Americans wanted full-size automobiles, preferably dripping with chrome trim and boasting large, eight-cylinder engines, regardless of low gas mileage. Car sales, overall, soared into the millions, and the paltry 20,000 or so Crosleys that dealers managed to sell each year could not compete; their image—small, tinny, noisy, and cheap—did not fit the image of what buyers wanted in a new car.

A good idea whose time never came, the various Crosleys built from 1939 to 1952 provide a footnote to American automotive history of the 1940s. Collectors' clubs have kept the name alive, and every so often one can be spotted, usually with the top down, on the open road.

See also: Aviation; Motorsports; Technology

Selected Reading
"Crosley Cars." www.geocities.com/motorcity/garage/7896/crosley.htm
McClure, Rusty, with David Stern and Michael A. Banks. *Crosley.* Cincinnati: Clerisy Press, 2008.

D

DANCE

Dance has always been a part of the American scene, and the 1940s proved to be an active decade for its advancement both as a social outlet and a performing art. In the popular culture arena, Hollywood continued its tradition of producing numerous musical films with lots of dancing, while new stars got a start at the Cotton Club, a Harlem nightclub, and new dances and steps traveled from another Harlem spot, the Savoy Ballroom, to downtown New York and across the United States. In the performing arts, Broadway frequently offered musical plays; in ballet, themes of everyday life occasionally replaced the traditional classic topics. As a previously distinct individual form of dance, ballet sometimes combined with modern and popular dance movements.

In the midst of all of this activity, celebrities emerged, and some became giants of dance, such as Fred Astaire (1899–1987), Gene Kelly (1912–1996), Hermes Pan (1909–1990), George Balanchine (1904–1983), Agnes de Mille (1905–1998), Martha Graham (1894–1991), and Jerome Robbins (1918–1998). Group acts, including the Nicholas Brothers, the Berry Brothers, and the Four Step Brothers, also gained popularity and recognition for their talent. Likewise, Broadway musicals, such as *Pal Joey* (1940), *Oklahoma!* (1943), and *Annie Get Your Gun* (1946) featured much dancing and experienced commercial success followed by even more popularity in the 1950s as **movies.**

Two male dancers, Fred Astaire and Gene Kelly, one already established, the other just starting, surpassed all others. Astaire's career had begun in 1917 and extended over seven decades. He excelled as a stage and film dancer, choreographer, actor, and singer. Already a Broadway veteran, he made his motion picture debut (as himself) in 1933's *Dancing Lady.* By 1940, he had appeared in 10 more movies, dancing in all but one with Ginger Rogers (1911–1995) and always bringing elegance, grace, originality, and precision to the screen.

In the 1940s, Astaire added 11 more movie musicals to his resume, starting with *Broadway Melody of 1940* and *Second Chorus,* both in 1940, and ending with *The Barkleys of Broadway* in 1949, his last film performance with Ginger Rogers. His other notable partners during the 1940s included Paulette Goddard (1910–1990) in *Second Chorus,* Rita Hayworth (1918–1987) in *You Were Never Lovelier* (1942), Ann Miller (1923–2004) in *Easter Parade* (1948), and Eleanor Powell (1912–1982) in *Broadway Melody of 1940.*

Gene Kelly, new on the dance scene at the beginning of the 1940s, soon garnered enthusiastic attention from the American public. In addition to dancing, he worked as an actor, singer, and choreographer. His first venture as a professional dancer occurred in 1938 on Broadway in Cole Porter's (1891–1964) *Leave It to Me.* One year later, he danced again on Broadway to his own choreography in *The Time of Your Life.*

A leading role in *Pal Joey* by Richard Rodgers (1902–1979) and Lorenz Hart (1895–1943), propelled Kelly to stardom and offers from Hollywood. Known for his energetic and athletic dancing style, Kelly made his Hollywood debut in *For Me and My Gal* (1942), directed by Busby Berkeley (1895–1976). Berkeley, a very busy choreographer and director during the 1930s and 1940s, gained much fame for his elaborate musical productions, which often involved large numbers of showgirls dancing in geometric patterns.

Kelly, like Astaire, went on to appear in a total of 11 Hollywood musicals during the decade, ending with *Take Me Out to the Ball Game* and *On the Town,* both in 1949. Astaire and Kelly partnered in a Metro-Goldwyn-Mayer (MGM) production of *Ziegfeld Follies* (1946), dancing in a number titled "The Babbitt and the Bromide," a song and dance routine performed to music and lyrics by the renowned George and Ira Gershwin (1898–1937; 1896–1983).

While Astaire and Kelly advanced their careers with relative ease, talented black performers encountered discriminatory practices. Nevertheless, a few black dancers managed to embark upon or maintain careers throughout the 1940s. One, Bill "Bojangles" Robinson (1878–1949), famous with years of work as a tap dancer, headed a black cast for the 1939 show *The Hot Mikado,* a jazz version of the Gilbert and Sullivan's 1885 operetta, *The Mikado.* The more modern interpretations appeared first on Broadway and then at the 1939–1940 New York World's Fair. Robinson managed two other performances on Broadway during the 1940s, *All in Fun* (1940) and *Memphis Bound* (1945), as well as three movies, *Let's Scuffle* and *By an Old Southern River,* both in 1942, and *Stormy Weather* (1943), a production featuring an all-black cast.

The Nicholas Brothers, Fayard (1914–2006) and Harold (1921–2000), a black dancing duo, had been tap dancing since childhood, and their journey to stardom included performing at Harlem's Cotton Club, on Broadway, and in Europe. They skillfully incorporated tap, acrobatic, and ballet moves to jazz rhythms. Success clearly came when choreographer George Balanchine invited them in 1943 to dance in the Rodgers and Hart musical *Babes in Arms.* The brothers also appeared in *Stormy Weather.* In five other Twentieth Century-Fox musical releases during the decade, they were billed as "specialty dancers" (a standard Hollywood practice, or code, concerning black entertainers in movies giving top billing to white performers).

The three Berry Brothers, Ananias "Nyas" (ca. 1913–1951), James (ca. 1915–1969), and Warren (1922–1996), had danced before audiences as children. Initially taking turns to form a duo, by 1940, they were working as a trio with an acrobatic soft shoe (no taps) and cane-work routine. They frequently executed a step called freeze and melt, whereby they would have a moment of immobility followed by a sudden dance movement. They performed in numerous venues such as the Cotton Club and the Savoy Ballroom, had a dancing competition with the Nicholas Brothers with no clear winner, and performed in several movies from the 1940s—*Lady Be Good* (1941), *Panama Hattie* (1942), *Boarding House Blues* (1948), and *You're My Everything* (1949).

Another group called themselves the Four Step Brothers, although they were not actually related and the members of the group changed over the years. They played nightclubs and theaters throughout the United States. Starting as three dancers, Maceo Anderson (1909–2001), Al Williams (1909–1981), and Red Walker (active 1920s–1960s), the trio added, off and on, a number of other talented dancers to form a quartet. Sometimes dubbed the Eight Feet of Rhythm, they excelled in fast tap routines, aerobic leaps, and **boogie-woogie** jitterbug. The Four Step Brothers received credit as being the first black act to perform at Radio City Music Hall and appeared in four Hollywood pictures during the decade: *Hi Buddy, It Ain't Hay, Rhythm of the Islands* (all 1943), and *Greenwich Village* (1944). They danced on the 1948 **television** variety show, ***The Texaco Star Theater***, hosted by Milton Berle (1908–2002), as did the Berry Brothers.

Of all the black dancers from the 1940s, Sammy Davis Jr. (1925–1990) rose to the greatest fame. He had performed as a child with his father and uncle, billing themselves as the Will Masten Trio. He served in an integrated Special Services entertainment unit with the army during World War II. After the war, he rejoined the trio, which appeared in the movie *Sweet and Low* (1947). As a solo performer and singer, he cut some albums, and in the 1950s his career soared with the addition of Broadway, television, and casino shows in Las Vegas. In the 1960s, he became a member of the Rat Pack, a group of entertainers led by his friend singer **Frank Sinatra** (1915–1998).

Dancers dance and choreographers create dance movements, but choreographers also direct and stage dance productions. The 1940s witnessed a number of outstanding choreographers on both the East and West Coasts. In Hollywood, dancer Hermes Pan started out in the 1930s as an uncredited assistant dance director and soon became the primary dance director for Fred Astaire and Ginger Rogers. Pan won a 1937 Academy Award for his work on *A Damsel in Distress* and advanced to the position of choreographer and dance director. Much in demand, he provided choreography and direction for 26 musicals during the 1940s.

Choreographer George Balanchine arrived in New York City from the Soviet Union in 1933, and immediately founded a ballet school. In 1946, he organized the Ballet Society and two years later took up residency at the New York City Center for Music and Drama, which shortly thereafter became known as the New York City Ballet. In addition to his ballet activities, he served as a choreo-grapher for Broadway productions every year of the decade. He worked with such notable composers as Irving Berlin (1888–1989) on *Louisiana Purchase* (1940–1941) and Vernon Duke (1903–1969) on *Cabin in the Sky* (1940–1941) and *The Lady Comes Across* (1942).

The genius of the choreographer can be linked to the quality of the musical composition. Early in 1940, **Aaron Copland** (1900–1990) emerged as a notable composer

Lee Dixon leads the male members of the 1943 cast of Oklahoma! *in a sprightly number choreographed by Agnes de Mille. The musical, the first Broadway production for the team of Richard Rodgers and Oscar Hammerstein II, made dance an integral part of its story. (Photofest)*

of ballet and collaborated with two outstanding choreographers, Agnes de Mille on *Rodeo* (1942) and Martha Graham on *Appalachian Spring* (1944). Both works celebrate the pioneering spirit of early American settlers and appealed to a broader audience than more traditional classical ballets. The composer-choreographer partnerships for these two productions significantly advanced the careers of Copland, de Mille, and Graham.

Agnes de Mille became a charter member of the Ballet Theatre (founded in 1939 and today known as the American Ballet Theatre) in 1940. Two years later, the Ballet Russe de Monte Carlo, an influential company founded in 1933, asked her to create a ballet that resulted in the dances performed to Copland's score of *Rodeo*. The ballet's success influenced the decision by composers Richard Rodgers and Oscar Hammerstein (1895–1960) to ask de Mille to choreograph *Oklahoma!* Dance serves as a vital force in this play, which presents a positive view of the American experience and coincided nicely with the upsurge of patriotism occurring across the country because of World War II. Box office lines at the theater extended to the far end of the block for over a year. Other hit **Broadway shows (musicals)** of the 1940s choreographed by de Mille included *Bloomer Girl* (1944), *Carousel* (1945), *Brigadoon* (1947), *Fall River Legend* (1948), and *Gentlemen Prefer Blondes* (1949).

Martha Graham, known, like de Mille, as one of the 20th century's greatest choreographers, became interested in creating dances on the theme of American history in the early 1930s and excelled in her choreography for Copland's *Appalachian Spring*. She also danced the lead role in the opening night performance on October 30, 1944. Throughout the 1940s, she produced, choreographed, and performed on Broadway along with her company, the Martha Graham Dance Group, which she had founded

1929. Her accomplishments during a career as both a dancer and teacher spanned seven decades and focused on interpretations and expression rather than traditional, stiff movements causing some to call her the "mother of modern dance."

Graham and de Mille, however, were not the first to explore interpretative dance movements. Dancers such as Isadora Duncan (1877–1927), Ruth St. Denis (1879–1968), and Doris Humphrey (1895–1958) had laid a foundation for broader acceptance of modern dance movements. From their work, Helen Tamiris (1905–1966), a major dancer and choreographer, took inspiration. She first appeared in a solo performance of modern dance in 1927 and created a suite of dances called *Negro Spirituals* (between 1928 and 1941) using jazz and spirituals to explore social themes via dance. The choreography for musical theater that Tamiris created during the 1940s included *Showboat* (1946), *Annie Get Your Gun,* and a Tony Award for her work on *Touch and Go* (1949). She also choreographed *Up in Central Park,* a 1948 movie.

Meanwhile, Balanchine, de Mille, and Graham not only experienced success in their own right but, through their work, influenced others. Jerome Robbins had danced in several Broadway shows by the late 1930s, one being the short run of *Keep Off the Grass* (1940), choreographed by Balanchine. In 1941, Robbins returned to ballet performances and appeared as a soloist with the American Ballet Theatre. Noting the success of *Oklahoma!* and intrigued by de Mille's accomplishments in making dance an integral part of musicals, Robbins conceived his first ballet. In 1944, he choreographed and danced in *Fancy Free,* a story about sailors on leave in New York, performed at the Metropolitan Opera. It featured a score written by Leonard Bernstein (1918–1990) that displayed the influences by **jazz** and symphonic music, particularly Igor Stravinsky (1882–1971) and Copland.

Robbins' storyline for *Fancy Free* served as the basis for a Broadway production titled *On the Town,* which ran from December 1944 to February 1946. The show, while introducing popular songs such as "New York, New York," with music by Bernstein and lyrics by Betty Comden (1917–2006) and Adolph Green (1914–2002), also uses dance as a fundamental part of the storytelling. In 1949, *On the Town* achieved considerable success as a movie starring Gene Kelly and Frank Sinatra.

The decade continued to be an active one for Robbins. Other Broadway productions included *Billion Dollar Baby* (1945); *High Button Shoes* (1947), which won him a Tony Award for his choreography; and *Look, Ma, I'm Dancin'!* While working on these shows, Robbins also choreographed new works for the American Ballet Theatre. In 1948, he left this company to join Balanchine's newly formed New York City Ballet as a dancer and choreographer. Before the decade ended, Robbins collaborated with composer Irving Berlin (1888–1989) and playwrights Robert E. Sherwood (1896–1955) and Moss Hart (1904–1961) on a new musical called *Miss Liberty* (1949); Robbins' choreography drew the only favorable reviews. He went on to even greater success in succeeding years, especially for his direction and choreography for *West Side Story* (1957).

Broadway was not the only dance show in New York. The Rockettes, a precision dance company that originated in Missouri in 1925, performed at the opening night of Radio City Music Hall in 1932. Working in a chorus line and executing a basic tap and eye-high kick in perfect unison, they received thunderous accolades and became a tradition at Radio City that has continued into the 21st century. They are perhaps best known for their spectacular annual Christmas show.

When the United States entered World War II on December 7, 1941, the **music** played by big bands had for some time entertained Americans, both for listening and dancing. **Swing,** a blending of jazz and popular music, was king and attracted all ages to the dance floor. Carried over from the 1930s, swing dancing in the 1940s included the lindy hop, the shag, and the jitterbug. The lindy hop, something of an aerobic dance and a precursor to the jitterbug, involved steps that appeared to duplicate the taking off and landing associated with flying and derived its name from Charles "Lindy" Lindbergh (1902–1974) and his famous solo flight across the Atlantic Ocean in 1927.

The better-known jitterbug, a term that could be used to refer to a swing dancer or to various kinds of swing dancing, enjoyed enormous popularity from the mid-1930s until well after the end of World War II. During the 1930s and 1940s, the Savoy Ballroom in Harlem became the hub for all that was happening with the jitterbug. The dance needs a medium or upbeat tempo—the faster the better—and involves many steps and constant motion, so much so that the Savoy had to replace its hardwood floors every three years. World War II facilitated the spread of the jitterbug to Europe. In the 1950s, the dance became the basic framework for couples dancing in the early days of rock 'n' roll.

Cartoons and shorts out of Hollywood reflected the jitterbug craze. *Mighty Mouse in Krakatoa* (1945) ends with Krakatoa Katy, the hottest dancer of all, leading Mighty Mouse and others in a jive-chanting jitterbug scene. The short, *Cavalcade of Dance* (1943), features ballroom dancers performing the various dance **fads** of the 20th century.

In the late 1940s, the jitterbug and the shag, the latter a dance with fancy footwork while the upper body and hips hardly move, blended into what has come to be called East Coast swing, a dance with simple steps that can be executed to various jazz tempos. Another form, Western Swing, sometimes called country swing, resembles East Coast swing but adds variations from other **country music** dances, primarily the country or Texas two-step.

With growing interest in social dancing, many young people and adults desired instruction. Dance teacher and businessman Arthur Murray (1885–1991), along with his wife and partner Kathryn (1907–1999), had opened a dance school in the mid-1920s offering personal dance instruction. By the 1940s, this simple operation expanded into group lessons taught at hotels and finally to a highly successful enterprise with Arthur Murray School of Dancing franchises across the country. At each school, trained instructors provided lessons in the latest dancing fad, along with proven dances such as the fox trot and waltz, as well as what was popular in that locality. Starting in 1950, the Murrays hosted a television show known as *The Arthur Murray Party* (first aired as *Arthur Murray Party Time*). Over its 10-year run, it appeared on all four television networks—NBC, CBS, ABC, and **DuMont.** Each week the couple demonstrated a mystery dance, and the viewer who correctly identified it qualified for two free lessons at a local Arthur Murray studio.

In the closing years of the 1940s, television emerged as a major entertainment venue and adopted a proven radio format—the weekly variety show—providing employment opportunities for performers and contributing to the selling of thousands of television sets. The first such show, the pioneering *Hour Glass,* seen on NBC in limited markets from May 1946 to February 1947, laid many of the foundations for television variety. *The Texaco Star Theater* hosted by Milton Berle in June 1948, held true to the standard formula of dancers, singers, and comics, with the addition of a well-known star as host.

Dancers moved more to the forefront of the variety show when choreographer June Taylor (1917–2004) and her troupe, known as the June Taylor Dancers, made their debut in 1948 on **The Toast of the Town** starring Ed Sullivan (1901–1974). Two years later, they joined Jackie Gleason's (1916–1987) *Cavalcade of Stars* and continued with him on *The Jackie Gleason Show* (1952–1970), which employed an opening shot from an overhead camera of the June Taylor Dancers making geometric patterns reminiscent of Busby Berkeley's choreography. Others appearing in early TV variety shows included the accomplished Marge and Gower Champion (b. 1919; 1921–1980), a husband-wife team that also had successful movie careers with MGM during the 1940s and 1950s.

Great musicians inspire great dancers, and vice versa. The 1940s experienced a wide range of both talented musicians and dancers, who entertained and inspired a country, first at war and then in postwar prosperity. In the performing arts, ballet made inroads where it had never traveled before. Movies, with dancers such as Fred Astaire and Gene Kelly, inspired many young people to take tap dancing lessons, while adults rushed to the Arthur Murray studio for social dancing lessons. As television sets arrived in more and more homes, even more Americans were exposed to the art of dance.

See also: *ASCAP vs. BMI* Radio Boycott and the AFM Recording Ban; Musicals (Film); Race Relations and Stereotyping; Youth

Selected Reading
Frank, Rusty E. *Tap! The Greatest Tap Dance Stars and Their Stories, 1900–1955.* New York: Da Capo Press, 1994.
Long, Robert Emmet. *Broadway, the Golden Years: Jerome Robbins and the Great Choreographer-Directors, 1940 to the Present.* New York: Continuum, 2001.
Reynolds, Nancy, and Malcolm McCormick. *No Fixed Points: Dance in the Twentieth Century.* New Haven, CT: Yale University Press, 2003.
Stearns, Marshall, and Jean Stearns. *Jazz Dance: The Story of American Vernacular Dance.* New York: Macmillan, 1992.

D-DAY

During the spring of 1944, Allied forces, under the overall command of **General Dwight David Eisenhower** (1890–1969), assembled the greatest land-sea-air armada the world has ever seen. Stationed throughout southern England, soldiers, sailors, and airmen, plus countless tons of equipment, gathered in ever-increasing numbers to wait out the weeks, days, hours, and minutes before they received the signal that Operation Overlord, the invasion of Europe, would commence. After developing plans for over two years prior to the actual invasion, strategists for General Eisenhower had determined to launch the strike in May, but incomplete preparations and an unseasonable spring and unpredictable weather kept postponing the final date. With the onset of June, no one knew exactly when forces could move from England, cross the Channel, and storm the beaches of Normandy, France.

Weather ships stationed in the Atlantic gave grim predictions for conditions on the continent in early June, except for a brief break from winds and storms around the fifth and sixth of the month, but even these dates utilized estimates, not firm promises. To confuse the German defenders along the Normandy coast, elaborate acts of subterfuge had been practiced, trying to keep them guessing. The Germans knew an invasion was in the offing, but where would they land? Calais? Farther north in Holland? As distant as Norway? Uncertain, the Germans had to disperse their formidable forces, trying to avoid having weak, undefended areas, but not overprotecting sites, either. But the longer the Allies postponed the landings, the more likely the enemy would learn where they planned to invade.

In standard military parlance, orders from headquarters identify the date, or day (D), and the time in hours (H) and minutes (M) for an operation. For Overlord, this approach meant that on D-Day, at H-Hours and M-Minutes, the operation would begin. Eisenhower, realizing that he might soon lose any weather advantage for some time, decreed that Tuesday, June, 6, 1944, would be the date. With that decision, and in the

This picture, with its mass of men and machines, suggests why historians call the Normandy invasion of 1944 the largest single military undertaking in the history of warfare. (Columbia Pictures/Photofest)

predawn darkness, some 5,000 ships, carrying over 160,000 troops, set sail for the nearby French coastline. Overhead, thousands of Allied aircraft began endless sorties, pummeling German shore defenses. The much-anticipated Operation Overlord had begun.

Soon thereafter, the initial reports of the ongoing battle went out to **newspapers** and **radio** stations around the world. Reporters and writers at first naturally referred to this momentous event as Overlord, its official name. But within a short time they adopted traditional military usage, dubbing the invasion D-Day. A minority view, now discarded, had the letter *D* signifying deliverance, or Deliverance Day, but it never attracted much of a following. In strict grammatical terms, D-Day without a specific date means the redundant "Day-Day," a meaningless construction, but one that quickly took on a meaning of its own. Since then, there have been other D-Days in other wars, but once launched, none have been called that; in historical and symbolic terms, D-Day in the popular mind signifies but one thing, the invasion of Normandy on June 6, 1944.

See also: Radio Programming: News, Sports, Public Affairs, and Talk; War Films

Selected Reading
Ambrose, Stephen E. *D-Day, June 6, 1944: The Climatic Battle of World War II.* New York: Pocket Books, 2002.
Ryan, Cornelius. *The Longest Day: June 6, 1944.* New York: Simon & Schuster, 1959.

DESIGN

The 1920s and 1930s witnessed an emphasis on machine-based design, a modernistic approach that subordinated organic, or living, forms for smooth, hard-edged shapes, items that suggested efficiency, mass production, and ease of replication. From 1939 to 1940, the New York World's Fair, a last bubble of optimism as World War II was breaking out in Europe and Asia, presented the work of a pantheon of leading designers, decorators, and architects of the late 1930s that championed modernism, or streamlining, as the preferred style for the new decade.

The two memorable symbols of the fair, the tall (700 feet), angular Trylon and the round (200 feet in diameter) Perisphere, the work of the architectural firm of Harrison & Fouilhoux (Wallace Harrison and Jacques-Andre Fouilhoux, 1895–1981 and 1879–1945, respectively), greeted visitors at the entrance to the grounds at Flushing Meadows, outside New York City. Inside the Perisphere, designer Henry Dreyfuss (1904–1972) had created Democracy, a model of a planned, streamlined metropolis of tomorrow; rotating balconies took viewers on a tour, while a score by composer William Grant Still (1895–1978) accompanied them. Designer Norman Bel Geddes (1893–1958) and architect Albert Kahn (1869–1942) created the General Motors Pavilion, a sinuous complex of stark white buildings, virtually windowless, the interiors of which showed Futurama, a popular view of a circa 1960 city with automated superhighways and no traffic problems. Walter Dorwin Teague (1883–1960) took credit for the Ford Motor Company Exposition, wherein visitors could tour its displays in sample Ford cars. The Chrysler Corporation countered with two soaring, winglike pylons and a film about a rocketport that would effortlessly transport passengers to London. Numerous other distinguished designers and architects also contributed to the sweeping streamlined modernity that characterized the vast exposition.

A few isolated hints at changing design concepts nonetheless appeared at the fair, such as the Finnish Pavilion, the work of Alvar Aalto (1898–1976). The building presented a rather boxlike exterior, but the interior consisted of curving slatted wood walls and warm, natural finishes. This approach, one that stressed a flowing simplicity of line, would later become known as Scandinavian modern (also called Danish modern and Swedish modern) in the postwar era and enjoy considerable popularity. By 1940 and the close of the fair, however, World War II had put a virtual stop to innovative design—at least for the consumer market—and not until 1946 and thereafter did the creation of new styles again receive emphasis. Changes, some subtle, some obvious, had by that time occurred in American design, and streamlining, so fresh in the late 1930s, had been supplanted by a new and evolving postwar aesthetic.

During the conflict, the government recruited many top designers to work on various products related to the war effort. For example, the husband-wife team of Charles and Ray Eames (1907–1978; 1912–1988) developed a molded plywood leg splint for wounded military personnel. Widely used because of its strength and light weight, it demonstrated the versatility of plywood; following the war, laminated furniture, particularly that designed by the Eameses, gained wide acceptance with both designers and consumers. Henry Dreyfuss created the situation room for the U.S. Joint Chiefs of Staff, including a huge globe for them to follow changing events, while Norman Bel Geddes worked extensively with military models and **photography,** and Walter Dorwin Teague found employment with the Bendix Corporation in the area of missiles and rocketry. A number of designers experimented with improving camouflage patterns; their efforts usually involved organic patterns that imitated nature and would be difficult to discern from any distance. These same patterns would later be reflected in consumer products like wallpaper, textiles, and countertops.

The reasons behind this shift came from different sources. In the arts, the work of Jean (Hans) Arp (1886–1966), a French-German surrealist/dadaist painter-sculptor had been admired by critics. Surrealism and expressionism had grown in importance in Europe prior to the war, and these influences then percolated into the American mainstream during the 1940s. Arp's creations emphasized organically shaped free forms, and their soft and flowing lines were reflected in designs at this time.

In 1932, the Cranbrook Academy of Art was founded in Bloomfield Hills, Michigan, a Detroit suburb. Finnish architect Eliel Saarinen (1873–1950), already famous in the arts and crafts movement, served as its first director. Cranbrook attempted to supplant the mechanical functionalism its faculty saw in much contemporary design, stressing instead a more expressive, natural approach. Saarinen's son Eero (1910–1961) joined the institution in 1936 and added his own organic motifs to the curriculum. Together, the Saarinens introduced a variety of furniture designs that reinforced the Scandinavian modern concepts then beginning to attract considerable attention. The Museum of Modern Art in New York City mounted a 1941 show, *Organic Design in Home Furnishings,* that featured Eero Saarinen and others, but the onset of World War II blocked any substantial commercialization of its themes for several years.

When victory finally came within sight, retailers wanted to have modern, innovative products ready for war's end. They foresaw a vast new consumer market that would move beyond mere utility with the arrival of peace in 1945. With cash in their pockets and deprived of many goods during the war, Americans were eager to spend money on housing, appliances, furnishings, **fashion, automobiles,** and just about anything else that struck their fancy. And manufacturers, along with the design community, stood ready to fulfill those postponed wants.

In the area of housing alone, new home starts leaped from 200,000 in 1945 to over 1 million in 1950. New car sales similarly climbed, from just over 2 million in 1946 (the first year following the war that new vehicles came off assembly lines in any quantity) to over 6.5 million in 1950. Consumers wanted designs featuring softly curving contours and forms that evoked a sense of humanity and supplanted the more aggressive machinelike angles and hard-edged shapes that had previously dominated. In some respects, they were responding to the horrors of World War II and what people wanted in a post-Holocaust, post-Hiroshima/Nagasaki age. As a result, American design in general became warmer, more fluid and undulating, providing a contrast to the colder rationalism of machine design.

In the area of architectural styles, the West Coast, especially in trendsetting Southern California, began to see what came to be called "Googie" **architecture** in the late 1940s. For a brief while, these designs also went by the terms doo-wop, coffee-shop modern, populuxe, jet age, space age, and atomic age. Architect John Lautner (1911–1994), a pioneer in this area, had designed a Hollywood coffee shop in 1949 that bore the name Googie's. Lautner and others had already built a number of commercial establishments in the Los Angeles area, but the name Googie shortly encompassed any buildings that incorporated upswept roofs for maximum window exposure, cantilevered extensions, and unusual organic shapes, such as **advertising** signs formed like boomerangs, amoebae (also called woggles and wigglies in popular parlance), starbursts, and atomic nuclei—the last usually a spherical nucleus surrounded by smaller exploding atoms. Not missing a beat, motels began to feature kidney-shaped swimming pools as early as 1948.

These design trends did not remain exclusively in California. Isamu Noguchi (1904–1988), well known as an artist and sculptor, designed a free-form ceiling in St. Louis for the American Stove Company in 1947–1948 that included hidden lighting. Architect Morris Lapidus (1902–2001) did a Bond Store in Cincinnati with an elaborate kidney-shaped ceiling motif in 1949, the first of many progressive designs that he created, mainly in the 1950s. Alexander H. Girard (1907–1994), a prominent architect and interior designer of the period, likewise employed this approach in a number of modern restaurant layouts.

Sizable commercial office buildings and most government construction rejected organic themes. Large corporations, conservative by nature, favored the crisp, unadorned lines of the International Style. It therefore held sway for the majority of tall structures well into the 1950s, since most architectural firms strove to please their clients.

Frank Lloyd Wright (1867–1959), never one to sit idly by in the midst of change, had commenced working on the Jacobs Solar Hemicycle House in Middleton, Wisconsin, in 1943. It reached completion in 1948. Built in a large curving shape, sided with rusticated stone, and set into a hillside, it showed a new side to Wright's endless imagination and fit in well with the growing emphasis on organic shapes in architecture and design. His interest in curves would culminate with the Guggenheim Museum in New York City, a project he began planning in the 1940s, but one that did not reach completion until 1959, several months after the architect's death. But Wright's architectural colleagues often viewed him as a vestige of the past, the architect-artist who curried no corporate favor, and few individuals rose to take his mantle.

By the same token, and despite the interest shown in organic forms, most residential buildings of the immediate postwar era remained resolutely traditional. As the suburbs grew and large subdivisions took shape outside cities, conventional Cape Cods and rectangular ranches led the way. In keeping with the popularity of anything that echoed the nation's past, stock Colonial homes (but fully equipped with modern conveniences) continued to attract numerous buyers. The movie industry, alert to all trends, in 1948 released *Mr. Blandings Builds His Dream House,* a comedy with Cary Grant (1904–1986) about the pitfalls that accompany a move to the suburbs. Incidentally, Mr. Blandings chooses a New England Colonial instead of anything the least bit contemporary.

Only in the layout of these suburban tracts did organic design manifest itself. Many of the developments featured gently curving streets—a break from the rigid grid patterns of the past—and many of them ended in cul-de-sacs. In blueprints and from the air, these street plans revealed a strong curvilinear layout, and designers frequently referred to this approach as organic planning. Similarly, the cloverleaf intersections of primary highways, many of which transported suburbanites to their new homes, have a distinctive, organic look, especially when seen from above.

The interiors of many homes showed a greater willingness to experiment with modern design than did the exteriors. A Colonial house might well have molded plywood or fiberglass furniture, and Scandinavian designs caught on toward the end of the 1940s. The Herman Miller Company, a furniture manufacturing firm based in Zeeland, Michigan, took the lead in introducing modernism into American homes. Founded in 1923 to make reproductions, the company began to change under the leadership of designer Gilbert Rohde (1894–1944). He joined the organization in 1930 and moved to introduce a more modern line of products. He added clean-lined wooden cabinets for clocks and radios, storage units, and recessed lighting.

In 1946, George Nelson (1907–1986) took over from Rohde and led the Miller organization until 1970. Dissatisfied with what he saw as antiquated methods of production and marketing in the furniture industry, he attempted to make it more up to date. Along with Henry Wright (1910–1986), he published *Tomorrow's House* in 1946, a book that accurately predicted a number of postwar design trends. Kidney-shaped coffee tables, soft boomerang and amoebalike shapes that broke with angular geometric design in wallpaper and textiles received coverage in this influential publication. Many of the patterns that Wright and Nelson showed would become commonplace during the 1950s, the heyday for organic designs.

Nelson created several notable products. The rise of the family room in many homes, along with unparalleled abundance, caused him to introduce the concept of a storage wall and other built-ins in the late 1940s. He also created the Ball Wall Clock in 1947;

it suggested the atomic age, complete with a center nucleus and atoms representing the hours. It has since become a classic of 1940s design.

During his tenure, Nelson also acquainted countless Americans with the best in modern design. He hired Isamu Noguchi to create glass and wood tables in various organic shapes as well as design paper lantern lighting. Charles and Ray Eames came on board in 1946 with a dining chair constructed of molded plywood that could be inexpensively mass produced. The couple followed that with a popular folding plywood screen in 1947. They also devised a molded plastic armchair in 1949 that sold well. Using their own 1949 house in Pacific Palisades as a laboratory, they showed that many of its details were off the rack from hardware and building supply stores, a demonstration of economy and ease in modern building.

The success of the Herman Miller Company naturally attracted the attention of other furniture makers. Hans Knoll (1914–1955) in 1938 founded a firm under his own name in New York City. Architect-designer Florence Schust Knoll (b. 1917) joined the group in 1943; she and Hans Knoll married in 1946, and the company became Knoll Associates. Their partnership formed a rival to Herman Miller in the area of contemporary design, and they hired several top names, such as Eero Saarinen and Harry Bertoia (1946–1948).

Saarinen contributed his popular Womb chair in 1948, a design that featured a cushioned fabric over a reinforced fiberglass shell. It has remained available ever since its introduction. Bertoia became noted for his Diamond chair, which came out around 1949 to 1950. Made of welded steel wire arranged in a latticework pattern, it too gained a wide following. The Knolls in 1947 also acquired rights to manufacture Jorge Ferrari-Hardoy's (1914–1977) Butterfly chair (also known as a Hardoy chair), a design that the Argentinian-born architect created in 1938. A simple steel frame of plain metal rods supports fabric that has been slung over it; it contains no upholstery, no padding, and no cushions but retains considerable comfort. Florence Schust Knoll, as an architect, designed minimalist cabinetry, often blending woods, metal, and glass. She received numerous commissions for her work, usually in the area of the International Style during the 1940s.

To accompany these new lines of furniture, various companies introduced complementary textiles, wallpapers, and floor and counter coverings. Formica laminates pioneered in patterns that emphasized organic elements; colorful amoebalike forms on a neutral background proved particularly influential. Textiles often were made with hand weaving that employed unusual color combinations that caught the eye. Because of wartime shortages of certain materials such as silk, natural materials like burlap and jute provided cruder, rougher surfaces. For example, sisal carpeting became stylish, as did later shag carpets.

Glassware, table settings, and ceramics likewise reflected the latest design trends. Russel Wright (1904–1976) created the American Modern line of dinnerware that enjoyed phenomenal popularity and also earned the praise of china connoisseurs. Introduced in 1939, it sold over 80 million pieces before being discontinued in 1959 and attracted a middle-class clientele with its reasonable prices and organic forms. Wright also designed stainless flatware with plastic handles. His Iroquois casual china, which appeared in 1946, remained available until the late 1950s, but his later Russel

Wright line of bowls and such that came out in the late 1940s proved too modern for many tastes and did not do well. At roughly the same time, Eva Zeisel (b. 1906) created Town and Country dinnerware for Minnesota-based Red Wing Pottery. Its amusing humanoid shapes resembled the Shmoo, a wildly popular comic strip creation by cartoonist Al Capp (1909–1979) that first appeared in his *Li'l Abner* series in 1948. Some items in these and other competing lines demonstrated a crossover between art and popular culture.

Architect Alvar Aalto in 1936 designed a series of organically styled glass vases he called the Savoy series; in continuous production ever since, they did well on the U.S. market during the later 1940s. Similarly, Peter Schlumbohm (1896–1962) created the classic glass Chemex coffeemaker in 1941. Its simple design, involving two cones meeting at their points, used a more free-form motif than in the past for such a utilitarian device. Finally, Majilis (Maija) Grotell (1899–1973), who worked and taught at the Cranbrook Academy of Arts, emerged as one of the most influential ceramicists working in postwar era. Her vessels—bowls, cups, pitchers—usually relate to nature, and the decorative glazes she applied to them involve organic shapes and earthen colors.

The attention given to designers in the 1940s resulted in the formation of the American Craftsmen's Cooperative Council in 1942, followed by the Society of Industrial Designers two years later and renamed the Industrial Designers Institute in 1949. The Detroit Institute of Arts put on a show called *For Modern Living* in 1949 that sought to recognize the contributions of designers in contemporary American culture. In it, Charles and Ray Eames, Alexander Girard, Florence Schust Knoll, George Nelson, Isamu Noguchi, Eero Saarinen, and others displayed their latest creations, giving the postwar trends in interior decoration prominent billing.

It took Detroit automakers longer to recover from the effects of the war and respond to new trends in American design. Their factories, which had turned out tanks, trucks, and other motorized military vehicles, had not produced any civilian automobiles for the duration of the conflict. They thus had to completely revamp their assembly lines beginning in 1946, which meant that the best they could initially do, in terms of design, would be to slightly alter prewar models. The Studebaker Corporation, a smaller company based in South Bend, Indiana, got the jump on Chrysler, Ford, and General Motors—the Big Three—by introducing the 1947 Studebaker Champion Starlight Coupe ("First by Far with a Post-war Car"). The result came from designs overseen by Virgil Exner (1909–1973), not the better-known Raymond Loewy (1893–1986) as commonly thought. Studebaker, recognizing good publicity, did little to dissuade the public about this error. The Starlight Coupe featured a curving rear window that in some ways resembled a front windshield, prompting the joke that "you can't tell if it's coming or going." A radical departure in automotive design, it spurred Detroit automakers to rush into production several models ahead of schedule, although they offered nothing quite as daring as Studebaker's coupe.

In 1948, Cadillac, once the top-of-the-line leader among General Motors cars, displayed nascent fins on its rear fenders. They did not grow much until the 1950s and then sprouted significantly throughout the decade, culminating in the 1959 models. The concept of fins, such a hallmark of the 1950s, evolved from the vision of chief designer Harley Earl (1893–1969). He had seen a sleek Lockheed P-38 Lightning fighter at an airfield, and he particularly admired the tail assembly. Earl would emerge as an important figure in the world of automotive design later in the 1950s.

Aircraft also had an influence on other aspects of the automobile industry. Dreamers envisioned postwar cars that could fly, and the idea of a combination car and airplane blossomed, although it basically remained a dream. Henry Dreyfuss convinced the Consolidated Vultee Aircraft Corporation to invest in his 1947 ConvAIRCAR. An ungainly machine, it actually flew in tests but never reached the production stage. In the meantime, the car companies decided to begin referring to their designers as stylists, perhaps with the idea that the term sounded more sophisticated. With the exception of Studebaker, however, most 1940s American cars remained rather stodgy, and it would not be until the early 1950s that the designers/stylists unveiled truly new and modern vehicles.

In all, the postwar era witnessed a flood of new consumer items, many of which sported modern lines. The challenge facing producers involved creating good designs that simultaneously possessed broad consumer appeal. Should a product possess warm, embracing shapes (womblike, feminine), or should it possess sharp, geometric lines (aggressive, masculine)? Should it encourage meditation or display? Should a design be simple or complex? Although aestheticians created elaborate theories about the relationship between organic design and the higher purposes of art (form determined by function, from functionalism to style, geometric forms versus forms from nature, etc.), manufacturers quickly translated their ideas into popular consumer goods that bore no discernable connections to **art.** The postwar consumer society was on a buying binge, and such questions mattered little.

See also: Abstract Expressionism; Aviation; Baby Boom; Classical Music; Comic Strips; Fads; Levittown and Suburbanization; Magazines; Newspapers; Sculpture

Selected Reading
Meikle, Jeffrey L. *Design in the USA.* New York: Oxford University Press, 2005.
Pulos, Arthur J. *The American Design Adventure, 1940–1975.* Cambridge, MA: MIT Press, 1988.
Rapaport, Brooke Kamin, and Kevin L. Stayton. *Vital Forms: American Art and Design in the Atomic Age, 1940–1960.* New York: Harry N. Abrams, 2001.
Smith, C. Ray. *Interior Design in 20th-Century America: A History.* New York: Harper & Row, 1987.

DESSERTS, CANDY, AND ICE CREAM

A sweet taste at the end of a meal, such as a dessert, candy, or ice cream, has long appealed to Americans. Sugar, a key ingredient of such treats, flowed as a cheap and abundant commodity during the Great Depression, but the events of World War II created a different story. Even before the December 7, 1941, attack by the Japanese on Pearl Harbor, rumors of impending **rationing** sent some people scurrying to stores to buy and hoard sugar. By early 1942, imports from the Philippines had ceased, and this event, coupled with a shortage of ships for transporting Cuban or Puerto Rican crops to the States, did indeed mean a limited supply of the sweetener.

Making desserts, as well as jams, jellies, and other items that cry for sugar, became a challenge. For five years (1942 to 1947), sugar appeared on the Office of Price Administration's (OPA) ration list, with each citizen initially receiving 8 ounces per week, a small amount when you realize the incidental daily use plus recipes such as the popular Depression cakes from the 1930s call for anywhere from 1-1/2 to 2 cups of it. Eventually the rationed portion rose to 12 ounces a week, still not enough to completely lessen the challenge.

The **food** editor at the *New York Times* calculated that each person's weekly share in 1942 equaled about seven teaspoons a day. The article suggested amounts that could be a prudent distribution over three daily meals, along with possible substitutions, so as to enable the household to still have enough sugar for weekly desserts of at least one pie and one cake.

Most citizens responded positively to living with reduced amounts of sugar. Cooks baked less and altered recipes to use molasses, maple syrup, corn syrup, or honey. Butter, another key dessert ingredient, also made it to the ration lists, while eggs, milk, and shortening frequently proved hard to find.

Food writer M. F. K. Fisher (Mary Frances Kennedy Fisher Parrish, 1908–1992), in her 1942 *How to Cook a Wolf*, offers two special cakes—War Cake and Tomato Soup Cake. Although they require a little sugar, these cakes do not call for eggs, milk, or butter. Shortening provides the needed fat and, if it should be unavailable, she advises using bacon grease because the heavy proportion of spices called for will hide its taste. General Mills' Betty Crocker's in *Your Share: How to Prepare Appetizing, Helpful Meals with Foods Available Today* (1943), also offers a war cake recipe, but the book proposes that the cook continue to use traditional ingredients, just make smaller cakes, half or less of a recipe.

Many people, in order to stretch their sugar supply, purchased desserts requiring the ingredient from their neighborhood baker, who, because it constituted a business necessity, received extra allotments. For home-baked dishes, housewives frequently attempted to add extra flavor by using a sugarless boiled frosting made from egg whites, light corn syrup, salt, and vanilla or, when chocolate was available, a no-sugar icing of marshmallows, unsweetened chocolate, and evaporated milk. Bisquick, a General Mills product dating from 1931, and originally promoted as an easy way to make biscuits, now found use in shortcakes, fruit rolls, and cobblers.

Nothing is more American than apple pie. Along with other kinds of pies, this old standard suffered in a number of ways. Scarce supplies of shortening, a basic ingredient for pie crust, caused cooks to forego two crusts and be satisfied with a one-crust pie or pursue a different route entirely with a graham cracker crust. Fruit pies without sugar can be sour and offered another challenge. But tapioca added to apples or other fruits helps to cut the tartness.

The lack of sugar, and an occasional scarcity of eggs, reduced the frequency of homemade cream pies. Jell-O pudding could have served as a quick and easy way to prepare a quasi-cream pie, but in 1942, the sugar shortage restricted Jell-O production, so much so that the company stopped sponsoring *The Jell-O Program* on NBC (National Broadcasting Company) radio, a show that starred Jack Benny (1894–1974). After the war, American housewives quickly resumed making their favorite Jell-O dishes, and for a slightly different treat, in 1948, Jell-O tapioca pudding appeared in **grocery stores and supermarkets** in three flavors: vanilla, chocolate, and orange-coconut.

Around 1940, two companies, Dromedary of New Jersey and Pillsbury in Minneapolis, in hopes of providing rations to U.S. troops, submitted rudimentary cake mixes to the military for consideration. An inadequate shelf life prevented commercial sales. Research continued, however, resulting in a much improved product. Dromedary introduced a gingerbread mix in 1947, and the following year Pillsbury advertised two mixes: a white cake and a chocolate fudge cake. General Mills, not to be outdone, offered two ready-mix grocery items in 1948: Betty Crocker ginger cake mix and Betty Crocker pie crust mix. Dromedary responded with a devil's food cake mix in 1949, and Charles Lubin (1904–1988), founder of the Kitchens of Sara Lee, introduced Sara Lee cheese cake. Commercial cake mixes, like many convenience foods, in the postwar years, hit markets in quantity following the scarcities brought about by the war.

For easy cakes, there must be an easy topping, and in 1946 Aaron S. Lapin (1914–1999) developed Reddi-Wip in an aerosol can. He founded the Reddi-Wip company, and in 1948, milkmen in Lapin's hometown of St. Louis delivered this new product door to door. Just one year later, this mixture of pasteurized cream, flavored and sweetened with vanilla, could be found in retail stores.

Desserts received a lot of publicity when Pillsbury, hoping for a good marketing tool, played host on December 13, 1949, to its first Bake-Off at the Waldorf-Astoria Hotel in New York City. General Electric had installed 100 stoves for the 100 finalists—97 women and 3 men—in this national recipe contest. The rules allowed the cooks to prepare their dish as many times as they wished, just as long as they submitted their final efforts to the panel of judges by 5:00 p.m. Nine prizes ranged from $500 to $50,000 (around $4,400 and $436,000 respectively in 2008 money). First Lady **Eleanor Roosevelt** (1884–1962) presented Mrs. Theodora Smafield (active 1940s) with a check for her first-place winner, No-Knead Water-Rising Twists, at a luncheon the next day. Realizing its expected public relations coup, Pillsbury decided to hold the Bake-Off again in 1950 and added a junior division. The competition continues today as a biannual event awarding $1 million to the winner.

Candy, another popular sweet and easily carried in a pocket, can be eaten on its own as a treat or snack and provides an immediate sweet taste and sugar boost. During World War II, candy bars and blocks of chocolate did just that for U.S. troops, and a number of companies landed contracts with the government to supply the armed forces with their specialties. These items appeared as a part of mess hall meals as well as in the different rations that the troops carried on them: C rations (balanced meals during combat), D rations (quick energy survival packs), and K rations (emergency balanced meals). Government contracts meant priority sugar allotments, and several well-established candy manufacturers directed either all or most of their production to military distribution. This meant many U.S. candy items went missing on store shelves for purchase by citizens on the home front.

The Brown & Haley Candy Company of Tacoma, Washington, sent its Almond ROCA Buttercrunch Toffee in tin packages to military personnel stationed overseas, and the Hershey Corporation likewise had a deal to provide chocolate for the troops. In March 1941, Forrest E. Mars Sr. (1904–1999) of Mars, Incorporated, and Bruce Murrie (active 1940s) at Hershey formed a partnership and patented Mars' design for a candy-coated milk chocolate drop. They called this new candy M&Ms for the first initials of their last names and jointly started production using a cardboard tube for packaging. It proved to be an instant hit with soldiers. In 1945, Mars bought out Murrie to take sole ownership of the M&Ms brand, and it became available to the general public.

The Sweets Company of America supplied Tootsie Rolls, another popular treat dating back to 1896, especially because of the candy's ability to withstand severe weather conditions, plus it provided a quick energy lift. The Williamson Candy Company manufactured Oh Henry! candy bars, a high-selling sweet that has rolled off production lines since the mid-1920s. Despite sugar rationing, this product set a sales record in 1943, but more than half the bars went to military personnel. The Heath Candy Company's Heath Bar, with its long shelf life, provided a tasty contribution to soldiers' rations.

The Wrigley Company assembled the final ration packs for the military; they included a stick of gum, along with essential food items, sugar tablets, caramels, a chocolate bar, hard candies, and candy-coated peanuts or raisins sent by other manufacturers. To meet the military's chewing gum demand, Wrigley removed its Spearmint, Doublemint, and Juicy Fruit flavors from the civilian market early in the war.

A successful regional operation in York, Pennsylvania, called the York Cone Company, manufactured ice cream cones and waffles, along with some confectionary items. In 1940, it introduced a new product, the York Peppermint Patty, and managed to continue to distribute the patty to its customers in its home state as well as Ohio, Indiana, and New England throughout the war. After many years of satisfying regional customers, the Peppermint Patty became available nationwide in 1975.

For several candy makers, candy bars and chewing gum became bigger businesses than ever during the postwar years. Military personnel returned home somewhat hooked on chocolate and other candies and spread the word about their favorites. As a result, Brown & Haley, with its Almond ROCA Buttercrunch, advanced from a strong Northwest reputation to one that embraced the entire country. M&Ms grew in popularity and, in 1948, came in improved brown plastic pouches similar to those provided today. Tootsie Rolls saw production increases and immediately surpassed prewar levels. Wrigley brought its products back on the market, first Spearmint and Juicy Fruit in 1946 and Doublemint in 1947.

In 1940, the Just Born Company, operating out of Bethlehem, Pennsylvania, had manufactured its first fruit-flavored, chewy sweets called Mike and Ike, named for twins in a newspaper comic strip, *Mike and Ike (They Look Alike),* created in 1907 by cartoonist Rube Goldberg (1883–1970). The candy came in two flavors, root beer and licorice. In 1950, Just Born added a cinnamon flavor called Hot Tamales and has continued to increase its product line, all available today nationally.

Snickers candy bars, a 1929 creation of Mars, Inc., and hand-wrapped until 1944, did not appear in military rations despite growing popularity. This sweet made a big leap with sponsorship of one of the first **television** programs for children, ***The Howdy Doody Show*** from 1949 until 1952; Snickers soon became known as one of the best-selling chocolate bars of all times, a position it strives to maintain today.

The Connecticut-based Peter Paul Candy Manufacturing Company has experienced continuous success with its Mounds Bar, first put on the market in 1922. During the war, the firm dropped most of its other offerings to concentrate on this hit. In 1946, it returned to prewar production and added the Almond Joy, which quickly produced high sales on its own.

The last new candy to appear during the 1940s was James O. Welch Company's Junior Mints, making its debut in 1949. Industry lore reports that the name derives from Sally Benson (1897–1972) stories that first appeared in *New Yorker* magazine and then were adapted into a theatrical play titled *Junior Miss* (1941–1943). Supposedly, the play ranked as one of the favorites of Mr. Welch (1906–1985), the originator of the candy and, thus, the pun, Junior Mints. A soft-mint center drenched in dark chocolate, Junior Mints soon became a popular candy at movie concession stands, leading the manufacturer to produce a three-ounce box marketed as the Junior Mint Theater Size Concession Candy.

Perhaps more so than desserts or candy, ice cream is considered by many as an essential part of American life, dating back to the second half of the 19th century, when nearly everyone could purchase and enjoy it. Before that, only the wealthy indulged. Technological advancements of the first half of the 20th century raised ice cream to a thriving business. Some acknowledge it to be an adequate dessert, and certainly a special snack, while others demand that a scoop always accompany a piece of cake or a slice of pie. Somewhere along the way, it became a strong American symbol, right alongside apple pie.

In 1941, as the U.S. government faced the eventuality of war and began preparing to impose rationing, it declared ice cream a nonessential food. But intense lobbying by the International Association of Ice Cream Manufacturers and the National Dairy Council caused a reversal of the ruling as well as placement of ice cream on the Basic Seven Foods Chart, a government effort to show the nutritional value of different foods. Even with this inclusion of ice cream, most of the wartime production went to the military. This, coupled with the rationing of sugar and the occasional scarcity of milk, created ice cream shortages back home.

The armed forces, however, wherever their location, had ice cream to soothe both the palate and nerves. Doctors even prescribed it for cases of combat fatigue, and many praised ice cream as a "morale food." The military considered it so important that the navy, in 1945, commissioned the world's first floating ice cream parlor, a concrete barge with the sole responsibility of producing ice cream for U.S. sailors serving in the Western Pacific.

As a high-status product for the troops, ice cream kept some businesses afloat. For example, Howard Johnson's, which served 3 flavors from 1 ice cream stand in 1925, grew to 107 sites dispensing 28 choices in 1939, had dropped to only 12 businesses by 1944. Food and gas rationing had taken its toll. Contracts, however, to provide commissary food including ice cream to military installations, defense plants, and schools allowed Howard Johnson's to stay in operation. By 1947, the company had reopened most of its closed **restaurants,** built 200 new ones, and continued to specialize in ice cream, as well as other food.

Desperate to stay in business during the war, ice cream sellers without government contracts looked for ways to get around the scarcity of necessary ingredients. Some pushed sherbet, which contains less butterfat, as a healthy alternative, while others offered half-and-half sundaes made with one scoop of sherbet and one of ice cream. A successful nationwide marketing campaign promoted Victory Sundaes. Vendors added a dime ($1.20 in 2008 dollars) to the cost of each ice cream treat and the buyer received a savings bond stamp. The sundaes themselves varied from shop to shop.

Even before the United States became involved in the war, creative entrepreneurs were experimenting with new ways to serve ice cream. The father-son team of J. F. and Alex McCullough (both active 1930s and 1940s) owned a dairy shop in Davenport, Iowa, and found that they preferred semisolid ice cream, that state before it goes through a hardening process. They spent several years attempting to create a machine that would produce a semifrozen, thick ice cream that was soft but not runny. By 1938, they felt they had a good product and conducted two trial runs offering soft ice cream in seven Illinois shops. At both events, and with rave reviews, they depleted their supply quickly. Encouraged, they continued to perfect their continuous freeze process, and the first Dairy Queen opened in 1940 in Joliet, Illinois, under a franchise agreement with Sherb Noble (1908–1991).

With the establishment of this franchise, the McCulloughs planned for expansion, but wartime rationing and shortages created difficulties, and finally their growth stopped completely when materials for the manufacture of their freezers had to be redirected to defense plants. After the war, public interest in soft ice cream enabled Dairy Queen expansion to begin again in earnest. The McCulloughs developed standards to ensure uniformity of the ice cream and added new products such as malts and shakes to the menus. Today, as it successfully continues, Dairy Queen offers a wide range of products and facilities.

Although Dairy Queen amassed the largest number of franchised outlets following World War II—17 by 1946 and 2,600 by 1955—other roadside ice cream operations also boomed in the postwar era. Thomas Carvel (1906–1990), founder of Carvel Ice Cream Company (1934), also invented an electric freezer that produced soft ice cream; by 1939, he operated three ice cream stores. During World War II, he remained successful by placing his freezers in PXs (post exchanges), government-run stores found on military bases. After the war, Carvel decided to develop his business as retail stores instead of ice cream stands and became the first to franchise such an operation for ice cream. In 1949, in an attempt to improve the profitability of his franchises, he inaugurated the Carvel College of Ice Cream Knowledge, an 18-day intensive training institute referred to by its attendees as "Sundae School."

While soft-serve ice cream, which includes frozen custard and iced milk, created a large market in postwar United States, premium ice cream also successfully moved into the picture. A notable 1940s beginning came under the directorship of brothers-in-law Burton Baskin (1913–1967) and Irvine Robbins (1917–2008). Both settled in California after discharge from the military, each opening an ice cream shop—Baskin in Pasadena and Robbins in Glendale. They soon owned six stores between them and began to sell franchises, reaching a total of 40 by 1949. In 1953, they merged their businesses to form Baskin-Robbins and advertised 31 flavors, outnumbering Howard Johnson's offerings as well as having a different flavor for each day of the month.

Desserts, candy, and ice cream hold a special place in American cuisine as an important part of festive occasions as well as being a comfort food in times of stress.

Shortages and rationing during World War II made these previously common treats scarce luxuries for those on the home front, while for the military they became symbols of support essential for maintaining troop morale. After the war, appetites for anything and everything—including sweets—seemed unstoppable. Pudding cake, chiffon cake, chiffon pie, and chocolate chip cookies ranked among the favorites. Candy became a bigger business than ever with strong national brands such as Snickers, Hershey's, and M&Ms dominating. Soft serve, big news for ice cream lovers, became a booming business, as did some premium brands.

See also: Baseball; Comic Strips; Fast Food; Magazines; Newspapers; War Bonds

Selected Reading
Broekel, Ray. *The Great American Candy Bar Book.* Boston: Houghton Mifflin, 1982.
Funderburg, Anne Cooper. *Chocolate, Strawberry, and Vanilla: A History of American Ice Cream.* Bowling Green, OH: Bowling Green State University Press, 1995.
Ice Cream for the Troops. *New York Times,* November 21, 1943, December 16, 1943, April 9, 1945. www.proquest.com
Lovegren, Sylvia. *Fashionable Food: Seven Decades of Food Fads.* New York: Macmillan, 1995.

DISNEY, WALT

Born in Chicago, Walter Elias Disney (1901–1966) will be remembered by millions simply as Walt Disney, the creator of Mickey Mouse and an accompanying cast of cartoon characters. He moved to the West Coast in 1923, along with his brother Roy (1893–1971), and there they founded The Walt Disney Company. Initially the business operated in a tiny space in Hollywood and utilized a small group of creative artists. They produced their first sound short, *Steamboat Willie,* featuring Mickey Mouse, in 1928. Mickey's popularity soared and the studio was on its way to success.

Experimenting with ways to expand the business, Disney in 1937 took a calculated risk and produced the first of several full-length cartoon feature films. *Snow White and the Seven Dwarfs,* made with sound and shot in color, proved an enormous success. It even won an honorary 1939 Academy Award for its innovation—one full-size statuette and seven miniature ones. By 1940, Disney's business had completed construction of a first-rate facility in Burbank with a staff of more than 1,000 artists, animators, technicians, and other necessary personnel. Walt Disney himself had also become a public figure known for his creation of cartoon personalities.

Generally referred to as Disney Productions, or just Disney, the growing enterprise turned out three more full-length films before the United States officially entered World War II. They included *Pinocchio* and *Fantasia* (both 1940) and *Dumbo* (1941). *Fantasia* features animation set to **classical music** with no dialogue and presents live-action segments of conductor Leopold Stokowski (1882–1977) leading the Philadelphia Orchestra. Their symphonic concert contains eight sequences, including Peter Tchaikovsky's (1840–1893) "The Nutcracker Suite," Amilcare Ponchielli's (1834–1886) "Dance of the Hours," and Modest Petrovich Mussorgsky's (1839–1881) "Night on Bald Mountain." Disney's staff even devised a stereo system they called Fantasound,

A photograph of Walt Disney sitting at his desk with figures representing characters from his cartoon features. Starting with Mickey Mouse, Disney created an entertainment empire during the 1930s and 1940s. (Disney Pictures/Photofest)

which required movie theaters to install special sound equipment. Because of this expense, *Fantasia* initially opened in only 14 theaters equipped to show it.

In 1941, RKO Radio Pictures took over distribution of *Fantasia* with a monophonic sound track so that more theaters could offer it to their patrons. RKO next cut the film to 81 minutes (it originally ran over two hours) and released it yet again in early 1942. It did not do well at the box office, however, and disappeared from public view that same year, leaving Disney in a straitened financial condition. The movie was re-released in 1946, did better, and eventually became one of the most highly regarded creations of Disney Productions, a reputation it continues to hold into the present.

Reeling from the financial losses incurred by *Fantasia,* Disney rushed into production *The Reluctant Dragon* in 1941. A curious mix of live action and animation, it purports to tell about the studio and how the staff creates cartoons. The title piece, based on a story by Kenneth Grahame (1859–1932), author of *Wind in the Willows,* a children's classic published in 1908, receives the full Disney animation treatment, but most of the remainder of the film possesses a dated quality. Dumbo, on the other hand, presents a sweet story of a flying elephant that charms most audiences. Often overlooked when assessing Disney's animated features, this short movie—just over an hour in length—presents circus lore, clowns, and dancing pink elephants; Disney himself claimed it as his particular favorite.

Immediately after the United States entered World War II on December 7, 1941, most U.S. industry converted to defense production, and the Disney Company proved no exception. It devoted over 90 percent of its facilities to special government work, primarily the making of training films for the armed services, morale-boosting shorts such as the classic Donald Duck cartoon called *Der Fuehrer's Face* (1943; originally titled *Donald Duck in Nutzi Land*), and a noncartoon feature called *Victory Through Air Power* (1943).

Der Fuehrer's Face, an anti-Nazi propaganda piece, stars Donald Duck as an assembly line worker in a Nazi-controlled factory screwing caps onto artillery shells. Mixed in with the shells are portraits of the Fuehrer's face; each time his picture appears, Donald must do a mandatory "Heil Hitler" salute. Tension mounts, and Donald suffers a nervous breakdown; the story ends with him awakening in his own bed and realizing it had all been a nightmare. The animation concludes with a caricature of an angry-faced Hitler. Before the film opened, the popular **Spike Jones** (1911–1965) and His City Slickers band released, to much acclaim, their version of the film's theme song, "Der Fuehrer's Face," admittedly in a more humorously offensive version.

Victory Through Air Power, a propaganda film shown at the height of World War II, attempts to convince the American public of the practicality of long-range strategic bombing. It provides humorous animation that gives the story of the development of air warfare and includes U.S. Major Alexander de Seversky (1894–1974), a strong proponent of military air power, illustrating how precision bombing could win the war for the Allies. Although the film, a departure for the Disney organization, did not do well at the box office, it nonetheless made the public more aware of the destructive potential of aerial bombardment.

Bambi, a film with no references to the ongoing war, premiered in London in August 1942. It tells the story of a fawn that grows up with friends Thumper, a rabbit, and Flower, a skunk. A coming-of-age story, Bambi suffers the death of his mother, falls in love, and barely escapes a spectacular forest fire before becoming the Great Prince of the Forest. Work on this feature-length film started in 1937, shortly before the release of *Snow White and the Seven Dwarfs,* and took the studio in a new direction with an all-animal cast, great attention to detail and realism, and a serious story leavened with humor.

The project's complexity delayed its release for five years while Disney artists heard lectures from animal experts, studied live animals at the Los Angeles Zoo, watched nature films shot in the woods of Maine, and observed the movements of two fawns given to the studio. Release of *Bambi* came at a difficult time, with the United States well into World War II. It lost money during its initial theatrical run, but recouped costs in a 1947 re-release, and profited thereafter. The story has endured and been shown in theaters seven separate times: 1942, 1947, 1957, 1966, 1975, 1982, and 1988. Undeniably one of Walt Disney's most charming pictures, it came out on video in 1989 and on DVD in 2005.

When not working on government projects, Disney employees engaged in producing comedy **cartoons,** a total of 89 for the years 1940 through 1945. Moving from wartime government contracts to postwar commercial work required Disney Productions to concentrate on reorganizing so as to regain its prewar status. During this time, they also made *Saludos Amigos* (premiered in Rio de Janeiro in 1942, followed by its U.S. release in 1943) and *The Three Caballeros* (1944). Known as package films, both consisted of several short pieces that, when combined, result in a feature-length compilation. Each film urges close relations with South America and Mexico.

Once back in full operation after World War II, Disney Productions between 1945 and 1949 produced 94 cartoons and 4 packaged features: *Make Mine Music* (1946), *Fun and Fancy Free* (1947), *Melody Time* (1948), and *The Adventures of Ichabod and Mr. Toad* (1949). *Make Mine Music* offers a contemporary version of *Fantasia* that utilizes popular music instead of the classics. *Melody Time* likewise consists of several sequences set to popular and folk music. Singers Frances Langford (1913–2005), the Andrews Sisters (Patty [b. 1918], Maxene [1916–1995], LaVerne [1911–1967]), Fred Waring (1900–1984) and the Pennsylvanians, and cowboy and movie star Roy Rogers (born Leonard Slye, 1911–1998) with his horse Trigger enliven the proceedings. Dennis Day (1916–1988), radio's popular tenor on *The Jack Benny Program,* serves as the picture's narrator and also sings. *Fun and Fancy Free* consists of two tales, *Bongo* and *Mickey and the Beanstalk*. Jiminy Cricket (voiced by singer Cliff Edwards, 1895–1971) hosts the stories, and Walt Disney provides Mickey's voice.

The final package, *The Adventures of Ichabod and Mr. Toad* presents two animated stories. *The Adventures of Ichabod* retells the Washington Irving (1783–1859) classic, "The Legend of Sleepy Hollow" (1820), and receives narration by the popular actor Basil Rathbone (1892–1967). Kenneth Grahame's *The Wind in the Willows* (1908) provides the basis for *Mr. Toad,* and none other than **Bing Crosby** (1903–1977) does the reading.

These four package movies, collections of various bits and pieces from the Disney studios created during the difficult war years or shortly thereafter, along with *Song of the South,* were uneven productions. Some of the episodes stand among his finest work, while others can be classified, generously at best, lackluster. They collectively rank as commercial disappointments, but they provided the studio some time to work on new productions that everyone hoped would do better at the box office and again put the Disney organization back on a firm financial footing.

The company in 1946 also ventured into a full-length dramatic film that mixed live action and animated scenes. *Song of the South* (1946), based on the Uncle Remus stories by Joel Chandler Harris (1848–1908) is seldom seen today in its entirety because of uncomfortable racial stereotyping. Two years later, the studio returned to the live action–animation mix with *So Dear to My Heart*. More or less forgotten in subsequent years, and never re-released until 1986, the story revolves around a boy's quest to have a champion lamb shown at the county fair. The film's musical theme, *Lavender Blue,* an English folk song dating to the 17th century, received an Academy Award nomination for best song. It, however, lost to *Baby, It's Cold Outside,* a tune from *Neptune's Daughter,* a competing musical.

By 1948, the company decided to move in yet another new direction and offered a series of live-action nature documentaries titled *True-Life Adventures*. They began with the release of *On Seal Island*. In 30 minutes, this piece captures the saga of life on Seal Island, a tiny dot in the Bering Sea. It gained the Oscar for best short subject, two-reel, in 1949.

While its live-action documentaries began to gain audiences, the studio's animation shorts had dipped in popularity. Warner Bros., with its raucous cartoon star Bugs Bunny, rose as the company's main competitor. Mickey Mouse's days of stardom faded, and Disney turned to Donald Duck as a box office draw. Donald's fiery temper appealed to movie audiences and made him a competitor to Bugs Bunny; by 1949, he had become the studio's top star, surpassing Mickey Mouse in the number of cartoons reaching theaters across the country. In the meantime, the new postwar emphases and direction achieved renewed financial stability for Disney Productions, allowing them to return to producing full-length features, a line of the business that had been put on hold because of the war and its aftermath. *Cinderella* came out in 1950, followed by *Alice in Wonderland* (1951), *Peter Pan* (1953), and a host of other features in succeeding years.

In 1932, early in his career, Walt Disney won the first of many Oscars in the category best short subject, cartoons, from the Academy of Motion Picture Arts and Sciences (founded in 1927). That year, the Academy also gave him an honorary award for the creation of Mickey Mouse. He did not receive any nominations in 1933, but for each year from 1934 through 1940 and then again in 1942 and 1943, he picked up Oscars in the best short subject, cartoons, category that included *Ugly Duckling* (1939), *Lend a Paw* (1941) and *Der Fuehrer's Face* (1942). He also received a special Academy Award for *Fantasia* in 1940. He won for best song in 1947 for the *Song of the South* theme, *Zip-A-Dee-Doo-Dah,* music by Allie Wrudel (1905–1973) and lyrics by Ray Gilbert (1912–1976).

The Motion Picture Alliance for the Preservation of American Ideals, founded in 1944 by conservative Hollywood personalities to protect the industry from Communist infiltration, included Disney as one of its prominent members. In 1947, during the early years of the **Cold War,** he testified before the **House Un-American Activities Committee (HUAC),** identifying some former animators as members of the Communist party. His actions caused controversy in the Hollywood community.

Both Walt Disney and Disney Productions exerted monumental influence on the entertainment industry. Soon after the arrival of sound for **movies** in the late 1920s, he had begun experimenting with ways to coordinate both sound and music with moving images. His cartoon shorts, first with Mickey Mouse, and later with Donald Duck, along with full-length features, proved highly successful and established a firm base for growth after World War II. An entrepreneur, Disney constantly looked for ways to expand his business. At the time of his death, the company, in addition to cartoon shorts and animated features, had produced live-action movies, nature documentaries, **television** programs, big-budget screen musicals, and operated two successful theme parks.

See also: Autry, Gene, and Roy Rogers; Aviation; Country Music; Musicals (Film); Race Relations and Stereotyping; Technology

Selected Reading
Disney Archives. www.disney.go.com/vault/archives/today.html
Finch, Christopher. *The Art of Walt Disney: From Mickey Mouse to the Magic Kingdoms.* New York: Harry N. Abrams, 1975.
Schickel, Richard. *The Disney Version: The Life, Times, Art and Commerce of Walt Disney.* New York: Avon, 1968.

DRAMA (FILM)

One of the most all-encompassing areas of film, drama can include elements of comedy, pathos or tragedy, realism or fantasy, politics or history, or almost any other category of storytelling. A rootin' tootin' Western almost certainly contains dramatic components, as does the most imaginative adventure in outer space. The stories that connect the songs in musicals, the revelation of the monster in horror films, the plotting behind a crime in mysteries—all of these examples reinforce the idea that drama, in its broadest sense, can be found in virtually any type of motion picture.

For ease of classification, however, drama has long been considered a separate film genre, even though other recognized genres employ dramatic formats in their narrative construction. Those **movies** generally considered to fit the category of drama better than anywhere else tend to focus on emotional involvement and strong characterization while avoiding an emphasis on physical action and special effects. They usually eschew sweeping vistas, elaborate sets, and showy costumes in favor of the story itself. Love and romance of all kinds, character studies, and biographies (both fictional and real) tended to predominate in the 1940s.

All the King's Men, *one of the outstanding films of 1949, dramatized the 1947 Pulitzer Prize–winning novel by Robert Penn Warren. Actor Broderick Crawford, shown here, deservedly won an Academy Award for his portrayal of Willie Stark, a thinly veiled character based on Louisiana politician Huey Long. (Photofest)*

World War II and its effects on the lives of diverse characters naturally received considerable cinematic play during the period 1940 to 1945, but a surprising number of motion pictures ignored the conflict entirely, thereby offering audiences a respite from headlines and news broadcasts. The postwar era for the most part increased this avoidance; most studios turned to nontopical dramatic films, although the Cold War between the Communist bloc and the Western alliances that commenced at the end of decade brought forth a smattering of anti-Communist movies such as *I Married a Communist, The Red Danube,* and *The Red Menace* (all 1949). For the most part, however, Hollywood refrained from messages or propaganda in its dramatic offerings.

TABLE 48.   Representative Dramatic Films, 1940–1949

Year	Film Titles	Stars
1940	*Abe Lincoln in Illinois*	Raymond Massey, Ruth Gordon
	All This, and Heaven Too	Bette Davis, Charles Boyer
	Boomtown	Clark Gable, Spencer Tracy
	Dr. Ehrlich's Magic Bullet	Edward G. Robinson, Ruth Gordon
	The Grapes of Wrath	Henry Fonda, Jane Darwell
	Kitty Foyle	Ginger Rogers, Dennis Morgan
	The Long Voyage Home	John Wayne, Thomas Mitchell
	Our Town	William Holden, Frank Craven
	Rebecca	Laurence Olivier, Joan Fontaine
	Waterloo Bridge	Vivien Leigh, Robert Taylor
1941	*Citizen Kane*	Orson Welles, Joseph Cotton
	The Devil and Daniel Webster	Edward Arnold, Walter Huston
	Hold Back the Dawn	Charles Boyer, Olivia de Havilland
	The Little Foxes	Bette Davis, Herbert Marshall
	Manpower	Marlene Dietrich, Edward G. Robinson
	Meet John Doe	Gary Cooper, Barbara Stanwyck
	One Foot in Heaven	Fredric March, Martha Scott
	Penny Serenade	Cary Grant, Irene Dunne
	Shepherd of the Hills	John Wayne, Ward Bond
	Tobacco Road	Charley Grapewin, Gene Tierney
1942	*Across the Pacific*	Humphrey Bogart, Sidney Greenstreet
	Casablanca	Humphrey Bogart, Ingrid Bergman
	I Wake Up Screaming	Betty Grable, Victor Mature
	In This Our Life	Bette Davis, Olivia de Havilland
	Johnny Eager	Robert Taylor, Lana Turner
	Kings Row	Ann Sheridan, Ronald Reagan
	The Magnificent Ambersons	Joseph Cotton, Agnes Moorehead
	Now, Voyager	Bette Davis, Paul Henreid
	Random Harvest	Ronald Colman, Greer Garson
	Tortilla Flat	Spencer Tracy, Frank Morgan
1943	*The Constant Nymph*	Joan Fontaine, Charles Boyer
	Flesh and Fantasy	Charles Boyer, Edward G. Robinson
	Forever and a Day	Ray Milland, Claude Rains
	Happy Land	Don Ameche, Frances Dee

(continued)

TABLE 48. (continued)

Year	Film Titles	Stars
	The Man in Grey	James Mason, Helen Hayes
	The Moon and Sixpence	George Sanders, Herbert Marshall
	Old Acquaintance	Bette Davis, Miriam Hopkins
	Shadow of a Doubt	Joseph Cotton, Teresa Wright
	The Song of Bernadette	Jennifer Jones, Charles Bickford
	Watch on the Rhine	Paul Lukas, Bette Davis
1944	*The Adventures of Mark Twain*	Fredric March, Alexis Smith
	The Bridge of San Luis Rey	Louis Calhern, Lynn Bari
	Gaslight	Charles Boyer, Ingrid Bergman
	Guest in the House	Ralph Bellamy, Anne Baxter
	The Hairy Ape	William Bendix, Susan Hayward
	Keys of the Kingdom	Gregory Peck, Thomas Mitchell
	None but the Lonely Heart	Cary Grant, Ethel Barrymore
	Summer Storm	Linda Darnell, George Sanders
	Wilson	Alexander Knox, Geraldine Fitzgerald
	When the Lights Go on Again	Jimmy Lydon, Regis Toomey
1945	*A Bell for Adano*	John Hodiak, Gene Tierney
	Brief Encounter	Trevor Howard, Celia Johnson
	The Clock	Judy Garland, Robert Walker
	The Corn Is Green	Bette Davis, John Dall
	Leave Her to Heaven	Gene Tierney, Cornel Wilde
	The Lost Weekend	Ray Milland, Jane Wyman
	Mildred Pierce	Joan Crawford, Ann Blyth
	The Picture of Dorian Gray	George Sanders, Hurd Hatfield
	The Southerner	Zachary Scott, J. Carrol Naish
	A Tree Grows in Brooklyn	Dorothy McGuire, Peggy Ann Garner
1946	*The Best Years of Our Lives*	Fredric March, Myrna Loy
	Humoresque	Joan Crawford, John Garfield
	It's a Wonderful Life	James Stewart, Donna Reed
	A Matter of Life and Death	David Niven, Kim Hunter
	Of Human Bondage	Paul Henreid, Eleanor Parker
	The Postman Always Rings Twice	John Garfield, Lana Turner
	The Razor's Edge	Tyrone Power, Anne Baxter
	The Stranger	Edward G. Robinson, Loretta Young
	Three Strangers	Sidney Greenstreet, Peter Lorre
	To Each His Own	Olivia de Havilland, Mary Anderson
1947	*Black Narcissus*	Deborah Kerr, Jean Simmons
	Body and Soul	John Garfield, Lilli Palmer
	Crossfire	Robert Young, Robert Ryan
	A Double Life	Ronald Coleman, Shelly Winters
	The Farmer's Daughter	Loretta Young, Joseph Cotton
	Forever Amber	Cornel Wilde, Linda Darnell
	The Fugitive	Henry Fonda, Ward Bond
	The Gangster	Barry Sullivan, John Ireland
	Gentleman's Agreement	Gregory Peck, Dorothy McGuire
	The Hucksters	Clark Gable, Deborah Kerr

Year	Film Titles	Stars
1948	*All My Sons*	Edward G. Robinson, Burt Lancaster
	Another Part of the Forest	Fredric March, Edmund O'Brien
	Apartment for Peggy	Jeanne Crain, William Holden
	The Boy with Green Hair	Pat O'Brien, Dean Stockwell
	Enchantment	David Niven, Teresa Wright
	I Remember Mama	Irene Dunne, Barbara Bel Geddes
	Johnny Belinda	Jane Wyman, Lew Ayres
	Portrait of Jennie	Jennifer Jones, Joseph Cotton
	Rope	James Stewart, Farley Granger
	The Treasure of the Sierra Madre	Humphrey Bogart, Walter Huston
1949	*All the King's Men*	Broderick Crawford, Mercedes McCambridge
	Caught	James Mason, Barbara Bel Geddes
	Champion	Kirk Douglas, Arthur Kennedy
	Come to the Stable	Loretta Young, Celeste Holm
	The Heiress	Olivia de Havilland, Montgomery Clift
	Intruder in the Dust	Claude Jarman Jr., David Brian
	A Letter to Three Wives	Jeanne Crain, Linda Darnell, Ann Sothern
	Madame Bovary	Jennifer Jones, Van Heflin
	Pinky	Jeanne Crain, Ethel Barrymore
	The Reckless Moment	James Mason, Joan Bennett

Three exceptional dramatic movies from the mid-1940s illustrate the depths American filmmaking could reach in this genre. In 1946, RKO Radio Pictures released **The Best Years of Our Lives,** a poignant study about veterans returning from World War II. Superior in every way, it won multiple Academy Awards, including best picture, and gave the studio a box-office success. Everyone identified with the stresses and dislocations brought about by the war, and it foretold the adjustments ahead for both civilians and soldiers in the postwar era.

The following year, 1947, Hollywood tackled prejudice in U.S. society, a topic swept under the rug during the war and one censors looked at carefully. That summer saw the release of RKO Radio's *Crossfire,* an explosive examination of anti-Semitism in the armed forces. A hate crime against a young Jewish soldier propels the plot, and the dark, **film noir photography** adds to the mood of this benchmark picture. At the end of 1947, another potentially controversial film, *Gentleman's Agreement,* came to theaters. More cerebral than *Crossfire,* it also deals with anti-Semitism, but focuses on the subtler aspects of bigotry. Together, *Crossfire* and *Gentleman's Agreement* caused the moviegoing public to reassess its attitudes.

The 1940s overall proved a rich decade for dramatic movies and often pointed to a growing maturity in the industry. The war, of course, affected the content of many pictures—soap-opera plotting plagued more than one romantic offering, and cheap melodramatics took away from others—but, by and large, the 1940–1949 period gave moviegoers a varied menu of movies that fit the drama designation.

Alcoholism, something of a taboo topic for Hollywood films of the 1940s, received a grim portrayal in The Lost Weekend. *Ray Milland, on the left, received critical acclaim and an Academy Award for his role as a man battling his addiction. (Paramount Pictures/Photofest)*

See also: Broadway Shows (Comedy and Drama); Horror and Thriller Films; Musicals (Film)

Selected Reading
Higham, Charles, and Joel Greenberg. *Hollywood in the Forties.* New York: A. S. Barnes, 1968.
Muller, Jurgen. *Movies of the 40s.* Cologne, Germany: Taschen, 2005.
Thomas, Tony. *The Films of the Forties.* Secaucus, NJ: Citadel Press, 1975.

DRIVE-INS: MOVIE THEATERS, RESTAURANTS, AND BANKS

Soon after the first automobile rolled out of a factory, Americans declared it their preferred means for **travel.** Even in the depths of the Great Depression, many individuals claimed ownership of a car to be more important than a home, telephone, electrical lighting, or indoor plumbing. Entrepreneurs, always ready for new opportunities, began to look for ways to capitalize on this romance with **automobiles** and early on developed drive-in theaters, **fast food** eateries, and drive-in banking. A listing for contemporary times, of course, contains more kinds of drive-ins.

Drive-in theaters. **Movies,** at their inception, grabbed the attention of just about everyone and quickly became one of the most popular forms of entertainment in the United States. In 1933, Richard Hollingshead Jr. (1900–1975), of Camden, New Jersey, who receives credit as an inventor and manufacturer of chemicals, was involved with the family auto products business. He sometimes worked outdoors at his home, searching for a means to watch movies from the comfort of the family car. Descriptions of his activities indicate an experimental approach: to test for achieving the best image, he took a projector he had placed on the hood of his automobile and aimed it at his garage as well as at a sheet stretched across adjoining trees. To test whether the sound seemed to come from the picture and could be clearly heard, he put a **radio** behind the sheets and checked what happened with car windows up and car windows down. He supposedly even used a lawn sprinkler to simulate rain.

Satisfied with the results, Hollingshead and his cousin, W. Warren Smith (active 1930s), opened the first drive-in theater, the Automobile Movie Theater, in Camden on June 7, 1933, locating it in an area that would accommodate 400 cars on eight terraced rows facing a 30-by-40-foot screen. Sound came from speakers hung at the screen. The following year, other enterprising individuals in Orefield, Pennsylvania, and Galveston, Texas, followed suit.

During the early days of drive-in movies, most people who lived in urban areas had homes or apartments within walking distance of businesses and movie theaters,

A photo of a Los Angeles drive-in theater taken in the early 1940s. Instead of individual speakers for each car, rows of synchronized speakers in front of the parked vehicles blasted out the movie's sound and drivers had to roll down their windows in order to hear dialogue clearly. (Hulton-Deutsch Collection/CORBIS)

causing the early drive-in theaters to grow slowly. Technical problems involving both the quality of the sound system and some distortions of the picture also contributed to the initially poor public reception. Some additional outdoor theater construction did occur in the states of Massachusetts, Rhode Island, Maine, New York, California, Florida, Ohio, and Michigan. Chicago, in 1941, welcomed its first drive-in movie theater, sited in an area large enough to accommodate 1,160 cars. But the nation's December 7, 1941, entry into World War II brought a halt to most building projects not related to the country's defense. Approximately 100 drive-ins in 27 states showed movies before World War II; by 1945, however, the number had declined to about 25.

When the war ended and soldiers returned home, Americans eagerly sought ways to enjoy the return to peace. **President Franklin Delano Roosevelt** (1882–1945) signed the **GI Bill (Servicemen's Readjustment Act of 1944)** into law on June 13, 1945; it provided eligible military personnel the means for obtaining, among other things, loans for the construction or buying of homes. Soon thereafter, middle-class Americans moved in record numbers to the suburbs, and at their new homes, a car adorned each driveway. Drive-in theaters appeared in nearby farmers' fields at a phenomenal rate—some 800 by 1948, reaching totals of 2,200 in 1950 and 4,000 in 1958.

Improvements in the sound systems at drive-in theaters came in 1946, when RCA offered the first in-car speakers, cast-metal boxes that hung on the car window and directed the dialogue to the passengers. A prototype unit had been ready for production in 1941, but its use was delayed because of resources being diverted to the war effort. Given the tiny speakers enclosed in the boxes, the audio portion of the movie continued to be scratchy. But the ease and casualness of taking the family to a drive-in theater apparently outweighed an inferior sound system. People seemed to love the convenience of not dressing up, not even combing their hair, and having the children already in their pajamas. An evening of fun without the hassle of finding or paying a babysitter could be had for a small admission charged in a variety of ways—a flat fee that included everyone in the car, a small amount for the car and an additional charge for each passenger, or a graduated price by age, such as these 1946 figures: 50 cents for adults, 35 cents for high school students, and 20 cents for children (approximately $5.50, $3.90, and $2.20, respectively, in 2008 dollars).

As the number of drive-in theaters grew and competition for the business increased, owners offered additional attractions: playgrounds, baby bottle warmers, horseshoes, merry-go-rounds, picnic areas, and elaborate concession stands that sold hamburgers, soft drinks, popcorn, candy, hot dogs, and many other refreshments. Some even had laundry services. Along with families, dating teenagers found drive-in theaters enticing, especially for the privacy and safety offered each couple in their car, giving rise to outdoor theaters being known as "passion pits."

A former navy pilot, Edward Brown Jr. (active 1930s–1950s), offered perhaps the most unusual drive-in. He opened the Fly-In Drive-In Theater on June 3, 1948, in Asbury Park, New Jersey. In addition to room for 500 cars, this facility offered space for 25 airplanes, which could land at an airfield next to the drive-in and then taxi to the last row of slots large enough to accommodate them. When ready to leave, a Jeep towed the planes back to the airfield.

Eventually, the nuisance of foggy windows, cold, and distorted sound, coupled with increasing numbers of homes with **television** sets, reduced the number of drive-in theater attendees. By the 1960s, the original facilities needed capital improvements, and many owners chose not to invest, especially since rising land values offered them more profitable ventures. During the 1970s and 1980s, audience figures continued to decline, and drive-in theaters proved unprofitable as families stayed home and watched movies on cable television, VCRs and DVD units, or played video or computer games. But not all closed, and in 2007, some 400 survivors continued to regularly show movies. In addition, a handful of new drive-ins had been built.

Drive-in restaurants. The first fast-food businesses of the 20th century offered simple menus for a walk-in trade and could be found in the downtown sections of a city. They consisted of taverns, coffee shops, tea rooms, diners, sandwich shops, automats, soda fountains, luncheonettes, and **food** carts and stands. As cars became more affordable and popular, the owners of many of these ventures transplanted their eateries to the side of heavily traveled roads.

Recognizing the value of catering to automobile travelers, proprietors of some of these fast-food establishments offered curb service provided by young men and women dressed in uniforms and known as carhops. In 1940, two brothers, Maurice (1902–1971) and Richard McDonald (1909–1998) converted their walk-in food stand business in San Bernardino, California, to McDonald's Barbeque Restaurant with drive-in service provided by 20 carhops. In 1948, they dismissed their carhops, closed their restaurant for two months, and reopened with speedy service at a counter. By the mid-1950s, their efficient fast-food procedure plus drive-in capability attracted the attention of Ray Kroc (1902–1984) who first assisted the brothers with selling franchises. He eventually bought them out and created the first McDonald's, expanding it in time to include locations across the United States and around the world.

The same year—1948—that the McDonald brothers changed from carhops to counter service, Harry and Esther Snyder (1913–1976; 1920–2006), in Baldwin Park, California, opened their In-N-Out Burger. They provided a speaker box similar to those that had become available for drive-in theaters, enabling customers to remain in their cars and place their orders directly to attendants in the building. Some other fast-food businesses, instead of having an attendant bring the order to the car, created the drive-thru (this informal spelling of "through" became popular at this time), with purchasers moving to a window for pickup after giving their orders over a speaker.

The development of fast-food businesses utilizing curb and drive-thru services occurred primarily after World War II and experienced sporadic success. Their accomplishments were sufficient, however, to lay a strong foundation for their phenomenal growth in the 1950s and following decades.

Drive-in banking. Led by the City National Bank of South Bend, Indiana, the financial industry had its first bank curb service in 1936 for customers wishing to makes deposits or withdrawls. City National Bank offered a teller at an exterior window to utilize its otherwise useless alleyway. The practice, however, did not spread to other banks until after World War II.

The First National City Bank of New York (the name changed to Citibank in the mid-1970s) experimented with a mechanical cash dispenser in 1939 but removed it after six months because of a lack of use. The Exchange National Bank of Chicago opened drive-through tellers' windows protected by bullet-proof glass and sliding drawers for conducting business in 1946 and almost doubled its deposits during its first two years of operation. Its traffic flow grew from 50 cars daily to more than 600 by late 1948. At the same time, drive-in banking had spread to approximately 250 banks in 18 states. At some institutions, services had expanded to include loan payments, foreign exchange, bond purchases, and the like. The successful automated teller machine (ATM), which could be found worldwide at the beginning of the 21st century, was invented in 1971.

The automobile may have entered American society primarily as a means of **transportation,** but it quickly evolved to offer the family a pleasurable Sunday afternoon drive. The romance grew and, as it did, clearly encouraged the creation of a variety of car-related business opportunities. In the 1940s, the owners of theaters, fast-food restaurants, and banks found ways to increase their bottom line by interacting with customers who remained in their cars. The technique evolved over the following decades to include other businesses, such as libraries, dry cleaners, and movie rental operations. The possibilities proved endless.

See also: Architecture; Beverages; Desserts, Candy, and Ice Cream; Leisure and Recreation; Levittown and Suburbanization; Restaurants.

Selected Reading
Drive-in Theater Statistics. www.drive-ins.com
Hoffman, Frank W., and William G. Bailey. *Fashion Merchandising and Fads.* New York: Haworth Press, 1994.
———. *Sports & Recreation Fads.* New York: Haworth Press, 1991.
Segrave, Kerry. *Drive-in Theaters: A History from Their Inception in 1933.* Jefferson, NC: McFarland, 1992.

DUMONT NETWORK

Most individuals, when considering **television** networks in the days before cable, probably think of three: **ABC (American Broadcasting System),** CBS (Columbia Broadcasting System), and NBC (National Broadcasting Company). But a fourth network tried to make a go of it against such formidable opposition: the DuMont Network. Allen B. DuMont (1901–1965; several variations in the spelling of his surname exist, including Dumont and Du Mont), the founder of that enterprise, was an American engineer, inventor, and visionary business entrepreneur. He created DuMont Laboratories in 1931 to explore opportunities in the new field of television after being employed for a time with the Westinghouse Corporation and the De Forest Radio Company. Working out of his garage, DuMont's labs constructed cathode ray tubes of his design that functioned and sold well, thereby providing working capital for his other projects.

To finance a dream of owning and operating the first television network, DuMont in the mid-1930s raised additional funds in an agreement with Paramount Pictures. He had also designed a home receiver that he hoped to sell and keep his network plans afloat. The first DuMont set, the Model-180, rolled off assembly lines in 1938, ahead of those manufactured by other competing firms. A quality component—most experts rank the Model-180 above anything then coming onto the market—it carried a hefty price tag of $395 (slightly over $6,000 in 2008 dollars). Housed in several available wood cabinets, this early DuMont product boasted an 8-by-10-inch picture, large for its time.

Informative brochures, along with newspaper and magazine **advertising,** touted DuMont television sets, but their large initial cost, coupled with the limited availability of programming—and that only in selected metropolitan areas with TV broadcast facilities—sharply limited sales. When World War II intervened and halted the fledgling television industry until 1946, Allen DuMont continued to plan for his network. In 1942, he had acquired license rights to W2XWV, an experimental television station in New York City. Shortly thereafter, its call letters became WABD, DuMont's initials. By 1945, he owned W3XWT in Washington, DC, later calling it WTTG. With the addition of WDTV in Pittsburgh, plus lining up a number of affiliates, he had the makings of a bona fide operation. In August 1946, the DuMont Network commenced broadcasting, arguably the first postwar American commercial television network.

A pioneer television network, the DuMont organization attempted to compete with giants CBS and NBC during the late 1940s. With the beginning of commercial television broadcasting, it premiered a variety series called Cavalcade of Stars, *which in turn introduced audiences to the comedic talents of Jackie Gleason (1916–1987). He can be seen here in a typical segment. (Photofest/DuMont Television Network)*

While DuMont moved ahead, NBC and CBS (and later ABC), fat with revenues from their **radio** operations, worked to activate television networks of their own. Realizing that if he were to compete against NBC and CBS, DuMont strove to cobble together a reasonable schedule of shows that would cover the broadcast day. But with no radio stars he could transfer to his new television network and lacking deep cash reserves, he found he could not afford expensive, top-ranked talent that would draw audiences and attract sponsors. He tried to expand and offer additional programming, but other stations, realizing DuMont's dilemma, were reluctant to sign on with him. The network thus had difficulty growing, whereas NBC and CBS gathered new stations with relative ease, given their advantages in programming.

During the later 1940s, the DuMont Network nevertheless carried several shows that won considerable acclaim. In 1949, it advertised *Cavalcade of Stars,* a variety show that introduced viewers to the comedic talents of Jackie Gleason (1916–1987). During his tenure on the program, Gleason created the first episodes of *The Honeymooners,* a series within the series that later became a major part of *The Jackie Gleason*

Show (CBS, 1952–1957) and an important entry in any history of American television comedy. Unfortunately for DuMont, *Cavalcade of Stars* ran only until the fall of 1952, whereupon CBS, offering more money and greater exposure, took over the show.

Life Is Worth Living, featuring the telegenic Fulton J. Sheen (1895–1979), a Catholic bishop, served as another star in DuMont's somewhat skimpy crown. Sheen, who had risen to fame by hosting *The Catholic Hour* on NBC radio from 1930 to 1950, dispensed easy-to-swallow religious advice on his program, and he attracted a large, devoted audience. The DuMont Network carried *Life Is Worth Living* from 1952 to 1955, when Sheen moved to ABC.

Captain Video premiered on the network in 1949. A space serial, it featured the Captain (Richard Coogan, b. 1914; replaced in 1950 by Al Hodge, 1912–1979) and his Video Rangers, a group of youthful agents set on saving humanity from extraterrestrial villains. The Captain's endless array of novel gadgets made their efforts possible. One of DuMont's longest-running offerings, it stayed with the network until 1955.

The Original Amateur Hour joined DuMont in 1948. Hosted by the genial Ted Mack (1904–1976), this talent show had its origins with *Major Bowes Amateur Hour,* a radio program that began in 1934 with Edward Bowes (1974–1946). The premise of both the radio and television productions involved bringing previously unknown amateur entertainers on stage to display their talents, or lack thereof. The level of the acts ranged from very good to truly awful, and audiences for many years enjoyed this wide variety.

Mack, who had been Bowes's talent coordinator, took over in 1946, immediately following Bowes's death. *The Original Amateur Hour* continued on radio until 1952 and on television until 1970. Mack guided the show onto television in 1948, with the DuMont Network picking it up; DuMont, however, had it only until 1949, when NBC took it away. Later CBS, and then ABC, carried the production, by that time known as *Ted Mack's Original Amateur Hour,* until its demise in 1970.

In one switch from ongoing patterns, DuMont actually gained a show from a rival network. In 1950, ABC premiered *The Arthur Murray Party.* Murray (1895–1991) had gained fame as a popular instructor and owner of an extensive **dance** school franchise. His program consisted of ballroom dancing and a bit of humor. ABC initially put it on its schedule as a summer replacement show in 1950; with the fall season, DuMont ran it for a year and it gained additional viewers. Its renown caused ABC, in a game of musical chairs, to try *The Arthur Murray Party* a second time for 1951–1952; CBS then took it for the summer 1952 season, and DuMont regained the show for 1952–1953, its last appearance on that network. NBC and CBS, however, decided to continue the confusion until 1960, when *The Arthur Murray Party* was cancelled once and for all.

Aside from those four headliners, the DuMont Network had few memorable series to offer the public, although it did pioneer some genres of drama. A show like *Mary Kay and Johnny* (1947–1948) has been called the first TV sitcom, but little else is known about it. *Faraway Hill* (October to December 1946), one of the network's earliest series, has been referred to as the first TV soap opera, but again, its brief run and lack of any surviving episodes make reliable information difficult to locate. Finally, *Rocky King, Inside Detective* ran for four years, 1950 to 1954. It starred Roscoe Karns (1891–1970), a busy actor and familiar face who had appeared in dozens of B movies in the 1930s and 1940s as a fast-talking private eye. But, like *Mary Kay and Johnny* and *Faraway Hill,* it never generated much of a following and disappeared as did most of DuMont's offerings.

At its peak in 1954, the DuMont Network could claim only six primary stations. In contrast, NBC and CBS by that time boasted over 40 each. DuMont had some 200 affiliates, but they had the freedom to pick and choose what they ran, including shows from rival networks. Ironically, beginning in 1951, Allen DuMont had been forced to cut back production of his TV sets—a major source of income for continuing his network—because of a lack of buyers. With revenues down, seemingly unable to expand the network, and faced with a stockholder rebellion, DuMont had to throw in the towel. In 1955, the DuMont Network went off the air.

See also: Religion; Technology

Selected Reading
Television History. www.MZTV/mz.asp
Weinstein, David. *The Forgotten Network: DuMont and the Birth of American Television.* Philadelphia: Temple University Press, 2004.

E

EDGAR BERGEN/CHARLIE MCCARTHY SHOW, THE

On December 17, 1936, an unusual duo made their **radio** debut as guests on the NBC (National Broadcasting Company) network's *Royal Gelatin Hour.* The pair consisted of Edgar Bergen (1903–1978), a ventriloquist, and his dummy, Charlie McCarthy (created ca. 1916). It might seem strange that such an act, depending as it does on the visual illusion that a ventriloquist does not move his lips when the dummy talks, would attempt any routines on the aural medium of radio. But Bergen and McCarthy soon erased any doubts with their quips and rapid-fire repartee. Both the studio audience and the many unseen radio listeners loved them. Crooner Rudy Vallee (1901–1986), the host and star of the *Royal Gelatin Hour,* promptly invited them back for a 13-week stint on the program.

Bergen, no newcomer to show business, had labored in vaudeville and performed on nightclub circuits but could never become a national headliner. Most booking agents—and most of the public as well—looked on ventriloquism as a novelty act and little more. But Vallee, himself a major radio and recording star, saw them perform at a club and took the chance with his hugely popular radio show. The gamble paid off.

NBC promptly signed Bergen to a contract that gave him his own show, *The Chase and Sanborn Hour,* a comedy-variety program that premiered in the spring of 1937. In 1939, recognizing their popularity, the network changed the name to *The Edgar Bergen/Charlie McCarthy Show.* In the early 1940s, it became *The Charlie McCarthy Show,* a title it would carry throughout the decade. It left the air in 1956 after a remarkable 19-year run, successful to the end.

During that time, merchandisers took advantage of the show's popularity. Charlie McCarthy dolls became a hot item in department stores, despite their price tag of $9.98 (roughly $150 in 2008 dollars). Hollywood likewise wanted the two for **movies,** such as *The Goldwyn Follies* (1938), *Charlie McCarthy, Detective* (1939), and

The two stars of The Edgar Bergen/Charlie McCarthy Show, *ventriloquist Edgar Bergen and his dummy, Charlie McCarthy (initially made around 1916), traded quips over the air from the 1930s to 1956. They are shown here in Pilgrim get-up, presumably for a Thanksgiving broadcast, although only the studio audience could see their costumes. (NBC / Photofest)*

You Can't Cheat an Honest Man (1939), with comedian W. C. Fields (1880–1946). A frequent guest on their radio show; Fields and McCarthy had an on-air feud that consisted mainly of hilarious ad libs between the two. In the 1940s, Charlie and Bergen appeared with other radio stars in *Look Who's Laughing* (1941), *Here We Go Again* (1942) and *Stage Door Canteen* (1943), a film designed to pump up spirits and sell **war bonds.** *Fun and Fancy Free* (1947), an animated film from Walt Disney (1901–1966), features Bergen/McCarthy as they comment on and link two cartoon stories.

Since radio listeners could not see him, it would seem that it mattered little whether Bergen moved his lips or not, nor how Charlie appeared for his broadcasts. But Bergen, a clever showman, cultivated Charlie's persona. He dressed him in top hat, white tie, and tails, and even added a monocle as the finishing touch. In their conversations, Bergen played the straight man, asking Charlie questions and discussing various topics with him. Charlie, the consummate wise guy, answered in clipped, sarcastic comebacks. He usually referred to the ventriloquist as simply Bergen and ceaselessly made fun of his appearance, even lampooning him when his lips moved. Audiences quickly forgot that anything Charlie might say originated with Edgar Bergen.

In time, Bergen created several other dummies. Mortimer Snerd remains the best remembered, a slow-talking oaf that Charlie teased unmercifully. Effie Klinker, a stereotypical old maid, came along in 1944, but Bergen used her infrequently. Charlie reveled in being the undisputed star, and he often reminded Bergen of the fact. In addition, English bandleader Ray Noble (1903–1978) provided the music and frequently joined in the banter, his accent a target for Charlie's jibes.

At the start of World War II, in an attempt to spur enlistments, Charlie joined the Army Air Corps in 1942, shortly after Pearl Harbor. He then tried to sign up with the U.S. Marines, an act that brought forth a court-martial skit broadcast from a California army base. Leading actor Jimmy Stewart (1908–1997), who then served in the U.S. Air Force as a lieutenant, made an appearance as a military defense lawyer for Charlie. All good fun, the series reflected how the entertainment industry threw itself into the war effort.

An adequate ventriloquist, but never an outstanding one (he did not perform stunts like drinking a glass of water while Charlie spoke, whistling while talking, and the like), Bergen relied on his writing skills and ability to interact with Charlie. His quick wit and ability to ad lib more than made up for any deficiencies in skills as a ventriloquist. After the decline of network radio, Bergen made little attempt to appear on **television.** He briefly hosted *Do You Trust Your Wife?* in the mid-1950s but, aside from guest appearances on other shows, seldom appeared on the small screen. Married to radio, he overcame any disadvantages the medium might offer an essentially visual comedian. For most of the 1940s, *The Charlie McCarthy Show* ranked as one of the most consistently popular programs on the air. In his will, Edgar Bergen gave Charlie McCarthy to the Smithsonian Institution, where the pine and hickory celebrity now rests, resplendent in his dress clothes.

See also: *ASCAP vs. BMI* Radio Boycott and the AFM Recording Ban; Comedies (Film); Radio Programming: Comedy Shows; Radio Programming: Music and Variety Shows

Selected Reading
Dunning, John. *On the Air: The Encyclopedia of Old-Time Radio.* New York: Oxford University Press, 1998.
Grams, Martin, Jr. *The Edgar Bergen and Charlie McCarthy Show: An Episode Guide and Brief History.* http://www.old-time.com/otrlogs2/charlie_mg.html

EDUCATION

The 1940s proved to be a significant decade in the history of American education. Enrollment in high schools, colleges, and universities declined during the war years but eventually increased once peace and veterans returned to the United States. Teacher shortages became a major home-front problem both during the war and postwar years. The process of recruiting millions of citizens to fight in World War II brought high illiteracy figures, especially for minority groups, to public attention and resulted in discussions by armed forces personnel on how best to address the issue. Before the decade ended, both blacks and women gained educational opportunities lacking in past decades, a situation that opened new doors for them. Efforts to promote international understanding widened, indicating a change in Americans' willingness to be more informed about the rest of the world. Finally, these trends grew from questions raised about the role of the federal government in the education of its citizenry.

The establishment of schools accompanied the founding of the United States. By 1918, every state in the union had passed laws requiring children to attend elementary school to study at least reading, writing, and arithmetic. Compulsory attendance ages varied among the states with most opting for ages 6 through 14. Facilities also differed in size and amenities. Many small communities and rural areas with limited resources could provide only one- or two-room schools, not always the best of conditions, and the problem continued into the 1940s.

Towns and large cities usually had separate buildings for the elementary and high school grades, and enrollments at some secondary schools included young people coming from nearby areas with only elementary schools. Despite limitations, 10.6 percent of 14- to 17-year-olds enrolled in high school in 1900, a statistic that gradually increased to 51.1 percent in 1930, 71.3 percent in 1940, and 85 percent in the early 1950s. Graduation rates for this same age group, however, lagged behind, although they rose from 6.3 percent in 1900 to 28.8 percent in 1930, 49 percent in 1940, and 52.4 percent in 1950.

After the country's entry into World War II, educational institutions at all levels faced challenges. Even with decreases in high school enrollments at the beginning of the war, both elementary and high schools experienced an immediate shortage of teachers when the draft took those who were younger. As early as January 1942, **newspapers** across the country reported an additional nationwide educational crisis caused by teachers leaving for higher-paying wages in defense industries. A survey conducted in December 1942 by the *New York Times* indicated an immediate need across the country for 75,000 instructors. In an attempt to fill the gap, many school systems initiated a campaign to lure those who had left the profession to return. Also, temporary teaching certificates were awarded to individuals, many of whom lacked the necessary training, putting less than satisfactory teachers in classrooms.

Decreases in college and university enrollments occurred as men, and some women, turned from educational pursuits to either enlist or be drafted into the armed forces. Businesses and industries likewise faced serious manpower shortages. Thus, women and adolescents were urged to go to work, and many teenagers quit school, causing a decrease in high school enrollments—a situation that continued throughout the war years and concerned educators. The U.S. Office of Education attempted to address this situation with a National Go-to-School Drive for the 1944–1945 academic year. A return to higher enrollments and increased high school completion rates did not occur, however, until 1947.

Slogans such as "Study, Sacrifice, Save, and Serve" appeared in high school classrooms to remind those still enrolled that they had responsibilities for preserving democracy. Some schools allowed older students to accelerate their studies by going to summer school and graduating in three years, an effort that would enable them to receive a high school diploma before, instead of after, they reached draft age. High school courses varied widely from rigorously academic to fundamentally commercial or vocational, as well as variations in between. Boys now received hard training in physical education in order to be in good condition for becoming a soldier. Subjects suitable for those who would eventually join a branch of the armed forces could also be taken—navigation, military math, physics, preflight aeronautics, and military drill, for example.

In many communities, schools also served as sites for distributing ration books, selling **war bonds** and stamps, and receiving donations from **scrap drives.** These activities, along with routine air raid drills, provided reminders of the hardships that had to be assumed by all those on the home front. School publications expanded beyond the usual curriculum information, sports updates, and school gossip to include articles about the war effort, especially on regulations contained in the **Selective Training and Service Act of 1940 (Selective Service, or Draft).** Guidance departments broadened their programs to help students learn about local war service and industrial opportunities as well as clarifying draft requirements. Some also offered assistance to those experiencing emotional strain through counseling and helped to increase social activities available after school and on weekends. Students were urged to be active and take a part in a school play, participate in school sports, attend school-sponsored dances, or join activities within the community offered by various **youth** organizations and community centers.

But these conditions existed primarily in segregated white schools. Before World War II, the level of education offered most minorities living in the United States ended with elementary school. When the nation entered the war, three-quarters of the black population resided in the South, where segregated school systems provided few high schools for minorities. Thus, many blacks—twice as many as whites—who registered under the Selective Training and Service Act of 1940 failed to meet the minimum educational requirements of reading and writing at the fourth-grade level.

The U.S. Army, uncertain about whether to draft educationally nonqualifying applicants, initially waffled and accepted between 5 and 10 percent in this group. In November 1942, in order to be more definitive about induction decisions, the United States Armed Forces Institute asked the American Council on Education to develop a battery of tests that would measure high school–level knowledge and skills. Known today as the GED (General Equivalency Diploma), its introduction clarified educational questions and gave those soldiers and sailors returning home from war the academic credentials they needed to pursue a college education or get civilian jobs.

Also in 1942, the Department of War and the Office of Education attempted to address the illiteracy problem another way and collaborated on offering a preinduction training program for selective service registrants who had their draft deferred because of educational deficiencies. Any interested high school and college students under draft age could also attend. It was hoped that this would qualify more minorities for service as well as decrease military training time for both whites and blacks once in the military.

The army soon realized, despite efforts being made to strengthen registrants educationally, that rejection rates were jeopardizing attainment of draft quotas needed for the armed forces and on June 1, 1943, lifted the restrictions. It also established Service Training Units (STUs), organized as efficient school systems, to assist those who needed to improve their basic educational skills. For these classes, the army developed a four-part program featuring Private Pete, while the navy employed Sailor Sam. Over 400,000 men—black, white, Asian, Hispanic, and Native American—moved from these units to regular army service.

In addition to addressing illiteracy through the STUs, the federal government and the Department of War underwrote extensive instructional programs where soldiers learned, among other things, foreign languages and how to become radio men, engineers, mechanics, airplane pilots, and medics. After the war, thousands of soldiers returned home with knowledge and skills that allowed for a variety of educational and vocational choices. Almost 8 million decided to take advantage of the college scholarships that constituted a part of the Servicemen's Readjustment Act, commonly known as the **GI Bill,** signed into law in June 1944 and offered to all who received an honorable discharge. By 1947, veterans accounted for almost half of the nation's college students, while many others enrolled in technical and vocational training programs. Together, these educational experiences allowed veterans to move beyond the limits of their prewar lives.

World War II also opened up many new possibilities for women in the areas of a college education or a job with better pay than the stereotypical teacher, secretary, or nurse. From the first years of the 20th century, increasing numbers of girls had attended high school and in 1940 represented more than half of that population. Women also enrolled in colleges and universities in record numbers and represented a little less than one-half of all college enrollments by 1920, a figure that rose slightly during the 1930s. During the first half of the 1940s, because of war-depleted male enrollments, female students constituted a majority of the student body and accounted for 40 percent of the graduates. To the benefit of women, various all-male institutions looked to them for survival. Male-only Harvard University, for example, entered into an agreement in 1943 with neighboring women-only Radcliffe College to allow its students to attend classes at Harvard for the first time, an event that eventually led to the 1977 merger of these two esteemed centers of learning.

After the war, women experienced increased competition for college acceptance from men benefiting from the GI Bill. Between 1947 and 1950, the proportion of women enrolled relative to men declined, but at the same time their numbers as degree recipients grew at all levels—bachelor's, master's, doctorates, and professional—enabling them to pursue careers previously closed to them.

Along with the challenges presented by decreasing wartime enrollments of men at most colleges and universities, World War II also provided some unique opportunities for these institutions. To meet the wartime demand for technically trained individuals, higher-education curricula underwent rapid revisions that placed a greater emphasis on technological courses and allowed students to receive college degrees in less than the traditional four years. This led to many discussions about the value of a liberal arts education versus practical courses, a debate that continues today.

Whatever the emphases of the institution's curriculum, the postwar years brought growth. On March 20, 1950, the *New York Times* reported that 150 colleges and universities had been added to the U.S. Office of Education's list, giving a total of 1,808 recognized institutions of higher learning for the academic year 1948–1949, an increase greater than any comparable period in the nation's history. Two-year junior and community colleges, fairly new kids on the block, accounted for approximately 50 percent of this expansion.

In addition to heightened interest in higher education in the United States, the postwar years saw educational ventures taking place internationally. The independent, nonprofit Institute of International Education, founded in 1919, both then and today provides experiences in international education and training for undergraduates, graduate students, college faculty, professionals, teachers, and technical trainees. In 1949, more than 2,000 foreign and American recipients, representing a 42 percent increase over the previous year, received fellowships and scholarships for their studies.

The federal government became an active player in international exchanges when Arkansas Senator J. William Fulbright (1905–1995) introduced legislation to initiate and finance certain international educational programs. Signed into law on August 1, 1946, it became known as the Fulbright Act. The program, in 1946–1947, provided for the exchange of 74 teachers from the United States and Great Britain. Funding for these individuals came from the sale of surplus U.S. war property. By 1949, agreements had been reached with seven countries for the exchange of graduate students, college and university professors, and researchers, with a total of 648 Fulbright scholarships available. In 1961, the revised Fulbright-Hays Act broadened the program and sources of funding and today it carries the honor of being the largest U.S. exchange program.

Problems in education, along with many other domestic issues, had been put on a partial hold during the war years but returned to the forefront of national attention during the second half of the 1940s. Population shifts brought about by the concentration of defense plants and military bases in certain parts of the country, coupled with the predicted 5 million **baby boom** children destined to enter elementary school between 1947 and 1957, caused many to regard new classroom construction and recruitment and retention of quality teachers as urgent needs.

Local communities faced uncertainty in how to finance school building programs along with hiring the necessary staff for increased enrollments. In 1946, Ohio Senator Robert Taft (1889–1953) saw mass education as essential to the country's economic welfare and the only defense for liberty against totalitarianism; he introduced a bill for federal aid to education as a possible solution. Released from committee in 1947, it passed in the Senate in 1948 but stalled in the House of Representatives that year as well as the next. The principal point involved religious issues relating to the inclusion or exclusion of private and parochial schools receiving federal funds. It would not be until the 1960s that federal aid for education became a reality.

Education has always been viewed by Americans as the cornerstone of democracy—a concept strengthened during the 1940s as secondary education gained ground as a universal right for all, while at the same time the country saw a sharp rise in the numbers attending college. Since 1921, the week before Thanksgiving has been celebrated as American Education Week. Originally sponsored by the NEA (National Education Association) and the American Legion, it sought to raise public awareness of the importance of this right. Themes during the 1940s reflected the perceived role of education during challenging times. They included "Education for a Strong America" (1941), "Education in a Democracy at War" (1943), "Education for the Atomic Age"

(1946), "Strengthening the Foundation of Our Freedom" (1948), and "Making Democracy Work" (1949).

See also: Civil Defense; Juvenile Delinquency; Rationing; Religion; Roosevelt, Eleanor

Selected Reading
"Education." *New York Times,* November 5, 1940; November 9, 1941; August 23, 1942; July 18, 1943; November 5, 1943; July 30, 1944; March 20, 1950. www.proquest.com
Fass, Paula S. *Outside In, Minorities and the Transformation of American Education.* New York: Oxford University Press, 1989.
Knight, Edgar W. *Education in the United States.* Rev. ed. New York: Ginn, 1951.
"Teacher Shortages." *New York Times,* January 25, 1942; December 13, 1942; June 29, 1946; February 27, 1949. www.proquest.com

EISENHOWER, GENERAL DWIGHT DAVID

Born David Dwight Eisenhower (1890–1969) in Denison, Texas, and raised in Abilene, Kansas, he changed the order of his given names when entering West Point in 1911. While there, Eisenhower received the nickname Ike. After graduating in 1915, he married Mamie Geneva Doud (1896–1979) the following year; they had two sons, Doud Dwight Eisenhower (1917–1921) and John Sheldon Doud Eisenhower (b. 1922).

In the years following World War I, he never saw combat. He instead carried out a series of low-key assignments, one of which included writing a guidebook to American battlefields in France and another serving as an aide to **General Douglas MacArthur** during the 1932 Bonus Army incident in Washington, DC.

When the Japanese bombed Pearl Harbor on December 7, 1941, Colonel Eisenhower had 25 years of service with the U.S. Army. This attack took the United States into a war already raging in Europe and Asia and signaled the beginning of a remarkable climb in the military for Eisenhower. After Pearl Harbor, Army Chief of Staff **General George Catlett Marshall** (1880–1959), recognizing strong organizational and administrative abilities in Eisenhower, called him to Washington, DC, to head the Pacific and Far Eastern Section of the War Department's War Plans Division. Eisenhower, now a brigadier

General of the Army Dwight D. Eisenhower, walking away from an airplane, with Lt. General Lucius Clay, architect of the later Berlin Airlift. (Library of Congress)

general, quickly distinguished himself with his skills related to planning and follow-through: thoroughness of analyses, sound rationales behind decisions, and clarity in reports. In June 1942, Marshall selected Eisenhower, recently made a major general, over 366 other senior officers to command all U.S. forces in the European theater. This preferment became the first of many, each leading to new roles that allowed him to add strong leadership and diplomacy skills to his other abilities.

Promoted to lieutenant general soon thereafter, Eisenhower advanced from commanding general of the European Theater of Operations, to supreme commander, Allied forces, North African Theater of Operations. Next he moved to commander not only of the North African Theater, but across the entire Mediterranean basin, which included the British Eighth Army. With this position, Eisenhower advanced a plan that successfully cleared North Africa of Axis forces; he then oversaw the invasion of southern Italy.

As a leader, Eisenhower demonstrated brilliance in developing successful military strategies. At the same time, he acknowledged soldiers' needs and the importance of instilling an atmosphere of positive morale. A case in point: In 1943, in an attempt to address the dryness of the North African heat and his men's accompanying thirst as well as their constant longing for reminders of home, he requested the building of 10 Coca-Cola bottling plants supplied with enough syrup to provide his troops 6 million bottles a month. General Marshall immediately gave Eisenhower, and all other theater and area commanders, authority to set up soft-drink bottling operations and to request personnel to operate the facilities. In record time, Coca-Cola arrived at the battlefield.

Hollywood reported that General Eisenhower supposedly said that next to guns and ammunition, what "the boys need most is **movies** and more movies." Right after Pearl Harbor, Hollywood filmmakers agreed to produce 16-millimeter prints of their motion pictures and make them available to military services without charge. The Army Overseas Motion Picture Service estimated that, by 1945, some 2,400 films were shown nightly in the European and Mediterranean areas alone.

In December 1943, Eisenhower's responsibilities increased when he became supreme Allied commander in Europe, as well as supreme Allied commander of the Allied Expeditionary Force. He also took charge of all U.S. forces on the Western front north of the Alps and he supervised the detailed planning that led to the much-anticipated Allied assault on Normandy known as Operation Overlord, in June 1944. He followed that with the subsequent invasion of Germany and liberation of Western Europe. In recognition of his senior position and outstanding accomplishments, Eisenhower, on December 20, 1944, received a fifth star as general of the army, the highest attainable rank.

He returned to the United States in November 1945 as a hero and assumed the position of chief of staff, U.S. Army, a rank he held until 1948. As such, he took charge of the postwar demobilization of U.S. soldiers. Probably unaware of it at the time, Eisenhower's distinctive short uniform jacket—appropriately named after him—became popular with both soldiers and civilians. It had first became available to troops in 1943. After the war, women borrowed the basic design as a **fashion** accessory; variations on the Eisenhower jacket began appearing in department stores in 1946, and retailers advertised it as "short and snappy."

In 1947, with the passage of the National Security Act, Eisenhower became the army's first commanding officer to participate in the newly formed Joint Chiefs of Staff. The following year, he retired from service and published his highly acclaimed memoir, *Crusade in Europe*. From the military he moved to academia, becoming president of New York City's Columbia University in 1948.

Immensely popular with U.S. troops during World War II, Eisenhower instilled confidence in them and, in turn, with those back home. Always ready with his famous grin, Ike epitomized the effective leader and found that he could not disappear from the public stage. As postwar Europe struggled with recovering from the ravages of World War II, it faced possible economic collapse. Realizing the dangers, the United States, Canada, and 10 European and Scandinavian countries signed the North Atlantic Treaty on April 4, 1949. This pact, created with the onset of the **Cold War,** formed a military alliance known as the North Atlantic Treaty Organization (NATO), a response to the threat posed by Russian forces in Eastern Europe.

President Harry S. Truman (1884–1972) recalled Eisenhower at the end of 1950, asking him to assume the role of Supreme Allied Commander for NATO troops. Taking a leave of absence from Columbia, Eisenhower accepted and again demonstrated strong leadership as he successfully promoted a sense of partnership among the NATO membership nations while creating a multinational force able to shield Western Europe from Communist aggression.

In 1952, he retired from active service a second time and returned to Columbia University. Still a popular individual, many viewed Dwight Eisenhower as a man ideally suited for the White House. "Draft Eisenhower" movements started as early as 1948 among both Democrats and Republicans, since he had never announced any party affiliation. The Republican Party finally persuaded him to run for president in 1952. "I like Ike" became an irresistible slogan propelling Eisenhower to a sweeping victory against Adlai Stevenson (1900–1963) as the 34th president of the United States. Four years later, he was reelected for a second term. Following his retirement from the presidency in 1960, he and Mamie moved to Gettysburg, Pennsylvania, and a quieter life. He died in 1969.

See also: Beverages; D-Day; Roosevelt, President Franklin Delano; Selective Training and Service Act of 1940 (Selective Service, or Draft); United Nations

Selected Reading

Doherty, Thomas. *Projections of War: Hollywood, American Culture, and World War II*. New York: Columbia University Press, 1993.

Eisenhower, Dwight David. www.whitehouse.gov/about/presidents/DwightDEisenhower/

Kennedy, David M. *Freedom from Fear: The American People in Depression and War, 1929–1945*. New York: Oxford University Press, 1999.

ELLINGTON, DUKE

Nicknamed Duke in childhood by friends who noticed his innate savoir faire and dapper way of dressing, Edward Kennedy Ellington (1899–1974) was born in Washington, DC. Raised in a musical home, he became an accomplished piano player at an early age. He studied art in high school, but a growing love for music and performance determined him to move in that direction. He had formed his first small group by 1917, playing mainly for private social functions in the Washington region.

In the early 1920s, Ellington moved to Harlem, anxious to participate in the active **jazz** scene found there. Several long-term engagements at local clubs allowed him to concentrate on developing a distinctive style while he gathered some outstanding musicians around him. He made a number of recordings on various labels during this period and received an important booking at Harlem's famous Cotton Club in 1927, one that included remote broadcasts for **radio.** His fame spread throughout the 1920s and into the 1930s; when not performing, he could be found composing, creating a remarkable legacy of American music (Ellington disdained labels like "jazz" or "popular") that remains one of the glories of 20th-century songwriting, regardless of category.

As **swing** became the dominant format in pop music during the 1930s, Ellington and his orchestra stood at the forefront. One enduring hit after another flowed from his pen during this time, such as "Mood Indigo" (1931), "Sophisticated Lady" (1933), "Solitude" (1934), "Stompy Jones" (1934), "In a Sentimental Mood" (1935), "Azure" (1937), "I Let a Song Go Out of My Heart" (1938), and others too numerous

By the time the 1940s rolled around, Edward Kennedy "Duke" Ellington had long since established his fame as a composer, pianist, and orchestra leader. The passage of time, however, did not slow him down, and he fronted some of his best aggregations and wrote some of his finest music throughout the decade. This picture shows him in a familiar role, at the grand piano, enjoying the playing of his sidemen. (Photofest)

to mention, assuring Ellington a secure place among the era's favorite composers and performers. At the same time, his orchestra became an extension of his genius, and his flair for texture and tonality placed him on a unique plane; no one else duplicated the Ellington band's sound, making his music instantly recognizable.

Constant traveling, including tours to Europe, club dates, concerts, broadcasts, and a steady stream of recordings, kept Ellington and his sidemen in front of audiences and further broadened his appeal. At the end of the 1930s, well-established and reasonably prosperous despite the competition of dozens of other bands, he hired a young pianist-arranger named Billy Strayhorn (1915–1967). The 1940s may have marked the decline of the Swing Era, but the decade also witnessed the unique collaboration between Ellington and Strayhorn, establishing a new era of creativity for the orchestra. Strayhorn alone during the 1940s contributed the classics "Day Dream" in 1940, "Passion Flower" and "Chelsea Bridge" in 1941, "A Flower Is a Lovesome Thing" in 1946, and "Lush Life" in 1949 (probably composed in the mid-1930s), among many others.

Ellington's writing, no doubt spurred on by Strayhorn, took on a complexity seldom seen or heard in popular music, and yet the band swung with the best of them, and dancers continued to take to the floor when he played his new, innovative arrangements. In a burst of inspiration in 1940, Ellington penned "Jack the Bear," "Ko-Ko," "Cottontail," "In a Mellotone," "Harlem Airshaft," along with several other standards, all of which immediately became part of the orchestra's book. The following year, 1941, Strayhorn composed "Take the 'A'-Train," a piece that virtually overnight became the band's theme; Ellington contributed "I Got It Bad (and That Ain't Good)" and "Subtle Slough" (better known as "Just Squeeze Me" in its vocal version).

As an orchestra leader, Ellington demanded the best of anyone who played for him. Some refer to his orchestras of the late 1930s and the World War II period as a golden era for the leader, since so many memorable numbers and performances are associated with that time. Even during the war years, despite some inevitable personnel shifts, the band's lineup remained remarkably stable. One thing remained unchanged: the Ellington bands included some of the best instrumentalists of the day, sidemen capable of reading a complex chart for one number and improvising brilliantly on another.

The 1940s were also a period when Duke Ellington began to reach out and try some new directions in his music, especially in terms of extended-length compositions. The 78-rpm record, the standard recording and playback medium until the 1948 advent of the long-playing record, normally had a playing time of only 3 to 4 minutes per side on a regular 10-inch disk. As a result, almost all American jazz and popular music of the day had to fit within those confines. Occasionally, a songwriter would create a longer piece that required two or more consecutive sides, but such compositions, outside of classical music, were rare. Ellington, for example, in 1931 recorded "Creole Rhapsody" on two sides, and "Reminiscing in Tempo" (1935) consisted of four parts for a total of more than 12 minutes of playing time; it required four sides, or two disks.

Undeterred, Ellington in 1942 composed *Black, Brown and Beige,* a three-part concert work that, in its entirety takes about 45 minutes. It premiered in January 1943 at New York's prestigious Carnegie Hall. Because of the recording ban then in effect, no one recorded the concert commercially, and it was assumed lost. Over the years,

TABLE 49. The Duke Ellington Orchestra, Early 1940s (an Approximation)

Instrument	Musician
Reeds	Johnny Hodges (1906–1970) alto saxophone Otto Hardwicke (1904–1970) alto saxophone Ben Webster (1909–1973) tenor saxophone Barney Bigard (1906–1980) tenor saxophone, clarinet Harry Carney (1910–1974) baritone saxophone
Trumpets	Rex Stewart (1907–1967) Ray Nance (1913–1976; also violin) Wallace Jones (1906–1983)
Trombones	"Tricky" Sam Nanton (1904–1946) Lawrence Brown (1907–1988) Juan Tizol (1900–1984)
Rhythm Section	Ellington or Strayhorn piano Jimmy Blanton (1918–1942) bass Fred Guy (1897–1971) guitar (also banjo) Sonny Greer (1895–1982) drums
Vocals	Ivie Anderson (1905–1949) Kay Davis (b. 1920) Al Hibbler (1915–2001)

Ellington released new arrangements of sections from *Black, Brown and Beige* on record, especially "Come Sunday" and "The Blues," but in 1977, staff members at Carnegie Hall discovered a complete version of the performance on acetate disks and restored them. That same year, the entire original event finally became available on record.

In many ways, the inspiration for *Black, Brown and Beige* came from a stage musical Ellington created in 1941 called *Jump for Joy*. An unabashed paean to black life in the United States, it featured an all-black cast and some splendid Ellington music. It ran from July into September in Los Angeles, but theater owners in New York saw it as too progressive, too concerned with civil rights and a history of racial wrongs, to risk a Broadway production. The onset of World War II also overshadowed *Jump for Joy* and it languished, lost amid the many other Ellington tunes then being written.

The popularity of the 1943 concert caused Carnegie Hall to schedule annual appearances by Ellington and his orchestra, which allowed him to introduce extended works. For 1944, he premiered *The Perfume Suite*. He had a banner year in 1947, giving both *The Liberian Suite* and *The Deep South Suite* their debuts. Maintaining his compositional pace, he brought forth *The Tattooed Bride* in 1948.

While he worked on his longer pieces, Ellington did not neglect the more traditional three-minute works that had brought him to fame. "I'm Beginning to See the Light," a popular hit, came out in 1944, as did "Main Stem." "I'm Just a Lucky So-and-So" arrived in 1945, "Esquire Swank" and "Pretty Woman" the next year, and "Love You Madly," Duke's phrase for his audiences, closed out the decade.

No stranger to film, Ellington and his orchestra also appeared in a number of **movies.** Hollywood displayed his talents in over a half-dozen motion pictures during the 1930s, and the 1940s showed no letup. Two 1942 musical shorts, *Flamingo* and *Jam Session,* feature Ellington and the band. Singer Herb Jeffries (b. 1913; a sometime vocalist with the orchestra) also had a role in *Flamingo.* The documentary *Upbeat in Music,* an episode of *The March of Time* series, displayed the talents of many musicians, as did *Reveille with Beverly* (both 1943). The latter, however, received distribution as a full-length commercial musical, with a plot and a cast of Hollywood stars. Ellington also plays a significant role in *Cabin in the Sky* (1943), a much-ballyhooed version of the 1940 hit Broadway musical of the same name. With an all-black cast but aimed at general audiences, it gave the band, performing an Ellington number called "Going Up," a chance to be seen by a wide public. In a more unusual light, *Date with Duke,* a 1947 animated short, has pianist Ellington playing and leading a group of stop-motion figures in a performance of his *Perfume Suite.*

Even with concerts and movies, the later 1940s proved a difficult time for Ellington and his orchestra, just as they did for almost all American big bands, at least those that remained active. Changing musical tastes, especially a sharp decline in the popularity of swing, and the rise of small groups and vocalists caused straitened economic circumstances. A number of his long-time musicians sought greener pastures, and people like Johnny Hodges (alto sax; 1906–1970), Lawrence Brown (trombone; 1907–1988), and Sonny Greer (drums; 1895–1982) departed. He primarily relied on club dates and occasional other appearances to see him through, along with recording royalties.

Music veteran that he was, Ellington survived this dark period, and by the mid-1950s, fortune came around again, particularly in the form of the Newport Jazz Festival of 1956. He electrified the crowds, and a best-selling recording of the event resurrected his stagnating career. For the next 20 years, the songs and the extended compositions poured forth, and the rediscovery of his earlier work by a new generation of fans made Duke Ellington once more a mainstay of American music.

See also: ASCAP *vs.* BMI Radio Boycott and the AFM Recording Ban; Broadway Shows (Musicals); Musicals (Film)

Selected Reading
Dance, Stanley. *The World of Duke Ellington.* New York: Charles Scribner's Sons, 1970.
Jewell, Derek. *Duke: A Portrait of Duke Ellington.* New York: W. W. Norton, 1977.
Tucker, Mark, ed. *The Duke Ellington Reader.* New York: Oxford University Press, 1993.

F

FADS

This term refers to an all-abiding public interest that becomes quickly popular for a brief period and then generally fades into obscurity. Often called crazes, manias, rages, fashions, trends, obsessions, and vogues, fads occasionally establish themselves as a lasting part of the culture. Each decade of U.S. history has witnessed many fads, and the 1940s fits this pattern well. Jitterbug dancing, wearing bobby socks ("sox") or a zoot suit, collecting Shmoo and Kigmy paraphernalia, doodling "Kilroy was here," admiring a pinup girl, competing in blowing bubbles with bubble gum, using slang and World War II lingo—all enjoyed their moment at some point between 1940 and 1949. In addition, some facets of **fashion, food,** and music of the decade could be classified as fads.

Jitterbug dancing. Popular during the Swing Era (1935–1945) and on into the 1950s, the jitterbug, although based on **dance** routines from the 1920s such as the Charleston and the lindy hop, achieved its own distinctive style with various breakaway moves, jumps, lifts, and air steps. First identified with swing music in the 1930s, the jitterbug dispensed with formal rules and allowed for individual expression, a revolutionary feeling that appealed to **youth.**

World War II and the widespread drafting and enlistment of men into the armed forces interrupted the Swing Era, but the jitterbug, which could be danced alone and—particularly for women, given the shortage of men—even with a person of the same gender, survived as a dance favorite throughout the war and immediate postwar years. If unable to attend a dance, women jitterbugged at home to records or **radio** broadcasts, and GIs tripped the light fantastic with hostesses and movie stars at **canteens** in both the United States and abroad. And what better way to celebrate the end of the war and the beginnings of prosperity than by dancing the jitterbug?

Bobby-soxers. Coined in the 1940s, this term describes adolescent girls in general, especially those who sported loafers or two-tone saddle shoes and socks (sox) rolled down to ankle level, thus "bobbing" or cutting short this particular item of footwear. It also applied to the overly zealous, screaming fans of popular crooners, such as those who followed **Frank Sinatra** (1915–1998). They would line up for hours to obtain a ticket for a concert by this rising star.

Shirley Temple (b. 1928), who had started her career as a child star, graduated into adolescence costarring with the considerably older actors Cary Grant (1904–1986) and Rudy Vallee (1901–1986) in a silly comedy, *The Bachelor and the Bobby-Soxer* (1947). Hollywood's portrayal of this stereotypical variety of teenager helped to extend the fad's popularity.

Zoot suits. If girls could wear bobby sox, young men could distinguish themselves with a long, fitted jacket that featured outsize lapels, rakishly padded shoulders, and multibutton sleeves. The accompanying trousers boasted a high waist and legs cut full in the thigh and pegged to ankle-hugging tightness. The zoot suit first appeared in the early 1940s among West Coast minority populations—especially blacks, Filipinos, and Mexican Americans. The ultimate finishing touch for the ensemble occurred when a zoot-suiter donned a wide-brimmed hat or one that came to be called the porkpie style. Zoot suits, gaining more headlines than wearers, never attained the universal appeal of bobby sox. The attire still had enough of a following to signify adolescent rebellion, which made it a subject of concern for many. Whatever the origin and reason for wearing them, the baggy, pegged pants made the suit perfect for dancing a rousing jitterbug.

Popular entertainers helped spread the image of the zoot suit nationally. When orchestra leader **Duke Ellington** (1899–1974) performed a number called "Jump for Joy" at the Orpheum Theatre in Los Angeles in 1941, he and all his sidemen sported the flashy outfits. Band leader Cab Calloway (1907–1994) likewise donned a similar costume for his appearance in the 1943 film, *Stormy Weather*.

Preachers decried the outfit and government officials condemned it. In 1943, U.S. sailors on leave and carousing through the streets of Los Angeles assaulted any man wearing this fashion to the end that service personnel lost visiting privileges in the city. But the final demise of zoot suits happened when the War Production Board (WPB) restricted the amount of material that could be used in men's clothing; big, oversized suits had to go, and this unique style of dress never made a comeback.

Fashionable apparel, especially for some young men living on the West Coast, involved the flamboyant zoot suit. The style can be seen in this shot taken of bandleader Cab Calloway for the 1943 movie, Stormy Weather. *(20th Century Fox/Jagarts/Photofest)*

Shmoos and the Kigmy. Cartoonist Al Capp (1909–1979) created the Shmoo for *Li'l Abner,* his popular newspaper comic strip, in August 1948. A cuddly, roly-poly, mustachioed white blob with a perpetual smile, Shmoos resembled a bowling pin that easily tipped over. They reproduced spontaneously, loved everyone, provided everything a person needed to survive, and would happily roll over and die for you. Among a wide range of abilities, they could lay eggs and produce milk, cheese, and butter. Further, Shmoos turned into a tasty steak when broiled or an equally delicious chicken when fried; the hide, sliced thin, served as fine leather, and when cut thick and dried, it made high-quality lumber. Moreover, the Shmoos's whiskers supplied everyone with splendid toothpicks, and the eyes made excellent buttons. In addition to satisfying all of the world's needs, the Shmoos also provided entertainment and companionship.

Almost immediately after the introduction of Shmoos, an array of licensed Shmoo merchandise became available for the millions of *Li'l Abner* readers and interested others. Dolls, toys, glasses, wallpaper, belts, books, jewelry, balloons, clocks, ashtrays, canisters, salt and pepper shakers, banks, belts, ear muffs, and even an official Shmoo fishing lure could be purchased. Capitalizing on its popularity, Capp's publishers put together an anthology of his **comic strips,** *The Life and Times of the Shmoo* (1948). By 1950, the book had sold 700,000 copies, and sales of Shmoo memorabilia had grossed $25 million (about $225 million in 2008 dollars). On November 6, 1948, artist Capp, along with his characters Abner, Daisy Mae, and two Shmoos, appeared on the cover of *Time* magazine.

The Shmoo existed as a metaphor for American abundance, but it also represented a utopia that could not stand. Ironically, the lovable and selfless Shmoos ultimately brought misery to humankind because people with a limitless supply of self-sacrificing Shmoos stopped working and society broke down. Eventually, piggish Dogpatch resident J. Roaringham Fatback had them eliminated in 1948 (but a pair escaped, just in case); and with their symbolic extinction the craze died.

In 1949, Capp followed the demise of the Shmoo with the short-lived *Kigmy,* a strange, dark, big-nosed creature that loved to be kicked. While the Kigmy did not enjoy the commercial success of the Shmoo, merchandisers soon created inflatables and other Kigmy goods, allowing humans to take out their frustrations on this hapless critter.

"Kilroy was here." A number of stories exist concerning the origin of this popular piece of graffiti, an icon of World War II. Much of the credit probably belongs to James J. Kilroy, a government employee at a naval shipyard. His job involved inspecting the welds and rivets in the bulkheads of vessels under construction. At the end of the day, he would mark the extent of his inspection with a chalked "Kilroy was here." Legend has it that workers would sneak in after Kilroy had left and erase his signature, replacing it with a facsimile in another location, thus misleading supervisors and lightening the workload of those coming in for the next shift. Whatever the truth of this, servicemen sailing aboard these ships would see the cryptic "Kilroy was here" above their bunks and adapted it to their own uses.

In various theaters of combat, the phrase began to appear on walls, vehicles, cartons, and anything else where U.S. troops had passed. The slogan also gained a visual representation, a simple line cartoon featuring the head of a wide-eyed, bald,

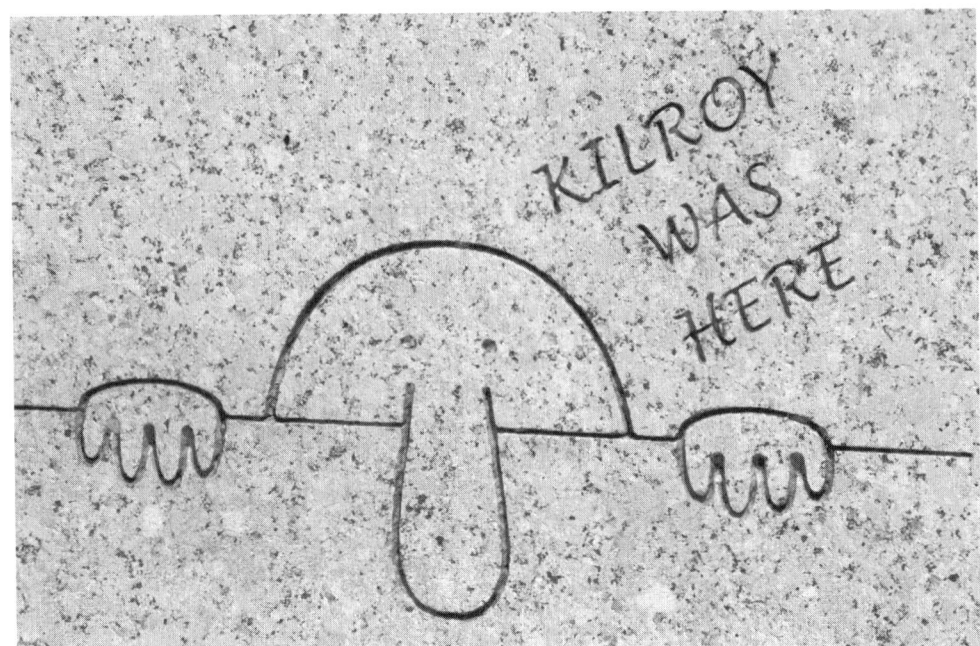

A familiar piece of graffiti throughout the war, Kilroy—as pictured here—appeared everywhere, from shipping cartons to vehicles to the sides of buildings. Stonecutters at the World War II memorial in Washington, DC, have commemorated the long-nosed figure in out-of-the-way places, so tourists often overlook him. (KAREN BLEIER/AFP/Getty Images)

droopy-nosed man peering over a wall, with the three immortal words beneath him. This aspect of Kilroy had originated in the British Isles before the war as "Mr. Chad." Many attribute Mr. Chad to English cartoonist George Edward Chatterton (n.d.). The words "Wot, no...?" normally accompany the drawings, and the phrase means, variously, "What, no petrol?" "What, no sweets?" "What, no meat," and anything else then in short supply.

Mr. Chad may have been seen by U.S. troops based in England and given the name Kilroy. Their version, however, did not refer to shortages, but just the fact that U.S. soldiers had been in a particular place. Whatever the true origins of the Kilroy graffiti, it quickly emerged as an internationally known phenomenon during the decade. It lives on at the massive World War II memorial that now commands one section of the National Mall in Washington, DC. This imposing structure, which opened in 2004, surprises sharp-eyed visitors with a bit of impish humor. There, among all the formal stonework, Kilroy peeks out, a reminder of the enduring humor found among soldiers even in the midst of a bloody conflict.

Pinup girls. Art work depicting beautiful women dates back to antiquity. The 1940s equivalents display carefully airbrushed celebrities and starlets flashing brilliant smiles and striking sexy poses. Often dubbed "cheesecake" (an early 20th-century term for similarly unclothed women; the etymological roots are hazy, but the term does suggest pretty, sweet, and so on), the practice of featuring feminine pulchritude has a long history, especially in **magazines** and **newspapers**. *Esquire* magazine, in the early 1930s, began running the work of illustrator George Petty (1894–1975), whose specialty included this kind of art. *Time* magazine even offered such a rendering of movie star Rita Hayworth on its November 10, 1941 cover. When the United States became involved in World War II, pictures of attractive, bathing-suit and lingerie-clad women were pinned up, taped, and pasted throughout the military communities—barracks' lockers, inside helmets, even on airplanes and bombs. *Yank,* the army's weekly newspaper, coined the term "pinup girl" in its April 30, 1943, issue, and the Petty Girls, as well as the Vargas Girls produced by another *Esquire* artist, Alberto Vargas (1896–1982), became staples and contributed to the war effort as morale boosters.

Pinups were also called Forties Girls, and the most famous photographs of this wartime industry came from the ever-alert Hollywood studios. One of the best-known of these, taken in 1943, shows movie star Betty Grable (1916–1973) dressed in a bathing suit and looking over her right shoulder at the camera. Seen as an all-American girl radiating come-hither innocence and optimism, this classic pose gave servicemen a vision of what they were fighting for; coupled with her movie income, Betty Grable earned $300,000 (about $3.5 million in 2008 dollars) in that one year.

Many other Hollywood stars posed for pinup pictures as well as participated in war bond and USO (United Service Organizations) tours. Lana Turner (1921–1995), Ava Gardner (1922–1990), Hedy Lamarr (1914–2000), Jane Russell (b. 1921), and Rita Hayworth (1918–1987) offered Grable the most competition. Hollywood furthered its involvement with this craze when, in 1944, it produced two films. In Columbia Pictures' *Pin Up Girl,* Betty Grable works as a canteen hostess and becomes engaged to almost all the fellows who obtain her autographed photo; Twentieth-Century Fox gave movie audiences *Cover Girl,* starring Rita Hayworth as a beautiful showgirl who becomes a magazine's front-page subject. The story has it that air force personnel affixed her photo to the **atomic bomb** dropped on Hiroshima in 1945.

Along with *Esquire,* men's magazines such as *True* and *Argosy* often managed to decorate their pages with similar illustrations. Both during the war and postwar years, most photographs and drawings of pinup girls featured a slight exaggeration of the model's long, attractive legs and could be found on calendars, advertisements, and billboards. A fad that started with soldiers became a national phenomenon.

Bubble gum. The bane of school administrators and a continuing delight for kids, bubble gum has been around since the first third of the 20th century. The Fleer Chewing Gum Company of Philadelphia most likely invented the chewy substance, and in 1938 one of its employees, Walter Diemer (1904–1998), brought it to its present form. He even made the product in its characteristic pink; he found some pink coloring agent in his limited work area, and it quickly became the standard for Fleer's and its competitors.

Called Dubble Bubble from the outset, Fleer's soon developed a sizable market; kids liked the elasticity of the gum and the huge bubbles it made. To entice its youthful clientele further, the company wrapped individual pieces in tissue imprinted with comics. *Dub & Bub* led the way, replaced by the more familiar *Pud* in the 1940s. During World War II, Fleer's even put bubble gum squares in the ration kits issued to GIs so they would not lose the taste of home. For civilians, however, bubble gum proved hard to come by in the war years; with the scarcity of sugar, only limited amounts of gum could be manufactured.

When the conflict ended in 1945, a rival company, Topps, attempted to gain a portion of this growing lucrative market. They called their gum Bazooka, and the name came either from the famous antitank weapon or the humorous musical instrument Bob "The Arkansas Traveler" Burns (1890–1956) featured in his stage act. Regardless of which story people believe, Topp's Bazooka bubble gum quickly rivaled Fleer's Dubble Bubble. Topps likewise offered tiny comics with Bazooka, and *Bazooka Joe* made his debut in 1947.

In the immediate postwar period, with sugar, gum, and candy again plentiful, children went on a mini-binge with bubble gum. Sales soared, bubble-blowing contests, both informal and sponsored, were the rage in the late 1940s. That aspect fizzled out after a short time, but the consumption of bubble gum has remained substantial. The addition of trading cards, often of sports figures, resumed in the late 1940s with the lifting of restrictions on paper consumption.

Slang and World War II influences. Slang generally refers to words and figures of speech that are deliberately used in place of standard terms and may include jargon, colloquialisms, neologisms, and vulgar words. Traditionally popular with youth, but employed by all levels of society, slang proves one's membership in a certain group, that a person belongs and knows the various linguistic codes.

A small sampling of the slang used during the 1940s follows. Some examples did not necessarily originate during this decade but continued in common usage from earlier times; others stand as unique for the period. The desire of all teenagers was (and is) to be "cool"–that is, clever, fashionable, really "with it." An "able Grable" or a "ready Hedy" referred to the popular movie stars Betty Grable and Hedy Lamarr and meant a girl possessed sex appeal, while "whistle bait," "angel cake," or "slick chick" signified any pretty girl. A boy thought attractive by girls would be known as a "mellow man," "a hunk of heart break," or a "glad lad," and pictures of such males received the label "beefcake" to complement "cheesecake." On the other hand, "puss" and "phiz" meant an ugly face. And no young woman wanted to date a "drip," "jerk," "square," or "geek." When life did include a date, girls might "put on the dog" and dress up in fancy clothes. To save money, a couple might attend a "rent party," a gathering where guests chipped in cash to help pay for the refreshments and the host's apartment.

"Hi-de-ho" served as a greeting of hello, thanks to bandleader and trendsetter Cab Calloway. If a person's comments or demeanor appeared silly or boring, "corny" functioned as an all-purpose putdown. Enthusiastic volunteers earned the title "eager beaver," while those who shrugged their responsibilities "passed the buck." A despicable person became a "creep," a condition perhaps worse than being a "fuddy-duddy," or old-fashioned.

Slang also incorporates phrases, and many people looked for "pennies from heaven," that easy money that would help them "keep up with the Joneses" and enjoy a lifestyle or socioeconomic status comparable to the people next door. "Grandstanding" meant showing off, but when times got difficult and "the chips were down," many rendered the advice, "if you can't beat 'em, join 'em"; after all, some things are not "the end of the world."

Events and people can cause the creation of new slang. With World War II clearly the biggest event of the decade, a number of words that dealt with the war and military personnel appeared as slang and then permanently entered the language. "Bazooka" immediately entered vocabularies as the name for the military's new five-foot-long antitank rocket gun, which resembled an improvised musical instrument of that name created by comedian Bob Burns. The term may possess some arcane Dutch roots, or it could refer to the sounds emitted from Burns' horn when he played it ("bazo-o-oom"). In any case, bazookas of the explosive variety soon became a staple with the infantry.

A "burp gun" came to mean any submachine gun; it received the name from the belchlike sound emitted by several varieties of German machine gun then in service. A similar weapon, the American M3 submachine gun, was dubbed a "grease gun" because of its resemblance to a device used to lubricate cars. Those unfortunate enough to die in action "bought the farm," a term referring to the automatic insurance policies issued by the government. Beneficiaries received $10,000 (about $120,000 in 2008 dollars), or enough to pay off the mortgage on a small farm. Sometimes, a soldier did not suffer a wound but instead endured the "creeping crud," another term for "jungle rot," unpleasant skin conditions (rashes, itching, etc.) experienced by troops serving in tropical climates. A lucky soldier might endure a "million-dollar wound," a non–life threatening injury but severe enough to send him back to the United States; said to be worth a million dollars.

The Eisenhower jacket, a fitted, belted, waist-length military coat introduced by **General Dwight David Eisenhower** (1890–1969), caught on as a popular design for a woman's article of clothing immediately following the war. "Geronimo!" was the exuberant shout of U.S. paratroopers as they "hit the silk" (actually, parachutes could be made of either nylon or silk) by leaping from an airplane; today it connotes surprise. "Gobbledygook" means nonsensical bureaucratic jargon; it originated from a reference to official language in a Congressional committee report issued in 1944 and indicates the gobbling utterances of turkeys. "Mae West," a canvas inflatable rubber life vest issued to airmen, derived its name from the Hollywood star of the same name whose chest measurements made her look as if she were wearing an inflated vest. If a soldier got sick or wounded in the field, he received the ministrations of a "bedpan commando," or platoon medic. And if the services did not meet his satisfaction, he could always "bellyache," or complain, to someone. And if the wound or symptoms were truly severe, the "Holy Joe," or chaplain, might be called.

Some slang depicted conditions specific to the war. *Ersatz,* a German word meaning replacement or artificial, became a word for English-speaking people that signified any item that replaced a natural one because of wartime shortages. Cooks created ersatz coffee from chicory and ersatz bread from potato peels. Since the war, it simply denotes anything fake and inferior. And the list could go on—java and joe (both mean coffee, as in "a cuppa joe," and soldiers christened really strong coffee "battery acid"), Kraut (a German), Nip (a Japanese), walkie-talkie (a portable two-way radio), squawk box (electronic speaker), SOS (in slang, not a distress signal but a GI term for poor food, s—on a shingle), Flying Fortress (an American heavy bomber), and wolf pack (groups of German submarines traveling together in search of enemy vessels)—to name but a few.

Acronyms such as POW for prisoner of war, radar (or radio detecting and ranging, a military device for locating aircraft aloft), sonar (or sound navigation and ranging, a military device for detecting submarines beneath the sea), WAAC (Women's Army Auxiliary Corps, and usually shortened to WAC for Women's Army Corps), and WAVES (Women Accepted for Voluntary Emergency Service) came into popular usage in the forties. Sometimes women in the armed forces gained the complementary title of GI Jane.

"G.I." (with periods) originally meant government issue and could be found stamped on many military supplies. Soldiers, with their dark humor, considered themselves a type of government issue, and the initials spread and entered everyday speech. As is always the case with slang, the meanings for GI expanded and the periods disappeared, as more and more troops swelled the armed forces. If a soldier complained of stomach discomfort, it meant he had the "GIs," or a gastrointestinal illness. To "GI a place" meant cleaning up a site, probably under supervision. A "GI haircut" meant short on the sides and back of the head.

"Joe," meaning an average sort of guy, dates to the 19th century; "Joe College" and "regular Joe" probably emerged in the 1930s; in 1942, "GI Joe," referring to any regular enlisted man, made its debut in cartoons drawn by Dave Breger (1908–1970) for *Yank, the Army Weekly.* Hollywood picked up on the term and offered *A Guy Named Joe* in 1943, and Joe can be any of the soldiers depicted on screen. The popular war correspondent Ernie Pyle (1900–1945) immortalized foot-slogging infantrymen in his dispatches, and the film *The Story of G.I. Joe* (1945) recaptures much of Pyle's reporting. Cartoonist Bill Mauldin (1921–2003) also contributed to the image of the U.S. soldier with his cartoons depicting Willie and Joe, two tired, wise-cracking enlisted men. His book, *Up Front* (1945), a collection of cartoons about Willie and Joe, made the best-seller lists.

Along with the development and use of slang during the war, the postwar years offered even more. As in all decades, various popular culture venues—movies, radio, music, even cars—inspired new slang terms. By 1949, music had contributed bop, **bebop,** and rebop, while a retooling of old cars provided the nation with **hot rods.** Whatever the source, the words and phrases of slang, both past and present, enrich the language, some momentarily, while others remain in the mainstream of American English.

See also: ASCAP *vs. BMI* Radio Boycott and the AFM Recording Ban; Best Sellers (Books); Desserts, Candy, and Ice Cream; Games; Illustrators; Leisure and Recreation; Photography; Toys

Selected Reading
Panati, Charles. *Panati's Parade of Fads, Follies, and Manias.* New York: HarperCollins, 1991.
Rottman, Gordon L. *Fubar: Soldier Slang of World War II.* London: Osprey, 2007.
Sickels, Robert. *American Popular Culture through History: The 1940s.* Westport, CT: Greenwood Press, 2004.
Wallechinsky, David. *David Wallechinsky's Twentieth Century, History with the Boring Parts Left Out.* Boston: Little, Brown, 1995 [Previously published as *The People's Almanac Presents the Twentieth Century*].

FASHION

The announcement on January 5, 1941, that New York City had received the title of Fashion Center of the World caused considerable excitement. This coup came, however, at a time of tragedy and sacrifice in Europe. Paris, long the mecca of clothing design, had fallen under the thumb of Nazi Germany in 1940, thus abdicating its influence in the world of fashion. New York, already recognized as the leader in the manufacture of clothing, now also hosted the majority of both established and new designers. To acknowledge this turn of events, the posh Hotel Astor played host on January 8 to the first of two showings of "Fashion Futures."

Prior to this event, Hollywood, through its screen imagery, had for many years played a role in setting fashion trends for Americans. Gilbert Adrian (1903–1959), a premier costume designer for the **movies,** introduced fashion to millions of American women by dressing such stylish stars as Greta Garbo (1905–1990) and Joan Crawford (1904–1977) during the 1930s. Square-shouldered clothes for Crawford became his trademark, and in 1941 he established his own line of women's clothes under Adrian, Ltd. to offer fashionable ready-to-wear and custom-designed clothes.

But war and material shortages soon curtailed the glory of the United States as a fashion leader and its fashion future. In December 1941, the country entered World War II, and on January 16, 1942, by executive order, **President Franklin Delano Roosevelt** (1882–1945) established the War Production Board (WPB). This group's activities touched fashion, along with nearly every other aspect of the American consumer economy; it set regulations on the allocation of crucial materials and issued directives to production and consumption to accommodate war needs.

Limiting Order L-85, one of many from the WPB issued in 1943, placed restrictions on the kind and amount of fabrics that could be used for clothing and guaranteed that changes would not occur in fashion manufacturing equipment, techniques, or labor—an important consideration for a country needing to focus all its retooling on defense work. WPB orders also limited the use of wool in civilian clothing. Expensive or showy dressing soon became taboo, which contributed to a somewhat universal dressing down across the country.

The degree of influence caused by L-85 varied in reference to women's and men's clothing. Women merely retained the popular silhouette style, but men experienced a significant change in what they wore because suits underwent modifications. Americans willingly made the necessary sacrifices in both clothing and other facets of life in order to win the war, but once it ended they welcomed new fashion styles. Women eagerly filled their dresser drawers with nylon stockings and applauded the "New Look" introduced by Christian Dior (1905–1957), while clothing for teenagers emerged as distinctive to that age group. For after work hours, men appreciated more casual attires.

Men and women in uniform. When designing military uniforms, fabric durability, drying qualities, and the climate conditions where an outfit could be worn receive primary consideration. During World War II, a U.S. infantryman in Europe during inclement weather typically dressed in an olive drab wool service shirt and trousers and a greenish water-repellant M43 field jacket, along with an overcoat when needed. By 1943, a short Eisenhower jacket, named for **General Dwight David Eisenhower** (1890–1969), became available and military restrictions said that it could only be worn outside the continental United States or by those returning stateside from overseas duty. Originally intended for combat wear, soldiers soon elected to use it for dress-up occasions.

In addition to the outward articles of clothing, the soldier's wardrobe included pile liners and woolen sweaters for extra warmth in inclement weather. Knitted woolen stocking caps covered the head beneath the helmet, and high-laced combat boots with a buckled ankle flap protected the feet. For summer fighting and battles in the Pacific, soldiers dressed in lightweight khaki shirts and trousers made of twill, along with a light garrison cap and boots.

Naval officers wore either navy blue or white lapel coats with epaulettes, trousers, white shirts, and hats. For sailors below the grade of chief petty officer, the basic garment consisted of a loose-fitting shirt known as a jumper adorned with a black silk neckerchief rolled and draped around the neck under a square collar and tied below the neck opening. For summer dress, officers donned white, short-sleeved shirts and white trousers. Khaki uniforms served as working outfits for navy personnel.

Capitalizing on one navy outfit, composer Moe Jaffe (1901–1972) in 1944 wrote "Bell Bottom Trousers," a tune that some claim to be a cleaned-up version of an old sea chantey. Jaffe's words refer to the flared trousers worn by enlisted men. In essence, his rendition offers lyrics suitable for public performances and it became an instant hit. Five music studios released recordings performed by well-known groups, and all five made it to *Billboard*'s best-seller chart: Guy Lombardo (1902–1977) Orchestra on Decca Records, April 20, 1945; Tony Pastor (1907–1969) Orchestra on RCA Victor Records, May 10, 1945; Kay Kyser (1905–1985) Orchestra on Columbia Records, June 7, 1945; Louis Prima (1910–1978) Orchestra on Majestic Records, June 7, 1945; and Jerry Colonna (1904–1986) on Capitol Records, July 26, 1945.

More than 350,000 women served in the U.S. armed forces and most worked as typists, clerks, mail sorters, drivers, and nurses. They had their own branches, including, for the army, the Women's Auxiliary Corps (WAC; originally the Women's Army Auxiliary Corps). The Women Air Force Service Pilots (WASP) worked with the Army Air Corps, and the Women Accepted for Volunteer Military Services (WAVES) served with the U.S. Navy. Women also joined the Marines Corps Reserves, while those affiliated with the Coast Guard became known as SPARS, an acronym taken from that division's motto *Semper Paratus*, "Always Ready."

Soon after women became actively involved in the war, Fiorello LaGuardia (1882–1947), the colorful mayor of New York City, appointed a committee of New York designers to submit ideas for uniforms suitable for women serving in the various military branches. They contributed ideas for the designs, with the famous Mainbocher (born Main Rousseau Bocher, 1891–1976), an American designer recently back home from Paris, greatly influencing the final outfits. Colors for the uniforms consisted of dark or olive drab for winter; khaki dominated outfits for summer wear, except for women in the navy, who wore that service's navy blue or white coats. In addition to a jacket and skirt, women were issued a heavy topcoat, hooded raincoat, tan oxfords, tennis shoes, galoshes, and bedroom slippers. They also followed regulations requiring neat, above-the-collar hairstyles.

Women's civilian clothing. Early in the war, the WPB's Limiting Order L-85 dictated the maximum amounts of fabric that could be utilized in making different civilian garments, with no more than three-fourths of a yard serving as the allowance for a dress. Other WPB orders restricted metals available for zippers and buttons, silk for stockings, and leather for shoes. Clothing styles, by necessity, featured straight cuts and simple lines without ruffles or pleats. Manufacturers limited most daywear to conservative colors or the classic navy or black. Evening dress usually featured a long, flowing sheath of soft shades. Dresses, suits, and jackets still included shoulder pads, giving the wearer a wide look that tapered to a tailored waist over a narrow skirt.

Dresses and skirts fell just below the knees and could have a circumference of no more than 72 inches. Evening wear allowed longer lengths. For hems, the WPB set the maximum at two inches. The length of jackets had to stop at 25 inches, and blouses became plain with no turned-back cuffs, double yokes, sashes, scarves, or hoods. Some women spent the war years dressed in tailored gabardine shirtwaist dresses considered to be a "town and country" look, while others opted for the peasant look featuring dress tops and blouses using a drawstring neckline, small puffed sleeves, and a gathered narrow skirt.

For most, simplicity and modesty became patriotic guidelines, and accessories consisted mainly of gloves, plain jewelry, and small head covers such as turbans, snoods, scarves, and berets that could remain in place without elastic. Ribbons, bows, braids, and pigtails served as hair adornments. Women applied mascara only on their top lashes, groomed their eyebrows to follow the natural arch, and used rouge that matched and blended with their complexion. Brilliant shades of lipstick and nail polish gave brightness to an otherwise dull presentation.

Fashion dictated shoulder-length hair; slightly longer hair could be curled or rolled and pulled back. During the war, side reverse rolls worn to cascade up the head and end closely together on the top created a V shape called "victory rolls." A wavy look accomplished by pin curls made in rows and brushed through also proved to be popular. A few, however, dared to follow the example of movie star Veronica Lake (1922–1973), who appeared in *I Wanted Wings* (Paramount Pictures, 1941) with long blonde hair that swept across her forehead and daringly covered an eye. Alternately called the strip-tease style, the peek-a-boo style, the sheep-dog style, and the bad-girl style, it prompted hair discussions across the United States about the relationship between hair fashions and morals.

Arranging one's hair proved fairly simple; dealing with the lack of stockings presented a more difficult problem. Even before the formation of the WPB, escalating prices set in the late 1930s by Japan, the largest producer of silk in the world, had made silk stockings a scarce item. In 1938, DuPont introduced nylon fiber, a synthetic that could replace silk in hosiery and other products. Sears sold nylon stockings in its 1940 catalog; they also appeared for the first time in New York stores in May 1940. An instant success, women purchased 64 million pairs the first year, and nylons immediately became the generic name for silklike hosiery products. Their availability changed in December 1941, when the U.S. government commandeered nylon for war production, particularly for use in parachutes, airplane tires, netting, and tents. In a state of desperation about not having this necessary article of clothing for proper dress, many women resorted to applying makeup to their legs and then taking a pen and drawing a line down the back of the calf so it appeared as if they were wearing seamed stockings. An impractical solution, ankle socks emerged as a substitute. To the relief of many, nylon stockings became readily available soon after the war ended.

The WPB placed rigid restrictions on the use of leather for civilian footwear, forcing shoe manufacturers to search for alternatives. A variety of materials such as reptile skins and molded mesh became successful substitutes. Cork, rope, and plastic served as materials for the soles of cold-weather shoes, and a wooden wedge heel became popular for summer wear. Most Americans, however, had to make do with the shoes they already owned because the purchase of a new pair required a government certificate showing need. For shoes manufactured during the war, trims and embellishments had to be held to a minimum, causing some women to use household items such as cellophane and pipe cleaners to create a festive shoe decoration. Fabrics substituted for leather whenever possible in pocketbooks and belts.

As the war progressed and shortages of clothing increased, *Vogue* magazine and other fashion publications suggested a "Make Do and Mend" campaign. Fashion periodicals had long kept American women informed on the newest trends and now offered suggestions on how to creatively recycle existing garments. For example, one could make a bra out of an old tablecloth and outfits out of feed and flour sacks or curtains. *McCall's* magazine produced patterns that showed how to cut men's suits into ladies' suits and women's dresses into children's clothing. Designers introduced the concept of separates, which, if kept to a color scheme, allowed for coordination of these pieces to create the illusion of more outfits than one actually had. Even the U.S. Department of Agriculture got into the act with *Fitting Dresses,* a pamphlet describing the importance of making or buying clothes that fit and hints on how to be sure that the article under consideration could be worn. It lists 20 common faults of dresses that do not fit along with a remedy for each.

Eventually more than 16 million men fought in World War II, creating a labor shortage in the United States. Businesses and industry turned to those men, women, and teenagers left at home; before the war ended, more than 6 million women went to work for the first time. Some held traditional women's positions as clerks, teachers, and health care workers, while many took jobs in war-related industries such as aircraft factories, shipyards, and armaments industries.

Some working women readily adopted the clothes worn by their male counterparts—sturdy overalls, thick-soled shoes, and hard hats. But many, concerned about maintaining their femininity, resisted. Their skirts and dresses, however, quickly became workplace hazards, with parts of the outfits getting caught in heavy machinery.

Muriel King (1900–1977), a Hollywood costume designer during the 1930s and 1940s, created four work uniform designs, each displaying a wing motif, for women employees at Boeing Aircraft. These "Flying Fortress" fashions pleased everyone. The company immediately saw a decrease in accidents because the outfits lacked the large sleeves and cuffs to catch in equipment. The women applauded the cuts, which featured slimming waistlines, flattering high-cut bosom lines, and trim slacks. King also included a simple shirtdress for office workers. By 1943, *Life* magazine described this clothing as a new West Coast fad, with many appreciating that slacks did not require the wearing of expensive or unavailable stockings. Nevertheless, most working women, after punching their factory time cards at the end of the day, returned home to dress in a more traditional way.

Perhaps the fad status of the King design had been helped by a 1942 poster by an American graphic artist named J. Howard Miller (ca. 1915–1990) titled "We Can Do It!" The painting features an attractive woman dressed in a Boeing-type outfit with her hair pulled back in a scarf and sporting bright lipstick and pink-painted fingernails.

Frequently used as an image of a working woman, this depiction has been mistakenly called ***Rosie the Riveter,*** the title given to a painting by Norman Rockwell (1894–1978) that appeared on the cover of *The Saturday Evening Post* on May 29, 1943. Both presentations became national cultural icons and helped in the recruitment of women into traditional men's jobs. Both renderings of a working woman show a hairstyle that can easily be tucked into a scarf, snood, turban, or bandanna. Loose hair, like some articles of clothing, could easily be caught in industrial machinery and cause serious accidents. By this time, Hollywood had Veronica Lake styling her famous peek-a-boo long hair by pulling it back from her face in two films, *So Proudly We Hail* (1943) and *The Hour Before the Dawn* (1944).

With the end of the war and the lifting of government controls and restrictions, the availability of fabrics returned to prewar levels, and designers on both sides of the Atlantic Ocean began experimenting with more frivolous and feminine fashions. Many women scanned the first ideal-weight charts published by the Metropolitan Life Insurance Company in the early 1940s to determine what they should aim for in order to look best in the postwar clothing styles. Department stores advertised clothing under the banner of the "American Look," an attempt to promote American designers. One of these, Claire McCardell (1905–1958), became a leading force in ready-to-wear fashions, simple, functional, mass-produced pieces that retained a sense of style.

One highly controversial piece of recreational clothing came in 1946 from French fashion designer Louis Reard (1897–1984). He created a bathing suit made from two miniscule pieces of fabric that left little to the imagination. During the war, the scarcity of cloth had eliminated bathing suits with the billowing skirts of the 1930s and produced slightly more revealing wear in both one-and two-piece styles, but they did not begin to be as scandalous as this new item called the bikini. Some suggested that the name of this startling piece of clothing came from the tiny Pacific atoll where the United States conducted nuclear testing that same year, suggesting a "split" of a previously more modest one-piece swimwear into something as small as atoms.

An explosive furor surrounded the introduction of the bikini. Only the most daring donned the tiny bathing suit at public beaches. Churches condemned both bikinis and their wearers, fashion magazines wagged an editorial finger at the style (while running pictures that boosted circulation), and cultural critics on both sides of the issue made much of the commotion. Many places explicitly banned bikinis, while officials at other locations told patrons to dress in more modest attire.

A combination of enthusiasm and protest also accompanied Christian Dior's 1947 introduction of the New Look, an attempt to turn away from the angular silhouette style of World War II. Shoulder pads disappeared, giving way to a more fitted appearance with soft, full collars and sleeves; a padded bust; tight waist; and rounded hipline. Girdles became essential accessories for pinching the waist and obtaining the required curves. Longer and fuller skirts swept to between 8 and 10 inches from the floor, and tailors cut coats containing much more cloth. High price tags placed Dior originals outside the reach of many consumers, but mass clothing vendors such as Sears offered the long look at cheaper prices.

As the New Look swept across the country, outcries against it matched the excitement for it. Some women with attractive legs, and not eager to hide them in longer dresses, joined men voicing disappointment about being deprived of the pleasurable sight and bombarded the press with letters of opposition. Some said it may have been right for Fifth Avenue but not Main Street. A Texas housewife who felt strongly about keeping the shorter clothes founded the Little Below the Knee Club and recruited fellow protestors across the Lone Star State and soon boasted members in all 48 states. But most of America was ready for a change, and the New Look, despite this brief objection, grew in popularity.

American designers, such as Ceil Chapman (d. late 1970s) and Anne Fogarty (b. 1919), followed Dior's lead in their designs for Hollywood starlets and teenagers. Accessories also took on a new, feminine look. The squared, plain, comfortable low-heeled shoes of the first half of the decade changed to pointed toes and narrow high heels. Hairstyles became more casual, sometimes curled high on the head in front and worn to the shoulders in the back, or short with modest curls, and, for some, bangs. Hats, dressy and decorated, both large and small, continued as a necessary accessory, as did gloves. Longer dresses drew the eye to the ankles, and shoe manufacturers offered daring styles showing a lot of the foot with straps in a variety of designs, including a broad T-strap, two straps circling the ankle, or a narrow diagonal strap.

Nylon, now released from its previous use in defense production, significantly influenced postwar fashion. In addition to displacing silk in stockings, the DuPont synthetic appeared in lingerie, negligees, blouses, scarves, gloves, sweaters, and even toothbrushes. It could be blended with other fibers, resulting in material that washed easily and required little, if any, ironing. Initially, manufacturers of luxury clothing considered nylon of inferior quality for high fashion, but soon its ease of care and ability to retain shape won over most of the public.

Immediately following the end of World War II, products such as nylon stockings, handbags, and lingerie continued to have limited availability, sometimes creating problems in finding the perfect gift for mothers, sisters, wives, and sweethearts. As fast as possible, cosmetic companies produced a plethora of new beauty and toilet products that offered fathers, brothers, husbands, and boyfriends alternative gift ideas. Artificial eyelashes had long been used in Hollywood but now became available commercially, along with eyeliner, eye shadow, and waterproof mascara. Eyelash curlers helped those who did not want to use artificial lashes. The application of beauty spots returned to many faces, and burnt orange shades of lipstick joined the reds and pinks. Toward the end of 1948, the *New York Times* reported estimated sales of beauty and toiletry aids for the year to be at least $800 million (approximately $7 billion in 2008 dollars).

Men's civilian clothing. In order to save millions of pounds of wool a year during World War II, the WPA ordered the elimination of vests, patch pockets, cuffs, and an extra pair of trousers in men's suits. Thus masculine dress changed from generous three-piece, double-breasted suits featuring pants with multiple pleats and cuffs to fabric-conserving outfits with single-breasted jackets and trousers with no pleats or cuffs for the duration of the war. Fancy jackets displaying a long pleat down the back and gathered slightly at the waist, an item that had been popularized by actor Clark Gable (1901–1960), and double-breasted dinner suits could no longer be purchased.

But, just as American women desired a new look following the war, so did men. Male service personnel, weary of uniforms, rushed to stores for new civilian garb only to find the shelves bare. By late 1946, supply finally caught up with demand and included new designs. Men quickly appreciated the loose-fitting clothes made from lots of material and returned to broad-shouldered jackets, long coats, full-cut trousers with generous pleats, deep patch pockets, and cuffs. Double-breasted suit jackets designed with center vents and peaked lapels, along with hand-painted ties decorated in festive patterns and colors showing skyscrapers, exotic foliage, and sunsets, returned a sense of fun and luxury to men's clothing.

One of the most daring wardrobe additions following the war involved the introduction of a casual shirt called the aloha shirt. Claiming a Hawaiian ancestry and first seen at California and Florida beaches, this item displayed patterns of ocean flora, hula dancers, island flowers, or flames. Even **President Harry S. Truman** (1884–1972), who always wore a business suit when seen in public, became enamored with openly wearing tropical sport shirts when he went on working vacations at the Little White House in Key West, Florida. Across the country, an attitude of casualness about dress spread to sports coats and slacks. In 1949, Sears, Roebuck advertised a leisure coat for men to be worn during those "carefree hours…designed for complete ease of action with the tailoring you expect in suits."

Before the decade ended, men not wearing jackets and hats could sometimes be seen on the streets of New York. Informality also appeared in the form of blue jeans. Denim had originally been used for men's work wear, but Western movies during the 1930s shifted the association of denim pants or jeans from laborers to cowboys, such as Hollywood stars John Wayne (1907–1979) and Gary Cooper (1901–1961). Some soldiers took jeans with them to war for off-duty wear and, once back home, often preferred denim for leisure activities.

But just as veterans found time to be casual and play, they quickly became serious about their work and role as breadwinner of the family. By 1949, contrary to the growing acceptance of casualness, many had adopted a somber work uniform, usually a gray flannel suit or a dark blue alternate. The outfit consisted of a three-button, single-breasted jacket with narrow shoulders, small lapels, flaps on the pockets and accompanying pants without pleats. Simple, crisp white cotton shirts with slim, striped ties, plus shiny shoes and a conservative fedora (a style of felt hat), completed the ensemble. In 1955, author Sloan Wilson (1920–2003) lamented America's sartorial sameness in a world dominated by business with a best-selling novel, *The Man in the Gray Flannel Suit*.

Children's and youth clothing. The material restrictions assigned to adult clothing contained exceptions for infants' and children's wear for those up to four years of age. Nevertheless, new clothes for babies and young children tended to be scarce during the war, and stores did not regain an adequate inventory until 1946. Thus, outfits for children tended to be their older siblings' hand-me-downs or pieces restyled from adult clothes. By 1943, junior military styles became available for both sexes. Boys could dress representing various ranks—army officer, naval commander, aviator, marine, and sailor—while girls could deck themselves out in a facsimile of either a WAC or WAVES uniform.

When new clothes could be found, they looked similar to those of the 1930s. For boys, knickers, pants that ended just below the knee and tucked into high argyle socks, remained popular. In 1940, before rationing, the Sears, Roebuck catalog advertised suits with either one or two pairs of knickers, each with the addition of a long pair of pants. Boys often wore scaled-down versions of their fathers' suits, although with short pants. Jackets also resembled those of adults, and long pants with attached suspenders were worn for school and play.

Just as men's clothing took on a more casual air after the war, so did boys'. Dress-up, two-piece suits continued to be popular as did sports outfits for the "little fellow." Again, the styles mimicked those for men, offering broad-shouldered jackets with wide lapels and slacks with pleats and cuffs. Gabardine and blue denim pants cut in a Western style, including wide, rolled-up cuffs were popular. Just as men donned Hawaiian shirts, boys appeared at the beach or pool in swimwear consisting of matching trunks and shirts in bright colors and patterns advertised as "styled in the California manner."

Little girls, as in previous decades, dressed like children. They wore dresses with natural waistlines, full skirts, and puffed sleeves, sometimes decorated with embroidery trimming. Favorite materials included gabardine, cotton, flannel, wool, chambray, or corduroy. Pinafores, sun suits, and playsuits held great appeal, as did occasional matching mother-and-daughter dresses made in the same style from the same fabric. A popular money-saving gimmick after the war involved dressing all the children in a family alike.

Toward the end of the decade, playsuits for children under school age featured Walt Disney cartoon characters such as Mickey Mouse and Donald Duck. Playwear for young girls came in one-piece and two-piece outfits of both gay and plain prints. Some had short skirts, others fell just to the knee, and some consisted of shorts with a cover dress. Casual pants had lengths that ranged from that of shorts, to just below the knee, to a couple of inches above the ankle, to the floor. For both boys and girls alike, T-shirts gained popularity.

Clothing for youth underwent more drastic changes. Two prominent **fads** originated in the 1940s. Adolescent girls called bobby-soxers and known as enthusiastic fans of crooner **Frank Sinatra** (1915–1998) sported loafers or two-tone saddle shoes and socks rolled down to ankle level. At the same time, a handful of teenage boys and young men made news wearing zoot suits—a long, fitted jacket with padded shoulders and multibutton sleeves worn with trousers with a high waist and legs cut full in the thigh and pegged at the ankle. The restrictions surrounding materials and the manufacture of clothing helped to bring this last fad to an end because it used too much cloth. Condemnations from preachers and government officials also hastened its demise. The zoot suit did, however, influence the cut and fullness of men's coats produced after the war.

During the later 1940s, many felt that the dress of adolescent boys conformed to a pattern of sloppiness. A typical classroom uniform consisted of a flannel shirt with tail flapping and opened enough to show the white T-shirt worn underneath, blue jeans with rolled cuffs, white socks, and loafers. For Saturdays, the outfit would change a little with a tailless sport shirt over a regular shirt and saddle shoes. Attire for a date consisted of a V-necked sweater over a shirt or a jacket and tie, a hat, and oxford shoes. Whatever the outfit, standard equipment included a comb in the back pocket for keeping a wavy pompadour in place.

Adolescent girls became their own entity in the world of fashion; **advertising** built a case that they were neither children nor women and needed their own appropriate sizes and styles. Department stores began to cater to this age group with clothing sections devoted to them. In 1944, a new periodical titled *Seventeen* appeared on newsstands and successfully advanced the concept of an identifiable teenage market, especially for girls.

Sweater sets worn over narrow skirts that flared at the knee and influenced by the appearance of Lana Turner (1921–1995) in films in the late 1930s, particularly *Love Finds Andy Hardy* (MGM, 1938), became a necessity for young women. Turner would later be seen as alluring and provocative, dressed in tight-fitting sweaters, and quickly became known as the "Sweater Girl" and sweater sets rose in popularity and retained that status into the 1950s.

College-bound women showed partiality to clothes provided by the B. H. Wragge Company (1920–1971), manufacturers of a collection of separates—jackets, skirts, vests, blouses, jumpers, shirtwaist dresses, and coats—which allowed for a lot of mixing and matching, an important feature of the growing American ready-to-wear fashions and the college student desiring to be well dressed.

Fashions during the 1940s experienced a number of changes. In 1941, the manufacturing of war goods took center stage as the U.S. government directed most of its resources toward winning the war. Thus, every yard of cloth, every button, and every silk and nylon stocking became crucial to victory. After restrictions and willing sacrifices during the war, Americans eagerly embraced new designs, and the fashion world responded with clothes just as exciting as their new homes, new cars, and prosperous way of life.

See also: Atomic Bomb, The; Leisure and Recreation; Magazines; Rationing; Westerns (Films); Women in the Military: WACs, WASPs, WAVES, SPARS, and Others.

Selected Reading

Clothing Regulations and Availability: *New York Times,* January 5, 1941; April 9, 1942; October 18, 1942; August 1, 1942; February 2, 1945; November 25, 1946. www.proquest.com

Mulvey, Kate, and Melissa Richards. *Decades of Beauty: The Changing Image of Women, 1890s–1990s.* New York: Checkmark Books, 1998.

Olian, JoAnne, ed. *Everyday Fashions of the Forties: As Pictured in Sears Catalogs.* New York: Dover, 1992.

Wartime and postwar fashions: *Life magazine.* "Flying Fortress Fashions," May 17, 1943; "Teen-Age Boys," June 11, 1945; "Life Presents a Review of Fall Fashions," May 22, 1947.

FAST FOOD

Sometime in the late 1940s or early 1950s, the words "fast food" entered everyday American speech. The term refers to **food** that can be prepared easily and served quickly. An industry built around fast food developed throughout the 20th century, beginning with simple-menu, quick-eating establishments—taverns, coffee shops, tea rooms, diners, automats, sandwich shops, soda fountains, luncheonettes, and food carts and stands. Before the automobile became the primary source of **transportation** for Americans, these eateries tended to be in the downtown sections of a city or other areas where large numbers of people congregated, such as industrial sites. With the growing use of cars, fast food businesses began appearing on highway shoulders or set back on lots adjacent to the road.

White Castle, a pioneer hamburger stand and the first major fast-food chain, opened its earliest walk-in site in 1921. Located in Wichita, Kansas, and close to factories, it easily accommodated those who had arrived in the area by trolley, bus, or foot. Its immediate success prompted founders Edgar W. Ingram (Billy, 1880–1966) and Walter L. Anderson (1880–1963) to expand, and soon other White Castles dotted the city and nearby communities. The chain offered a limited menu that emphasized hamburgers and inexpensive, good-tasting food with consistent quality. Operating 24 hours a day, these stands employed distinctive, bright, white architectural motifs that reflected their name; they soon became a model for other urban food stands. White Tower (1926), Krystal (1932), Steak 'n Shake (1934), Rockybilt (1936), Bob's Big Boy (1936), and Royal Castle (1938) all trace their lineage back to the original White Castles.

With the increased affordability and popularization of **automobiles,** establishments such as roadside diners, **restaurants,** and food stands could easily be patronized by growing numbers of people. From 1930 to 1940, motor vehicle miles driven in the United States jumped from 206 billion to 302 billion annually. As the miles grew, so did the demand for road food. Both the war and postwar years witnessed a strong emergence of food stands in three varieties: walk-ins, drive-ins, and drive-throughs. Initially, they all served primarily hamburgers and/or hot dogs.

Food and labor shortages during World War II, along with **rationing,** caused hardships for businesses, and many of the smaller food stands closed their doors. On the other hand, the war and good fortune coincided when Carl and Margaret Karcher (1917–2008 and 1915–2006) purchased a hot dog stand across from a Goodyear Factory in Los Angeles, five months before the United States entered the conflict in December 1941. Employment at the plant soared, and the Karchers did a booming business; soon one cart became five. In 1944, they opened a family restaurant and, in 1956, moved into another level of the fast-food industry with Carl's Jr., a hamburger chain that still operates on the West Coast.

Understanding the wisdom of catering to automobile travelers, many fast-food establishments during the late 1930s and early 1940s operated as drive-ins and offered curb service provided by young men or women dressed in uniforms. Called carhops, they brought the food to the customers who had remained seated in their cars, the ultimate in convenience at the time.

Two brothers, Maurice and Richard McDonald (1902–1971; 1909–1998), moved to California from New Hampshire in 1920. In 1937, they entered the walk-in food stand business with the Airdrome in Arcadia, California, a place where they sold hot dogs, orange juice, coffee, and tea. The McDonald brothers soon realized the value of running the business as a drive-in and, in 1939, moved their operation to a location in San Bernardino that would accommodate this approach. In 1940, they held a grand opening for McDonald's Barbeque Restaurant. It featured a 25-item menu that included barbeque ribs and beef and pork sandwiches served by 20 carhops to customers waiting in their cars.

The McDonalds struggled during the war but managed to stay open. Their expenses grew, caused primarily by employee wages, and the output of the carhops dissatisfied them. As a result, the McDonalds studied ways to improve business. After some research, they settled on what they saw as two essential components—hamburgers and young families. They discovered that 80 percent of their sales came from a single ground beef patty served on a bun, and they foresaw that growing numbers of postwar households would constitute a significant market. The **baby boom** had begun, and young families would be looking for efficient, economical, and easy ways to eat.

Moving forward on their findings, the McDonalds closed their barbeque restaurant in 1948 and two months later reopened as a self-service facility. They used the concepts of speed, lower prices, and volume to formulate a new approach to food preparation and service. The newly named McDonald's featured a "Speedee Service System" selling hamburgers at a bargain 15 cents apiece ($1.29 in 2008 dollars; the competitive price was then 30 cents [$2.58]), cheeseburgers, three soft drink flavors, milk, coffee, potato chips, and pie. Soon French fries for 10 cents (86 cents in 2008 money) and milkshakes could also be purchased. The McDonald brothers changed from the use of carhops to counter service and reengineered the stainless steel kitchen for mass production, using efficient assembly-line procedures. The fast-food industry, as it is known today, was born.

The McDonald brothers did not see an immediate and significant growth with their redesigned San Bernardino site, but by the mid-1950s, they had achieved close to double the volume of their previous drive-in business, coupled with a corresponding increase in annual revenues. They had also expanded to nine franchises. Because they quickly filled orders, the McDonalds attracted the attention of salesman Ray Kroc (1902–1984), a man who envisioned an eatery that mass produced many more items than hamburgers and milkshakes. He convinced the brothers he should be their franchising agent and, by the late 1950s, had purchased the entire chain, along with their name, a business deal that ultimately resulted in McDonald's in locations all across the United States and throughout the world.

Franchising had been practiced since the early 1900s, mainly by automobile manufacturers, gasoline companies, and soft drink producers. The system grants independently owned businesses the right to sell the manufacturer's products. This method provided entrepreneurs such as Howard Johnson (1896–1972) in the 1930s and the McDonald brothers, Ray Kroc, and William Rosenberg (1916–2002) of Dunkin Donuts in the 1940s a way to expand retail operations without expending too much precious capital. It also allowed people in communities around the country to start their own business without risking everything on a new, and possibly unknown, venture. For the consumer, fast food franchise networks guaranteed three features: a recognized trademark, a uniform product, and fast service.

Additional entrepreneurs entered the fast-food industry during the 1940s, but they did not achieve enduring stability until the 1950s. Harry and Esther Snyder (1913–1976; 1920–2006) greeted their first customers at In-N-Out Burger in Baldwin Park, California, in 1948 with the unique feature of ordering over an intercom system. This gave customers a means to speak directly to an attendant in the building. Others soon created the drive-through, whereby after ordering over a speaker, the driver moved to a window for pick-up.

The Snyders' menu of hamburgers, cheeseburgers, French fries, sodas, and milkshakes elicited a good response, and in 1951 they opened a second site. By 1976, In-N-Out Burger had grown to 18 locations, a low number in the fast-growing fast-food industry, because the Snyders' decided not to franchise their additional sites. Harmon Dobson (d. 1967) founded a similar chain, Whataburger, in 1950 in Corpus Christi, Texas. One of the few fast-food restaurants to initially open outside California, Whataburger continues today to operate franchises primarily in the South and Midwest.

Following the success of the McDonald brothers, much of the early fast-food industry grew up in southern California. But it quickly spread eastward, and as it did so, the food selection broadened beyond hot dogs, hamburgers, and cheeseburgers. In 1940, Harland Sanders (1890–1980), better known as Colonel Sanders (an honorary rank bestowed on him in 1935 by the governor of Kentucky) had perfected his Kentucky Fried Chicken recipe, something he first sold in a restaurant in Corbin, Kentucky, throughout the 1930s. He moved into the chain business when, in 1952, a Salt Lake City businessman opened the first Kentucky Fried Chicken franchise. Today, Kentucky Fried Chicken (or KFC) can be bought both nationally and internationally and offers a variety of chicken items as well as other kinds of food.

The success stories in American fast food are many. William Rosenberg founded Industrial Luncheon Services in 1946 in suburban Boston. He sold sandwiches, coffee, and baked goods from trucks. By 1948, his enterprise had grown to 140 trucks, and he discovered that doughnuts were a consistent seller. To better concentrate on this commodity, Rosenberg opened a small shop called The Open Kettle in Quincy, Massachusetts, in 1948. Two years later and with five stores, he changed the name to Dunkin' Donuts and sold his first franchise in 1955. Like many other providers of fast food, this chain can be found throughout the United States and around the world.

Similarly, Winchell's Donut House, owned and operated by Verne Winchell (1915–2002), first opened in Temple City, California, in 1948. It continues today as a successful West Coast chain with a few international sites. Known as the home of the Warm 'n Fresh Donut, Winchell's serves over 70 varieties of doughnuts and bakery products and earned for its founder the nickname, "the Donut King."

J. F. McCullough and his son Alex (both active 1930s and 1940s) owned a dairy shop in Davenport, Iowa, where they made a soft ice cream. Based on their successful 1938 introductory sale of this soft frozen product, they continued to perfect their continuous freeze process and, in 1940, Sherwood (Sherb) Noble (1908–1991) opened a Dairy Queen franchise in Joliet, Illinois. World War II defense industries needed the materials used in manufacturing the machines for producing soft ice cream and caused a wartime halt to expansion. After the war, Dairy Queen made a quick comeback and boasted 17 franchises by 1946. Two years later, the business expanded to include malts and milkshakes. Banana splits joined the menu in 1953, and, by 1955, Dairy Queen boasted 2,600 sites. Today it offers a variety of venues ranging from seasonal roadside ice cream stands to walk-ins, drive-ins, drive-throughs, and sit-down dining for a multitude of soft serve items, as well as hamburgers, hot dogs, and fries.

Irvine Robbins (1917–2008), newly out of the military in 1945, opened the Snowbird Ice Cream Shop in Glendale, California. Just one year later, his brother-in-law, Burton Baskin (1913–1967), founded Burton's Ice Cream Shop in Pasadena, California. By 1948, the two owned six stores between them and, in 1953, decided to consolidate and form Baskin-Robbins. They offered complimentary taste spoons for customers to sample their 31 flavors, enough kinds of ice cream to outnumber Howard Johnson's famous 28, and provided ice cream connoisseurs with a different taste each day of the month. Like Dairy Queen, this chain can be found worldwide.

The advancement of the fast-food industry during the 1940s perhaps marks the most far- reaching development in food and dining for the decade. It laid a firm foundation for phenomenal growth in the 1950s. Of the many entrepreneurs who at the time ventured into this new business, several immediately expanded their operations. Those who imitated White Castle's simplicity and consistency and McDonald's speed and efficiency usually realized sustained success. Hot dogs and hamburgers, along with fried chicken, ice cream, and doughnuts, established a basic menu that proved popular. Later, pizza, fish, ethnic foods, and submarine sandwiches joined in leading to a contemporary array that also includes tacos, prepackaged salads and sandwiches, and even espresso.

See also: Beverages; Desserts, Candy, and Ice Cream; Travel

Selected Reading
Jakle, John A., and Keith A. Sculle. *Fast Food: Roadside Restaurants in the Automobile Age.* Baltimore: Johns Hopkins University Press, 1999.
Smith, Andrew F. *Encyclopedia of Junk Food and Fast Food.* Westport, CT: Greenwood Press, 2006.
Witzel, Michael Karl, and Tom Steil. *Classic Roadside Americana.* New York: MBI, 2006.

FILM NOIR

One particular style, or genre, of motion picture always associated with the 1940s carries a French name, *film noir,* which roughly translates as "black movie." The "black/noir" refers to the darkness, both psychological and visual, that permeates such productions. The films that fall into this category overrode all the gangster, detective, police procedural, and whodunit **movies** of the day in both audience appeal and critical acclaim. Although the film noir movement lasted only about a dozen years—approximately 1940 until the early 1950s—the pictures falling under its umbrella have come to be among the top-rated ones of the decade, especially in the area of **crime and mystery films.**

A typical film noir scene can be described in a few words: nighttime in an urban setting, with flickering neon signs haloed in misty rain; a figure wearing a trench coat, water dripping off a battered fedora, stands beneath a dim streetlight. Shadows and smoke curling from a cigarette mask his face, but passing headlights create sharp contrasts with the surrounding darkness. He doubtless waits for a woman, a femme fatale, who will in the end do him no good.

By the end of the film noir cycle, such scenes had become virtual clichés, as did the battered hero (or antihero, in many cases). A distinct style in terms of cinema aesthetics, film noir grew out of the gothic romanticism of the 19th century, early 20th-century European expressionism, the pulp **magazines** and mystery stories of the 1920s, and the dark horror pictures so popular in the 1930s. Almost always shot in black and white, the genre presents a threatening, uncertain world, a milieu in which characters experience at best limited success, and the differences between good and evil can be as murky as the stylistics.

The possibilities of capturing the ambiguities of crime appealed to a number of directors, some of whom emerged as box office draws in their own right. Many of them had come to the United States from Europe prior to World War II and, given events in their homelands, perhaps brought with them a darker, gloomier view of human nature than that espoused by their cheerier U.S. counterparts. For example, the celebrated directors listed in Table 50, all European emigrants and all contemporaries, at one time or another in their careers worked in the film noir genre, creating some of the major achievements within the category.

Tough guys, sultry dames, guns, and exaggerated shadowing are among the characteristics of film noir, a motion picture genre that gained its greatest fame in the 1940s. This publicity shot for 1942's The Glass Key *shows Alan Ladd and Veronica Lake providing just such dramatic interest. (Sunset Boulevard/Corbis)*

Carol Reed (1906–1976), another outstanding director from abroad, was born in London and did not move to the United States. Although he remained in England, his films were widely seen in the States and significantly influenced the development of the genre, most notably *Odd Man Out* (1947) and *The Third Man* (1949).

Numerous American directors working in film noir also significantly influenced the genre; Table 51 identifies some of the leaders in the field. As far as concerns the films themselves, the following titles merit attention. It can be seen in Table 52 that the movement begins slowly in the first years of the decade but, by the mid-1940s, has gathered considerable momentum, maintaining a full-blown production schedule through 1949, and would continue that pace into the early 1950s. Following the widespread use of color instead of black-and-white **photography,** plus such innovations as wider screens and more special effects, the dark, almost claustrophobic imagery of film noir fell out of favor, and it ceased to be a significant component of Hollywood productions in the later 1950s. A number of the titles listed below can also be found in the Crime and Mystery Films, **Drama (Film),** and **Horror and Thriller Films** entries elsewhere in this encyclopedia. Many film noir pictures focus on either crimes or mysteries, and virtually all of them involve tense, dramatic situations.

TABLE 50. Notable Foreign-Born Directors Working in American Film Noir

Director	Place of Birth	Selected Films
Michael Curtiz (1886–1962)	Budapest, Hungary	*Casablanca,* 1942 *Mildred Pierce,* 1945 *The Unsuspected,* 1947 *Flamingo Road,* 1949
Alfred Hitchcock (1899–1980)	London, England	*Suspicion,* 1941 *Shadow of a Doubt,* 1943 *Notorious,* 1946 *Rope,* 1948
Boris Ingster (1903–1978)	Riga, Latvia	*Stranger on the Third Floor,* 1940
Fritz Lang (1890–1976)	Vienna, Austria	*Ministry of Fear,* 1944 *The Woman in the Window,* 1944 *Scarlet Street,* 1945 *Secret Beyond the Door,* 1948
Anatole Litvak (1902–1974)	Kiev, Russia	*The Long Night,* 1947 *The Snake Pit,* 1948 *Sorry, Wrong Number,* 1948
Rudolph Mate (1898–1964)	Cracow, Poland	*The Dark Past,* 1948 *D.O.A.,* 1950
Lewis Milestone (1895–1980)	Kishinew, Russia	*The Strange Love of Martha Ivers,* 1946
Otto Preminger (1906–1986)	Vienna, Austria	*Laura,* 1944 *Fallen Angel,* 1945
Robert Siodmak (1900–1973)	Dresden, Germany	*Phantom Lady,* 1944 *Christmas Holiday,* 1944 *The Strange Affair of Uncle Harry,* 1945 *The Spiral Staircase,* 1946 *The Killers,* 1946
Josef von Sternberg (1894–1969)	Vienna, Austria	*The Shanghai Gesture,* 1942
Jacques Tourneur (1904–1977)	Paris, France	*The Leopard Man,* 1943 *Out of the Past,* 1947 *Berlin Express,* 1948
Edgar G. Ulmer (1904–1972)	Olmutz, Austria	*Detour,* 1945 *The Strange Woman,* 1946 *Ruthless,* 1949
Billy Wilder (1906–2002)	Sucha, Austria	*Double Indemnity,* 1944

TABLE 51. Notable American-Born Directors Working in Film Noir

Director	Selected Films
George Cukor (1899–1983)	*Gaslight,* 1944
Edward Dmytryk (1908–1999; born in Canada)	*Murder My Sweet,* 1944 [also known as *Farewell My Lovely* in the United Kingdom] *Cornered,* 1945 *Crossfire,* 1947
Howard Hawks (1896–1977)	*To Have and Have Not,* 1944 *The Big Sleep,* 1946
John Huston (1906–1987)	*The Maltese Falcon,* 1941 *Key Largo,* 1948
Nicholas Ray (1911–1979)	*They Live by Night,* 1948 *Knock on Any Door,* 1949 *A Woman's Secret,* 1949
Frank Tuttle (1892–1963)	*The Glass Key,* 1935 [remade in 1942 with director Stuart Heisler (1896–1979); see below] *This Gun for Hire,* 1942
Orson Welles (1915–1985)	*Citizen Kane,* 1941 *The Stranger,* 1946 *The Lady from Shanghai,* 1948

TABLE 52. Representative Film Noir Movies, 1940–1949

Year	Film Titles	Stars
1940	*Rebecca*	Laurence Olivier, Joan Fontaine
	Stranger on the Third Floor	Peter Lorre, Elisha Cook Jr.
	They Drive by Night	Humphrey Bogart, George Raft
1941	*Among the Living*	Albert Dekker, Susan Hayward
	Citizen Kane	Orson Welles, Joseph Cotton
	High Sierra	Humphrey Bogart, Ida Lupino
	I Wake Up Screaming	Betty Grable, Victor Mature
	The Maltese Falcon	Humphrey Bogart, Mary Astor
	Suspicion	Cary Grant, Joan Fontaine
1942	*Casablanca*	Humphrey Bogart, Ingrid Bergman
	*The Glass Key**	Alan Ladd, Veronica Lake
	Johnny Eager	Robert Taylor, Lana Turner
	The Shanghai Gesture	Gene Tierney, Victor Mature
	This Gun for Hire	Alan Ladd, Veronica Lake
1943	*Journey Into Fear*	Orson Welles, Joseph Cotton
	The Leopard Man	Dennis O'Keefe, Margo
	Shadow of a Doubt	Teresa Wright, Joseph Cotton

Year	Film Titles	Stars
1944	*Christmas Holiday*	Deanna Durbin, Gene Kelly
	Double Indemnity	Barbara Stanwyck, Fred MacMurray
	Gaslight	Ingrid Bergman, Charles Boyer
	Laura	Gene Tierney, Dana Andrews
	Ministry of Fear	Ray Milland, Dan Duryea
	Murder My Sweet [also known as *Farewell My Lovely* in the United Kingdom]	Dick Powell, Claire Trevor
	Phantom Lady	Franchot Tone, Elisha Cook Jr.
	To Have and Have Not	Humphrey Bogart, Lauren Bacall
	The Woman in the Window	Edward G. Robinson, Joan Bennett
1945	*Cornered*	Dick Powell, Walter Slezak
	Detour	Tom Neal, Ann Savage
	Fallen Angel	Dana Andrews, Linda Darnell
	Lady on a Train	Deanna Durbin, Ralph Bellamy
	Leave Her to Heaven	Gene Tierney, Cornel Wilde
	Mildred Pierce	Joan Crawford, Zachary Scott
	The Red House	Edward G. Robinson, Judith Anderson
	Scarlet Street	Edward G. Robinson, Joan Bennett
1946	*The Big Sleep*	Humphrey Bogart, Lauren Bacall
	The Dark Corner	Lucille Ball, Clifton Webb
	Decoy	Jean Gillie, Robert Armstrong
	Gilda	Rita Hayworth, Glenn Ford
	The Killers	Burt Lancaster, Ava Gardner
	Notorious	Cary Grant, Ingrid Bergman
	Somewhere in the Night	John Hodiak, Lloyd Nolan
	The Spiral Staircase	Dorothy McGuire, Ethel Barrymore
	The Strange Affair of Uncle Harry	George Sanders, Geraldine Fitzgerald
	The Strange Love of Martha Ivers	Barbara Stanwyck, Kirk Douglas
	The Stranger	Orson Welles, Edward G. Robinson
	Undercurrent	Katharine Hepburn, Robert Mitchum
1947	*Born to Kill*	Lawrence Tierney, Claire Trevor
	Brute Force	Burt Lancaster, Hume Cronyn
	Calcutta	Alan Ladd, William Bendix
	Crossfire	Robert Young, Robert Ryan
	Fear in the Night	Paul Kelly, DeForest Kelley
	Lady in the Lake	Robert Montgomery, Audrey Totter
	The Long Night	Henry Fonda, Vincent Price
	Nightmare Alley	Tyrone Power, Joan Blondell
	Out of the Past	Robert Mitchum, Kirk Douglas
	They Won't Believe Me	Robert Young, Susan Hayward
	T-Men	Dennis O'Keefe, Wallace Ford
	The Unsuspected	Claude Rains, Joan Caulfield

(continued)

TABLE 52. *(continued)*

Year	Film Titles	Stars
1948	*Act of Violence*	Robert Ryan, Van Heflin
	Berlin Express	Robert Ryan, Merle Oberon
	The Dark Past	William Holden, Lee J. Cobb
	Force of Evil	John Garfield, Marie Windsor
	Key Largo	Humphrey Bogart, Edward G. Robinson
	The Lady from Shanghai	Orson Welles, Rita Hayworth
	Moonrise	Dane Clark, Gail Russell
	The Naked City	Howard Duff, Barry Fitzgerald
	Raw Deal	Dennis O'Keefe, Claire Trevor
	Ruthless	Zachary Scott, Louis Hayward
	Sorry, Wrong Number	Barbara Stanwyck, Burt Lancaster
	They Live by Night	Farley Granger, Cathy O'Donnell
1949	*C-Man*	Dean Jagger, John Carradine
	Criss Cross	Burt Lancaster, Yvonne De Carlo
	Flamingo Road	Joan Crawford, Zachary Scott
	Knock on Any Door	Humphrey Bogart, John Derek
	Manhandled	Dorothy Lamour, Sterling Hayden
	Thieves' Highway	Lee J. Cobb, Richard Conte
	The Third Man	Orson Welles, Joseph Cotton
	Tokyo Joe	Humphrey; Bogart, Alexander Knox
	White Heat	James Cagney, Virginia Mayo
	The Window	Bobby Driscoll, Paul Stewart
	A Woman's Secret	Maureen O'Hara, Melvyn Douglas

* This version, directed by Stuart Heisler (1896–1979), came after Frank Tuttle's (1892–1963) production of 1935; many consider the Tuttle interpretation a pioneering example of film noir.

A brief moment in movie history, and one primarily limited to the 1940s, film noir has exerted a lasting influence on motion pictures. Visually, the dark, expressionistic frames of a classic film noir tale can still be found in many productions, particularly mysteries. The pessimistic, often amoral stories have likewise carried over into many postnoir films, perhaps reflecting the continuing anxieties of the present.

See also: Best Sellers (Books); Fashion

Selected Reading
Naremore, James. *More than Night: Film Noir and Its Contexts.* Berkeley: University of California Press, 1998.
Robson, Eddie. *Film Noir.* London: Virgin Books, 2005.
Silver, Alain, and Elizabeth Ward. *Film Noir: An Encyclopedia of the American Style.* Woodstock, New York: Overlook Press, 1992.

FM RADIO

Although most developments in the 20th-century history of **radio** broadcasting came about because of numerous group efforts, the rise of FM (frequency modulation) can be attributed primarily to one man, Edwin H. Armstrong (1890–1954). A brilliant engineer with several radio-related inventions to his credit, Armstrong became wealthy through his improvements in radio circuitry, and it allowed him to work independently. The concept of modulating frequency had been understood since the 1900s, but most engineers of the day thought FM would introduce distortion into a signal and eventually dropped the idea. They instead believed that ever-stronger AM (amplitude modulation) signals could overpower distortion, and so they looked to boosting the strength of existing stations.

In the late 1920s, Armstrong came to the realization that the standard channel for an AM signal, which measured 10 kilohertz (kHz, a measurement for defining the number of cycles per second), proved too narrow to eliminate static from radio broadcasts. He widened the channel to 200 kHz and found that static and interference from adjacent channels disappeared. He also discovered that FM, contrary to then-common belief, can faithfully reproduce a wide range of accurate sound while using relatively low power. He quickly applied for patents on his findings and how he achieved them in 1930; he received patent protection in 1933. He then convinced the Radio Corporation of America (RCA) of the feasibility inherent in FM signals, despite RCA's dominance in traditional AM broadcasting. At first, RCA seemed receptive to his ideas but eventually began to view any improvements in Armstrong's inventions as threatening to its extensive network of AM stations. As a significant stockholder in the corporation, he had often utilized RCA facilities for his research, until the corporate giant in 1935 denied him further access to company **technology** and equipment.

On his own and confident, Armstrong went ahead with plans for FM broadcasting, and the Federal Communications Commission (FCC) in 1935 authorized 13 experimental channels for tests. He built a prototype station in Alpine, New Jersey, across the Hudson River from New York City, constructing a transmission tower from which he sent FM signals to associates with receivers capable of picking them up. These tests proved successful, and soon over 20 other test stations were on the air, and the future of FM looked bright. By this time, the Yankee Network, a loose confederation of AM stations in New England, considered emergent FM in a favorable light and, using Armstrong's technology, opened its first FM station in 1939. A number of others also commenced operation later that year and into 1940, leading several electronics firms to begin manufacturing FM receivers. With such encouraging results, Armstrong persuaded the FCC to approve the broadcasting of commercial FM signals at the beginning of 1941. RCA, wanting to squash this potential threat to its networks, offered to buy out Armstrong's FM patents, but he refused. At the end of 1941, World War II engaged the energies of the United States and brought most nondefense radio experimentation and expansion to a halt.

Despite the war, the FCC approved FM as the sound medium for **television** broadcasting and allocated new, wider bandwidths (the markings on a radio dial represent these channels) for this purpose in 1944. In making this allocation, the FCC specified bandwidths different from those that had been utilized in the later 1930s. The commission's move effectively rendered obsolete any older transmitters, along with some 400,000 receivers built prior to the war. When the final cessation of hostilities occurred in the autumn of 1945, Armstrong challenged the FCC decisions, which resulted in a long, drawn-out legal battle that lasted until 1948. RCA, waiting in the wings, jumped at this opportunity and claimed to have developed its own FM circuitry independent of Armstrong; the company began to utilize its FM components in the sound receivers found in its postwar TV sets. Armstrong again went to court, this time against RCA. Legal fees and the lack of royalties from his previous patents for his earlier FM inventions worked to destroy Armstrong's health. The inventor of modern-day FM committed suicide in 1954. Ironically, the courts in 1967 eventually decided the lawsuits in his favor.

While all the legal wrangling went on, various entrepreneurs applied for FM licenses in the postwar years. These applicants foresaw a booming market for FM in the later 1940s, but most would be disappointed. The FCC doled out over 80 percent of its broadcast licenses to those parties already associated with AM broadcasting. These owners convinced officials that any start-up risks involved were lessened by those actively engaged in broadcasting, plus they could immediately duplicate the programming already found on their AM stations until their FM colleagues were up and running on their own. To rein in expenses, many applicants initially continued to broadcast regular network AM shows over FM and then slowly substituted "good music" (primarily classical) on their FM franchises. Few, however, attempted to produce any original programming for FM outside of recordings, a factor that discouraged potential sponsors. They knew full well that the postwar FM audience, generally older listeners interested in serious music, constituted a demographic that caused them to withhold their **advertising** dollars, spending them instead on a more youthful mass AM market.

Despite what appears to be prodigious growth in FM stations, 1949 marked the high-water mark for postwar FM start-ups. In subsequent years, the number would fall off sharply as existing stations folded and no new ones came along to replace them. In 1958, as a point of reference, the number of FM stations grew to 548, the first increase since 1949 but well behind that year's figure.

Given the limited menu available on FM in the late 1940s along with the high cost of new, compatible FM receivers, few listeners wanted to make the investment. The enthusiasm found among the first flurry of station applicants also died down, while AM radio and television outlets continued to grow rapidly. The revival of FM would not occur until the later 1950s and early 1960s, a time when the FCC sanctioned FM stereo signals and forbade the duplication of AM programming on the FM band. A radio medium attracting a distinct niche audience, FM struggled during this difficult postwar period, whereas AM and TV became the reigning electronic media.

TABLE 53. The Postwar Growth of AM and FM Radio Stations, 1945–1950

Year	AM Stations on the Air	FM Stations on the Air
1945	931 (24 additional authorized)	46 (19 additional authorized)
1946	961 (254 additional authorized)	55 (401 additional authorized)
1947	1,298 (497 additional authorized)	238 (680 additional authorized)
1948	1,693 (331 additional authorized)	587 (433 additional authorized)
1949	2,006 (173 additional authorized)	737 (128 additional authorized)
1950	2,144 (159 additional authorized)	691 (61 additional authorized)

See also: *ASCAP vs. BMI* Radio Boycott and the AFM Recording Ban; Classical Music; Radio Programming: Music and Variety Shows

Selected Reading
Barnouw, Erik. *A History of Broadcasting in the United States.* Vol. 1, *A Tower in Babel.* New York: Oxford University Press, 1966.
———. *A History of Broadcasting in the United States.* Vol. 2, *The Golden Web.* New York: Oxford University Press, 1968.
Sterling, Christopher H., and John M. Kitross. *Stay Tuned: A Concise History of American Broadcasting.* Belmont, CA: Wadsworth, 1990.

FOLK MUSIC

In 1940, RCA Victor Records issued *Dust Bowl Ballads,* a collection of songs written and performed by rural folk singer Woody Guthrie (1912–1967), telling about his life during the Great Depression. Many numbers in the collection, such as "Dust Bowl Blues" and "I Ain't Got No Home in This World Anymore" (both ca. 1935–1938), "The Ballad of Pretty Boy Floyd" (1939), and "So Long, It's Been Good to Know Yuh (Dusty Old Dust)" (1940) rank among his best and contributed to the growing popularity of folk music during the 1940s.

This musical genre originated through the oral transmission of a story of some importance or a lesson about everyday life. For the United States, much folk music can be traced to the Appalachian Mountains of the Southeast during the early colonial period. By the 1920s, when **radio** and recordings enabled songs to be widely disseminated, some individuals saw commercial value in folk tunes and ventured into the southern Appalachian mountains to record folk musicians. From these efforts, interests in songs about economic hardship, such as the ones by Guthrie, and protest numbers about labor injustices in Kentucky and West Virginia enjoyed a following. Performers like Sarah Ogan Gunning (1910–1983) and Florence Reese (1900–1986) also attracted attention and demonstrated the increased popularity of this musical tradition.

Guthrie, in addition to cutting *Dust Bowl Ballads,* recorded four hours of songs and stories for folklorist Alan Lomax (1915–2002) and his Library of Congress Archive of American Folk Song project at around the same time. Two years later, the first record album from Lomax's work became available for purchase. While collaborating with Lomax, Guthrie also wrote what may be his best-known piece, "This Land Is Your Land" (1940, originally titled "God Blessed America for Me"), in reaction to Tin Pan Alley composer Irving Berlin's (1888–1989) "God Bless America" (1938), which Guthrie considered unrealistic. A prolific composer, Guthrie in 1941 gained a commission from the U.S. Department of the Interior to write numbers for a public information film promoting the building of the Bonneville Dam on the Columbia River. From this collection of 26 songs, came such well-known pieces as "Roll On Columbia," "Hard Traveling," and "Pastures of Plenty."

After moving to New York City in 1940, Guthrie actively participated in a folk music reawakening occurring there, which led to his joining the Almanac Singers, a folk trio formed by Pete Seeger (b. 1919), Lee Hays (1914–1981), and Millard Lampell

(1919–1997). Throughout the trio's brief history, other singers floated in and out of the group, many of them active in left-wing politics and/or the Communist Party. The Almanac Singers held their first major public appearance in May 1941 at Madison Square Garden for the striking Transport Workers' Union. Highly successful, they next recorded four albums—one of antiwar songs (released before the December 7, 1941, attack on Pearl Harbor), one of union songs, and two of traditional folk songs. They also embarked upon a road trip singing at colleges, union meetings, migrant camps, antifascist rallies, and on street corners.

Once back home from their travels, the Almanac Singers established the Almanac House, a co-op apartment in Greenwich Village, where they lived and held weekly hootenannies, an old word revived in Seattle and brought to New York by Guthrie and Seeger. It describes lively evenings of music. For these gatherings, the music also often contained political commentary. But when the United States officially entered World War II, the focus of their music changed from labor and political protest to support of the country's war efforts. To validate their seriousness, Seeger joined the army, where he entertained troops, and Guthrie enlisted in the Merchant Marine.

After World War II, Seeger returned to New York City and helped form People's Songs, Inc., a union of folksingers and songwriters. He worked as the national director and oversaw the publication of *People's Song,* the first magazine devoted exclusively to folk music. In 1949, *People's Song* went bankrupt; Seeger had been a member of the Communist Party since 1942, and in the emerging **Cold War** atmosphere between the United States and the Soviet Union, organized labor turned against radicalism and anyone seemingly involved with the USSR.

A folk magazine may have gone out of business, but folk music did not die. Seeger and Lee Hays cowrote "If I Had a Hammer" (1949), and Seeger formed a musical quartet, this time composed of himself, Hays from the defunct Almanac Singers, Fred Hellerman (b. 1927), and Ronnie Gilbert (b. 1926). The foursome called themselves The Weavers, the title of an 1892 tragedy by German playwright Gerhart (Johann Robert) Hauptmann (1862–1946), first performed in 1893. Their songs' lyrics were clearly folk oriented, while their arrangements leaned more to pop, thus bringing an entirely new audience to folk music. The Weavers soon landed a six-month contract at the Village Vanguard, a popular New York City nightclub that featured music, usually **jazz.** They had a hit with their own *Kisses Sweeter Than Wine* in 1951, and throughout the 1950s their popularized versions of traditional folk songs, such as "So Long, It's Been Good to Know Yuh (Dusty Old Dust)" and "On Top of Old Smoky," gave them several best-selling recordings.

Moses (Moe) Asch (1905–1986), founder in 1948 of the Folkways record label, made a major contribution toward strengthening the place of folk music in the American musical mainstream. Early on, Asch recorded Guthrie, Seeger, and others considered at the time to be at the center of a folk music revival. In 1952, Folkway Records released a six-LP *Anthology of American Folk Music,* and today the Center for Folklife and Cultural Heritage, administered by the Smithsonian Institution in Washington, DC, holds all of Asch's Folkways recordings and business files.

Burl Ives (1909–1995), another performer active in New York City in the early 1940s, also contributed to the growth of folk music at that time. Interested in acting and singing, Ives contracted with both NBC (National Broadcasting Company) and CBS (Columbia Broadcasting System) radio networks for weekly shows. Airing on various days in many time slots, he used several different program names—*Back Where I Came From, The Burl Ives Coffee Club, God's Country,* and the title he used most often, *The Wayfaring Stranger.* During these programs, Ives sang and told stories from his extensive travels across the United States during the 1930s. He popularized several traditional folk songs such as "Lavender Blue," "Foggy Foggy Dew," and "The Erie Canal." During the postwar years, Ives published an autobiography, *The Wayfaring Stranger,* in 1948; he made his film debut as a singing cowboy in *Smoky* (1946), and appeared in several **Broadway shows (musicals)** and additional **movies.**

From its origins, folk music has focused on important issues of a given time. With the Great Depression, the genre experienced a resurgence in the 1930s because of how it reflected the difficulties of that decade. Unsatisfactory labor conditions gave rise to protest songs, setting the stage for Woody Guthrie and Pete Seeger to be among the leading promoters of the style during the 1940s. The formation of the Almanac Singers offered the first group of trained musicians who got together for the purpose of singing folk music in a commercial context. Next came the Weavers and the first folk-pop singers who made an effort to divorce themselves from politics. The Weavers enjoyed considerable popularity and became one of the most influential groups in folk music history. Others followed in the 1950s and 1960s, carrying folk music forward. Over these decades, individuals such as Alan Lomax and Moe Asch recorded this rich musical history, preserving it for generations to come.

See also: ASCAP vs. BMI Radio Boycott and the AFM Recording Ban; Best Sellers (Books); Boogie-Woogie; Country Music; Labor Unrest; Magazines; Radio Programming: Music and Variety Shows

Selected Reading
Denisoff, R. Serge, and Richard A. Peterson, eds. *The Sounds of Social Change.* New York: Rand McNally, 1972.
Ewen, David. *All the Years of American Popular Music.* Englewood Cliffs, NJ: Prentice Hall, 1977.
Santelli, Robert, Holly George-Warren, and Jim Brown, eds. *American Roots Music.* New York: Harry N. Abrams, 2001.

FOOD

Most Americans had recovered from the hardships of the Great Depression by the end of the 1930s, and they expected a growing economy to offer a more promising future. The entry of the United States into World War II, however, changed life drastically. In particular, food and diets during the first half of the 1940s contrasted sharply with both the pre- and postwar years.

During the conflict, people on the home front experienced some shortages, although no one went hungry. **Rationing, victory gardens,** canning and preserving, nutrition, the Basic Seven, and recommended daily allowances (RDAs) served as ways of coping. With a resurgent economy and flourishing consumer culture, the postwar years brought about unparalleled abundance. This included huge jumps in the variety of processed, convenience, frozen, and **fast food**s. New appliances in new kitchens, including backyard barbecue equipment, allowed homemakers a variety of ways to prepare this outpouring of products. Finally, over the decade, prewar regional differences in food consumption gradually shifted to somewhat homogeneous eating patterns across the country.

After the 1941 attack on Pearl Harbor, in an effort to energize public opinion, governmental publications and commercial **advertising** presented a common theme of women playing a crucial role in winning the war. Slogans such as "There's a War Job in Every Kitchen" underscored the idea that cooking nutritious food from victory gardens and the wise use of rationing quotas served as an attractive way to sustain good health and moral strength, necessary elements for carrying out daily tasks that would lead the country to victory.

A massive educational program attempted to improve the health of all Americans. It was one of the first tasks for the Office of Health Defense and Welfare created in 1941 by President Franklin Roosevelt. By 1943, posters such as this one could be found displayed in a wide variety of establishments across the United States. (Library of Congress)

Wartime messages to women focused on their getting a job outside of the home. From one-quarter of the workforce, 13 million women, at the war's beginning, their numbers rose to 18 million, or one-third, in 1945. Many more served as volunteers for the Red Cross and similar organizations. This movement to employment, however, did not lessen women's responsibilities at home, and, for some, their duties became more difficult because domestic workers left many households for more lucrative jobs in defense plants.

Early in the decade, a series of events brought the nation's attention to the well-being of its citizens. It began in September with the call of the first 1 million men for induction into military service under the **Selective Training and Service Act of 1940.** Some 40 percent of those conscripted, or about 400,000 men, were rejected for service. Much to the alarm of federal officials, nutritional deficiencies of one form or another caused 132,000 men, or one-third of those rejected, to fail their physical examinations.

President Franklin Delano Roosevelt (1882–1945), after reading a report on this matter, concluded that unhealthy eating habits left the country with men who lacked the necessary stamina for battle and also hindered defense workers and housewives from adequately performing important jobs on the home front. He took immediate action and directed Paul V. McNutt (1891–1955), then head of the newly formed Federal

Security Agency (FSA; it included the Board of Social Security, Public Health Service, Food and Drug Administration, Office of Education, and a number of other agencies), to improve the nutritional well-being of all U.S. citizens.

McNutt in turn established study committees to develop a remedial plan as fast as possible. A research group under McNutt, headed by Lydia J. Roberts (1879–1965), a prominent home economist with the University of Chicago, reviewed the number of calories and amounts of protein and other nutrients needed by people of different ages. From this data they developed a table of recommended daily allowances of basic nutrients and suggested that a healthy eating program could come from following this information.

The president accepted this approach and, on September 3, 1941, announced the creation of the Office of Health Defense and Welfare to be directed by McNutt, who, when interviewed by the *New York Times,* stated that his appointment amounted to "a reorganization so as to use the RDA table for 'putting more teeth' in health, welfare, educational, nutritional and recreational activities." But many women, the primary cooks in most American households, reported confusion when trying to determine which foods had which nutrients and how to guarantee all meals to be healthy. To clarify the information and ease their frustration, the Food and Nutrition Board (FNB), operating under the Office of Health Defense and Welfare, organized the material into a table with eight food rules.

By 1943, these rules had been pared down to seven numbered and named groups, with all items in each category containing the same nutrients. Illustrated in a circle as slices of pie, this diagram became known as the Basic Seven, and it encouraged users to strive to eat something from each group every day: (1) leafy, green, and yellow vegetables; (2) citrus fruit, tomatoes, raw cabbage; (3) potatoes and other vegetables and fruits; (4) milk, cheese, ice cream; (5) meat, poultry, fish, eggs, dried peas, beans; (6) bread, flour, cereals—whole grain, enriched, or restored; and (7) butter and fortified margarine.

The Office of Health Defense and Welfare officially launched a national nutrition campaign with the release of a poster offering the slogan "America Needs You Strong" and a list of the Basic Seven. With the hope of encouraging participation by defense workers, nonworking women, and children, **posters** and pamphlets became a primary educational tool.

Artists with the Works Projects Administration (a New Deal agency that operated until 1943) at local and state levels quickly developed additional posters that outlined what to eat every day, along with menus. Schools displayed posters that promoted good eating habits for children, and Lydia Roberts published a well-received booklet titled *The Road to Good Nutrition* (May 1942). It sold for 15 cents (approximately $2 in 2008 dollars) and describes the meals children should eat from earliest infancy to maturity. In 1946, Congress passed the National School Lunch Act that requires school-provided meals to be nutritionally balanced with minimum amounts from the seven food groups.

In addition to posters and printed materials, McNutt and his staff, through conferences, letters, and announcements, contacted health professionals such as physicians and nutritionists, as well as executives in the food industry, for assistance. In many communities, nutritionists responded by offering classes and materials for both housewives and industrial workers that promoted foods that guaranteed nutritious meals and snacks. They also provided specific menus that came from the Basic Seven. An example for a "dinner pail meal" (meals taken by defense workers in a lunch box to their jobs) included milk or creamed soup made of vegetables, coleslaw, potato salad, sandwiches made of whole wheat bread and sliced meatloaf, peanut butter and crackers, a piece of fruit, and oatmeal cookies.

The FNB asked industries to be mindful of the nutrition level of the food served in their cafeterias and encouraged those processing food to use the government's system that would show endorsements on those particular items that met nutritious standards. A logo similar to *Good Housekeeping*'s Seal of Approval shows Uncle Sam holding a forkful of food to his mouth with the slogan, "U.S. Needs US Strong, Eat Nutritional Food"; it could be displayed on products that measured up to government standards.

The War Activities Committee of the Motion Picture Industry produced brief films as educational tools. *Food and Magic* (1943), *America's Hidden Weapon* (1944), and *Something You Didn't Eat* (1945) deal with food conservation and healthy eating. Metropolitan Life Insurance, in cooperation with the U.S. Public Health Service, made a short color motion picture titled *Proof of the Pudding,* another attempt to educate the public about the importance of regularly eating from the Basic Seven. The agency encouraged community groups and movie theaters to show these films.

Recipes in cookbooks, pamphlets, **magazines,** and **newspapers** promoted food for fitness and greatly affected what appeared on American tables. Articles illustrated and explained the Basic Seven alongside menu ideas that included at least one food from each of the groups for each day of the week. Illustrative pieces in the *New York Times* food column included "Grocers Being Taught How to Help Housewife Make Purchases" (March 24, 1941), "Budgeting Our Seven Basic Foods" (October 3, 1943), and "Well-Balanced Diet Makes Use Each Day of One Item from Each of 7 Basic Groups" (February 5, 1944). Likewise, ads for various foods indicated their placement in the Basic Seven and the value of their consumption.

Along with the nutrition campaign, governmental officials, health professionals, and leaders in the food industry debated the merits of injecting vitamins into commercial foods and offered a new slogan: "Vitamins Vital for Victory." Popular possibilities included vitamin A added to margarine, lard, vegetable oils, and butter and vitamin D added to milk. Conversations about and interest in the importance of vitamins had occurred during the 1930s, when a laboratory synthesis of vitamins permitted their incorporation in pills sold on the shelves of **grocery stores and supermarkets.**

In late 1942, the American Medical Association (AMA), a major opponent of injecting vitamins into foods, agreed to an infusion in flour and milk but no other foods, and a government mandate in January 1943 resulted in about 75 percent of the nation's bread being made with enriched flour, which meant the addition of calcium, iron, niacin, riboflavin, and thiamin. As a sidelight, this mandate also included a ban on the selling of sliced bread, because defense industries needed the metal used in manufacturing the slicing machines. Some authorities insisted that a whole loaf of bread lasted longer than a sliced one and cut down on waste, an important practice during the war and another reason for the regulation. But housewives voiced loud dissatisfaction when they discovered that poor slicing techniques caused increased waste. This, along with numerous complaints from bakers and restaurant owners, influenced Secretary of Agriculture Claude R. Wickard (1893–1967) to rescind the ban on March 8, 1943, just two months after its inception.

The various approaches tried during the early 1940s to improve eating habits and the health of Americans had only a small impact on the diet of those on the home front. A different story existed in the military. In 1941, the army developed a master list of menus of nutritious meals to be served to all soldiers no matter where in the world they were stationed, and in fact U.S. soldiers did eat well. Dehydration and freezing facilities in the United States produced dried vegetables, fruits, juices, milk, powdered eggs, and meat for the armed forces' K rations. These consisted of ready-to-eat, balanced meals for a day that could fit in a soldier's pocket and received their name from physiologist Ancel Benjamin Keys (1904–2004), the person responsible for developing them. The army also created D (for dry) rations for emergencies and C (for combat) rations. Such products became available back home only after the conclusion of the war. The military's adherence to the Basic Seven and the specially preserved foods, along with supplies available because of rationing on the home front, enabled the U.S. military to have the best-fed soldiers in the war.

Once the United States officially entered World War II, the country faced runaway prices and shortages of a variety of products. Some food scarcity, however, occurred before the attack on Pearl Harbor, when, in the spring of 1941, spices such as sage from Greece and Yugoslavia, thyme from France, paprika from Hungary and Spain, and saffron from Spain nearly vanished from grocers' shelves. As the war progressed, more serious items disappeared from markets, causing Americans to decrease their consumption of sugar, coffee, butter, cheese, canned goods, and meat. These conditions changed the specific foods Americans ate far more than the information about the Basic Seven and vitamins but did not significantly alter the three-meals-a-day pattern.

Similar to meals in the previous decade, breakfast tended to be juice, cereal, and toast, but now with enriched bread and no eggs and bacon. An alternate possibility consisted of fruit such as applesauce and pancakes or waffles with syrup. For lunch, most Americans consumed soup and/or salad, a sandwich, or just bread, and fruit; they ended the day with a dinner of a meal-in-one-dish such as meatball stew or tuna casserole with bread and pudding for dessert. A carryover from the 1930s included a meat (not a choice cut) and vegetables from their victory gardens or, in winter, vegetables that had been canned during the peak of summer growth. These meals concluded with a sugarless dessert or something that had been sweetened with honey, molasses, or maple or corn syrup.

The government instituted a wartime system of price controls and rationing of consumer goods in January 1942. April saw sugar as the first table item to be placed on the ration list, followed by coffee in November; meat from the butcher, as well as canned products—meat, fish, milk, fruit, vegetables, jams, and jellies—in 1943. With the scarcity of canned foods, the frozen food industry, led by Birds Eye, boomed. During the first year of canned goods rationing, 140 companies provided households with 60 kinds of frozen food.

Shortages of many nonrationed foods also periodically occurred, often caused by a lack of **transportation** or storage problems. In 1942, a shopper could find lots of apples but no citrus fruit. The next year saw a brief decrease in the egg supply followed in the winter with no onions. By spring 1944, an oversupply of eggs had home economists searching for new ways to use them, and the only way to get string beans, a scarcity item at the time, was to also load up on onions, a product now readily available.

Hearty meat dishes had ranked high among the favorite foods for many Americans before the war. This commodity became one of the most heavily rationed foods during the conflict but still allowed roughly 5-1/2 ounces for each person per day, an adequate amount. The sacrifice came not with giving up red meats but doing without expensive choice cuts.

At the time, less desirable ground beef required fewer ration stamps than steaks and roasts and frequently appeared on plates as hamburgers, meat loaf, pinwheel meat rolls, baked meat loaf potatoes, or beef casserole or stew. Those desiring to appear more sophisticated served stuffed meat loaf featuring a line of hard-boiled eggs baked in the middle of the loaf, or meat loaf covered with mashed potatoes, or an emergency steak—ground beef shaped to resemble a steak with a cooked carrot inserted to represent the bone. Despite having food on the table every day, a fear of scarcity caused some anxious citizens to hoard and others to resort to buying from the **black market,** operations largely confined to beef partly because of Americans' love for this product and a willingness to pay whatever the price, even in an activity viewed as unpatriotic.

Those who decided to remain legal with their shopping had many sources of help in solving food challenges they might be facing. First, various publications offered specific recommendations, such as weekly menus should be prepared alongside a list of the Basic Seven chart, the family's available points, and food budget. Information also covered how to conserve, not waste, and recipes emphasized how to use leftovers effectively and stretch both rationed and nonrationed foods to their maximum.

A cook could easily find a number of articles with creative ways to make do with less—sugarless cookies, eggless cakes, and meatless meals. Wartime menus intentionally included recipes for foods that required the smallest number of ration stamps and highlighted items not on the ration lists such as oatmeal, unbuttered sweet rolls bought at the bakery, vegetable soup with cottage cheese and tomato sandwiches, chicken giblets and mushroom gravy, brown rice, and maple custard. Hints on how to stretch various items included adding honey to butter when used as a spread, whipping together equal amounts of butter and margarine, and preparing one-dish meals with a lot of macaroni, potatoes, or rice and a little beef added to vegetables and other ingredients as a flavoring,

Cookbooks likewise emphasized the centrality of the kitchen and food to both the home and winning the war. The vegetable sections of popular cookbooks increased in size while some publishers quickly offered specialty volumes and pamphlets on salads and vegetables. Betty Crocker's wartime publication by General Mills, *Your Share: How to Prepare Appetizing, Healthful Meals with Foods Available Today* (1943), along with a wartime pamphlet from the National Livestock and Meat Board, provided helpful recipes, including some that dealt with the preparation of less appealing cuts of meat, such as French Fried Liver, Creole Kidney, and Jellied Tongue.

In a similar vein, a January 11, 1943, article in *Life* magazine on "How to Prepare Variety Meats" offered suggestions for attractive ways to serve pigs' feet and ears, oxtails, and beef hearts, along with graphic pictures, so no one would mistake these cuts in the butcher's showcase. For some, frankfurters, stretched with fillers of soybeans, potatoes, or cracker meal, were preferable to horse meat, muskrat, rabbit, hog jowls, lamb necks, sweetbreads (the pancreas, usually of a young calf or lamb), and tripe (the lining of a cow's stomach).

Spam, a Hormel Food Corporation product named for its combination of "spicy ham," first appeared on grocery shelves in 1937. During the war, as a nonrationed, easily transportable meat product high in fat and salt, and boasting an indefinite shelf life, Spam gained popularity, both on the home front and abroad with the U.S. military and its Allies. Creativity abounded in different ways to serve Spam, ranging from a simple sandwich to an entrée with spaghetti.

After the war, the company established the Hormel Girls, a troupe of 12 musically talented women who came from all branches of the armed forces. They traveled across the country from 1946 to 1953, serving as door-to-door salespeople and as a performing musical group along the way. With their growing popularity, the organization expanded into a 60-piece aggregation, and network **radio** broadcast a weekly "Hormel Girls' Band and Chorus" during those years. Spam continued as a best-selling meat product into the postwar years, a position it retains today.

A cheap white-colored fat called margarine had appeared on the market as an import from France at the end of the 19th century. Considered by the dairy industry as too much of a competitor for butter, margarine had been heavily taxed and prohibited from having the characteristic yellow appearance of real butter. With the rationing of butter, margarine gained in popularity, and some states repealed the tax. Manufacturers even provided a separate packet of yellow dye that consumers kneaded into margarine once purchased—an important 1940s chore for children. Shortly after the war, the courts relaxed restrictions on yellow margarine, which meant consumers could purchase it already colored.

An anticipated return to a peacetime lifestyle without shortages and rationing did not immediately occur. Black markets continued to flourish as sugar, butter, and the better cuts of meat remained on ration lists. Severe shortages of food in Europe and other parts of the world grew at the same time as Americans cried for a cessation of rationing, especially on meat. Life without restrictions was on the upswing in the United States, and people generally did not give much thought about conditions in the rest of the world.

In November 1945, the U.S. government acknowledged pressure from all fronts at home and relented by removing all ration mandates except for sugar, followed by a lifting of meat price controls in July 1946. This action put more meat in grocery stores, but demand continued to increase from a large number of citizens who had money to spend; the average cost of meats rose by some 70 percent in just two months. Thus, a reinstatement of price controls on this item occurred on September 1, 1946. A meat-crazed market protested vehemently, and, by October 14, the controls were lifted again. At the same time, in order to send much-needed wheat overseas, Americans were urged to make the small sacrifice of voluntarily forgoing three slices of bread and one tablespoon of fat per day.

The situation abroad remained serious, and, in hopes of sending more aid, **President Harry S. Truman** (1884–1972) requested that no meat be eaten on Tuesdays and no poultry and eggs on Thursday, that everyone decrease daily bread consumption by at least one additional slice, and that **restaurants** serve bread and butter only on request. Many reported compliance to these various steps, but statistics indicated otherwise. Continued demand for meat brought about another price increase in 1948, and many people had to return to eating cheaper cuts. This created a new meat fad for Swiss steak, easily cooked on Reynolds Wrap, a new aluminum foil product from Reynolds Metal Company. Ads proposed preparation as a meal-in-one—just cook the steak along with frozen vegetables and potatoes on foil in a pan in the oven or on the grill. Then for after-serving ease of cleanup, just throw the foil away.

As the country changed from wartime production to a more balanced state of supply and demand, Americans moved into an environment of technological advancement and sustained economic growth. Prosperity appeared in many ways, offering an American dream of a new home in the suburbs with new appliances and a new car in the carport. Pantries and attics now held the unused canning jars and pressure cookers as housewives returned to the grocery store and supermarkets for food shopping and happily purchased the convenience products that soon became available.

The final lifting of the rationing of meat and a stabilization of costs ended with an almost manic rush to purchase and devour meat, especially beef roasts and thick T-bone and porterhouse steaks. Hamburgers and hot dogs reigned as popular economical meals and the preferred fare at the growing number of fast-food eateries.

Meat at home, whatever the cut, often seemed to demand outdoor cooking. Outside the house, victory gardens became lawns, while flower beds adorned the outdoor patio, the latter frequently outfitted with a fireplace or a grill. Barbecues had gained some popularity in the late 1930s and then boomed in the postwar era. Kingsford charcoal had provided the necessary fuel since the 1920s, and James Beard (1903–1985), a rising chef and food writer, stimulated interest with his 1941 publication of *Cook It Outdoors*. Ads for portable grills and special grills with spits appeared in newspapers before the April 1943 rationing of meat, and products such as Coca-Cola and various beers were linked to the enjoyment of outdoor cooking and dining.

The kinds of grills available after the war broadened, as seen in a June 1947 ad for Macy's department store in New York City; it contains descriptions of five kinds of grills ranging in price from $2.29 to $55.75 (approximately $22 to $538 in 2008 dollars) as well as other items—stainless steel cutlery, hot dog salt and pepper sets, ice cream freezers, wire popcorn poppers, plastic plates with nested cups—all designed to add to the festivities.

During the war and after, a number of innovations assisted cooks. Many recipes called for the use of herbs and spices instead of butter as flavoring. Spice Islands, a distributor of seasonings, in 1941 introduced a line of herbs, spices, and wine vinegars much needed for wartime cooking. With periodic shortages of eggs, new breakfast foods such as Cheerios (introduced in 1941 as Cheerioats; the name changed in 1946) and Kellogg's Raisin Bran became available. Other new products included Dannon yogurt, Sunbeam bread, and Maytag blue cheese.

Much of the research that preceded production of these new food items occurred in an attempt to enhance the quality and supply of food sent to fighting troops abroad. In late 1945, filled with a yen for good living, American shoppers found an array of new products, particularly convenience foods, on the market: frozen concentrated orange and grapefruit juice, instant mashed potatoes, Ragu spaghetti sauce, Kraft single slices of cheese, Pace Foods picante sauce, Mrs. Paul's frozen deviled crabs, Pet-Ritz foods, self-rising cornmeal, Nesquik chocolate flavoring for milk, V8 vegetable juice, Maxwell House instant coffee, and easy-to-prepare breads and desserts, to name but a few. A Maxwell House advertisement that reads, "For People Who Like Good Things The Easy Way," indicates postwar attitudes.

Other breakthroughs addressed packaging issues and the preparation of food. In 1940, the A&P Grocery chain sold cellophane-wrapped meat, which introduced pre-wrapped cuts available from a self-service case. Roy J. Plunkett (1910–1994) received a patent for Teflon in 1941, the same year that saw the introduction of garbage disposers. Earl Tupper (1907–1983) started working on Tupperware objects in the early days of the decade, and, in 1947, *House Beautiful* featured these clever, airtight kitchen containers obtainable by mail order. Just before the decade ended, electric dishwashers became widely available for purchase.

Throughout the 1940s, entertaining around food remained an important part of American life. Cocktail parties, popular before the country entered the hostilities, continued during the conflict and afterward. James Beard's first book, *Hors d'Oeuvres and Canapés* (1940), offered recipes for strongly flavored finger food and classic drinks, including America's favorite at the time, the martini. Once at war, the media offered strategies for working within the rationing and shortages limitations. A progressive dinner party allowed each household to serve one course and not strain its ration books too much. Magazines such as *Good Housekeeping* published articles that emphasized that, even with rationing and loved ones away at war, holiday meals could be joyful and nutritious. Families frequently invited soldiers or sailors from neighboring camps or on leave to join them for the festivities, and they packed nonperishable items, such as Kellogg's Rice Krispies Marshmallow Treats, first advertised in 1940, to send to family members not able to attend. Wartime weddings also meant a time for celebration and at least light refreshments.

Victory certainly called for a party; in fact, many parties were held from the time of Germany's surrender in May 1945 until the Japanese capitulation in August 1945. Postwar prosperity and the excitement of building a new home gave rise to barbecue parties that celebrated groundbreaking at the building site. Guests brought their own meat, and the hosts offered the grill, along with side dishes, iced tea, and coffee.

When the veterans came home, they brought with them the experience of eating not individualized regional or ethnic foods but a standard, basic, well-balanced menu. Busy wives of returning servicemen had learned to cook quick and easy dishes from magazines and newspapers and now preferred time-saving products instead of recreating their mothers' favorite recipes from scratch. A country that had held on to regional eating preferences now saw many moving to a national American style.

But servicemen and -women also brought back to the United States an exposure to the foods of the countries where they had been stationed. An interest in gourmet dining, which meant foreign dishes, had been developing among some since the 1930s, especially with the New York World's Fair in 1939–1940 offering visitors samplings of the foods of the world. *Gourmet* magazine, first published in 1941, presented enticing articles and recipes for those interested in this kind of eating. James Beard published *The Fireside Cook Book* in 1949; it offered recipes with a gourmet slant.

Other avenues of popular culture also made references to food. CBS (Columbia Broadcasting System) radio in 1945 offered print copies of *The Cookbook of the Stars;* it featured many recipes, such as Edward R. Murrow's Oatmeal Scones and George Burns and Gracie Allen's Lamb Terrapin. In addition, the networks and their affiliates broadcast numerous programs that included cooking and household hints, and most enjoyed long radio lives. For example *Betty Crocker* ran from 1924 to 1953, *Women's Exchange* from 1928 to 1942, John MacPherson's (1877–1962) *The Mystery Chef* from 1930 to 1948, *The Mary Lee Taylor Program* from 1933 to 1954, and *Neighbor Nell* from 1934 to 1943.

Biologist **Alfred C. Kinsey** (1894–1956) published *Edible Wild Plants of Eastern North America* in 1943, although he undoubtedly became better known for his 1948 publication, *Sexual Behavior in the Human Male*. United Fruit Company created a long-running hit, "Chiquita Banana," both as a song and advertising jingle in 1944. Sylvester the Cat first tried to have Tweety Bird for lunch in a 1947 Warner Bros. cartoon. Singer Kate Smith (1907–1986) aired two network shows on radio during the 1940s. One, *Kate Smith Speaks* (1939–1951), could be heard weekdays at noon. The show featured a news and commentary format and was considered to be a big morale booster for women on the home front. They seemed to especially enjoy her talking about favorite recipes for a variety of cakes, particularly the rich chocolate ones given in the second half of the decade when everyone rushed to indulge in everything that had been missing during the war.

The 1940s served as a bridge between the 1930s and 1950s. Consumer buying power was virtually nonexistent during the Great Depression and severely curtailed throughout World War II. With victory and the lifting of rationing and price controls, the story changed. Americans embarked on a spending spree. In reference to the food they ate, 22 percent of their cash income went for food in 1941; by the early 1950s, it had jumped to 26 percent. For comparison, in 2005, it had fallen to roughly 13 percent (does not include dining out).

During World War II, a large number of Americans grew their own fruits and vegetables; some even raised livestock or owned or co-owned a cow. They canned, preserved, and conserved, using everything in some way. The table did not always contain choice cuts and the eaters' preferences, but no one went hungry. The postwar years contrasted sharply by serving abundant amounts of good food, frequently with built-in convenience and new dishes, a trend that has continued ever since.

See also: Beverages; Desserts, Candy, and Ice Cream; Frozen Foods; Health and Medicine; Leisure and Recreation; Radio Programming: Educational Shows; Technology

Selected Reading
Hayes, Joanne Lamb. *Grandma's Wartime Kitchen*. New York: St. Martin's Press, 2000.
Hooker, Richard J. *Food and Drink in America: A History*. Indianapolis: Bobbs-Merrill, 1981.

Levenstein, Harvey. *Paradox of Plenty: A Social History of Eating in Modern America.* New York: Oxford University Press, 1993.

National Nutrition Campaign. *New York Times,* March 24, 1941; September 4, 1941; December 8, 1941; April 5, 1942; May 25, 1942; January 11, 1943; October 3, 1943; November 19, 1943; February 5, 1944; October 6, 1944; May 13, 1945; June 1, 1947; August 20, 1947. www.proquest.com.

FOOTBALL

With the onset of World War II and discussions of how life would change because of the conflict, debate about the merits of football took on new significance, especially its role at the college level, the most popular version of the sport. Articles in the *New York Times* in 1941 and 1942 expressed a commonly held belief that a combative sport such as football served as excellent preparation for fighting. Many writers stated that football places a premium on personal contact, aggressiveness, and quick thinking, and it therefore provides qualities needed by men serving in the armed forces; the game should occupy an important place in educational institutions and community recreational programs.

Colleges responded by emphasizing the sport, although by 1944, many could no longer field full teams because of the large numbers of college age men fighting in the war. The United States Military Academy at West Point, New York, and the United States Naval Academy in Annapolis, Maryland, were exceptions. Providing both a college education and training for soldiers and sailors, they easily attracted talented athletes and during the war stood out as strong football institutions. Each year, the nation eagerly awaited the two schools' annual post-Thanksgiving football contest.

Nevertheless, throughout the 1940s, football as a popular spectator sport lagged behind **baseball.** The collegiate version of the game, which can be traced to 1869, drew larger crowds than the slightly younger professional format, which began in 1892. The payment of money to a player in a contest between the Allegheny Athletic Association and the Pittsburgh Athletic Club constituted the first professional football game.

Collegiate football. Throughout the 1940s, Americans true to their alma mater, along with those who simply liked watching football, flocked to college games. Fans unable to cheer on their favorites in person could sometimes listen to a game in the comfort of their homes thanks to **radio** remote capabilities. Whether shivering in the stadium on a fall afternoon or at home in their favorite easy chair listening to a broadcast of the play-by-play, they applauded their favorite school on to victory hoping for enough wins to allow the team to play in one of five annual college bowl games—Orange, Sugar, Rose, Sun, or Cotton.

Following the attack on Pearl Harbor on December 7, 1941, the U.S. Army, citing security concerns, canceled all large gatherings, especially on the West Coast. This action caused the oldest college championship game, the Rose Bowl, to be moved out of Pasadena, California, for the only time in its history. The two teams scheduled for this January 1, 1942, contest, Duke University and Oregon State, agreed to meet in Durham, North Carolina, where the undefeated Duke Blue Devils lost 20–16 to Oregon's Beavers. Likewise, a December 1941 professional football game between the Chicago Bears and a National Football League All-Stars team switched from Los Angeles to the Polo Grounds in New York. By 1943, the army had relented on these kinds of restrictions, and the Rose Bowl returned to Pasadena.

In addition to striving to play in a bowl game, college teams and fans hoped that one of their team members would be selected to receive the Heisman Memorial Trophy, an annual presentation to the nation's outstanding college football player. Established by the Downtown Athletic Club of New York City in 1935, a poll of sportswriters and sportscasters made the determination. In 1936, the National Collegiate Athletic Association (NCAA)—founded in 1906 to set rules to govern the game so as to be safer—added a second distinction, an award to what they called the national college champion as determined by press association polls of writers and coaches.

Based on the winners of these two awards, 10 players and 7 collegiate teams, as shown in the tables below, stand out as the best during the 1940s. Notre Dame dominated by being recognized as the national football champion for four years of the decade, while three of its players received the Heisman Trophy. Army and Minnesota followed close behind. In 1944 and 1945, the army won the title of national football champion, while members of its team took home the Heisman. Players from Michigan, Georgia, Ohio State, and Southern Methodist received the Heisman trophy, and Minnesota, Ohio State, and Michigan completed the ranks on being named the national champion.

TABLE 54. Heisman Trophy Winners, 1940–1949

Year	Heisman Trophy Recipient	Team
1940	Tom Harmon (1919–1990)	Michigan
1941	Bruce Smith (1920–1967)	Minnesota
1942	Frank Sinkwich (1920–1990)	Georgia
1943	Angelo Bertelli (1921–1999)	Notre Dame
1944	Les Horvath (1921–1995)	Ohio State
1945	Doc Blanchard (b. 1924)	Army
1946	Glenn Davis (1924–2005)	Army
1947	John Lujack (b. 1925)	Notre Dame
1948	Doak Walker (1927–1998)	Southern Methodist
1949	Leon Hart (1928–2002)	Notre Dame

Source: www.heisman.com/winners/hsmn-winners.html

TABLE 55. Teams Declared National College Football Champions, 1940–1949

Year	Team
1940	Minnesota
1941	Minnesota
1942	Ohio State
1943	Notre Dame
1944	Army
1945	Army
1946	Notre Dame
1947	Notre Dame
1948	Michigan
1949	Notre Dame

Source: www.infoplease.com/ipsa/A0908943.html

During the first half of the 1940s, all of the players winning the Heisman Trophy went on from college to serve in a branch of the armed forces. For the decade as a whole, with the exception of 1945 winner Doc Blanchard (1924–2009), 9 played professional football and all 10 eventually won election to the College Football Hall of Fame. Established in 1951, in South Bend, Indiana, it honors outstanding college players.

In the late 1930s, fledging **television** stations tested various broadcast venues; the first televised college football game took place on September 30, 1939, a contest between Fordham University and Waynesburg College. NBC (National Broadcasting Company) transmitted the game to a limited audience within a 50-mile radius of New York City.

Coaches and college administrators for some time voiced concern that any sport activities transmitted by a mass medium would lower attendance and thus approached televised games with caution. By the 1940 season, however, television had moved from an experimental phase to a commercial entity, and Philco, a manufacturer of both radios and televisions, on October 5, 1940, sponsored the first college game under this new status, a contest between the University of Maryland Terrapins and the University of Pennsylvania Quakers.

The postwar years saw both college and professional teams becoming more and more receptive to being televised, especially as they realized any financial gains that might accrue from the airing of games. In 1948, the first Rose Bowl was telecast in Los Angeles, and, by 1950, a small number of the more prominent colleges that offered football had entered into contracts with networks to show their games.

Professional football. Following the historic Pittsburgh and Allegheny game of 1892 in Pennsylvania, football contests featuring paid players spread to small towns and eventually to large cities, primarily in the Midwest. The professional version of the sport tended to be a game with no player protection, so severe injuries such as broken bones and even death were always a possibility. In addition, underhanded deals and straight out stealing of other teams' players emerged as a problem.

In an attempt to bring structure and order to professional football, interested businessmen and promoters organized the American Professional Football Association in 1920 with an initial membership of seven teams—Canton, Cleveland, Akron, and Dayton, Ohio; Buffalo and Rochester, New York; and New York City. The group soon thereafter changed its name to the American Professional Football League and, by 1922, had acquired its current name, the National Football League (NFL).

In 1933, the NFL divided its teams into two groups—the Eastern and Western Divisions—nomenclature that remained in place until 1949. They then changed to the American and National Conferences. The NFL, also in 1933, initiated the recognition of an annual champion from a postseason playoff that pitted the top team from each division. In 1936, the first NFL annual draft of college players took place, bringing a new pool of players to pro football.

Six teams won the NFL championship during the 1940s. As seen in Table 56, the Chicago Bears dominated with five appearances, including four straight times for 1940 to 1943. The Washington Redskins played four years but won only once, while the Philadelphia Eagles made it to the championship game three times and achieved two victories. The Chicago Cardinals and the Cleveland Rams managed one win out of two

TABLE 56.   NFL Championships, 1940–1949

Season	Winning Team	Losing Team
1940	Chicago Bears	Washington Redskins
1941	Chicago Bears	New York Giants
1942	Washington Redskins	Chicago Bears
1943	Chicago Bears	Washington Redskins
1944	Green Bay Packers	New York Giants
1945	Cleveland Rams	Washington Redskins
1946	Chicago Bears	New York Giants
1947	Chicago Cardinals	Philadelphia Eagles
1948	Philadelphia Eagles	Chicago Cardinals
1949	Philadelphia Eagles	Los Angeles Rams

Source: www.4nflpicks.com/NFL%20Championship%20Games.html

appearances, and the Green Bay Packers won the only time they played. The only team always to be in the losing column, the New York Giants nonetheless made the playoffs in three tries.

National radio had set the stage for the airing of a championship game back in 1934, when it broadcast a professional football game between the Detroit Lions and Chicago Bears on Thanksgiving Day. Ninety-four stations across the country had signed up for the game, creating a financial success. The radio industry took note and began to expand its coverage so that, by 1940, most NFL teams had their own radio outlet. **MBS (Mutual Broadcasting System)** broadcast the Chicago Bears' 73–0 victory over the Washington Redskins on December 8, 1940, an event that enhanced the popularity of the sport and interest in the annual championship game.

A quiet media event on October 22, 1939, eventually had an even greater impact on the success of the NFL. On that day, a small crowd of about 13,000 fans had gathered for a game between the now defunct Brooklyn Dodgers and the Philadelphia Eagles, while an estimated 1,000 TV sets in New York City enabled an untold number of viewers to watch the first televised broadcast of a professional football game by NBC. Eventually, it would be the power of television that would push professional football to the status it holds today.

Before it enjoyed success, however, pro football had to weather the storm created by World War II. Attendance initially dropped in 1942 as Americans living on rationed gas stayed close to home for **leisure and recreation.** The next year, fans seeking distraction from the war turned out in larger numbers. The draft and voluntary enlistments, however, drained the rosters of both players and team staffs, causing the Cleveland Rams to suspend operations for the 1943 season, while teams in Philadelphia and Pittsburgh merged. Some other one-year adjustments occurred during the war, but the league held on, offering some games every year of the war, as well as continuing its championship game.

With the end of the war and the return of servicemen again desirous to play pro football, recruitment improved. The requirement of wearing helmets increased safety.

Rule changes and innovations such as the T formation meant a faster-paced, higher-scoring game, conditions that appealed to many spectators; attendance at games began to rival that at college games.

In 1946, the NFL faced a new problem, the formation of the All-America Football Conference (AAFC). The existence of two pro football leagues created fierce competition for the best players, a situation that necessitated higher salaries and a more costly sport. The AAFC, like the NFL, divided itself into two divisions, Eastern and Western, and offered an annual championship game. As a newcomer, the conference faced more difficulties than its well-established rival and, by 1949, had folded.

But competition and media coverage can be good for business, and soon pro football began to rival the college game for both attendance and fan enthusiasm. A 1945 NFL decision to expand beyond its original Eastern and Midwestern regions resulted in the Cleveland Rams locating in Los Angeles as the first big-league franchise on the West Coast, a move that exposed more Americans to the pro version of the game. In 1950, the NFL accepted three teams from the defunct AAFC, bringing the total to 13 clubs and more games in more cities.

Both collegiate and professional football had its ups and downs throughout the 1940s. One measurement of the popularity of any facet of American life is its inclusion, or lack thereof, in Hollywood motion pictures. Although football received a reasonable amount of exposure during the 1930s, it fell off as a subject during the 1940s. An animated short by Walt Disney Productions titled *How to Play Football* (1944), a Pete Smith (1892–1979) *Football Thrills of 1944* (1945), another animated short by Terrytoons, *Peace Time Football* (1946), and a full-length movie, *Father Was a Fullback* (1949) starring Fred MacMurray (1908–1991) and Maureen O'Hara (b. 1920) comprise a short list of football fare both during World War II and the postwar years.

During most of the decade, television waited in the wings, hoping its moment would come. By the late 1940s, more people had acquired more receivers, and the networks and independent stations increased their telecasts of games. Football, especially pro football, slowly earned its place as a major sport during the 1950s.

See also: Movies; Radio Programming: News, Sports, Public Affairs, and Talk

Selected Reading
Football. *New York Times,* December 31, 1941; July 28, 1942. www.proquest.com
Peterson, Robert. *Pigskin, the Early Years of Pro Football.* New York: Oxford University Press, 1997.
Rader, Benjamin G. *American Sports, From the Age of Folk Games to the Age of Spectators.* Englewood Cliffs: Prentice Hall, 1983.

FROZEN FOODS

In the early 1920s, Clarence Birdseye (1886–1956) received a patent for a method to flash-freeze **food.** He then founded the General Seafoods Company and worked with the DuPont Chemical Company to develop wrapping that allowed foods to be frozen quickly. He also desired packaging that did not disintegrate as the food thawed. DuPont's moisture-proof cellophane fit both needs. General Seafoods became a part of the General Foods Corporation in 1929, and the following year, under the brand name of Birds Eye, 27 kinds of frozen products including fruits, vegetables, fish, and meats appeared in a test market of 18 stores in Springfield, Massachusetts.

Birds Eye frozen foods soon became available in other areas of the country, but sales during most of the 1930s remained low for two reasons: first, consumers showed only moderate interest in a product that was often tasteless and soggy; second, home refrigerators and ice boxes did not contain a space with temperatures low enough to keep a package frozen. The food had to be eaten the day of purchase. General Foods nevertheless predicted eventual success for its Birds Eye division and engaged in a wide range and variety of **advertising** and marketing approaches, culminating with its hosting the only frozen food exhibit at the 1939 New York World's Fair.

The entrance of the United States into World War II immediately changed the focus of American manufacturing facilities from turning out products for consumers at home to assembling supplies for the troops. For example, two days after the attack by the Japanese on Pearl Harbor, meatpackers in Chicago boned and froze 1 million pounds of meat to be shipped to military facilities. By 1943, the amount had reached 70 million pounds.

Supplies needed by the troops and scarcities at home steadily increased, putting frozen and canned fruits and vegetables on **rationing** lists in March 1943. Frozen food manufacturers immediately protested their inclusion and successfully convinced the government that their products qualified as essential to the war effort. Rationing boards removed this commodity from their lists, enabling some 140 companies such as Birds Eye, Honor Brand, Stokely-Van Camp, and Pratt to continue to provide both the military and the home market with their 60 varieties of frozen foods. For those at home, this meant the availability of products otherwise missing because of the rationing of canned goods. Suddenly, food shortages in some commodities made the purchase of frozen items both necessary and patriotic.

A major contribution toward the popularity and growth of the frozen food industry came from the wartime and postwar work of the National Research Center. Throughout the war, this organization experimented with ways to provide the military with easily transported foods. For example, in 1945, the center organized Florida Foods Corporation to find a way to produce a powder for making orange juice. But the war ended just as this work commenced, and the corporation's research immediately shifted to the commercial market with a focus not on a powder but on a frozen orange juice concentrate. They soon met with success and introduced Minute Maid frozen orange juice on April 15, 1946. Extensive advertising made this frozen product a top-selling item by the end of the decade.

With victory in hand and soldiers coming back home, the number of Americans with some familiarity with frozen food had increased. At the same time, improved refrigerator **technology**—including a specific space with the necessary low temperature for frozen foods—along with a drop in the price of this appliance put appropriate home storage units in more homes. The stage was set for the arrival of the frozen TV dinner.

Some report that this phenomenon started in 1944, a time before the wide popularity of **television,** with Maxson Food Systems, Inc., a company that manufactured the first complete frozen meal. It consisted of three parts: meat, vegetable, and potato, each nestled in its own special compartment. These frozen dinners, first called Sky Plates and later Strato Plates, were taken aboard airplanes, heated, and served to military and civilian passengers. Because of a lack of funding and the death of the founder of the company shortly after introducing this new line, the concept never hit larger retail markets.

A couple of years later, two other businesses attempted similar dinners. Jack Fisher's Fridgi-Dinners appeared in bars and taverns in a small geographic area, while Albert and Meyer Bernstein's (both active 1940s) Frozen Dinners first sold in a limited Pennsylvania area but eventually expanded to other eastern localities. The two brands reached limited markets, a factor that prevented national recognition and renown as the first official frozen dinner.

That honor goes to C. A. Swanson and Sons, a subsidiary of the Campbell Soup Company. In 1951, Swanson sold frozen turkey pot pies nationally and three years later enlarged the line to include turkey dinners in stamped aluminum trays divided into sections that held the meat with dressing, potatoes, and buttered peas, soon to be followed by roast beef, fried chicken, and ham glazed with raisin sauce. To reinforce the idea that the meal had been created to be eaten while watching television, Swanson designed the container to resemble a TV screen and coined the phrase "TV dinner." A massive advertising campaign, including leaflets with the government's 1943 Basic Seven nutritional chart, tied this product to healthy eating. These events secured success for both the product and the company, transforming frozen meals and other food items into standard fare in freezer containers in **grocery stores and supermarkets.**

The technological foundation of the frozen food industry had been laid in the 1930s and early 1940s. The postwar drive for prosperity produced rapid expansion and growth in many businesses. The success experienced by frozen foods, especially Swanson TV dinners, accompanied two growing postwar trends: fascination with the new medium of television and the lure of time-saving food products and modern appliances.

See also: Fast Food; Health and Medicine

Selected Reading
Bernstein, Leilan. "Birth of a Frozen Food Nation," *Los Angeles Times,* January 24, 2001. www.articles.latimes.com/2001/jan/24/food/fo-16097
Panati, Charles. *Panati's Parade of Fads, Follies, and Manias.* New York: HarperCollins, 1991.
TV Dinners. www.loc.gov/rr/scitech/mysteries/tvdinner.html

G

GAMES

Available leisure time increased during the 1930s, enabling many Americans to engage in a variety of nonwork activities, interests that continued in some fash throughout the 1940s. All ages played a variety of games; children especially enjoyed hide-and-seek, jacks, hopscotch, jump rope, tiddlywinks, and marbles. Following the 1941 attack on Pearl Harbor, people welcomed entertainment of just about any kind as a brief respite from worries and concerns about the war. With victory, Americans played games for the pure pleasure they offered.

National surveys showed card playing to be the favorite pastime during the war years. *Hobbies* magazine in 1942 reported that someone in the household played cards in over 87 percent of American homes and that, in 83 percent of those dwellings, the entire family gathered around a table to play card games. Among all the possible choices, bridge ranked as the most popular in the 1942 survey.

Charles H. Goren (1901–1991) had emerged from the 1930s as the nation's ultimate expert on the game. His 1936 book, *Winning Bridge Made Easy,* initiated a long list of his publications that sold well during the 1940s and beyond. The Goren titles covered a wide range of topics: *Better Bridge for Better Players: The Play of the Cards* (1942), *Contract Bridge Complete* (1942; revised editions in 1944 and 1947), *Standard Book of Play* (1942), *Standard Book of Bidding* (1944; revised in 1947), *Contract Bridge in a Nutshell* (1946; revised in 1947), and *Bridge Quiz Book* (1949). All these books, along with his long-running newspaper column, "Goren on Bridge," appealed to players at every level of expertise.

Bridge continued to hold first place among card players until 1947, when a completely unanticipated change took place. A poll by the American Institute of Public Opinion (more familiarly known as the Gallup Poll) in that year reported that only 56 percent of a national sample either regularly or occasionally played bridge—a huge, virtually overnight, drop. Canasta, an imported, rummylike card game for two or four players, had brought about this upheaval.

The name canasta comes from the Spanish word for basket and refers to a tray or basket used to hold both unused cards and discards. Developed in Uruguay and popularized in Argentina, canasta had a remarkable start and quickly became a fad. As interest in the game grew, **newspapers,** which already regularly carried columns about bridge, began to devote space to canasta. Reporting highlighted the publication of three nonfiction **best sellers** for 1949, Oswald Jacoby's (1902–1984) *How to Win at Canasta,* Ottilie Reilly's (1898–n.d.) *Canasta: The Argentine Rummy Game,* and Josefina Artayeta de Viel's (active 1940s) and Ralph Michael's (active 1940s) *The Official Rules and Play of Canasta.* Newspapers also kept the American public informed about celebrity players. On August 28, 1949, the *New York Times,* in a lengthy update on the game, announced that former President Herbert Hoover (1874–1964) "when recently traveling east from California spent a five-hour stop-over in Chicago playing and winning canasta games with friends at the Drake Hotel."

Easy to learn, canasta required only two regulation decks of cards plus jokers. Canasta clubs and canasta parties soon became commonplace. Plastic holders (the canasta basket itself), "official canasta mugs," as well as ashtrays and other canasta paraphernalia flooded the market. A peak in playing card sales, over 80 million decks, occurred at the end of the 1940s. The initial excitement over the game held well into the 1950s but, like all **fads,** died out by the 1960s. Millions continue to play canasta, but newer games have since come along and now outshine this humble South American import.

Along with their strong preference for cards, Americans also played time-tested board games such as chess, checkers, Monopoly, and Parcheesi. In 1940, Milton Bradley, a major manufacturer of a variety of games, released several new titles, including the Horse Racing Game, The Merry Game of Fibber McGee, and The Adventures of **Superman**. These games capitalized on current interests such as the Kentucky Derby, popular radio celebrities, and comic book figures. On a more educational level, the company's 1940 Game of the States focused on the country's products and resources and at the time served as an educational tool for teaching children about the states and their industries.

Parker Brothers, one of Milton Bradley's strongest competitors, in 1940 brought out innocuous games such as Citadel, a game of blocks called Hi-Lo, and reissued Pollyanna, a popular board game dating back to 1915. The company's hugely successful Monopoly continued to be a big seller. A little-known firm, Northwestern Products, sold Tactics: A Game of World Strategy, which allowed the players to suggest ways for addressing international problems. Jaymar chose a lighter approach with Snuffy Smith's Hootin' Holler Bug Derby board game, based on the daily comic strip then running in newspapers.

With the outbreak of World War II, producers of games attempted to stockpile materials they could use for future production and managed to continue to offer some of the old favorites, as well as introduce a very small number of new ones. Manufacturers of board games that required metal, rubber, or petroleum products had to search for other materials and frequently utilized wood and cardboard as substitutes. The best that the game industry could do during the war years was hope that its limited output would satisfy most demand. But these struggles did not prevent a show of patriotism; many placed a facsimile of a Victory stamp or the slogan "buy war bonds" on their game boxes to encourage purchasers to participate in efforts toward victory.

Thinking that timely themes would sell, Northwestern Products in 1943 issued a game called Victory Rummy. Employing a pack of 63 cards, players tried to obtain sequences of five cards consisting of three dots, a dash, and a V (...—V) all in one color, or five Axis cards. Five hundred points won the game. (The three dots and a dash make up V, or Victor, in Morse code and became a familiar theme for the Allies during the war; the first four notes of Beethoven's *Fifth Symphony,* composed in 1808, make this same progression and were widely used to symbolize victory.)

Jayline Manufacturing Company used a somewhat similar approach with its Ration Board Game (1943), which allowed children to play the role of the local board and ration items on the home front. The firm employed the slogan, "Fun You Can Hoard!" for a not particularly funny subject. Milton Bradley countered with an adaptation of its 1931 Battleship game, calling it Broadsides, The Game of Naval Strategy. It also manufactured Milton Bradley's Game Kit for Soldiers, a much-revised version of a product it first produced during the Civil War. It proved to be Milton Bradley's biggest wartime success, although its adaptation of Snakes and Ladders, a game that had originated in ancient India and deals with good versus evil, has successfully survived into the present. Renamed Chutes and Ladders, it focuses on good deeds and rewards, along with bad behavior and its consequences, teaching children right from wrong and good from bad.

Jigsaw puzzles experienced a golden age during the 1920s and early 1930s, waned slightly by 1940, and returned to a craze level during World War II. Because they were cut from cardboard or wood, manufacturers did not suffer from any shortages of materials. Offering images of military might along with more traditional imagery, jigsaw puzzles complemented the tremendous support for the war felt by Americans. They provided inexpensive home entertainment for many age groups during anxious times.

The Upson Company, with its beautiful Tuco puzzles, offered vivid battle scenes as well as patriotic images of Uncle Sam, the American flag, the Statue of Liberty, and Washington, DC, landmarks. Jaymar puzzles went the extra step with some of the pieces cut into war-related shapes such as bombs, jeeps, flags, and guns. Map puzzles that featured information about the progress of U.S. armed forces abroad appealed to a large number of people back home.

Immensely popular during the 1930s and 1940s, jigsaw puzzles provided inexpensive entertainment for everyone. This scene from Citizen Kane *(1941), depicts a bemused Kane (Orson Welles) observing his bored wife (played by Dorothy Comingore) assembling the pieces in Xanadu, their California castle. (RKO Radio Pictures Inc./Photofest)*

Jigsaw puzzles also benefited the troops. Shortly after the attack on Pearl Harbor, volunteer groups distributed jigsaw puzzles, books, and **magazines** to soldiers on **trains** as well as gave them to **USO (United Service Organizations)** clubs. Submariners even took puzzles on their missions. After 1945 and peace, puzzle makers continued carrying war-related themes, but they became general military ones instead of battles specific to World War II.

After World War II, popular wood jigsaw puzzles went into a decline since sharply rising wages made their time-consuming production costly. At the same time, improvements in lithography and die cutting allowed cardboard puzzles to be more attractive and cheaper to produce and buy.

By 1948, American life had regained some semblance of normality, and the Production & Marketing Company issued what would become one of the most popular board games of the 20th century, Scrabble. The game, first invented in 1931 by Alfred Mosher Butts (1899–1993), experienced little initial success. In 1947, James Brunot (1902–1984) gave Butts a small royalty for the game and obtained legal rights in 1948, when he changed its name from its original Lexico (also called Lexiko, and later Criss-Cross Words), to a name that he felt served as a description of the activity of the game, players "scrabbling" to fit words onto the board.

Scrabble can be played by two to four participants and utilizes single-letter wooden tiles to form words. The letters carry varying point values, and the player accumulating the highest number of points for words spelled wins. The game experienced only limited success throughout the later 1940s. Macy's Department Store in New York City placed Scrabble on its shelves in the early 1950s, and the firm of Selchow and Righter gained the license to market and distribute it in the United States and Canada. From then on, Scrabble enjoyed unprecedented success across the country and became a standard board game, just like Monopoly.

Minnesotan William Herbert Schaper (active 1940s) whittled an odd shape out of some scrap wood in 1948 and thus gave birth to the first Cootie, a combination toy and game. The word, originally from the Malay *kutu,* denoting a biting body louse, around World War I evolved into British naval slang meaning any parasitic, biting insect. From there the term passed into general usage and carried a similar meaning. Herb Schaper's design consisted of a body, a head, six legs, two eyes, two antennae, and a slender feeding organ. Together, these parts formed an insect; Schaper's game included enough body parts to construct four such creatures. A dice roll determines which part a player can acquire in an attempt to be the first to build a complete Cootie. Originally all carved by hand, the need for mass production made that approach impractical. In 1949, the inventor formed W. H. Schaper Game Company, based in Minneapolis, and the firm did so well that Milton Bradley acquired it in 1978.

Candy Land premiered in the late 1940s, gained popularity rapidly during the 1950s, and, along with Scrabble, went on to be identified in a list of most popular games of the last 100 years published by *Forbes* magazine in December 2005. Candy Land, designed in 1946 for young children by Eleanor Abbott (active 1940s) while recuperating from polio, utilizes a board with a winding, linear track made of 134 spaces of rainbow colors. Abbott submitted Candy Land to Milton Bradley Company, which manufactured and distributed it starting in 1949.

Clue, invented in 1944 as Cluedo by Anthony E. Pratt (1904–1994), first appeared in stores in England in 1948 under the aegis of Waddington's Games. Parker Brothers purchased the rights to distribute this whodunit board game in the United States. They changed Cluedo to Clue, and it made its American debut in 1949. Initially marketed as "the Great New Sherlock Holmes Game," the object of the play is to identify who did it—Colonel Mustard, Miss Scarlet, Professor Plum, Mrs. Peacock, Mrs. White, or Mr. Green—with which weapon—rope, lead pipe, knife, wrench, candlestick, or revolver—and in which part of a nine-room Victorian mansion. The game immediately became a best seller and has since remained one of America's favorites. In 1985, Hollywood produced *Clue,* a mystery-comedy based on this popular board game, featuring an all-star cast.

Games have always provided a means of play and entertainment for children and adults. During the 1930s and 1940s, with the recognition of childhood and adolescence as specific developmental experiences, parents began to look to leisure activities as a way to teach values and critical thinking, and game and toy manufacturers responded accordingly. Although World War II caused a declined in the production of both old favorites and new games, Monopoly remained popular during the conflict, and the postwar years saw the introduction of Scrabble, a highly successful word game.

See also: Comic Books; Comic Strips; Hobbies; Leisure and Recreation; Movies; Rationing; Toys

Selected Reading
Hoffmann, Leah, "Most Popular Toys of the Last 100 Years." *Forbes,* December 2, 2005.
Irving Crespi. "Card Playing as Mass Culture." In *Mass Culture: The Popular Arts in America,* eds. Bernard Rosenberg and David Manning White, 418–422. New York: Free Press, 1957.
Walsh, Tim. *Timeless Toys: Classic Toys and the Playmakers Who Created Them.* Kansas City, MO: Andrews McMeel Publishing, 2005.
Williams, Anne D. *The Jigsaw Puzzle: Piecing Together a History.* New York: Berkley Books, 2004.

GI BILL (SERVICEMEN'S READJUSTMENT ACT OF 1944)

The National Resources Planning Board (NRPB) had been operating out of the executive office of **President Franklin Delano Roosevelt** (1882–1945) since 1939, performing special duties related to national defense. Anticipating that the war would come to a successful end soon, the NRPB, in June 1943, recommended a series of programs for honorably discharged military personnel. It based its suggestions on three concerns: (1) the inability of the U.S. economy to quickly absorb large numbers of returning veterans into the workforce, (2) the accompanying possibility of lower wages, and (3) the resulting gap between large inventories of products for sale and citizens without the money to buy them.

President Roosevelt, in a **radio** address to the nation in 1943, presented the NRPB's proposal for a bill of veteran benefits that would educate and prepare members of the armed forces for a successful return to civilian life. The American Legion, a veterans' organization, immediately endorsed the idea and became a major participant in deciding the bill's wording. Officially known as the Servicemen's Readjustment Act, a strong publicity campaign carried out by the American Legion coined what became the colloquial title, the GI Bill, and helped to bring about a speedy passage.

On January 10, 1944, the two ranking Democratic and Republican members of the House of Representatives Veteran Affairs committee, Congressman John Rankin (1882–1960) of Mississippi and Congresswoman Edith Nourse Rogers (1881–1960) of Massachusetts, introduced the legislation. The next day, Democratic Senator Joel Bennett Clark (1933–1945) of Missouri, the chairman of the Senate Veterans Subcommittee, took the bill to the Senate floor, where it passed in a 50–0 vote on March 24, 1944. The bill got stuck in a House Committee, which delayed passage there until May 18, 1944, with a vote nonetheless of 387–0. As is true with most pieces of legislation, the bill that passed the Senate and House had picked up modifications and amendments in each chamber. A committee composed of senators and congressmen worked on resolving these issues, and the Servicemen's Readjustment Act received its final approval from the House on June 13, 1944, and from the Senate on June 14, 1944. President Roosevelt signed it into law that same day.

The bill assigned the Veterans Administration (VA)the responsibility to carry out the law's key provisions, including (1) loans for buying small businesses or farms and constructing or buying homes; (2) scholarships for **education** or technical training, including refresher and retraining courses, along with a monthly living allowance while pursuing studies; and (3) weekly unemployment payments up to a maximum period of one year for those unable to find jobs. The bill also authorized construction of necessary hospital facilities for the sick and wounded and established a mechanism for effective job counseling.

On May 7, 1945, Germany signed a document of surrender, followed by Japan in early September, and thus brought World War II to an official end. Throughout the war, numerous veterans with honorable discharges had returned home, and in October 1945, the final process moved ahead in order to reach completion by June 1946. In the end, about 15.5 million surviving veterans found themselves living in a country eager to celebrate their victory and reward their efforts.

Before World War II, a college education and homeownership were unreachable dreams for many Americans. At the end of almost four years of conflict, the GI Bill allowed millions of veterans who would have flooded the job market to instead take steps toward realizing those dreams. Many opted for education and in 1947 accounted for almost 50 percent of college admissions. From 1944 to 1952, the VA backed nearly 2.4 million home loans for these honorably discharged service personnel. Because a majority of the veterans accepted the education and home loan benefits, less than 20 percent of the funds set aside for unemployment pay were used. The concern about soldiers flooding the workforce and causing high unemployment figures had been abated.

This legislation, which ran until 1956, benefited 7.8 million veterans, mostly men, since women made up less than 3 percent of those in the armed forces. But the bill did not assist all who came home. Draftees who, after special educational help, still could not meet the minimum educational requirements received dishonorable discharges and thus could not enjoy the benefits outlined in the bill. For minorities who qualified for assistance, housing, job, and educational discrimination barred many of them from realizing what the bill had intended. Nevertheless, the Servicemen's Readjustment Act contained some of the most sweeping social reforms in the nation's history and it contributed immeasurably to the prosperity of the postwar era.

See also: Selective Training and Service Act of 1940 (Selective Service, or Draft); Truman, President Harry S.; V-E and V-J Day

Selected Reading
GI Bill Statistics. www.gibill.va.gov/GI_Bill_Info/history.htm
Kaledin, Eugenia. *Daily Life in the United States, 1940–1959: Shifting Worlds.* Westport, CT: Greenwood Press, 2000.
National Resources Planning Board. www.archives.gov/research/guide-fed-records/groups/187.html

GODFREY, ARTHUR

Nicknamed "the Ol' Redhead" for his shock of red hair, Arthur Godfrey (1903–1983) emerged as one of the major **radio** personalities of the 1940s. Born in New York City, his family fell on hard times, and the young Godfrey left home and eventually ended up in the U.S. Navy at age 17 by lying about his age. While in the service—with both the navy and the coast guard—Godfrey received radio training that turned him toward pursuing a career in the medium.

Upon his discharge from the Coast Guard in 1930, Godfrey obtained a job as an announcer for a Baltimore station. He moved on to Washington, DC, announcing and doing a morning talk program, *Arthur Godfrey's Sundial Show,* on which he occasionally sang or strummed a ukulele, an instrument he enjoyed playing. His casual, folksy manner while on the air contrasted with the more formal delivery favored by most of his counterparts, and his program attracted listeners. The late 1930s found him modestly successful in New York City where he briefly served as announcer for Fred Allen's (1894–1956) radio version of *Texaco Star Theater,* but he soon thereafter returned to Washington.

In 1945, Godfrey finally attracted a large national audience. At the time, he served as morning host for the local CBS (Columbia Broadcasting System) affiliate, and he covered **President Franklin Delano Roosevelt**'s (1882–1945) funeral cortege then proceeding through the capital. Unlike other reporters, Godfrey created a moving, personal account of events, and the network picked up the feed and broadcast it across the nation. His emotions caught up with him, and be began to weep while talking. Listeners appreciated his warmth and subjective approach to an ongoing news event so much that CBS promptly offered him a show of his own. Thus, in 1945, *Arthur Godfrey Time* took to the airwaves.

An overnight success for the network, *Arthur Godfrey Time,* a five-days-a-week production usually heard in the late morning, ran from 1945 until 1972 (an evening version made its debut in 1950; it also appeared on **television** schedules beginning in 1952). Informal, with Godfrey chatting about almost anything, sometimes with guests, other times in extended, impromptu monologues, the show mixed music and talk in an atmosphere that appealed to the public. Carmen Lombardo (1903–1971), a brother of the famous bandleader Guy Lombardo (1902–1977), in 1945 composed a theme song for the show called "Seems Like Old Times." It soon became well-known in its own right, and today many people consider the tune a standard.

Godfrey's growing popularity led CBS to offer him an evening program in 1946. Instead of relying just on talk, producers came up with *Arthur Godfrey's Talent Scouts*, a series that introduced new entertainers to the public, and Godfrey served as its genial host. It premiered on radio in 1946 and lasted until 1956. Spurred by success, CBS created a television version in 1948; its final telecast took place in January 1958.

Participants, amateurs all, were chosen by people who knew them and had some acquaintance with their particular talents. During a broadcast, an audiometer in the studio recorded levels of applause for each performer; the winner received a professional booking in a club. Over the years, among the hundreds of entertainers heard or seen on the program, singers Tony Bennett (b. 1926) and Rosemary Clooney (1928–2002), along with comedians Don Knotts (1924–2006) and Jonathan Winters (b. 1925), graced the *Talent Scouts* stage.

As if the foregoing shows were not enough, Godfrey also undertook a separate television broadcast of *Arthur Godfrey and His Friends* in 1949. A musical variety series that showcased countless acts over its life, the "friends" could be Godfrey regulars from other shows or celebrity guests invited to appear. It stayed on the air until 1957. He also found time to make a few recordings. One novelty number, "The Too Fat Polka (She's Too Fat for Me)," which he recorded in 1947, made its way up the charts and became a minor hit.

By the end of the 1940s, Arthur Godfrey sat astride a small radio-television empire that he would continue to expand during the early 1950s. Sponsors, many of which he gently ribbed over the air, lined up to advertise their products on his various shows. Lipton Tea, in particular, boasted a long relationship with the entertainer. A series of unfortunate decisions on his part, however, gradually destroyed much of that empire in ensuing years. Despite his easygoing exterior, Arthur Godfrey possessed a mercurial temperament and a large ego. He would not be overshadowed by staffers or guests, and he could, in the blink of an eye, fire associates of long standing. As the public learned of this dark side to his personality, audiences began to fall away. He lost his last remaining show, *Arthur Godfrey Time*, when it went off the air in 1972.

See also: Advertising; *ASCAP vs. BMI* Radio Boycott and the AFM Recording Ban; Beverages; Radio Programming: Music and Variety Shows; Radio Programming: News, Sports, Public Affairs, and Talk

Selected Reading

Dunning, John. *On the Air: The Encyclopedia of Old-Time Radio*. New York: Oxford University Press, 1998.

Singer, Arthur J. *Arthur Godfrey: The Adventures of an American Broadcaster*. Jefferson, NC: McFarland, 1999.

GOLF

First played in 1754 at St. Andrews, Scotland, golf since the late 1800s has enjoyed a rich history in the United States. It thrived during the 1920s, especially as a sport for the wealthy people who played at private country clubs. With the Great Depression, only a few could continue to pay club membership dues, and the number of golfers momentarily declined. But to the benefit of nonclub members, private clubs, anxious to continue in existence, opened their links to public play. In addition, the Works Projects Administration (WPA) built many city-owned municipal courses. Suddenly golf became available to the average citizen. On August 5, 1940, a *Time* magazine article reported that 6,500 public golf courses (out of a total of 9,900 in the United States), allowed more people to play golf than had 10 years earlier.

At the same time that average citizens took up golf for recreation, professional golf grew as a news item and as a spectator sport. Four men's tournaments, often referred to as "the majors," provided the most prestigious annual competitions: (1) the British Open Championship, established in 1860 and frequently called The Open outside the United Kingdom; (2) the United States Open Championship, 1895, and commonly known as the U.S. Open; (3) the PGA (Professional Golfers' Association) Championship, 1916; and (4) the Masters Tournament, 1934. Reputations grow from winning various invitation-only matches that occur each season, and the declaration of the best player for the year rests on the number of championship victories accumulated from these four events. For example, in 1941, Craig Wood (1901–1968), who would retire in 1946, made a final splash after an outstanding two-decade career, when he ended a string of runner-up finishes in major events by winning the Masters and the U.S. Open.

Crooner Bing Crosby loved the game of golf and frequently lent his name to its promotion. The first Crosby National Pro-Amateur PGA tournament took place in Rancho Sante Fe, California, in 1937. Suspended in 1942 because of the war, Crosby and the PGA revived it in 1947 on three courses at Pebble Beach, California. (Photofest)

But World War II caused cancellation of the British Open in 1940, and it would not resume until 1946; the other three tournaments soon followed suit. Officials placed the U.S. Open on hold from 1942 to 1945, and the Masters from 1943 to 1945; the PGA Championship fared better, missing only the 1943 event. Other changes occurred because of the war. The Augusta National Golf Club, founded by golfer Bobby Jones (1902–1971) in 1933 and the home of the Masters Tournament, became a turkey farm to ease wartime **food** shortages. Both amateur and professional golfers as well as many caddies and groundskeepers either enlisted or were drafted for military service. Among the outstanding players of the 1940s, Sam Snead (1912–2002) joined the navy in 1942, followed by Ben Hogan's (1912–1997) enlistment in the Army Air Corps in 1943.

The United States government halted the manufacture of golf balls and equipment, a move that greatly affected the play for both the pros and the average citizen, and even led to draining golf course lakes to retrieve lost balls. Some country club courses were ploughed under to be **victory gardens** for their members. Where golf courses still existed, players raised millions of dollars for the war effort—sometimes in unique ways, such as paying a fine every time a ball landed in a sand trap.

Along with the majors, the Ryder Cup matches, first played in 1926 but suspended by the war from 1939 to 1945, register as another important event for professional golfers. Held every two years, alternating between a golf course in the United States and one in England, and founded on prestige, not prize money, this competition originally pitted a team of players from the United States against a team from Britain and Ireland; this changed in 1979 to include players from continental Europe. During the war, the United States retained the trophy it had won in 1937, and U.S. professional golfers continued the spirit of the Ryder Cup by organizing teams to participate in events to raise funds for the American Red Cross and other war-related efforts. With resumption of the Ryder Cup matches in 1947, the U.S. team remained victorious until 1957.

After the war, American professional golfers Ben Hogan, Sam Snead, and Byron Nelson (1912–2006), born within six months of one another, easily established themselves as the "big three," gaining nationwide recognition by dominating both minor and major tournaments. The table below shows these players, along with Craig Wood, as the winners of the majors and members on the Ryder Cup teams during the 1940s. In addition to these accomplishments, Nelson ended his career in 1945 with a record-breaking win of 18 tournaments, 11 in a row. Hogan added 10 victorious tournaments in one year to his fame in 1948, and Snead maintained recognition as a top player in the world for almost four decades.

Snead and Hogan continued playing during the 1950s, with Snead adding three more majors to his record, but never the U.S. Open. He also had two documentaries highlighting his career—*Sport Thrills: Saving Strokes with Sam Snead* (1940) and *Slammin' Sammy Snead* (1951). Hogan, generally considered one of the greatest golfers of all time, won six more majors in the early 1950s, a miraculous feat considering that an automobile accident in 1949 left him unable to walk and play that season. Winning the 1953 British Open made him the second player to win all four of the

TABLE 57. U. S. Men's Professional Golf Champions during the 1940s

Year	Sam Snead	Ben Hogan	Byron Nelson	Craig Wood
1940			PGA	
1941				The Masters
				U.S. Open
1942	PGA		The Masters	
1945			PGA	
1946	British Open	PGA		
1947	Ryder Cup Team	Ryder Cup Team	Ryder Cup Team	
1948		PGA		
		U.S. Open		
1949	PGA			
	The Masters			
	Ryder Cup Team			

majors. The biographical Hollywood film, *Follow the Sun* (1951), starring Glenn Ford (1916–2006) as Hogan, depicted his life.

Individual playing was not limited to the major tournaments, because golf associations across the country regularly staged professional events with large purses as well as amateur matches offering a trophy to the winner. The United States Golf Association (USGA), in addition to the U.S. Open, has sponsored the U.S. Men's and Women's Amateur tournaments since 1895, the U. S Women's Open, 1946, and the U.S. Senior's Open, 1980. The Western Golf Association has offered the Western Open since 1899. These tournaments, however, are not considered a part of the majors.

Two celebrities, crooner **Bing Crosby** (1903–1977) and former heavyweight **boxing** champion **Joe Louis** (1914–1981), loved the game of golf and lent their names and influence to its promotion. In 1937, the first Crosby National Pro-Amateur, a PGA tournament, took place in Rancho Sante Fe, California. Suspended in 1942 because of the war, Crosby revived it in 1947 on three courses at Pebble Beach, California, where it continues as an annual event. Crosby also teamed with comedian **Bob Hope** (1903–2003) and professional golfer Byron Nelson, who had been classified as 4-F (not qualified for military service) because of slow-clotting blood, in exhibition games designed to raise money for war-related causes.

Louis played golf with celebrities such as Crosby, Hope, and singer **Frank Sinatra** (1915–1998), but supposedly preferred games with close friends and the top black golfers of the day. In 1928, a group of black professional players had formed the United Golf Association (UGA) for the purpose of holding tournaments for blacks during the era of racial segregation when the PGA's by-laws contained a whites-only clause. Louis became a major supporter of the UGA and, in 1941, sponsored the first of eight Joe Louis Open Tournaments at Detroit's Rackham Municipal Golf Course.

Women, as well as men, participated in amateur matches as early as 1895 but did not gain a professional tournament of their own until 1930, with the forming of the Western Open for Women. The PGA added a U.S. Open for Women to its roster of events in 1946, but throughout the decade tournaments were few and far between, with just two qualifying as major events. In 1950, leading women golfers, including Babe Didrikson Zaharias (1911–1956), Patty Berg (1918–2006), Betty Jameson (1919–2009), and Louise Suggs (b. 1923), established the Ladies Professional Golf Association as an organization to govern women's professional golf.

Throughout the 1940s, Zaharias attracted as much public attention as her male counterparts. She easily drew crowds to watch her play and in the process helped to popularize women's golf. Before taking up the game, she had gained recognition as an outstanding athlete in other areas with an all-American status in **basketball** and the recipient of two gold medals and one silver in track and field events from the 1932 Los Angeles Olympic Games. By 1950, Zaharias had won five major tournaments, giving her every golf title available to women and a winning total of 82 when combining amateur and professional tournaments.

Berg accumulated 15 major title wins over three decades of playing. She also served in World War II as a lieutenant with the Marines. Jameson won three major tournaments and a total of 13 professional titles. Suggs, who first played golf at age 10, quickly developed into a strong competitor with a high degree of accuracy and a

TABLE 58. U. S. Women's Professional Golf Champions during the 1940s

Year	Babe Didrikson Zaharias	Patty Berg	Betty Jameson	Louise Suggs
1940	Women's Western Open			
1941		Women's Western Open		
1942			Women's Western Open	
1943		Women's Western Open		
1944	Women's Western Open			
1945	Women's Western Open			
1946		U.S. Women's Open		Women's Western Open
1947			U.S. Women's Open	Women's Western Open
1948	U.S. Women's Open	Women's Western Open		
1949				U.S. Women's Open, Women's Western Open

consistent swing, traits that helped her easily accumulate a career record of 58 professional victories; 11 of those tournaments qualified as majors.

Scotland may be considered the traditional home of golf, but since the conclusion of World War II, the United States has become the dominant nation. Over golf's history, several American players have achieved star status for their ability to raise the standards and excitement of the game. During the 1940s, three professional male players—Bryon Nelson, Ben Hogan, and Sam Snead—and four women—Babe Didrikson Zaharias, Patty Berg, Betty Jameson, and Louise Suggs—stand out as establishing a foundation from which the sport grew in popularity during the next two decades.

See also: Race Relations and Stereotyping; Rationing

Selected Reading
Dawkins, Marvin P., and Graham Charles Kinloch. *African American Golfers during the Jim Crow Era.* Westport, CT: Greenwood Publishing Group, 2000.
Grimsley, Will. *Golf: Its History, People, and Events.* Englewood Cliffs, NJ: Prentice Hall, 1966.
Strege, John. *When War Played Through: Golf during World War II.* New York: Gotham Books, 2005.

GROCERY STORES AND SUPERMARKETS

The 1940s proved to be a period of both challenges and opportunities for the **food** industry. Throughout the previous decade, chain grocery stores, such as A&P (Great

Atlantic & Pacific Tea Co.), Kroger, Safeway, Giant Food Store, and Piggly Wiggly, to name a few, had opened across the country in America's first, but rough, version of a supermarket. By 1940, some chains had started to consolidate smaller operations into more spacious buildings, both remodeled and new, in efforts to remove a warehouse look that dominated during the 1930s and to add conveniences such as self-service and parking lots. These larger stores proved at the time to be cost effective and resulted in lower grocery prices, more shoppers, and larger profits.

A number of innovations to aid the cook and put new stock on grocery shelves also took place. In 1937, A&P had created its own publishing company to print *Woman's Day* magazine. Originally free, the content focused on recipes and menu planning. By 1940, it had expanded to feature articles on food and cooking, nutrition, crafts, home decoration, health, needlework, and child care. Available exclusively in A&P stores, it sold for two cents (approximately 30 cents in 2008 money) and had achieved a circulation of 3 million by 1940. The next year, the Spice Islands Company introduced a line of herbs, spices, and vinegars that could add zest to otherwise bland dishes. Other new products in this year included Cheerioats (the name changed in 1946 to Cheerios), and M&M Plain Chocolate Candies.

The December 7, 1941, attack by the Japanese on Pearl Harbor, however, changed all aspects of life in the United States. For grocery stores, shortages of both food and

During the postwar years, the American housewife readily turned away from the family's wartime victory garden to shop at a new supermarket that offered an abundance of choices and low prices. (Library of Congress)

manpower, along with **rationing,** adversely affected the nature of selling and buying. Grocery store owners and customers had to contend with limited supplies, hoarding by some citizens, and **black market** operators functioning outside the law to supply items otherwise scarce or unavailable. On the positive side, during the 1930s, self-service, which required a smaller labor force and made for easier shopping, had been available in some stores in dry and canned groceries as well as dairy departments. By 1942, this approach had expanded to include fruits and vegetables. For women, employment opportunities increased and, as opposed to many defense factories, continued after the war. The exodus of male employees to military service saw women in grocery stores and supermarkets working at all levels—checkers, butchers, bakers, warehouse workers, as well as department heads and managers.

With the entry of the United States into World War II, the food industry, like the rest of the nation, did all it could to convert to a wartime economy. In this undertaking, grocery stores collected ration stamps, sold **war bonds,** promoted **scrap drives,** and created and posted menus that used readily available foods requiring a minimum of ration points to purchase. Stores also kept patrons advised about items no longer needing stamps, such as coffee after July 1943 and canned goods in the summer of 1944. Many merchants used their **advertising** space in the store and ran newspaper ads to support the war effort by explaining rationing or offering nutritional tips. Also, in response to a wartime paper scarcity, grocers conducted campaigns reminding shoppers to supply their own bags.

As the war continued, many grocery stores and supermarkets lost money. A series of governmental anti-inflation measures, introduced in 1942, included rent ceilings and wage and price freezes. For some grocers, frozen prices occurred when they were selling certain items at loss-leader margins—that is, a product priced lower than actual cost as an enticement to get customers into the store. At the same time, operating expenses steadily increased because of more clerical work required for rationing reports and other government regulations. For those stores not located in population centers, gas rationing caused a decrease in the number of shoppers. Most larger stores struggled to stay open, while many small family-owned operations closed their doors.

With the end of World War II and a return to peace, the grocery industry continued to cope with supply uncertainties and contrasts. For example, there would be periods of widespread shortages of several items, especially meat, followed by an unexpected abundance of the commodities. Governmental controls alternated—first in place, briefly lifted, then reinstated, and finally, removed completely. By 1948, business returned to some normalcy, and merchants felt more confident as Americans arrived at their doors ready to buy not only food necessities but luxury items as well.

Along with the uncertainties, some conditions boded well for grocery stores and supermarkets. The average annual percent change in the U.S. population growth almost doubled from 1945 to 1950, going from 1.10 percent to 2.05 percent. This expansion meant a greater need for food and more business for food vendors. At the same time, many families took advantage of the mobility offered by **automobiles** and improved highway systems and moved to the suburbs. The leading grocery chains continued to close smaller stores and replaced them with modern-day supermarkets, many located in new suburban shopping malls. These larger markets offered a wider selection of popular merchandise but continued competitive pricing.

In marketing efforts to move consumers away from mom-and-pop establishments to chain supermarkets, companies diverted considerable funds to advertising and other promotional ploys. Between 1945 and 1950, money spent on supermarket advertising rose from $3 billion to $6 billion. Special sales, giveaway contests, in-store advertising with **posters,** and expanded available merchandise drew customers to stores with many new features: (1) more self-service than ever before, making shopping faster and easier; (2) cellophane prepackaging of a wider variety of items including meat, poultry, and cheese; (3) **frozen foods** in redesigned display cases allowing for larger displays and convenient selection; (4) health and beauty-aid products, heretofore limited to drugstore shelves; (5) books and **magazines;** and (6) housewares, including small appliances.

With a massive expansion of available products, store features such as space, convenience, and efficiency became important considerations. This caused a ripple effect that created business for others. Various equipment manufacturers responded with adjustable shelving, streamlined refrigerated display cases and coolers, price-computing scales, packaging machines, and belt-driven checkout counters.

At the beginning of the 1940s, the American supermarket found itself in a position to become the nation's primary source for groceries. Involvement in World War II and a shift to a wartime economy slowed that growth but led to a new understanding of methods to improve the business, such as self-service, large inventories, and plenty of free parking. After the war, gradual consumer acceptance of this format, coupled with a desire for convenience and affordability, paved the way for the supermarket boom that occurred between 1950 and 1965.

See also: Architecture; Desserts, Candy, and Ice Cream; Labor Unrest; Levittown and Suburbanization; Newspapers

Selected Reading
Gwynn, David. Grocery Stores and Supermarkets. www.groceteria.com/about/host.html
"History of Supermarkets." *Progressive Grocer* 66 (12) (December 1987): 53.
Mathews, Ryan. "1926–1946: The Mass Market Comes of Age: How the Great Depression, the Rise of Mass Media and World War II Helped Create a Mass Consumer Market." *Progressive Grocer* 75 (12) (December 1996): 47.
Population Statistics. www.npg.org/facts/us_historical_pops.htm

H

HEALTH AND MEDICINE

In 1941, a group of physicians, working with Harper Brothers Publishing, issued a series of little books on five diseases collectively titled *Help Your Doctor to Help You*. Each volume sold for 95 cents (approximately $14 in 2008 dollars) and could be purchased in book stores and at newsstands, drugstores, and railroad stations. The resultant popularity of these publications underlined a growing interest among Americans in maintaining good health, a concern that, in 1946, the *New York Times* reported ranking as one of 12 basic human interests along with items such as achievement, faith, and recreation,

From 1900 to 1930, average life expectancy at birth for U.S. citizens increased from 47.3 to 59.7 years because of improved public health services and a reduction in death rates from infectious diseases. Increased awareness of the importance of cleanliness also came into play; after all, Procter & Gamble had been successfully selling soap for over 100 years. By 1950, average life expectancy had climbed to 68.2 years, largely as a result of better nutrition, a growing interest in physical fitness, World War II and postwar medical innovations and breakthroughs, and continuing attention to improved personal hygiene and sanitation practices.

Healthier **food** had emerged as a popular cause during the 1930s, contributing to the 1938 passage of a revised and expanded Pure Food and Drug Act. It called for, among other things, more extensive labeling and testing of food products that would ensure safer and better eating. That same year, the laboratory synthesis of vitamins permitted their incorporation into pill form. By 1940, vitamins could easily be purchased over the counter at pharmacies and **grocery stores and supermarkets** and used as nutritional supplements to one's diet.

Despite increased information about healthy eating, many Americans apparently continued to engage in unhealthy practices as revealed in 1941, when the military services rejected a high percentage of conscripted men because of nutritional deficiencies. A concerned government embarked on ways to improve the health of all of its citizens. Public health authorities, building on a growing wave of patriotism, used periodicals such as *Parents' Magazine* to inform everyone that "it is patriotic to stay healthy" and suggested that effective steps included eating well-balanced meals, practicing sanitary personal hygiene, and having regular physical examinations and dental checkups.

The Food and Nutrition Board (FNB) in 1943, operating under the Office of Health Defense and Welfare, focused just on healthy eating and, through various media outlets, distributed a table of seven basic food groups to choose from each day. As with most federal government promotions at the time, the FNB emphasized a link to the war, that cooking and eating nutritious food bought at grocery stores or grown in **victory gardens** better enabled those on the home front to do their part in bringing a quick and victorious end to the conflict.

Just how much civilians improved their eating habits depended on personal initiative and probably proved minimal. A different story existed in the army, where soldiers eating in the mess halls and on the battlefields were served from menus that adhered to the new governmental guidelines. After the war, most of these men and women wanted to continue their healthy habits, and, indeed, the postwar years saw an increase in the serving of nutritious food.

In the United States, calisthenics, play, sports, or exercise periods had been a part of most school days since the early 1800s and, by the 1920s, some states had even passed legislation requiring physical **education.** Along with World War I, and again with World War II, the emphases of physical education curricula switched from games and sports to physical conditioning, necessitated by clear evidence that many of those drafted or enlisted were not fit for combat.

Important contributions to improve fitness came during the 1940s, specifically from "the father of physical fitness," Thomas K Cureton (1901–1992), professor, researcher, and director of the Physical Fitness Research Laboratory, founded in 1944 at the University of Illinois. Under his leadership, researchers developed methods to test motor fitness and to appraise human physique, cardiovascular fitness, and aquatic performance. Cureton also established programs for teaching adults, children, and **youth** the importance of exercise, along with correct techniques—information that became the basis for exercise programs put in place in schools, colleges, and universities across the country. In 1947, recognizing the value of Cureton's work, Olympic athletes from throughout the Midwest participated in a series of tests at the laboratory.

Despite increased emphasis on good eating and regular and appropriate exercise, people still got sick, and, because of a short supply of physicians, hospitals, and nurses, those on the home front had to cope as best they could. Forty percent of the country's physicians would soon serve in the military, and many nurses would join their ranks, resulting in many communities lacking properly staffed clinics and hospitals. Even medical research would now concentrate on military-related projects.

Most of the doctors who remained at home engaged in solo general practices and frequently made house calls as opposed to seeing everyone in their office. In small towns, some opened clinics or hospitals with limited services in an attempt to be more efficient in the delivery of their medical skills. Most large communities boasted at least one hospital, often founded by a religious group, which offered operating rooms, X-ray equipment, diagnostic laboratories, and nurses to care for patients. After the war, the number of hospitals across the country greatly increased thanks to the Hill-Burton Act of 1946, which, through funds and planning assistance, expanded the Veterans Administration (VA) hospitals for the millions of returning soldiers who would need medical attention and also provided aid to the nation's community hospitals.

During World War II, higher-paying defense jobs usurped the normal pool of practicing and prospective practitioners. In hopes of countering any shortage of nurses, the U.S. government enacted the Nurse Training Act of 1943, which established the Cadet Nurse Corps within the United States Public Health Service (PHS) and allowed for the granting of scholarships and stipends to educate qualified applicants in exchange for their providing military or essential civilian nursing services for the duration of the war.

An active publicity campaign to help achieve a yearly quota of 65,000 nurse recruits included advertisements in **newspapers** and **magazines,** discussions about the corps on **radio** programs, and displays of film stars posing with cadets in ads and **posters** in a variety of stores and facilities across the country. In 1944, Metro-Goldwyn-Mayer distributed a U.S. Office of War Information documentary titled *Reward Unlimited;* it stars Dorothy McGuire (1916–2001) as Cadet Nurse Peggy Adams, along with James Brown (1920–1992), Aline MacMahon (1899–1991), and Spring Byington (1886–1971). Scenes of actresses donning cadet nurse uniforms can be observed in other features such as Shirley Temple's (b. 1928) *Kiss and Tell* (1945). The corps continued until 1948 and graduated a total of 124,000 nurses.

The demands of being at war brought about increased financing and coordination between the U.S. government and medical research, which resulted in many significant changes in the practice of American medicine. While military doctors and nurses focused on efficient delivery of life-saving procedures, scientists perfected miracle drugs such as sulfonamides and penicillin, the insecticide DDT (dichlorodiphenyltrichloroethane), and invented new medical technologies based on the use of radioactive isotopes produced from the atomic pile at Oak Ridge, Tennessee.

Experiments with Prontosil, the first sulfa drug, had begun in 1932 with hundreds of manufacturers producing large amounts of sulfa in various forms. The death of at least 100 people caused by a toxic derivative served as a major factor in the passage of the Food and Drug Act of 1938, which established guidelines for testing and approval of new drugs before their distribution to the public. Despite the temporary setback with sulfa drugs, at the beginning of World War II, sulfa became the first antibiotic available to military physicians and their patients, and soldiers' first aid kits contained sulfa powder to be immediately sprinkled on any open wound.

But a more effective antibiotic stood in the wings ready to make its appearance before the war ended. Scottish scientist Alexander Fleming (1881–1951) had discovered penicillin in 1928. Eleven years later in England, Australian Howard Florey (1898–1968) and German-born Ernst Chain (1906–1979) isolated its active ingredient so that it could be produced in a powdery form. By 1943, the required clinical trials had been completed and production on a large scale began, allowing the use of penicillin for treating Allied soldiers wounded on **D-Day,** the June 6, 1944, invasion of Europe by Allied forces. Considered a miracle drug at the time, the three men responsible for its discovery and development shared the honor of receiving the Nobel Prize in Physiology or Medicine in 1945. At that same time, the perfection of oral penicillin had been achieved and made available to the American public. Other antibiotics produced during the 1940s included streptomycin (1944), chloramphenicol (1947), aureomycin (1948), and neomycin (1949).

In 1939, Swiss chemist Paul Muller (1899–1965) discovered insecticidal powers in DDT, first synthesized in 1874 from chlorine, alcohol, and sulfuric acid. DDT stopped a typhus epidemic in Naples, Italy, in 1944, by killing lice, the carrier of the disease. It also proved effective in controlling malaria and yellow fever. The army and DDT manufacturers announced other amazing qualities such as clearing areas of fleas, bedbugs, mosquitoes, moths, roaches, termites, and flies—all of this in addition to various varmints that could do major damage to agricultural crops. Muller received the Nobel Prize in Physiology or Medicine in 1948 for his contribution, and Americans looked at DDT as a great scientific gift. The fascination changed to a sense of horror when biologist Rachel Carson's (1907–1964) study, *Silent Spring* (1962), revealed its devastating effects on the natural environment. Authorities banned its use in the United States in 1973.

Drugs obviously helped medical personnel carry out their priority of immediate care for battlefield injuries in an attempt to return as many soldiers as possible to duty quickly. The availability of safe blood transfusions also contributed to quick recovery of the wounded. In 1940, physician Charles Drew (1904–1950) devised a way to separate plasma from the rest of human blood, which allowed for safe preservation, storage, and shipment for longer periods of time. Shortly after his discovery, Drew became the medical director of the first Red Cross blood bank. He resigned this post in 1942, after the United States War Department issued a directive that blood taken from white donors should be separated from that of black donors. Drew left the Red Cross to head the Department of Surgery at Howard University, a segregated college for blacks, as well as to serve as the chief of surgery at nearby Freedman's Hospital. The National Association for the Advancement of Colored People (NAACP) awarded him its prestigious Spingarn Medal in 1944 for his pioneering work on blood plasma.

The European theater of the war allowed quick and complete treatment of wounded military personnel more easily than did the Pacific. Army medics rendered first aid at the battle site before transporting the casualties to a battalion aid station. Division hospitals received those needing additional stabilization or surgery. In the Pacific theater, however, long distances from the area of fighting to a hospital posed a challenge. To this end, the army, navy, and War department operated a total of 39 hospital ships staffed by military medical personnel who offered modified treatment while speeding to a full-service military hospital. Anticipating heavy casualties in the D-Day invasion, the navy converted a number of LSTs (landing ship tanks)—vessels originally created to support amphibious operations by carrying vehicles, cargo, and troops directly onto shore—to serve as small hospitals.

Loss of life on the battlefield clearly posed a major threat to those fighting the war. Back home, citizens viewed sexually transmitted diseases (venereal) and polio (infantile paralysis) as the most frightening health challenges. Two forms of venereal disease—gonorrhea and syphilis—created a serious adult public health problem. Gonorrhea, less damaging than syphilis, impairs the well-being of the victim, whereas untreated syphilis can lead to insanity and severe damage to the cardiovascular and nervous systems. By 1940, many physicians viewed venereal diseases as both a health and social problem needing government intervention. The U.S. military took action through the development of an antidisease protocol involving education, control of prostitution, and medical treatment. For both military personnel and civilians, the use of antibiotics developed during the decade—sulfa for gonorrhea and penicillin for syphilis—led to a dramatic drop in disease rates.

In the area of polio, a British doctor, Michael Underwood (1737–1820), had provided the first clinical description of the disease in 1789, and the United States reported its first major epidemic in 1894. Incidents of polio and related concerns grew over the decades. **President Franklin Delano Roosevelt** (1882–1945), who had contracted the disease in 1921, announced the creation of the National Foundation for Infantile Paralysis in 1937, and entertainer Eddie Cantor (1892–1964) used the phrase "March of Dimes" to urge radio listeners to march—that is, send their spare change to the White House for the foundation to use in its fight against polio. The term stuck for future fundraisers.

The foundation in 1939 commenced mass distribution of tank respirators, usually referred to as iron lungs, to assist polio victims who experienced difficulty with breathing. Epidemics, always in the summer, had occurred in different states before the 1940s but now came with more regularity. For example, Texas, California, Washington, Kansas, and New York reported enough cases in 1943 to warrant epidemic status, and New York, North Carolina, Kentucky, Pennsylvania, and Virginia experienced the same in 1944. The U.S. Public Health Service declared in August 1946 that the nation had the worst infantile paralysis outbreak since 1916.

Many communities during these years operated in a state bordering on panic; they closed schools and **swimming** pools, while parents kept their children at home in hopes of preventing further spread of the disease. In 1947, physician and medical researcher Jonas Salk (1914–1995) accepted a position at the University of Pittsburgh School of Medicine and one year later, thanks to four research grants, devoted himself to developing a vaccine against polio. A nationwide epidemic in 1949 that claimed over 30,000 victims, and the worst up to that time, added pressure to Salk's work. The early 1950s saw the greatest number of polio cases ever reported in the United States, with more deaths than from any other communicable disease. Jubilation followed the announcement on April 12, 1955, of the discovery of an effective vaccine.

Equally exciting, in June 1946, Major General Leslie R. Groves (1896–1970), the primary military leader for the Manhattan Project, stated that radioactive isotopes would be available for medical and biological research giving birth to what some called atomic medicine. The medical community now had materials that would greatly expand their ability to study the human body and develop revolutionary diagnostic procedures and new ways to treat diseases, especially cancer.

Psychiatric medicine also made advances. The successful treatment of large numbers of soldiers hospitalized for psychiatric disorders during World War II persuaded

Congress to pass the National Mental Health Act in 1946, with funds available for the education of thousands of psychiatrists, psychologists, social workers, and nurses. Three years later, the government created the National Institute of Mental Health (NIMH), a division of the National Institutes of Health (NIH), founded in 1887 to conduct and support medical research.

The rising costs of medical services, both before and after World War II, could not be afforded by all Americans. The first group health insurance plan went into effect in 1929, when a contract for teachers in Dallas, Texas, called for Baylor Hospital to provide room, board, and medical services for a fee. By the 1930s, several large insurance companies entered the field, as did nonprofit groups called Blue Cross, or Blue Shield, organizations that negotiated discounted contracts with doctors and hospitals.

Looking for a way to include all citizens under a comprehensive plan, President Franklin Roosevelt, in 1939, asked Congress for a national health care program; the request did not pass, and Roosevelt promised to try again after the conclusion of the war. By November 1945, when his successor, **Harry S. Truman** (1884–1972), sent a similar bill to Congress, the American Medical Association had organized to prevent what physicians saw as a government attempt to regiment medicine and control their freedom of practice and fee schedules. Despite some favorable reaction across the nation, many voters and members of Congress believed the plan an attempt to introduce socialized medicine into the country, and again a call for national health insurance met defeat.

The 1940s laid a groundwork for many changes in the practice and benefits of medicine, including an expansion of knowledge among both practitioners and their patients, increased availability of blood and plasma for transfusions, effective new drugs, improvement of equipment and diagnostic procedures, the building of hospitals, many of which became centers providing specialized medicine, and an enhanced public image of psychiatry, to name only a few. Existing and new federal agencies, such as the Centers for Disease Control and Prevention (CDC; 1946) and the National Heart Institute (NHI; 1948) provided increased expertise in the prevention and treatment of diseases. Building on the accomplishments of the 1940s, advances continue, resulting in a projected probability of life expectancy for those born in 2010 to be 75.7 years for men and 80.8 for women, or a combined average of 78.3 years.

See also: Advertising; Movies; Race Relations and Stereotyping; Radio Programming: News, Sports, Public Affairs, and Talk; Technology

Selected Reading
Cadet Nurse Corps. www.lhncbc.nlm.nih.gov/apdb/phshistory/resources/cadetnurse/nurse.html
Health, Medicine, Physical Fitness. www.oxfordreference.com; www.ahs.uiuc.edu/history/cureton.htm
Kaledin, Eugenia. *Daily Life in the United States, 1940–1959: Shifting Worlds.* Westport, CT: Greenwood Press, 2000.
Life Expectancy. www.census.gov/compendia/statab/cats/births_deaths_marriages_divorces/life_expectancy.html

HOBBIES

Americans in 1940 pursued their interest in hobbies—specific nonwork, pleasurable activities—at the same level of popularity as they did during the Great Depression. The full employment brought on by World War II quickly put free time at a premium and reduced the necessity of having a hobby, unlike the 1930s, when people had idle hours they needed to occupy. Despite the pressures of the war years, the value of an enjoyable activity outside of work continued to be a relevant aspect of American life.

Statistical records kept during the 1940s did not include the numbers of children and adults with a hobby. Documentation of community hobby shows indicates an interest in leisure pursuits. The New York Stock Exchange sponsored its first such show in 1941, an event that continued annually until 1954. Groups such as the Union League Club, the New York Real Estate Board, and the New York Medical College followed suit. The Hobby Guild of America and the American Hobby Federation, as well as schools, recreation groups and centers, and community associations across the country also underwrote such exhibitions.

Attention paid by the media can be another indicator of popularity and relevance. *Hobby Lobby,* a **radio** program on the CBS (Columbia Broadcasting System) network, started in 1937 with Dave Elman (1900–1967) as host; he interviewed people who pursued unusual interests. The show had an uninterrupted run until 1943, the height of World War II. It resumed for the 1945–1946 season, then went off the air again, and made its last regular season appearance in 1949, finally finishing with a summer series in 1950 on NBC (National Broadcasting Company). Its disappearance from scheduled programming did not indicate a lessening interest in hobbies but more the reduced scale of radio broadcasting in the face of growing competition from **television**.

In the area of print, *Hobbies* magazine debuted in 1931; throughout the 1940s, it served as "the magazine for collectors." It typically contained stories about potential hobby sources, such as glass and china items, gems, miniatures, postcards, firearms, coins, stamps, and so on. It also carried a range of advertisements directed at enthusiasts.

In 1941, *Popular Science* magazine identified **photography,** stamp collecting,

Model airplanes could be built by almost anyone; they ranged from simple kits to detailed assemblies that required special tools. Casual surveys conducted during the 1940s indicate model making to be one of the period's favorite hobbies. (Library of Congress)

music, model making, and home workshops as the five most popular hobbies for Americans but offered no definitions or statistical documentation. Likewise, a 1948 book titled *Guide to Popular Hobbies,* by Geoffrey Mott-Smith (1902–1960), provided basic information on photography, magic, collecting stamps, coins, buttons, model airplanes, ships, and the like. Just one year earlier, Dave Elman had declared to a *New York Times* reporter that the collecting of autographs ranked as the most popular American hobby, with photography a close second, which suggests some changes from the beginning of the decade.

Whether first or second in popularity, photography could, by 1940, be enjoyed by many individuals, regardless of their skill levels. The Eastman Kodak Company had manufactured a simple, easily operated Brownie camera to commemorate the 1939–1940 New York World's Fair, and a price of $1.25 (about $19 in 2008 dollars) made it generally affordable. With experience and more sophisticated cameras, the amateur photographer could take quality pictures and might even earn some extra money from a variety of potential markets.

The advent of World War II disrupted the normal patterns of American life, and photography became a way for families to stay connected. Snapshots kept everyone visually informed about important personal activities—births, weddings, family gatherings—and other everyday events. Recognizing this value and the growing interest in photography, Kodak produced three versions of the Brownie during the war years followed by four more in the postwar era. In 1948, however, another company, the Polaroid Corporation, made a significant contribution to popular photography and challenged Kodak's traditional dominance in the field.

The company had been founded in 1937 by Edwin Land (1909–1991), a scientist and inventor. Land developed a new concept for still photography and publicly marketed a device he labeled a Polaroid camera ("Polaroid" has no real meaning; it merges the word "polarize" and the suffix "-oid" to create a trademarked word). Land's design allowed a person to take a picture and then in no time have a partially developed print emerge from the camera. A dab of polymer fixative preserved the image, and the photographer experienced instant gratification with a finished picture. For the remainder of the decade, Polaroid instant photography fascinated consumers who bought the cameras as quickly as the company could manufacture them. The basic model retailed for the relatively high cost of $89.75 (or roughly $775 in 2008 dollars), but the price seemed not to deter public enthusiasm at all.

While advancements in **technology** enabled some hobbyists to snap pictures, other pursuits acknowledged a natural inclination to collect objects, which in turn becomes the basis for a hobby. By the 1940s, the collecting of coins and stamps had long served as a source of pleasure and an identifiable pursuit for many. For collectors, an important milestone occurred in 1892, when the United States Mint issued its first commemorative coin and the postal service released a series of commemorative stamps to mark the 400th anniversary of the arrival of Christopher Columbus (1451–1506) in the Americas. Since then, many other nations have likewise minted coins and printed stamps specifically for the purpose of being saved, a practice that continues into the 21st century.

Both during and after World War II, basic coin collecting required little in the way of supplies and cost. Keeping some special denominations such as one-cent pieces of all possible years of issue from the loose change that passed through one's hands each day served as an initiation into the hobby. From this simple beginning, an enthusiastic numismatist could next acquire knowledge about coin values and conditions and increase the size and value of the collection by making purchases from a dealer.

In 1940, Richard S. Yeoman (1904–1988), a commercial artist and coin collector working for the Whitman Publishing Company, made the life of a novice coin collector easier with an inexpensive cardboard coin holder that continues to be available. Yeoman's version features fold-out panels and an assortment of titles—pennies, nickels, dimes, etc.—that allows for a wider variety of denominations to be stored. He also compiled two authoritative coin price guides: the *Handbook of United States Coins* (1942; known as the Blue Book) and *A Guide Book of United States Coins* (1946; known as the Red Book). Both receive regular updating.

Stamp collecting was another popular hobby, especially after the many favorable endorsements made by the era's best-known philatelist, **President Franklin Delano Roosevelt** (1882–1945). While collectors on the home front continued their involvement with the hobby, the **USO (United Service Organizations)** encouraged them to donate stamps, albums, catalogs, and accessories for a program called Stamps for Servicemen. This activity let those in the armed forces either to continue an already established hobby or acquire a new one.

Soon after the entry of the United States into the war, the U.S. Department of the Treasury urged citizens of all ages to support the effort by buying federal savings stamps that ranged in cost from a dime to five dollars per stamp, although most schoolchildren bought either 10-cent or 25-cent denominations. These stamps differed from those used for postage in that they earned interest and could be pasted in bond books designed for that purpose. A full book, which contained $18.75 in stamps (or approximately $225 in 2008 dollars) could be turned in for a $25 Series E savings bond. The Scott's Standard Postage Stamp Catalogue, the foremost authority on philately, in the fall of 1942 requested that collectors purchase as many savings stamps as they could for "victory, duty, protection and recreation," an appeal that worked, although some hobbyists doubtless added a savings stamp or two as permanent additions to their collections.

Collecting as a hobby during the 1940s hardly limited itself to coins and stamps. For those with the curiosity and interest, other items—buttons, small animal figurines, dolls, autographs, documents, salt and pepper shakers, objects of art or nature—received attention as potential hobbies. Whatever the focus, they all involved acquiring a knowledge base, collecting, housing, cataloguing, and preserving.

For many, in addition to collecting, the word "hobby" means handicraft pursuits that require an assortment of tools and defined skills. During the 1940s, along with interests in photography and collecting, these pursuits occupied the leisure time of many. At home they could be as simple as sewing articles of clothing that included decorative touches done by hand. Knitting, crocheting, and quilting also flourished. Decoratively painting household objects such as waste baskets, wall trim, and serving trays brought out the artist in many.

With a steady increase in middle-class home ownership, workshops located in the garages or the basements of houses grew in popularity as more and more men gained confidence to take on do-it-yourself tasks. The term had first appeared in a

Suburban Life magazine article back in October 1912, and its application grew in the intervening years. By the 1930s, Sears, Roebuck and Company had created a building materials catalog offering everything needed to construct, remodel, modernize, or repair a house, activities that most people then viewed as a man's hobby and domain. During the 1930s, for those who did not live in a house or could not afford a workshop, schools and recreational centers opened their shop doors to would-be woodworkers.

The onset of war and the deployment of soldiers to foreign shores did not change the theory that home maintenance and building projects were a man's responsibility. But the absence of men forced many women to use their husband's or brother's or father's tools. Once women began to practice these skills, the number of do-it-yourselfers grew significantly. During the war, however, these efforts by women frequently came more from the necessity of making home repairs than as a hobby.

Anyone unsure about woodworking as a leisure pursuit during the 1940s could easily turn to **magazines** and books for help. Both *Popular Mechanics* and *Popular Science* regularly published articles about tools and projects for casual woodworkers and also assembled these articles into books such as *Forty Power Tools You Can Make* (1941, 1943, 1944, 1948; articles excerpted from *Popular Mechanics*) and *How to Get the Most Out of Your Home Workshop with Hand and Power Tools* (1946; articles taken from *Popular Science*). *Woodworking for Everybody* (1944, 1945, 1946, 1947, 1970), by John Gerald Shea (1906–1980) and Paul Nolt Wenger (active 1940s), provided useful information and served as hands-on manuals. The postwar phenomenon of many Americans moving to the suburbs and the accompanying building boom further promoted the acquisition of practical skills and set the stage for the do-it-yourself craze that blossomed in the 1950s.

Both during and after the war, many psychologists encouraged involvement with handicrafts for office workers and professional people as an effective means of relieving stress. In early 1943, the American Red Cross Hospital Recreation Corps assisted with instruction for wounded servicemen in various forms of art, woodworking, leather craft, metal craft, basket weaving, ceramics, weaving, and macramé. This approach to occupational therapy significantly contributed to the formation of hobbies for wounded soldiers on the mend. Acknowledging the success of this program, the army and navy decided to launch similar campaigns to encourage hobbies among its active members in hopes of forestalling unwanted attitudes and behaviors. Military facilities created craft centers, and the army held an exhibition of GI crafts at New York's Metropolitan Museum of Art in 1945. Many a soldier established a postwar career based on craft skills acquired while in the service.

Model making as a handicraft certainly had a place in the hierarchy of popular leisure activities both during and after the war, thanks to the availability of prefabricated materials and the ease of participating in this hobby, whatever one's degree of expertise. At the simplest level, some kits could be purchased that only required assembling the object. At the other end of the spectrum, basic materials could be purchased that called for the hobbyist to have both the tools and skills needed to follow a plan to form parts, bring those parts together as a whole, and paint or otherwise finish the model. This acquisition of necessary tools and skills allowed for a wide range of ages to enjoy making models of every description. Because of the lack of metal and plastic for anything other than the war effort, paper modeling saw some popularity during World War II.

Many other leisure activities of the 1940s could also be considered hobbies. During the war, the cultivation of **victory gardens** became a necessity to combat the scarcity and **rationing** of certain foods. It also served as an introduction to a new hobby for many. Likewise, the building of homes and accompanying lawns and gardens established lawn care as an ongoing activity and a hobby for some. A fad involving tinkering with **automobiles** to alter their appearance, as well as increase speed, created a subculture of **hot rods** and yet another postwar hobby. Finally, old-time favorites like reading, crossword puzzles, model railroading, ceramics, drawing, and painting should also be mentioned.

And in good American consumer style, by the end of the 1940s, hobbies had taken on a new dimension. Shops that supplied kits and materials became successful businesses achieving new profit records, and hobbyists, for the first time, felt increasingly comfortable making money from their new avocations.

See also: Aviation; Best Sellers (Books); Fads; Lawns, Lawnmowers, and Fertilizers; Leisure and Recreation; Levittown and Suburbanization; Newspapers; Toys; War Bonds

Selected Reading
Gelber, Steven M. *Hobbies and the Culture of Work in America.* New York: Columbia University Press, 1999.
Mott-Smith, Geoffrey. *Guide to Popular Hobbies.* Chicago: J. G. Ferguson, 1948.
Photography. *New York Times,* February 22, 1942. www.proquest.com

HOCKEY

In contrast to the grace and precision of figure skating, the sport of ice hockey offers a fast-paced test of skill, endurance, and teamwork. Brought to the New World by European settlers, the history of ice hockey primarily dates back to the 18th and 19th centuries in Canada. An outdoor game originally limited to those localities sufficiently cold for consistent ice coverage, the advent of indoor ice rinks advanced hockey to a year-round activity in many major metropolitan areas. Numerous variations on ice hockey have developed over time, and street and field hockey, played on paved or other hard-surfaced areas, enjoy considerable popularity. Because they do not rely on cold weather and ice, street and field hockey can be played in any season; some enthusiasts even play the game wearing roller skates. Many schools and colleges boast organized field hockey teams, whereas street hockey has always been played as a more impromptu sport. Whatever the variation, the object of the game remains the same: to place a puck, or hard disk—a ball in field hockey—in a goal. The term "hockey" usually applies to the game played on ice.

Given its more northern setting and climate, Canada became the home of most ice hockey during the 19th century. Rules were agreed upon and teams organized. The first amateur hockey league formed in Ontario in 1885 but succeeded in gaining only a small following. Frederick Arthur Stanley (1841–1908), known as Lord Stanley of Preston, and a governor general of Canada, in 1893 donated a competitive trophy cup to the Montreal Hockey Club, which he called the Dominion Challenge Cup, for the teams then actively participating in the game. In time, his gift became known as the Stanley Cup and emerged as the top prize in professional hockey league play.

These humble beginnings generated interest in the sport; during the 1890s, U.S. skaters began playing hockey at several New England colleges as well as other wintry sites. The National Hockey Association emerged in 1909 but suspended operations in 1917 after most of the qualified players had been drafted for fighting in World War I. The National Hockey League (NHL) came into being in 1917, and the organization now dominates the professional side of the sport. Ice hockey became a part of the Olympic Games in 1920.

By 1942, World War II had severely impacted the NHL because a majority of the players served in the military. Some league officials suggested suspending operations for the war's duration, but government and military leaders considered the continuation of professional sports good for public morale and urged the NHL to function as best as it could.

Membership declined to six teams, called "the original six," and remained that way throughout the 1940s. Four, the Boston Bruins, Chicago Black Hawks, Detroit Red Wings, and New York Rangers, came from the United States; the other two, the Montreal Canadiens and the Toronto Maple Leafs, from Canada. Despite the majority of teams being from the United States, most players claimed Canada as their home. In addition, the two Canadian teams won more Stanley Cups than their U.S. counterparts during the 1940s, with the Toronto Maple Leafs dominating the series.

Leaders in the NHL decided in 1943 to establish an ice hockey hall of fame in Kingston, Ontario, the site of North America's first hockey league. Problems and disagreements developed about location and cost, which resulted in the completion of a building in 1961, not in Kingston but in Toronto, using a refurbished bank. Since 1943, six U.S. players have been inducted. One, Frank Brimsek (1913–1998), played from 1938 to 1950 for the Boston Bruins and in 1941 made significant contributions to his

TABLE 59.   NHL Teams and Stanley Cup Winners, 1940–1950

Year	Team
1939–1940	New York Rangers
1940–1941	Boston Bruins
1941–1942	Toronto Maple Leafs
1942–1943	Detroit Red Wings
1943–1944	Montreal Canadiens
1944–1945	Toronto Maple Leafs
1945–1946	Montreal Canadiens
1946–1947	Toronto Maple Leafs
1947–1948	Toronto Maple Leafs
1948–1949	Toronto Maple Leafs
1949–1950	Detroit Red Wings

team's winning of the Stanley Cup. In 1973, a similar U.S. museum opened its doors in Eveleth, Minnesota, Brimsek's hometown. Hollywood made a comical contribution to ice hockey in 1945 with the release of a Walt Disney cartoon, *Hockey Homicide,* that featured Goofy on skates.

With the widespread availability of **television** in the 1950s, hockey found a new audience. People in warmer climates, who perhaps had never been on ice, finally experienced the excitement and continuous action that characterize ice hockey. Since then, new franchises have been developed, new rinks constructed, and "the fastest game on ice" has steadily risen in popularity.

See also: Cartoons (Film); Skating (Figure); Skating (Roller)

Selected Reading
McFarlane, Brian. *Brian McFarlane's History of Hockey.* Champaign, IL: Sagamore, 1997.
Stewart, Mark. *Hockey: A History of the Fastest Game on Ice.* New York: Franklin Watts, 1998.

HOPE, BOB

Born of British parents in Eltham, England (a part of greater London), Leslie Townes Hope (1903–2003), or Les to his friends, moved with his family to Cleveland, Ohio, in 1908. He discovered a gift for humor at an early age and parlayed those talents into vaudeville as a song and dance man while still in his teens. During the 1920s, Les Hope enjoyed modest success on the various vaudeville circuits then crisscrossing the United States. At some point around 1928, he decided on Bob as a more stage-friendly name, and it endured for the remainder of his long life. With the advent of World War II, Bob Hope became one of the most popular and beloved entertainers of the decade.

With his new name and some improved routines, the early 1930s found Hope playing New York City's Palace Theatre, the pinnacle of success for vaudevillians. He also landed a role in the ensemble casting of *Smiles,* a 1930 Broadway musical. It served as a steppingstone; after *Smiles,* he appeared in *Ballyhoo of 1932,* a short-lived revue, and then took an important part in Jerome Kern's (1885–1945) production of *Roberta* in 1933. The once-anonymous member of the chorus successfully moved to the important character of Huckleberry Haines, a bandleader, and he got to sing "You're Devastating," as well as participate in several other numbers. Critics generally liked Hope's performance, and *Roberta* would lead to significant work in other entertainment areas, as well as a continuing presence on Broadway. In 1936, he shared star billing with Ethel Merman (1908–1984) and Jimmy Durante (1893–1980) in Cole Porter's (1891–1964) *Red, Hot and Blue,* another musical comedy. Along with his acting chores, he sang Porter's inimitable "It's Delovely."

The mid-1930s also found Hope performing on network **radio,** mainly doing revue-style programs. But audiences enjoyed his comedic routines, and he eventually landed his own series, *The Pepsodent Show, Starring Bob Hope.* It premiered in 1938 with the new fall season on Tuesday nights over NBC (National Broadcasting Company); the program would remain there, along with Pepsodent toothpaste as its sponsor, until 1948. During those years, *The Pepsodent Show* became a listening ritual for millions

With a varied show business career already behind him, Bob Hope, accompanied by Bing Crosby and Dorothy Lamour, embarked on a series of comedies ostensibly set in exotic locales. This illustration shows a still from Road to Singapore, *the first of the so-called Road pictures, with the trio clowning for the camera. (Paramount Pictures/Photofest)*

of fans. Swan Soap took over sponsorship from late 1948 through the spring of 1950, when various other sponsors underwrote the broadcasts until 1955, a time when **television** had all but vanquished network radio programming.

But Hope had anticipated the rise of television; in 1953, *The Bob Hope Show* made its NBC-TV debut, running until 1956. After that, he could be found as a guest on countless programs, plus he hosted his own comedy specials for many years thereafter. Hope made his final television appearance in 1996.

While becoming established on stage and in radio, Hope also emerged as a prominent comedian in the **movies.** He began his film career in the mid-1930s with a number of forgettable musical shorts, such as *Going Spanish* (1934), *Calling All Tars* (1935), and *Watch the Birdie* (1935). He made his full-length feature debut with *The Big Broadcast of 1938.* With a cast mainly made up of popular radio personalities, Hope acquits himself well. He sings "Thanks for the Memory" (1937) in a duet with Shirley Ross (1913–1975); the tune went on to win the 1938 Academy Award for best song. In light of that, "Thanks for the Memory" became Hope's theme song: he used it on both his radio shows and later television appearances. Given the commercial success of *The Big Broadcast of 1938,* Paramount Pictures reunited the two in *Thanks for the Memory,* a lesser film from that same year designed to capitalize on the popularity of the previous movie. Despite its title, Hope and Ross instead sing "Two Sleepy People," another excellent melody but probably not the anticipated song. At this point, however, Hope had established himself as both a radio and movie star.

Among his wide circle of friends, Hope counted **Bing Crosby** (1903–1977) as one of his closest and best. The two would make a number of comedies during the 1940s and after, and moviegoers took to their brand of humor. Crosby's easygoing demeanor proved the perfect foil to Hope's machine-gun delivery of jokes and wisecracks. With the opening of the decade, Hope's first film for 1940 bore the title *Road to Singapore*. It also served as his first pairing with Crosby.

In addition to the five Road pictures noted below, Hope, Crosby, and Lamour would also collaborate on *Road to Bali* in 1952 and *The Road to Hong Kong* in 1962, for a total of seven comedies using a road to somewhere as their collective theme. These motion pictures created a category all their own. Uneven at times, and going from hilarity to boring stretches, they present the threesome at their cinematic best.

Hope's movie career clearly moved along in high gear during the 1940s, with 19 releases in 10 years. Most of them, in retrospect, have not aged well. Quickly made and generally mediocre, they provide some chuckles but tend to lack any memorable routines that would elevate them to the realm of classic comedies. A handful of the 19 films, however, provide a look at just how good Hope really was, both in terms of his own skills and those of strong costars, gifted directors, and sharp screenwriters.

TABLE 60. Bob Hope Feature Films, 1940–1949

Year	Title	Notes
1940	*Road to Singapore*	with Bing Crosby, Dorothy Lamour (the first Road picture)
	The Ghost Breakers	with Paulette Goddard
1941	*Road to Zanzibar*	with Bing Crosby, Dorothy Lamour (the second Road picture)
	Caught in the Draft	with Dorothy Lamour
	Nothing But the Truth	with Paulette Goddard
	Louisiana Purchase	with Victor Moore
1942	*My Favorite Blonde*	with Madeleine Carroll
	Road to Morocco	with Bing Crosby, Dorothy Lamour (the third Road picture)
1943	*They Got Me Covered*	with Dorothy Lamour
	Let's Face It	with Betty Hutton
1944	*The Princess and the Pirate*	with Virginia Mayo, Bing Crosby (cameo)
1946	*Road to Utopia*	with Bing Crosby, Dorothy Lamour (the fourth Road picture)
	Monsieur Beaucaire	with Joan Caulfield
1947	*My Favorite Brunette*	with Dorothy Lamour
	Where There's Life	with Signe Hasso, William Bendix
	Road to Rio	with Bing Crosby, Dorothy Lamour (the fifth Road picture)
1948	*The Paleface*	with Jane Russell
1949	*Sorrowful Jones*	with Lucille Ball
	The Great Lover	with Rhonda Fleming

For example, in 1948's *The Paleface,* he portrays a patented Hope character, in this case "Painless" Peter Potter, a timid dentist in the Wild West. The picture plays as a straight Western, except that Hope and Jane Russell (b. 1921) spoof the genre's conventions, often self-consciously, but to good effect. In addition, Hope gets to sing "Buttons and Bows," a cute tune—itself something of a spoof—penned by Ray Evans (1915–2007) and Jay Livingston (1915–2001) for the movie. It earned an Academy Award for best movie song of 1948.

In like manner, *The Ghost Breakers* (1940) takes the horror picture genre and gives the audience some genuine chills. But Hope's string of quips and the able support of Paulette Goddard (1910–1990) also allow for strong comedy elements. Willie Best (1913–1962), an underappreciated black actor of the period, provides additional humor, albeit some of it fitting racial stereotypes, but he nonetheless assumes a major role in the picture. *The Ghost Breakers* followed close on the heels of 1939's *The Cat and the Canary,* another mix of comedy and horror that had done well at the box office.

Movies, radio programs, and stage appearances aside, the reason Americans held Bob Hope in such high esteem can be attributed to his ceaseless humanitarian efforts, especially for U.S. military personnel. Even before the first shots had been fired against the Axis powers, Hope and his staff began planning for ways the entertainer could take his shows to the troops. By the spring of 1941, he had performed for the **USO (United Service Organizations)** at California bases. Once war had been declared in December 1941, he and his entourage were off and running to places around the globe—wherever U.S. troops could be found. He traveled to remote islands in the Pacific, war zones in Europe and North Africa, stateside bases, and isolated posts in Alaska, always with good cheer, a supply of wisecracks about military life, and several attractive Hollywood starlets for soldiers a long way from home.

Since the war usually found them far from the NBC studios in California, *The Pepsodent Show, Starring Bob Hope* usually broadcast from wherever Hope and his crew might be. Despite the technical problems such programs might face, audiences appreciated the fact that these entertainers voluntarily chose to be on the front lines instead of in a secure network studio.

The recipient of virtually every award a grateful nation could bestow, Hope returned to the front line for the Korean War in the 1950s, Vietnam in the 1960s and 1970s, and even to the Middle East for the first Gulf War in 1990–1991 at the age of 87. He also campaigned for the Hollywood Canteen in the 1940s, helped raise money for **war bonds,** and visited military hospitals whenever and wherever he could.

The Academy Award for best actor proved to be the one honor that eluded Bob Hope, and it became the source of a continuing series of gags. Hope hosted the Academy Award ceremonies a record 18 times between 1939 and 1977 (during the 1940s, the network broadcast them from Hollywood). Despite his popularity as a comedian, his movies seldom forced him to do any serious acting of a caliber that might make him an eligible recipient, and he, of course, realized that. The Academy of Motion Picture Arts and Sciences (AMPAS) was also aware of this situation because of his countless contributions to the industry; to rectify the situation, he received formal recognition on four separate occasions from this prestigious group. In 1940, he was given a medal for his achievements in film; in 1944, AMPAS granted him honorary life membership in the organization. In 1952, he finally received an Academy statuette, or Oscar, not for acting, but for his contributions to the industry, and in 1965 another gold medal came his way. These recognitions were in addition to the many professional accolades he earned from other organizations.

Bob Hope lived to be 100. Although he had become something of a national icon in his later years because of his endless good works, he probably gained his greatest popularity as an entertainer during the 1940s and 1950s, thanks primarily to his movie and radio endeavors.

See also: Advertising; Broadway Shows (Comedy and Drama); Broadway Shows (Musicals); Canteens; Comedies (Film); Horror and Thriller Films; Race Relations and Stereotyping; Radio Programming: Music and Variety Shows; Westerns (Film)

Selected Reading
Faith, William Robert. *Bob Hope: A Life in Comedy.* New York: DaCapo Press, 2003.
Grudens, Richard. *The Spirit of Bob Hope: One Hundred Years, One Million Laughs.* Stony Brook, NY: Celebrity Profiles, 2004.

HORROR AND THRILLER FILMS

These two movie genres have much in common: they are meant to get audiences on the edge of their seats, arouse excitement, and create a collective feeling of suspense—what will occur next, and how will it happen? Although virtually all horror films can be seen as a subcategory of the thriller, few thrillers, by themselves, qualify as traditional horror **movies.**

The reason for this seeming paradox arises from the content of the two types. Horror pictures feature bizarre characters or once-human figures such as mummies or zombies that create fear or loathing on the part of the beholder. Often these movies introduce alien life forms, such as mutated animals or weird creatures not of this world, but always the emphasis in the presentation rests in creating a sense of terror or dread. Directors bring this about through special effects and plotting that minimize story and characterization and instead generate a creepy setting designed to frighten the audience. A ghoul slogging through a murky bog in pursuit of some hapless, screaming victim just ahead should arouse even the most lethargic viewers who can neither warn nor assist the intended prey.

A well-wrought thriller, on the other hand, seldom introduces strange, grotesque people or things, nor does it rely on special effects to any great degree. Instead, the thriller presents a story in which tension grows and audience anxiety rises, reactions that result from stories that place realistic people in realistic situations. A werewolf or a vampire can frighten viewers, but so can a psychotic killer or a ticking time bomb; one achieves its effect from a blend of fantasy and a willing suspension of disbelief, whereas the other creates an actuality that fits within the audience's realm of possibilities. A car careening down a hillside, out of control, while the driver, hands bound, works furiously to untie the knots in time to grab the steering wheel may be imaginative cinematically but hardly the stuff of horror movies. And yet the situation will grip the viewer who once again helplessly watches, unable to do anything as the scene unfolds. The emotional effects achieved by horror and thriller films have much in common.

The 1930s marked the heyday of the American horror film, with classics like *Dracula* (1931) *Frankenstein* (1931), and *King Kong* (1933), but the 1940s nevertheless managed to produce a respectable number of pictures. Originality and shock value, however, qualities so much in abundance in the preceding decade, were frequently replaced by repetitiveness and an overreliance on cheap special effects during the war years and immediately thereafter. The studios also placed great faith in the box office appeal of a handful of actors, such as Boris Karloff (1887–1969), Bela Lugosi (1882–1956), Lon Chaney Jr. (1906–1973), and John Carradine (1906–1988), placing them in one mediocre tale after another, an effort that probably diluted their already-limited popularity instead of enhancing it.

The opening years of the decade actually saw a number of fairly effective releases in the genre; pictures like *Black Friday* (1940), *The Wolf Man* (1941), *Cat People* (1942), and *Son of Dracula* (1943) contain the same terror-inducing elements their illustrious predecessors boasted just a short time earlier. But tastes change, especially in the midst of inferior efforts in a category, and thrillers moved up as horror films dipped in popularity around mid-decade. An occasional horror standout still came along—*Isle of the Dead* (1945), for example—but most must be seen as mere shadows of past glories. Perhaps the best evidence of their decline came about with the 1948 release of *Bud Abbott and Lou Costello Meet Frankenstein.* The two slapstick comedians (Abbott, 1895–1974; Costello, 1906–1959) make a mockery of iconic horror characters and conventions. In addition to Frankenstein, they also encounter Dracula and the Wolf Man and gleefully reduce what once induced fear to parody.

The new generation of thrillers that began around mid-decade to replace horror films on theater marquees demonstrated considerable box office appeal, always the primary measure of success for Hollywood. Led by a host of suspenseful mysteries and a new style, **film noir,** they quickly filled the gap left by the fading horror genre. With the Second World War looming and on everyone's minds, tense, topical motion pictures like *Foreign Correspondent* and *Night Train to Munich* (both 1940) drew audiences as their heroes strove to keep out the clutches of Nazi villains. After Pearl Harbor, the industry settled into more traditional fare, such as *The Glass*

The horror and thriller genre of movies attracted audiences throughout the decade. This still from The Beast with Five Fingers *(1946) shows Andrea King discovering a disembodied human hand in a wall cabinet. Thanks to special effects, audiences were treated to the requisite thrills and chills. (Warner Bros./Photofest)*

Key (1942) and *Shadow of a Doubt* (1943), movies that kept audiences guessing and anxious.

By the middle 1940s, film noir, with its use of eerie black-and-white **photography** and rumpled, tired heroes, began to make inroads into traditional thriller territory. Films like *Dark Waters* and *Double Indemnity* (both 1944), *Cornered* and *Detour* (both 1945), and *The Blue Dahlia* and *The Postman Always Rings Twice* (both 1946) paved the way to a veritable deluge of film noir/thriller offerings. Most of the 1947 to 1949 entries in the table below fall under this combined category. Horror films, on the other hand, are notable by their absence after 1946.

This imbalance would persist on into the 1950s, at which time film noir would lose its previous novelty and dominance, replaced by brighter, less gloomy thrillers that utilized Technicolor, wide screens, and more positive characterizations. The dark, nail-biting stories of the later 1940s and early 1950s mark a brief moment in film history—one that continues to be loved by aficionados, but a moment nonetheless.

TABLE 61. Representative Motion Pictures in the Horror-Terror Genres, 1940–1949

Year	Film Titles	Stars
1940	The Ape	Boris Karloff, Maris Wrixon
	Before I Hang	Boris Karloff, Evelyn Keyes
	Black Friday	Boris Karloff, Bela Lugosi
	Dark Eyes of London	Bela Lugosi, Hugh Williams
	The Door with Seven Locks	Lilli Palmer, Leslie Banks
	Foreign Correspondent	Joel McCrea, Laraine Day
	The Mummy's Hand	Dick Foran, Wallace Ford
	Night Train to Munich	Rex Harrison, Paul Henreid
	Rebecca	Joan Fontaine, Laurence Olivier
	Stranger on the Third Floor	Peter Lorre, Elisha Cook Jr.
1941	Among the Living	Albert Dekker, Susan Hayward
	The Black Cat	Basil Rathbone, Bela Lugosi
	The Devil Commands	Boris Karloff, Amanda Duff
	Dr. Jekyll and Mr. Hyde	Spencer Tracy, Ingrid Bergman
	High Sierra	Humphrey Bogart, Ida Lupino
	I Wake Up Screaming	Betty Grable, Victor Mature
	The Invisible Ghost	Bela Lugosi, Polly Ann Young
	King of the Zombies	Dick Purcell, Mantan Moreland
	Suspicion	Cary Grant, Joan Fontaine
	The Wolf Man	Lon Chaney Jr., Claude Rains
1942	The Boogie Man Will Get You	Boris Karloff, Peter Lorre
	Bowery at Midnight	Bela Lugosi, Tom Neal
	Cat People	Simone Simon, Kent Smith
	The Corpse Vanishes	Bela Lugosi, Luana Walters
	The Glass Key	Alan Ladd, Brian Donlevy
	The Ghost of Frankenstein	Lon Chaney Jr., Bela Lugosi
	I Wake Up Screaming	Betty Grable, Victor Mature
	The Man with Two Lives	Edward Norris, Frederick Burton
	Nightmare	Diana Barrymore, Brian Donlevy
	Night Monster	Bela Lugosi, Lionel Atwill

(continued)

TABLE 61. (continued)

Year	Film Titles	Stars
1943	The Black Raven	George Zucco, Robert Livingston
	Dead Men Walk	George Zucco, Dwight Frye
	Frankenstein Meets the Wolf Man	Lon Chaney Jr., Bela Lugosi
	The Ghost Ship	Richard Dix, Russell Wade
	I Walked with a Zombie	Frances Dee, Tom Conway
	The Leopard Man	Dennis O'Keefe, Jean Brooks
	Phantom of the Opera	Claude Rains, Nelson Eddy
	The Seventh Victim	Tom Conway, Kim Hunter
	Shadow of a Doubt	Joseph Cotton, Teresa Wright
	Son of Dracula	Lon Chaney Jr., Robert Paige
1944	Bluebeard	John Carradine, Jean Parker
	The Climax	Boris Karloff, Susannah Foster
	The Curse of the Cat People	Simone Simon, Kent Smith
	Dangerous Passage	Robert Lowery, Phyllis Brooks
	Dark Waters	Merle Oberon, Franchot Tone
	Double Indemnity	Barbara Stanwyck, Fred MacMurray
	House of Frankenstein	Boris Karloff, Lon Chaney Jr., John Carradine
	Jungle Woman	J. Acquanetta, Carrol Naish
	The Lady and the Monster	Erich von Stroheim, Richard Arlen
	The Uninvited	Ray Milland, Gail Russell
1945	And Then There Were None	Barry Fitzgerald, Walter Huston
	The Body Snatcher	Boris Karloff, Bela Lugosi
	Cornered	Dick Powell, Walter Slezak
	Dead of Night	Mervyn Johns, Roland Culver
	Detour	Tom Neal, Ann Savage
	Fallen Angel	Alice Faye, Linda Darnell
	House of Dracula	Lon Chaney Jr., John Carradine
	Isle of the Dead	Boris Karloff, Ellen Drew
	A Place of One's Own	James Mason, Margaret Lockwood
	Spellbound	Gregory Peck, Ingrid Bergman
1946	The Beast with Five Fingers	Robert Alda, Peter Lorre
	Bedlam	Boris Karloff, Anna Lee
	The Blue Dahlia	Alan Ladd, Veronica Lake
	Dragonwyck	Gene Tierney, Walter Huston, Vincent Price
	The Face of Marble	John Carradine, Claudia Drake
	A Game of Death	John Loder, Audrey Long
	The Postman Always Rings Twice	John Garfield, Lana Turner
	Shock	Vincent Price, Lynn Bari
	The Spiral Staircase	Dorothy McGuire, Ethel Barrymore
	The Verdict	Sidney Greenstreet, Peter Lorre
1947	Fear in the Night	Paul Kelly, DeForest Kelley
	Framed	Glenn Ford, Barry Sullivan
	The Long Night	Henry Fonda, Vincent Price
	Lured	George Sanders, Lucille Ball
	Odd Man Out	James Mason, Robert Newton

Year	Film Titles	Stars
	Out of the Past	Robert Mitchum, Kirk Douglas
	The Red House	Edward G. Robinson, Judith Anderson
	Riffraff	Pat O'Brien, Walter Slezak
	Scared to Death	Bela Lugosi, George Zucco
	They Won't Believe Me	Robert Young, Susan Hayward
1948	*Caged Fury*	Richard Denning, Buster Crabbe
	The Lady from Shanghai	Orson Welles, Rita Hayworth
	Moonrise	Dane Clark, Gail Russell
	Night Has a Thousand Eyes	Edward G. Robinson, Gail Russell
	Raw Deal	Dennis O'Keefe, Claire Trevor
	Road House	Ida Lupino, Cornel Wilde
	Ruthless	Zachary Scott, Louis Hayward
	Secret Beyond the Door	Joan Bennett, Michael Redgrave
	Sorry, Wrong Number	Barbara Stanwyck, Burt Lancaster
	Unknown Island	Virginia Grey, Phillip Reed
1949	*Black Magic*	Orson Welles, Akim Tamiroff
	C-Man	Dean Jagger, John Carradine
	The Man on the Eiffel Tower	Charles Laughton, Franchot Tone
	Manhandled	Dorothy Lamour, Sterling Hayden
	Obsession	Robert Newton, Sally Gray
	Take One False Step	William Powell, Shelly Winters
	Thieves' Highway	Lee J. Cobb, Richard Conte
	The Third Man	Orson Welles, Joseph Cotton
	White Heat	James Cagney, Virginia Mayo
	The Window	Bobby Driscoll, Paul Stewart

See also: Crime and Mystery Films; Drama (Film); Radio Programming: Action, Crime, Police, and Detective Shows; Radio Programming: Drama and Anthology Shows; Serial Films

Selected Reading

Clarens, Carlos. *An Illustrated History of the Horror Film.* New York: Capricorn Books, 1967.
Huss, Roy, and T. J. Huss. *Focus on the Horror Film.* Englewood Cliffs, NJ: Prentice Hall, 1972.
Naremore, James. *More Than Night: Film Noir and Its Contexts.* Berkeley: University of California Press, 1998.
Robson, Eddie. *Film Noir.* London: Virgin Books, 2005.

HORSE RACING

Winning is a crucial goal in any sport. For horse owners, trainers, and jockeys, monetary stakes accompany the satisfaction and adrenalin flow of a win; for spectators, in addition to the excitement, gambling on a possible winner puts money in the pockets of some and takes it out of others. These elements have supported the growth of horse racing as a sport since the first crude track on Long Island, New York, in 1665.

The presence of criminal activities during horse racing's early development as a national sport came close to curtailing its success, but the formation of the American Jockey Club in 1894, and its subsequent assumption of responsibility for pedigree registration in *The American Stud Book,* brought rules and oversight that eliminated much of the corruption at over 300 racetracks across the country. By the early 1900s, however, strong antigambling sentiment reigned, and the number of active race tracks had dwindled to 25.

In 1908, the Kentucky legislature, in an attempt to turn around this serious decline in the popularity of horse racing, sanctioned pari-mutuel betting on the Kentucky Derby, perhaps the most famous of all American races. This system has all bettors wagering among themselves, not against the house, and the track then takes a percentage of money out of the pool to cover expenses before awarding the payoffs. This form of gambling turned out to be a crowd pleaser, and soon other state legislatures agreed to allow pari-mutuel betting in exchange for a cut of the money wagered. Horse racing once again flourished as a popular spectator sport and even drew good crowds during the dark days of the Great Depression (1929–1933).

During the late 1930s, Seabiscuit (1933–1947), a winning horse popular to the level of celebrity and named American Horse of the Year in 1938, furthered his place in the history books in 1940. A leg injury had kept him out of racing in 1939, but sufficient recovery encouraged his owner, Charles S. Howard (1877–1950), to register him in the La Jolla (California) Handicap on February 9, 1940. Although Seabiscuit only placed third, it was enough for him to continue racing, and a month later jockey Red Pollard (1909–1981) rode him to victory over his training partner, Kayak II (1935–n.d.), before a cheering crowd of 78,000 at California's Santa Anita Handicap. Seabiscuit officially retired on April 10, 1940, as horse racing's all-time leading money winner at the time, with $437,740 (approximately $6.75 million in 2008 dollars).

The United States' entry into World War II on December 7, 1941, changed life on the home front in many ways, eventually including horse racing. During the first full year of the war, the sport continued with business as usual and set records in paid taxes, attendance, and purses. But a lack of jockeys and other track workers because of military service or work in defense plants, along with **rationing** and a curtailment of public **transportation,** took their toll. Races became subject to approval by local War Manpower Commissions. Saratoga Springs Race Track in upstate New York, a premier thoroughbred site since 1863, closed after the 1942 season and remained dark until 1946, when it hosted a record opening-day crowd. Many other tracks, however, managed to continue operations. They often designated Army-Navy Days for fundraising and, even with reduced attendance, collectively made major contributions to war relief—a little over $3 million in 1942 followed by more than $4 million in 1943 (approximately $42 million and $50 million in 2008 dollars, respectively). The first full season following the war broke all gross revenue records, and racing income continued to rise through 1948.

During the development and growth of American thoroughbred horse racing, sometimes referred to as the "sport of kings," three events always drew significant attention: the Kentucky Derby at Churchill Downs, in Louisville, Kentucky (opened 1875), the Preakness Stakes at Pimlico Race Course in Baltimore, Maryland (1870), and the Belmont Stakes at Belmont Park in Elmont, New York (1905). In 1919, a horse named Sir Barton (1916–1937) won all three events in a single season, creating a new racing tradition and making him the first Triple Crown winner. A five-week schedule beginning with the first Saturday in May with the Kentucky Derby and ending in early June with the Belmont Stakes, along with each race covering a different distance, offers a tremendous challenge for a horse.

Over the course of Triple Crown racing history, 11 horses have held the title, 4 of them in the 1940s. There have been no winners since 1978. Before the country entered World War II, Whirlaway (1938–1953) ridden by Eddie Arcaro (1916–1997) earned the honor in 1941. Two years later, Johnny Longden (1907–2003), atop Count Fleet (1940–1973), achieved the feat. Next came Assault (1943–1971) in 1946, with the reins held by Warren Mehrtens (1920–1997). In 1947, Citation (1945–1970) gave the Triple Crown spot for a second time to Arcaro, who remains the only jockey to be in the saddle for two Triple Crowns. The term "Triple Crown" also appears in **baseball;** it means a hitter who leads in the league in three areas: home runs, batting average, and runs batted in and a pitcher who leads in earned run average, wins, and strikeouts during a single major league baseball season.

All of the above-mentioned horses—Whirlaway, Count Fleet, Assault, and Citation—received the American Horse of the Year award the years they won the Crown. Whirlaway, always a crowd favorite, also gained the title again in 1942. The award, the highest honor given in American thoroughbred racing to a horse, irrespective of age, recognizes the performance deemed the best during the season. Whirlaway continued to race to age five and won 32 out of 60 contests. Over his career, he earned $561,161 (approximately $7 million in 2008 dollars). Count Fleet, with 16 victories out of 21 races and purses totaling $250,300 (approximately $3 million in 2008 money), stopped racing at age three because of an injury. Both Whirlaway and Count Fleet spent many years as studs producing other winning thoroughbreds. Assault retired at age four, but unable to sire a foal, returned to the sport until age seven. He had a record of 18 wins out of 42 races and amassed $675,470 (approximately $6.5 million in 2008 dollars) for his owners.

Citation became a high-profile stallion during his career. As a two-year-old, he won eight of nine events and was named the champion two-year-old. By the end of his third year, he had 27 victories and two second places, as well as a 15-race winning streak. He did not compete in 1949, but won his first comeback contest in 1950, giving him 16 victories in a row. His owner retired him at age six, having reached a goal of earnings that exceeded $1 million—$1,085,760 (approximately $16.75 million in 2008 dollars).

In addition to highly publicized thoroughbred racing, other forms of the sport exist in the United States. Harness racing, where standard-bred horses, sometimes called trotters, run in a specified gait and pull a two-wheel cart, dates back to ancient times and earned considerable popularity in the United States in the days before **automobiles.** Known as the "sport of the people," it frequently served as a major attraction at local and state fairs. Interest dropped as cars replaced horses and the country became more urbanized. Harness racing regained a significant following in 1940, when Roosevelt Raceway in New York moved the event to the evening, under lights, with pari-mutuel betting. This enabled harness racing to attract larger crowds and, like thoroughbred racing, soon had an impressive following across the country. Since 1955, harness racing has offered a Triple Crown to three-year-old trotters that in the same year win the Hambletonian, held at Meadowlands, New Jersey; the Yonkers Trot, at Yonkers, New York; and the Kentucky Futurity at Lexington, Kentucky.

The steeplechase, a race over a two- or four-mile course that features obstacles such as brush fences, stone walls, timber rails, and water jumps, gained recognition in the United States in the late 1800s and since then has experienced shifts in popularity and uneven media coverage. The Iroquois Steeplechase, held for the first time in Nashville, Tennessee, in 1941, has been an annual event at Percy Warner Park, with the exception of one year off during World War II. In the late 1940s, the Broad Hollow Steeplechase Handicap, held on Long Island, New York, the Brook National Steeplechase Handicap and the Grand National, both at Belmont Park, served as the Triple Crown events for steeplechase racing with American Way (n.d.) winning in 1948 and Trough Hill (n.d.) in 1949. Frank David "Dooley" Adams (1927–2004) started his career as a steeplechase jockey in 1941 and went on to set records in a number of races won within a year.

The sports sections of larger **newspapers** provided betting odds and detailed statistics on thoroughbred racing. On the funny pages, a few **comic strips** featured horse racing as part of their storyline, but they constituted a distinct minority. Cartoonist Kenneth Kling (1895–1970) wrote and drew *Joe and Asbestos,* a series focusing on characters that spent most of their time around tracks. It circulated only in major metropolitan dailies where racing had its biggest following, but within those limitations enjoyed success. It ran from 1926 to 1966. A more humorous take appeared with Billy De Beck's (1890–1942) *Barney Google,* which premiered in 1919. The misshapen Google owns a bumbling horse he calls Spark Plug, a creature that never wins a race. Their misadventures color the strip through several decades, although Google's hillbilly pal, Snuffy Smith, comes to dominate the tales in the 1940s. It continues to run, but with new artists and under the name *Snuffy Smith.*

Regarding **radio** coverage, Clem McCarthy (1882–1962), an NBC (National Broadcasting Company) sportscaster and public address announcer, gained fame for his commentaries on horse races and prizefights. Known for his gravelly voice and dramatic style, McCarthy described most of the Kentucky Derby races until 1950. In announcing for the Preakness Stakes in 1947, he mistakenly identified the winner when a crowd standing on a platform blocked his view just as two horses switched places. Despite the embarrassment, he readily acknowledged his error. **Television** also viewed horse racing as a broadcasting opportunity; in 1948, CBS (Columbia Broadcasting System) televised the Preakness Stakes for the first time. The following year, the Kentucky Derby received similar coverage on a limited basis by a local station.

Hollywood probably embraced horse racing the most enthusiastically, cranking out a number of B **movies** during the 1940s. Two, *Black Gold* (1947) starring Anthony Quinn (1915–2001) and *The Story of Seabiscuit* (1949) starring Shirley Temple (b. 1928), feature McCarthy as a track announcer. *National Velvet* (1944), an A picture with Mickey Rooney (b. 1920), Elizabeth Taylor (b. 1932), and Anne Revere (1903–1990), details a simple story of a boy, a girl, and a horse. It won two Academy Awards, Anne Revere for best actress in a supporting role, and Robert Kern (1885–1972) for best film editing. *The Winner's Circle* (1948), presented in somewhat of a documentary format with a narrator, tells the life story of a famous race horse, in all likelihood a fictionalized Seabiscuit, with Johnny Longden playing himself. It includes film footage of many champion horses, including Whirlaway, Assault, Sir Barton, and even some frames with Seabiscuit.

Many elements go into making a horse a winner and champion, all with a goal of speed. Owners, champion jockeys, and expert trainers come and go, but their speedy champion thoroughbreds such as Seabiscuit, Whirlaway, and Citation, stay with us as a part of America's culture and heritage.

See also: Best Sellers (Books); Radio Programming: News, Sports, Public Affairs, and Talk

Selected Reading
Horse Racing and World War II. *New York Times,* December 22, 1940; May, 25, 1942; January 1, 1943; December 26, 1943; August 6, 1946. www.proquest.com
Robertson, William H. P. *The History of Thoroughbred Racing in America.* Englewood Cliffs, NJ: Prentice Hall, 1964.
Simon, Mary. *Racing through the Century: The Story of Thoroughbred Racing in America.* Irvine, CA: Bowtie Press, 2002.

HOT RODS AND DRAG RACING

The hot rod, a seemingly ordinary, but older, automobile possessed of a powerful engine and stripped of all unnecessary items, fascinated many Americans almost from its first appearance some time in the 1930s, although no name other than "fast car," "race car," "modified car," "roadster," and so on existed then to identify these vehicles. The etymology of "hot rod" remains vague at best; certainly "hot" suggests speed, but "rod" has never been a synonym for an automobile, but the term began appearing in the early 1940s and quickly caught on, first with automotive and racing fans and then with the general public, and has long since entered the language.

As car ownership became widespread following World War I, tinkering with an automobile evolved as a rite of passage for many young men, turning into a hobby for some and even a passion for a few. A long-lived comic strip, *Gasoline Alley* (1918 to present), celebrated this interest in its early years, and doubtless many readers identified with its mechanically inclined characters. Both in fiction and real life, significant numbers of males, young and old, souped up their vehicles and took them out to quiet back roads to test their capabilities, to see what they could do. Hot rods in all their manifestations gained a particularly strong following in Southern California during the late 1930s and early 1940s, where a type of competition called drag racing caught on. A drag race, in its simplest form, consists of several cars, usually two at a time, that accelerate from a standing start over a quarter-mile track. The track might actually be a straight stretch of deserted highway, and the driver who reaches the finish line first can claim to be the winner.

Naturally, law enforcement officials took a dim view of these activities, so in an attempt to sanction what many saw as an illegal sport, the Southern California Timing Association (SCTA), which had been founded in 1937, developed sophisticated timing devices. The group offered driving classes and promoted safe racing, urging would-be racers to speed in sanctioned events on the flat, hard surfaces that abounded in the dry lakebeds of the Mojave Desert. The SCTA attempted in this way to discourage racing on the residential streets of California towns and cities, particularly in the greater Los

Angeles area. In 1941, the SCTA introduced a monthly publication called *Throttle Magazine*. It intended to track racing results, run features on some of the better cars, and report on new safety and speed concerns. The attack on Pearl Harbor in December of that year, however, caused *Throttle* to fold shortly thereafter; gas-guzzling cars suddenly lost favor in the midst of fuel shortages and **rationing**.

World War II may have closed down the pioneering magazine, but the fascination and mystique of hot rods kept drag racing alive, if only in memory. The route for servicemen headed to the war in the Pacific often took them through California. While on leave, they occasionally witnessed modified cars careening through the city streets. Throughout the conflict, GIs native to the West Coast told exciting stories and showed pictures about these activities to any other soldiers wiling to listen. As a result, many servicemen became intrigued with the possibility of owning a hot rod and eventually experiencing the thrill of racing for themselves. When these youthful veterans returned to the States, they often had gained the mechanical skills, along with sufficient money, needed for creating such a vehicle. Their overseas dreams could become a reality.

But these same young men, when behind the wheel of a hot rod, often found themselves stereotyped as unsavory hoodlums, not war-weary veterans. Disregard for laws, especially speeding, along with a demeanor that some judged to be outlaw behavior, created reams of negative publicity that soon snowballed into national coverage. In

A 1950 Hollywood production called Hot Rod *highlighted a growing fad among teenagers and young men. They drove customized fast cars, the ultimate status symbol for that group. (Monogram Pictures/Photofest)*

January 1948, in an attempt to counter this kind of image, the SCTA sponsored its first Annual Automotive Equipment Display and Hot Rod Exposition at the National Guard Armory in Los Angeles.

For this event, Robert E. "Pete" Petersen (1926–2007), a youthful car enthusiast, published the first issue of *Hot Rod* magazine, a periodical that recognized hot-rodding as more than a fad or questionable hobby, but as a legitimate endeavor. The premier issue of *Hot Rod* had an initial print run of 5,000 copies; by 1950, Peterson was producing 200,000 copies each month. Recognizing early on that hot-rodding reflected not just fast cars, but a growing interest in **automobiles** generally, Petersen in 1949 inaugurated *Motor Trend,* a magazine that appealed to a much broader range of drivers. Both publications have long since established enthusiastic readerships that have continued into the 21st century.

By the end of the 1940s, hot rods and drag racing had advanced from the days of back roads and street racing. No longer limited to older cars, the sport saw a wide variety of models, particularly Fords, Mercuries, Studebakers, Chevrolets, Oldsmobiles, and Cadillacs. Some of the better drivers could push their deceptive vintage cars to speeds in excess of 100 miles per hour in the space of a quarter-mile.

To meet the demands of a growing number of hot rod and racing fans, a second group, the Russeta Timing Association (RTA), organized in 1948. Working with the SCTA, the two organizations held classes and speed events at the desert lakebeds. In addition, many small military airports had been constructed throughout the United States during the war, and their long, straight runways often became available when peace returned. Some drag racing fans yearned for even faster events, and, in 1949, they saw their wishes granted; southern Utah hosted the first National Speed Trials. A gathering designed specifically for hot rods, the trials utilized the vast surfaces found at the Bonneville Salt Flats. This venue offered longer runs that virtually guaranteed faster times.

While the RTA and SCTA had given structure to the events at the dry lakes and airfields, a new group, the National Hot Rod Association (NHRA) came along in 1951. It, too, monitored and promoted drag racing with an emphasis on getting racing off the streets and onto designated tracks. Headed by Wally Parks (1913–2007), one of the original founders of the SCTA and editor of *Hot Rod,* NHRA finally brought respectability to a sport that had been viewed as dangerous and also vindicated its participants, who many saw as rebellious. NHRA sent hot-rodders across the country to speak at clubs and law enforcement gatherings about the merits of legal drag racing and sanctioned events, and they usually enjoyed success in spreading their message.

While the hot rod hobby was gaining legitimacy and respect on the West Coast, a group of automobile enthusiasts worked to achieve similar ends on the East Coast. In 1947, after a decade or more of pursuing their passion on small dirt tracks scattered throughout the Southeast, the National Association of Stock Car Auto Racing took shape at Daytona Beach, Florida. Most people know this organization as NASCAR, today the largest automotive racing group in the United States.

Stock cars, unlike heavily modified hot rods, attempted to be true to their name, particularly in the formative years of NASCAR. Regular factory models of standard Detroit brands—Chrysler, Ford, and General Motors—competed in small races before small crowds. Drivers sometimes drove their own vehicles to these events, raced them, and, if still operable, drove them home. That would all change in the 1950s and later, of course, but in the 1940s, stock car racing had to define itself.

Hot rods or stock cars and sensing profits to be made, publishers, recording companies, and the **movies** looked for opportunities to connect with these growing sports. Success for the entertainment industry would come in the early 1950s, when the hot rod and stock car phenomenon had become more acceptable elements of American popular culture. Author Henry Gregor Felsen (1916–1995), who had written detective stories before joining the Marine Corps, proved pivotal in this regard. During the war, he contributed articles for *Leatherneck* magazine, but once back home in Iowa, he wrote *Hot Rod* (1951), a novel about the sport and the people associated with it. Designed for adolescent readers, *Hot Rod* struck a nerve, although not all school libraries would place the book on their shelves, deeming it inappropriate for their audience. Nevertheless, the book climbed on lists of best-selling literature for teenagers and remained a strong favorite for nearly 30 years.

On the music side of things, many songs have been recorded with the words "hot rod" in the lyrics, but they too were late in coming. One of the first, "Hot Rod Race" (ca. 1950), spawned a number of imitations, so pinpointing details about them poses problems. Several individuals have, from time to time, taken credit for "Hot Rod Race," but Arkie Shibley (1914–1975) and/or George Wilson (n.d.; the name may be a pseudonym for Shibley) receive the most mention as composers, although the correct answer remains in doubt. Regardless, the tune tells the story of a race between two cars, a Ford and a Mercury (variants employ other makes). A 1950 recording by Shibley and His Mountain Dew Boys reached the No. 5 spot on *Billboard*'s Country Charts in 1951. Other songs about hot rods date mainly from the 1950s and beyond. "Hot Rod Lincoln" (1955) retells the action of "Hot Rod Race" and has become much better known. In this later song, a Lincoln and a Cadillac replace the previous cars.

Like the recording business, Hollywood slowly capitalized on the widespread interest shown in hot rods, drag racing, and stock cars. Monogram Pictures Corporation, a small studio, released a motion picture titled *Hot Rod* in 1950, but its cast of unknowns failed to stir much interest. By the mid-1950s, however, the industry had realized the potential of such pictures, and produced a spate of films, such as *Dragstrip Girl* (1957), *Hot Rod Girl* (1956), and *Joy Ride* (1958), which they marketed directly at teenagers. As the titles suggest, virtually all of these cheaply-made pictures unfortunately reinforce the worst stereotypes about the sport.

In the postwar years, adolescents and young adults discovered a new freedom and self-importance when driving a unique automobile. To be seen at the local drive-in restaurant or on downtown streets in a customized hot rod epitomized "cool" in the 1940s slang of the younger generation.

See also: Best Sellers (Books); Drive-Ins: Movie Theaters, Restaurants, and Banks; Fads; Hobbies; Leisure and Recreation; Magazines; Technology; Youth

Selected Reading
Felsen, Henry Gregor. www.lib.uiowa.edu/spec-coll/MSC/ToMsC650/MsC601/felsen.html
Hot Rods. www.hotrod.com/index.html

Moorhouse, H. F. "The 'Work' Ethic and 'Leisure' Activity: The Hot Rod in Post-War America," in Glickman, Lawrence B., ed. *Consumer Society in American History: A Reader,* pp. 277–297. Ithaca, NY: Cornell University Press, 1999.

NHRA. www.nhra.com/aboutnhr/history.html

HOUSE UN-AMERICAN ACTIVITIES COMMITTEE (HUAC)

When the war ended in 1945, the reality of the **Cold War** soon squashed any hopes for an extended period of peace and tranquility. Two former Allies, the United States and the Soviet Union, now found themselves as adversaries and at loggerheads over politics, military might, and the general conduct of affairs in postwar Europe. This tension between the two powers soon manifested itself in a number of ways, especially the fear that Communism might gain a foothold in the Western Hemisphere.

Such apprehension about alien influence in American life has marked several periods in the 20th century: following World War I, a "Big Red Scare" galvanized many to oppose anyone harboring leftist, liberal, or what came to be called Bolshevist beliefs; between 1919 and the early 1920s, the U.S. Constitution frequently hung in tatters as civil liberties were frequently overrun by courts, politicians, and other zealous supporters of nativist policies.

The advent of the Great Depression in the 1930s, coupled with concerns about the growing threat of another world war, brought a resurgence of xenophobia, and it often focused on perceived Communist infiltration of American institutions. In response, Congress in 1934 formed the Special Committee on Un-American Activities. It originally investigated Communist, fascist, and Nazi-leaning organizations. Also called the McCormack-Dickstein Committee (John McCormack, 1891–1980; Samuel Dickstein, 1885–1954), it evolved into the House Committee Investigating Un-American Activities in 1938. Still considered a special committee, Martin Dies Jr. (1900–1972), a conservative Democratic congressman from Texas, chaired this group, often called the Dies Committee, from 1937 until 1944. Under his leadership, the membership continued to look into the operations of any parties deemed inimical to the interests of the United States, with special attention paid to possible Communist links.

The Dies Committee generated considerable controversy with its heavy-handed attempts to find evidence of infiltration or subversive activities within the country. During World War II, the exigencies of the war itself tended to overshadow many of the committee's activities. But old attitudes die hard, and with the return of peace and the simultaneous growth of the Cold War, a new Red Scare was poised to make a reappearance. When Dies resigned his chairmanship, the status and name of the group changed, becoming the House Committee on Un-American Activities, or HUAC, in 1945. (Although HCUA would be technically more correct, HUAC, for House Un-American Activities Committee, has long been the more popular abbreviation.) It moved from a special committee to a permanent, or standing, one, and it gained the power to carry on probes for years at a time, which, for the postwar era, meant that HUAC would grow in influence.

Following the 1946 elections, Republicans took control of the 80th Congress, and the chairmanship of the House Un-American Activities Committee passed in early 1947 to New Jersey's J. Parnell Thomas (1895–1970), an avowed anti-Communist. Under his leadership, HUAC led numerous colorful, and frequently contentious, investigations. Thomas had to relinquish his post in 1948 after being convicted of taking kickbacks from his staff. Despite this complication, the work of the committee went forward for the remainder of the decade and on into the 1950s.

With reports of Russian spies operating brazenly within the United States and the specter of an Iron Curtain snuffing out freedom in Eastern Europe, many felt the times cried out for strong opposition to anything remotely suggesting sympathy for Communist ideology. Chairman Thomas, convinced that the Communist Party of the United States and other left-wing conspiracies had successfully infiltrated organized labor, the federal government, and the film industry, ordered the committee to examine the content of American **movies.** The probe even went back to the war itself, when the Soviet Union appeared to be a staunch U.S. ally, and found fault with a number of pro-Soviet pictures, including *Mission to Moscow* (1943), *The North Star* (1943), *Days of Glory* (1944), *Song of Russia* (1944), and *Counter-Attack* (1945). The committee accused the filmmakers of sneaking in dialogue that supports Marxism, socialism, and collectivism; that these films reflect the wartime alliance between the United States and the Soviet Union seemed immaterial in their quest to weed out anything that, in their estimation, might be construed as harmful or anti-American.

Thomas traveled to Hollywood in 1947 to meet with studio executives and discuss the topic. Upon his return to Washington, Thomas and his committee in September subpoenaed 41 individuals then working in the film industry to answer questions about their political affiliations. Of that number, 19 said they would be "unfriendly witnesses"—that is, they would refuse to testify on the subject. Their protests notwithstanding, the committee called 11 of the 19 to testify. One of them, the noted playwright Bertolt Brecht (1898–1956), briefly spoke before the House members and the next day left the country. The remaining 10 carried out their vow, and Thomas's group held them all in contempt of Congress. In time, they would become known as the Hollywood Ten and would pay heavily for their collective defiance.

Over the space of two years, the 10 individuals refused to testify about their political leanings and would not divulge the names of others who might or might not

TABLE 62. The Members of the Hollywood Ten

Producer-Director Herbert Biberman (1900–1971)
Director Edward Dmytryk (1908–1999)
Producer-Screenwriter Adrian Scott (1912–1973)
Screenwriter Alvah Bessie (1904–1985)
Screenwriter Lester Cole (1904–1985)
Screenwriter Ring Lardner Jr. (1915–2000)
Screenwriter John Howard Lawson (1894–1977)
Screenwriter Albert Maltz (1908–1985)
Screenwriter Samuel Ornitz (1890–1957)
Screenwriter Dalton Trumbo (1905–1976)

have Communist connections. Eight of the 10 received $1,000 fines (approximately $9,300 in 2008 dollars) and one-year prison sentences. Two (Biberman and Dmytryk) received $500 fines (approximately $4,600 in 2008 dollars) and six-month sentences. The discrepancy in punishment has never been adequately explained. The Ten had violated no written laws but were nonetheless convicted of wrong thinking, of siding with a political ideology that many at the time thought threatened the United States. The Ten appealed, but the courts, including the Supreme Court, rejected their arguments. In the anxious postwar years, national security and the perceived Communist threat often overrode logic and law.

During the span of the hearings, several noteworthy events occurred: First, two future U.S. presidents, Richard Nixon (1913–1994; president, 1969–1974) and Ronald Reagan (1911–2004; president, 1981–1989) participated in the 1947 investigation. Nixon served as a member of HUAC, and Reagan, as president of the Screen Actors Guild, testified about the dangers of Communism.

Second, **President Harry S. Truman** (1884–1972; president, 1945–1952), in order not to be seen as "soft on Communism," and with the 1948 elections looming, instituted loyalty checks for potential government employees. Anyone found with Communist affiliations would be denied federal jobs, not unlike the studio blacklisting practices.

Third, Hollywood, which had not, up until the time of the hearings, released any feature films with blatantly anti-Communist themes, rushed into production several titles during the late 1940s: *The Iron Curtain* (1948), *The Red Menace* (1949), and *I Married a Communist* (1949). The studios clearly hoped that such features would demonstrate the film capital's resistance to subversive elements. Many more such motion pictures followed in the early 1950s.

The hearings would drag on until 1958 and then quietly disappeared with no real evidence that any motion pictures ever knowingly served as a vehicle of political propaganda and attempted to seduce the population with disinformation and lies. They did, however, bring about the unfortunate practice of blacklisting (identifying persons who should not be hired or otherwise accepted) in the film industry. The studios fired more than 300 people and effectively ruined countless careers or forced individuals to seek work under assumed names. Not until much later—the 1970s and 1980s—were the Ten returned to the good graces of Hollywood, and many grudges and bitter memories on both sides have remained and festered. Amid growing dissatisfaction with the committee and its methods, and with its prestige dimmed, Congress eventually disbanded HUAC in 1975.

See also: Copland, Aaron; Drama (Film); Political and Propaganda Films; War Films

Selected Reading
Ceplair, Larry, and Steven Englund. *The Inquisition in Hollywood: Politics and the Film Community, 1930–1960.* Urbana: University of Illinois Press, 2003.
Cogley, John. *Report on Blacklisting I: The Movies.* New York: Fund for the Republic, 1956.
———. *Report on Blacklisting II: Radio-Television.* New York: Fund for the Republic, 1956.
Dick, Bernard F. *Radical Innocence: A Critical Study of the Hollywood Ten.* Lexington: University Press of Kentucky, 1989.
Kanfer, Stefan. *A Journal of the Plague Years: A Devastating Chronicle of the Era of the Blacklist.* New York: Atheneum, 1973.

HOWDY DOODY SHOW, THE

One of the first **television** shows to attract a significant audience came on the air at 5:30 in the afternoon and featured a puppet, a clown, and a cowboy. These unlikely elements nevertheless charmed millions of children while introducing them to Howdy Doody, Clarabell, and Buffalo Bob. *The Howdy Doody Show* made its debut at the end of 1947 and bore the name *Puppet Playhouse Theater.* It initially ran for an hour on Saturdays, but so few households had access to television at the time that no one remembers those early telecasts or the show's original title. In August 1948, it moved to a daily schedule and shortly thereafter appeared on screens as *The Howdy Doody Show* in a half-hour format, 5:30–6:00 p.m., Mondays through Fridays, on the NBC (National Broadcasting Company) network. An immediate success, the late afternoon program ran, with a few time changes, until 1960. In 1976, it reappeared in a syndicated version but failed to generate the enthusiasm enjoyed by the original and disappeared that same year.

Bob Smith (1917–1998; ne Robert Emil Schmidt) came to the show after hosting a children's program, *The Triple B Ranch,* on NBC **radio.** He greeted his listeners with an enthusiastic "howdy doody." With an eye to the future, Smith convinced network executives that a similar production, but featuring puppets, would do well on television, given its visual qualities. NBC-TV, in need of programming to fill its broadcast hours, agreed. Smith and his staffers set the show in Doodyville, supposedly a circus town. They then created a cast of characters, with Howdy, Smith himself as Buffalo Bob, the great white leader of the Sigafoose tribe, and Clarabell Hornblow, a mute clown that "spoke" with horns and seltzer water, as the lead players. Other citizens of Doodyville included Chief Thunderthud of the Ooragnak tribe (Kanagaroo spelled backward), an Indian chief noted for his exclamations of "Cowabunga!" Princess Summerfall Winterspring, a lovely Tinka Tonka Indian; Oil Well Willie; Cornelius Cobb, a storekeeper; Dilly Dally, a local carpenter; Phineas T. Bluster, Doodyville's cantankerous mayor; plus a host of other characters that evolved with the show. Some appeared as puppets, while costumed humans took the remaining roles.

For example, in the first years of the program, Bob Keeshan (1927–2004) took the role of Clarabell, unrecognizable in a clown costume. He would later go on to considerable fame as the title character in the long-running (1955–1984) children's show called *Captain Kangaroo.* He clearly learned how to interact with youngsters during his years on *The Howdy Doody Show.*

Howdy himself, something of a country bumpkin marionette with a perpetually smiling, freckled face, usually resided on Buffalo Bob's lap. Although it would be impossible to tell, given the usually fuzzy picture that then came over viewers' TV sets, Howdy's face possessed 48 carefully painted freckles, one for each of the then-continental United States (Alaska and Hawaii had not been granted statehood at the time). He also had a sister, Heidi Doody, and a twin brother, Double Doody, but the producers wisely limited their appearances, allowing Howdy center stage.

In time, commercials and product tie-ins became an important aspect of *The Howdy Doody Show.* Sponsors were initially leery of a program involving puppets, clowns, and a middle-aged cowboy. But success quickly dispelled those misgivings, and agents

This picture shows most of the important cast members of the pioneering children's television program, The Howdy Doody Show. *From the left, Buffalo Bob Smith (also the amiable host), Howdy himself, Mr. Bluster (a minor character), and Clarabell (played by Bob Keeshan, later to gain fame as Captain Kangaroo in the 1950s). (Photofest)*

representing a variety of products soon appeared at NBC's offices looking for available time slots. In addition, companies strove to get licensing rights to market records, clothing, toys, and other items bearing Howdy's name and countenance. *The Howdy Doody Show* served as one of television's first series to demonstrate the **advertising** potential of the new medium.

Because everything seen on TV in its early days came to audiences live and unedited, mistakes of course occurred, but no one minded. Part of the audience in the studio consisted of children; they sat on bleachers and were dubbed the "Peanut Gallery"; their unrehearsed enthusiasm and antics, frequently caught on camera, endeared them to viewers and helped immeasurably to make *The Howdy Doody Show* a major television hit.

See also: Children's Films; Radio Programming: Children's Shows, Serials, and Adventure Series

Selected Reading
Davis, Stephen. *Say Kids! What Time Is It? Notes from the Peanut Gallery.* Boston: Little, Brown, 1981.
Rautiolla-Williams Suzanne. "The Howdy Doody Show." www.museum.tv/archives/etv/H/htmlH/howdydoodys/howdydoodys.htm

I

ILLUSTRATORS

Americans may have been only dimly aware of the many artists active during the 1940s, but that does not mean the public lacked exposure to significant paintings and drawings. Illustrators displayed an array of work in **magazines,** books, **posters,** calendars, and **advertising,** thus sustaining a tradition begun in the 19th century and creating a contemporary body of work that merits attention. Over the course of the decade, they turned out thousands of pictures that ranged from the frankly amateurish to compositions that could stand beside anything produced by their more "serious" counterparts.

In any assessment of American illustrators active during the 1940s, one name overshadows the rest: Norman Rockwell (1894–1978). From his warm, realistic, narrative-style paintings appearing as covers on the *Saturday Evening Post,* to his distinctive, elegantly lettered signature that usually appeared in the lower right corner of each work, Rockwell set a standard of excellence that the public came to love. He knew how to stop action at just the right moment, revealing just enough of an ongoing story that viewers find it easy to make sense of the composition.

Born in New York City, he studied at the Chase School of Fine and Applied **Art,** the National Academy of **Design,** and the Art Students League. While still in his teens, Rockwell worked at *Boys' Life,* the magazine published by the Boy Scouts of America, which led to numerous other magazines and freelance advertising assignments (over 150 commercial firms eventually sought his services), and finally to Curtis Publishing and the *Saturday Evening Post;* at the age of 22, Rockwell completed his first cover for the venerable magazine, one of the most popular and widely circulated periodicals in the country. He would eventually paint 322 covers for the *Post*—71 in the 1940s alone—between 1916 and 1963, whereupon he moved to *Look* magazine and continued painting until his death in 1978. Because of the *Post*'s high circulation, each cover was seen, on average, by 4 million people, giving him the largest cumulative audience ever enjoyed by an artist.

During the war years, Rockwell created Willie Gillis, a boyish-looking young man entering the U.S. Army in October 1941; the artist proceeded to track his character for 11 *Post* covers, with KP (kitchen police) duty; in church; his happy return home in May 1945; and, finally, a studious Gillis in college, his framed discharge papers hanging on a wall in his dormitory room (October 1946). Rockwell wisely chose not to show Gillis in combat—the public had enough of that with daily newspaper headlines and the gold and blue **service flags** hanging in neighborhood windows (a gold star meant a family member lost while serving the country, blue signified a family member in active service).

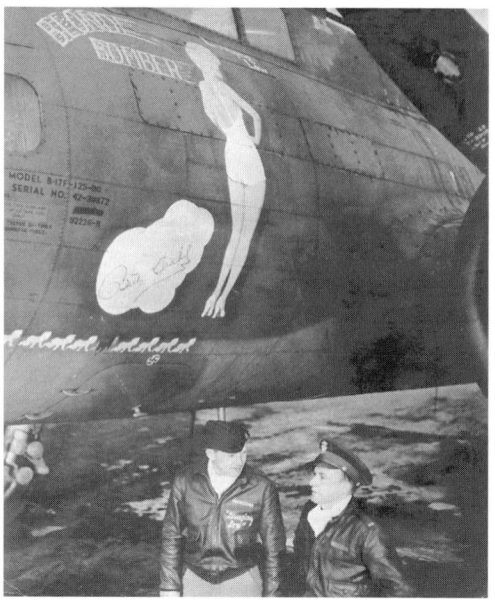

An anonymous airman painted this picture of pinup favorite Betty Grable, called here "Blonde Bomber," on the forward section of a military airplane. This custom, called nose art, became common during the war, and images of every kind abounded. (Photofest)

The closest Rockwell came to depicting actual fighting appeared in a poster he executed for the army, "Let's Give Him Enough and On Time" (n.d.). In darkness, a GI huddles over his machine gun, firing away at an unseen enemy. Empty shell casings litter the ground, and the weapon spits a yellow flame. A powerful illustration, it ranks among the best in World War II military art. He also painted for the May 29, 1943, *Post* a classic portrait of **Rosie the Riveter,** the iconic defense plant worker, in all her glory, her feet resting on *Mein Kampf* and munching a sandwich.

On January 6, 1941, just 11 months before the attack on Pearl Harbor and the active entry of the country into World War II, **President Franklin Delano Roosevelt** (1882–1945) delivered a somber State of the Union address to Congress that has come to be known as the "Four Freedoms Speech." In it, he enumerated (1) freedom of speech, (2) freedom of worship, (3) freedom from want, and (4) freedom from fear—beliefs that have long defined the United States. He further said that, as the clouds of war grew ever darker, it might become necessary to defend these beliefs, a duty for all men of good will. His words struck a chord with Rockwell, too old for service himself, and he decided to create a quartet of paintings depicting the Four Freedoms as he perceived them.

Upon their completion, he offered them to the government, but bureaucratic wrangling canceled any expressions of official interest. Rockwell then turned to his friends at the Curtis Publishing Company and they readily accepted an offer to run the pictures. The covers of four consecutive issues of the *Saturday Evening Post*—February 20, 1943 (speech), February 27, 1943 (worship), March 6, 1943 (want), and March 13, 1943 (fear)—carried his paintings, and to loud acclaim. At this point, the U.S. Department of the Treasury and the Office of War Information (OWI) belatedly decided to participate, with the result that "The Four Freedoms War Bond Show" went on the road in April, traveling to 16 cities. Well over a million spectators saw Rockwell's work, and the tour raised over $130 million (roughly $1.6 billion in 2008 dollars) for **war bonds,** making his set of four illustrations one of the most successful vehicles for patriotic fundraising of the entire war. In addition, countless reproductions and postcards found eager buyers at the time and for years afterward.

The postwar years saw no slowdown in the prolific artist's output. The *Saturday Evening Post* covers continued to appear with regularity, although references to the war had been replaced with a lighter, nostalgic touch about the passing American scene reminiscent of his earlier paintings of the 1920s and 1930s. Rockwell returned to the small towns and their citizens that he enjoyed painting, filling his canvases with anecdotal details. About his closest brush with topicality occurs in the fall of 1949, as he depicts a hapless homeowner risking life and limb as he wrestles with an early **television** antenna atop his roof. During these sometimes anxious years following World War II, he provided pictorial reassurances, suggesting that social and political rituals such as family vacations, senior proms, and voting had meaning, as did all the traditional holidays.

Over time, a consensus has arisen that Rockwell, a superb technician and stylist, produced his best and most memorable works during the 1930s and 1940s. Certainly he set high standards for illustration for over 60 years, yet throughout much of the 20th century, academic critics have shunted aside most American illustrators, maintaining that their work, too narrative or too commercial, lacks a high seriousness of purpose. But this kind of derisive attitude has been the bane of all popular culture; it often seems difficult for elitist critics to accept work aimed at a mass audience. For whatever reasons, the problem worsens if the work achieves great success and has a large, receptive audience. If so many people like it, can it possibly be worthwhile? Similar arguments surface with **best sellers,** hit **movies,** Broadway blockbusters, top-rated TV shows, and the like.

Table 63 presents a cross-section of artists, all of whom worked in a manner similar to that employed by Rockwell (i.e., realistic, usually with a narrative element that suggests a story or an ongoing event), since that dominated the field of illustration throughout the 1940s. Their pictures appeared in books, magazines, as well as a variety of advertising formats. Because of the large number of illustrators at work during the decade, the list should be thought introductory, but hardly conclusive.

Lest it be thought that all American illustrators imitated Norman Rockwell at one time or another, mention should be made of Boris Artzybasheff (1899–1965) and Constantin Alajalov (1900–1987). Each worked in a boldly stylized and personalized manner that rendered their work instantly recognizable. Artzybasheff concentrated on creating machines that resembled humans (or humans that resembled machines), often choosing famous individuals and assigning them mechanical qualities that fit their personalities. His covers for *Time* magazine remain classics for this unique approach.

The Russian-born Alajalov, on the other hand, utilized the trademark geometrics used in cubism and sometimes found in modern abstraction. He also imported techniques taken from comic strips, especially the element of caricature when depicting real persons. Despite its predilection for traditional art, the *Saturday Evening Post,* along with several other large-circulation magazines, did not hesitate to run his paintings for covers.

TABLE 63. Some Representative American Illustrators Active during the 1940s

Name and Dates	Comments
Ernest Hamlin Baker (1889–1975)	During a lengthy career, Baker painted almost 400 cover portraits for *Time* magazine, including virtually all the wartime political and military leaders.
McClelland Barclay (1891–1943)	Created many posters and illustrations on behalf of the U.S. Navy during the war and lost his life while in action in the Pacific.
Dean Cornwell (1892–1960)	Throughout World War II, Dean Cornwell, nicknamed "the Dean of Illustrators" by his peers, painted countless illustrations for advertisers depicting both a product and U.S. armed forces in action. He also won commissions from most of the major magazines of the day and became a noted muralist in addition to all his other commercial activities.
Douglass Crockwell (1904–1968)	Like Rockwell, Crockwell contributed covers for the *Saturday Evening Post,* and their styles could easily be confused. He often signed his paintings "Douglass," given the similarity of their names and techniques.
Floyd MacMillan Davis (1896–1966)	Davis served as a correspondent-artist for the War Department, visiting various combat zones. *Life* magazine ran a number of his paintings during the war.
Steven Donahos (1907–1994)	After working with the Federal Arts Project during the 1930s, Donahos moved to commercial art and found success in many areas. A prolific painter, he even executed the designs for dozens of U.S. postage stamps and Christmas Seals.
John Falter (1910–1982)	The covers of more than 200 issues of the *Saturday Evening Post* were created by Falter, all in a style reminiscent of Norman Rockwell's work, with small towns and folksy humor being major themes. He also boasted extensive advertising contacts, and *Reader's Digest* commissioned him to illustrate a number of its condensed books.
Fred Freeman (1906–1988)	After serving as a lieutenant commander in the Navy during the war, Freeman took his maritime expertise and created the illustrations for an official history of U.S. submarine operations.
Hamilton Greene (1904–1966)	Although he initially worked with pulp and men's magazines in the 1930s, Greene became an artist-correspondent for the American Legion's magazine in World War II. On the front lines in order to cover combat operations in Europe, he was shot but survived the wound. With the outbreak of the Korean conflict in 1950, he again returned to drawing battles up close, and his on-the-spot sketches from both wars have become highly prized.
Peter Helck (1893–1988)	A skilled technician, Helck specialized in automotive art and attracted an enthusiastic following.

Name and Dates	Comments
Frances Tipton Hunter (1896–1957)	Among the few women active in the field of illustration, Tipton displayed a talent for painting children; in addition to popular advertisements, she also created numerous covers for the *Saturday Evening Post.*
Tom Lovell (1909–1997)	An exacting craftsman, Lovell received commissions from most of the major magazines published in the 1940s. He also created an illustrated wartime history of the Marine Corps war that has become part of that branch's permanent collection.
Ronald McLeod (1897–1977)	The *Saturday Evening Post* was not alone in publishing covers by good illustrators; *Collier's,* a competing weekly, ran many McLeod covers for more than 20 years.
Al Parker (1906–1985)	Noted for a long series of "mother-daughter" covers he executed for the *Ladies' Home Journal* in the 1940s, Parker possessed the unique ability to work in a variety of styles, from traditional to modern—a trait that endeared him to magazine publishers and advertising agencies. He remains best remembered for his stylish women, immaculately coiffed and always clad in the latest fashions.
Martha Sawyers (1902–1988)	At the onset of World War II, *Collier's* magazine dispatched Sawyers to the Far East to chronicle life and events there, with the result that her illustrations and posters about Asia proved popular with the U.S. public, which did not know much about that part of the world.
Mead Schaeffer (1898–1980)	A personal friend of Norman Rockwell, Scheaffer painted in a similar, realistic way. During the war, he created a series of covers for the *Saturday Evening Post* that depict the different branches of the U.S. armed forces; in this effort, he received the full cooperation of the War Department and access to ships, planes, vehicles, and uniforms in order that all details be accurate and correct.
Jon Whitcomb (1906–1988)	Like his colleague Al Parker, Whitcomb had a gift for portraying glamorous, attractive women. He gained a modicum of fame in the 1940s for an ongoing series entitled "Home for Keeps." It depicts wives and sweethearts welcoming back husbands and boyfriends returning from active service. His own military experiences involved naval duty in the Pacific as a combat artist assigned to record several island engagements.

In addition, George Petty (1894–1975) and Alberto Vargas (1896–1982) carved out a distinctive niche for themselves by creating curvaceous pinup girls for the delectation of males around the globe. Although beautiful women have been the subject of artists since time immemorial, Petty and Vargas mass-produced hundreds of images, mainly watercolors that have been carefully air-brushed to depict a kind of idealized femininity—voluptuous, but all in good taste. They became extremely popular during the 1940s, especially for servicemen. Bomber crews frequently decorated their aircraft with Petty and Vargas look-alikes—called "nose art"—that injected a bit of humor into their deadly business.

Petty began his career with *Esquire,* a sophisticated men's magazine. It regularly carried one of his pinups, or "Petty Girls," throughout the later 1930s. After a falling-out, the magazine lost no time and soon ran Vargas pinups during the 1940s, called "Vargas Girls," within its pages long before the days of *Playboy* (although Vargas also drew—albeit more explicitly—for that magazine in the 1960s). Petty, in the meantime, went with *True,* another men's periodical, until the 1950s.

Hollywood paid tribute to the pinup's popularity with a 1950 musical called *The Petty Girl.* Actor Robert Cummings (1910–1990) portrays Petty as a painter noted for his cheesecake art. A decorous affair, it boasts a soundtrack by the renowned composer Harold Arlen (1905–1986) and lyricist Johnny Mercer (1909–1976). The two even wrote a song called "The Petty Girl," and the studio correctly assumed people would know to what it referred.

As the foregoing list would suggest, the names of most of the illustrators who practiced their craft in Norman Rockwell's time—the 1920s until the 1960s—have largely been forgotten. People may continue to admire their work when encountering it in dusty magazines, crumbling advertisements, or an old calendar, but their signatures will not be familiar (if any appear at all, since many commercial illustrators labored in relative anonymity and did not sign their work). Rockwell and his art have been remarkably enduring, successfully blurring the line between high and low culture by appealing to a large, diverse mass of people; his public acceptance has ensconced him as the most popular American artist of all time.

The 1940s were a rich decade for illustration, and it is unfortunate that too many skilled practitioners of the craft have been forgotten or remain anonymous. Much of their output contributed to raising the public consciousness about art in general, and certainly they achieved a level of sophistication in illustration that anyone can admire. As a gesture of acknowledgement for the contributions American illustrators have made over the years, the United States Postal Service in 2001 issued a set of 20 commemorative stamps, each honoring a different artist. Of the 20 individuals chosen, 14 were active illustrators during the 1940s, suggesting the increasing role illustration took in visual culture as the decade progressed.

See also: Abstract Expressionism; Automobiles and the U.S. Automotive Industry; Aviation; Cold War, The; Fads; Fashion; GI Bill (Servicemen's Readjustment Act of 1944); Hobbies; Musicals (Film); Newspapers; Selective Training and Service Act of 1940 (Selective Service, or Draft); *Seventeen;* Songwriters and Lyricists

Selected Reading
Buechner, Thomas S. *Norman Rockwell: Artist and Illustrator.* New York: Harry N. Abrams, 1970.
Hennessey, Maureen Hart, and Anne Knutson. *Norman Rockwell: Pictures for the American People.* New York: Harry N. Abrams, 1999.
Reed, Walt, and Roger Reed. *The Illustrator in America, 1880–1980.* New York: Society of Illustrators, 1984.
Stoltz, Donald Robert, Marshall Louis Stoltz, and William B. Earle. *The Advertising World of Norman Rockwell.* New York: Madison Square Press, 1985.

INTERNMENT CAMPS (RELOCATION CENTERS)

Aircraft from the Japanese Imperial Navy attacked Pearl Harbor on December 7, 1941. The next day, the United States Congress declared that a state of war existed between the government of Japan and the government and people of the United States. **Newspapers** soon printed stories of spies and sabotage activity along the West Coast, causing widespread hysterical fears of more Japanese attacks. These reports turned out to be false rumors. Hollywood's Twentieth Century-Fox nevertheless contributed to the paranoia of the hour with the release of *Little Tokyo, U.S.A.* in July 1942. The film presents the Japanese American community as a vast army of volunteer spies and ardent admirers of Japan's emperor.

With the nation at war, **President Franklin Delano Roosevelt** (1882–1945) signed several executive orders to establish boards and mechanisms for managing the conflict. Executive order 9066, presented as a military necessity to protect the country from internal attacks of espionage and sabotage, authorized Secretary of War Henry L. Stimson (1867–1950) and appropriate military commanders to identify military areas within the United States from which any or all persons, regardless of their citizenship, could be excluded.

The War Relocation Authority, established in March 1942, oversaw the confinement of over 100,000 Japanese Americans during World War II. This picture, taken in September 1942 at the Tanforan Assembly Center, shows the first step in the relocation process. From the civilian assembly centers, individuals went to 1 of 10 internment camps, sometimes called relocation centers, and remained there until the end of the war. (CORBIS)

The War Relocation Authority (WRA), established on March 18, 1942, and headed by Milton S. Eisenhower (1899–1985), brother of **General Dwight David Eisenhower** (1890–1969), had the responsibility to oversee any such actions. Vaguely worded, the order could have been applied to any group or nationality, but with just a few exceptions, the only ones subjected to this directive were Japanese Americans living on the West Coast. In November 1942, Paramount Pictures and the Office of War Information (OWI) produced *Japanese Relocation,* a documentary short written by Milton Eisenhower that attempted to present reasons for interning Japanese American citizens, a film clearly seen in modern times to be blatant propaganda in support of the government.

By the time the studio released the movie, the relocation of between 110,000 and 120,000 persons of Japanese ancestry had been completed. Officials first sent them to temporary facilities called civilian assembly centers. Most of these individuals possessed U.S. citizenship or qualified as legal permanent resident aliens; children accounted for half of the population. Beginning on March 21, 1942, and continuing into early October, 10 bleak and remote camps surrounded by barbed wire and armed guards opened in five states to house these citizens, most for four years. In some cases, family members found themselves separated and in different facilities.

As the relocation took place, short notice became the rule. For example, the first group to be ousted from their homes lived on Terminal Island near Los Angeles Harbor and had 48 hours to prepare. This practice resulted in heavy financial losses as homes, farms, and businesses had to be liquidated or quickly entrusted to a neighbor or acquaintance. Homes and personal property left unprotected fell to vandalism and theft despite government promises of protection.

Once at a camp, residents had to endure unacceptable and unhealthy conditions. Living space consisted of shoddy wooden barracks covered by tar paper and mostly divided into one-room apartments, originally intended for four, but usually housing more. In the desert and swamp camps, temperature extremes and poisonous snakes and wildlife created discomfort and danger. At some camps, people arrived before sewer

TABLE 64. The Internment Camps for Japanese Americans, 1942–1946 (Listed Chronologically by Opening Date)

Camp Locations	Opened	Closed	Peak Population
Manzanar, California	March 21, 1942	November 21, 1945	10,046
Poston (Colorado River), Arizona	May 8, 1942	November 28, 1945	17,814
Tule Lake, California	May 27, 1942	March 20, 1946	18,789
Gila River, Arizona	July 20, 1942	November 10, 1945	13,348
Minidoka, Idaho	August 10, 1942	October 28, 1945	9,397
Heart Mountain, Wyoming	August 12, 1942	November 10, 1945	10,767
Amache (Granada), Colorado	August 24, 1942	October 15, 1945	7,318
Topaz (Central Utah), Utah	September 11, 1942	October 31, 1945	8,130
Rohwer, Arkansas	September 18, 1942	November 30, 1945	8,475
Jerome, Arkansas	October 6, 1942	June 30, 1944	8,497

Source: PBS. *Children of the Camps: Internment History.* 1999. www.pbs.org/childofcamp/history/camps.html

systems had been built. Women giving birth usually had little or no professional help. Guards tended to shoot and ask questions later, conditions that resulted in unjustified woundings and deaths. Some of those incarcerated died in the camps because of inadequate medical care and emotional stress.

In addition to confinement, other injustices occurred. Within 48 hours of the attack on Pearl Harbor, over 1,000 men identified as leaders in their Japanese American communities had been arrested by local authorities and the Federal Bureau of Investigation (FBI). Most spent the war years in confinement. The FBI arrested another 2,000 Japanese Americans for a variety of reasons and kept them in Department of Justice detention camps. Only one, whose offense involved forgetting to register as a business agent of a Japanese importing firm, received a conviction, that of imprisonment.

Despite the inhuman aspect of the rounding up and internment of Japanese Americans by the War Relocation Authority, the agency in the summer of 1942 organized the National Japanese American Student Relocation Council. Public officials, civic organizations, and other groups worked with colleges and universities as the council relocated Japanese American college students to institutions of higher learning away from the West Coast in hopes of keeping them out of camps and enrolled in colleges. Participating schools had to be approved by the army and navy. Those attending high school and planning to enroll in college were included in the approximately 3,000 students assisted by this effort.

To document the relocation program, Milton Eisenhower had retained photojournalist Dorothea Lange (1895–1965), known for her Depression-era pictures taken for the Farm Security Administration (FSA). Because of restrictions placed upon Lange, most of her internment photographs cover Manzanar, the first camp to open. Even here, she could not photograph the wire fences, watchtowers with search lights, or the armed guards.

Ironically, her earliest pictures chronicle children of Japanese ancestry obediently pledging allegiance to the U.S. flag at Raphael Weill Public School in San Francisco, California. The rest of her almost 800 shots show the injustice of people being uprooted and forced to live in deplorable conditions, an honest pictorial story disturbing enough that, by early 1943, the U.S. Army had confiscated both her photographs and negatives. With the word "impounded" stamped on many of Lange's pictures, her work continued to be suppressed for the duration of World War II. Soon thereafter, the government quietly gave the pictures to the National Archives.

One year after Lange's visits to Manzanar, another famous photographer, Ansel Adams (1902–1984), went there at his own expense. Between October 1943 and July 1944, Adams made four trips to interview and photograph detainees in activities that emphasized their pro-American beliefs. As his last visit approached, announcements about the possible closing of camps had been made.

Adams published his pictures in an inexpensive book ironically titled *Born Free and Equal* (1944) in hopes that his portraits would enable ordinary Americans to be more tolerant of the return of the Japanese Americans to their homes and communities. The book sold well in San Francisco but had poor distribution to other parts of the country. Despite his efforts, California officials recorded 59 acts of violence against returning Japanese Americans. In 1968, Adams gave his pictures to the Library of Congress.

Even with ongoing internment programs, a little over 17,500 Japanese Americans served in the U.S. Army. In mid-1942, those in Hawaii were put into a segregated unit named the 100th Infantry Battalion. The group saw bloody and heavy fighting in Europe, and members earned over 900 Purple Hearts, giving it the nickname the Purple Heart Battalion. In the summer of 1944, the 100th Battalion became attached to the 442nd Regimental Combat Team, home for Japanese American mainlanders since 1943. Because of its previous honors, it continued to be called the 100th Battalion. In 1944, working together, these two groups gained world recognition for rescuing another U.S. unit trapped behind enemy lines for eight days, at the heavy cost of losing nearly half, over 800, of its men.

In 1946, **President Harry S. Truman** (1884–1972) received the 442nd Regimental Combat Team on the White House lawn. He stated, "You fought not only the enemy but you fought prejudice—and you have won." Hollywood joined in giving accolades by telling the story of the Japanese American soldiers of World War II in the movie *Go for Broke* (1951). In contrast to these honors, back in the internment camps, 106 young men were arrested in 1944 for refusal to participate in combat training as a protest about treatment of their impounded families. Twenty-one received convictions and served prison time before being paroled in 1946.

Some Japanese Americans were allowed to leave their camps and return home before the war officially ended. The Relocation Center at Jerome, Arkansas, closed in June 1944, and in December, authorities declared all the camps would be closed. A slow process, it took until March 1946 before the last detainees left. This final operating site, Tule Lake, had housed the largest number of people, leaving some 5,000 individuals to move during its last month of operation. Many were elderly, impoverished, or ill, which caused difficulties in completing the relocation process, and some had no place to go.

Returning home involved continued difficulties. Rude receptions including homes being shot into and signs reading "No Japs Allowed" greeted a few. As a group, they had suffered around $400 million in income and property losses (approximately $4.8 billion in 2008 money).

Cries for justice increased as more and more U.S. citizens became aware of the unwarranted internment and atrocious living conditions inflicted on fellow citizens during World War II. On July 2, 1948, President Truman signed the Japanese American Evacuation Claims Act, a measure to compensate individuals for economic losses attributable to their forced internment. This act, however, contained limitations. The bill required a lengthy and costly process to prove a claim, which became costly to the government. Also, evidence of economic losses frequently no longer existed. Personal papers had been lost; even the Internal Revenue Service had destroyed tax returns for the years 1939 to 1942. These problems would not be rectified until 1988, when President Ronald Reagan (1911–2004) signed into law a bill that provided individual payments of $20,000 (a little over $36,000 in 2008 money) to each surviving person who spent time in an internment camp. The bill also established a $1.25 billion **education** fund (approximately $2.3 billion in 2008 money).

The internment of Japanese Americans during World War II stands as one of the worst violations of civil liberties in wartime America and a huge embarrassment to a nation devoted to individual rights and freedom. The experience created financial difficulties and psychological trauma for many of the detainees, much of it permanent.

See also: Atomic Bomb, The; Axis Sally and Tokyo Rose; Movies; Photography; Race Relations and Stereotyping

Selected Reading
Gordon, Linda, and Gary Y. Okihiro. *Impounded: Dorothea Lange and the Censored Images of Japanese American Internment.* New York: W. W. Norton, 2006.
Kashima, Tetsuden, and the United States Commission on Wartime Relocation and Internment of Civilians. *Personal Justice Denied: Report of the Commission on Wartime Relocation and Internment of Civilians.* Washington, DC: U.S. Government Printing Office, 1996.
Lingeman, Richard. *Don't You Know There's a War On? The American Home Front, 1941–1945.* New York: Thunder's Mouth Press, 1970.
O'Brien, Kenneth Paul, and Lynn Hudson Parsons, eds. *The Home-Front War: World War II and American Society.* Westport, CT: Greenwood Press, 1995.

IT'S A WONDERFUL LIFE (FRANK CAPRA)

This film, released in 1946, remains one of the most popular Christmas **movies** ever produced, although its renowned director, Frank Capra (1897–1954), did not intend it as merely a holiday motion picture. He and several studio writers had adapted "The Greatest Gift," a 1939 short story by Philip Van Doren Stern (1900–1984), into a screenplay. An all-star cast headed by Jimmy Stewart (1908–1997), Donna Reed (1921–1986), and Lionel Barrymore (1878–1954), manages to explore a gamut of emotions, from pathos to humor, with the script. Although it did not do particularly well at the box office in its first year, the picture slowly attracted a growing audience and a reputation as good, family-oriented entertainment. In time, *It's a Wonderful Life* evolved into a perennial favorite, especially with repeated **television** showings, videotapes, and DVDs, and audiences began returning to it season after season.

In the story, banker George Bailey (Stewart), after living a good and sensible life, feels his accomplishments amount to little, especially when a financial crisis threatens the very existence of his tiny savings and loan company. A dastardly competitor, played to the hilt by Barrymore, leads him to consider suicide, but a helpful guardian angel intercedes and gives him a little commonsensical heavenly advice. He also shows him the influence he has had over his friends and town, Bedford Corners, New York, and then presents him a nightmarish vision of what life for others would have been like without Bailey in the picture. This what-might-have-been revelation changes Bailey's mind, he returns to his home, and all ends well. Although this extended concluding sequence properly belongs in the realm of fantasy, the details of the larger story are firmly grounded in economic reality, especially in light of bank failures in the recent Great Depression of the 1930s. Capra's recurring theme of the lonely individual against the crowd becomes apparent when townspeople at first turn against Bailey after it appears his firm will fail. But Capra can also turn the tables, by showing those same neighbors supporting Bailey by raising cash to keep the savings and loan solvent and out of the hands of Barrymore's character. In this way, Capra balances American idealism with the actual postwar world.

At its release, a number of critics dismissed *It's a Wonderful Life* as too sentimental, too saccharine, but they tended to overlook a decidedly darker side it harbors until its sunny conclusion. Visually, much of the film takes place in wintry gloom, reinforcing the grim thoughts in Bailey's mind. This device works especially well in black and white, Capra's preferred métier (a colorized version also exists, but loses some of the dark, shadowy drama of the original). And, despite opening at Christmas time, usually a profitable season for new movies, its solemn subject matter caused it to show only mediocre box office returns. Its reputation as a cinema classic would take several years to establish.

Capra came to *It's a Wonderful Life* with an enviable track record. He had delighted audiences prior to World War II with such classics as *It Happened One Night* (1934), *You Can't Take It with You* (1938; Jimmy Stewart's debut motion picture with the director), *Mr. Deeds Goes to Town* (1936), *Mr. Smith Goes to Washington* (1939; Stewart again teamed with Capra), and *Meet John Doe* (1941). A veteran of World War I, Capra found himself back in uniform when the U.S. Army Signal Corps commissioned him as a major and gave him the job of creating a series of films about American goals in World War II. Between 1942 and 1945, he created seven documentaries that received the collective title of *Why We Fight: Prelude to War* (1942), *The Nazis Strike* (1943), *Divide and Conquer* (1943), *The Battle of Britain* (1943), *The Battle of Russia* (1944), *The Battle of China* (1944), and *War Comes to America* (1945). In addition, Capra also directed *The Negro Soldier* in 1944, a demonstration of the worthiness of black troops in an era of military segregation. The overall experience exhausted and saddened him, and it challenged the idealism he had exhibited in the 1930s.

When he returned to commercial filmmaking with *It's a Wonderful Life,* his attitudes about human experience became tinged with anxiety and gave his subsequent movies a heightened maturity. At times, some critics have cynically referred to the director's innate populism and belief in the honorable side of humanity as "Capra-corn," a clever pun, perhaps, but one that relies on a shallow reading of his work.

Just prior to the 1946 release of *It's a Wonderful Life,* Capra, along with fellow directors George Stevens (1904–1975) and William Wyler (1902–1981) and Columbia Pictures executive Samuel J. Briskin (1896–1968), formed Liberty Films as a production company. The three directors, all veterans of World War II, expressed reluctance to return to the then-existing Hollywood studio system; they agreed to grant RKO Radio Pictures distribution rights for any films Liberty produced. Because of chronic financial problems, however, the fledgling studio released only two films under its banner, *It's a Wonderful Life* (1946) and *State of the Union* (1948), and then broke up.

In an ironic twist, William Wyler, despite his ongoing association with Liberty, directed **The Best Years of Our Lives** in 1946 for the Samuel Goldwyn Company. When the Academy Awards for 1946 were announced, *It's a Wonderful Life* received nominations for best picture and best director, as did *The Best Years of Our Lives.* Unfortunately for Capra and Liberty Studios, *The Best Years of Our Lives* won in both categories. For his part, although he would go on making movies until the early

1960s, Frank Capra never regained the prominence he had achieved in the 1930s and 1940s.

See also: Comedies (Film); Drama (Film); Louis, Joe; Political and Propaganda Films; Race Relations and Stereotyping; War Films

Selected Reading
Capra, Frank. *The Name above the Title.* New York: Macmillan, 1971.
McBride, Joseph. *Frank Capra: The Catastrophe of Success.* New York: Touchstone Books, 1992.

Index

AAA (American Automobile Association), 726
AAA Championship Trail Races, 485
AAFC. *See* All-American Football Conference
Aalto, Alvar, 23–24, 262
Abbott, Bud, 172, 203, 204*t*
Abbott, George, 151
Abbott, Senda Berenson, 87
ABC (American Broadcasting Company), **1–4**, 21, 183, 286, 287, 288, 459, 692
abstract expressionism, **4–8**, 7*t*–8*t*, 30
Academy of Motion Picture Arts and Sciences (AMPAS), 384
Acaro, Eddie, 391
Action Comics, 208, 664
Acuff, Roy, **8–10**, 9 (photo), 230
Adams, Ansel, 411, 510, 515, 516*t*
Adams, Frank David "Dooley," 392
Adams, Franklin Pierce, 568
Adrian, Gilbert, 313
Adventures in Good Eating (Hines, Duncan), 109–110, 588, 727
The Adventures of Ichabod and Mr. Toad, 276
advertising, 5, **11–15**, 37, 75, 121

automobile, 52
baseball and, 77
Citizen Kane and, 174
Coca-Cola, 107
design, 263
fashion and, 321
grocery stores and, 366, 367
on *The Howdy Doody Show*, 400–401
on *The Jack Benny Program*, 419
jukeboxes, 429–430
Kraft Television Theatre and, 438–439
lawns and, 447–448
on *The Lone Ranger*, 461
magazines and, 468
newspapers, 501
Pepsi-Cola, 107–108
radio and, 332
in *Seventeen*, 628
Sexual Behavior in the Human Male (Kinsey), 436
Spam, 659
stereotyping and, 538–539
war bonds, 753, 755
water skiing, 669
women's role in winning war, 336
to youth, 783

Advertising Council, 753
AEC. *See* Atomic Energy Commission
aerosol spray cans, 677
AFL. *See* American Federation of Labor
AFM. *See* American Federation of Musicians
AFR. *See* Armed Forces Radio
AGF. *See* Army Ground Forces
Airgraph, 510
Alajalov, Constantin, 405
Alison, Joan, 166
All My Sons (Miller, Arthur), 139 (photo)
All the King's Men, 278 (photo)
All-American Football Conference (AAFC), 349
All-American Girls Professional Baseball League, 78–79, 79*t*
Allen, Fred, 3
all-girl orchestras, **15–19**, 18*t*, 673
Almanac Singers, 333–334, 442–443
Almond Joy, 271
Almond ROCA Buttercrunch, 270
AMA. *See* American Medical Association
Amalgamated Clothing Workers, 47
Amateur Softball Association (ASA), 650
Ameche, Don, 482
America First Committee, 788
American Automobile Association. *See* AAA
American Bowling Congress, 128, 129
American Bricks, 711–712
American Broadcasting Company. *See* ABC
American Federation of Labor (AFL), 441, 443 (photo), 504–505
American Federation of Musicians (AFM), **40–41**, 91, 634–635, 674
American Jockey Club, 389
American Medical Association (AMA), 338
American Motorcycle Association, 488
American Newspaper Guild, 504–505

American Society of Composers, Authors, and Producers. *See* ASCAP
The American Stud Book, 389
American Theatre Wing, 139, 150
American Way, 392
AMI. *See* Automatic Music Instrument Company
Amos 'n' Andy, 550
AMPAS. *See* Academy of Motion Picture Arts and Sciences
Anchors Aweigh, 635
Anderson, Eddie, 418, 536
Anderson, Elmer "Elbows," 596
Anderson, Marian, 598
Anderson, Walter L., 322
Andrews, Dana, 187 (photo), 522
The Andrews Sisters, **19–21**, 19 (photo), 20*t*, 112, 124, 229, 249
Andriola, Alfred, 221–222
Andy Hardy, 172, 199*t*
Annenberg, Walter, 627–628
Annual Automotive Equipment Display and Hot Rod Exposition, 395
AP. *See* Associated Press
Appalachian Spring (Copland), 223, 616
Apple Mary, 216
Aquacade, 668–669
aqualung, 678
Arapaho Basin, 645
architecture, **22–28**, 263, 738
Argetsinger, Cameron, 486
Arlen, Harold, 408
Arlen, Michael, 244
Armed Forces Radio (AFR), 183, 453, 558
Armstrong, Edwin H., 330–333
Armstrong, Louis, 422, 423
Army Ground Forces (AGF), 777
Army Service Forces (ASF), 776
Arnheim, Gus, 247
Arnold, Eddy, 231
Arnold, Edward, 783
Arnold, Kenneth, 736

Arp, Jean (Hans), 262
Arriola, Gus, 214
The Arrow, 208
Arsenic and Old Lace (Kesselring), 139, 146–147
art, 4, 6, 30, 53, 404 (photo)
   See also abstract expressionism; design; illustrators; painting; sculpture
Arthur Godfrey Time, 359–360
The Arthur Murray Party, 288
Artists for Victory, 29
Artzybasheff, Boris, 405
"As Time Goes By," 168–169
ASA. *See* Amateur Softball Association
ASCAP v. BMI, **32**, **37–40**, 674
Asch, Moses, 334
ASF. *See* Army Service Forces
Assault, 391
Associated Press (AP), 505, 509
Astaire, Fred, 249, 253–254, 496, 499, 538, 774
Astor, Mary, 118 (photo)
Atherton, John C., 527
atomic bomb, 24, **42–46**, 44 (photo), 63t, 466, 474, 581, 678, 731–732, 744, 792–793
   Hayworth, Rita, on, 309, 453
   New Yorker and, 473
   newspapers and, 503–504
   Soviet Union and, 45–46, 179–180, 191, 733, 798
   technology, 191
Atomic Energy Commission (AEC), 45
Atwater, Edith, 139
Auerbach, Artie, 418
Austin, Gene, 249
automated streetlights, 678
Automatic Music Instrument Company (AMI), 427
automatic washer, 678
automobiles, 13–14, **46–53**, 48t, 49t, 74, 720–721
   postwar demand for, 723
   sales and travel, 726t

Autry, Gene, 25, **53–61**, 57t, 170, 223, 231, 547, 769
Avedon, Richard, 514–515
Avery, Milton, 5
Avery, Sewell, 189
Avery, Tex, 166
aviation, **61–70**, 63t–65t, 68t–69t, 721, 724–725
   jet, 682
   See also Berlin airlift
Axis Sally, **70–72**
Ayers, E. Duran, 540

B. H. Wragge Company, 321
Babes on Broadway, 496
baby boom, **73–76**
   education and, 75, 297
   fast food and, 323
   movies and, 491
   suburbanization and, 455
Bacall, Lauren, 120–121, 122
The Bachelor and the Bobby-Soxer, 306, 783
Back at the Front, 532
Bad Boy, 495
Baer, Buddy, 131, 463
Baker, George, 214
Balanchine, George, 255, 256
Ballew, Smith, 54
ballpoint pen, 678
Bambi, 275
Banks, Henry, 485
barbecues, 342
Barbera, Joe, 165–166
Barfield, Johnny, 124
Barnaby (Johnson, Crockett), 215
Barney Google (De Beck), 392
Barris, Harry, 247
Barrymore, Lionel, 199, 413
Baruch, Bernard, 188
baseball, **76–82**, 81t, 184, 345, 478, 789
   television, 697
   Triple Crown, 391
   war bonds and, 757

Basie, Count, 17, **82–85**, 82 (photo), 84*t*, 419
basketball, **85–88**, 363
Baskett, James, 520
Baskin, Burton, 325
Baskin-Robbins, 272, 325
Batman, 208
Battle of the Bulge, 534, 792
Battle of Waterloo Road (Capa), 511
Battleship, 355
Bazooka Joe, 310
Beard, James, 112, 342, 343
The Beast with Five Fingers, 386 (photo)
bebop (bop), 84, **88–92**, 194, 420, 591
Beemer, Brace, 459 (photo), 460
Begley, Ed, 242, 537
Bell, Benny, 48
Bell and Howell Company, 730
Belle of the Yukon, 630
Belluschi, Pietro, 23, 26
Belmont Stakes, 390
Beneke, Tex, 481, 676
Bennett, Joan, 518
Bennett, Robert Russell, 758
Benny, Jack, 196, 417–419, 550 (photo)
Benso, Catherine, 747
Benson, Sally, 271
Berg, Patty, 363
Bergen, Edgar, 291–293, 292 (photo), 552
Berger, Bob, 784
Bergman, Ingrid, 167, 167 (photo)
Berkeley, Busby, 254, 482
Berle, Milton, 2, 255, 259, 426, 644, **705–707**, 706 (photo)
Berlin, Irving, 56, 151, 156, 249, 496, 587, 619, 648, 657, **773–775**, 790
Berlin airlift, **93–95**, 190, 796–797
Bernhardt, Sarah, 525
Bernstein, Artie, 420
Bernstein, Leonard, 183, 184
Berry Brothers, 255
Bertoia, Harry, 265
Best, Willie, 384

best sellers (books), **95–97**, 98*t*–103*t*, 125, 435–437, 506, 660–661
Best Western, 729
The Best Years of Our Lives, 97, **104–106**, 104 (photo), 105 (photo), 176, 281, 414, 520
Betz, Pauline, 701
The Beulah Show, 536
beverages, 11, **106–113**, 159, 579
Beyond Glory, 494–495
Big Little Books, 207
The Big Sleep, 121
Big Town, 507
Bigelow, Ruth, 111
Biggers, Earl Derr, 241–242, 537
bikini, 45, 317, 670–671
Billboard, 591
Billy the Kid (Copland), 223
Birdland, 92
Birds Eye, 350
Birdseye, Clarence, 349–350
birth rates, 73–74, 74*t*
Bisquick, 268
Black, Brown and Beige (Ellington), 302–303
Black, Johnny S., 41
black market, **113–115**, 445, 578, 580
  food, 114, 340, 341
  grocery stores and, 366
blackouts/brownouts/dim-outs, **115–117**, 177, 578
Blake, Eurbie, 193
Blanc, Mel, 418, 425
Blanchard, Doc, 347
Blitzstein, Marc, 183
Block, Martin, 559 (photo)
Blockade, 517
Blondie, 172, 201–202, 201*t*, 214 (photo), 216, 218
blood transfusions, 372
The Blue Ghost: A Photographic Log and Personal Narrative of the Aircraft Carrier U.S.S. Lexington in Combat Operation (Steichen), 509

Blue Grass Boys, 232
blue jeans, 319
BMI v. ASCAP, **32**, **37–40**, 674
BMP. *See* Bureau of Motion Pictures
The Bob Hope Show, 382
bobby-soxers, 306, 320, 633–634, 782, 783
Boettiger, Anna Roosevelt, 599
Bogart, Humphrey, **117–123**, 118 (photo), 119*t*, 167, 167 (photo)
Bohannon, David Dewey, 25
BOMC. *See* Book-of-the-Month Club
Bonavita, Rosina, 606
Bonneville Salt Flats, 395, 484, 486–487
Bonney, Betty, 78
boogie-woogie, 15, 21, **123–125**, 591
book clubs, 97, **125–127**, 451
Book-of-the-Month Club (BOMC), 125
Borglum, Gutzon, 613
Born Free and Equal (Adams, Ansel), 411
Bosch, Carl, 448
Boston Blackie, 240–241, 241*t*
Boston Symphony Orchestra, 185
Boswell Sisters, 20
Boulanger, Nadia, 223
Bourke-White, Margaret, 511, 512*t*
Bow, Clara, 669
Bowery Boys, 205, 206*t*
Bowes, Edward, 288, 632
bowling, **127–129**, 449, 697
boxing, **129–134**, 462–464, 697
The Boy with Green Hair, 521
Boyce, Westray Battle, 777
Boyd, Edward F., 109
Boyd, William (Hopalong Cassidy), 25, 58, **134–138**, 137*t*–138*t*, 769
Boyle, Jack, 240–241
Bracken, Eddie, 196
Braddock, James J., 462
Bradley, Will, 124
Brashun, Midge "Tuffy," 595 (photo), 596
Bread and Butter Magazine, 577

Brecht, Bertolt, 398
Breger, Dave, 214
Brennan, Francis E. (Hank), 526
Breuer, Marcel, 24, 27
The Brick Foxhole (Brooks, Richard), 520
bridge, 353–354, 449
Brimsek, Frank, 380
Bringing Up Father (McManus), 215
Briskin, Samuel J., 414
British Open Championship, 361
Broad Hollow Steeplechase Handicap, 392
Broadcast Music Incorporated. *See* BMI
Broadway Melody of 1940, 496
Broadway shows
    comedy and drama, **138–145**, 141*t*–145*t*
    musicals, **148–156**, 152*t*–155*t*, 256, 798
    See also specific shows
Brook National Steeplechase Handicap, 392
Brooks, Richard, 520
Brown, Edward, Jr., 284
Brown, Johnny Mack, 54
Brown, Les, 78, 674–675
Brown & Haley Candy Company, 269, 270
Brown v. Board of Education, 541
Bruce, Nigel, 240
Brunot, James, 356, 452
bubble gum, 309–310
Bud Abbott and Lou Costello Meet Frankenstein, 386
Budge, Don, 699–700
Built-Rite Toys, 709
Bunshaft, Gordon, 24
Bureau of Motion Pictures (BMP), 762
Burnett, Murray, 166
Burnette, Smiley, 55
Burns, Bob "The Arkansas Traveler," 310, 311, 424
Burns, Ralph, 421–422
Bush, Vannevar, 42

Button, Richard "Dick," 639, 640
Buttram, Pat, 55–56
Butts, Alfred, 356, 452
Byrnes, James F., 743
Byron, Robert "Red," 487

C. A. Swanson and Sons, 351
CAA. *See* Civil Aeronautics Administration
Cabin in the Sky (Duke), 149, 304
Cadet Nurse Corps, 371
Cagney, James, 494
Calder, Alexander, 613–614
Call Me Mister, 156
Calloway, Cab, 306, 306 (photo), 310
Calvert, John, 244
canasta, 354
Candoli, Pete, 422
Candy Land, 356
Caniff, Milton, 222, **702–705**
canteens, 12, 21, 109, 139, **157–161**, 305
  teen, 433
Cantor, Eddie, 12, 373, 629–630
CAP. *See* Civil Air Patrol
Capa, Robert, 511, 512*t*
Capitol Records, 194
Capp, Al, 214, 218, 307
Capra, Frank, 413–415, 763
The Captain and the Kids, 215
Captain Video, 288
Carl's Jr., 322
Carney, Don, 547
Carson, Jack, 158 (photo)
Carson, Rachel, 372
Carvel Ice Cream Company, 272
Casablanca, 106, 120, **166–169**, 167 (photo), 176
Casey, Crime Photographer, 507
The Catholic Hour, 584
Catlett, Sid, 423
Cavalcade of Stars, 287–288, 287 (photo)
CBS (Columbia Broadcasting System), 1, 37, 136, 184, 286, 287, 692

CCA. *See* Comics Code Authority
CCC. *See* Civilian Conservation Corps
CDC. *See* Centers for Disease Control and Prevention
Centers for Disease Control and Prevention (CDC), 374
Central Intelligence Agency (CIA), 189, 795
Cerdan, Marcel, 131
Chain, Ernst, 371
"A Challenge to American Sportsmanship" (Roosevelt, E.), 598
The Chamber Music Society of Lower Basin Street, 629, 630
Chambers, Whittaker, 192
Champion, Gower, 151, 259
Champion, Marge, 259
Chandler, Raymond, 121
Chaplin, Charlie, 170, 518
Chapman, Ceil, 318
Charles, Ezzard, 132*t*, 464
Charlie Chan, 241–242, 242*t*, 537
Charlie McCarthy, 291–293, 292 (photo), 552
Charteris, Leslie, 243
Chase, Mary, 147
Chatterton, George Edward, 308
Cheret, Jules, 525
Chiang Kai-shek, 190–191, 733
Chicago Roller Skate Company, 642
Chicago Symphony Orchestra, 185–186
Chicago World Fair, 649
child care centers, 599
"Chiquita Banana," 344
Christian, Charlie, 420, 421
Christian, Sara, 487
Christie, Agatha, 96
"The Christmas Song," 195
Christy, June, 422
Chrysler, 46, 50*t*
Churchill, Henry, 25, 601 (photo), 603
Churchill, Winston, 187, 188, 794
Chutes and Ladders, 355
CIA. *See* Central Intelligence Agency

CIO. *See* Congress of Industrial Organizations
Cisco Kid, 772
Citation, 391
Citizen Kane, **173–176**, 174 (photo), 355 (photo)
Civil Aeronautics Administration (CAA), 66*t*
Civil Air Patrol (CAP), 178
civil defense, 116, **176–180**, 191
　youth and, 430–431
Civil War, 618
Civilian Conservation Corps (CCC), 447
Civilian Defense Corps, 178
Civilian Public Service (CPS), 618
Clark, Joel Bennett, 358
Clark, Tom, 433
classical music, **180–186**, 222–226, 273–274
　lacking copyright protection, 460
　radio and, 181, 185*t*, 332, 561–562
Clay, Lucius, 93, 298 (photo)
Cleveland Orchestra, 185, 186
Clifton, Nathaniel "Sweetwater," 87, 535
Clue, 357
Coachman, Alice, 535
Coast-to-Coast on a Bus, 546–547
Coates, Robert, 4
Coca-Cola, 11, 107–109, 299
Cochran, Jacqueline, 778
A Code of Wartime Practices for the American Press, 503
coin collecting, 376–377, 662–663
Cold War, 46, 69*t*, 93, 179, **187–193**, 277, 300, 397–399, 446, 474, 499, 519, 620, 733, 793
　movies and, 492–493
　newspapers and, 504
　See also Soviet Union
The Cold War (Lippmann), 188
Cole, Nat King, 52, **193–196**
Colley, Sarah Ophelia, 230–231
Collins, Ted, 646
Collyer, Bud, 476 (photo)

Columbia Broadcasting Company. *See* CBS
Columbia Records, 83, 184
The Columbia Symphony Orchestra, 184
comic books and strips, 25, 52, **207–213**, 210*t*–211*t*, **213–222**, 217*t*–218*t*, 219*t*, 220*t*–221*t*, 307, 460, 702
　atomic bomb in, 44, 45
　boxing, 133
　horse racing and, 392
　juvenile delinquency and, 212, 432–433
　scrap drives, 610
　serial films and, 623
　stereotyping in, 537
　youth and, 782
Comics Code Authority (CCA), 433
Comingore, Dorothy, 175, 355 (photo)
The Common Sense Book of Baby and Child Care (Spock), 660–661
Community Facilities Grants, 599
computers, 678–679, 680, 794
Condon, Eddie, 423
Congress of Industrial Organizations (CIO), 441, 446, 504–505
Conn, Billy, 131, 463
conscientious objectors (COs), 587, 618
Consolidated Edison Company, 443 (photo)
Constant Comment, 111
Conway, Tom, 244
Cook, Willa Worthington McGuire, 670
Cook It Outdoors (Beard), 342
Cooke, Sarah Palfrey, 701
Cooper, Charles "Chuck," 87, 535
Cooper, Gary, 319
Cooper, Jackie, 200
Cootie, 356
Coplan, Aaron, 181, 183, **222–226**, 224 (photo), 256, 616
Coppertone, 687
Corley, Bob, 536
Cornell, Joseph, 614–615
Correll, Charles, 536, 550

cortisone, 679
COs. *See* conscientious objectors
Costello, Lou, 172, 203, 204*t*
Cotton Club, 301
Council of National Defense, 36
Count Fleet, 391
country music, 8, 38, 55, **229–236**, 258
Cousy, Bob, 87
Cover Girl, 309
CPS. *See* Civilian Public Service
Crain, Jeanne, 521
Cranbrook Academy of Art, 262
Crawford, Broderick, 278 (photo)
Crawford, Joan, 54, 313
Crazy Horse (Chief), 613
The Crimson Avenger, 208
Crocker, Betty, 268, 340
Crockett, Johnson, 215
Crosby, Bing, 2, 10, 19 (photo), 21, 40, 111, 202–203, 229, **246–251**, 247 (photo), 248*t*, 276, 382 (photo), 383, 424, 437, 496, 538, 774
    golf and, 361 (photo), 363
    top-rated songs performed by, 250*t*
Crosley automobiles, **251–252**
Cross, Milton, 546–547
Crossfire, 281, 520
Crusade in Europe (Eisenhower, D.), 300
Culinary Institute of America, 590
Cummings, Robert, 408
Cunningham, Briggs, 486
Cunningham, Imogen, 515
Cureton, Thomas K., 370
Curtiz, Michael, 167
cybernetics, 679
Cypress Gardens, 669–670

Daffan, Ted, 234
Dailey, Dan, 156
Dairy Queen, 272, 324
Dale, Virginia, 538
Dameron, Tadd, 91
dance, 39, 150, **253–259**, 496
Dance Index, 615

DAR. *See* Daughters of the Revolution
Dark Legend (Wertham), 432
A Date with Judy, 483
Daughters of the Revolution (DAR), 598
Davidson, Jo, 613
Davies, Marion, 175
Davis, Bette, 158 (photo)
Davis, Elmer, 511, 762
Davis, Miles, 91
Davis, Sammy, Jr., 255–256
Day, Dennis, 418
Day, Doris, 19, 675
Day, Dorothy, 779–780
Day, Ned, 129
Daytona 500, 488
D-Day, **259–261**, 260 (photo), 299, 372, 480
DDT, 372, 680
de Graff, Robert, 96
de Mille, Agnes, 151, 223, 256 (photo), 256
Dead End Kids, 205, 206*t*, 432
Death of a Salesman (Miller, Arthur), 146
DeBeck, Billy, 392
Defense Savings Stamps, 752–753
Dell, Gabriel, 205
DeMille, Cecil B., 134, 228
Department of Defense, 189
design, 13, 23, **261–267**, 456
desserts/candy/ice cream, **267–273**
DeSylva, Buddy, 194
Detective Comics, 208
Dewey, Thomas E., 733
Dexter, Al, 233–234
Diamond, David, 182
Dick Tracy, 221–222, 246
Dies, Martin, Jr., 397
Dies Committee, 397
Dietrich, Marlene, 740 (photo)
Dietz, Howard, 156
DiMaggio, Joe, 78, 559 (photo)
"Dinah," 629
The Dinah Shore Show, 629, 631
Dior, Christian, 313, 317–318

Dirks, Rudolph, 165–166
Disney, Walt, 161–163, **273–277**, 274 (photo)
    See also Walt Disney
Dix, Dorothy, 507
Dixon, Lee, 256 (photo)
DNA, 680
Dobson, Harmon, 324
Doby, Larry, 80, 535
do-it-yourself tasks, 377–378
Dole, Charles, 644–645
Dollar Book Club, 125
dolls, 712–713
Donald Duck, 275, 277, 320
The Dooleys Play Ball (Renick), 651
Dorsey, Tommy, 124, 559 (photo), 633–634
Doubleday & Company, 125
Dowd, Elwood P., 147
Down Argentina Way, 481–482
Doyle, Arthur Conan, 239–240
Doyle, Geraldine Hoff, 606
draft. *See* Selective Training and Service Act of 1940
drag racing, 52, **393–397**
Dragnet, 546
Dragstrip Girl, 396
Drew, Charles, 372
Dreyfuss, Henry, 261, 262, 267
Driscoll, Bobby, 520
drive-ins, 53, **282–286**
    banks, **285–286**
    theaters, **282–285**, 283 (photo)
Duff, Howard, 544
Duke, Vernon, 149, 304
DuMont network, **286–289**
Duncan, Isadora, 257
Dunkin' Donuts, 324
DuPont, Margaret Osbourne, 701
DuPont Chemical Company, 315, 349–350
Durante, Jimmy, 635
Durham, Eddie, 17–18, 83
Dust Bowl Ballads (Guthrie), 333
Dykstra, Clarence, 619–620

Eames, Charles, 26, 262, 265
Eames, Ray, 26, 262, 265
Earl, Harley, 266–267
East Side Kids, 205, 206t
Eastman, George, 510
Eastman, Joseph B., 722
Eastman Kodak Company, 376, 510, 730
Eberle, Ray, 479
Ebony, 538
EC Comics, 212
Eckstine, Billy, 89, 90
The Ed Sullivan Show, 708
The Eddie Cantor Show, 630
Eddy, Nelson, 183
Ederle, Gertrude, 669
Edgar Bergen/Charlie McCarthy Show, **291–293**, 552
Edible Wild Plants of Eastern North America (Kinsey), 344
Edison, Harry, 84
Edison, Thomas, 427
education, 14, 85, **293–298**, 358
    baby boom and, 75, 297
    film as tool for, 338
    health, 336 (photo)
    Japanese American fund for, 412
    money for college, 74
    physical, 370
    radio, **555–557**, 557t
    sex behavior and, 436
Edward B. Marks Music Company, 38
Edwards, James, 522
Edwards, John Paul, 515
Eerie, 211–212
Eichler, Joseph, 26
Einstein, Albert, 42
Eisenhower, Dwight D., 108, 259, **298–300**, 298 (photo), 534
    fashion and, 299, 311, 313
Eisenhower, Milton S., 409–411
Eldred, William T., 644
Eldridge, Roy, 421
Ellington, Duke, 91, **300–304**, 301 (photo), 303t, 306

Elliott, Bill, 772
Ellison, James "Jimmy," 136
Elman, Dave, 375, 376
Emde, Floyd, 488
Emergency Price Control Act, 576
Emergency Rescue Committee, 597
Emerson, Faye, 779–780
Erector Sets, 712
Escape, 518, 555
Espionage Act, 503
Esquire, 308–309, 407–408, 469
Etiquette (Post), 506
Evans, Dale, 58, 60, 547
Evans, Redd, 606
Evans, Walker, 511, 512*t*, 514
Everybody Comes to Rick's (Burnett & Alison), 166
Ewell, Tom, 532
Exner, Virgil, 48, 266

Fadiman, Clifton, 568
fads, **305–312**, 320
Fair Employment Practices Committee (FEPC), 535–536, 598, 620
Fairbanks, Mabel, 638–639
Fairfax, Beatrice, 507
The Falcon, 244, 244*t*
Falk, Lee, 537
Famous Funnies, 207
Fanfare for the Common Man (Copland), 225
Fantasia, 162–163, 180, 273–274
FAP. *See* Federal Arts Project
Faraway Hill, 288
Farley, James A., 601
Farm Security Administration (FSA), 514
fashion, 263, **312–321**, 611
  atomic bomb and, 45
  Eisenhower, D., 299, 311, 313
  Miranda, Carmen, 482 (photo), 484
  photography, 514–515
  Seventeen and, 627
  youth, 319–320, 785
fast food, **321–325**, 336, 590
The Fat Man, 544

Fatool, Nick, 420–421
Faulkner, William, 120, 121, 521
Faye, Alice, 482, 496
FBI. *See* Federal Bureau of Investigation
FCC. *See* Federal Communications Commission
Federal Arts Project (FAP), 29, 115 (photo), 525–526
federal budget, 787
Federal Bureau of Investigation (FBI), 411
Federal Communications Commission (FCC), 1, 331, 693, 694, 748
Federal Housing Authority (FHA), 455
Federal Interagency Committee, 450
Federal Security Agency (FSA), 336–337
Federal Theatre Project (FTP), 139
Federal-Aid Highway Act, 723, 729–730
Feller, Bob, 77–78
Fellig, Arthur. *See* Weegee
Fender solid-body electric guitar, 680
FEPC. *See* Fair Employment Practices Committee
Fermi, Enrico, 43
Ferrer, Mel, 521
Field, W. C., 292
Finegan, Bill, 39
The Fireball, 596
First Motion Picture Unit of United States Army Air Forces, 66
The First Nighter Program, 553
Fischer, Leo, 649
Fisher, M. F. K., 268
Fisher-Price, 711
fishing, 449
Fitzgerald, Ella, 19
Flagg, James Montgomery, 527
Flaherty, Robert, 14
Flanders, Charles, 460
Flatt, Lester, 232
Fleer Chewing Gum Company, 309
Fleischer, Max, 163
Fleming, Alexander, 371

Flock, Truman Fontell "Fonty," 487
Florey, Howard, 371
fluoridation, 680–681
FM radio, **330–333**, 332t, 556, 693
FNB. *See* Food and Nutrition Board
Fogarty, Anne, 318
Foggy Mountain Boys, 232
Foley, Clyde "Red," 231
folk music, **333–335**
   labor unrest and, 442–443
Folkway Records, 334
Follow the Band, 606–607
Follow the Boys, 630
Fonda, Henry, 517
food, 93, 150, **335–345**, 361, 364–367
   black market, 114, 340, 341
   fast, **321–325**, 336, 590
   frozen, 339, **349–351**, 367, 681–682
   health and, 369
   posters, 526 (photo)
   rationing, 339–342, 579–580, 589
   See also beverages; desserts/candy/ice cream
Food and Drug Act of 1938, 371
Food and Nutrition Board (FNB), 337, 370
football, 81, **345–349**, 478, 697
   war bonds and, 757
Ford, Gerald, 72
Ford, John, 773
Ford, Ruth VanSickle, 531
Ford Corporation, 46, 47 (photo), 50t–51t, 67, 721
Foreign Correspondent, 518
Fortune, 469, 514
Foster, Dan, 489
Foster, Stephen, 39
Fouilhoux, Jacques-Andre, 261
Four Sons, 518
France, William "Bill," 487, 488
franchising, 323–324
Fraser, Gretchen, 645
Fraser, James Earle, 612
Frazee, Jane, 607
Frisbee, 452, 681, 716

From Here to Eternity, 636–637
frozen food, **349–351**, 367
   complete meal, 351, 681–682
FSA. *See* Farm Security Administration; Federal Security Agency
FTP. *See* Federal Theatre Project
Der Fuehrer's Face, 161–162, 275, 425
Fulbright, J. William, 297
Fulks, Joe, 87
Fuller, Charles E., 584–585
Fuller, Mary, 622
Fuller, Paul M., 428, 429
Fun and Fancy Free, 276
Funnies on Parade, 207
Funny Pages, 208

Gable, Clark, 318
Gaines, William M., 212
games, **353–357**, 449
Gang Busters, 543
The Gang's All Here, 482
Garbo, Greta, 313
Gardner, Ava, 309, 453
Gardner, Erle Stanley, 96
Garfield, John, 158 (photo)
Garland, Judy, 496
Gasoline Alley (King, Frank), 52, 214, 393
Gaynor, Charles, 156
Gebhard, Paul, 435
GED (General Equivalency Diploma), 295
Geddes, Norman Bel, 261, 262, 721
General Electric Company, 45
General Equivalency Diploma. *See* GED
General Foods Company, 349–350
General Maximum Price Regulations, 576
General Motors, 46, 51t, 721
Gentleman's Agreement, 281
The Ghost Breakers, 384
GI Bill (Servicemen's Readjustment Act of 1944), 25, 74, 86, 106, 284, 296, **357–359**, 791
   suburbanization and, 455

Gibson, Althea, 535
Gibson, Walter B., 476–477, 663–664
Gilbert, Peggy, 15–16
Gilbert, Ronnie, 334
Gillars, Mildred, 70–72
Gillespie, John Birks "Dizzy," 89, 89 (photo), 91, 92, 422
Girard, Alexander H., 263
Giuffre, Jimmy, 92
The Glass Key, 326 (photo)
The Glass Menagerie (Williams, Tennessee), 146
Gleason, Jackie, 259, 287–288, 287 (photo)
Glory for Me (Kantor), 97, 104
GNP. *See* gross national product
Go for Broke, 412
GOC. *See* Ground Observer Corps
"God Bless America," 587, 648
Goddard, Paulette, 254, 384
Godfrey, Arthur, **359–360**
Gold, Bill, 529
Goldberg, Rube, 270
golf, **360–364**, 362*t*, 364*t*, 452
   Crosby and, 361 (photo), 363
   Louis, Joe, and, 363
Gonzales, Pancho, 700
Goodman, Benny, 10, 16, 92, 182, 225, 419–420
Goosens, Eugene, 183
Gorcey, Leo, 205
Gordon, Dorothy, 431–432
Gordon, Ruth, 139
Gosden, Freeman, 536, 550
Gould, Chester, 221–222, 246
Gould, Morton, 181–182
Grable, Betty, 156, 309, 310, 404 (photo), 453, 482
Graham, Billy, 437, 584, 585–586
Graham, Martha, 223, 256–257, 615–616
Grahame, Kenneth, 274
Grand Ole Opry, 229–235
Grant, Cary, 199, 306, 507, 507 (photo), 761, 783

Graves, Jackie, 133
Gray, Harold, 214
Grayson, Carl, 425
Grayson, Kathryn, 635
Graziano, Rocky, 129, 131, 132*t*, 133
"The Greatest Gift" (Stern), 413
Green, Johnny, 420
Green, William, 441
The Green Hornet, 208, 460
Greenberg, Clement, 5, 6
Greenberg, Hank, 77–78
Greenwich Village, 482–483
Greyhound Bus Company, 723
Griffith, Clark, 77
Griswold, Frank, Jr., 486
grocery stores/supermarkets, 113, 338, **364–367**, 365 (photo)
Groebli, Werner, 640
Grofe, Ferde, 183
Gropius, Walter, 24
gross national product (GNP), 787
Grotell, Majilis (Maija), 266
Ground Observer Corps (GOC), 178–179
Groves, Leslie R., 42, 373
Guarnieri, Johnny, 420
Guertin, M. K., 728–729
Gustavson, Paul, 208
Guthrie, Woody, 333, 442–443

Haber, Fritz, 448
Hall, Huntz, 205
Hallaren, Mary A., 777
Halop, Billy, 205
Hammerstein, Oscar, III, 149, 151, 156, 256 (photo)
Hammett, Dashiell, 544
Hammond, John, 83, 124
Hampton, Lionel, 420
Hancock, A. G., 670
Handy, George, 422
Hanna, William "Bill," 165–166
Hansen, Howard, 182
Harding, Ann, 783
Hardy, Oliver, 205

Hargrove, Marion, 619
Harley-Davidson, 488
Harman, Fred, 537
Harper's Bazaar, 515
Harriman, W. Averell, 188, 644
Harris, Bill, 422
Harris, Harwell H., 26
Harris, Joel Chandler, 276
Harris, John H., 640
Harris, Roy, 181
Harrison, Wallace K., 23, 261
Hart, Lorenz, 149
Hartley, Fred, 445
Harvest Show, 747
Harvey (Chase), 147
Haskell, William N., 177
Haugdahl, Sig, 487
Hawkins, Coleman, 420
Hawks, Howard, 120
Hayden, Russell, 136
Hayes, Clancy, 423
Hayes, George "Gabby," 58, 136
Hayes, Helen, 139
Haymes, Dick, 19, 40, 41
Hays, Lee, 333–334, 442–443
Hayworth, Rita, 254, 309
    on atomic bomb, 309, 453
Head, Howard, 645
health, **369–374**
Hearst, William Randolph, 173–179
Heatter, Gabriel, 477
Hedda Hopper Show, 506
Hefti, Neal, 421–422
Heggen, Thomas, 147
Hellerman, Fred, 334
Help Your Doctor Help You, 369
Hemingway, Ernest, 120
Henderson, Fletcher, 420
Henie, Sonja, 638, 640, 644
Henry Aldrich, 199–200, 200*t*
Herlihy, Ed, 439
Herman, Woody, 92, 421–422, 423
Herman Miller Company, 264, 265
Herriman, George, 215
Herrmann, Bernard, 175–176

Hersey, John, 473
Hershey, Lewis, 620
Hershey Corporation, 269–270
The Hidden Persuaders (Packard), 14
High Sierra, 118
Hill, George Washington, 13
Hill-Burton Act of 1946, 371
Hillman, Sidney, 47
Hines, Duncan, 109–110, 588, 727
Hines, Earl, 89
Hirohito (Emperor), 48, 467
His Girl Friday, 507, 507 (photo)
Hiss, Alger, 192, 798
Hitchcock, Alfred, 518
Hitler, Adolph, 425, 518, 743
Ho Chi Minh, 190
hobbies, **375–379**
    Roosevelt, Franklin Delano, 601
Hobbies, 375
Hobby, Oveta Culp, 776
Hobby Lobby, 375
hockey, **379–381**, 640
Hoffman, Hans, 4
Hogan, Ben, 361, 362
Holgate Toy Company, 711
Holiday, 729
Holiday, Billie, 83, 423
Holiday Inn, 249, 496, 538, 657, 774
Holiday on Ice, 640
Hollingshead, Richard, Jr., 282–283
Hollywood Canteen, 159, 183, 742
Hollywood Cavalcade, 757
Hollywood Hotel, 506
Hollywood Production Code, 517
Hollywood Ten, 398–399, 398*t*, 492, 525
Hollywood Victory Caravan, 757
Holman, Bill, 735
Home Country (Pyle), 530
Home of the Brave, 521–522
Home Sweet Home, 71
Hoosier Hot Shots, 231
Hoover, Herbert, 354, 465
Hope, Bob, 196, 202, 248, 363, **381–385**, 382 (photo), 383*t*–384*t*

Hormel, George A., 658
Hormel Foods Corporation, 657–660
Horn, Ted, 486
Horne, Lena, 521
Hors d'Oeuvres and Canapés (Beard), 343
horse racing, **389–393**
Horwitt, Arnold B., 156
Hot Rod, 394 (photo)
hot rods, 52, 312, 379, **393–397**, 431, 682
Hour of Charm Orchestra, 16 (photo), 17
House and Garden, 448, 614
House Un-American Activities Committee (HUAC), 191–192, 277, **397–399**, 492, 504, 522, 524–525, 795
How Green Was My Valley, 173
How to Cook a Wolf (Fisher), 268
Howard, Charles S., 390
Howard Johnson's, 271, 325, 588–590
The Howdy Doody Show, 270, **400–401**, 401 (photo)
Howe, Louis, 601
HUAC. *See* House Un-American Activities Committee
Hubley Manufacturing Company, 709
Hull, Cordell, 605
Hull, Josephine, 139
Humes, Helen, 83
Hummert, Anne, 572
Hummert, Frank, 572
Humphrey, Doris, 257
Hungerford, Cyrus C., 528
hunting, 449
Hupfeld, Herman, 168–169
Hurt, Marlin, 536
Huston, John, 119, 121
Hutton, Ina Ray, 15, 16
Hutton, Marion, 479
Hutton, Robert, 783
Hyams, Marjorie, 15

I Wanted Wings, 315
Ibsen, Don, 669
Ice Capades, 640
Ice Follies, 640
Ickes, Harold L., 605
Idiot's Delight, 517
If You Ask Me (Roosevelt, E.), 599
"I'll Never Smile Again," 633
illiteracy, 295, 296
illustrators, **403–408**, 406*t*–407*t*, 526
  USO club, 740
  war bonds and, 758
Indian Motorcycle Company, 488
Indian Reorganization Act of 1934, 539
Indianapolis 500-Mile Race, 484, 485–486
Industrial Designers Institute, 266
Information Please!, 568
Ingram, Edgar W., 322
Inner Sanctum Mysteries, 554
In-N-Out Burger, 285, 323–324
INS (International News Service), 509
Inside U.S.A. (Schwartz & Dietz), 156
Institute of International Education, 297
International Confederation of Free Trade Unions, 446
International Mobile (Calder), 614
International News Service. *See* INS
International Skating Union (ISU), 638
International Sweethearts of Rhythm, 17, 18
internment camps (relocation centers), **408–413**, 410*t*, 539, 598, 604, 615, 789
Intruder in the Dust, 521
The Iron Curtain, 187 (photo), 522
Iroquois Steeplechase, 392
ISU. *See* International Skating Union
It Happened in Brooklyn, 635–636
It's a Wonderful Life, **413–415**
Ives, Burl, 151, 156, 334–335
Ives, Charles, 180–181

J. P. Seeburg Corporation, 428
Jack, Beau, 132*t*, 534
The Jack Benny Program, **417–419**, 536
Jaffe, Moe, 314
James, Henry, 633

James O. Welch Company, 271
Jameson, Betty, 363
Janie, 783
Jannus, Tony, 61
Japanese American Evacuation Claims Act, 412
Japanese Relocation, 410
jazz, 5, 39, 82, 88, 123, 193, 301, 304, **419–424**, 591
Jeep, 682
Jell-O, 200, 268–269, 419
Jenkins, David Abbott "Ab," 484
Jepson-Turner, Gladys Lyne, 639
Jet, 538
jigsaw puzzles, 355–356, 355 (photo), 449
jitterbug, 258, 305, 673 (photo)
job training, 74
Joe and Asbestos (Kling), 392, 537
John Gabel Manufacturing Company, 427
Johnson, John H., 538
Johnson, Pete, 123 (photo)
Johnson, Philip, 24, 27
Jolson, Al, 2
Jones, Bobby, 361
Jones, Isham, 421
Jones, Spike, 275, **424–426**
Jordan, Bobby, 205
Jordan, Louis, 592–593
Joy Ride, 396
"Juke Box Saturday Night," 428
jukeboxes, 229, **427–430**, 427 (photo), 480, 592
Jump, Larry, 645
Jump for Joy (Ellington), 303
Junior Mints, 271
juvenile delinquency, **430–434**, 784
   comic books and, 212, 432–433
   movies and, 432, 495

Kahn, Albert, 22–23, 261, 721
Kaiser, Edgar F., 599
Kane, Bob, 208
Kantor, MacKinlay, 97, 104

Kapp, Jack, 247
Karcher, Carl, 322
Karcher, Margaret, 322
Karloff, Boris, 243
Karns, Roscoe, 288–289
The Katzenjammer Kids, 215
Kayak II, 390
Kaye, Sammy, 568–569
Keefe, Mary Doyle, 607
Keeshan, Bob, 400
Kefauver, Estes, 799
Kelly, Gene, 253–254, 635, 636
Kelly, Joe, 569
Kelly, Walt, 215–216
Kennan, George F., 188, 189
Kenton, Stan, 422
Kentucky Derby, 390, 392
Kentucky Fried Chicken, 324
Kern, Jerome, 182, 381, 635
Kerry Drake, 221–222
Kesselring, Joseph, 139, 146–147
Key Largo, 122
Keys, Ancel Benjamin, 339
Kid Boots, 629
Kidd, Michael, 151
Kiefer, Adolph, 671
Kieran, John, 568
Kilroy, James J., 307
"Kilroy was here," 307–308, 308 (photo)
King, Andrea, 386 (photo)
King, Frank, 52, 214
King, Martin Luther, Jr., 541
King, Muriel, 316
King, Pee Wee, 233
King, Scott, 728
Kinsey, Alfred C., 344, **435–437**
Kinsey Institute for Research in Sex, Gender, and Reproduction, 435
Kirstein, Lincoln, 223
Kiss Me Kate (Porter, Cole & Abbott, George), 151
Klamfoth, Dick, 488
Klein, Evelyn Kaye, 17
Kling, Kenneth, 392, 537
Knoll, Florence Schust, 265

Knoll, Hans, 265
Knox, Alexander, 737
Knudsen, William S., 46
Koerner, Henry, 528
Kool-Aid, 111–112
Korean War, 467, 621, 734, 739, 799–800
Kostelanetz, Andre, 182–183, 184
Kracken, Jack, 462
The Kraft Music Hall, 248, 249, 424, 437, 774
Kraft Television Theatre, **437–439**
Kramer, Jack, 699, 700
Krazy Kat (Herriman), 215
Kroc, Ray, 323
Krupa, Gene, 421
Kubelsky, Benjamin, 417
Kubik, Gail, 183
Kyser, Kay, 568–569

La Guardia, Fiorello, 177, 216, 314
La Touche, John, 149
labor unrest, **441–446**, 504–505, 580, 732, 798
Ladd, Alan, 326 (photo), 494–495, 544
Ladies Home Journal, 455
Lake, Arthur, 201
Lake, Veronica, 315, 317, 326 (photo)
Lamarr, Hedy, 309, 310
LaMotta, Jake, 132*t*, 133
Lamour, Dorothy, 202, 382 (photo), 383
  war bonds and, 757
L'Amour, Louis, 135
Lampell, Millard, 333–334, 442–443
Land, Edwin, 376, 510
Landis, James M., 177
Lang, Fritz, 492
Lange, Dorothea, 411, 511, 512*t*, 514
Langley, Roger, 644
Lantz, Walter, 165
Lapidus, Morris, 263
Lapin, Aaron, 269
Lattimore, Owen, 799
Laurel, Stan, 205
Lautner, John, 263

lawns, lawnmowers, and fertilizers, **446–448**
Lawrence, Gertrude, 139
League of Nations, 737
Leatherneck, 396
Lee, Peggy, 19, 420
Lee, Russell, 514
leisure and recreation, 97, 348, **449–453**, 450*t*, 451*t*
Lembeck, Harvey, 532
Lend an Ear (Gaynor), 156
Lend-Lease Act, 575, 602–603
Lesnevich, Gus, 132*t*
Let Us Now Praise Famous Men (Evans, Walker), 514
Levitt, Abraham, 455–458
Levitt, Alfred, 455–456
Levitt, Helen, 511, 513*t*, 514
Levitt, William, 26, 455–458
Levittown, **453–458**, 457 (photo), 540
Levy, Julien, 614
Lewine, Richard, 156
Lewis, Fulton, Jr., 477–478
Lewis, Jerry, 205–206
Lewis, John L., 441, 444, 445, 580, 798
Leyvas, Henry, 540
Liberman, Alexander, 514
Liberty, 469
Liberty Films, 414
Life, 469, 509, 511
  rationing and, 580
The Life and Times of the Shmoo, 307
life expectancy, 369, 374, 787
Life is Worth Living, 288
Life with Teena, 628
Lights Out, 553
Light-Up Time, 635
Li'l Abner (Capp), 218, 307
Limiting Order L-85, 313, 314–315
Lincoln Logs, 711
Lionel Trains, 714–715
Lippmann, Walter, 188
Lipton Tea, 360
Liston, Melba, 15
Litchfield, Johnny, 645

Literary Guild, 125
Little Annie Rooney, 216
Little Caesar, 432
Little Orphan Annie, 216
"Little Steel Formula," 444
Little Tokyo, U.S.A., 409
Little Tough Guys, 205, 206*t*
Livingstone, Mary, 418
Lloyd, Earl, 87, 535
Loeb, John Jacob, 606
Loewy, Raymond, 13, 48–49, 266, 721
Log Building Sets, 711
Lomax, Alan, 333
Lombard, Carole, 418
   war bonds and, 756–757
Lombardo, Carmen, 359–360
Lombardo, Guy, 489
The Lone Ranger, 208, **459–462**, 459 (photo), 461 (photo), 476, 537
The Lone Wolf, 245, 245*t*
Longden, Johnny, 391
Look, 455, 511
Looney Tunes, 164–165
Loring, Eugene, 223
Lost Boundaries, 521
The Lost Weekend, 282 (photo)
Louis, Joe, 129, 130–131, 130 (photo), 132*t*, **462–464**, 462 (photo), 535
   golf and, 363
   war bonds and, 757
Louisiana Story, 14
Lovejoy, Frank, 544
Lowther, George F., 665–666
Loy, Myrna, 105 (photo), 783
Luce, Henry, 469
Lucky Strikes, 12–13, 419, 635
Luke, Keye, 243
Lundigan, William, 521
The Lux Radio theater, 553
Lydon, Jimmy, 200
Lytle, Betty, 642

M. M. Cole Publishing Company, 38
MacArthur, Douglas, 298, **465–467**, 466 (photo), 467, 734, 739, 791

Macfadden, Bernarr, 469
Mack, Ted, 288
Mack, Walter S., 108
Macon, Uncle Dave, 9
MAD. *See* mutual assured destruction
"Magazine War Guide," 433
magazines, 12, 56, 96, 107, 125, 128, **468–473**, 471*t*–473*t*
   atomic bomb in, 43
   Berlin airlift in, 94
   celebrating black culture, 538
   Cold War and, 192
   gardening, 448
   lifestyle reporting, 511
   pinup girls in, 308–309
   pulp, 326, 543, 663
   skating and, 642
   Spam and, 658
   suburbanization and, 454, 455
   victory gardens and, 745
   war bonds and, 756
   youth and, 782
Magic 8-Ball, 715
Mainbocher, 314, 778
Make Mine Manhattan (Lewine & Horwitt), 156
Make Mine Music, 276
Male Call, 703–704
The Maltese Falcon, 118 (photo), 119
The Man I Married, 518
The Man in the Gray Flannel Suit (Wilson, Sloan), 319
Mandrake the Magician (Falk), 537
Mankiewicz, Herman J., 173
Manship, Paul, 612
Mao Zedong, 190–191
Marble, Alice, 699
March, Fredric, 104, 105 (photo), 520
The March of Time, 763–764
March on Washington Movement (MOWM), 535–536, 541
Marciano, Rocky, 464
margarine, 341
Marin, John, 5
Marine Corps Women's Reserve, 779

Marks, Sadye, 418
marriage, 73, 74t
Mars, Incorporated, 269–270
Marshall, George C., 108, 189, 298, 299, **474–475**
Marshall Plan, 189, 474–475, 732, 796
Martin, Clarice, 594
Martin, Clyde, 435
Martin, Dean, 205–206
Martin, Freddy, 39
Marvel Comics, 209
Marx, Groucho, 2–3, 204–205, 483, 569
Marx Brothers, 204–205
Mary Kay and Johnny, 288
Masters Tournament, 361
Mathews, Billy, 488
Mattel, 715–716
Mauch, Hans, 640
Mauldin, Bill, 504, **530–533**
Mauriello, Tami, 464
Maxson Food Systems, 351
May, Cliff, 26
Mays, Rex, 486
MBS. *See* Mutual
McAfee, Mildred, 778
McCalls, 316
McCardell, Claire, 317
McCarthy, Clem, 392
McCarthy, Joseph, 192, 225, 799
McConnell, Ed, 547
McCormack-Dick Committee, 397
McCrea, Joel, 518
McCullough, Alex, 324
McCullough, J. F., 324
McDaniel, Hattie, 536
McDonalds, 285, 322–323, 588–589
McGrane, Paul, 428
McKay, Bernie, 594
McKinley, Ray, 124, 481
McLuhan, Marshall, 14
McManus, George, 215
McNutt, Paul V., 336–337, 620
McPherson, Aimee Semple, 584
McShann, Jay, 592
Meany, George, 446

medicine, **369–374**
Meet the Press, 478
Mehrtens, Warren, 391
Mellett, Lowell, 762
Melodears, 16
Melody Ranch, 55–56, 547
Melody Time, 276
Menninger, Karl, 437
Menotti, Gian Carlo, 182
Mercer, Johnny, 194, 247 (photo), 408, 652 (photo)
Meredith, Burgess, 531, 614
Merman, Ethel, 148 (photo)
Merrie Melodies, 164–165
Merrill, Gretchen, 639
Metcalf, Nelson C., Jr., 12
Metro-Goldwyn-Mayer. *See* MGM
Metronome, 194
MGM (Metro-Goldwyn-Mayer), 165–166, 490
Mickey Mouse, 162, 212, 273, 320
microwave oven, 683
Mies van der Rohe, Ludwig, 23, 24, 26–27
Mikan, George, 87
Mike and Ike, 270
Milland, Ray, 282 (photo)
Miller, Ann, 254
Miller, Arthur, 139 (photo), 140, 146
Miller, Glenn, 12, 39, 420, 428, **479–481**, 479 (photo), 482, 559, 644, 676
Miller, J. Howard, 316–317, 528, 606
Miller, Johnny, 193
Mills Brothers, 41
Milton Bradley, 354, 355
Minton, Henry, 88
Minute Maid, 111, 350
The Miracle of the Bells, 636
Miranda, Carmen, **481–484**, 482 (photo), 496
Mister Roberts (Heggen), 147
Mitchell, Joan, 639
Mitchum, Robert, 531
Mix, Tom, 548

M&Ms, 270
mobile telephone, 683
model making, 378–379, 711
Modernaires, 479
Mohr, Gerald, 245
Molded Products, 709
Moline Pressed Steel Company, 709
Monogram Pictures, 205
Monopoly, 354, 449
Monroe, Bill, 231–232
Monroe, Rose Will, 607
Monroe Brothers, 231–232
Montana Moon, 54
Montgomery, Bob, 534
Montgomery, George, 631
The Moon Is Down, 519
Moore, Clayton, 461 (photo)
Moore, Oscar, 193
Moorehead, Agnes, 477
The Moral Basis of Democracy (Roosevelt, E.), 597–598
Moran, Gertrude, 701
Morgan, Henry, 2
Morgan, Julia, 175
Morgenthau, Henry, Jr., 751
Morris, Chester, 240–241
The Mortal Storm, 518
motels, 728
Moten, Bennie, 83
Motion Picture Alliance for the Production of American Ideals, 277
Motley, Marion, 535
Motor Trend, 395
motorcycle races, 488
motorsports, **484–490**
Mounds Bar, 270–271
Mount, William Sydney, 456
Mount Rushmore, 613
Mountain Dew, 112
movies, 2, 21, 57*t*, 59*t*–60*t*, 82, 84, 119*t*, 134, 137*t*–138*t*, 148, 159, 166–176, 181, 195, 202–203, 204*t*, 218, 223–224, 291–292, 299, 382–384, 383*t*–384*t*, 398, 417–418, 426, 449, 450, 461, 463–464, 477, 480–483, **490–493**, 494–495, 531–532, 630, 635–638, 636*t*, 648, 668–669
  anti-Communist, 187 (photo), 192, 399, 522
  atomic bomb, 44
  attendance, 491
  aviation, 66–67
  baby boom and, 491
  baseball, 76–77
  black market and, 114
  blacklisting and, 399, 492, 525
  boxing, 133–134
  cartoons, **161–166**, 701, 746
  children's, **169–173**, 171*t*–172*t*
  comedies, **196–206**, 197*t*–198*t*
  costume/spectacle, **226–229**, 227*t*–228*t*
  crime and mystery, 120, **236–246**, 237*t*–239*t*
  drama, **278–282**, 279*t*–281*t*
  drive-in, **282–285**, 283 (photo)
  as education tool, 338
  fashion in, 313
  film noir, 119–120, 122, 281, **325–330**, 327*t*, 328*t*–330*t*, 386–387
  football, 349
  golf, 362–363
  horror and thriller, **385–389**, 387*t*–389*t*
  horse racing, 392
  juvenile delinquency and, 432, 495
  labor unrest, 443
  monopoly, 491
  music and, 656
  musicals, **495–500**, 497*t*–499*t*
  newspapers and, 492, 501, 507
  nursing, 371
  package, 276
  pinup girl, 309
  political and propaganda, **517–525**, 523*t*–524*t*
  posters, 529
  race, 538
  racial intolerance in, 520–522
  Roller Derby, 596

Rosie the Riveter, 606–607
Selective Service and, 619, 761
serial, 172, **621–626**, 623t–624t
skating, 638–640, 641–642
skiing, 644
softball, 650
sound technology, 54, 495
stereotyping in, 537–538
swimming, 668–669
television and, 491, 695
UFO, 736
war, **759–767**, 765t–766t
war bonds and, 757
westerns, 25, 53–61, 134, 170, **767–773**, 770t–772t
youth and, 785
See also specific movies
MOWM. *See* March on Washington Movement
"Mr. Chad," 308
Mr. Lucky, 761
Mr. Winkle Goes to War, 761
Mr. Wong, Detective, 242–243
Mulford, Clarence, 134–135
Muller, Paul, 372
Mundy, Jimmy, 83
Murphy, Audie, **493–495**
Murphy, George, 156, 496
Murphy, Gerry, 596
Murphy, Turk, 423
Murray, Arthur, 258
Murray, Gerry, 595 (photo)
Murray, Kathryn, 258
Murray, Philip, 442, 446
Murrow, Edward R., 115, 562–563
Museum of Modern Art, 22
music, 258
  about conflict, 656–657
  atomic bomb and, 45
  baseball, 76
  movies and, 656
  popular, 654t–656t
  race records, 591
  radio, **558–562**
  Rosie the Riveter, 606

Selective Training and Service Act of 1940 and, 618–619
standards, 652, 656
See also classical music; *specific songs*
Mutual (Mutual Broadcasting System), 1, 37, 60, 85–86, 136, 348, 426, 459, **475–478**, 583, 585
mutual assured destruction (MAD), 191
"My Blue Heaven," 249
"My Day" (Roosevelt, E.), 598, 599

NAACP. *See* National Association for the Advancement of Colored People
Naismith, James, 85
NASCAR (National Association for Stock Car Auto Racing), 53, 395, 487
National Association for the Advancement of Colored People (NAACP), 372, 533–534, 620
National Barn Dance, 231
National Basketball Association (NBA), 86–88
National Broadcasting Company. *See* NBC
National Collegiate Athletic Association (NCAA), 85, 346
national debt, 787
National Education Association (NEA), 75
National Football League (NFL), 347, 348t, 349
National Hockey League (NHL), 380
National Hot Rod Association (NHRA), 395
National Japanese American Student Relocation Council, 411
National Labor Union, 441
National Mental Health Act, 374
National Park Service (NPS), 727
The National Radio Pulpit, 583–584
National Screen Service (NSS), 529
National Security Act, 189, 300, 795

National Security Agency, 795
National Security Council (NSC), 189
National Security Resources Board (NSRB), 179
National Ski Patrol, 644–645
National Speed Trials, 395
National War Labor Board (NWLB), 41, 441
Native Land, 443
NATO (North Atlantic Treaty Organization), 190, 300, 475, 732, 797
"Nature Boy," 195
NBA. *See* National Basketball Association
NBC (National Broadcasting Company), 1, 2, 37, 85, 286, 287, 459, 692
The NBC Symphony Orchestra, 184
NCAA. *See* National Collegiate Athletic Association
NEA. *See* National Education Association
The Negro Soldier, 463, 535
Nelson, Byron, 362, 363
Nelson, George, 264–265
Nelson, Harriet Hilliard, 3
Nelson, Ozzie, 3
Neutra, Richard, 25, 26
New Orleans, 423
New York Drama Critics Circle Awards, 140, 151
New York Philharmonic, 185
New York World's Fair, 23, 46, 261–262, 344, 350, 490, 510, 612, 650, 692, 721–722
New Yorker, 473
newspapers, 4, 56, 96, 125, 128, 179–180, 201, 213, 460, **501–508**, 506*t*, 530, 665
  Berlin airlift in, 94
  canasta and, 354
  Citizen Kane and, 173–174
  Cold War and, 192, 504
  comic books and, 207
  D-Day and, 261
  education and, 294
  horse racing and, 392
  movies and, 492, 501, 507
  pinup girls in, 308–309
  reporters, 507, 507 (photo)
  scrap drives, 609
  skating and, 642
  travel and, 728
NFL. *See* National Football League
NHRA. *See* National Hot Rod Association
Nicholas Brothers, 255
"Night and Day," 632
Nixon, Richard, 399, 524
Noble, Edward J., 1–2
Noble, Ray, 91, 293, 479
Noble, Sherwood, 324
Noguchi, Isamu, 263, 615–616
North Atlantic Treaty Organization. *See* NATO
North Platte Canteen, 157–158
Noskowiak, Sonya, 515
NPS. *See* National Park Service
NSC. *See* National Security Council
NSRB. *See* National Security Resources Board
NSS. *See* National Screen Service
nuclear chain reaction, 678
Nurse Training Act of 1943, 371
NWLB. *See* National War Labor Board
nylon, 315, 318, 611

O. M. Scott and Sons, 447
OCD. *See* Office of Civil Defense
ocean liners, 725
O'Day, Anita, 421, 422
O'Donnell, Cathy, 104 (photo)
ODT. *See* Office of Defense Transportation
OEM. *See* Office for Emergency Management
O'Farrell, Chico, 92
Office for Emergency Management (OEM), 29, 177
Office of Censorship, 503, 504

Office of Civil Defense (OCD), 177, 180, 609
Office of Defense Transportation (ODT), 722
Office of Health Defense and Welfare, 337
Office of Price Administration (OPA), 114, 226, 576, 752, 788
Office of Production Management (OPM), 46–47
Office of Scientific Research and Development (OSRD), 42
Office of War Information (OWI), 168, 433, 504, 511, 526, 527, 748, 762, 763
Oh Henry!, 270
O'Keeffe, Georgia, 5
Oklahoma! (Rodgers, R. & Hammerstein), 149, 151, 156, 256 (photo)
Oland, Warner, 241
The Old-Fashioned Revival Hour, 584–585
On the Town, 636, 792
O'Neill, Eugene, 140, 146
OPA. *See* Office of Price Administration
OPM. *See* Office of Production Management
Oppenheimer, J. Robert, 42
The Original Amateur Hour, 288, 632
Osborne, Mary, 15
OSRD. *See* Office of Scientific Research and Development
Our New Music (Copland), 225
Outdoor Advertising Association of America, 527
Owen, Maribel Vinson, 638
Owens, Jesse, 535
OWI. *See* Office of War Information

Pabst Blue Ribbon, 112
Packard, Vance, 14
Page, Walter, 83
Pagoda Chinese Restaurant, 589
Paige, Satchel, 80, 535
painting, 5, **29–32**, 30*t*, 31*t*, 32*t*–35*t*

The Paleface, 383–384
Pan, Hermes, 256
Pan American Coffee Bureau, 110
Panama Hattie (Porter, Cole), 148 (photo)
paperbacks, 96
Paramount, 490
Parker, Charlie "Bird," 89, 90 (photo), 91, 92
Parker, Frank, 700
Parker Brothers, 354, 357
Parks, Bert, 3, 569, 797
Parks, Wally, 395
Parsons, Louella, 506
Pastor Hall, 518
Pat Novak, for Hire, 544, 546
Pauley, M. J., 649
Paulsen, Carl, 527–528
Peale, Norman Vincent, 584
Peale, Ruth Stafford, 584
Peanuts, 175
Pearl, Minne, 230–231
Pearson, Drew, 778
Peer, Ralph, 38
Penguin Books, 96
penicillin, 371–372, 683–684
Penn, Irving, 514–515
People's Book Club, 126
People's Song, 334
Pep, Willie, 132*t*, 133
Pepsi & Pete, 107–108
Pepsi-Cola, 11, 107–109, 160
The Pepsodent Show, Starring Bob Hope, 381–382, 384
Perkins, Frances C., 604–605
Perry, Antoinette, 140, 151
Perry, Lincoln, 537
Personal History (Sheean), 518
Peter Paul Candy Manufacturing Company, 270–271
Petersen, Robert E. "Pete," 395
Petrillo, James C., 40, 674
Petty, George, 309, 407–408
The Petty Girl, 408
Pfeifer, Friedl, 645
PGA Championship, 361

The Phantom (Falk), 537
Philadelphia Orchestra, 185, 273–274
Philip Morris, 183
Phillips, Irma, 572
photography, 30, 262, 376, **509–517**, 516*t*
   in *Citizen Kane*, 175
   film noir, 122, 281, 326, 387
   staying connected through, 376
   Technicolor, 228
   travel, 730
Physical Fitness Research Laboratory, 370
Pickett, Clarence, 597
Pidgeon, Walter, 607
Pied Pipers, 633
The Pilgrim Hour, 585
Pillsbury, 269
Pinky, 521
Pinocchio, 162
pinup girls, 308–309, 407, 453, 703–704
Piston, Walter, 182
Pittsburgh Orchestra, 186
Pizzeria Uno, 589
Playskool Manufacturing Company, 711
Plimpton, James Leonard, 641
Plunkett, Roy J., 343
Pocket Books, 96
Pogo (Kelly, Walt), 215–216
Polaroid Corporation, 376, 510–511, 684
polio, 373, 601
Pollard, Red, 390
Pollock, Jackson, 6, 30
Pomeroy, Wardell, 435
Pope, Richard, Jr., 670
Pope, Richard, Sr., 669
Popeye, 214
Popular Mechanics, 378
Popular Science, 375–376, 378
population, 787
Porter, Cole, 91, 148 (photo), 151, 381, 496
Porter, Del, 425
Porter, Edward, 510
Post, Emily, 506

posters, **525–530**, 526 (photo)
   grocery stores, 367
   scrap drives, 609, 610 (photo)
   victory gardens, 745
Potsdam Proclamation, 44
Powell, Dick, 544
Powell, Eleanor, 254, 496
Power in the Pacific: Battle Photographs of Our Navy in Action, 509
Poynter, Nelson, 762
Pozo, Chano, 91
Prairie View Co-eds, 18
Pratt, Anthony E., 357
Preakness Stakes, 390, 392
Preminger, Otto, 492
President's Committee on Equality of Treatment and Opportunity in the Armed Forces, 540–541, 621
President's Cup, 489
Price, Vincent, 243
Prince, Wesley, 193
Professional Tennis Association, 699
Prohibition, 110, 112, 113–114
Project Blue Book, 736
Prontosil, 371
Pulitzer, Joseph, 147
Pulitzer Prizes, 147
Punsly, Bernard, 205
Puppet Playhouse Theater, 400
Pure Food and Drug Act, 369
Putnam, George Carson, 586
Pyle, Ernie, 504, **530–533**

race relations, **533–541**
   movies and, 520–522
radar, 684
radio, 1, 8, 12, 17, 20, 25, 37, 52, 54, 70–71, 83, 85–86, 107, 136, 148, 184, 195, 196, 224–225, 283, 291–293, 301, 341, 359–360, 375, 381–382, 417–419, 449, 480, **541–542**, 602, 629–630, 646–647, 659, 665, 692, 748–749, 798
   action, crime, police, and detective shows, **543–546**, 545*t*–546*t*
   advertising and, 332

AM, 331–332, 332*t*, 541, 556
children's shows, **546–549**, 548*t*
classical music and, 181, 185*t*, 332, 561–562
comedy shows, **550–552**, 551*t*
D-Day and, 261
drama and anthology, **552–555**, 554*t*
educational, **555–557**, 557*t*
FM, **330–333**, 332*t*, 556, 693
folk music and, 333
football and, 345
horse racing and, 392
husband-wife teams, 550
music and variety, **558–562**, 560*t*–561*t*
news, sports, public affairs, and talk, **562–568**, 567*t*
newspapers and, 501, 507
notable newscasters, 563–566
propaganda, 71
quiz shows, **568–571**, 570*t*
religion, 582–586, 583*t*
Roller Derby and, 594
schedules, 542
scrap drives, 609
serial films and, 623
serials and adventure series, **546–549**, 549*t*
soap operas, 216, **571–574**, 573*t*–574*t*
stereotyping, 536
technology, 331
toys from, 713
two-way, 722
war bonds and, 755
youth and, 785
Radio Berlin, 70–72
Radio Bible Class, 583
Radio Corporation of America (RCA), 331
Radio Free Europe (RFE), 189, 748–749
Radio Liberty (RL), 748–749
Radio Tokyo, 70–72
Raeburn, Boyd, 422
Ralston, Vera, 639
Randell, Ron, 245
Randolph, A. Phillip, 464, 535–536, 540–541
Rankin, John, 358
Rathbone, Basil, 240
Ration Board Game, 355
rationing, 11, 110, 114, 183, 214–215, 226, 271, 379, **574–581**, 575 (photo), 619
 black market and, 114
 butter, 268
 canteens and, 159
 drag racing and, 394
 food, 339–342, 579–580, 589
 frozen food, 350
 gasoline, 29, 48, 125, 252, 484, 578–579, 722, 790
 grocery stores and, 366
 horse racing and, 390
 Life and, 580
 motor oils, 48
 motorsports and, 484
 paper, 97
 removing, 341, 342, 580–581
 restaurants and, 322
 skating and, 642
 softball and, 651
 Spam and, 658
 sugar, 108, 267–268, 579
 swing and, 674
 tires, 48, 577–578
 travel and, 726
 youth and, 430–431
Raymond, Alex, 214
RCA. *See* Radio Corporation of America
Reagan, Ronald, 66, 156, 399, 412, 464
Reard, Louis, 45, 317, 670–671
records, 681, 688
Red, Hot and Blue (Porter, Cole), 381
Red Cross clubmobiles, 110, 160
Red Ryder (Harman), 537, 772
Reed, Carol, 326
Reed, Donna, 413
Reeves, George, 666
refrigerator-freezer combination, 684–685

religion, **581–588**, 582*t*, 583*t*
relocation centers. *See* internment camps (relocation centers)
The Reluctant Dragon, 274
Renaldo, Duncan, 772
Renick, Marion, 651
Republic Pictures, 622–623
restaurants, 109, 271, **588–590**
   drive-in, **285**
   fast food, **321–325**
   rationing and, 322
Reuther, Walter, 446
Reynolds, Joyce, 783
Reynolds, Marjorie, 538
Reynolds Wrap, 342
RFE. *See* Radio Free Europe
rhythm and blues, 39, 426, **591–594**, 592*t*, 593*t*
The Rhythm Boys, 247
Riccardo, Ric, 589
Rice, Diana, 728
Richards, Johnny, 422
Richmond, Kane, 477
Rickey, Branch, 80
Rideout, Percy, 645
Riggs, Bobby, 700
Riggs, Tommy, 552
Rinker, Al, 246, 247
RL. *See* Radio Liberty
The Road to Good Nutrition (Roberts), 337
Road to Singapore, 202, 382 (photo), 383
Road to Victory, 509
Robbins, Irvine, 325
Robbins, Jerome, 151, 257
Roberta (Kern), 381
Roberts, Lydia J., 337
Robeson, Paul, 443
Robinson, Bill "Bojangles," 255
Robinson, Edward G., 122, 199, 761
Robinson, Jackie, 80, 463, 535
Robinson, Neil, 645
Robinson, Sugar Ray, 132*t*, 133, 463, 534–535
Rock, George, 426

Rockefeller, John D., Jr., 738
Rockefeller Center, 22
Rockefeller Foundation, 436
The Rockettes, 257–258
Rock-Ola Manufacturing Corporation, 428
Rockwell, Norman, 107, 317, 403–405, 528, 529, 607
   war bonds and, 404–405, 528, 758
Rocky King, Inside Detective, 288–289
Rodeo (Copland), 223, 224 (photo)
Rodgers, Jimmie, 230 (photo)
Rodgers, Richard, 149, 151, 156, 256 (photo)
Rogers, Edith Nourse, 358, 776
Rogers, Ginger, 253, 254, 499
Rogers, Roy, 25, **53–61**, 54 (photo), 59*t*–60*t*, 163, 170, 231, 547, 769
Rohde, Gilbert, 264
Roland, Gilbert, 772
Roller Blades (Sawyer), 642
Roller Derby, **594–596**, 595 (photo), 596, 698
Roller Skating Association, 641
Rooney, Mickey, 172, 199, 496, 596
Roosevelt, Eleanor, 269, 506, **597–600**, 597 (photo)
Roosevelt, Franklin Delano, 24, 41, 42, 46–47, 77, 86, 110, 159, 176–177, 188, 284, 313, 336, 357, 377, 409, 443–444, 466, 474, 504, 575–576, 581, **600–605**, 601 (photo), 617
   "Arsenal for Democracy" speech, 602, 788
   "Day of Infamy" speech, 603
   death of, 187, 359, 731, 792
   "Fireside Chats," 71, 602
   "Four Freedoms" speech, 404, 602, 788
   health care and, 374
   polio and, 373
   "A Prayer in Dark Times," 586–587
   race relations and, 533
Rose, Billy, 668–669
Rose, Fred, 9, 230

Rose, Mauri, 485
Rose, Wally, 423
Rose, William L., 529
Rose Bowl, 345, 347
Rosenberg, Harold, 5, 6
Rosenberg, William, 324
Rosenthal, Joe, 509–510
Rosie the Riveter, 11, 528, **605–608**, 619, 767
"Rosie the Riveter" (Rockwell), 317, 404, 607
Ross, Shirley, 382–383
Roswell, New Mexico, 736
Rountree, Martha, 478
Roventini, Johnny, 12
Royal Gelatin Hour, 291
RTA. See Russeta Timing Association
rubber, 610, 685
"Rudolph the Red-Nosed Reindeer," 56
Rudolph Wurlitzer Company, 428
Rugolo, Pete, 422
Runyon, Damon, 594–595
Rushing, Jimmy, 83
Rusk, Howard A., 436
Russell, George, 91
Russell, Harold, 104 (photo)
Russell, Jane, 309
Russell, Rosalind, 507, 507 (photo)
Russeta Timing Association (RTA), 395
Ruth, Babe, 710 (photo)
Ryder Cup Matches, 362

Saarinen, Eero, 24, 262, 265
Saarinen, Eliel, 24, 262
Saddler, Sandy, 132*t*, 133
The Saint, 243, 243*t*
Salk, Jonas, 373
Salvation Army, 160
Samuelson, Ralph, 669
San Francisco Ballet Company, 183
Sandburg, Carl, 224–225, 509
Sanders, Colonel, 324
Sanders, George, 243, 244
Sandrich, Mark, 774
Saroyan, Williams, 147

Saturday Evening Post, 403–405
Savoy Records, 91
Sawyer, Ruth, 642
Schaper, William Herbert, 356
Schauffler, Sandy, 645
Schilling, David C., 67
Schindler, Bill, 488
Schlaikjer, Jes Wilhelm, 527
Schlesinger, Leon, 164
Schlumbohm, Peter, 266
Schmeling, Max, 462, 463
Schmidt, Gottfried, 128
Scholastic Magazine, 609–610
Schulz, Charles, 175
Schuman, William, 182
Schwartz, Arthur, 156
Scobey, Bob, 423
Scott, Raymond, 675
Scrabble, 356, 452
scrap drives, 11, 295, **609–612**, 610 (photo), 619
    Crosby and, 249
    grocery stores and, 366
    youth and, 430–431, 609–610
Scruggs, Earl, 232
SCTA. See Southern California Timing Association
sculpture, **612–617**
Seabiscuit, 390
Seduction of the Innocent (Wertham), 432–433
See Here, Private Hargrove (Hargrove), 619
Seeger, Pete, 333–334, 442–443
Seiberling, Dorothy, 6
Seibert, Peter, 645
Selective Service. See Selective Training and Service Act of 1940
Selective Training and Service Act of 1940, 295, 336, 443–444, **617–621**, 673, 739–742, 776
    movies and, 619, 761
Seltzer, Leo, 594, 596
service flags (gold stars and blue stars), 404, **626–627**

Service Training Units (STUs), 295–296
Servicemen's Readjustment Act of 1944. *See* GI Bill
Sessions, Roger, 182
Seventeen, 321, **627–628**, 784–785
Sewell, Ike, 589
Sexual Behavior in the Human Female (Kinsey), 435–437
Sexual Behavior in the Human Male (Kinsey), 344, 435–436
The Shadow, 476–477, 543, 663–664
Shaw, Artie, 419
Shaw, Wilbur, 484, 485
Shearing, George, 92
Sheean, Vincent, 518
Sheen, Fulton J., 288, 584
Sheena, Queen of the Jungle, 209, 211
Sherlock Holmes, 239–240, 240t
Sherman, Harry, 134–135
Sherwood, Robert E., 104, 520
Shibley, Arkie, 52, 396
Shore, Dinah, **628–631**, 629 (photo)
Shuster, Joe, 163–164, 208, 476, 664
Siegel, Jerry, 163–164, 208, 476, 664
Silent Spring (Carson, Rachel), 372
Silly Putty, 685, 713
Silverheels, Jay, 461 (photo)
Simmons, Zalmon, Jr., 489
Simon, Abe, 131, 463
Simon & Schuster, 96
simulcasting, 685–686
Sinatra, Frank, 19, 40, 41, 195, 256, 306, 320, 363, **631–637**, 634t, 636t, 782
singing cowboy, 54, 60, 231, 496
Singleton, Penny, 201
Sir Barton, 390
skating
  figure, **637–641**
  roller, **641–643**
Ski, 644
Skidmore, Owings & Merrill. *See* SOM
skiing, **643–646**
  water, **667–672**
Slack, Freddie, 124

slang, 310–312
Sleight, Rae, 157–158
Sligh, Charles R., 670
Slinky, 686, 713
Smart, J. Scott, 544
Smith, Bob, 400
Smith, David, 616
Smith, George A., 587
Smith, Kate, 344, 587, **646–649**, 647 (photo), 757
Smith, Louise, 487
Smith, W. Eugene, 511, 513t, 514
Smith, W. Warren, 283
Smith, Willie "the Lion," 82
The Smithsonian Collection of Classical Country Music, 236
Smokey Stover (Holman), 735
Snead, Sam, 361, 362
Snickers, 270
snorkel, 686
Snow White and the Seven Dwarfs, 273
Snuffy Smith, 392
Snyder, Esther, 323–324
Snyder, Harry, 323–324
So Dear to My Heart, 276
So Proudly We Hail!, 780
Sockman, Ralph W., 584
softball, **649–652**
Soglow, Otto, 107
SOM (Skidmore, Owings & Merrill), 24–25
Something for the Boys, 483
sonar, 686–687
Song of the South, 276, 520
Songs by Sinatra, 635
songwriters and lyricists, **652–657**, 757
Sons of the Pioneers, 57
sound barrier, 67, 687
"The Sources of Soviet Conduct" (Kennan), 188
"South American Way," 481
South Pacific (Rodgers, R. & Hammerstein), 151
Southern California Timing Association (SCTA), 393–394, 395

Southern Music Publishing Company, 38
Soviet Union, 187–193, 397–399
    atomic bomb and, 45–46, 179–180, 191, 733, 798
    See also Cold War
Spam, 341, **657–660**, 658
SPARs, 779
Specht, Robert, 639
speedboat racing, 488–489
Spellman, Francis Joseph Cardinal, 467, 587
Spencer, Tim, 57
Spice Islands Company, 365
Spiegelhoff, John, 488
spies, 191, 192, 398, 409
The Spike Jones Show, 426
Spillane, Mickey, 95 (photo)
Spitalny, Phil, 15, 16 (photo), 17
Spivak, Lawrence, 478
Spock, Benjamin, 75, **660–661**
Spotlight Revue, 426
Springtime in the Rockies, 482
Stafford, Jo, 19
Stage Door Canteen, 139, 150, 159, 742
Stalin, Joseph, 187, 188, 601 (photo), 603
stamp collecting, 376–377, 408, 601
Standard Oil Company, 14
Stanley, Frederick Arthur, 380
Stanley Cup, 380, 380*t*, 381
Stars and Stripes, 531–532
"The Star-Spangled Banner," 648
steel pennies, 611, **661–663**
Steichen, Edward, 509
Steinbeck, John, 519
Steiner, Max, 168
stereotyping, **533–541**
    in war movies, 766–767
Stern, Philip Van Doren, 413
Steve Canyon, 222, 704
Stevens, Clifford Brooks, 428
Stevens, George, 414
Stevenson, Adlai, 300
Stewart, Jimmy, 293, 413, 518
Stewart, Redd, 233
Stieglitz, Alfred, 515
Still, William Grant, 181, 261
Stillman, Al, 428
Stimson, Henry L., 409, 618
Stirling, Linda, 623
stock cars, 395–396, 486–487
Stockwell, Dean, 521
Stokowski, Leopold, 162, 273–274
Stone, Edward Durrell, 22
Stone, Harlan Fiske, 605
Stone, Lewis, 199
Stop the Music, 569, 797
Stordahl, Axel, 634
Stormy Weather, 306, 306 (photo)
The Story of G.I. Joe, 531
"Straighten Up and Fly Right," 194
Strandlund, Carl, 27–28
Stratton, Dorothy C., 779
Strayhorn, Billy, 302
A Streetcar Named Desire (Williams, Tennessee), 146
Streeter, Ruth Cheney, 779
streptomycin, 372, 687
Strike Up the Band, 496
Striker, Fran, 459, 460
Strode, Woody, 535
Stubbins, Hugh, Jr., 24
Studebaker Corporation, 48–49, 266
STUs. *See* Service Training Units
Suburban Life, 377–378
suburbanization, **453–458**
Suggs, Louise, 363
Sullivan, Ed, 417, **707–708**, 707 (photo), 797
Sun Valley, 643, 644
Sundblom, Haddon, 107
suntan lotions, 687
Superman, 163–164, 208, 476, 476 (photo), 507, **663–667**
Suspense, 554–555
Swift, Henry, 515
swimming, **667–672**, 668 (photo), 671*t*
swimsuits, 670–671
    See also bikini

swing, 12, 16, 19, 83, 89, 124, 182, 194, 225, 232–233, 258, 301, 419, 420, 479, 591, 633, **672–676**, 673 (photo)
Swing, Raymond Gram, 478
Szilard, Leo, 42
Szyk, Arthur, 527

Taft, Robert A., 75, 297, 445
Taft-Hartley Act, 441, 445
Take Me Out to the Ball Game, 636
Tanforan Assembly Center, 409 (photo)
Tarzan, 172
taxis, 722
Taylor, Deems, 162
Taylor, June, 259
Taylor, Robert, 518
Teagarden, Jack, 423
Teague, Walter Dorwin, 261, 262, 721
technology, 184, **677–692**
   atomic bomb, 191
   chronological listing of achievements in, 691*t*
   Copland and, 225
   frozen food, 351
   magazines and, 468
   motorsports, 490
   sound, 54, 495
Teen Trouble, 431
Teflon, 343, 688
Tehran Conference, 603, 605, 790
television, 2, 12, 16, 21, 41, 54, 85, 128, 135, 140, 166, 168, 195, 200, 228–229, 233, 285–289, 293, 375, 382, 437–439, 450, 461, 477, 581, 631, 637, 647–648, 666, **692–698**, 705–708, 798
   anthology dramas, 437–439, 696
   baseball and, 697
   bowling, 697
   boxing, 134, 697
   camera setup, 679 (photo)
   children's, 696
   color, 678, 788
   FM radio and, 331–332
   football and, 347, 697
   game/quiz shows, 696*t*
   Golden Age of, 439
   hockey and, 381
   horse racing and, 392
   inspired toys, 716
   movies and, 491, 695
   news, 697
   newspapers and, 501
   Roller Derby, 596, 698
   variety shows, 695–696
   wrestling, 697–698
   See also specific programs
Temple, Shirley, 170, 306, 783
tennis, 452, **698–702**, 700*t*
Terry, Paul, 165
Terry and the Pirates, 214, 222, **702–705**
Terrytoons, 165
The Texaco Star Theater, 255, 259, **705–707**, 706 (photo), 797
Thank Your Lucky Stars, 630
"Thanks for the Memory," 382
That Night in Rio, 482, 496
theaters, 449
   drive-in, **282–285**, 283 (photo)
Theatre World Award, 140, 151
This Is the Army (Berlin), 151, 619, 790
Thomas, George, 123
Thomas, J. Parnell, 398, 524
Thompson, J. Walter, 437
Thomson, Virgil, 181, 183
Thornhill, Claude, 675
Three Stooges, 172, 203–204
Throttle Magazine, 394
Tide detergent, 688
Tierney, Gene, 187 (photo)
Tilden, Bill, 699
Till the Clouds Roll By, 635
Till the End of Time, 520
Tillie the Toiler (Westover), 779
Tillman, Floyd, 234
Time, 465, 467, 469
"Time After Time," 635
The Time of Your Life (Saroyan), 147

timeline (1940s), 787–800
Tinkertoys, 711
Tito, Josip Broz, 189
To Be or Not to Be, 196, 418
To Have and Have Not, 120
To Hell and Back, 495
Toast of the Town, **707–708**, 707 (photo)
The Toast of the Town, 259, 797
Todd, John, 460
Toguri, Iva, 70–72, 70 (photo)
Tokyo Rose, **70–72**
Toland, Gregg, 173
Toler, Sidney, 241, 537
The Tommy Riggs and Betty Lou Show, 552
Tonka, 714
Tony Award, 140, 151
Tootsie Rolls, 270
Topps, 310
Toscanini, Arturo, 183, 184
Tough Hill, 392
toys, 53, 94, **708–716**
Trading with the Enemy Act, 503
trains, 93, 157, **716–720**, 718*t*, 719*t*, 721, 733
  decline in, 720, 723
  military service, 719, 724
  toy, 714–715
Transcontinental Roller Derby, 594
transistors, 689
transportation, 46, 61, 75, 226, 286, **720–725**
  fast food and, 321–322
  food, 340
  horse racing and, 390
  labor unrest and, 444
  restaurants and, 590
  skiing, 643–644
  suburbanization and, 455
  swing and, 674
travel, 67, 94, 282, **725–730**, 726*t*, 727*t*
Travern, B., 121
Travis, Merle, 235–236
TravLodge, 728
The Treasure of Sierra Madre, 121–122

Trendle, George, 459, 460
Trotter, John Scott, 424
Troup, Bobby, 52
True Detective Mysteries, 543
True-Life Adventures, 276
Truman, Harry S., 4, 6, 44, 75, 93, 128, 177, 187, 189, 300, 319, 399, 412, 433, 445, 467, 474, 600, 621, **730–734**, 731 (photo), 739, 743, 797
  on food, 342
  health care and, 374
  race relations and, 540–541
  speedboat racing and, 489
Truman Doctrine, 189, 733, 795
Tubb, Ernest, 230 (photo), 235
Tupperware, 343, 689–690
Turner, Curtis, 487
Turner, Eugene, 639
Turner, Lana, 309, 321, 453
Tuskegee Airmen, 534, 534 (photo)
Twentieth Century-Fox, 490

UAW. *See* United Automobile Workers of America
U-boats, 116
UFOs (Unidentified Flying Objects), 735–736
UMW. *See* United Mine Workers of America
Underwood, Michael, 373
Unidentified Flying Objects. *See* UFOs
United Artists, 490
United Automobile Workers of America (UAW), 443
United Mine Workers of America (UMW), 444
United Nations, 621, 732, **736–739**
  Declaration of, 603, 737
  Educational, Scientific, and Cultural Organization, 182
  Human Rights Commission, 600
  Roosevelt, Eleanor, appointed to, 600
  Secretariat, 23
United Service Organizations. *See* USO (United Service Organizations)

United States Committee for the Care of European Children, 597
United States Information Agency (USIA), 189–190, 748
United States Public Health Service, 371
Universal Pictures, 622
Up Front (Mauldin), 532
Up in Arms, 630
Upson Company, 355
USA Today, 505
USIA. *See* United States Information Agency
USO (United Service Organizations), 12, 18, 21, 58, 84, 126, 150, 159, 183, 230, 384, 451, 499, 529, **739–742**

VA. *See* Veterans Administration
Valentine, Helen, 627
Vallee, Rudy, 291, 306, 783
Van Dyke, William, 515
Vance, Louis Joseph, 245
Vargas, Alberto, 309, 407–408
Varipapa, Andy, 128–129
Vaughan, Sarah, 89
V-Discs, 41, 558
V-E Day, **743–744**
vending, 112–113
Verdi, Giuseppe, 183
Veterans Administration (VA), 358, 371, 728
Victory Book Rallies, 97, 126
victory gardens, 370, 379, 452, 579, **744–748**, 745 (photo)
  golf and, 362
Victory Through Air Power, 275
View, 615
Village Vanguard, 334
vitamins, 369
V-J Day, **743–744**
V-Mail, 510
Vogue, 316, 514–515, 614
Voice of America (VOA), 189, **748–749**, 794–795

The Volga Boatman, 134
Vox Pop, 568

WAC. *See* Women's Auxiliary Corps
Wagner, George "Gorgeous George," 697–698
Wake Island, 760
Walcot, Jersey Joe, 130 (photo)
Wall Street Journal, 505
Wallace, Coley, 464
Wallace, Henry A., 600, 730–731
Waller, Fats, 82
Waller, Fred, 669
Wallichs, Glenn, 194
Walt Disney, 161–163, 172, 180, 212, 273–277, 425, 520, 712
Walter, Rosalind, 606
Wanger, Walter, 517
War Advertising Council, 11, 13, 753
war bonds, 11, 58, 140, 150, 295, 619, **751–759**, 752 (photo)
  boxing and, 129
  campaigns, 754*t*
  Crosby and, 249
  grocery stores and, 366
  Hope and, 384
  jukeboxes and, 430
  Rockwell, Norman, and, 404–405, 528, 758
  Smith, Kate, and, 647, 757
War Powers Act, 503
War Production Board (WPB), 48, 108, 313
War Ration Program, 576, 580
War Relocation Authority (WRA), 409, 409 (photo), 539
Warm 'n Fresh Donut, 324
Warner Bros., 164, 172, 212, 277, 490
Warren, Robert Penn, 278 (photo)
Washburne, Joe "Country," 425
Washington, Kenny, 535
WASPs. *See* Women Airforce Service Pilots
Watkins Glen Grand Prix, 486
Watson, Lucile, 139

Watters, Lu, 423
WAVES. *See* Women Accepted for Volunteer Military Services
Wayne, David, 532
Wayne, John, 54, 319, 769
WBA. *See* World Boxing Association
"We Can Do It!" (Miller, J. Howard), 316–317, 528, 606
Weaver, Winstead "Doodles," 425
Webb, Jack, 544, 546
Weegee, 511, 513*t*, 514
Week-End in Havana, 482, 496
Weir, Walter, 753
Weissmuller, Johnny, 667–668, 669
Welles, Orson, 71, **173–176**, 174 (photo), 183, 355 (photo), 477
Wells, Herman B., 436
Wertham, Fredric, 432
West, Mae, 311
Westinghouse War Production Co-Ordinating Committee, 528
Weston, Edward, 510, 515, 516*t*
Westover, Russ, 779
Wham-O, 716
"What Are We Fighting For?" (Roosevelt, E.), 598
What Happened to Mary?, 622
Whataburger, 324
"When the Moon Comes Over the Mountain, 648
Whirlaway, 391
White, Minor, 514
White Castle, 322
"White Christmas," 56, 249, 496, 657, **773–775**, 790
Whiteman, Paul, 246, 437
Why We Fight, 763
WIBC. *See* Women's International Bowling Congress
Wick, Claude R., 339
Wilder, Billy, 492
William, Warren, 245
Williams, Esther, 636, 667–669
Williams, Hank, 10, 234–235
Williams, Ike, 132*t*

Williams, Mary Lou, 15
Williams, Ted, 78, 78 (photo)
Williams, Tennessee, 140, 146
Willis, Bill, 535
Wills, Bob, 232–233
Wills, Royal Barry, 26
Wilson, 737
Wilson, Don, 418
Wilson, Dooley, 169
Wilson, George, 396
Wilson, Sloan, 319
Wilson, Woodrow, 737
Winchell, Verne, 324
Winchell, Walter, 3–4, 72, 506
Wings for This Man, 66
Winter, Roland, 537
Winters, Roland, 241
Wismer, Harry, 67
Woman's Day, 365
Women Accepted for Volunteer Military Services (WAVES), 314, 778
Women Airforce Service Pilots (WASPs), 314, 778
Women at War, 779–780
women in military, 314, **776–780**
Women's Armed Services Integration Act, 779
Women's Auxiliary Corps (WAC), 314, 776–778
Women's International Bowling Congress (WIBC), 127–128
Wood, Craig, 361, 362
Wood, Garfield, 489
Wood, Morrison, 112
Woodruff, Robert W., 108
woodworking, 378
Works Projects Administration, 29, 447, 612
World Boxing Association (WBA), 130
WPB. *See* War Production Board
WRA. *See* War Relocation Authority
wrestling, 697–698
Wright, Frank Lloyd, 22, 22 (photo), 23, 24, 27, 263–264
Wright, Henry, 264

Wright, Orville, 61
Wright, Russel, 265–266
Wright, Wilbur, 61
Wrigley, Phillip K., 78
Wrigley Company, 270
Wunder, George, 704
Wurster, William W., 26
Wyler, William, 104, 414, 520
Wyman, Jane, 158 (photo)

Yank, 309
Yeager, Charles E. (Chuck), 67
Yeoman, Richard S., 377
Yip Yap Yaphank (Berlin), 151, 156, 648
York Cone Company, 270
York Peppermint Patty, 270
You Bet Your Life, 569
Young, Chic, 172, 201–202, 214 (photo), 216, 218
Young, James Webb, 753
Young, Lester, 83

Your Hit Parade, 635
Your Share: How to Prepare Appetizing, Helpful Meals with Foods Available Today (Crocker), 268, 340
youth, 91, 305, 430–434, **781–786**
   civil defense and, 430–431
   fashion, 319–320, 785
   oriented agencies, 452–453
   rationing and, 430–431
   scrap drives and, 430–431, 609–610
   softball and, 650
Youth in Crisis, 432
Youth Runs Wild, 432

Zaharias, Babe Didrikson, 363
Zale, Tony, 129, 131, 132*t*, 133
Zamboni, 690
Zeisel, Eva, 266
Zero Hour, 71–72
Ziolkowski, Korczak, 613
zoot suits, 306, 306 (photo), 320, 431, 540, 783